Advanced V
Basic 6

Second Edition

Kip Irvine
Kaiyang Liang
Miami-Dade Community College-Kendall

Scott/Jones Inc., Publishers
P.O. Box 696, El Granada, CA 94018
scotjones2@aol.com
(650) 726-2436 or Fax: (650) 726-4693
http://www.scottjonespub.com

Advanced Visual Basic 6
Kip Irvine and Kaiyang Liang

ISBN: 1-57676-030-8

Composition: David Irvine
Book Manufacturing: Bawden Printing
Text Design: Kip Irvine
Cover Design: Bill Ulch, Art Central

2109 YXWV

Other Programming Language Texts by Scott/Jones

Assembly Language for the IBM-PC Family, 2nd Edition
William Jones

C by Discovery, 3rd edition
Foster & Foster

C Through Objects
John Connely

The Java Platform for Programmers
Computing with Java: Programs, Objects, Graphics
Arthur Gittleman

Problem Solving with C
Jones and Harrow

Starting Out with C++, 2nd Edition
Tony Gaddis

Additional Books in Visual Basic

Introduction to Programming Using Visual Basic 6
Gary Bronson

Visual Basic 6 CourseBook
Forest Lin

Visual Basic 6 with Applications, 2nd Edition
Mark Simkin

Additional Titles Of Interest From Scott/Jones

Building Applications with MS Office and Visual Basic
Ron Gilster and Karen Braunstein-Post

The Access 97 Guidebook
Concise Guidebook to Access 97
The Access 2000 Guidebook
Maggie Trigg, Phyllis Dobson

The Windows 98 TextBook – Extended Edition
The Windows 98 TextBook – Standard Edition
Short Course in Windows 98
Stewart Venit

ActiveX and the Internet
QuickStart in DOS for Windows 9X
QuickStart in JavaScript
Short Course in HTML
Forest Lin

HTML for WWW Developers
Client Side Programming for WWW Developers
Server Side Programming for WWW Developers
John Avila

This book is dedicated to

the many excellent students

at Miami-Dade Community College

who have helped us learn to teach

Visual Basic 6

Preface

It is a pleasure to bring out the Second Edition of this book and to have a chance to improve a book that has already been doing so well. With the introduction of Dr. Kai Liang as co-author, we bring a wider range of experience and expertise to the Second Edition.

Because of the many exciting changes in Microsoft Visual Basic 6.0, this new edition was a necessity. We learned a great deal by teaching from the first edition during the past year and a half, and I truly believe that we have made many excellent changes. Now, with the strong emphasis on Active Data Objects (ADO), we hope to keep up with the rapid pace of change and at the same time deliver a book that instructors and students will enjoy using in the classroom.

This book is targeted toward second and third semester courses in Visual Basic at the college and university level. At Miami-Dade Community College-Kendall, for example, the book is used in both the Intermediate and Advanced Visual Basic courses. We recommend that students using this book have already completed at least one semester programming course. The course could be in Visual Basic, C++, Delphi, or any modern programming language. It can also be used in High School level-2 honors computer classes.

Web Site

We maintain a fairly active student web site for this book, located at the following URLs:

www.pobox.com/~irvinek/books/vb6
www.nuvisionmiami.com/books/vb6

There is also an instructor web site, located at the following URL. It requires a password, which you can obtain if you are an adopting instructor:

www.nuvisionmiami.com/instructor/vbook

If for some reason you're having trouble getting through to these sites, please send email to Kip Irvine, at: **kip.irvine@pobox.com**. or to the publisher, Scott/Jones, at: **scotjones2@aol.com**. Or, if you just want to talk to us, we're happy to receive mail and phone calls. The publisher's phone number is (650) 726-2436.

Why This Book Was Written

During the last few years, colleges everywhere have found Visual Basic to be a popular and useful vehicle for teaching Windows Programming applications and concepts. At Miami-Dade, we began teaching the course in late 1995, using Visual Basic 3. Soon afterward, we realized that Visual Basic should be taught at the intermediate and advanced levels, to people who take programming *very* seriously. We immediately found professional programmers and would-be programmers filling the second-semester Visual Basic classes. For four years we have been creating and refining stacks of course handouts and sample programs for this course, and getting great help from students. To say that students have *taught us to program* in Visual Basic is an understatement, because so many of them have shared their considerable knowledge and skills.

New Topics in the Second Edition

We've included a lot more reference information and short examples in the second Edition, particularly for topics that were not in the first edition:

- ActiveX controls, including the ToolBar, ImageList, StatusBar, ListView, TreeView, CoolBar, Multimedia, Microsoft Chart, and ActiveMovie.
- ADO-related topics, including the ADO data control, Hierarchical FlexGrid, DataReport Designer, and DataEnvironment Designer.
- Increased coverage of the SQL query language, with many examples.
- Creating HTML Help files.
- Examples of in-process and out-of-process ActiveX servers.
- ActiveX Controls: Property Page Wizard, ActiveX Control Wizard, and creating data-aware controls.
- Internet programming: WinSock and Internet Transfer controls, Dynamic HTML, HTML Help, and ActiveX Documents.

Features of This Book

Every experienced instructor knows that students have a variety of learning styles. Some learn from manuals; others from sample programs; some prefer the "human" touch, being able to spend one-on-one time with an instructor; some learn from step-by-step exercises. To help address different learning styles, this book contains a number of pedagogical features that serve to reinforce each other during the learning process:

- ***Object-oriented programming.*** During the survey and reviewing process for this book, we found that many instructors wanted object-oriented programming to be emphasized much more strongly than in existing Visual Basic textbooks. I completely agree! Therefore, objects are used throughout the book, with special emphasis on ActiveX data objects in Chapter 5, class design in Chapter 8, ActiveX component design in Chapter 9, ActiveX servers in Chapter 10, and Internet objects in Chapter 12.
- ***Discussions about program design, coding style, object-oriented concepts***. These concepts are at the core of a solid computer science education.
- A ***short table of contents*** is displayed at the beginning of each chapter. People like to see what the chapter is about, at a glance.
- ***Pop-up programming tips*** that show up in gray-shaded boxes. The reader can ignore these without disturbing the flow of the main text body, and come back to them later. It's surprising how often these little tips become useful when programs won't work!
- ***Reference information*** on Visual Basic, ADO connections and recordsets, SQL query language, Data Report Designer, the Windows API, ActiveX components, and online help. The Microsoft manuals and online help are wonderful, but it's not easy to limit the scope of information. In this book, you find lots of tables and lists, just when you need to use them in a program.
- ***Hands-on programming examples*** that guide the reader while working at the computer. These are short and simple, designed to demonstrate concepts, and it's always nice to have something to do.
- ***One or two moderately complex applications*** that are specified, designed, and implemented. The source code for these programs is on the student disk. Anyone who has written real-

world applications can appreciate the importance of careful design and planning. Students, lacking that experience, should not be misled into thinking that all Visual Basic programs are trivial in size and complexity.

- ***Review questions*** at the end of each chapter. Some are no-brainers, some require thought. But you can trace the origin of every question back to a specific spot in the reading, in case you didn't read the chapter carefully enough the first time (who does?). Answers to the odd-numbered questions are located in Appendix C. Answers to the even-numbered questions are available on the Instructor Web.

- ***End-of-Chapter programming exercises*** that offer a variety of programming challenges, from easy to difficult. The solutions to these programs are available for download from the Instructor web site. In the writing of these programs, we gain valuable experience in problem solving. The programs can be fun, frustrating, exhilarating, aggravating, inspiring, and many other things. But they *do* teach you to program.

- ***A Visual Basic review tutorial*** for programmers who are experienced in other languages is available in Appendix A. This doesn't replace a beginning course in programming by any means, but it can be great for people who already know what they want to do, and just need the tools to do it. A tutorial on creating sequential and random access files is located in Appendix B.

- A ***competency exam*** located in Appendix A to help professors and students move more rapidly into Visual Basic. Students can judge their own mastery of fundamental topics, on their own time. Each question in the test is keyed to a particular topic in the Visual Basic review tutorial, also in Appendix A.

- ***Programs supplied on disk*** are indicated by the word *samples* in italics at the beginning of sections. For example, the Mozart Music Sales 1 program in Chapter 2 has a note at the beginning of the section indicating that the program is in the ch02\Mozart1 directory on the student CDROM shipped with the book:

    (samples: Mozart1)

A Quick Survey of Chapter Topics

- Chapter 1, **Designing and Coding Programs**, explains the application development cycle, user interface design, coding guidelines, error handling, and performance optimization.

- Chapter 2, **Building Applications,** introduces a number of useful ActiveX controls for user interface design, develops a point-of-sale application in several stages, introduces the CommonDialog control, and shows how to save and restore system registry settings.

- Chapter 3, **Objects and Collections,** introduces objects, collections, the ListView, TreeView, and CoolBar controls, and MDI applications.

- Chapter 4, **Data-Bound Controls,** shows how to use the ADO data control, data-bound fields, the DataList, DataCombo, and DataGrid controls, and perform sorting, searching, and filtering records.

- Chapter 5, **ActiveX Data Objects,** concentrates on direct programming with ADO object methods, properties, and events.

- Chapter 6, **Relational Databases and SQL,** shows how to design multi-table databases, create SQL queries for searching, sorting, define recordsets, modify recordsets, and use validation rules.
- Chapter 7, **DataReport, MSHFlexGrid, and MSChart,** shows how to create connections, commands, and reports using the DataEnvironment Designer and the DataReport Designer. Applications using the Hierarchical FlexGrid and MSChart controls are also presented.
- Chapter 8, **Creating Class Modules,** goes head-on into object-oriented programming, with classes, objects, methods, properties, collection classes, and a complete application for scheduling doctors office appointments.
- Chapter 9, **Creating ActiveX Components**, shows how to create ActiveX DLLs (in-process servers), stand-alone server components, and ActiveX controls. Most important, we show how an ActiveX component can implement the *data services* segment of a Visual Basic application.
- Chapter 10, **Using OLE and ActiveX Servers,** introduces object linking and embedding (OLE), showing how to integrate Visual Basic with Microsoft Word and Excel, using OLE containers and objects.
- Chapter 11, **Tapping into the Windows API,** focuses on calling DLL procedures and taking advantage of the Windows *application programmer's interface* (API).
- Chapter 12, **Internet Programming,** demonstrates the Internet Transfer control, the Winsock control, Dyanmic HTML applications, and HTML Help. Many useful examples are presented, with extensive reference information.
- Appendix A, **Visual Basic Review,** is a quick-start tutorial on the essentials of Visual Basic for readers who are already experienced programmers.
- Appendix B, **Sequential and Random Files,** shows how to read and write sequential access files as well as random-access files.
- Appendix C, **Answers to Odd-Numbered Review Questions**, provides answers to all odd-numbered review questions found at the ends of Chapters 1-12.

Chapter Sequence Flowchart. It is often more useful for professors to cover chapters in a different order from the sequence presented in the book. The following sequences of chapters are possible, given built-in dependencies between topics:

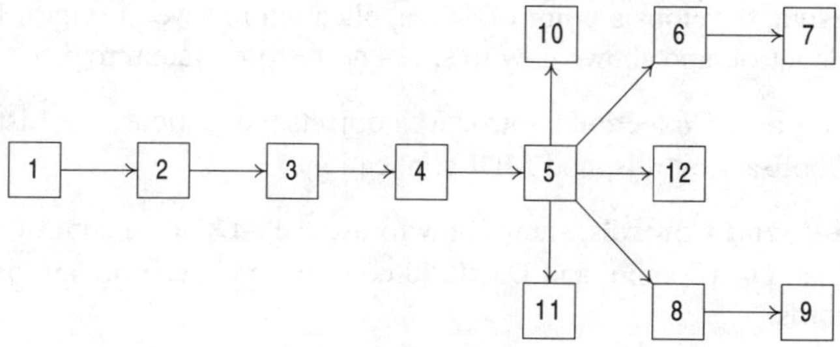

The first five chapters contain core information that is used throught the book. From there, you can emphasize object-oriented programming by covering chapters 8 and 9. Or, you can emphasize database applications by covering chapters 6 and 7. Chapters 10, 11, and 12 can be covered anytime after Chapter 5.

Supplemental Materials and Teaching Aids

The following learning aids are furnished with each copy of the book:

- Review Questions at the end of each chapter.
- Answers to the odd-numbered review questions in Appendix C.
- A CD containing all sample programs.
- Access to the student Web site. We post corrections to errors found in the text, udpates to program examples found in the book, and new information about Visual Basic as it becomes available.

The following teaching aids are furnished on the passsword-protected instructor Web site:

- A test bank of short-answer, multiple-choice and True/False questions, with a separate test for each chapter (also available on CD).
- Additional programming exercises designed to enhance the use of this book.
- Answers to all even-numbered review questions in the book (also available on CD).
- Sample course outlines, objectives, and semester lecture plans for two courses taught by the authors at Miami-Dade Community College: COP 2171 (Intermediate Visual Basic), and COP 2333 (Advanced Visual Basic).
- Solution programs for all programming exercises in the book.

Acknowledgements

First, let me warmly thank Richard Jones, the publisher, who provided a lot of the inspiration and guidance for this book. Through our many conversations, we developed the ideas that eventually brought this book to life. Cathy Baehler, of Baehler Editing, helped eliminate many typos and minor errors that slipped by me.

Kathy Blicharz, Professor, Pima College in Tucson, Arizona, was instrumental in testing and reviewing the first edition as it was under development during the first half of 1997. She had many fine suggestions that affected the book's design.

Merrill Parker, Professor, Chattanooga State Technical Community College, reviewed several chapters and created an excellent competency test for Visual Basic fundamentals, found in Appendix A.

Edward Wittke, Project Data Manager, University of Arizona, contributed a tremendous amount of time and energy to proofreading both the first and second editions. He provided many excellent suggestions for corrections, improvements and clarifications.

Many thanks to the following instructors who reviewed the book's outline and/or manuscript for the First Edition:

Mary Amundson-Miller, Greenville Technical College
Kamran Azad, Orangeburg Technical College
Collin Ballance, Nashville State Technical Institute
Allen Brooks, Linfield College
Jesse Cabrera, San Antonio College
Randolph Campbell, Morningside College
Brad Chilton, Tarelton State College
Alejandro Ferro, Miami-Dade Community College

Rob Fitzgerald, University of North Florida
Lee Hunt, Collin County Community College
Mozelle Johnson, Pima Community College
Jeffrey Kent, Los Angeles Valley College
Carol Peterson, South Plains College
Jeff Scott, Blackhawk Technical College
Cherie M. Stevens, South Florida Community College
Michael J. Walton, Miami-Dade Community College-North
Melinda White, Santa Fe Community College

The following persons classroom tested this book during 1997:

- Kathy Blicharz, Pima College
- Kai Liang, Miami-Dade Community College-Kendall, who also created some great programming projects involving financial calculations for the First Edition.
- David Victor, Miami-Dade Community College-Kendall

Thanks are due to Darren Lyn, who contributed ADO programming ideas while we were writing the second edition, and Eduardo Molieri, who wrote most of the solution programs for the chapter exercises in the first edition. Eduardo was also the co-author of the Instructor's Manual for the first edition.

TypeSetting

Typesetting of this book was done by David Irvine, using Adobe PageMaker 6.5. Any suggestions, criticism, and locations of misprints would be warmly appreciated. Please send e-mail to: **kip.irvine@pobox.com** or call Kip Irvine at **305-237-2806** (Miami-Dade Community College). The editor, Richard Jones, can be reached at: **Scotjones1@aol.com**.

About the Authors

Kip Irvine holds a Masters degree in Computer Science (1995) and a Doctor of Musical Arts (1982) from the University of Miami. He has been a Professor of Computer Information Systems at Miami-Dade Community College-Kendall since 1983. Published textbooks are *COBOL for the IBM Personal Computer* (Prentice Hall, 1987), *Assembly Language for Intel-Based Computers* (Prentice-Hall 1990, 1993, and 1999), *C++ and Object-Oriented Programming* (Prentice Hall, 1997), and *Advanced Visual Basic* (1998).

Kaiyang Liang holds both Masters and Doctoratoral degrees in Mathematics from the University of Miami. He has been a Professor of both Mathematics and Computer Information Systems at Miami-Dade Community College-Kendall since 1989. He also does work as a Visual Basic and Microsoft Access consultant.

Table of Contents

1 Designing and Coding Programs 1

1.1 APPLICATION DEVELOPMENT CYCLE 1
- 1.1.1 Interviewing Management and Users 1
- 1.1.2 Creating Program Specifications 2
- 1.1.3 Performing a Feasibility Review 2
- 1.1.4 Designing the Application 3
- 1.1.5 Design Goals 4
- 1.1.6 Implementing the Application 4
- 1.1.7 Testing the Application 5

1.2 USER INTERFACE DESIGN 5
- 1.2.1 Avoiding Crowding Forms 6
- 1.2.2 Setting the Tab Order 6
- 1.2.3 Keyboard Input 7
- 1.2.4 Using Standard Menus 8
- 1.2.5 Dragging and Dropping 9

1.3 CODING GUIDELINES 9
- 1.3.1 Declaring Variables and Constants 10
- 1.3.2 Naming Variables and Constants 10
- 1.3.3 Naming Controls 11
- 1.3.4 Naming Procedures and Methods 12
- 1.3.5 Indenting Code 12
- 1.3.6 Predefined VB Constants 14
- 1.3.7 Line Continuation 14
- 1.3.8 App Object Properties 15
- 1.3.9 Avoid Default Properties 15
- 1.3.10 Use General Procedures to Avoid Duplication 16

1.4 ERROR HANDLING 17
- 1.4.1 Causes of Errors 17
- 1.4.2 On Error GoTo Statement 18
- 1.4.3 Resume Statement 18
- 1.4.4 Using the Err Object 20

1.5 REDUCING CODE SIZE 21

1.6 IMPROVING EXECUTION SPEED 22
- 1.6.1 Code Optimization 22
- 1.6.2 Display Optimization 23
- 1.6.3 Perceived Speed Optimization 23

1.7 REVIEW QUESTIONS 24

1.8 CHAPTER EXERCISES 26
- 1.8.1 Changing Form Colors 26

1.8.2 Freight Forwarding Service (Design) 26
1.8.3 Freight Forwarding Service (Implementation) 27
1.8.4 Express Travel Agency (Design) 27
1.8.5 Express Travel Agency (Implementation) 27
1.8.6 Multiple-Choice Test (Design) 28
1.8.7 Multiple-Choice Test (Implementation) 28

2 Building Applications 29

2.1 USEFUL ACTIVEX CONTROLS 29
2.1.1 Tabbed Dialog Control 30
2.1.2 ProgressBar Control 31
2.1.3 ImageList Control 32
2.1.4 ToolBar Control 34
2.1.5 StatusBar Control 38
2.1.6 Multimedia Control 40
2.1.7 ActiveMovie Control 42

2.2 MOZART MUSIC SALES - 1 43
2.2.1 Objectives 44
2.2.2 Program Specifications 45
2.2.3 User Interface Design 45
2.2.4 Implementation: Module1.bas 47
2.2.5 Implementation: frmMain 48

2.3 MOZART MUSIC SALES - 2 52
2.3.1 Program Specifications 52
2.3.2 Program Design 53
2.3.3 Program Implementation 53

2.4 CREATING WIZARDS 57
2.4.1 College Registration Wizard Example 58

2.5 COMMON DIALOG CONTROL 59
2.5.1 ShowOpen, ShowSave Methods 60
2.5.2 Example: Selecting and Opening a File 61
2.5.3 Example: Saving a File 62
2.5.4 ShowColor Method 62
2.5.5 ShowFont Method 63

2.6 SAVING AND RETRIEVING REGISTRY SETTINGS 65
2.6.1 Viewing the System Registry 65
2.6.2 Visual Basic Procedures 67
2.6.3 SaveSetting Procedure 67
2.6.4 GetSetting Function 68
2.6.5 GetAllSettings Function 68
2.6.6 Example Program: Save/Retrieve Data Path 68

2.7 REVIEW QUESTIONS 69

2.8 CHAPTER EXERCISES 71
2.8.1 Mozart Music Common Dialog 71
2.8.2 Mozart Music Instruments 71

2.8.3 Mozart Music Color Settings 72
2.8.4 Mozart Music File and Directory Settings 72
2.8.5 Cleaning Equipment Rental Wizard 72
2.8.6 Hardbodies Health Club 73
2.8.7 Health Club Class Schedule 73
2.8.8 Depreciation Schedule 74
2.8.9 Time Clock Program 74
2.8.10 Classical Music Catalog - 1 76
2.8.11 Searching the Classical Music Catalog 76
2.8.12 College Registration Wizard 77

3 Objects and Collections 79

3.1 OBJECT VARIABLES 79
3.1.1 Declaring and Assigning Objects 80
3.1.2 Control Arrays 80
3.1.3 Creating a Control Array at Design Time 82
3.1.4 Filling a Control Array at Runtime 83

3.2 COLLECTIONS 84
3.2.1 Predefined Visual Basic Collections 84
3.2.2 Programmer-Defined Collections 85
3.2.3 Adding Objects to a Collection 86
3.2.4 Returning References to Members of a Collection 87
3.2.5 Removing Members of a Collection 88
3.2.6 Example: Resizing Controls on a Form 89

3.3 LISTVIEW CONTROL 91
3.3.1 Overview 91
3.3.2 Example: Music CD Collection Viewer 94

3.4 TREEVIEW CONTROL 96
3.4.1 Overview 96
3.4.2 Example: Interactively Building a Tree 98
3.4.3 Traversing and Saving the Tree 103
3.4.4 Attaching Icons to a TreeView Control 105

3.5 COOLBAR CONTROL 106
3.5.1 Properties 106
3.5.2 Example: CoolBar, ToolBar, ImageCombo, and Combo 106

3.6 CREATING MDI APPLICATIONS 112
3.6.1 Overview 112
3.6.2 Example: MDI Vehicle Reservations 115
3.6.3 Program Implementation 117

3.7 REVIEW QUESTIONS 119

3.8 CHAPTER EXERCISES 120
3.8.1 Jumping Button Program 120
3.8.2 The Buttons Control Array 120
3.8.3 Sorted Collection 121
3.8.4 Mozart MDI, Version 1 121
3.8.5 Mozart MDI, Version 2 122

3.8.6 Mozart MDI with a ListView 123
3.8.7 Mozart Music Using a CoolBar 123
3.8.8 Coolbar Editor - Version 1 123
3.8.9 Coolbar Editor - Version 2 123
3.8.10 Coolbar Editor - Version 3 123
3.8.11 Coolbar Editor – Version 4 124
3.8.12 Glossary Program - Version 1 124
3.8.13 Glossary Program - Version 2 126

4 Data-Bound Controls 127

4.1 TABLES AND DATABASES 127
4.1.1 Relational Databases 127
4.1.2 ActiveX Data Objects (ADO) 129
4.1.3 Using the ADO Data Control 130
4.1.4 Using Data-Bound Controls 131
4.1.5 ADODB Recordsets 133

4.2 SALES STAFF EXAMPLES 133
4.2.1 Displaying Records 134
4.2.2 Moving the Recordset Pointer 136
4.2.3 Adding, Deleting, and Updating Records 138
4.2.4 Sorting Records 139
4.2.5 Filtering Records 142
4.2.6 Using SQL to Create a Recordset 144
4.2.7 Using the Find Method 147
4.2.8 Displaying Images 149
4.2.9 ADO Control Events (optional) 151

4.3 DATAGRID, DATACOMBO AND DATALIST 153
4.3.1 Properties and Events 153
4.3.2 Example: Linking a DataList to a DataGrid 156
4.3.3 Example: DataCombo and DataGrid Controls 158

4.4 REVIEW QUESTIONS 160

4.5 CHAPTER EXERCISES 161
4.5.1 Mozart Music – 1 161
4.5.2 Mozart Music – 2 161
4.5.3 Mozart Music – 3 162
4.5.4 Mozart Music – 4 162
4.5.5 Mozart Music – 5 162
4.5.6 Mail-Order Computer Sales 163
4.5.7 Kyoshi Karate School - 1 163
4.5.8 Kyoshi Karate School - 2 166
4.5.9 Kyoshi Karate School – 3 168
4.5.10 Kyoshi Karate School – 4 169

5 ActiveX Data Objects (ADO) 171

5.1 USING THE DATA ENVIRONMENT DESIGNER 171

5.1.1 Hands-On Example 172

5.2 USING ACTIVEX DATA OBJECTS 174

5.2.1 Connections 175
5.2.2 Recordsets 177
5.2.3 Adding New Records 179
5.2.4 Modifying Existing Records 180
5.2.5 Deleting Records 181
5.2.6 Troubleshooting ActiveX Error Messages 182
5.2.7 SalesStaff Program Example 182
5.2.8 Loading SalesStaff into a ListView 185
5.2.9 Loading a ComboBox from a Recordset 188
5.2.10 Loading a TreeView from a Database 189
5.2.11 Creating Command Objects 192
5.2.12 Using Query Parameters 193

5.3 TRANSACTION PROCESSING 195

5.3.1 Example: Raising Employee Salaries 196

5.4 MULTI-USER DATABASE PROCESSING (OPTIONAL) 198

5.5 REVIEW QUESTIONS 200

5.6 CHAPTER EXERCISES 202

5.6.1 Products Table in a ListView 202
5.6.2 Products and Categories in a TreeView 202
5.6.3 Query Parameters 202
5.6.4 Doctors Office Scheduling – 1 202
5.6.5 Doctors Office Scheduling - 2 204
5.6.6 Doctors Office Scheduling - 3 205
5.6.7 Doctors Office Appointments - 4 205
5.6.8 Concert Hall Ticketing - 1 205
5.6.9 Concert Hall Ticketing - 2 207
5.6.10 Concert Hall Ticketing - 3 207
5.6.11 Concert Hall Ticketing - 4 207
5.6.12 Biblio TreeView 208
5.6.13 Computer Mail-Order Customer Data 208
5.6.14 Computer Mail-Order Invoice 208

6 Relational Databases and SQL 209

6.1 DATABASE DESIGN 210

6.1.1 Terminology 210
6.1.2 Designing a Database 210

6.2 USING THE SQL LANGUAGE 211

6.2.1 Structure of SQL Statements 212
6.2.2 A Sample Database 213
6.2.3 SELECT Statement 213
6.2.4 WHERE Clause 215
6.2.5 ORDER BY Clause 217
6.2.6 GROUP BY Clause 218
6.2.7 HAVING Clause 219

6.2.8 TOP Predicate 219
6.2.9 Calculated Columns 220
6.2.10 Logical Operators 221
6.2.11 Selecting from Multiple Tables 222
6.2.12 JOIN Clause 223
6.2.13 Creating Queries Using SQL Builder 225
6.2.14 Creating Queries in Microsoft Access 228

6.3 SQL DATA DEFINITION LANGUAGE (DDL) 229
6.3.1 CREATE TABLE 229
6.3.2 DROP TABLE/INDEX 230
6.3.3 ALTER TABLE 231
6.3.4 UPDATE 231
6.3.5 DELETE 232
6.3.6 INSERT INTO 232
6.3.7 CREATE INDEX 233

6.4 DDL PROGRAM EXAMPLE 234
6.4.1 Program Code 235

6.5 DESIGNING A CAR RENTAL DATABASE 238
6.5.1 Specifications 238
6.5.2 Vehicle Inventory 239
6.5.3 Models, Categories, and Status 240
6.5.4 Rental Prices 240
6.5.5 Customers, Reservations, and Invoices 242

6.6 VALIDATION RULES 242
6.6.1 Creating Validation Rules 244

6.7 TABLE RELATIONS 245
6.7.1 Creating Table Relations 247

6.8 DESIGNING THE INTERFACE 247
6.8.1 Running the Program 248

6.9 REVIEW QUESTIONS 251

6.10 CHAPTER EXERCISES 253
6.10.1 Stellar Car Rental - 1 253
6.10.2 Stellar Car Rental - 2 253
6.10.3 Stellar Car Rental - 3 253
6.10.4 Stellar Car Rental - 4 253
6.10.5 Stellar Car Rental – 5 253
6.10.6 Stellar Car Rental – 6 253
6.10.7 Doctors Office Scheduling - 1 254
6.10.8 Searching for Books with SQL 254
6.10.9 Yachting Regatta Program - 1 254
6.10.10 Yachting Regatta Program - 2 255
6.10.11 Yachting Regatta - 3 256

7 DataReport, MSHFlexGrid, and MSChart 259

7.1 DATA REPORT DESIGNER 259

7.1.1 DataReport Objects 260
7.1.2 Building a Report Application 262
7.1.3 Author Table Example 265
7.1.4 Building a Report Using SQL 267
7.1.5 Joining the Titles and Publishers Tables 268
7.1.6 Reports with Groups 270
7.1.7 Grouping by Creating Summary Fields 273
7.1.8 Showing Reports from ADO Connections in Program Code 275
7.1.9 One Record Per Page 278

7.2 HIERARCHICAL FLEXGRID CONTROL 278

7.2.1 Binding to a Data Environment 279
7.2.2 Properties and Methods 281
7.2.3 Displaying Hierarchical Data in a Report 283

7.3 MSCHART CONTROL 285

7.3.1 Simple MSChart Example 285
7.3.2 MSChart with Labels 286
7.3.3 Interactively Filling a Chart at Run Time 286
7.3.4 Binding a Chart to an ADO Control 291

7.4 REVIEW QUESTIONS 293

7.5 PROGRAMMING EXERCISES 295

7.5.1 NorthWind - 1 295
7.5.2 NorthWind - 2 296
7.5.3 NorthWind - 3 296
7.5.4 NorthWind - 4 296
7.5.5 NorthWind - 5 296
7.5.6 NorthWind – 6 297
7.5.7 Mail-Order Computer Sales 297
7.5.8 Kyoshi Karate School - 1 297
7.5.9 Kyoshi Karate School - 2 297
7.5.10 Kyoshi Karate School - 3 297
7.5.11 Kyoshi Karate School - 4 298
7.5.12 MSChart Interactive 298

8 Creating Class Modules 301

8.1 CLASSES AND OBJECTS 301

8.1.1 Object-Oriented Design 302
8.1.2 Class Modules 304
8.1.3 Creating Instances of a Class 305
8.1.4 Properties 306
8.1.5 Event Handlers 309
8.1.6 Methods 310

8.2 STUDENT CLASS EXAMPLE 310

8.2.1 Program Design 310
8.2.2 Program Implementation 311

8.3 STUDENT COLLECTION CLASS 314

8.3.1 Program Design 314

8.3.2 The Main Form 314
8.3.3 The CStudent Class 316
8.3.4 The CStudentCollection Class 316

8.4 CLIENT-SERVER EXAMPLE: RENTAL RATES 318
8.4.1 Client-Server Design 318
8.4.2 Client Program 319
8.4.3 CRentalPrices Class 320
8.4.4 Creating an ActiveX Server 321
8.4.5 Registering and Unregistering Components 323

8.5 DOCTORS OFFICE SCHEDULING 325
8.5.1 Program Specifications 325
8.5.2 User Interface Design 325
8.5.3 Class Interfaces 327
8.5.4 Class Relationships 328
8.5.5 Program Code 330

8.6 REVIEW QUESTIONS 340

8.7 CHAPTER EXERCISES 342
8.7.1 Student Collection: Searching for Names 342
8.7.2 Saving the Student Collection 342
8.7.3 Student Collection: Completed Courses 342
8.7.4 Student Collection: The CCourse Class 342
8.7.5 Object-Oriented Glossary Program 343
8.7.6 CMotor Class 343
8.7.7 CMotorCollection Class 344
8.7.8 Mozart Music: CInvoice Class 344
8.7.9 Object-Oriented Time Clock 344
8.7.10 E-Mail Address Book 344
8.7.11 Yachting Regatta – 1 345
8.7.12 Yachting Regatta - 2 345
8.7.13 Yachting Regatta - 3 347
8.7.14 Yachting Regatta - 4 347
8.7.15 Doctors Office Scheduling 347

9 Creating ActiveX Components 349

9.1 ACTIVEX COMPONENTS 350
9.1.1 Types of Objects Provided by Components 350
9.1.2 ActiveX Controls 351

9.2 STUDENTIDTEXT ACTIVEX CONTROL 352
9.2.1 Creating a Test Program 354
9.2.2 Adding Events to the Control 356
9.2.3 Resizing the Control 357
9.2.4 Making the Control Data-Bound 357
9.2.5 Using a DataRepeater Control 360

9.3 ADDAPPOINTMENT ACTIVEX CONTROL 361
9.3.1 Program Specifications 361
9.3.2 User Interface 362

9.3.3 Client Program 362
9.3.4 Saving and Restoring Properties 363
9.3.6 Implementing Property Procedures 365
9.3.7 AddAppointment Source Code 366
9.3.8 Client Program Listing 368

9.4 USING THE ACTIVEX CONTROL WIZARD 369
9.4.1 Running the Wizard 369
9.4.2 Wizard-Generated Source Code 371
9.4.3 Customizing the Source Code 374
9.4.4 Test Program 376

9.5 USING THE ACTIVEX PROPERTY PAGE WIZARD 377
9.5.1 Property Pages for the OptionGroup Control 377

9.6 CREATING AN ACTIVEX DLL 381
9.6.1 The DoctorSchedule DLL 381
9.6.2 Client Program Implementation 382
9.6.3 Instancing Property 384
9.6.4 Global Data 385
9.6.5 CSchedule Class 385
9.6.6 CAppointment Class 387
9.6.7 CPatient Class 388
9.6.8 Testing the Compiled Component 388

9.7 CREATING AN OUT-OF-PROCESS COMPONENT 389
9.7.1 Converting DoctorSchedule to ActiveX EXE Server 389
9.7.2 Where to Go from Here 390

9.8 REVIEW QUESTIONS 391

9.9 CHAPTER EXERCISES 393
9.9.1 StudentInfo Control - 1 393
9.9.2 StudentInfo Control - 2 393
9.9.3 AddAppointment Control - 1 393
9.9.4 AddAppointment Control - 2 393
9.9.5 AddAppointment Control - 3 393
9.9.6 Stellar Car Rentals - 1 394
9.9.7 Stellar Car Rentals - 2 394
9.9.8 Stellar Car Rentals - 3 394
9.9.9 Stellar Car Rentals - 4 394
9.9.10 OptionList Control – 1 394
9.9.11 OptionList Control – 2 395
9.9.12 OptionList Control – 3 395
9.9.13 OptionList Control – 4 395
9.9.14 Publisher ActiveX Control 395

10 Using OLE and ActiveX Servers 397

10.1 OLE CONTAINERS AND ACTIVEX SERVERS 397
10.1.1 Object Linking and Embedding 398

10.2 OLE CONTAINER CONTROL 399

10.2.1 Example: Creating an Embedded Word Object 399
10.2.2 Example: Creating an Embedded Excel Worksheet 402
10.2.3 Hands-on Chart Example 402
10.2.4 CreateLink Method 405

10.3 OLE CONTAINER PROGRAM 406
10.3.1 Creating a New Excel Worksheet 407
10.3.2 Inserting an Excel Worksheet 407
10.3.3 Inserting a Word Document 407
10.3.4 Program Implementation 407

10.4 USING MS-OFFICE CODE COMPONENTS 410
10.4.1 Visual Basic for Applications 410
10.4.2 Example: Creating a Word Document 410
10.4.3 Word Classes, Properties, and Methods 412
10.4.4 Using the Excel ActiveX Server 416
10.4.5 Excel: Statistical Score Analysis 417

10.5 COLLEGE ADMISSIONS PROGRAM 420
10.5.1 Program Specifications 420
10.5.2 Program Design 420
10.5.3 Program Implementation 423
10.5.4 Conclusion 428

10.6 REVIEW QUESTIONS 428

10.7 CHAPTER EXERCISES 430
10.7.1 Mozart Music Instruments 430
10.7.2 Hardbodies Health Club 430
10.7.3 Depreciation Schedule 431
10.7.4 Family Photo Album 432
10.7.5 Personal Stock Portfolio - 1 433
10.7.6 Personal Stock Portfolio - 2 434

11 Tapping Into the Windows API 437

11.1 DLL PROCEDURES 437
11.1.1 The Need for External Procedures 437
11.1.1 Static and Dynamic Linking 438

11.2 DECLARING AND CALLING DLL PROCEDURES 439
11.2.1 The Declare Statement 439
11.2.2 The API Viewer Utility Program 439
11.2.3 Example: Flashing a Window Caption 440

11.3 PARAMETERS IN DLL PROCEDURES 442
11.3.1 String Parameters 443
11.3.2 Numeric Parameters 443
11.3.3 User-Defined Types 444
11.3.4 Example: GetWindowsDirectory 445

11.4 GETTING DISK DRIVE INFORMATION 446

11.5 BLENDING COLOR ACROSS A FORM 450

11.6 SETTING TAB STOPS IN A LISTBOX 453
11.6.1 User Interface 454
11.6.2 Program Source Code 455

11.7 REVIEW QUESTIONS 457

11.8 CHAPTER EXERCISES 458
11.8.1 BlendColor Program 458
11.8.2 DriveInfo Program 458
11.8.3 Karate School MDI 458
11.8.4 Playing WAV Files 458
11.8.5 Selecting and Playing WAV Files 458
11.8.6 Keeping a Window On Top 458
11.8.6 Adjusting ListView Column Widths 459

12 Internet Programming 461

12.1 INTERNET TRANSFER CONTROL 462
12.1.1 Properties 462
12.1.2 Methods 462
12.1.3 Events 462
12.1.4 HTML Viewer Example 462
12.1.5 Downloading Files from an FTP Site 468
12.1.6 FTP Browser Program Implementation 468

12.2 DYNAMIC HTML 474
12.2.1 Overview 474
12.2.2 Dynamic HTML Events 474
12.2.3 Keyboard Events 475
12.2.4 Mouse Events 475
12.2.5 Focus and Selection Events 475
12.2.6 Other DHTML Events 476

12.3 USING THE DHTML PAGE DESIGNER 477
12.3.1 Creating the DHTML Pages 477
12.3.2 Coding a Command Button 478
12.3.3 Importing Existing HTML Pages 480
12.3.4 Managing Program State Between DHTML Pages 482

12.4 ACME CAR RENTAL EXAMPLE 483
12.4.1 Design 484
12.4.2 Car Rental Program, Page 1 485
12.4.3 Car Rental Program, Page 2 486
12.4.4 Car Rental Program, Page 3 487
12.4.5 Summary 488

12.5 WINSOCK CONTROL 488
12.5.1 Comparing TCP and UDP Protocols 488
12.5.2 Winsock Properties 489
12.5.3 Winsock Events 490
12.5.4 Winsock Client-Server Example 490
12.5.5 FrmSwitchboard Implementation 491
12.5.6 FrmClient Implementation 492

12.5.7 FrmServer Implementation 494

12.6 CREATING HTML HELP 495
12.6.1 Introduction 495
12.6.2 Creating HTML files with Microsoft Word 496
12.6.3 Creating the Main Help Window 497
12.6.4 Creating a Table of Contents 498
12.6.5 Creating an Index File 498
12.6.6 Compiling a Help Project 501
12.6.7 Hooking HTML Help to a Visual Basic Program 501
12.6.8 Creating a Frameset 501
12.6.9 Contents HTML File 502
12.6.10 Index HTML File 503
12.6.11 Visual Basic Host Program 503
12.6.12 Advantages to Using HTML Help 505

12.7 REVIEW QUESTIONS 505

12.8 PROGRAMMING EXERCISES 506
12.8.1 HTMLViewer - 1 506
12.8.2 HTMLViewer - 2 506
12.8.3 Winsock with Multiple Connections 506
12.8.4 Mortgage Calculator Program 507
12.8.5 Factoring a Number 508
12.8.6 Dynamic Changing HTML Page 508
12.8.7 Tic-Tac-Toe On Networked Computers 508

Appendix A: Visual Basic Review 511

A.1 COMPETENCY REVIEW TEST 512

A.2 DATA TYPES, VARIABLES, AND CONSTANTS 514
A.2.1 Data Types 514
A.2.2 Boolean 514
A.2.3 Byte, Integer, Long 514
A.2.4 Single, Double, Currency 515
A.2.5 String 516
A.2.6 Date 516
A.2.7 Object 517
A.2.8 Variant 517
A.2.9 Declared Constants 517
A.2.10 Static Arrays 518
A.2.11 Dynamic Arrays 518
A.2.12 Collections 519
A.2.13 User-Defined Types 519

A.3 IF STATEMENTS 520
A.3.1 Compound Expressions (And, Or, Not) 520
A.3.2 Block IF Statement 520
A.3.3 Using ELSE 520
A.3.4 Select Case 521

A.4 LOOPS 522

A.4.1 For-Next Statement 522
A.4.2 Do-While Statement 523
A.4.3 Do-Until Statement 523
A.4.4 While-Wend Statement 524

A.5 PROCEDURES 524
A.5.1 Declaring a Subroutine Procedure 524
A.5.2 Procedure Parameters 525
A.5.3 Declaring a Function Procedure 526
A.5.4 Passing Arguments by Reference 527
A.5.5 Passing Arguments by Value 528
A.5.6 Private and Public 528
A.5.7 Optional Parameters 529
A.5.8 Parameter Arrays 529

A.6 STRING HANDLING 530

A.7 FORMS 531
A.7.1 Form Properties 532
A.7.2 Form Methods 534
A.7.3 Form Events 536
A.7.4 Sample Form-Loading Program 539

A.8 STANDARD VISUAL BASIC CONTROLS 541
A.8.1 Label 541
A.8.2 Text 541
A.8.3 CommandButton 541
A.8.4 OptionButton 542
A.8.5 Frame 542
A.8.6 CheckBox 542
A.8.7 Image 543
A.8.8 Line 544
A.8.9 Timer 544
A.8.10 ScrollBar 544
A.8.11 ListBox and ComboBox 545

A.9 TOOLS FOR INPUT-OUTPUT 547
A.9.1 Print Method 547
A.9.2 Format Function 548
A.9.3 MsgBox Procedure 549
A.9.4 MsgBox Function 550
A.9.5 InputBox Function 551
A.9.6 Printer Object 552
A.9.7 Screen Object 553
A.9.8 Application Object 553

A.10 CREATING MENUS 554
A.10.1 Common Menu Types 554
A.10.2 Creating a Simple Menu 554
A.10.3 Menu Properties 555

A.11 ANSWERS TO THE COMPETENCY TEST QUESTIONS 557

Appendix B: Sequential and Random Files 561

B.1 SEQUENTIAL FILES 561
B.1.1 Basic Syntax 561
B.1.2 Reading From an Input File 562
B.1.3 Writing to an Output File 564

B.2 RANDOM ACCESS FILES 565
B.2.1 Opening a File 566
B.2.2 Writing Records 566
B.2.3 Reading Records 566

B.3 CUSTOMER ACCOUNTS PROGRAM EXAMPLE 567
B.3.1 Program Design 567
B.3.2 Program Implementation 568

Appendix C: Answers to Odd-Numbered Review Questions 571

C.1 CHAPTER 1 571

C.2 CHAPTER 2 572

C.3 CHAPTER 3 572

C.4 CHAPTER 4 573

C.5 CHAPTER 5 574

C.6 CHAPTER 6 575

C.7 CHAPTER 7 576

C.8 CHAPTER 8 577

C.9 CHAPTER 9 578

C.10 CHAPTER 10 579

C.11 CHAPTER 11 580

C.12 CHAPTER 12 580

Index 583

1 Designing and Coding Programs

Chapter Contents

Application Development Cycle
- Interviewing Mangagement and Users
- Creating Program Specifications
- Performing a Feasability Review
- Designing the Application
- Design Goals
- Implementing the Application
- Testing the Application

User Interface Design
- Avoiding Crowding Forms
- Setting the Tab Order
- Keyboard Input
- Using Standard Menus

Coding Guidelines
- Declaring Variables and Constants
- Naming Variables and Constants
- Naming Controls
- Naming Procedures and Methods
- Indenting Code
- Line Continuation
- App Object Properties

Error Handling
- Causes of Errors
- On Error GoTo Statement
- Resume Statement
- Using the Err Object

Reducing Code Size

Improving Execution Speed
- Code Optimization
- Display Optimization
- Perceived Speed Optimization

Review Questions

Chapter Exercises

1.1 APPLICATION DEVELOPMENT CYCLE

1.1.1 Interviewing Management and Users

Some programs are designed, coded, tested, and installed before their users even get to see the programs. Any suggestions or input are useless at that point, unless the design team is willing to re-engineer the programs. Needless to say, such programs do not generate a lot of support from the very people who will use them!

A good designer talks to the people who will actually use the software. The designer analyzes the application's requirements, and in many cases, involves one or more users in helping to design the program's visual interface. At the same time, a company's management will generally know what types of input and output information are needed for the application. Often, this knowledge will have to be built over a period of interviews, demonstrations, brainstorming sessions, and thoughtful analysis. Open and candid communication is essential between the designer and users at all levels.

1.1.2 Creating Program Specifications

Using the application requirements, the designer, along with management, will generate a list of specifications. The specifications spell out, item by item, what the program will do. For a very simple program, the specifications may be only a single paragraph; for a complex program, the specifications may resemble a legal document. Here, for example, are the specifications for a simple program that we will write in Chapter 2, called Mozart Music Sales:

The Mozart Music Store needs a simple invoice program that can be filled in by a store clerk (the *user*) when a compact disc or cassette tape is purchased. In our store, we use a 5-digit SKU number to uniquely identify all items.

On startup, the program displays the current date so that it may be verified by the store clerk. When the user selects a SKU number from an existing list of numbers, the program displays the album title that matches the number. The clerk looks at the item for a label indicating one of three price codes (A, B, or C) and enters the same code into the computer by clicking with the mouse. The clerk also selects the recording format (CD or tape). The program immediately calculates the sale amount, tax, and net price. The user can also click on a check box if the customer is entitled to a 10% discount. When the user decides to quit the program, the program confirms before terminating.

1.1.3 Performing a Feasibility Review

While the specifications are being developed, an experienced designer will be conducting an ongoing "reality check". This involves not only a knowledge of the application itself, but the strengths and weaknesses of Visual Basic. In addition, most designers do a considerable amount of research learning about the hundreds of third-party products that enhance the capabilities of Visual Basic.

Can the application requirements be met, given the available hardware and software? In general, 32-bit Visual Basic applications require 16 MB of RAM to run adequately, preferably on a Pentium or higher processor. Programs running on a network have more demanding database server requirements than stand-alone programs.

Is there enough time to design, code, and test the program? Deadlines should be set for each phase of the project: specifications, design, coding, and testing. If any of these steps end up being repeated, all subsequent deadlines must be renegotiated.

Are there enough programmers (particularly with experience in developing similar applications in Visual Basic) involved in the project? This is an important consideration, because every project needs a designer or programmer who can avoid the costly mistakes that result from inexperience. It is generally unwise to expect even an experienced programmer to learn Visual Basic and write a professional application at the same time. Invariably, code written at the beginning of the project will have to be rewritten near the end of the project, once the programmer has discovered better ways of doing things.

Extra time must be included for fixing bugs and providing for at least a minimal set of modifications that are outside of the original specifications.

1.1.4 Designing the Application

During the design phase of the project, the project specifications are translated into a detailed description of the program in terms that programmers can understand. Programmers are not expected to know anything about the application domain, for instance, so any special processing requirements must be spelled out. The design includes descriptions and examples of input/output data, illustrations of sample screens and reports, and data validation requirements.

Visual Design. Another aspect of the design is the visual component of the program. This can be achieved by creating the forms and controls even before any code has been written. This technique is called *prototyping*, and helps the client or user of the program visualize the finished product.

Procedural Design. The designer can use a procedural approach, which involves breaking down the program specifications into a hierarchy of high- and low-level *tasks*, or *processes*. This is the traditional method, used with success over the last 30-40 years, but it suffers from one major drawback: the program structure is greatly influenced by restrictions in the programming language, rather than being a reflection of the physical entities that make up the application. Procedural designs are gradually being replaced by object-oriented designs as computer languages evolve.

Object-Oriented Design. This approach to design focuses on the physical entities that make up an application problem. The design emphasizes the interactions between objects, as well as the responsibilities and characteristics of objects. In the design of a doctor's office scheduling program, for instance, the physical entities might be the Patient, Doctor, Schedule, and Appointment. Each of these could be translated into a class, with methods and properties. A Schedule class might have the following methods and properties:

Methods:

AddNewAppointment
RemoveAppointment
ShowAllAppointments
ShowAppointmentsByDoctor

Properties:

Appointments (a collection of Appointment objects)
NumberOfAppointments
LastUpdate (date when schedule was last updated)

A *method* represents an action that may be performed by the object, or a message that might be sent or received by the object. Methods are implemented as procedures. A *property* is a data value stored inside the object. Properties can have built-in validity checks, to make sure they always have reasonable values.

1.1.5 Design Goals

There are some basic goals to strive for when designing programs:

Simplicity. The design and user interface should be as *simple* as possible, while still fulfilling all of the program specifications. Avoid cluttering designs with lots of unnecessary features. A simple design can more easily be communicated between programmers and designers. In a Visual Basic program, simplicity is important in both the visual design and the design of the code inside modules, forms, and classes.

Flexibility. A well-executed design is *flexible* enough to accommodate the inevitable changes that will occur during the lifetime of the application. Changes may appear at the specification level, design level, or implementation level. Each change has a cascading effect on the levels after it, so a change to the program specifications will affect the design, which will in turn affect the implementation. On the other hand, a change to the program's implementation will generally not affect the design.

Extensibility. Well-designed software is *extensible,* meaning that additions of new features at both the large-scale level and at the detailed level are possible without destroying the original program. We extend Visual Basic programs by adding new modules, forms, and classes, and by modifying the procedures, methods, and properties of existing code.

Reusability. When the same code can be moved from one program to other programs, we say that it is *reusable*. This can be achieved in Visual Basic by encapsulating code inside class modules, and by loading these modules into multiple projects. In particular, the use of OLE automation servers and ActiveX controls makes it easier to allow many programs to share the same executable program code. The concept of *plug-in components* is fundamental to Visual Basic, beginning with the ActiveX controls in the toolbox window.

1.1.6 Implementing the Application

The *implementation phase* of a software project is usually what the programmers have been waiting for. The program design has been built from the specifications, the visual interface has been evaluated and approved by the users, and the project has been determined to be feasible. All projected deadlines are reasonable, adequate programming and testing personnel have been brought into the project, and any required software tools have been purchased and mastered.

Programming Teams. If a team of programmers is creating the application, each programmer will be assigned certain sections of the program to work on. Some might develop classes and objects that will be used by other project members. Others will be involved in fully developing the visual interface. Generally, a project leader will coordinate the actions of the programmers. Procedures will be established for the sharing of source code among the team, using library software such as *SourceSafe,* which is distributed with the Visual Basic Enterprise Edition. This software allows the tracking of changes made by programmers, rebuilding previous versions of the software, and checking source code modules in and out of a library. Strict coding guidelines are important at this phase, to ensure that all source code in the application has the same naming convention and a similar look and feel.

Allow for Changes. In the best of all possible worlds, once a program's specifications and design were approved by a client, no more changes would be made to the program. This would be great, but clients, who are usually not programmers themselves, often expect changes to be made at the last minute. If the consultant/programmer appears to be too rigid in not allowing changes to be made, the client may possibly dislike the final product. Most consultants get used to the idea that last-minute changes will be made, and build this cost into the original consulting fee. Fortunately, Visual Basic programs lend themselves well to visual modifications. Deeper, structural modifications are much more difficult, because they may involve moving large blocks of code between modules, creating new modules, redesigning classes, and so on.

1.1.7 Testing the Application

The testing phase of the application's development is in many ways the most important. This is the last point at which designers can verify that the program accomplishes the tasks outlined by the program specifications. Possible design flaws might be uncovered at this point, requiring a modification to the design and re-coding of certain parts of the program.

Companies with experience in developing high-quality software have strict procedures in place for the design, documentation, coding, and testing of software. Often a separate testing department will thoroughly test daily updates of the software, document each bug they find, and pass this information on to the programmers. After each bug is fixed, the same section of software must be re-tested, to ensure that new bugs were not created in the process of fixing existing bugs.

A *test suite* should be created for the program; this is a sequenced series of inputs designed to fully exercise the program and uncover any flaws. There are independent companies who only test other companies' software. They have considerable experience in developing high-quality test suites.

An ongoing problem in software development is the lack of adequate testing. Programming shops in small companies often have no formal testing procedures. In extreme cases, the programmer is given no assistance in the design, documentation, and testing phases of a project. Most programmers like to write programs, and are not likely to create great documentation and/or user manuals.

In small shops, the testing of the program is often left up to the programmer who wrote the actual code. This is a mistake, because most programmers tend to run their programs the same way, with the same types of inputs. A user who knows nothing about the program makes a much better tester, because he/she will provide unanticipated inputs and actions. Often, the intense pressure of constant deadlines imposed by management tends to make programmers release code into production before it is adequately tested.

1.2 USER INTERFACE DESIGN

The user interface of a program is that part of the program that interacts with users. It usually incorporates various types of input from the keyboard and mouse. Output will usually be to the screen or printer. Over the years, applications written for Windows 3.1, Windows 95, Windows 98, and Windows NT have established a standard look and feel. Microsoft publishes guidelines for the design of windows, menus, dialog boxes, and so on. Good sources of examples can be found in the Microsoft Office applications such as Word, Excel, Access, PowerPoint, and Project. The following topics consist of suggestions that you might want to follow.

1.2.1 Avoiding Crowding Forms

When you place controls too close together on a form, you give the impression of crowding, and the user has to work harder at focusing on information that is most important. If you really have a lot of information to display, or your program requires a great deal of input from the user, consider some alternatives.

Divide the form into several different forms, all accessible from a starting form. Use command buttons or a menu to let the user show the other forms. Provide hints on the starting form as to what the other forms contain, so the user will not have to spend a lot of time searching for the desired form.

Use the custom Microsoft Tabbed Dialog control (Figure 1) to overlay groups of controls on the same form. Each group of controls appears on a separate tab, similar to the tabs on a set of file folders. For example we can place a customer's address on one tab, and show his list of payments and credits on separate tabs. Any buttons that affect the entire form, however, should be separate from the Microsoft Tabbed Dialog control.

Watch Your Form's Size. A common problem occurs when you create a program on a computer with a high-resolution monitor, and then run the program on a low-resolution monitor. Many programmers work in 1024 x 768 mode (or higher), but their program users use a standard 640 x 480 VGA monitor. The result is that forms appear only partially on the screen, or are too large for the screen. Of course, you should always test your programs in standard VGA mode before delivering them to end-users. You can also calculate the size of any window at runtime, using the Width, Screen.TwipsPerPixelX, Height, and Screen.TwipsPerPixelY properties. For example, the following statements calculate the current form's height and width, in pixels, and display an error message if either is too large:

```
If (Width / Screen.TwipsPerPixelX) > 640 Then
  MsgBox "Form is too wide."
End If
If (Height / Screen.TwipsPerPixelY) > 480 Then
  MsgBox "Form is too tall."
End If
```

This code can be placed in the Form_Load event handler of a form. *Note:* you can optionally use the notation **Me.Height** to show that the Height property refers to the current form.

1.2.2 Setting the Tab Order

Every control that involves user input has a property called TabStop, which can be either True or False. If this property is True, the user can press the Tab key to move to this control when the program is running. The TabIndex property allows you to set the order in which

Figure 1. SSTab Control Example.

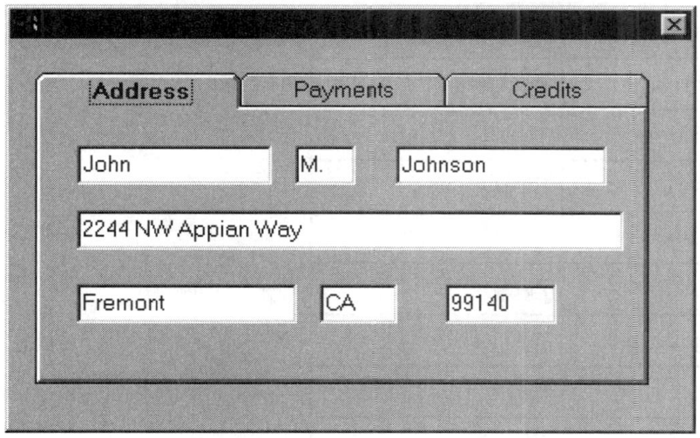

controls will receive the focus when the user tabs between controls. After all of the controls have been positioned on your form, you should give some attention to the order of tab stops. Start with the control that you want the user to begin with; set its TabIndex to 0. Then move to the next control in the desired tab order, and set its TabIndex to 1, and so on.

A group of OptionButton controls presents a special case when dealing with tab stops. The buttons should have their TabIndex values numbered sequentially. But when you run the program, notice that you can use the Tab key to move only to the first button in the group (the one with the lowest TabStop value). To move to the other buttons, you have to use the keyboard arrow keys. Pressing the Tab key will just take you to the next control following the group of option buttons.

1.2.3 Keyboard Input

When it has the focus, a control has the ability to respond to keyboard keys. The following event procedures trap keyboard events, shown here for a list box named List1:

```
Private Sub List1_KeyPress(KeyAscii As Integer)
Private Sub List1_KeyDown(KeyCode As Integer, Shift As Integer)
Private Sub List1_KeyUp(KeyCode As Integer, Shift As Integer)
```

The **KeyPress** event interprets ANSI characters only, so it is used for standard keyboard keys such as ‘A’, ‘7’, Enter, Tab, Backspace, and so on. If the user will be pressing an extended key (F1-F12, Ins, Del, arrow keys, Home, End, and so on), the KeyPress event will not be activated.

The **KeyDown** and **KeyUp** event procedures respond to the pressing and releasing of extended keyboard keys, respectively, ones that are generally non-displayable. When the key is pressed, the KeyCode parameter contains a numeric value that your program can act on. Table 1 shows a list of the more common keyboard constants along with their matching descriptions.

You can easily retrieve these values and paste them in your programs, using the View/Object Browser menu command. Look under “Visual Basic Objects and Procedures”, and look in the sub-category “KeyCodeConstants”. For example, the

Table 1. Keyboard Constants.

Constant	Description
vbKeyBack	Backspace
vbKeyTab	Tab
vbKeyReturn	Enter
vbKeyEscape	Esc
vbKeyPageUp	PgUp
vbKeyPageDn	PgDn
vbKeyEnd	End
vbKeyHome	Home
vbKeyLeft	Left arrow
vbKeyUp	Up arrow
vbKeyRight	Right arrow
vbKeyDown	Down arrow
vbKeyInsert	Insert
vbKeyDelete	Delete
vbKeyF1	F1 function
vbKeyF2	F2 function
...	...
vbKeyF12	F12 function

following event procedure would be activated if the user pressed a key while the list box had the focus:

```
Private Sub List1_KeyDown(KeyCode As Integer, Shift As Integer)
    If KeyCode = vbKeyDelete Then
        mnuMemberRemove_Click
    End If
End Sub
```

These statements call the mnuMemberRemove_Click procedure when the user presses the Delete key. All other keys are ignored. The Shift parameter can be used to check if the user was holding down the Shift, Ctrl and/or Alt keys.

1.2.4 Using Standard Menus

The menus of applications written for Microsoft Windows have a standard look and feel. This is in a large part due to the fact that many of the menu names are standardized. Microsoft Word, for example, contains the menus listed in Table 2. Of course, most Visual

Basic applications will not have the same menus; but whenever program operations can be logically grouped under these categories, standard menu names should be used.

1.2.5 Dragging and Dropping

The easiest way to move screen objects from one place to another has always been dragging and dropping, using the mouse. You can easily implement this kind of behavior in your own programs. When the uses clicks the mouse button, the first event to be generated is the **MouseDown** event, where it is customary to call the object's Drag method. In the following example, an Image control called **imgSource** responds to MouseDown by activating the Drag method and setting its DragIcon property to its own Picture value:

```
Private Sub imgSource_MouseDown(Button As Integer, Shift _
        As Integer, X As Single, Y As Single)
  imgSource.Drag
  imgSource.DragIcon = imgSource.Picture
End Sub
```

Any other icon or bitmap might have been used as the DragIcon, of course. This property controls what the user sees when dragging begins. The DragIcon can also be set at design time. Another essential event to trap is the **DragDrop** event, which is implemented for any control that will be receiving the dragged item. The Form itself can also respond to a DragDrop event.

Dragging Between ListBoxes. The DragDrop methods also work for ListBoxes. The user selects a line from a source ListBox and drops it in the destination ListBox. When the user holds down the mouse on an item in the source ListBox, we begin the **Drag** method:

```
Private Sub lstSource_MouseDown(Button As Integer, _
        Shift As Integer, X As Single, Y As Single)
  lstSource.Drag
End Sub
```

When the dragged item has found its source location, the **DragDrop** handler is active:

```
Private Sub lstDest_DragDrop(Source As Control, _
   X As Single, Y As Single)
  If lstSource.ListIndex = -1 Then Exit Sub
  lstDest.AddItem lstSource.Text
  lstSource.RemoveItem lstSource.ListIndex
End Sub
```

1.3 CODING GUIDELINES

Nobody writes perfect program code, of course, and among any group of experienced programmers one is bound to encounter a variety of opinions about what constitutes "good" coding style. But there are certain characteristics that seem to be universal: consistency, readability, and logical structure. The suggestions presented in this section are just that--suggestions, based on recommendations by Microsoft, ideas from other programmers and authors, and the authors' personal experiences.

Table 2. Microsoft Word Menu Sample.

Name	Description/Choices
File	New, Open, Close, Save, Save As, Print, Print Preview, file history list.
Edit	Undo, Cut, Copy, Paste, Clear, Select All, Find, Replace, Go To.
View	Lets the user switch between different formats, or views of the information in the current window.
Insert	Insert application-specific data into the current window.
Format	Change the style or appearance of data in the current window.
Tools	Application-specific tools, set program options.
Window	New, tile, cascade, split, show list of open windows.
Help	Contents, index, context-sensitive help, about the application.

1.3.1 Declaring Variables and Constants

It's easy to make a mistake when typing the names of variables and constants. If you use the **Option Explicit** command in the declarations section of all modules, Visual Basic will flag the misspelling before the program runs. If you omit this command, a brand-new variable will be created when the program runs, which is probably not what you intended. This type of error is quite difficult to catch, particularly in large programs. Option Explicit can be automatically placed in each new module as it is created: select the Tools/Options menu command, click on the Editor tab, and check the "Require Variable Declaration" option.

1.3.2 Naming Variables and Constants

For identifiers defined at the global or form level, always choose identifier names that are descriptive, because you will have to remember these names as you are writing the program, and later, when you or anyone else returns to the program to perform maintenance.

Table 3 contains both good and bad examples of variable names. Variable names inside procedures should also be meaningful if possible, particularly in longer procedures where the variable is used quite a bit. On the other hand, variables used for loop counters and those holding temporary values need not be descriptive. For example, a loop counter called j is perfectly acceptable because its usage is clear from the context:

```
Dim j As Integer
For j = 1 To QuestionCount
  '....
Next j
```

In the *Visual Basic Programmers Guide*, Microsoft recommends using standard prefixes at the beginnings of variables and constants that indicate their type (Table 4).

Table 3. Examples of Variable Names.

Good	Poor
lastName	lname
transactionCount	tcount
numQuestionsAsked	numQA
hourlyPayRate	rate
highestScore	high_s

Microsoft also recommends using a scope prefix at the beginning of identifiers: g = global, m = module, (no prefix) = local. Table 5 lists examples of variables that use both prefixes. The most important principle is that once you create a system, be consistent.

1.3.3 Naming Controls

It's a good idea to use standard prefixes for form, control, and menu names, to help identify them in program code. The default names given to controls such as Form1, Command1, and Option1 are not descriptive enough to be a help in understanding their

Table 4. Standard Prefixes for Variables.

Data Type	Prefix	Example
Boolean	bln	blnFound
Byte	byt	bytRasterData
Collection object	col	colWidgets
Currency	cur	curRevenue
Date (Time)	dtm	dtmStart
Double	dbl	dblTolerance
Error	err	errOrderNum
Integer	int	intQuantity
Long	lng	lngDistance
Object	obj	objCurrent
Single	sng	sngAverage
String	str	strFName
User-defined type	udt	udtEmployee
Variant	vnt	vntCheckSum

Table 5. Recommended Scope Prefixes.

Global	Module	Local
gblnFileFound	mblnFileFound	blnFileFound
gcurSalary	mcurSalary	curSalary
gstrLastName	mstrLastName	strLastName

purpose within the program. You definitely do not want to use names that look like ordinary variables. Table 6 contains a list of standard prefixes for forms, menus, and other controls, suggested by the *Visual Basic Programmers Guide*.

1.3.4 Naming Procedures and Methods

Procedures and methods are action statements, so their names should contain verbs. Can you tell which of the following procedure names correctly convey their meaning, and which names are somewhat cryptic?

```
1       CalculateWeeklyPay
2       WeeklyPay
3       AverageAllScores
4       AverageScore
5       LookUpPurchasePrice
6       LUPP
7       RandomizeButtons
8       RndButtons
9       AddNewRecord
10      NewRecord
```

Some of these names appear to be variables or constants, because they don't imply any action. If you guessed that the odd-numbered names were the best, you're right!

1.3.5 Indenting Code

Always indent statements inside loops and If statements. Nothing is more annoying to read than a program containing nested loops and If statements that does not use proper indentation. For example, the following code has no indentation. Does it make any sense?

```
Do While Not EOF(fileNum)
Input #fileNum, payRate, hours
If payRate > 0 Then
If hours > 0 Then
weeklyPay = hours * payRate
lblWeeklyPay = Format$(weeklyPay, "currency")
Else
MsgBox "Hours are invalid", vbInformation, "Error"
End If
Else
MsgBox "Rate is invalid", vbInformation, "Error"
End If
Loop
```

Table 6. Microsoft-Suggested Prefixes for Controls.

Control Type	Prefix	Example
3D Panel	pnl	pnlGroup
ADO data	ado	adoBiblio
Animated button	ani	aniMailBox
Check box	chk	chkReadOnly
Combo box, drop-down list box	cbo	cboEnglish
Command button	cmd	cmdExit
Common dialog	dlg	dlgFileOpen
Communications	com	comFax
Control (unknown type)	ctr	ctrCurrent
Data	dat	datBiblio
Data-bound combo box	dbcbo	dbcboLanguage
Data-bound grid	dbgrd	dbgrdQueryResult
Data-bound list box	dblst	dblstJobType
Data combo	dbc	dbcAuthor
Data grid	dgd	dgdTitles
Data list	dbl	dblPublisher
Data repeater	drp	drpLocation
Date picker	dtp	dtpPublished
Directory list box	dir	dirSource
Drive list box	drv	drvTarget
File list box	fil	filSource
Form	frm	frmEntry
Frame	fra	fraLanguage
Gauge	gau	gauStatus
Graph	gra	graRevenue
Grid	grd	grdPrices
Hierarchical Flex Grid	flex	flexOrders
Horizontal scroll bar	hsb	hsbVolume
Image	img	imgIcon
Image combo	imgcbo	imgcboProduct
ImageList	ils	ilsAllIcons
Label	lbl	lblHelpMessage
Lightweight check box	lwchk	lwchkArchive
Lightweight combo box	lwcbo	lwcboGerman
Lightweight command button	lwcmd	lwcmdRemove
Lightweight frame	lwfra	lwfraSaveOptions
Lightweight horiz scroll bar	lwhsb	lwhsbVolume
Lightweight list box	lwlst	lwlstCostCenters

Here is the same code, indented correctly:

```
Do While Not EOF(fileNum)
   Input #fileNum, payRate, hours
   If payRate > 0 Then
      If hours > 0 Then
         weeklyPay = hours * payRate
         lblWeeklyPay = Format$(weeklyPay, "currency")
      Else
         MsgBox "Hours are invalid", vbInformation, "Error"
      End If
   Else
      MsgBox "Rate is invalid", vbInformation, "Error"
   End If
Loop
```

Table 6 (continued). Microsoft Suggested Prefixes for Controls.

Control Type	Prefix	Example
Lightweight option button	lwopt	lwoptIncomeLevel
Lightweight text box	lwtxt	lwtxtStreet
Lightweight vert scroll bar	lwvsb	lwvsbYear
Line	lin	linVertical
List box	lst	lstPolicyCodes
ListView	lvw	lvwHeadings
MAPI message	mpm	mpmSentMessage
MAPI session	mps	mpsSession
MCI	mci	mciVideo
Menu	mnu	mnuFileOpen
Month view	mvw	mvwPeriod
MS Chart	ch	chSalesByRegion
MS Flex grid	msg	msgClients
MS Tab	mst	MstFirst
OLE container	ole	oleWorksheet
Option button	opt	optGender
Picture box	pic	picVGA
Picture clip	clp	clpToolbar
ProgressBar	prg	prgLoadFile
Remote Data	rd	rdTitles
Rich TextBox	rtf	rtfReport
Shape	shp	shpCircle
Slider	sld	sldScale
Spin	spn	spnPages
StatusBar	sta	staDateTime
SysInfo	sys	sysMonitor
Tab Strip	tab	tabOptions
Text box	txt	txtLastName
Timer	tmr	tmrAlarm
Toolbar	tlb	tlbActions
TreeView	tre	treOrganization
UpDown	upd	updDirection
Vertical scroll bar	vsb	vsbRate

Who would ever imagine that having beautiful code is important? But it's true—most experienced programmers have a distinctive coding style that could almost be called a "signature".

1.3.6 Predefined VB Constants

Whenever possible, use the Visual Basic predefined symbolic constants that apply to control properties. A few frequently used constants are listed in Table 7. The complete set of constants may be viewed by selecting **Object Browser** from the **View** menu.

1.3.7 Line Continuation

Avoid letting source code extend beyond the right edge of the screen, because it becomes almost impossible to read. If necessary, use the underscore (_) character to continue a line. The underscore must be preceded by at least one space, and must be the last character on the line. For example, we could break the line after a comma separating the procedure arguments:

Table 7. Selected Control Property Constants.

Control.Property	Symbol	Constant
CheckBox.Value	vbUnchecked	0
	vbChecked	1
	vbGrayed	2
Form.Windowstate	vbNormal	0
	vbMinimized	1
	vbMaximized	2
MousePointer	vbDefault	0
	vbHourglass	11

```
MsgBox "Hours worked must be greater than zero.", _
       vbExclamation, "Error"
```

It is not possible, however, to break a line in the middle of a string. The following would be an error:

```
MsgBox "Hours worked must be greater _
   than zero.", vbExclamation, "Error"
```

If you really must break a line within a string, create two strings and use the (&) concatenation operator to reconnect them. The following would be correct:

```
MsgBox "Hours worked must be greater " _
   & "than zero.", vbExclamation, "Error"
```

1.3.8 App Object Properties

Visual Basic creates a built-in App (application) object for each running program. These properties can be set at design time, by selecting **Project Properties** from the **Project** menu, and clicking on the **Make** tab (Figure 2).

Fill in the version number boxes, and from the Type listbox, select the element you wish to change; type a description into the Value text box. For example, you might want to assign values to Company Name, Product Name, and Legal Copyright. Notice that the executable program's icon can be selected from the list of icons already assigned to the various forms in the project.

1.3.9 Avoid Default Properties

You will probably encounter other Visual Basic programs that rely on default properties of controls because these defaults allow statements to be shorter. In this book, we almost always use explicit property names, so the reader is not forced to remember the default property name. This also helps to make the source code more self-documenting. So you can read other programs that use default properties, however, default properties of selected controls are shown in Table 8.

Figure 2. Visual Basic 6 Application Object Settings.

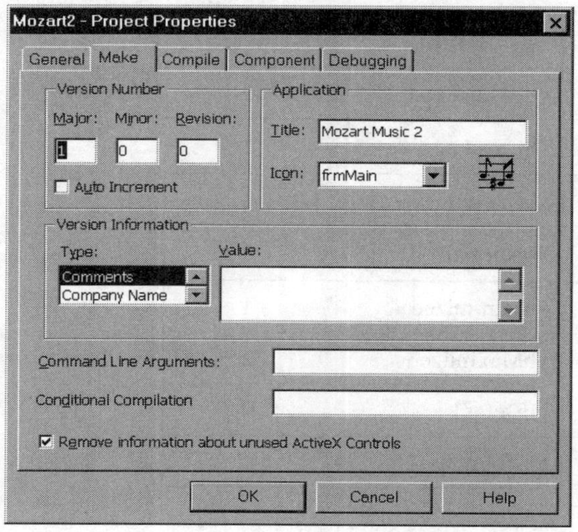

1.3.10 Use General Procedures to Avoid Duplication

When you have a lot of code to write in a program, store it in general procedures rather than in event handlers. It's very tempting, for example, to place all the statements that calculate the price on a sales invoice inside the command button called "Calculate". But problems occur later if the button is removed from the form. Instead, write a general procedure called something like CalculatePrice, and place all of your calculation statements inside of it. Then the command button's event handler can contain just a single statement:

```
Private Sub cmdCalculate_Click()
  CalculatePrice
End Sub
```

As it often turns out, you may decide later to call CalculatePrice when the user clicks on an OptionButton, a menu item, or CheckBox, or enters information that may require the

Table 8. Default Properties of Selected Controls.

Control	Default Property
Label	Caption
Frame	Caption
Text	Text
Image	Picture
Option Button	Value
Check Box	Value
Horizontal Scroll	Value
Vertical Scroll	Value

item's price to be recalculated. For example, when the "Discount" box is checked or unchecked, the following event handler executes:

```
Private Sub chkDiscount_Click()
  CalculatePrice
End Sub
```

Above all, remember that the final version of your program may be quite different from the one you started with. Anything you can do to make the program's code more flexible and easy to modify will end up saving you time in the long run.

1.4 ERROR HANDLING

Error handling is somewhat of an art among professional programmers, and many take pride in writing programs that are nearly "bullet-proof". On the other hand, it is nearly impossible to anticipate everything that can go wrong in a program, and one could spend an excessive amount of time writing error-trapping code. The managers of a project also affect the degree of error checking by pressuring programmers into deadlines that do not allow adequate time for testing and debugging.

1.4.1 Causes of Errors

Accidents happen, of course, and computer programs are no exception to the rule. Professional programmers spend a lot of their time planning for the inevitable runtime errors that can stop a program, and writing code that handles the errors in a reasonable way. Some runtime errors are caused by factors outside the programmer's control—hardware failure, for example. But programs still must recover from these errors and take whatever action is necessary. Here is a partial list of common errors that you are likely to encounter:

- An invalid numeric value is assigned to a numeric variable.
- An input file cannot be found.
- An attempt is made to read past the end of a file.
- An input file contains invalid data.
- An output file cannot be created.
- A function receives an invalid argument.
- A non-numeric value is used in a calculation.
- An attempt is made to divide by zero.
- An array subscript is out of bounds.
- A reference is made to a form name for which no instance exists.

Visual Basic provides a way to recover from runtime errors, so a program can take some or all of the following actions when an error has occurred:

- Diagnose the error.

- Notify the user that an error has occurred.
- Ignore the error and continue to the next program statement.
- Attempt to correct the error and continue the program.
- Abort the program.

1.4.2 On Error GoTo Statement

The **On Error Goto** statement enables an error handler and specifies the location of the error handler. An *error handler* is a block of code identified by a label, containing statements that attempt to report and/or deal with the error. For example, it might be as simple as displaying a message box.

In the following example, if the Open statement fails because the file was not found, the program immediately branches to the label OpenFileErr and an error message displays. On the other hand, if the file is opened successfully, the program continues to execute the statements following the Open, up to the Exit Sub statement:

```
Public Sub OpenFile( filename As String )
   Dim fileNum As Integer
   On Error Goto OpenFileErr
   fileNum = FreeFile
   Open filename For Input As fileNum
   MsgBox "File was opened."
   Close fileNum
   Exit Sub
OpenFileErr:
   MsgBox Error$, vbInformation, "OpenFile"
End Sub
```

Notice that we call the **Error$** function to get the error message passed by Visual Basic and place it in a message box. The **Exit Sub** statement prevents the program from "falling into" the error handler when no error has occurred. Functions use **Exit Function** and property procedures use **Exit Property.**

1.4.3 Resume Statement

In some situations, you might want to resume processing at the statement immediately following the one that caused the error:

```
OpenFileErr:
   MsgBox Error$,vbInformation,"OpenFile"
   Resume Next
```

Another possibility is to resume processing at the same statement that caused the error. In the next example, we call the **InputBox** function to ask the user for a new filename and attempt to open the file again:

```
Public Sub OpenFile( filename As String )
   Dim fileNum As Integer
   On Error GoTo OpenFileErr
   fileNum = FreeFile
   Open filename For Input As fileNum
```

```
    MsgBox "File opened successfully", vbInformation, ""
    Close fileNum
    Exit Sub
OpenFileErr:
    filename = InputBox("The file: " & filename & _
      " was not found. Please enter the " _
      & "correct filename.", "OpenFile Procedure")
    If Len(filename) > 0 Then Resume
End Sub
```

Figure 3 displays the dialog window seen by the user. If the Cancel button is clicked, a zero-length filename is returned, and we immediately exit the OpenFile procedure. In the absence of any On Error Goto statement, the program would display the default error window and halt, as in Figure 4.

Error handling is automatically disabled when execution leaves the current procedure. Error checking can also be turned off inside the current procedure by using the **On Error Goto 0** statement.

Automatic Backward Chaining. Sometimes you can purposely avoid handling an error, with the expectation that the error will be handled by the previous procedure in the current procedure call stack. Suppose that cmdOpen_Click called OpenFile, and the latter did not have any error handler. The error could still be handled inside cmdOpen_Click:

```
Private Sub CmdOpen_Click()
  On Error GoTo CmdOpenErr
  Openfile fileName
  Exit Sub
CmdOpenErr:
  MsgBox "The file: " & fileName & " could not be opened."
```

Figure 3. Dialog Box: File Not Found.

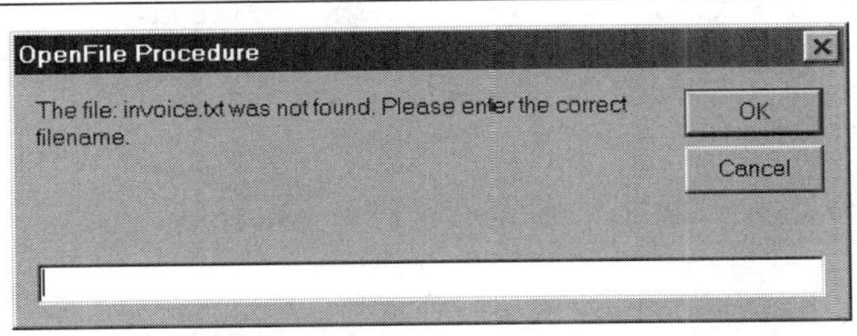

Figure 4. Unhandled Runtime Error.

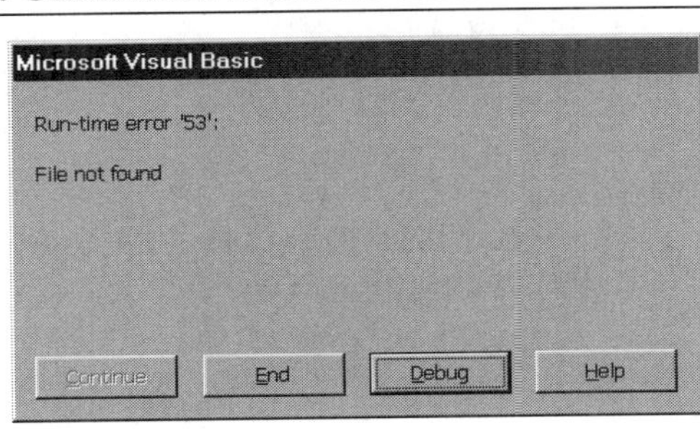

```
End Sub

Public Sub OpenFile( filename As String )
   Dim fileNum As Integer
   fileNum = FreeFile
   Open filename For Input As fileNum
   MsgBox "File opened successfully", vbInformation, ""
   Close fileNum
End Sub
```

If an error occurs inside OpenFile, control *immediately* leaves that procedure and branches to the error handler in cmdOpen_Click. In general, a procedure call stack can be unwound as far as necessary in order to locate an error handler, or if there are no more procedure calls left, the default error window is displayed and the program halts.

1.4.4 Using the Err Object

Visual Basic creates an object called **Err** whenever a runtime error occurs, and you can access the Err.Number and Err.Description properties separately:

```
OpenFileErr:
  MsgBox Err.Description, , "Error " & Err.Number
```

If the program could not open a file, "File Not Found" error message would be displayed, With "Error 53" as the message box caption.

The Err.Raise Method. An error handler can check for specific error codes and provide more specific help to the user. For example, we can revise the earlier example that displayed an input box when a file was not found. If error 53 occurs, we ask for a new filename; for all other errors, we display the error number, matching message, and exit the procedure:

```
OpenFileErr:
  Select Case Err.Number
    Case 53: filename = InputBox("The file: " & filename & _
             " was not found. Please enter the " _
             & "correct filename.", "OpenFile Procedure")
             If Len(filename) > 0 Then Resume
    Case Else
       MsgBox Err.Description, , "Error " & Err.Number
  End Select
```

The Err.Raise method is useful when testing error-handling code, because you can simulate the occurrence of a runtime error:

```
Public Sub OpenFile( filename As String )
  Dim fileNum As Integer
  On Error GoTo OpenFileErr
  fileNum = FreeFile
  Open filename For Input As fileNum
  Err.Raise 53                          'TEST the FileNotFound error
  MsgBox "File opened successfully", vbInformation, ""
  Close fileNum
  Exit Sub
```

To make programs more self-documenting, a good technique is to predefine useful runtime error constants. For example:

```
Const errFileNotFound = 53
```

Then your error handlers can be more descriptive:

```
OpenFileErr:
   Select Case Err.Number
     Case errFileNotFound: filename = InputBox("The file: " &
     (etc.)
     (etc.)
```

1.5 REDUCING CODE SIZE

There are a number of techniques you can use to reduce the size of a compiled Visual Basic program. This type of optimization can reduce the amount of memory used by the program, and help it to load more quickly. First, however, do not bother to reduce the length or number of identifier names, comments, or blank lines. Doing so will have no effect on the executable program size. The following suggestions appear in the Visual Basic *Programmers Guide*:

- Reduce the number of loaded forms. A form consumes a great deal of memory when loaded, so you can load forms only when they are needed, and unload them when unneeded. The Unload statement does not release all memory used by a form, unless you also set any references to the form to Nothing:

```
Unload frmCustomer
Set frmCustomer = Nothing
```

- Reduce the number of controls on each form. Rather than using a large number of separately named controls on the same form, use a control array.
- Use labels instead of text boxes when a value is simply being displayed.
- Keep data in disk files or resources and load only when needed. Large graphics and strings, for example, can be loaded from files at runtime.
- Organize your modules. Visual Basic loads modules "on demand", meaning that a module is only loaded into memory when one of its procedures or variables is referenced. If related procedures are grouped inside the same modules, fewer modules will be loaded at the same time.
- Consider alternatives to Variant data types. A Variant variable takes up at least 16 bytes of storage, so it should only be used when the type of data assigned to the variable cannot be known at compile time.
- Use dynamic arrays rather than fixed-size arrays. Dynamic arrays can be reduced in size or erased at runtime using the Erase and ReDim statements. When used on a fixed-size array, however, the Erase statement does not reduce memory usage.

- Reclaim space used by strings or object variables. Global strings and object variables, in particular, remain active for the entire life of a program. Setting a string variable to "" reclaims its storage, and setting an object variable to Nothing reclaims most of its storage.
- Eliminate dead code (code that is never executed). Debug.Print statements, incidentally, do not take up space in compiled programs.
- Reduce the number of unused variables.

1.6 IMPROVING EXECUTION SPEED

There are three types of speed: *code speed* (the actual time spent performing calculations and executing code), *display speed* (the time spent displaying graphics or painting the screen), and *perceived speed* (how fast your program appears to run).

A major factor in customer satisfaction with a program has to do with the program's *perceived* execution speed. The time spent waiting for such tasks as loading and displaying a form, loading a listbox from a database, for example, can be quite obvious. Of course, many performance factors are beyond the range of the programmer's control, such as CPU speed, memory size, disk access time, and so on.

1.6.1 Code Optimization

The *Visual Basic Programmers Guide* lists the following ways to optimize your programs' code:

- ***Avoid using variant variables.*** A variant variable has to be converted to the appropriate data type at run time, whereas typed variables do not require any conversion.
- ***Use long integer variables and integer math*** if only whole numbers are involved, rather than floating-point or currency variables. Because the native data type of the CPU is 32 bits, the Long data type is also more efficient than Integer or Byte.
- ***Store frequently used properties in variables.*** It takes less processing time to get and set the value of a variable than it does to access an object's property.
- ***Replace procedure calls with inline procedures.*** If a loop is executed hundreds or thousands of times, calling a procedure from within the loop slows the program down slightly. Instead, place the procedure body inside the loop.
- ***Use constants rather than variables whenever possible.*** The value of a constant never changes, so the compiler can substitute the same value into each place where the constant is referenced. A variable, on the other hand, can change value while a program is running, so the variable's value has to be retrieved whenever the variable is referenced.
- ***Pass arguments ByVal instead of ByRef***, unless the called procedure has to modify the passed argument.
- ***If you use optional arguments***, make them typed rather than Variant.

- ***Use collections properly.*** Use the For Each...Next statement rather than the For...Next statement. Avoid using Before and After arguments when adding objects to a collection. Use keyed collections rather than arrays for groups of objects of the same type.

1.6.2 Display Optimization

The Visual Basic Programmers Guide suggests the following ways to optimize a program's display speed:

- ***Set the ClipControls property*** of forms, picture boxes, and other containers to False. This will improve the speed at which forms containing a large number of controls are redrawn. ClipControls only needs to be True when using graphics methods such as Line or PSet.
- ***Set AutoRedraw to False*** if a program draws graphics on a form that must be redrawn frequently. When the form is covered up and then exposed again, place your graphics drawing statements inside the Paint method.
- ***Use image controls*** instead of picture box controls. Image controls are much simpler, use less memory, and display more quickly. They are ideal for displaying icons, bitmaps, and metafiles.
- ***Hide controls when setting control properties*** so that all modified controls on the same form can be repainted at the same time. Otherwise, the form repaints after each control is modified.
- ***Use Line instead of Pset*** when drawing graphics lines. Also, use shape and line controls for simple graphical elements, and use graphics methods for more complex drawings.

1.6.3 Perceived Speed Optimization

A program that seems to do its work quickly when the user is waiting will appear to run more quickly. Here are some techniques that you can use to improve this:

- ***Keep forms hidden but loaded.*** As we have already pointed out, keeping hidden forms in memory uses up more memory while the program is running. But it takes less time to show a form than it does to load it from disk and then show it.
- ***Preload data.*** Whenever the user already expects there to be a pause in the program, you can load all data that will be needed in the near future. This will eliminate delays during time-critical moments.
- ***Use timers that work in the background.*** If a program is waiting for a user input or action, it can perform background operations until the user responds. A timer control allows a program to activate a background processing routine at regular time intervals.
- ***Use progress indicators.*** The ProgressBar control can show the status of a slow operation, as is generally done by software installation programs. The progress bar will let the user know that the program has not simply frozen up. The hourglass mouse cursor may also be used during short delays. To use it, do the following:

```
Screen.MousePointer = vbHourglass
  (do the slow operations here)
Screen.MousePointer = vbDefault
```

- ***Speed the start of your application.*** Users hate to click on a program icon and stare at an empty screen for several seconds while all of the program DLLs load. Instead, you can use the Show method in the Form_Load event to show the program's startup form (called a *splash screen*). The startup form should be both simple and attractive. The program's other, larger forms can be loaded in the background while the user is reading the startup form. The Visual Basic documentation uses the following example, which would be in the startup form:

```
Sub Form_Load()
  Me.Show             ' Display startup form.
  DoEvents            ' Ensure startup form is painted.
  Load MainForm       ' Load main application form.
  MainForm.Show       ' Display main form.
  Unload Me
  Set frmSplash = Nothing
End Sub
```

The Professional and Enterprise editions of Visual Basic let you divide a program into an executable file and multiple DLL files. The executable file can be small, allowing it to load quickly.

1.7 REVIEW QUESTIONS

1. During which step in the application development cycle would you develop the user interface?
2. Why is it important for a program designer to speak to those persons who will use the final program?
3. Why is it important to review specifications for feasibility before proceeding to the design stage?
4. What is a common mistake made by companies developing programs in Visual Basic for the first time?
5. What is *prototyping*?
6. What is a major drawback of procedural design?
7. In what way is object-oriented design most different from procedural design?
8. Is the Visual Basic toolbox built around a procedural approach, or an object-oriented one?
9. What entities (objects) would be important in a doctor's office scheduling program? (This is an open-ended question, so your choices do not have to agree with those stated earlier in the chapter.)
10. How is a method different from a property?
11. For an Employee object, would PayRate be a method or a property?

12. Why is *flexibility* an important goal in application design?
13. What is meant by *extensibility* in the context of application design?
14. How does the concept of *reusability* apply to the way Visual Basic was designed?
15. When a programming team is working on a project, how can they be sure that two programmers will not inadvertently modify the same source code at the same time?
16. Which type of modification to a program design is usually more difficult to achieve: visual or structural? Why?
17. What is a common mistake made in small programming shops regarding the testing and validation of software?
18. What is *a test suite*, and why is it useful?
19. Why should a program not be placed into production immediately after several bugs have been fixed?
20. Which property is used to set the tab order for each of the controls on a form?
21. Which three events are triggered when the user presses and releases a key?
22. Which keyboard event procedure is best for ANSI characters?
23. What are several standard menu names found in Windows applications?
24. How does using Option Explicit help to catch programming errors?
25. What basic principles should you follow in naming variables?
26. What basic principles should you follow in naming procedures?
27. What are the recommended prefixes for variables of the following types: Integer, Long, String, Currency, Single, Boolean.
28. What are the recommended prefixes for names of the following controls? text box, list box, combo box, label, form, menu, command button.
29. What are the three types of identifier scope?
30. Explain the meaning of each of the following:

```
On Error GoTo <label>
On Error Resume Next
Error$
```

31. Name several of the most common types of runtime errors found in Visual Basic programs.
32. If you need to have a large number of controls on a form, what is one way that you can make more efficient use of memory?
33. Which type of control uses more memory: a label, or a text box?
34. Name several ways of helping Visual Basic programs use less memory.
35. How does grouping related procedures in the same module make more efficient use of memory?

36. Why are Variant type variables somewhat wasteful of memory?
37. What are the three main categories (mentioned by this chapter) of measuring execution speed?
38. Name several ways of optimizing the speed of a program's code.
39. Why would we want to store frequently-used object properties in ordinary variables?
40. How does the ClipControls property affect the optimization of a program's display?
41. Why would a programmer want to load several forms into memory before displaying them? How would this affect the program's use of memory?
42. How is a program able to perform background operations while waiting for user input?
43. How can a programmer give the illusion that a large program loads into memory quickly?

1.8 CHAPTER EXERCISES

1.8.1 Changing Form Colors

This programming exercise is just for fun: Select a program that you have already written; Add a Timer control to one of the program's forms, set the timer's interval property to 200, and place the following statement inside the timer's event handler:

```
BackColor = RGB(Rnd * 256, Rnd * 256, Rnd * 256)
```

This statement assigns a random background color to the current form. You should see the form's background change color five times per second. If this seems too easy, write statements that randomly select different controls on the current form (from the Controls collection) and change their foreground and background colors. And if you want to try something else, modify the timer event handler so the form gradually fades from one color to another.

1.8.2 Freight Forwarding Service (Design)

Design the visual interface for a program that will help a freight forwarding service keep track of small and medium-sized packages. All freight will be domestic, i.e., within the same country. The user should be able to perform the following tasks:

- Enter the following information about a package that will be sent from the current location to some other address: 5-digit package ID, recipient name, street, city, state, postal code, weight (in pounds), shipping cost, type of shipment (5-day, 2-day, overnight), and insured value.
- After all information for a package is entered, add the package ID and recipient name to a list box. Provide a way for the user to save all package information, along with today's date and time, in a file.
- Design a menu for the program; design a splash screen.

1.8.3 Freight Forwarding Service (Implementation)

Using the design from the previous exercise, implement the Freight Forwarding Service program. Save all package data in a file or database.

Provide the following validation before allowing a package to be saved:

- The package ID must be five digits long.
- The weight (W) must be in the range 0 < W <= 70.
- No fields may be blank.
- The insured value (I) must be in the range 0 <= I <= 1000.

1.8.4 Express Travel Agency (Design)

The Express Travel Agency needs to keep track of the vacation plans of its customers who are travelling by air. Design the visual interface for a program that lets a travel agent view and edit each customer's flight itinerary. The following information is required for each leg of the journey: Departure date and time, flight number, departure airport, airline, number of passengers in group, arrival date and time, arrival airport.

Here is a sample of the complete travel information for a customer named Carol Johnson, showing subsequent legs of the same journey from Miami to Los Angeles for four passengers:

```
Johnson, Carol
10/20/1999, 08:30, 456, MIA, AAL, 4, 10/20/1999, 11:45, DFW
10/20/1999, 12:30, 967, DFW, AAL, 4, 10/20/1999, 13:45, LAX
//
```

Design a splash screen for the program, and design a menu for the main window.

1.8.5 Express Travel Agency (Implementation)

Implement the Express Travel Agency program that was designed in the previous exercise. Add the following features:

- The flight information must be typed into a text file, random-access file, or database, and saved in such a way that it may be read and displayed by a Visual Basic program.
- Your program must read the flight information file, display the information, and allow the user to modify any of the fields. Provide a way for modified records to be saved in a separate file.
- Use the On Error GoTo statement to display a message if the flight information file cannot be found, and use the InputBox function to let the user enter a new file name. (The InputBox function is explained in Appendix A.)
- *Extra:* If you are using a database, save any modified records in their original input file (i.e., update the records).

1.8.6 Multiple-Choice Test (Design)

Design the visual interface for a simple program that administers a multiple-choice test. The test should display a sequence of questions, provide up to five answer choices, and let the user select an answer. When the user clicks a button to go to the next question, the question number and answer choice will be recorded in a file.

At the beginning of the test, let the student select his/her student ID number from a list box. This ID number will be saved in the output file, along with the answer given to each question.

Design the format of the input file, making sure that each question is numbered, contains a question stem (1 to 20 lines of text), and up to five answer choices. Each answer choice may be between 1 and 5 lines long.

1.8.7 Multiple-Choice Test (Implementation)

Implement the multiple-choice test program that was designed in the previous exercise. Be sure that all test questions will fit in the test window, and use scroll bars if necessary. Do not let the student skip a question without giving an answer.

Also, provide a separate program for the instructor to display the test results. This program must open the test results file, and display each student ID and corresponding list of answers. Provide a way for the instructor to search for a student ID.

2 Building Applications

Chapter Contents

Useful ActiveX Controls
- Tabbed Dialog Control
- ProgressBar Control
- ImageList Control
- ToolBar Control
- StatusBar Control
- Multimedia Control
- ActiveMovie Control

Mozart Music Sales - 1
- Objectives
- Program Specifications
- User Interface Design
- Implementation: Module1.bas
- Implementation: frmMain

Mozart Music Sales - 2
- Program Specifications
- Program Design
- Program Implementation

Creating Wizards
- College Registration Wizard Example

Common Dialog Control
- ShowOpen, ShowSave Methods
- Example: Selecting and Opening a File
- Example: Saving a File
- ShowColor Method
- ShowFont Method

Saving and Retrieving Settings
- Viewing the System Registry
- Visual Basic Procedures
- SaveSetting Procedure
- GetSetting Function
- GetAllSettings Function
- Example Program: Save/Retrieve Data Path

Review Questions

Chapter Exercises

2.1 USEFUL ACTIVEX CONTROLS

A number of excellent ActiveX controls are provided with Visual Basic that give you the opportunity to create applications with professional-looking user interfaces. In this section, we show how to use the Tabbed Dialog, ProgressBar, ImageList, ToolBar, StatusBar, Multimedia, and ActiveMovie controls. These can be combined in any number of ways, and your use of them will depend only on your own creativity and time spent mastering them.

2.1.1 Tabbed Dialog Control

The Microsoft Tabbed Dialog control provides a great way to place a lot of information on a single Form. This removes the need for the user to flip back and forth between forms, an activity which can be confusing and time-consuming. Most users can go about three levels deep into nested window displays without getting lost, so it makes sense for the visual designer to limit the stress on the user. To see an excellent example of a Tabbed Dialog, run Microsoft Outlook Express, and open up the Address book. Across the top is a row of tabs, each containing numerous input fields:

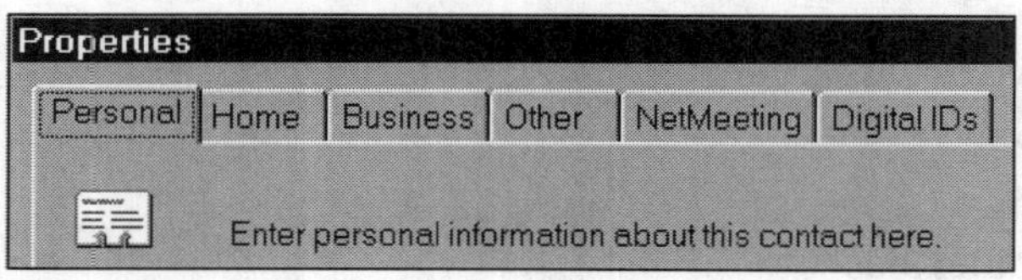

In Visual Basic, to place the Tabbed Dialog control in the ToolBox window, select "Microsoft Tabbed Dialog Control 6.0" from the **Project > Components** menu. Some important properties are listed here.

Tabs	Number of tabs to display
TabsPerRow	Number of tabs in each row of tabs
TabOrientation	Controls where the tabs appear, relative to the enclosing Form. The possible values are ssTabOrientationTop, ssTabOrientationBottom, ssTabOrientationLeft, and ssTabOrientationRight.

Figure 1 shows examples of Tabbed Dialogs with their TabOrientation set to top and left, respectively.

If you set the TabOrientation to left or right, be sure to choose a font style that supports rotation. TrueType fonts, for example, support rotation. To assign a caption to one of the tabs at design time, select the tab and enter a value into the Caption property.

Placing Controls on the Dialog. You can place controls on a Tabbed Dialog in one of two ways. If the control is to appear on only one pane, select that pane as the active pane before placing the control on the pane. If a control is to appear on all panes, deselect the Tabbed Dialog, place the control on the Form, and drag it into position on the Tabbed Dialog. This will make it appear to "float" above the individual panes, making it always visible. In Figure 2, the OK button remains visible when the user clicks on each of the tabs.

Manipulating Tabs at Runtime. You can manipulate a number of different properties for a single tab at runtime:

Tab	Select a tab as the active tab by assigning an integer in the range 0..(n-Tabs).
Tabs	Increasing the value of the Tabs property causes tabs to be added.

Figure 1. Microsoft Tabbed Dialog Control.

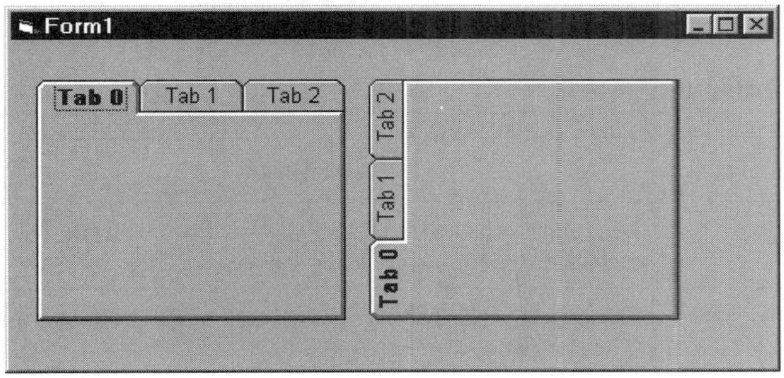

Caption   Change the caption of the currently selected tab.
Width   Change a tab's width.

The following statement sets the active tab by assigning a value to the Tab property:

```
SSTab1.Tab = 0                    'select the first tab
```

To add a tab at runtime, assign a larger value to the Tabs property than it already contains. For example, the following code inserts a new tab, makes it the active tab, and places a caption of "New Tab" on it:

```
With SSTab1
   .Tabs = .Tabs + 1
   .Tab = .Tabs - 1
   .Caption = "New Tab"
End With
```

2.1.2 ProgressBar Control

The ProgressBar control offers a convenient way for your programs to show the program's progress through a process or series of steps. Later in this chapter, for example, we will use a ProgressBar to track the steps in a simple Wizard application that registers students for

Figure 2. Floating a Command Button.

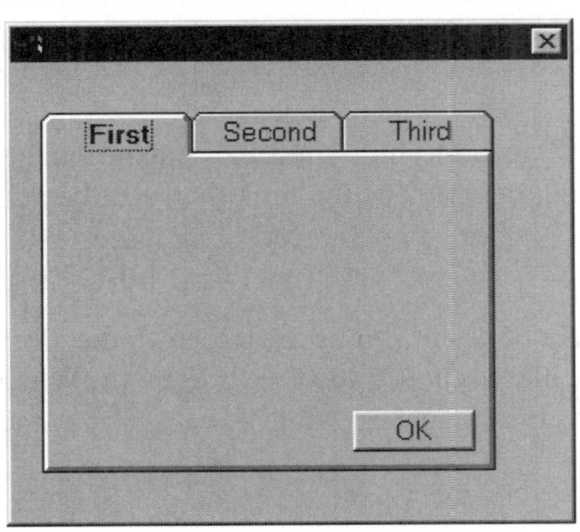

classes. The most useful properties are shown in Table 1. Figure 3 shows horizontal and vertical ProgressBar controls, segmented and smooth, in 3-D and Flat versions.

Table 1. ProgressBar Properties.

Property	Description
Appearance	Determines whether the ProgressBar is flush with the surface of the form (ccFlat) or sunken (cc3D).
Max	The largest value that may be assigned to the progress bar's Value property.
Min	The smallest value that may be assigned to the progress bar's Value property.
Orientation	Controls whether the scroll bar is horizontal (ccOrientationHorizontal) or vertical (ccOrientationVertical).
Scrolling	Controls whether the bar appears segmented (ccScrollingStandard) or solid (ccScrollingSmooth).
Value	Controls the position of the bar relative to the min and max values. Only available at run time.

Figure 3. ProgressBar Controls.

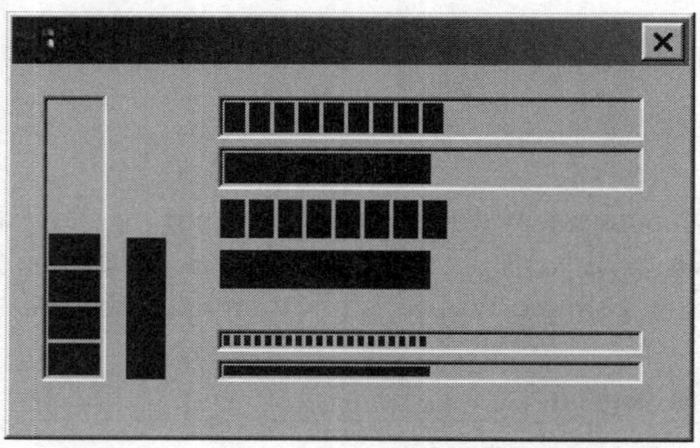

2.1.3 ImageList Control

The ImageList control is a container designed to hold multiple graphic images on a Form. The images do not have to be displayed, but most of the time they will be assigned to various other controls. Various types of images may be stored, including bitmaps (.bmp, .dib), cursors (.cur), icons (.ico), metafiles (.wmf), GIF (.gif), and JPEG (.jpg) files.

Before the ImageList control may be used, it must be added to the ToolBox window. From the Projects/Components menu, place a check next to "Microsoft Windows Common Controls 6.0". In the ToolBox window, the ImageList control looks like a stack of cards.

To add images to an ImageList, click on its Custom property to bring up the control's Properties page (see Figure 4). Click on the **Images** tab and click on the **Insert Picture** button. For example, you might want to use images relating to common commands used in Windows applications: Print, Open, New, and Save. It is also useful to assign a key value to each image so it may later be identified when attaching the ImageList to a ToolBar. For the four images shown, we set their Key property values to "print", "open", "new", and "save".

ListImages Collection. An ImageList keeps its images in a Collection called **ListImages**, allowing the images to be accessed using either an index or a key. Each member of the Collection is a **ListImage** object. Images can be inserted into the Collection at design time by clicking on the Custom property button in the properties window. For now, think of a Collection as being a kind of "super array". We will explain collections in detail in Chapter 3.

An image may be accessed at run time from the ListImages Collection. The index of the first image is 1. The following statement assigns the image at index position 1 in an ImageList to an Image control. The ImageList is named **ilsTest** and the Image control is named **Image1**:

```
Image1.Picture = ilsTest.ListImages(1).Picture
```

If the image has been assigned a key (a string), the key can be used to retrieve the image. If, for example, an image's key is "OpenFile", the following expression retrieves the image:

```
ilsTest.ListImages("OpenFile").Picture
```

A ListImage Object. The following are useful properties of a ListImage object:

Picture	A graphic image. May be set at design time, using the Properties page dialog. At runtime, this property can be set using the LoadPicture function.
Index	Identifies the image's position in the Collection. The first index is always 1.
Key	A unique string that identifies the image in the Collection.

Figure 4. Property Pages, ImageList Control.

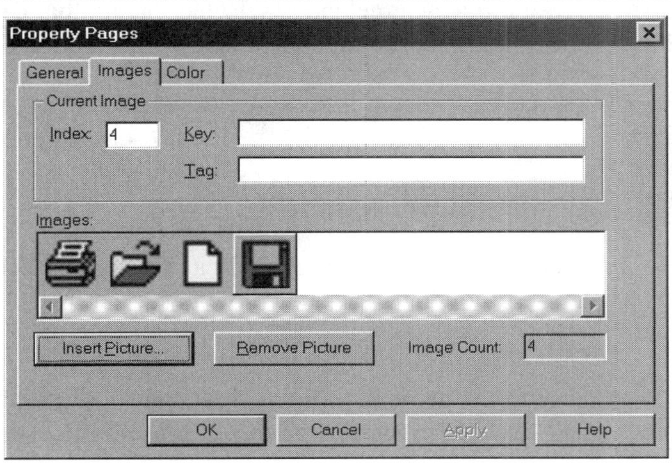

A default size can be set for all images in an ImageList, as long as the size is determined before inserting the first image. The **ImageHeight** and **ImageWidth** properties are designed for this purpose. If you do not set these before adding an image, the first image added to the Collection determines the size of all subsequent images that are added. If you plan to insert icons on buttons in a tool bar, for example, 16 x 16 images will be typical size. A 32 x 32 size will result in large buttons.

The ImageList is most effective when it is attached to other custom controls, including ListView, ToolBar, TabStrip, Header, and ImageCombo. Each of these has a property called **ImageList**, which is assigned the name of an ImageList control on the same Form.

Copying an ImageList from One Form to Another. You can copy an ImageList control from one Visual Basic project to another, using the Windows clipboard. Select the control from the source Form and copy it to the clipboard with the **Edit > Copy** menu command. Open the second project and paste the contents of the Clipboard onto a Form with the **Edit > Paste** command. All the images in the ImageList will be preserved. Within the same project, however, you would never want to duplicate the same ImageList on two different forms.

2.1.4 ToolBar Control

(samples: ToolBar)

The ToolBar control is a visual container into which you can insert buttons with text and/or images. Before images can be placed in the buttons, you must attach an existing ImageList control on the same Form to the ToolBar, using the latter's ImageList property. When this is done, each button on the ToolBar can automatically be assigned an image from the ImageList Collection.

Before you can use the ToolBar control, it must be added to the ToolBox window. From the **Projects > Components** menu, place a check next to "Microsoft Windows Common Controls 6.0".

By default, a ToolBar aligns itself to the top of its enclosing container, which is usually a Form. But a ToolBar can also be placed inside a Frame or a PictureBox. The Align property can be any of the following: vbAlignNone, vbAlignTop, vbAlignLeft, vbAlignRight, or vbAlignBottom. If vbAlignNone is selected, the toolbar can be any rectangular shape. The following toolbar, for example contains four buttons, and is aligned at the top of its containing Form:

Inserting Buttons. To insert buttons in a ToolBar, click on its Custom property to display the custom Properties page. The following steps show how to set the ImageList property and insert the first button:

1. Set the ImageList property to the name of an ImageList control. A combo list will let you view the names of all ImageList controls on the current Form .

Figure 5. Property Pages, ToolBar Control.

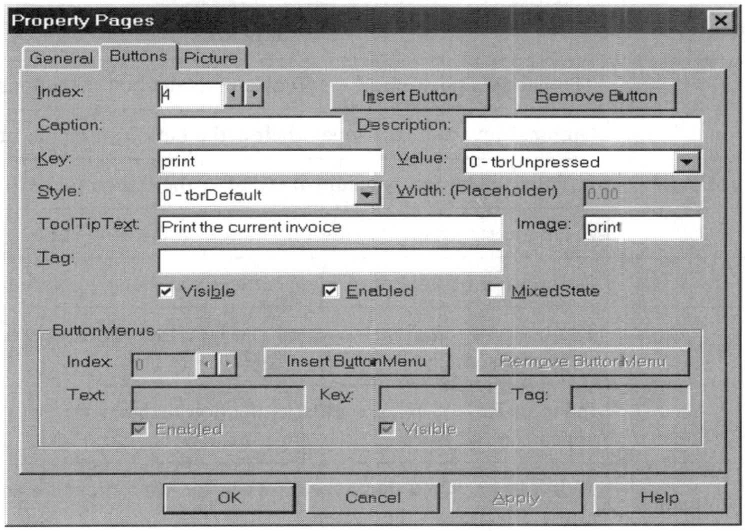

2. Click on the Buttons tab, then click on "Insert Button" (see Figure 5).
3. In the Image TextBox control, place either the index number of an image or the key of an image from the attached ImageList control. Usually it's best to use a key so you don't have to remember the index order of the images.

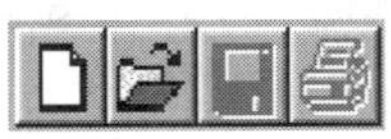

4. In the **Key** TextBox control, type a string that you want to use as the button's key. This will be useful later when you want to write code that responds to button clicks.
5. In the **ToolTipText** box, enter a string that you want to display when the user pauses the mouse over the toolbar button.

To insert additional buttons, repeat steps 2 through 4. Notice that various properties can be set for each button. Each object in the **Buttons** Collection is a Button object. Table 2 contains a summary of the most important Button properties. The Button's **Style** property has a number of useful options, shown in Table 3.

> ***Programming Tip:*** **ToolBar Maintenance**
>
> Usually, its best to plan ahead and insert all images into the ImageList that you will need for your attached ToolBar. Adding new images later is somewhat awkward. If you have to add or remove any images from an ImageList that is connected to a ToolBar, you must first clear the ImageList property from the ToolBar, then insert or remove the new images, and then reattach the ImageList to the ToolBar. Unfortunately, the Image property of each button must be set all over again, because the act of detaching the ImageList from the ToolBar cleared all of the Image values.

Table 2. ToolBar Button Properties.

Property	Description
Index	The button's position in the ToolBar's collection of buttons.
Caption	Optional text that can appear below the button's graphic image.
Enabled	If True, the button is enabled; If False, the button is disabled.
Key	A unique string identifying this button in the collection.
Style	Description of the button's appearance and behavior (see table).
Value	The button's initial state, which can be either tbrPressed or tbrUnpressed.
Image	Index or Key of an ImageList collection member that will appear on the button.
ButtonMenus	A dropdown menu that appears when the user clicks on an arrow attached to the button.
Visible	If True, the button is visible; if False, the button is invisible.

Enabling and Disabling Buttons. Most application programs selectively enable and disable toolbar buttons according to the current state of the program. For example, in a sales invoice program, the ToolBar might initially appear with only the New and Open buttons enabled:

Table 3. Button Style Properties.

Option	Description
tbrDefault	An ordinary, nonexclusive command button.
tbrCheck	When clicked, the button stays down. When clicked again, the button rises. This mimics the behavior of a CheckBox control.
tbrButtonGroup	All buttons having this property form a group in which only one button may be depressed at a time. This is identical to the behavior of a group of option buttons.
tbrSeparator	A blank space 8 pixels wide is left between the previous button and the following button. Can be used to delimit a button group so that any subsequent buttons will form a new group.
tbrPlaceholder	A blank space is left between the previous button and the following button. The width of the placeholder may be specified, using the unit of measurement defined in the Form's ScaleMode property.
tbrDropDown	Permits a small menu to drop below the button when the arrow icon is clicked. If you use this style, click on "Insert ButtonMenu" to create menu choices.

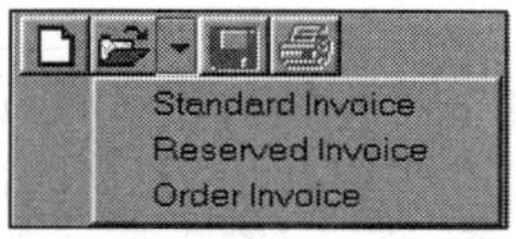

This is appropriate because if there is no current invoice, the Save and Print commands should not be enabled. The Enabled property of each button can be modified at design time by viewing the Properties page, selecting the Buttons tab, and then selecting or deselecting the Enabled check box.

After an invoice has been opened, we enable the Save and Print buttons using program code statements. Each refers to a member of the Buttons Collection, identified by the button's key value:

```
Public Sub OpenExistingInvoice()
'Open an invoice here...

'Enable the appropriate buttons:
   tlbTest.Buttons("save").Enabled = True
   tlbTest.Buttons("print").Enabled = True
End Sub
```

Writing Code for ToolBar Click Events. When the user clicks on a ToolBar button, your program must have an event handler procedure that receives the button information and responds accordingly. For example, if the ToolBar is called **tlbTest**, its ButtonClick event handler will have the following declaration:

```
Private Sub tlbTest_ButtonClick(ByVal Button As MSComctlLib.Button)
```

(Microsoft's suggested name prefix for a ToolBar control is **tlb**.) The single parameter is a Button object representing the button that was clicked. We can use its Key property to identify the particular button that was clicked. The following code uses a **Select Case** statement to call various procedures depending on the button's key:

```
Private Sub tlbTest_ButtonClick(ByVal Button As MSComctlLib.Button)
   Select Case Button.Key
     Case "new"
       Call CreateNewInvoice
     Case "open"
       Call OpenExistingInvoice
     Case "save"
       Call SaveCurrentInvoice
     Case "print"
       Call PrintCurrentInvoice
   End Select
End Sub
```

Dropdown Menus on ToolBar Buttons. The ToolBar control allows you to place a menu on any button. This may be done from the Properties page by clicking on **Insert ButtonMenu** and entering a text value and key value for each menu item. In Figure 6, for example, we have added a menu item for the **Open Invoice** button. Before you leave the Properties page, set the button's Style property to tbrDropDown. The following is an example showing a

Figure 6. ToolBar Button Dropdown Menu Properties.

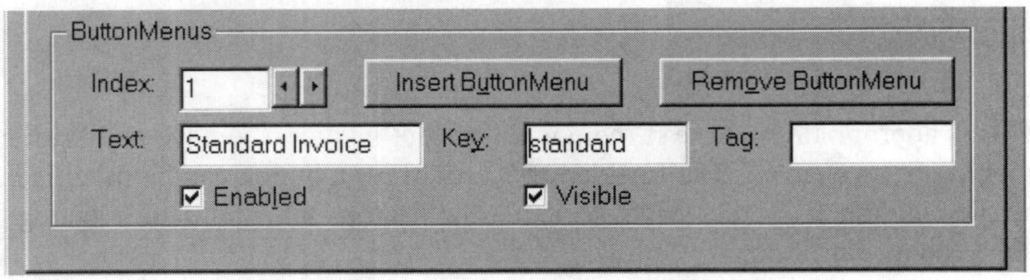

dropdown menu attached to the Open Invoice button as it appears at runtime. Notice that an arrow pointing downward appears next to any button that has a dropdown menu:

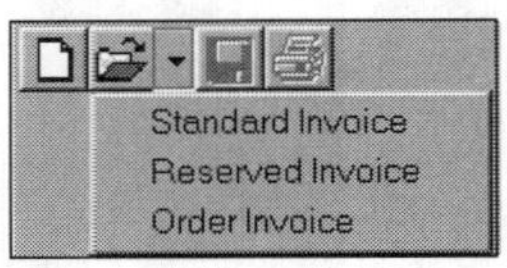

Working with Button Groups. A button group can be an effective way of letting the user select one item from a group. When the user clicks on a button, it stays down and any other buttons in the group pop up. Set each button's Style property to tbrButtonGroup. For example, we might have a shipping priority toolbar with buttons labeled Low, Med., and High:

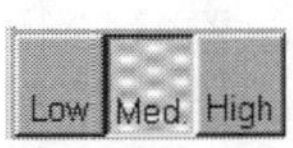

These buttons could either be on their own toolbar, or they could be placed on a toolbar with other types of buttons.

Copying a ToolBar from One Form to Another. You can copy a ToolBar control from one Form to another, by using the Windows clipboard. The two forms can also be in different projects. If the ToolBar is attached to an ImageList, copy the ImageList to the new Form first. Then copy the ToolBar to the clipboard, open the destination Form, and paste the ToolBar to the new Form. The link that existed between the ToolBar and ImageList on the source Form will be preserved.

2.1.5 StatusBar Control

The StatusBar control provides a way for your programs to display information such as the date, time, keyboard status, or program status messages. By default, a StatusBar is placed at the bottom of its enclosing container, but the Align property also allows it to be placed at the top, left, or right, or not aligned at all. Usually the enclosing container is a Form, but it can also be a PictureBox or Frame.

A **StatusBar** is divided into sections, each of which is called a *panel*. Each panel is represented as a Panel object, and the **Panels** property is a Collection that contains multiple Panel objects. Each panel can contain text and graphics, and there can be as many as sixteen panels on a single status bar. The **Style** property of a StatusBar determines whether or not it contains a single panel (sbrSimple) or multiple panels (sbrNormal).

Setting Panel Properties. To set individual Panel properties at design time, click on the Custom property to bring up the Properties page. After inserting a new Panel object into the Panels Collection, set each of the following properties, shown in Table 4.

The Panel's **Autosize** property takes one of the values shown in Table 5. The **Style** property of a Panel object can be set to one of the constants shown in Table 6.

The following is a StatusBar example containing the date, time, CapsLock flag, and a string indicating that the current file has been modified. The first three panels are updated automatically, and the fourth panel is updated by program code:

Table 4. Panel Control Properties.

Property	Description
Alignment	Affects the horizontal alignment of data in the panel. May be set to sbrLeft, sbrCenter, or sbrRight.
Autosize	Affects panel resizing behavior. See Table 5 for specifics.
Bevel	Affects the three-dimensional appearance of the panel. May be set to sbrNoBevel, sbrInset, or sbrRaised.
Style	Affects the type of data being displayed in the panel. See Table 6 for details.
Picture	Causes an image to be displayed in the panel.
Text	Inserts a string of characters in the panel.
Visible	Allows the panel to appear or disappear.
Key	A string that uniquely identifies the current panel in the Panels collection.

Table 5. Panel Autosize Properties.

Value	Description
sbrNoAutoSize	(default) The panel remains set to the size specified in the Width property. This may result in text being truncated.
sbrSpring	When the parent form resizes and there is extra space available, all panels with this setting divide the space and grow accordingly. The panel's width never falls below that specified by the MinWidth property.
sbrContents	The Panel is resized to fit its contents. The width will never fall below the width specified by the MinWidth property.

Table 6. Panel Style Property Values.

Value	Description
sbrText	(default) The panel displays text and/or a bitmap.
sbrCaps	The panel displays the state of the Caps Lock key.
sbrNum	The panel displays the state of the Number Lock key.
sbrIns	The panel displays the state of the Insert key.
sbrScrl	The panel displays the state of the Scroll Lock key.
sbrTime	The panel displays the current time in the system format.
sbrDate	The panel displays the current date in the system format.
sbrKana	The panel displays the letters KANA in bold when scroll lock is enabled, and dimmed when disabled.

2.1.6 Multimedia Control

The **Microsoft Multimedia** control, registered as a separate ActiveX control in Visual Basic, provides a simple, direct way to play sound and video files. It uses what is called the *Media Control Interface* (MCI) to support a number of different device types, shown in Table 7.

The Multimedia control has buttons that perform standard functions used by tape recorders and CD players. Table 8 lists the available commands. Here is a picture of the control, identifying each button:

When you place an Multimedia control on a Form, its control buttons are visible by default. You can hide the entire control by setting its Visible property to false, or you can hide, disable, or enable individual buttons.

To be sure, the Multimedia control is a simplified "wrapper" around the much more powerful MCI functions in the Windows runtime library. To use those commands, you must call DLL procedures directly. See Chapter 10 for examples of DLL calls.

Playing a MIDI File. When manipulating the Multimedia control with program code, call the Open method after you have specified certain properties. Suppose we want to play a MIDI music file called **mozart.mid** using a control called **mciMusic**. To open the file, we set the DeviceType, FileName, and Command properties as follows:

```
With frmSplash.mciMusic
   .DeviceType = "Sequencer"
   .FileName = "mozart.mid"
   .Command = "Open"
End With
```

Table 7. Device Types Supported by the Multimedia Control.

MCI Device Type	Description
AVIVideo	Audio Visual Interleaved video. File extension: .avi
CDAudio	CD audio player
DAT	Digital audio tape (DAT) player
DigitalVideo	Digital video in a window
Other	Undefined MCI device
Overlay	Overlay device
Scanner	Image Scanner
Sequencer	MIDI-capable device such as a sound card or music synthesizer. File extensions: .mid, .rmi
VCR	Video cassette recorder
Videodisc	Videodisc player
Waveaudio	Wave device, such as a sound card, that plays digitized waveform files. File extension: .wav

The **DeviceType** property must refer to one of the device names specified in Column 1 of Table 7. The **FileName** property identifies the file, if any, to be opened. The **Command** property sends any one of the commands shown in Table 8.

To begin playing the file, assign the string "Play" to the command property of the MCI control:

```
mciMusic.Command = "Play"
```

To pause or stop the music, assign the appropriate string to the Command property:

```
mciMusic.Command = "Pause"
mciMusic.Command = "Stop"
```

To resume playing the music, assign "Play" to the Command property. The last thing you should do with the MCI control is close the device:

```
mciMusic.Command = "Close"
```

There are a number of interesting applications you could write in Visual Basic that use the MCI control. For example, a Music CD cataloging program could let the user look up a song title, tell them which CD to insert in the computer, and play the requested track. Another application would be a program that lets you record speech from a microphone, store it in a WAV file, and insert the WAV file as an OLE object into an Access database. A music teacher could record short musical excerpts from various music CDs, save them in a database, and recall them in a classroom presentation or music appreciation test. (Of course, copyright laws apply in any cases where you copy excerpts from existing

Table 8. Multimedia Control Commands

Command	Description
Open	Opens an MCI device.
Close	Closes an MCI device.
Prev	Move to beginning of current track. If two Prev commands occur within three seconds, it moves to the beginning of the previous track.
Next	Move to the beginning of the next track.
Play	Plays an MCI device.
Pause	Pauses playing or recording.
Back	Step backward through available tracks.
Step	Step forward through available tracks.
Record	Enables recording of MCI device input.
Eject	Ejects Audio CD from CD drive.
Save	Save the audio file.

recordings.) There is also a Multimedia Development Kit available directly from Microsoft called DirectX, which provides a professional level of control over multimedia streams.

2.1.7 ActiveMovie Control

The ActiveMovie control, installed automatically with Internet Explorer, provides a convenient way to display movie files with both video and sound. You can give the user some degree of control over the playback parameters by displaying a default set of controls, or you can substitute your own controls.

To use the ActiveMovie control, select **Components** from the **Project** menu and place a check next to "Microsoft ActiveMovie Control". Select the control in the ToolBox and drag a rectangle onto a new Form. It has play and stop buttons, a time index LED display, and a slider control that lets the user position the playing point to any time index within the movie:

Bring up the Properties window, click on the FileName property, and select a movie file, looking for files with extensions of .avi, and .mpg. Resize the form to accommodate the size of the movie and run your program. When the program is running, click on the **Play** button to see the movie. Use the slider to move to a different position in the movie. You can find a number of AVI files (with no sound) in the Program Files\Microsoft Visual Studio\Common\Graphics\Videos\ directory. Also, from the Windows Start menu, select

Find, then select **Files or Folders**, and look for files with extensions of .avi and .mpg. The Internet, of course, is a great place to look for movie files.

Using Your Own Controls. You can set the ShowControls and ShowDisplay properties to False, which will cause only the video window to appear. If you place command buttons on the Form labeled Stop and Play, the following code can be placed in their Click event handlers:

```
Private Sub cmdStop_Click()
   acmMovie.Stop
End Sub

Private Sub cmdPlay_Click()
   acmMovie.Run
End Sub
```

Volume Level. You might also like to place a slider on the form to control the volume level. The slider control's value property works backwards to the way most of us perceive a slider: A slider in the "up" position has a value of zero, and the "down" position returns a value equal to the Max property. To try this, make sure you have selected "Microsoft Windows Common Controls 6.0" in the Project > Components menu, place a slider control on the Form, and set the following properties at design time:

Name = sldVolume
Orientation = ccOrientationVertical
Max = 3000
LargeChange = 200

The Max value (3000) represents the highest volume level that will be set for the movie. (Depending on your sound card's properties, you may have to adjust that value.) The following code should be placed in the Click event handler for the Slider control:

```
Private Sub sldVolume_Click()
   'The slider works backwards:
   acmMovie.Volume = sldVolume.Value * -1
End Sub
```

Your Form should appear as Figure 7, except that the initial frame of your movie will appear in the window. Run the program, click on Start, and click on the slider to change the volume level. The ActiveMovie control has many more properties than those shown here. One of the most exciting uses of ActiveMovie is on Web pages, when playing streaming video. The user can view a movie while the movie is still in the process of being downloaded from the Internet. To learn more about this control, search for "ActiveMovie" on the MSDN Library CD supplied with Visual Basic.

2.2 MOZART MUSIC SALES - 1

(samples: Mozart)

This chapter builds a Visual Basic application from the ground up, taking it through several revisions. The design concepts from the previous chapter will be applied here, as the

Figure 7. ActiveMovie Control.

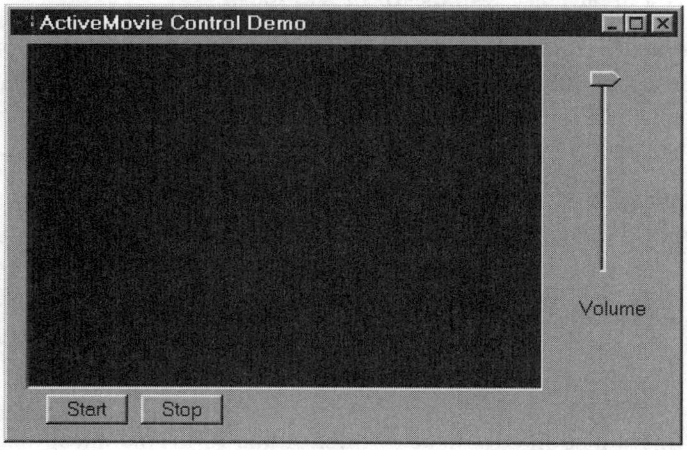

specifications are translated into a visual and functional design for a sales invoice program called *Mozart Music Sales*. The approach introduced here will serve as a model for other applications introduced later in the book.

2.2.1 Objectives

In this project, we hope to accomplish a number of important objectives. Many of the skills may be a review for you, but we want to establish a common base of program design, coding style, and error-handling techniques that will be used throughout the book. The objectives are as follows:

- Translating program specifications into a design.
- Implementing a program design.
- Retrieving and displaying the current date.
- Selecting items from a ComboBox control.
- Implementing a ToolBar with graphical buttons.
- Implementing a status bar.
- Grouping OptionButton controls within frames.
- Creating and manipulating an array of strings.
- Writing a general calculations procedure.
- Reading data from a text file and filling a ComboBox control.
- Using the On Error GoTo statement.
- Demonstrating effective coding techniques.

2.2.2 Program Specifications

The Mozart Music Store needs a simple sales invoice program that can be operated by a store clerk when a customer purchases a music album (compact disk or cassette tape). The clerk, whom we will call the *user*, selects a product number (called a *SKU*) from a list. The program immediately displays the album title that matches the number. This helps the user verify the album's title before the transaction is completed. Because the store has a frequent turnover of sales clerks, the program should be easy to learn and operate.

During a typical sales transaction, the user finds a colored label on the album indicating one of three price codes. He selects the price code on the computer by clicking an OptionButton control. The user also selects the recording format (CD or tape). The user can select one of several different discount rates, each affecting the sale amount. The program calculates the sale amount, discount, tax, and total price.

2.2.3 User Interface Design

Because users are expected to run our program with little or no training, we want it to have a simple, straightforward user interface, with a minimum of clutter. We want to focus the user's attention on a few vital pieces of information. A ComboBox lets the user select the product number from a list. Three OptionButton controls are grouped to let the user select the product price code, and two additional buttons are grouped to let the user select the album format. A ToolBar with grouped Command buttons allows the user to set the discount rate. The program automatically recalculates and displays the numeric amounts when the user changes the price code, format, or discount. The user may click on a ToolBar button to clear the current invoice and create a new one. Another button start and stops the background music.

Splash Screen. When the program starts up, it displays a splash screen, shown in Figure 8. The screen contains a picture of Mozart as a young man, the program title, software platforms (Win95, Win98, and Win/NT), program version number, and copyright information. The splash Form also has a Multimedia control that plays a selection from Mozart's *Magic Flute*. This music continues to play in the background after the splash screen closes.

Figure 8. Splash Screen.

Main Form. Figure 9 contains a sample of the main Form as it looks after a user has selected a SKU number, price code, format, and discount. Controls referenced by program code are labeled in the figure. The remaining controls use default names. There is also an invisible ImageList control on the Form called ilsTools that contains five graphic images for five of the toolbar buttons. A number of properties for frmMain and its controls are set at design time (see Table 9).

Menu Toolbar. The ToolBar below the menu, called tlbMenu, contains five buttons with properties shown in Table 10. The Image property of each contains the key property of an image in the ImageList control on the same Form. At design time, we have set the Enabled property of all buttons on the tlbMenu toolbar to False except the new button.

Input Files. When the program starts up, it opens a text file called "salesperson.txt" containing product SKU numbers and matching album titles. Here is a sample:

Figure 9. Mozart Music Main Form.

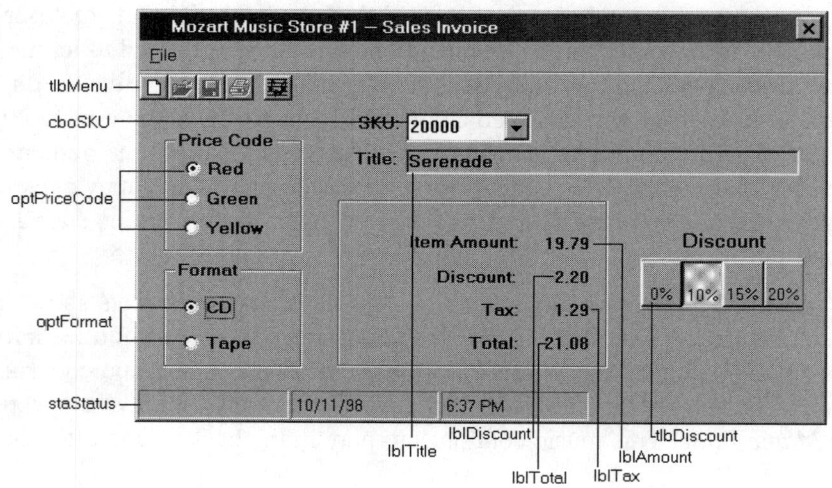

Table 9. FrmMain Properties.

Property	Value
frmMain.BorderStyle	Fixed Single
frmMain.StartupPosition	Center Screen
lblAmount.Alignment	Right Justify
lblDiscount.Alignment	Right Justify
lblTax.Alignment	Right Justify
lblNetTotal.Alignment	Right Justify

Table 10. Menu Toolbar.

Button Key	Image Key	Description
new	new	Create a new invoice
open	open	Open an existing invoice
save	save	Save the current invoice
print	print	Print the existing invoice
music	music	Play or Stop the background music

```
10000,"Marriage of Figaro"
20000,"Serenade"
22222,"Cosi Fan Tutti"
30000,"Requiem"
33333,"Symphony in G Minor"
40000,"Piano Concerto in C Major"
44444,"Sinfonia Concertante"
50000,"Mozart's Greatest Hits"
```

Project Properties. The following project properties are set for the Mozart Music program:

Title	Mozart Music 1
Company Name	Scott/Jones Publishing
Startup Object	Sub Main

2.2.4 Implementation: Module1.bas

A code module called module1.bas contains the following declarations. Notice that we consistently include the Option Explicit statement to force all variables to be declared. Otherwise, trivial misspellings of variables result in annoying, hard to catch logic errors:

```
Option Explicit
Public gblnMusicPlaying As Boolean
```

Incidentally, we will usually omit Option Explicit from program listings in the rest of this book, but be aware that they are always used in the sample programs.

The program starts executing with the Main procedure, showing frmSplash followed by frmMain:

```
Public Sub Main()
'Program entry point.
  frmSplash.Show vbModal
  frmMain.Show vbModal
  CloseMusic
  Unload frmSplash
End Sub
```

Multimedia Control. The LoadMusic and CloseMusic procedures initialize and shut down the control, respectively. The name of any standard MIDI music file can be substituted for the name used in this program:

```
Public Sub LoadMusic()
'Open the MIDI music file.

  With frmSplash.mciMidi
    .DeviceType = "Sequencer"
    .FileName = "mozart.mid"
    .Command = "Open"
  End With
End Sub

Public Sub CloseMusic()
'Stop the music and Close the MCI device.

  With frmSplash.mciMidi
    .Command = "Stop"
    .Command = "Close"
  End With
End Sub
```

The PlayMusic and StopMusic procedures are called whenever the user wishes to start and stop the music. This can be done with a check box on the splash window, or on the main window using a toolbar button:

```
Public Sub PlayMusic()
'Play the music.

  frmSplash.mciMidi.Command = "play"
  gblnMusicPlaying = True
End Sub

Public Sub StopMusic()
'Pause the music.

  frmSplash.mciMidi.Command = "stop"
  gblnMusicPlaying = False
End Sub
```

2.2.5 Implementation: frmMain

Declarations. Let's examine the declarations in frmMain. The constants MEDIA_FORMATS and PRICE_CODES represent the number of media formats and price codes that will be stored.

We declare the sales tax rate and title file name as constants because their values need not change. The mcollDiscounts Collection contains the various discount rates offered by the store. The mcollTitles Collection contains all album titles loaded from a data file. The two-dimensional sngItemPrice array contains the six possible album prices. mintPriceCode and mintMediaFormat are variables that contain the user's selection of a price code and media format. They are declared here to allow their values to be shared among the various procedures on this Form:

```
Const MEDIA_FORMATS As Integer = 2
Const PRICE_CODES As Integer = 3
Const SALES_TAX_RATE As Single = 0.065 ' standard sales tax rate
Const TITLE_FILENAME As String = "titles.txt"

Private mcollDiscounts As Collection ' Collection of discount rates
Private msngDiscountRate As Single    ' selected discount rate
Private mcollTitles                   ' Collection of album titles

Private sngItemprice(MEDIA_FORMATS, PRICE_CODES) As Single
Private mintPriceCode As Integer
Private mintMediaFormat As Integer
```

Initializing Private Variables. The Form_Initialize event occurs when the Form is created. It is here that programs usually create and initialize Form-level variables. For example, we create two collections and fill the two-dimensional array of album prices:

```
Private Sub Form_Initialize()
  Set mcollDiscounts = New Collection
  Set mcollTitles = New Collection
  mcollDiscounts.Add 0
  mcollDiscounts.Add 0.1
  mcollDiscounts.Add 0.15
  mcollDiscounts.Add 0.2
  msngDiscountRate = 0
  sngItemprice(0, 0) = 21.99
  sngItemprice(0, 1) = 15.99
  sngItemprice(0, 2) = 6.99
  sngItemprice(1, 0) = 10.99
  sngItemprice(1, 1) = 8.99
  sngItemprice(1, 2) = 5.99
End Sub
```

Loading the Form. In the **Form_Load** event handler, we tell the program to change the current directory to the same location as the project file, read the album titles from a file,

Programming Tip: **Declaring Constants**

To simplify program maintenance, it's a good idea to give names to constants at the beginning of a program. In the case of the discount rate, for example, it is much easier to modify a single constant definition rather than try to track down and change every place in the program that refers to the discount rate. To change the names of the files holding the album titles or the salesperson names, just change the constant definition.

and set the music button on the ToolBar according to whether or not the music is currently playing:

```
Private Sub Form_Load()
   ChDir App.Path
   LoadTitles        ' Load the file containing album titles
   If gblnMusicPlaying Then
      tlbMenu.Buttons("music").Value = tbrPressed
   Else
      tlbMenu.Buttons("music").Value = tbrUnpressed
   End If
   CreateNewInvoice
End Sub
```

The final statement in Form_Load calls a procedure that creates a new invoice.

Selecting a Product Number. When the user clicks on the ComboBox control to select a product number, we use the ListIndex property to locate the album's title from the mcollTitles Collection:

```
Private Sub cboSKU_Click()
   If cboSKU.ListIndex = -1 Then Exit Sub
   lblTitle.Caption = mcollTitles(cboSKU.ListIndex + 1)
End Sub
```

Calculating the Price. The calculations are placed in a general procedure called CalcPrice so it can be called from a number of event-handlers in the Form.

```
Private Sub CalcPrice()
   If mintMediaFormat < 0 Or mintPriceCode < 0 Then Exit Sub

   Dim sngPrice As Single
   Dim sngTax As Single, sngTotal As Single, sngDiscount As Single

   sngPrice = sngItemprice(mintMediaFormat, mintPriceCode)
   sngDiscount = sngPrice * msngDiscountRate
   sngPrice = sngPrice - sngDiscount
   sngTax = sngPrice * SALES_TAX_RATE
   sngTotal = sngPrice + sngTax
```

Programming Tip: Calculations Using Variables

Be careful to avoid the bad habit of performing calculations directly with text box values. Instead, convert them to numeric values and place them in numeric variables. Validity checks are particularly important in programs that allow for a variety of user input.

Most calculation procedures contains a standard sequence of steps:

- Declare local variables needed by the procedure.
- Copy numeric data from text boxes into the procedure's local variables.
- Perform validity checks on all data that will be used in calculations.

```
    lblAmount.Caption = Format(sngPrice, "standard")
    lblDiscount.Caption = Format(sngDiscount, "standard")
    lblTax.Caption = Format(sngTax, "standard")
    lblTotal.Caption = Format(sngTotal, "standard")
End Sub
```

Price Codes and Media Formats. There are two sets of OptionButton controls on the Form, one for price codes and the other for media formats. Each is a control array, so we use the Index parameter to set the module variables mintPriceCode and mintMediaFormat, respectively. Notice that we also call the CalcPrice procedure, which calculates the final invoice prices:

```
Private Sub optPriceCode_Click(Index As Integer)
    mintPriceCode = Index
    CalcPrice
End Sub

Private Sub optFormat_Click(Index As Integer)
    mintMediaFormat = Index
    CalcPrice
End Sub
```

Loading Album Titles. The **LoadTitles** procedure reads the album titles and SKU numbers from a text file, loading the titles into a Collection and the SKU numbers into a ComboBox control. Notice that we use **On Error GoTo** to trap for possible I/O errors:

```
Private Sub LoadTitles()
    Dim strSku As String, intFileNum As Integer, _
        strTitle As String
    On Error GoTo LoadTitlesErr
    intFileNum = FreeFile
    Open TITLE_FILENAME For Input As intFileNum

    Do Until EOF(intFileNum)
        Input #intFileNum, strSku, strTitle
        cboSKU.AddItem strSku
        mcollTitles.Add strTitle
    Loop
    Close intFileNum
    Exit Sub

LoadTitlesErr:
    MsgBox "Cannot load the Album Title file: " & _
        mstrTitleFilename, vbCritical, "Error"
End Sub
```

Creating a New Invoice. When the program starts, and when the user clicks on the **New Invoice** ToolBar button, the **CreateNewInvoice** procedure executes:

```
Private Sub CreateNewInvoice()
    Dim j As Integer
    mintPriceCode = -1
    mintMediaFormat = -1
    optPriceCode(0).Value = False
```

```
    optFcrmat(0).Value = False
    lblAmount = "0.00"
    lblDiscount = "0.00"
    lblTax = "0.00"
    lblNetTotal = "0.00"
    cboSKU.ListIndex = -1     'nothing selected
    lblTitle.Caption = ""
    tlbDiscount.Buttons(1).Value = tbrPressed  'no discount
    msngDiscountRate = 0
End Sub
```

Interpreting the Tool Bar Buttons. In this first version of the Mozart Music program, only the New and Music buttons will be enabled. When the user clicks on a button, a Select Case statement checks the Button.Key property and calls the appropriate procedure. This can easily be expanded to handle any number of buttons:

```
Private Sub tlbMenu_ButtonClick(ByVal Button As MSComctlLib.Button)
  Select Case Button.Key
    Case "new"
      CreateNewInvoice
    Case "music"
      If Button.Value = tbrPressed Then
         frmSplash.mciMidi.Command = "play"
      Else
         frmSplash.mciMidi.Command = "pause"
      End If
  End Select
End Sub
```

Menu Commands. The **File > Exit** and **File > New** commands are duplicated on the menu, along with the **File > Exit** command:

```
Private Sub mnuFileExit_Click()
  Unload Me
End Sub

Private Sub mnuFileNew_Click()
  CreateNewInvoice
End Sub
```

2.3 MOZART MUSIC SALES - 2

2.3.1 Program Specifications

Let's improve the Mozart Music program and correct some of the first version's limitations. We're going to add a modest list of new features:

- The program must generate a unique number for each invoice. Invoices must be sequentially numbered.
- The program must append the current invoice to a text file that contains all previously saved invoices.

- Before closing the program, if the current invoice has not been saved, the program must ask the user if they want to save the invoice.
- The program must be able to print the current invoice to a window and to the default printer.

2.3.2 Program Design

The main form and splash screen look exactly the same as in the first version. One new Form, called frmReport has been added. After completing all necessary input for an invoice, the user clicks on the printer button to display the Form shown in Figure 10. This report appears on the printer when the printer button in the lower right corner of this Form is clicked.

Figure 10. Mozart Music Invoice Report.

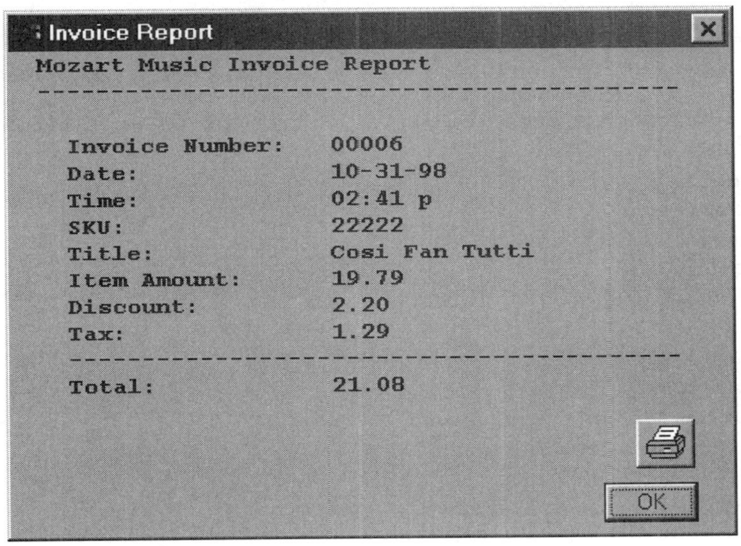

2.3.3 Program Implementation

The frmMain Form. The following lines have been added to the Form declarations area of the main Form (frmMain). The first is set to True when an invoice has been modified. The second is the current invoice number, stored as a string, and the third is a filename:

```
Private mblnInvoiceModified As Boolean
Private mstrInvoiceNumber As String
Const INVOICE_FILENAME As String = "invoices.txt'
```

The cboSKU_Click procedure has an additional line that sets mblnInvoiceModified to True:

```
Private Sub cboSKU_Click()
  If cboSKU.ListIndex = -1 Then Exit Sub
  lblTitle.Caption = mcollTitles(cboSKU.ListIndex + 1)
  mblnInvoiceModified = True
End Sub
```

The Form_Initialize event handler has one additional line of code:

```
mblnInvoiceModified = False
```

One new line has been added to the end of CalcPrice, setting mblnInvoiceModified to True whenever the user performs an action that results in calculating the price:

```
mblnInvoiceModified = True
```

Unloading the Form. The Form_Unload event handler checks the mblnInvoiceModified variable, and if the invoice has been modified, calls a procedure that asks the user if they want to save the invoice:

```
Private Sub Form_Unload(Cancel As Integer)
   If mblnInvoiceModified Then AskToSaveInvoice
End Sub
```

Menu ToolBar. The ButtonClick event handler for the tlbMenu toolbar has been expanded to include the Save and Print commands. Each has a unique button key value:

```
Private Sub tlbMenu_ButtonClick(ByVal Button As MSComctlLib.Button)
  Select Case Button.Key
    Case "new"
    CreateNewInvoice
    Case "save"
      SaveCurrentInvoice     ' save the invoice
      CreateNewInvoice       ' create a new one
    Case "print"
      PrintCurrentInvoice
    Case "music"
      If Button.Value = tbrPressed Then
         frmSplash.mciMidi.Command = "play"
      Else
         frmSplash.mciMidi.Command = "pause"
      End If
  End Select
End Sub
```

Saving the Invoice. The SaveCurrentInvoice procedure lets the user append the invoice currently shown on the screen to a file. It begins by making sure a SKU number was selected from the ComboBox control. It then opens a file in append mode, writes the invoice number, date, SKU number, sale amount, tax, and total to a single record:

```
Private Function SaveCurrentInvoice() As Boolean
  SaveCurrentInvoice = False
  On Error GoTo SaveInvoiceErr

  If cboSKU.ListIndex = -1 Then
    MsgBox "A SKU number must be selected before the " _
      & "invoice can be saved.", vbInformation, ""
    Exit Function
  End If

'Append the invoice to the invoice file.
```

```
Dim iFileNum As Integer
iFileNum = FreeFile
Open INVOICE_FILENAME For Append As iFileNum

Write #iFileNum, mstrInvoiceNumber, Format(Now, "mm-dd-yy"), _
  cboSKU.Text, CSng(lblAmount.Caption), _
  CSng(lblDiscount.Caption), _
  CSng(lblTax.Caption), CSng(lblTotal.Caption)
Close iFileNum

SaveCurrentInvoice = True
mblnInvoiceModified = False
MsgBox "Invoice #" & mstrInvoiceNumber & " has been saved.",
   vbInformation, ""
Exit Function

SaveInvoiceErr:
  MsgBox Error$, vbInformation, "SaveCurrentInvoice"
End Function
```

The **AskToSaveInvoice** procedure asks the user if they want to save the current invoice before discarding it:

```
Public Sub AskToSaveInvoice()
  Dim intChoice As Integer
  intChoice = MsgBox("Do you want to save the current invoice " _
    & "before discarding it?", vbYesNo + vbQuestion, _
    "Invoice Modified")

  If intChoice = vbYes Then SaveCurrentInvoice
End Sub
```

New Invoice Number. When the user creates a new invoice, one of the things the program has to do is create a new, unique invoice number. The GetNextInvoiceNumber function looks up the previous invoice number, adds 1, and returns the new number as a string:

```
Public Function GetNextInvoiceNumber() As String
  Dim iFileNum As Integer, strInvNum As String
  Dim f2, f3, f4, f5, f6, f7    'field placeholders
  iFileNum = FreeFile
  Open INVOICE_FILENAME For Input As iFileNum

'Loop through the file, find the last invoice number.
  Do Until EOF(iFileNum)
    Input #iFileNum, strInvNum, f2, f3, f4, f5, f6, f7
  Loop
  Close iFileNum

'Add 1 to the number, convert to a formatted string, and
'return it as the function result.
  GetNextInvoiceNumber = Format(Val(strInvNum) + 1, "00000")
End Function
```

Printing the Invoice. The PrintCurrentInvoice procedure takes all of the invoice information and displays it in report-like fashion on a separate Form. The user has the option of clicking on a Command button that sends the report to the printer:

```
Private Sub PrintCurrentInvoice()
  frmReport.Text = "    Mozart Music Invoice Report" & vbCrLf _
  & "  ____________________________" & vbCrLf _
  & vbCrLf _
  & "      Invoice Number:      " & mstrInvoiceNumber & vbCrLf _
  & "      Date:                " & Format(Now, "mm-dd-yy") & vbCrLf _
  & "      Time:                " & Format(Now, "hh:mm a/p") & vbCrLf _
  & "      SKU:                 " & cboSKU.Text & vbCrLf _
  & "      Title:               " & lblTitle.Caption & vbCrLf _
  & "      Item Amount:         " & lblAmount.Caption & vbCrLf _
  & "      Discount:            " & lblDiscount.Caption & vbCrLf _
  & "      Tax:                 " & lblTax.Caption & vbCrLf _
  & "  ____________________________" & vbCrLf _
  & "      Total:               " & lblTotal.Caption & vbCrLf
  frmReport.Show vbModal
End Sub
```

The frmReport Form. It is not possible to print to a Form until the Form is visible, so in the main window we assign a string containing all printed output to a public variable called Text on frmReport. When the Form appears, a statement in its Form_Activate event handler uses the Print method to print the string on the Form. Here is the code listing:

```
Public Text As String

Private Sub Form_Activate()
  Print Text
End Sub

Private Sub cmdOK_Click()
  Unload Me
End Sub

Private Sub cmdPrinter_Click()
'Print the current report to the printer. Set the font size
'and font type to values appropriate for printing.

  Screen.MousePointer = vbHourglass
  With Printer
    .Font.Size = 12
    .Font.Name = "Courier New"
```

Programming Tip: Using a Tabbed Dialog

You can use a Tabbed Dialog Control to group all of the wizard panels on a single form, rather than showing and hiding separate forms. This does, however, allow the user to skip steps by selecting tabs out of sequence. You might want to use the Tabbed Dialog when the order of choices is not critical.

```
        Printer.Print vbCrLf & vbCrLf & vbCrLf & Text
        .EndDoc
      End With
      Screen.MousePointer = vbDefault
    End Sub
```

2.4 CREATING WIZARDS

The Mozart music program was relatively straightforward from the user's point of view. All that was required was the selection of a product number, a price code, a media format, and a discount rate. The program was designed to accept input in any order, and calculate accordingly. There are many situations, however, when input cannot be supplied in random order. A program may be forced to generate error messages if the user enters data in an unexpected sequence. This can cause users to become annoyed, and it makes much more work for the programmer. A solution to this problem is to create a type of program or subprogram called a wizard. Wizards have certain characteristics in common:

- Wizards lead the user through a series of sequential steps, each shown on a different *panel*, or window.
- User choices may lead to alternate paths through the wizard.
- The user is allowed to back up and reenter choices and other information.
- The wizard may supply helpful information explaining each step.
- There are certain exit points when the wizard has collected enough information to finish using default values.

Wizards are useful when a program's user input requires a relatively high level of expertise or precision. Microsoft Windows uses wizards to help users install hardware and software, for example. In a later chapter, we will find that the *Simple Query Wizard* in Microsoft Access is extremely useful when constructing SQL queries that involve linking multiple tables. To create such queries in straight SQL code is quite difficult without serious study of the language.

Place an identical set of navigation buttons on each panel, in the same position. Also, try to place the Previous and Next buttons in the same positions on each panel. Ideally, the user should be able to move forward or backward between panels by clicking the mouse in the same position in the panel. For example, Figure 11 shows a set of Command buttons that appear on each panel of the Microsoft Access Simple Query Wizard.

Figure 11. Command Buttons from the Simple Query Wizard.

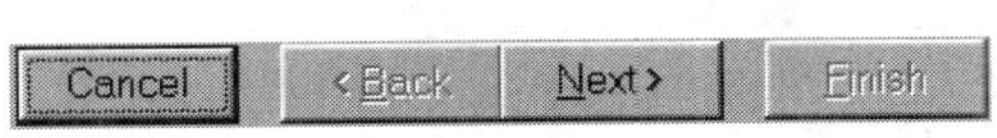

In Table 11, we see that the enabled buttons on each panel depend on which panel in the sequence is being displayed. The Finish button is typically enabled if all subsequent inputs are optional.

Table 11. Enabling/Disabling of Buttons.

Panel	Cancel	Back	Next	Finish
First panel	enabled	disabled	enabled	(either)
Second panel through next to last panel	enabled	enabled	enabled	(either)
Last panel	enabled	enabled	disabled	(either)

To preserve information entered on each Form, use the Hide method rather than Unload when removing a Form from the screen. When you show the Form again, the information entered into its controls will still be there.

2.4.1 College Registration Wizard Example

(samples: Wizard)

To demonstrate some of the Wizard design concepts discussed in this section, let's look at a simple interactive program that helps students register for classes. Let's call it the Course Registration Wizard, shown in Figure 12. Notice that we use a ProgressBar control to help track the user's progress through the steps. Visual cues such as this give the user an idea of how long the steps will take.

The second panel (Figure 13) shows the student's name and major. This is accomplished by looking up the student ID number in a database. In this panel, the user enters a five-digit advisor code and selects one of three actions: add, drop, or view.

Suppose the user clicks on the "Add a Class" button. The third panel appears (Figure 14), asking for a five-digit identifier called a *sequence number*. The user also identifies a particular campus within the college. The computer looks up the course in a database, displays detailed information, and asks for confirmation from the user. The user can back up and select a different course, or click on Next to confirm the choice (see Figure 15).

When the student has finished adding courses to the schedule, the summary screen displays the list of courses, tution fees, and total amount due (see Figure 16).

Figure 12. Course Registration Wizard, Panel 1.

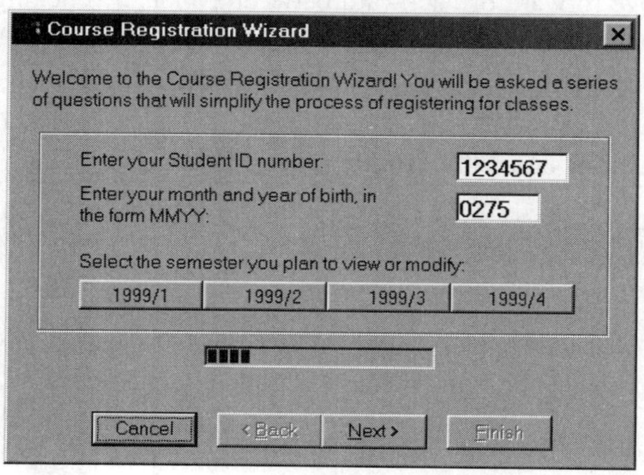

Figure 13. Course Registration Wizard, Panel 2.

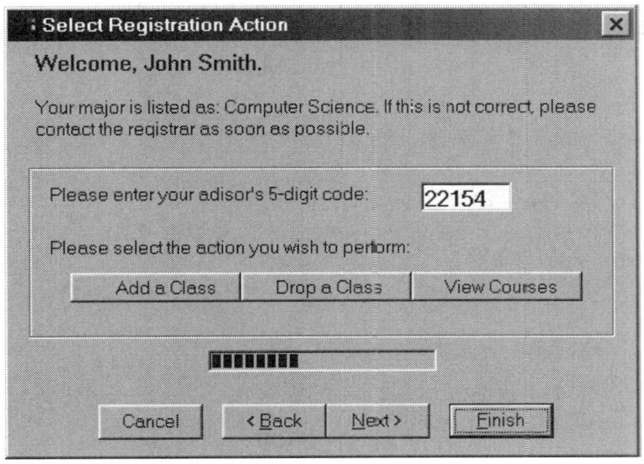

Figure 14. Course Registration Wizard, Panel 3.

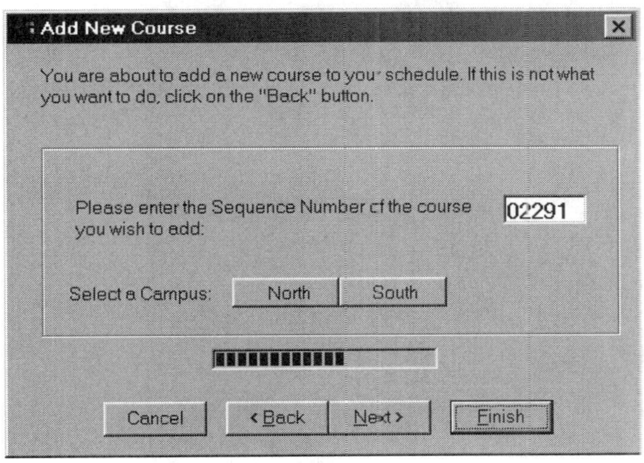

Optionally, we could allow the user to cycle back to the first panel, enter a new student number, and start over. Or, we could return the second panel and add more classes to the schedule. (The implementation of this program is a chapter exercise.)

2.5 COMMON DIALOG CONTROL

(samples: CommonDialog)

The Common Dialog control lets you create standard Windows dialog boxes for opening and saving files, selecting colors and fonts, printing documents, and displaying help files. The common dialog control icon appears on a Form only at design time. At runtime, you determine which type of window will be displayed by calling one of the following methods associated with the control:

- ShowColor: Display a color palette.

Figure 15. Course Registration Wizard, Panel 4.

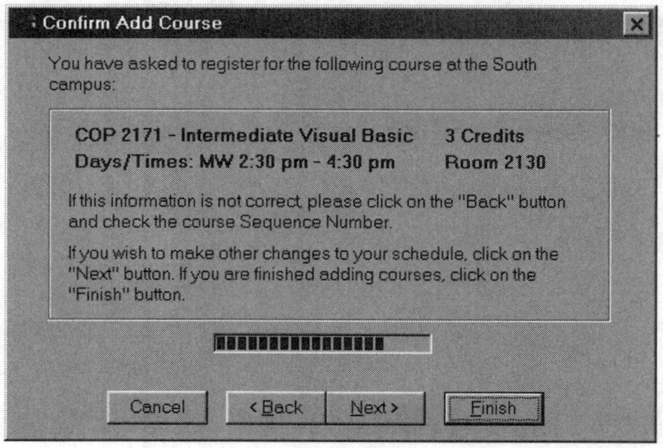

Figure 16. Course Registration Wizard, Summary Panel.

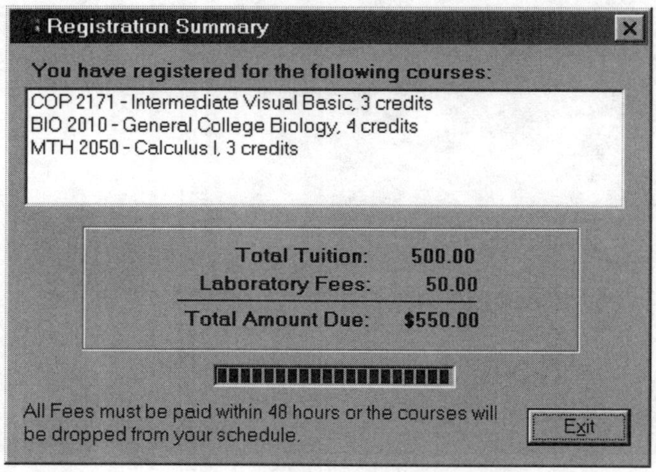

- ShowFont: Display a font dialog.
- ShowHelp: Display a help topic.
- ShowOpen: Display a File/Open dialog.
- ShowPrinter: Display a printer dialog.
- ShowSave: Display a File/SaveAs dialog.

2.5.1 ShowOpen, ShowSave Methods

The ShowOpen and ShowSave methods display the same dialog seen in all Windows applications when the user is asked to select a file. Before calling either of these methods, you should set certain properties in the Common Dialog control. Table 12 contains a list of the properties used most often. For complete descriptions of all file dialog properties, see

Table 12. File Open/Save Dialog Properties.

Property	Description
CancelError	When set to True, a trappable error will occur when the user clicks on the Cancel button (default value = False).
DefaultExt	If the user types a filename with no extension, the default extension will be automatically appended to the filename. This is useful when calling the ShowSave method.
DialogTitle	The title that appears at the top of the dialog window.
FileName	Before the dialog is shown, this can be a default filename. After the dialog closes, this is the complete path and filename selected by the user.
FileTitle	Just the filename selected by the user, with no path.
Filter	A list of file types and default extensions. This makes it easier for the user to know what types of filenames are being displayed.
FilterIndex	The starting position in the list of file types specified by the filter property, starting with 1, which is the default.
Flags	An integer value that refines the behavior of the window.
InitDir	The initial directory to be used when the dialog first appears.
MaxFileSize	The maximum length of a filename that may be entered by the user (the default is 256 characters).

the help topic "Common Dialog Control," click on the *Properties* hyperlink and click on "File Dialog Properties."

2.5.2 Example: Selecting and Opening a File

In the next example, a function called OpenFile uses a Common Dialog control named **dlgOpen** to display a list of Access database files. The modal dialog window appears when ShowOpen is called, so the statements following it are not executed until the window closes:

```
Private Function OpenFile() As String
  On Error GoTo OpenFileCancel
  With dlgOpen
    .CancelError = True
    .DialogTitle = "Opening Microsoft Access Database"
    .Filter = "Access databases|*.mdb|All files|*.*"
    .FilterIndex = 1
    .Flags = cdlOFNFileMustExist
    .ShowOpen
    OpenFile = .Filename
  End With
  Exit Function
OpenFileCancel:
  OpenFile = ""
End Function
```

The Flags property in this example was set to the predefined constant **cdlOFNFileMustExist**, which causes an error message to be displayed if the user enters a nonexistent filename (see Figure 17). For a list of predefined constants that may be used in the Flags property, enter the help topic "Flags Property (Open, Save As Dialogs)" in the MSDN index pane.

Figure 17. File Doesn't Exist Error.

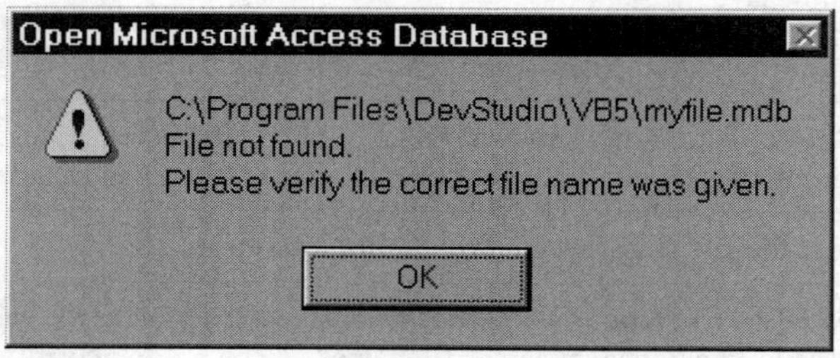

2.5.3 Example: Saving a File

You can use the Common Dialog control to let the user select a filename and directory when saving a file. The user can browse to the correct folder and enter a filename. The flag property **cdlOFNOverwritePrompt** is useful here, to warn the user that an existing file is about to be overwritten. The following GetSaveFilename function returns the filename selected by the user, or if the user cancels, the function returns an empty string:

```
Private Function GetSaveFilename() As String
  On Error GoTo SaveCancel
  With dlgSave
    .DialogTitle = "Select Filename for Saved Invoice"
    .CancelError = True
    .Filter = "Access databases|*.mdb|All files|*.*"
    .Flags = cdlOFNOverwritePrompt
    .ShowSave
    GetSaveFilename = .FileName
  End With
  Exit Function
SaveCancel:
  GetSaveFilename = ""
End Function
```

If the user clicks on "Cancel", a trappable error is generated; the On Error GoTo statement tells the program to jump to the **SaveCancel** label. Figure 18 shows a sample of the dialog window.

By default, the first filename mask in the Filter property determines the type of files displayed in the window. If the user clicks on "All files", the window shows all files in the directory matching "*.*".

2.5.4 ShowColor Method

A common dialog control can make it easier for the user to customize a program's appearance (see Figure 19). The **ShowColor** method implements the Common Dialog as a

Figure 18. Open Database Dialog.

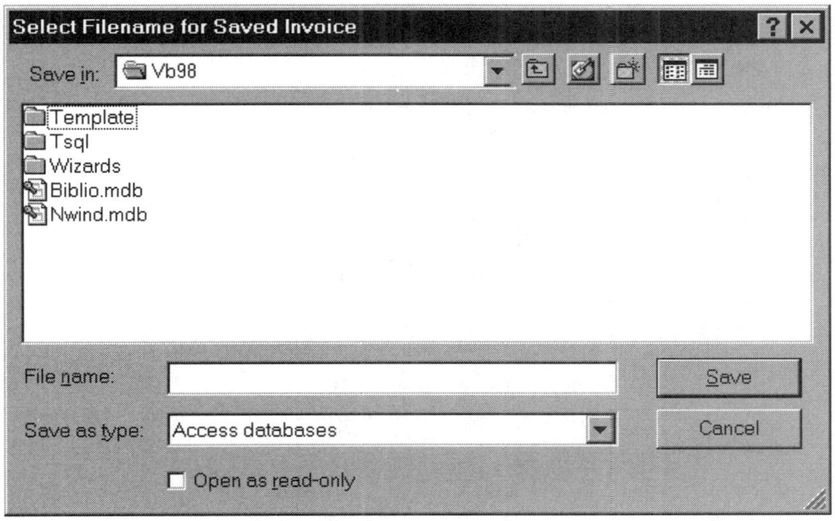

color palette, identical to the one used when we set the ForeColor or BackColor properties of controls at design time. In addition to the properties used with ShowOpen and ShowSave, the Color property may be set before the dialog is shown, and may be queried after the dialog is closed. Some useful flag values are:

cdlCCFullOpen	Enable the custom colors Command button, letting the user define a custom color.
cdlCCRGBInit	Set the initial color value for the dialog box before it is shown.
cdlCCPreventFullOpen	Disable the custom colors Command button.

The DialogTitle property is not used with ShowColor. A useful value to place in the Flags property is the predefined constant **cdlCCRGBInit**. The following statements let the user select the background color for the current Form:

```
Private Sub SelectBackColor()
   On Error GoTo BackColorCancel
   With dlgColor
      .CancelError = True
      .Flags = cdlCCRGBInit
      .Color = Me.BackColor   'get current color
      .ShowColor
       BackColor = .Color   'set the current Form color
   End With
   Exit Sub
BackColorCancel:
   'no action: user clicked "Cancel"
End Sub
```

2.5.5 ShowFont Method

The **ShowFont** method lets the user select a font and its various attributes. Some of the more commonly used properties of the Font dialog box are listed in Table 13.

Figure 19. Windows Color Dialog.

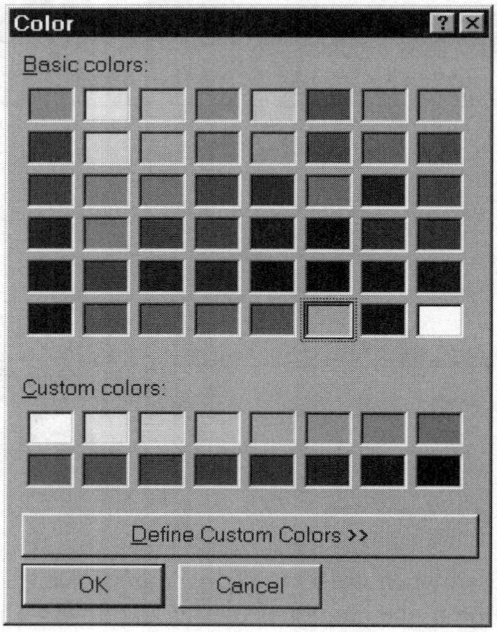

Table 13. Font Dialog Properties.

Property	Description
FontBold	Each character appears in bold type.
FontItalic	Each character appears in italic type.
FontName	Sets the name of the font.
FontSize	Sets the size of the font, in points.
FontStrikethru	Each character is overtyped with a horizontal line.
FontUnderline	Each character is underlined.

One of the following constants must be assigned to the Flags property before showing the font dialog: **cdlCFScreenFonts**, **cdlCFPrinterFonts**, or **cdlCFBoth**. The first tells the control to list only the screen fonts; the second lists only printer fonts; and the third lists both screen and printer fonts. The **cmdFonts_Click** procedure in the next example displays all available screen fonts and lets the user select a fontname and attributes. The procedure then applies these properties to a TextBox named Text1:

```
Sub cmdFonts_Click()
  On Error GoTo ShowFontsCancel
  With dlgFont
    .CancelError = True
    .Flags = cdlCFScreenFonts
    .ShowFont
```

```
        Text1.Font.Name = .FontName
        Text1.Text = .FontName + " " & .FontSize _
             & " point."
        Text1.Font.Size = .FontSize
        Text1.Font.Bold = .FontBold
        Text1.Font.Italic = .FontItalic
    End With
    Exit Sub
ShowFontsCancel:
' user cancelled - no action taken
End Sub
```

Figure 20. Font Dialog Example.

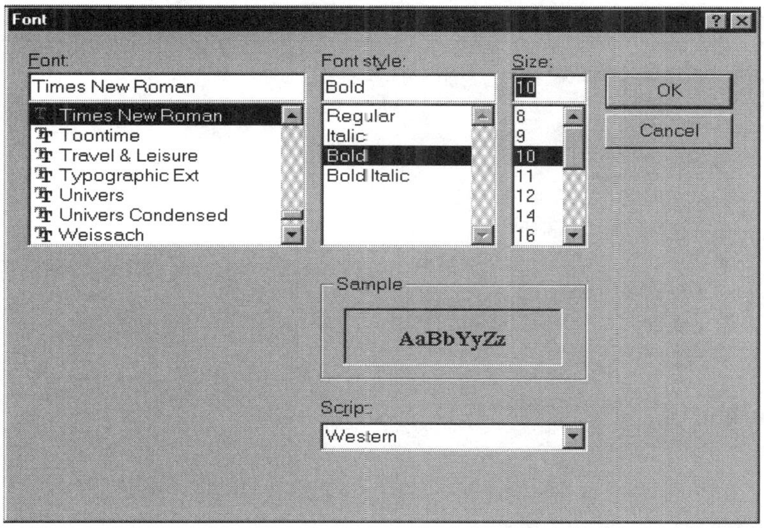

The procedure also prints some text in the TextBox, demonstrating the new Font style. Figure 20 contains a sample of the dialog window that would be displayed by the preceding code.

2.6 SAVING AND RETRIEVING REGISTRY SETTINGS

Application programs need to save certain configuration information on an ongoing basis, and the Windows System Registry is an ideal place for this. The information might include size, location, color, and font settings for the program's windows, locations of data used by the program, and other user configuration options.

2.6.1 Viewing the System Registry

The *system registry* is a hierarchical database that Windows uses to keep track of the associations between objects and applications, as well as configuration information for both the operating system and application programs. The system registry also contains classes, properties, and methods that have been *exposed* (made public) by other applications. You can view the system registry by running the **RegEdit** program that is supplied with Windows. From the **Start** menu, click on **Run** and enter the name **RegEdit** (see Figure 21).

This outline may be expanded by double-clicking first on HKEY_CURRENT_USER, then on Software. Figure 22 shows the topics that appear. If you expand the *Microsoft* topic, note that Windows saves quite a bit of information about you—the user who installed Microsoft products (Figure 23).

The system registry should not be directly modified by anyone other than an expert. The system registry is not intended to take the place of an application database that typically holds a much larger amount of data. You would not, for instance, place an

Figure 21. Registry Editor Example.

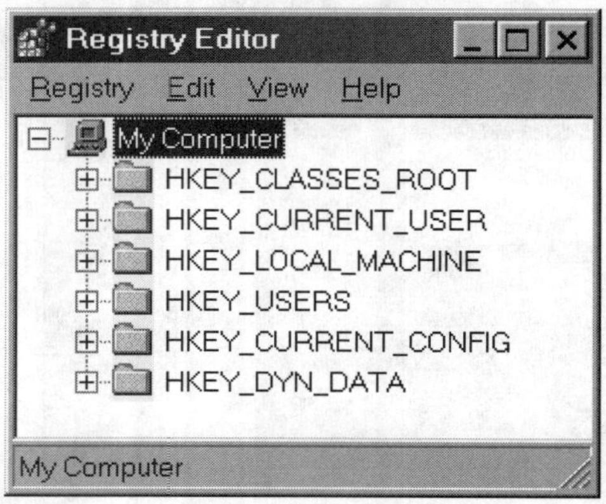

Figure 22. Registry: Software Entry.

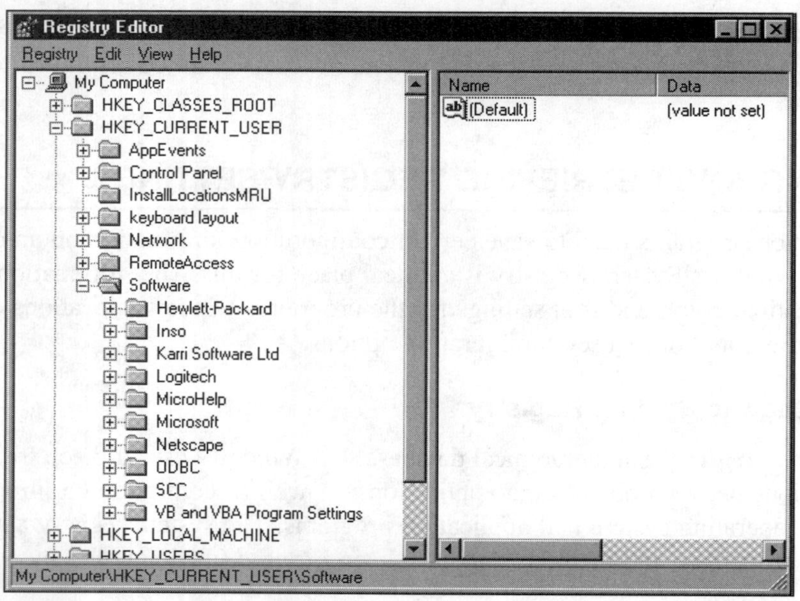

Figure 23. Registry: Software/Microsoft/User Information.

Registry Entry:

HKEY_CURRENT_USER
Software
Microsoft
User information

Name	Data
(Default)	(value not set)
Additional Address	"CIS Department"
Application Name	"MS Office 97 Professional"
CD-ROM	""
City	"Miami"
Company Name	"Microsoft"
Country	"1"
Date	"03/26/1997"
Daytime Phone	" "
Default Company	""
Default First Name	"Kip R."
Default Last Name	"Irvine"
Display Color Depth	"256"
Display Resolution	"1024 x 768"
E-mail Address	"kip.irvine@pobox.com"
Include Products	"1"
Include System	"1"

employee salary history in the system registry. But, you might place the file path of the employee database in the registry so your program can find it when it starts up.

2.6.2 Visual Basic Procedures

Visual Basic has four procedures that deal with the registry: SaveSetting, GetSetting, GetAllSettings, and DeleteSetting. All deal with a specific section of the registry that has been reserved for Visual Basic applications. If you need to access other parts of the registry, you have to call Windows API DLL procedues (See Chapter 10).

2.6.3 SaveSetting Procedure

The SaveSetting procedure saves a string value associated with a key in a specified section of an application's configuration. The syntax is:

```
SaveSetting appname, section, key, setting
```

appname is a string containing the name of the program or application; *section* is a string containing the name of the section where the information is located; *key* is the name of the key being saved, and *setting* is the value that will be displayed next to the key. An error occurs if the key setting could not be saved for any reason.

For example, we might want to save the location of data files used by the Mozart Music Sales program. The section is called **Directories**, the Key is **InvoiceFile**, and the path to the file is "C:\Mozart\Data\invoices.txt":

```
SaveSetting App.Name, "Directories", _
     "InvoiceFile", "C:\Mozart\Data\invoices.txt"
```

This creates the Directories section name and key if they did not already exist.

2.6.4 GetSetting Function

The GetSetting function returns a string value associated with a key from a program's registry entry. The syntax is:

```
GetSetting(appname, section, key [,default]) As String
```

appname is the program name, *section* is the section name, *key* is the name of the key, and *default* is the value to be returned by the function if a matching key cannot be found or if the value is empty. If *default* is omitted, it is assumed to be an empty string. The return value of GetSetting is a string containing the key's value.

When the Mozart Music program starts up, for example, it could retrieve the location of the invoice file used by the Mozart Music Sales program. The section name is **Directories**, and the Key name is **InvoiceFile**:

```
Dim InvoiceFilePath As String
InvoiceFilePath = GetSetting(App.Name, _
    "Directories", "InvoiceFile")
```

2.6.5 GetAllSettings Function

The GetAllSettings function returns a list of key settings and their respective values from an application's system registry entry. The syntax is:

```
GetAllSettings(appname, section) As Variant
```

appname is a string containing the name of the application, *section* is a string containing the name of the section. The return value is a two-dimensional array of strings containing all the keys and their respective values in the specified section. Or, if either *appname* or *section* does not exist, the function returns an uninitialized Variant. It is a good idea to call the Visual Basic **IsEmpty** function to prevent a runtime error that would be caused by trying to access the function's empty return value. For example, the following code retrieves all system registry settings for the VisData program, section VISDATA5, and displays them in a ListBox control:

```
Dim MySettings As Variant
Dim j As Integer, st1 As String * 20
MySettings = GetAllSettings("VisData","VISDATA5")
If IsEmpty(MySettings) Then
  MsgBox "No Settings were found.", , ""
Else
  For j = LBound(MySettings, 1) To UBound(MySettings, 1)
    LSet st1 = MySettings(j, 0)
    List1.AddItem st1 + MySettings(j, 1)
  Next j
End If
```

2.6.6 Example Program: Save/Retrieve Data Path

We can write a simple program that demonstrates the GetSetting and SaveSetting procedures. When the program starts, the user enters a path in a TextBox control that identifies the location of the program's data files (see Figure 24).

Figure 24. Program Settings Window.

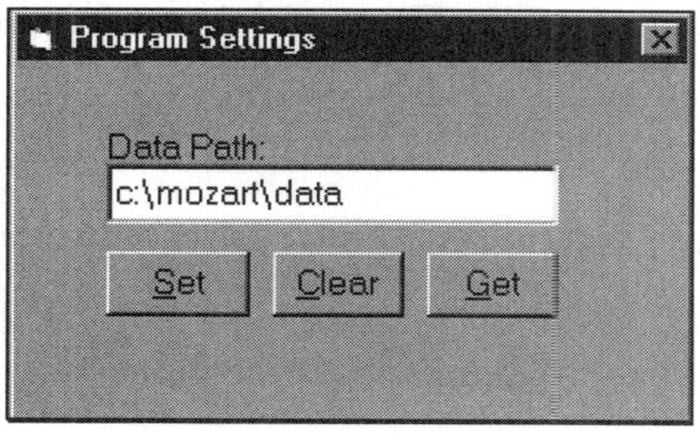

After clicking on the **Set** button, click on the **Clear** button to clear the TextBox control. Click on the **Get** button to retrieve the Data Path setting from the registry. The original data path (c:\mozart\data) should appear in the TextBox control. Using the **RegEdit** program, we can verify the Mozart—Settings—DataPath entry:

```
HKEY_CURRENT_USER
  Software
    VB and VBA Program Settings
      Mozart
        Settings
               DataPath="c:\mozart\data"
```

Here is the program listing:

```
Private Sub cmdClear_Click()
   txtDataPath.Text = ""
End Sub

Private Sub cmdGet_Click()
'Get the DataPath value.
   txtDataPath.Text = GetSetting(App.Name, "Settings", _
     "DataPath", "(not found)")
End Sub

Private Sub cmdSet_Click()
'Set the DataPath value.
   SaveSetting App.Name, "Settings", "DataPath", _
     txtDataPath.Text
End Sub
```

2.7 REVIEW QUESTIONS

The following questions refer to Version 1 of the Mozart Music Sales program:

1. In the Mozart Music Sales program, what determines the price of an album?
2. How many different prices are there?
3. How does the program retrieve the title of an album?
4. How does the program obtain the list of SKU numbers and matching titles?

5. In what way is the program's calculation of an album price somewhat inflexible?
6. Which BorderStyle property prevents the user from re-sizing the main window?
7. What modification would have to be made to this program so that it could be used in different states of the U.S.?
8. What types of validity checks does the program perform on the input values for the calculation of the album price?
9. Which Visual Basic function (used in this program) causes the numeric values to print with two digits after the decimal point?
10. Which event handlers call the CalcPrice procedure?
11. Which property of the cboSKU control is essential when locating the album title?
12. How does the program ensure that the user will not forget to select a price code (A, B, C) and recording format (CD, tape)?
13. What does the FreeFile function do?
14. How is the Error$ function used in this program?

The following questions refer to Version 2 of the Mozart Music Sales program:

15. How is Version 2 of Mozart Music Sales different from Version 1?
16. What output file is created by this program, and what does it contain?
17. What happens if the user does not click the mouse on the splash window?
18. How are *shortcut keys* used in this program?
19. Which input fields cannot be blank when an invoice is saved?
20. In order to modify the Text property of a ComboBox control, what must be the value of its Style property?
21. How do you open a text file so that new records can be added to the file without erasing existing records?
22. What does vbModal mean? What is its opposite?

The following questions refer to the Common Dialog Control:

23. How is the CancelError property used? Does it signify an error on the programmer's part?
24. Which method is used for opening files?
25. How is the FileTitle property different from the FileName property?
26. How can multiple file types be placed in the Filter property?
27. If the user enters a filename that doesn't exist, how is the FileOpen dialog able to display an error message?
28. Which method is used when displaying a color palette?
29. How can the Font dialog box be made to show both screen and printer fonts?

The following questions refer to saving and retrieving program settings:

30. What happens in the SaveSetting procedure if the application name or section name does not exist?
31. Which section of the system registry stores settings of Visual Basic programs?
32. How many key values can be stored in a single section, using SaveSetting?
33. What does GetSetting return if the key name cannot be found in the specified section?
34. What is the structure of the data returned by the GetAllSettings function?

2.8 CHAPTER EXERCISES

2.8.1 Mozart Music Common Dialog

Using the Mozart Music program as a guide, add a procedure that lets the user select the name and location of the file containing album titles. Use a Common Dialog control. Also, create a procedure that lets the user select the filename and directory to use when saving the current invoice.

2.8.2 Mozart Music Instruments

The Mozart Music store has decided to computerize its sales of musical instruments. Each instrument has both a purchase price and a monthly rental rate (see Table 14). These instrument names and prices should be kept in a file and loaded by the program at runtime.

Add a new Form to the program that allows the user to select an instrument from a ComboBox control, select from Purchase and Rental OptionButton controls, and enter the number of rental months. The program should display the cost of the purchase or rental and print an invoice (on the printer or screen) containing the customer name, instrument, address, phone, date, and rental or purchase amount.

Table 14. Instrument Price Table.

Instrument	Purchase Price	Monthly Rental Rate
Flute	415	40
Alto Saxophone	500	55
Tenor Saxophone	600	75
Bb Clarinet	425	42
Oboe	675	68
Bassoon	654	75
Violin	289	28
Viola	225	38
Cello	375	45
Electric Guitar	425	36

2.8.3 Mozart Music Color Settings

In the Mozart Music Sales program, add an **Options > Colors** menu selection that displays a color Common Dialog window and allows the user to select the background color of the main window and its controls. As soon as the user selects the new color, the BackColor properties of the Form and controls should be updated. Save the colors in the system registry whenever they are changed by the user. Load the color settings from the system registry when the program starts up.

2.8.4 Mozart Music File and Directory Settings

Create system registry entries for the Mozart Music Sales program that keep track of the following information:

- Complete path to the Album Title file.
- Complete path to the Invoice file.

Provide an **Options > Files** menu selection that will allow the user to customize these settings and save changes. When the program starts up, let it load the settings from the system registry. Use a common dialog control that will let the user browse the disk and select filenames.

2.8.5 Cleaning Equipment Rental Wizard

A *wizard* is a popular type of user interface tool used in computer applications today that guides the user through a short series of logical steps in solving a problem. Wizards are a subset of a larger class of problem-solving and advice-giving software called expert systems. In Microsoft Access, for example, the *Database Wizard* helps a user to design a new database; there are wizards to help you import and export data, build a Form, and so on. Along the way, the user makes decisions that affect the wizard's path through the process. A wizard ensures that the following are done:

- A user who is new to the software will be able to build an application component or complete a multi-step task.
- Critical steps will be carried out in the correct order.
- All necessary information will be collected.
- Steps can be retraced and repeated without disturbing the logical sequencing of information.
- The user is being educated along the way; various possibilities and options are presented in a logical manner.

Cleaning Equipment Rental Wizard. For this project, you must create a program that contains an Equipment Rental Wizard. The program will gather all information needed for selecting the items to be rented, the rental duration, price, date, delivery instructions, and customer data. Here are the steps to follow in filling out the rental reservation Form:

1. Select the device to be rented. The program should help the user narrow down the choices. Present a list of common household tasks, let the user select one, and ask the user pertinent questions about the scope or size of the task.
2. Enter the number of rental days. Various options might be presented, showing how a discounted rate can apply as the rental duration grows.
3. Select home delivery or customer pick-up. Home delivery might carry a surcharge for the larger items.
4. Verify that the customer was trained in the use of the equipment (this might be an insurance requirement for the store).
5. Get the customer's name, address, phone, and credit card data.
6. Compute the total rental charge, including sales tax and delivery.
7. Print a customer invoice.

Equipment. To avoid making the wizard become too complicated, limit the choices to the following equipment:

300 psi water pressure cleaner
1000 psi water pressure cleaner
10-gallon steam industrial-quality carpet cleaner
5-gallon steam carpet cleaner for medium-sized jobs
hand-held carpet cleaner for small jobs
10-gallon shop vacuum
home carpet vacuum
floor polisher

2.8.6 Hardbodies Health Club

Write a program that will manage the membership list of a health club. For each member who joins the club, the user will enter the following information: member ID, last name, first name, middle initial, date joined, street, city, state, zip, home phone, and membership fee. The membership fees are determined by the following schedule:

Paid yearly in advance:	$350.00
Paid quarterly in advance:	$450.00
Paid monthly in advance:	$650.00

When all data have been added to the Form, print an invoice for the customer and append all information to a text file. Optionally, you can use a database to store the information.

2.8.7 Health Club Class Schedule

Write a program that keeps track of the class schedules for the Hardbodies Health Club. Display a ListBox control containing the instructor names that have been read from a text file. Display another ListBox control containing the days and times of individual classes. Let the user select an instructor, select a class, and click a button called **Schedule** that matches the instructor to the class. When the program ends, write all information to a text file in such a way that the program can load and display the list of scheduled classes. When you run the program again, it should display the saved schedule.

2.8.8 Depreciation Schedule

Create a program that displays a tax depreciation schedule for items purchased by a business. Load a listbox containing item names from a sequential file. Load an array of matching prices from the same file. When one of these items is clicked, its depreciation schedule appears in the listbox on the right side of the Form. The depreciation occurs over a five-year period. There are two forms of depreciation: straight-line and accelerated. The straight-line method lets you deduct up to 20% of the cost of the item per year. The accelerated method allows 40% the first year, 25% the second, 20% the third, 10% the fourth, and 5% the fifth year. Figure 25 contains a sample of the program.

When the user changes an OptionButton control, the depreciation schedule recalculates. You can also add new items to the ListBox on the left, by typing in the small text controls near the bottom, and by clicking on "Add Item". Notice the frame around the ListBox and OptionButton controls on the right side of the window.

2.8.9 Time Clock Program

Write a program that keeps track of the amount of billable time you spend on consulting projects. The program will read the Client file as input, and it will append records to the Billing file:

Client: Id (Long), ClientName (String)
Billing: BillingDate, ClientId (Long), StartTime, StopTime

All dates and times are stored in Date/Time variables. The Client file should contain at least five names. The Billing file should be empty. When you start working on a project, click on the Start button; when you stop, click on the Stop button. At that moment, the

Figure 25. Depreciation Main Window.

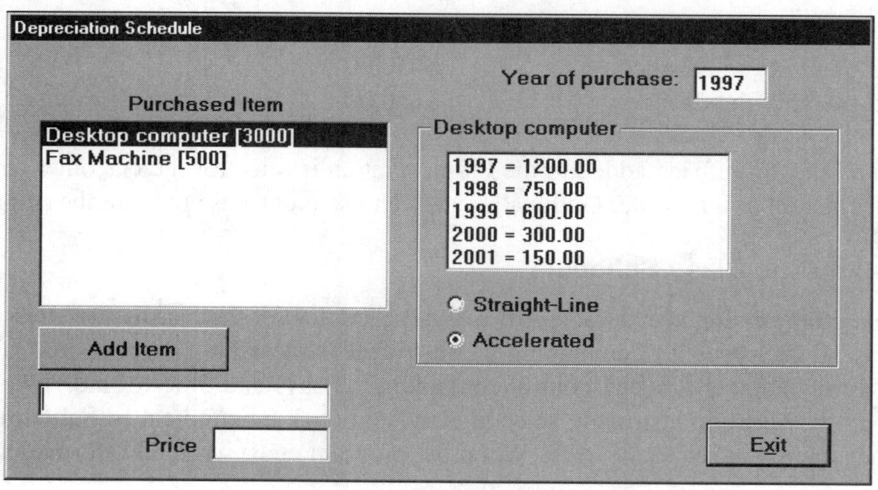

program shows the number of elapsed minutes, and writes a record to the Billing file. Here are two sample records:

Date	CustID	Start	Stop	Elapsed
02-01-1999	1101	21:51	22:10	19
02-02-1999	2034	10:20	12:25	125

Figure 26 shows a sample of the main window. The name of the selected client should appear in the window caption.

It is important to coordinate the command buttons carefully to make sure the user cannot click out of sequence. The following table shows the two possible program states that affect the buttons. The program is in State 1 when it starts; after clicking on Start, the program enters State 2:

State	Start	Stop	Exit
1	Enabled	Disabled	Enabled
2	Disabled	Enabled	Enabled

When the user clicks on the Start button, display a status message "Billing in Progress..." to clearly show that the clock is running. You can use a timer control to vary the ForeColor property of this status message once every 1/2 second. When the Stop button is clicked, the stop time and the number of billable hours and minutes are displayed.

Billing File. The program must append a new record to the Billing file when the Stop button is pressed. The client name is chosen from a ComboBox control. All times are displayed as 24-hour clock values. The following expression returns time of day in hh:mm format:

```
Format$(Now, "hh:mm")
```

Select an icon for the main window, possibly a clock. Compile the project to an EXE program so it can be run as a stand-alone program. ***Hint:*** The Visual Basic Timer() function returns the number of seconds that have elapsed since midnight.

Figure 26. TimeClock Program.

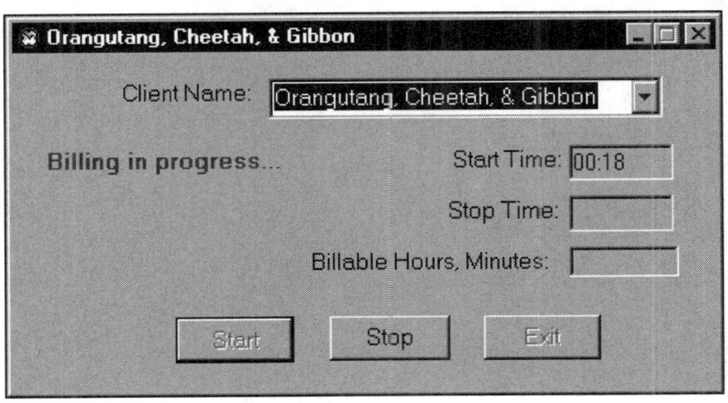

2.8.10 Classical Music Catalog - 1

Anyone who collects classical music CDs often encounters an annoying problem: it is nearly impossible to remember exactly which recordings of which compositions are in the Collection. To help remedy this problem, you can create a cataloging program suited to your needs.

There are a number of shareware programs for cataloging CDs available on the Internet and ther online services, but nearly all are oriented towards popular music. For example, they often represent an entire album as a single data entity. Or, they organize data entries according to star performers. The composers of the songs themselves may only be a footnote. In the proposed CD cataloging system, each composition is assigned a separate entry. Your instructor will determine whether the information is to be stored in (1) a sequential file, (2) a random-access file, or (3) a database.

From the user's point of view, the greatest inconvenience in using a music cataloging program is having to enter a large amount of data. To help reduce typing for the user, you can use ComboBox controls for the composer, instrumentation, soloist, and conductor fields. Store these values in text files or database tables, and load the ComboBox controls at runtime. New names can be added to the files whenever necessary. Figure 27 shows a sample of the program's main window; feel free to design a more interesting one of your own. Not all entries will have a soloist, as is the case in this sample containing Symphony No. 5 by Beethoven. The **Save** button saves the information in a file or database, and the **Close** button closes this window and ends the program.

2.8.11 Searching the Classical Music Catalog

Using the Music Cataloging program from the previous exercise, allow the user to search for records using any *one* of the following fields: CD number, Composer, Title, Instrumentation, Soloist, Conductor. The user should be able to select the search value from one of the ComboBox controls shown here. The program will then build a list of composition names and CD numbers and place it in a ListBox control. For example, if the user wants to find all compositions by J.S. Bach, the composer's name is selected before clicking on the **Find** button (see Figure 28).

Figure 27. Classical Music Catalog, Main Window.

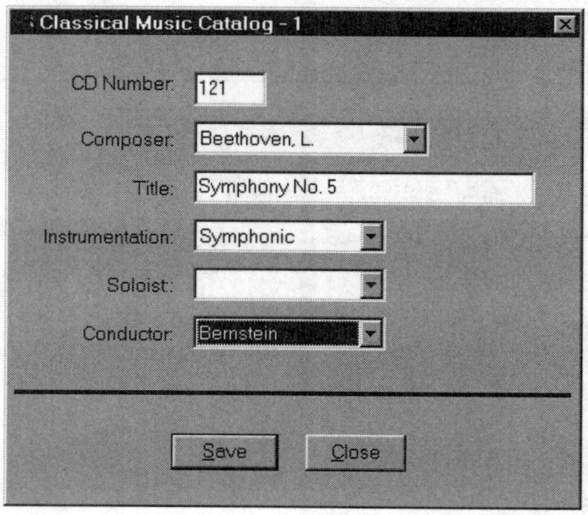

The program then builds a list of compositions by that composer. Optionally, the list can be sorted alphabetically by title (see Figure 29). If the user selects one of the titles by double-clicking in the ListBox control, the program should return to the main window and display all the details of the selected title. Suppose the user selected *Air on the G String*; the details might be displayed as in Figure 30.

Figure 28. Searching for a Single Composer's Compositions.

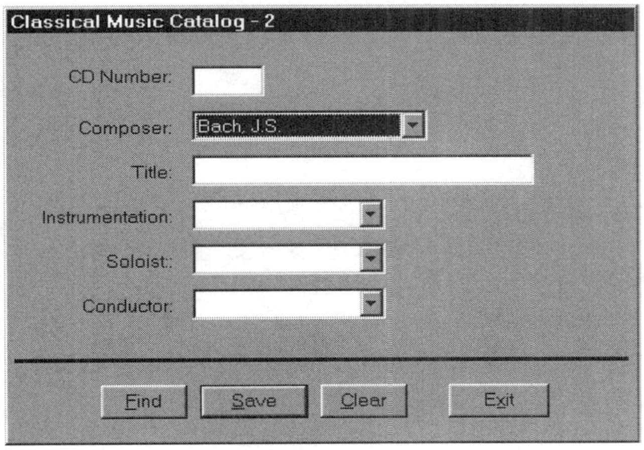

Figure 29. Found: Compositions by J.S. Bach.

Figure 30. Details of a Single Title.

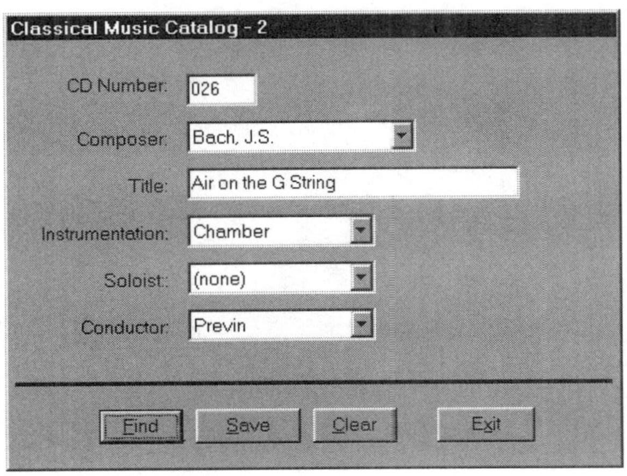

2.8.12 College Registration Wizard

Implement the complete College Registration Wizard program shown earlier in Section 2.4.1.

3 *Objects and Collections*

Chapter Contents

- Object Variables
  - Declaring and Assigning Objects
  - Control Arrays
  - Creating a Control Array at Design Time
  - Filling a Control Array at Runtime
- Collections
  - Predefined Visual Basic Collections
  - Programmer-Defined Collections
  - Adding Objects to a Collection
  - Returning References to Members of a Collection
  - Removing Members of a Collection
  - Example: Resizing Controls on a Form
- ListView Control
  - Overview
  - Example: Music CD Collection Viewer
- TreeView Control
  - Overview
  - Example: Interactively Building a Tree
  - Traversing and Saving the Tree
  - Attaching Icons to a TreeView Control
- CoolBar Control
  - Properties
  - Example: CoolBar, ToolBar, ImageCombo, and Combo
- Creating MDI Applications
  - Overview
  - MDI Vehicle Reservations
  - Program Implementation
- Review Questions
- Chapter Exercises

3.1 OBJECT VARIABLES

In Visual Basic, as in any programming language, an object is an instance of a class. A class, on the other hand, is a definition of a data type that includes properties, methods, and optionally, events. Forms are objects, as are all the controls displayed on forms. In this chapter we show how to create objects using program code, because this opens up a whole new area of programming in Visual Basic. Objects can be created, their properties modified, and their methods called without their even being visible. You can also create an array or Collection of objects, using a single object as a prototype.

3.1.1 Declaring and Assigning Objects

A number of object types are predefined in Visual Basic. All forms in a project are automatically defined as object types. For example, suppose that the frmEdit Form had already been added to the current project; the following code would create a new instance of frmEdit, assign a value to its caption, and display the Form:

```
Dim frmTemp As New frmEdit
frmTemp.Caption = "New Form"
frmTemp.Show vbModal
```

Visual Basic controls are predefined object types. Some of the more common types are CheckBox, CommandButton, Control, ComboBox, DataGrid, DataCombo, DataList, Frame, HScrollBar, Image, Label, ListBox, OptionButton, PictureBox, TextBox, Timer, and VScrollBar. If you need to pass one of these objects to a procedure, for example, you can declare the parameter type as the control's type. The following Toggle procedure, for example, reverses the state of any CheckBox control:

```
Private Sub Toggle(chk As CheckBox)
  If chk.Value = vbChecked Then
    chk.Value = vbUnchecked
  Else
    chk.Value = vbChecked
  End If
End Sub
```

The following procedure, called **ShowForm**, takes any Form object as its first parameter and a Boolean value as its second:

```
Public Sub ShowForm(frm As Form, IsModal As Boolean)
  If IsModal Then
    frm.Show vbModal
  Else
    frm.Show vbModeless
  End If
End Sub
```

The following **RandomMove** procedure moves a CommandButton object to a random location on the current Form. The Height and Width variables used here refer to the Height and Width properties of the current Form:

```
Private Sub RandomMove(btn As CommandButton)
  btn.Left = Rnd * (Width - btn.Width)
  btn.Top = Rnd * (ScaleHeight - btn.Height)
End Sub
```

3.1.2 Control Arrays

We often use unique names for all controls placed on the same Form because the names clearly identify the controls' meanings. For example, a Form containing an employee record might contain text boxes named txtID, txtLastName, txtFirstName, txtSalary, and so on. But many programmers prefer to assign a single name to a group of text boxes,

OptionButtons, CheckBoxes, or some other type of control. A subscript is used to select individual members of a control array.

Imagine that an employee record might be represented by an array of text boxes named txtEmployee. One could use a loop to check for missing input, clear the boxes, write them to a file, and so on. A control array uses less memory than the same number of separately named controls. Similarly, an array of OptionButtons or check boxes can streamline the process of querying the control values, or of clearing the control values. In general, it is very easy to carry out the same operation on each element of a control array.

A control array can be created in two ways:

- At design time, you can assign a value to the Index property of a control.
- In run mode, you can use the Load statement to create new instances of an existing control.

Using program code, you can also declare arrays of controls and forms:

```
Dim formList(0 to 10) as Form
Dim cmdQuest(0 to 50) as CommandButton
Dim allOptions(0 to 10) as OptionButton
```

The **Set** statement must be used when assigning an existing object to a control array:

```
Set formList(0) = frmMain
Set cmdQuest(j) = cmdChoiceA
```

In other words, frmMain would have to be the name of a Form that was already part of the current project, and cmdChoiceA would have to be a Command button that was created at design time.

Manipulating an Array of Text Boxes. When using an array of objects, you can easily manipulate the properties and methods of all members of the array. For example, to clear an array of TextBox controls on the same Form, a loop simplifies the task:

```
Dim j As Integer
For j = 0 to 9
   txtEmployee(j).Text = ""
Next j
```

The same operation on separately named controls is not as concise:

```
txtID.Text = ""
txtLastName.Text = ""
txtMiddleInit.Text = ""
txtFirstName.Text = ""
txtSalary.Text = ""
txtPhone.Text = ""
txtStreetAddress.Text = ""
txtCity.Text = ""
txtState.Text = ""
txtZip.Text = ""
```

Enumerated Constants. Experienced programmers often declare enumerated constants identifying the fields and use the constants as subscripts when referencing individual text boxes. Here is a declaration that would work for the txtEmployee array:

```
Private Enum EmployeeFields
  Id = 0
  LastName = 1
  MiddleInit = 2
  FirstName = 3
  '...etc.
End Enum

Sub ShowNames()
   Print txtEmployee(Id).Text
   Print txtEmployee(LastName).Text
   '...etc.
End sub
```

If the Enum declaration is within a Form or class module, it must be declared Private. If it is in a code module, it may be declared either Public or Private.

3.1.3 Creating a Control Array at Design Time

At design time, you can create a control array that contains multiple instances of the same type of control. For example, three OptionButtons named optColor(0), optColor(1), and optColor(2) are a control array. Each has a different value in its Index property (0, 1, 2). In fact, when the index property of a control is given a value, even zero, the control automatically becomes part of a control array.

You can use the Windows clipboard to copy and paste multiple instances of the same control onto a form by following these steps:

1. Create the first instance of the control by dragging it from the ToolBox onto a Form.
2. Select the control with the mouse and copy it to the Windows clipboard.
3. Paste the clipboard contents onto the Form. When you are asked whether you want to create a control array, answer Yes. The control will appear in the upper left corner of the Form.
4. Use the mouse to drag the new control to its desired location.
5. Repeat steps 3 and 4 to create more instances of the control.

Once properties such as Font, ForeColor, BackColor, and Alignment have been set for the first instance of a control, each copy of the control pasted onto the Form is automatically assigned the same properties. In Figure 1, for example, the Form contains an array of text controls named **txtArray**.

Only a single event handler is required for an entire control array. For example, the Change event for **txtArray** has a parameter called **Index** that identifies which member of the array has had its contents changed:

Figure 1. Control Array of Text Boxes.

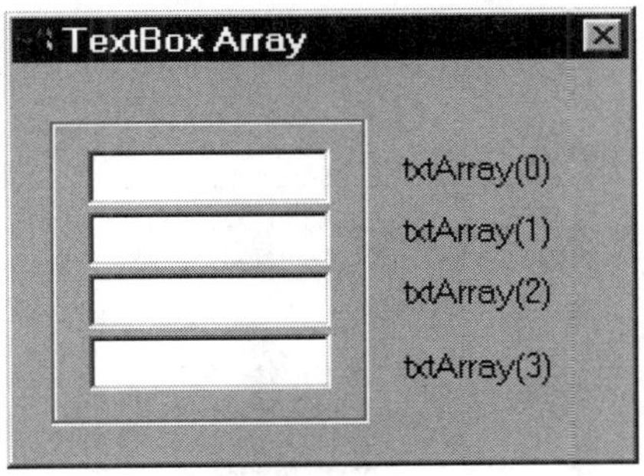


```
Private Sub txtArray_Change(Index As Integer)
   txtArray.Text(Index) = Ucase(txtArray.Text(Index))
End Sub
```

3.1.4 Filling a Control Array at Runtime

(samples: Buttons)

A control array can be filled with new controls at runtime, as long as a single instance of the control array already exists. For example, let's create an array of Command buttons called cmdBtn. Each would automatically have the same properties as cmdBtn(0):

```
For j = 1 To 9
  Load cmdBtn(j)          'create a button
Next j
```

The original instance of cmdBtn placed on the Form must be the first element of a control array, accomplished by setting its Index property to zero. Any new buttons added to the array automatically have the same properties, so the buttons are placed on top of each other, except that the new button's Visible property is False. Therefore, so see the new buttons, each new button is positioned just to the right of the previous one, and its Visible property is set to True. The following procedure adds nine buttons to a control array called cmdBtn, aligning them horizontally:

```
Private Sub cmdStart_Click()
  Dim leftpos As Integer, j As Integer
  Dim buttonWidth As Integer

  'Get the size and position of the first button.
  leftpos = cmdBtn(0).Left
  buttonWidth = cmdBtn(0).Width

  'Position the other buttons and make them visible.
  For j = 1 To 9
    Load cmdBtn(j)
    leftpos = leftpos + buttonWidth + 30
    cmdBtn(j).Left = leftpos
    cmdBtn(j).Caption = j
    cmdBtn(j).Visible = True
  Next j
End Sub
```

Figure 2 shows the running program before and after the user clicks on "Start" to create the buttons.

Figure 2. Filling a CommandButton Array at Runtime.

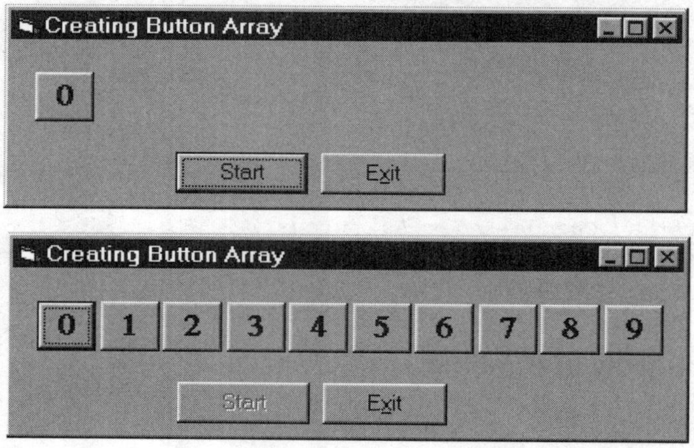

3.2 COLLECTIONS

3.2.1 Predefined Visual Basic Collections

Collections are the powerful relatives of arrays in Visual Basic. A Collection can contain strings, numbers, forms, buttons, and other types of objects. The objects in a Collection are called **members**. Every Collection has a **Count** property that returns the number of items in the Collection.

Visual Basic creates several standard collections. One, called **Forms**, contains all forms that have loaded into memory. Another, called **Controls**, contains all of the controls on a single Form. The following statements print the names of all currently loaded forms, using a subscript to refer to each member of the Collection:

```
Dim j As Integer
For j = 0 To Forms.Count - 1
   Debug.Print Forms(j).Name
Next j
```

Similarly, every Form contains a **Controls** Collection. The following statements loop through the controls in frmMain and display their names:

```
Dim j As Integer
For j = 0 To frmMain.Controls.Count - 1
   Debug.Print frmMain.Controls(j).Name
Next j
```

The following code does the same thing, using a **For Each** loop. This loop does not require a loop counter, but we do have to declare an object variable that matches the general type of all of the controls:

```
Dim ctrl As Control
For Each ctrl In frmMain.Controls
   Debug.Print ctrl.Name
Next ctrl
```

All controls have a **Name** property, so the reference to **ctrl.Name** is valid.

A Visual Basic program does not terminate until all of its forms have been unloaded. For that reason, it is often useful to execute a loop when the program ends that unloads all members of the Forms Collection:

```
Dim frm As Form
For Each frm In Forms
   Unload frm
   Set frm = Nothing
Next frm
```

3.2.2 Programmer-Defined Collections

You can create your own collections, called *programmer-defined collections*, and take advantage of their power and convenience. In general, collections are easier to use than arrays, particularly when elements must be inserted and removed at runtime. Collections also have a built-in search mechanism. To both declare and create a Collection object, use the **Dim** statement with the **New** operator:

```
Dim mcollFriends as New Collection
```

Or, you can first declare a variable that will refer to the Collection, and at a later time, use the **New** operator to create the actual Collection object. This separation of tasks lets you determine exactly when the Collection is created, a feature called *late binding*. In the following example, the **mcolFriends** Collection is initialized during the Form_Load event:

```
Option Explicit
Private mcolFriends as Collection

Private Sub Form_Load()
   Set mcolFriends = New Collection
End Sub
```

There is one important difference between built-in collections and programmer-defined collections: The indexes (subscripts) of the former begin at 0, whereas the indexes of the latter begin at 1.

Using Keys to Identify Members. The members of a Collection can be accessed using numeric indexes, or each member can be associated with a unique string, called a *key*. No two members can have the same key value, and the key must be a string expression. For example, we might want to create a Collection in which each person's social security number is the key and the person's name is the member:

SSN (key)	Name (member)
222-33-4444	Jones, S.
987-65-4234	Chong, A.
123-65-4321	Gonzalez, J.
879-56-3435	Schwartz, E.

To destroy a Collection, set its identifier to **Nothing** (a Visual Basic keyword):

```
Set mcolFriends = Nothing
```

Collections have a property called **Count** that returns the number of members in the Collection. You can use it, for example, to determine the number of items to be processed in a loop:

```
For j = 1 to mcolFriends.Count
   Print mcolFriends(j)
Next j
```

Notice in this example, that an index can be used to access each Collection item, just as a subscript can be used to access array elements.

3.2.3 Adding Objects to a Collection

To add a member to a Collection, call the **Add** method. The syntax is:

```
object.Add( member, key, before, after )
```

The object must be a Collection object. *member* is the object to be added; it is the only required parameter. *key* is a unique string value that is associated with the item, and can be used to look up a specific member. The optional *before* and *after* parameters can be used to specify a relative position in the Collection. It actual practice they are rarely used. The Add method generates a runtime error if an attempt is made to insert a new member whose key is already in the Collection, so you should provide an On Error GoTo statement to trap the error. The following are both valid calls to the Add method:

```
With mcolFriends
   .Add "Baker, G."
   .Add "Jones, S.", "222-33-4444"
End With
```

Any type of object can be inserted in a Collection, and the members of a Collection need not be the same type. The following Collection contains various types of information, which might not be particularly useful:

```
With mcolMiscellaneous
.Add 26
.Add 284.5
.Add "Fish"
.Add Form1
.Add True
End With
```

3.2.4 Returning References to Members of a Collection

Collections are designed to enable searching for members, as long as the member key values are known. The **Item** property returns a reference to the member that is associated with the key value. There are two ways to access the Item property. The first is using an integer that identifies the member's index position in the Collection. The second is using a key value. The two formats are shown here:

```
target = object.Item( index As Integer )
target = object.Item( key As String )
```

User-defined collections are indexed from 1 to Count. If a string is passed as an argument, the Item property searches for a member with a matching key value. Accessing the Item property generates a runtime error if no matching member is found in the Collection. In the following example, when we search for the key "123654321", the value "Gonzalez, J." is assigned to nameFound:

```
mcolFriends.Add "Gonzalez, J.", "123654321"
'(...add other members...)

Dim nameFound As String
nameFound = mcolFriends.Item( "123654321" )
```

If *target* is an object variable, the Set statement must be used when assigning the value returned by Item. For example, we retrieve a Form object from a Collection and assign it to a Form variable:

```
Dim frmTemp As Form
Set frmTemp = collMyForms.Item( index )
```

Because Item is the default property of a Collection, a shorthand way of referring it is to use parentheses. The following two expressions are equivalent:

```
mcolFriends.Item("123654321")
mcolFriends("123654321")
```

Copies and References. It is important to understand the difference between making a copy of a member versus assigning a reference to the member. If a Collection contains a member that is a fundamental data type such as Integer, Single, or String, the Item property returns a copy of the Collection member. Any subsequent changes you make to the copied variable do not affect the corresponding member in the Collection. In the next example, colNames contains a person's name. The Item property returns a copy of the name and sets it to an empty string:

```
Dim strTemp As String
mColNames.Add "Sam"
strTemp = mColNames.Item(1)
strTemp = ""
Debug.Print mColNames.Item(1)        ' "Sam" appears
```

You can see that the name stored in the Collection did not change. But this is not the case when a Collection contains objects. Here is another example, in which we insert a Form object in a Collection, assign the Collection item to another Form variable, and modify the latter's caption:

```
Private mcolMyforms As New Collection

Private Sub Form_Load()
   mcolMyforms.Add Form2
   Form2.Show
End Sub

Private Sub cmdRefForm_Click()
   Dim frmTemp As Form
   Set frmTemp = mcolMyforms.Item(1)
   frmTemp.Caption = "Actual Form"
End Sub
```

When we assign the Collection member to frmTemp, the later simply contains a reference (or *pointer*) to Form2 rather than creating a new Form. When we appear to modify only the caption of frmTemp, we are actually modifying the caption of Form2. This can be easily tested, and is shown by the demonstration program on the student disk in the FormColl directory.

3.2.5 Removing Members of a Collection

Use the **Remove** method to remove a member of a Collection. The syntax is:

object.**Remove** *index*

As with the Item property, *index* may either be an integer expression or a string value that matches one of the keys in the Collection. For example,

```
mcolFriends.Remove 5
mcolFriends.Remove "222334444"
```

The **Remove** method generates a runtime error if no matching member is found in the Collection. The standard error message generated by Visual Basic, "Invalid procedure call or argument," can be somewhat ambiguous. Instead, trap for the specific value in Err.Number, which is 5, and display your own message. The following procedure, called **RemoveItem**, takes a Collection and a key as input parameters, and returns True if the item was successfully removed. If the item is not found, a message is displayed and the function returns False:

```
Private Function RemoveItem(coll As Collection, _
   strKey As String) As Boolean
   On Error GoTo RemoveItemErr
   coll.Remove strKey
   RemoveItem = True
   Exit Function

RemoveItemErr:
   If Err.Number = 5 Then
     MsgBox "The key you requested, '" & strKey & _
        "' cannot be found in the Collection"
   Else
```

```
    MsgBox Error$
  End If
  RemoveItem = False
End Function
```

Removing All Collection Members. The following **ClearCollection** procedure is a general-purpose loop that removes all members of a user-defined Collection object:

```
Public Sub ClearCollection(coll As Collection)
  Dim obj As Variant
  For Each obj In coll
    coll.Remove 1
  Next obj
End Sub
```

3.2.6 Example: Resizing Controls on a Form

(samples: Resize)

You may have noticed that some Windows applications are able to adjust the height and width of controls on a Form when it is resized by the user. One way to do this is to compare the new dimensions of the window to its previous dimensions, and use this ratio to scale the positions and dimensions of all of the controls in the window.

Let's write a general-purpose procedure in Visual Basic that adjusts the width and horizontal positions of all controls on a Form when the Form is resized. Figure 3 shows a sample Form as it appears before the user resizes it.

When the user drags the corner of the Form, all controls automatically adjust their Left and Width properties (Figure 4). The Stretch property of the Image control is set to True.

Figure 3. Before Resizing the Form.

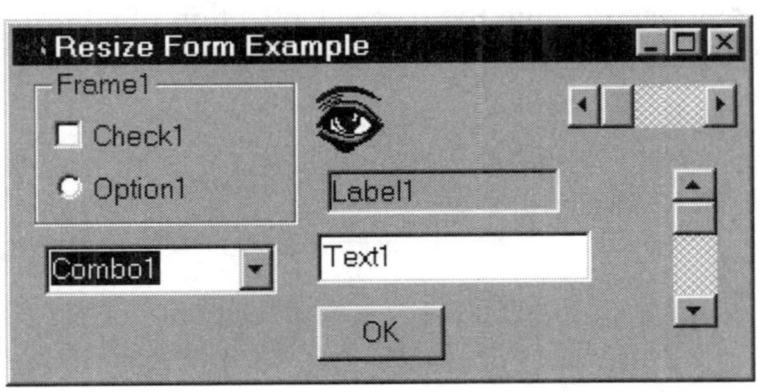

Program Code. Here's how to do it: First, we save the current height and width in module variables, in the Form_Activate event handler, which fires before the Form_Resize event:

```
Private mintSaveWidth As Integer
Private mintSaveHeight As Integer

Private Sub Form_Activate()
  mintSaveWidth = Me.Width
  mintSaveHeight = Me.Height
End Sub
```

Figure 4. After Resizing the Form.

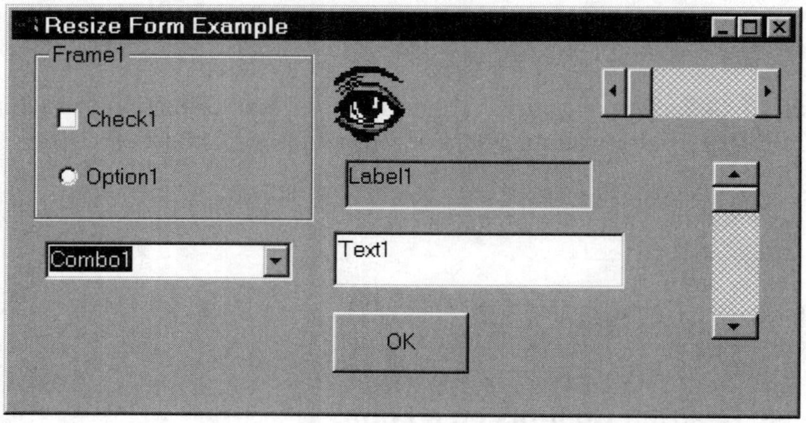

A **Form_Resize** event is generated when a Form is first shown, and when the user resizes the Form with the mouse. In the event handler procedure it calls ResizeControls, passing a reference to the current Form (called **Me**) along with the saved width and height of the current Form:

```
Private Sub Form_Resize()
   ResizeControls Me, mintSaveWidth, mintSaveHeight
End Sub
```

All that remains, then, is to create the ResizeControls procedure that takes the current Form and its previously saved height and width, and resizes the form's controls.

The **ResizeControls** procedure is placed in a general code module so it can be called from anywhere in a program. It calculates the ratios between the old and new heights and widths of the Form. Then, we iterate through the form's Collection of controls and recalculate each control's position and size:

```
Public Sub ResizeControls(ByRef frm As Form, _
   ByRef oldWidth As Integer, oldHeight As Integer)
   'Don't try to adjust a minimized Form.
   If frm.WindowState = vbMinimized Then Exit Sub
   Dim ratioW As Single, ratioH As Single
   ratioW = frm.Width / oldWidth
   ratioH = frm.Height / oldHeight

   On Error Resume Next
   Dim ctrl As Control
   For Each ctrl In frm.Controls
     With ctrl
        .Width = .Width * ratioW
        .Left = .Left * ratioW
        .Height = .Height * ratioH
        .Top = .Top * ratioH
     End With
   Next ctrl
   oldWidth = frm.Width
```

```
    oldHeight = frm.Height
End Sub
```

Some types of controls such as Timer and CommonDialog do not have Height and Width properties, so the On Error Resume Next statement lets the loop continue when an invalid property is referenced. Of course, we have only resized and moved the controls. You can augment this procedure so it adjusts the font sizes of the controls.

3.3 LISTVIEW CONTROL

3.3.1 Overview

(samples: ListView)

The ListView control is one of the most widely used ActiveX controls appearing in Windows applications today. It has a number of advantages:

- Data can easily be aligned in columns, without the need for tabs.
- Columns can be resized by the user, by dragging the column borders with the mouse.
- Column widths can be set at runtime, by program statements.
- Column headers respond to click events.
- Text appearing in columns can be centered, left justified, or right justified.
- List items are stored in a Collection and can be assigned Key values, making it easy to find individual items.

To add the ListView control to a project's ToolBox window, select **Components** from the **Project** menu and place a check next to **Microsoft Windows Common Controls 6.0**.

The most well known example of the ListView control can be seen when you open the "My Computer" window in Microsoft Windows. You can display the filenames and icons in several formats: Large Icons, Small Icons, List, and Details. All of those display formats can be configured in your own programs. Along with the TreeView control, the ListView control is one of the most complex and powerful ActiveX controls and takes some time to master. But it is well worth the effort, as it can give your programs a distinctly professional appearance.

The ListView control stores each row of its display in a ListItem object. All of the rows belong to a Collection called ListItems. Each column heading is represented by ColumnHeader object, and the ListView contains a Collection called ColumnHeaders. Table 1 shows the most important ListView properties, Table 2 shows ListView methods, and Table 3 shows ListView events.

ListItem Object. A ListItem object can contain both text and pictures. Pictures, if any, must be stored in an ImageList control that is associated with the ImageList. Each ListItem contains a key value that can be used to locate and display that item. A list of ListItem properties appears in Table 4 and a list of methods appears in Table 5.

Creating Column Headings. To create column headings for a ListView control, call the ColumnHeaders.Add method. The parameters are: index, key, text, and width. The index

Table 1. ListView Properties.

Property	Description
CheckBoxes	If set to True, allows a check box to appear next to each item.
ColumnHeaders	Collection of ColumnHeader objects, each of which describing a column's appearance.
DropHighLight	If True, a ListItem is highlighted when the cursor moves over it.
LabelEdit	If set to lvwAutomatic, allows the user to interactively edit labels.
ListItems	Collection of ListItem objects, determines the contents of the rows appearing in the ListView.
SelectedItem	Returns a reference to a ListItem that has been selected by the user.
Sorted	If set to True, allows the ListView to be sorted. By default, the first column will be the sort key.
SortKey	Determines which column, will be used to sort the items.

and key are optional, the text is a string that will be the displayed heading, and the width is the width of the displayed column, in Twips.

```
With lvwSample
   'Add method: (index,key,text,width)
   .ColumnHeaders.Add , , "Name",(.Width / 3)
   .ColumnHeaders.Add , , "Phone",(.Width / 3)
   .ColumnHeaders.Add , , "Email",(.Width / 3)
   .View = lvwReport          'show all column details
End With
```

Inserting a ListItem. Call the ListView.ListItems.Add method to create and append a ListItem object to the ListView control. You can then assign any number SubItems to the ListItem. The following statements do this, storing a person's name, phone, and email

Table 2. ListView Methods.

Method	Description
FindItem	Finds and returns a reference to a ListItem. Syntax: FindItem (string, value, index, match) As ListItem.
GetFirstVisible	Returns a reference to the first visible ListItem.
HitTest	Returns a reference to the ListItem located at given x, y coordinates. Syntax: HitTest (x As Single, y As Single) As ListItem.
StartLabelEdit	Enables a user to edit a label. (Only used when the LabelEdit property is set to manual.)

Table 3. ListView Events.

Event	Description
AfterLabelEdit	Occurs immediately after the user has edited the label of a ListItem.
BeforeLabelEdit	Occurs when the user attempts to edit the label of a ListItem.
ColumnClick	Occurs when the user clicks on a column header.
FullRowSelect	If set to True, a row can be selected by clicking anywhere in the row.
ItemCheck	Occurs when the user clicks on a checkbox next to a ListItem.
ItemClick	Occurs when a ListItem is clicked.

Table 4. ListItem Properties.

Property	Description
Count	Indicates the number of elements in the SubItems array.
Ghosted	Boolean value. If True, the ListItem is dimmed (unavailable).
Item	Returns a specific string from the SubItems array.
Selected	Returns True if a ListItem has been selected by the user.
SubItems	An array of strings representing the ListItem's data.
Text	A string containing the item's displayed text.

Table 5. ListItem Methods.

Method	Description
Add	Add a new ListItem to the ListItems collection.
Clear	Removes all objects from the ListItems collection.
CreateDrag	Create a drag image using a dithered version of an object's associated image.
EnsureVisible	Make sure a ListItem is visible, scrolling the ListView control if necessary.
Remove	Remove a ListItem from the ListItems collection.

address in each ListItem. The person's employee ID is the ListItem's key string, which cannot begin with a digit:

```
Dim mItem As ListItem
Set mItem = lvwSample.ListItems.Add(, "K" & strEmployeeId)
```

```
mItem.Text = strName              'first column
mItem.SubItems(1) = strPhone      'second column
mItem.SubItems(2) = strEmail      'third column
```

In this example, when we called the Add method, the first parameter (Index) was left blank. This automatically causes the item to be appended to the list. If you want to insert an item at a specific point in the ListItems Collection, you can supply an integer value for the Index parameter.

Using CheckBoxes. You can ask the ListView to display a checkbox at the beginning of each line, allowing the user to easily select individual items. To do this, set CheckBoxes property to True:

```
lvwSample.Checkboxes = True
```

The ItemCheck event is triggered whenever the user clicks on a checkbox. The Item parameter contains a reference to the corresponding ListItem:

```
Private Sub lvwSample_ItemCheck(ByVal Item As MSComctlLib.ListItem)
   MsgBox Item.Text & " has been checked"
End Sub
```

Selecting Items. When the user clicks on the first column of a ListItem, the ListView's Click event is triggered, and you can use its SelectedItem property to find out which item was selected.

```
Private Sub lvwSample_Click()
'The user clicked on a list item.
   MsgBox lvwSample.SelectedItem.Text & " has been selected"
End Sub
```

If you set the FullRowSelect property to True, the user can click anywhere in a row to select the row.

Note: Selecting items and clicking on their check boxes are two independent operations, each with their own event handlers.

Editing Labels. If you set the LabelEdit property to lvwAutomatic, the first click on an object will select it; a second (single) click on the highlighted object will initiate the label editing operation. You may find that you get better results by displaying a popup menu when the user right-clicks a label. You can initiate editing manually by calling the StartLabelEdit method. This is how the Windows Explorer lets users rename files and directories, for example.

3.3.2 Example: Music CD Collection Viewer

(samples: ListView)

To demonstrate a useful example of the ListView control, let's create a program that lets the user input music CD titles, select a style category, and add each title to the list. A list of titles can also be loaded from a text file. Figure 5 shows a sample of the program when running. The program uses a ToolBar control along the bottom of the Form to display each available musical style category. When the user clicks on the button containing the check icon, the title is added to the ListView control.

Figure 5. Music CD Collection Example (ListView).

Program Code. Because of space limitations, we won't show all of the program source code here, but you can always load the program from the sample program disk. The ListView control in this example is called lvwTitles.

Two module-level variables are shared by various procedures:

```
Private mintAlbumID As Integer      'Album ID number
Private mstrStyle As String         'Musical style
```

In the Form_Load event handler, we create the column headers and enable sorting:

```
'Set up the column headers with titles and default widths.
  With lvwTitles
    .ColumnHeaders.Add , , "CD #", 600     'index,key,text,width
    .ColumnHeaders.Add , , "Title", 3800
    .ColumnHeaders.Add , , "Style", (.Width - 800 - 3800)
    .View = lvwReport                      'show all column details
  End With

'Allow the sort order to be changed at runtime.
  lvwTitles.Sorted = True
```

Adding Items. The **AddListItem** procedure adds a new ListItem to the ListView control by incrementing the album ID and calling the Add method from the ListItems Collection:

```
Private Sub AddListItem(strTitle As String, strStyle As String)
  Dim mItem As ListItem, strKey As String
  mintAlbumID = mintAlbumID + 1
  strKey = Format(mintAlbumID, "000")
  With lvwTitles.ListItems
    Set mItem = .Add(, "K" & strKey)      'index,key
    mItem.Text = strKey                   'album ID
    mItem.SubItems(1) = strTitle          'album title
    mItem.SubItems(2) = strStyle          'musical style
  End With
End Sub
```

The cmdLoad_Click event handler loads all the album titles from a text file and calls AddListItem:

```
Private Sub cmdLoad_Click()
   Dim fileNum As Integer, strTitle As String, _
       strStyle As String
   On Error GoTo LoadFileErr
   fileNum = FreeFile
   Open App.Path + "\titles.txt" For Input As fileNum
   Do Until EOF(fileNum)
      Input #fileNum, strTitle, strStyle
      Call AddListItem(strTitle, strStyle)
   Loop
   Close fileNum
   Exit Sub
LoadFileErr:
   MsgBox Error$, vbCritical, ""
End Sub
```

Sorting. When the user clicks on a column header, we modify the sort key accordingly. The ListView immediately sorts by the new column, in ascending order:

```
Private Sub lvwTitles_ColumnClick(ByVal ColumnHeader As _
    MSComctlLib.ColumnHeader)
    lvwTitles.SortKey = ColumnHeader.Index - 1
End Sub
```

When the user clicks on the ToolBar showing the different musical styles (Classical, Rock, etc.), we copy the ToolBar button's key value into the mstrStyle variable:

```
Private Sub tlbStyle_ButtonClick(ByVal Button As _
        MSComctlLib.Button)
'The button key is the musical style.
   mstrStyle = Button.Key
End Sub
```

3.4 TREEVIEW CONTROL

3.4.1 Overview

The TreeView provides a hierarchical view of information in a Form that is familiar with anyone who uses Microsoft Windows applications. The Windows Explorer, for example, uses a TreeView to display the directory structure of a computer in the left side of its window (see Figure 6). A plus sign icon indicates that the current level can be expanded by clicking on the icon or by double clicking on the folder name next to it. A minus sign icon can be closed up by clicking on it. The TreeView control is part of the same Microsoft Windows Common Controls library as the ListView control.

A list of important TreeView properties is shown in Table 6, a list of methods appears in Table 7, and a list of TreeView events appears in Table 8. The sheer power of the TreeView control seems overwhelming when you look at the number of properties and methods, not only of the TreeView, but also of the associated Collection of nodes. But

Figure 6. Windows Explorer Example.

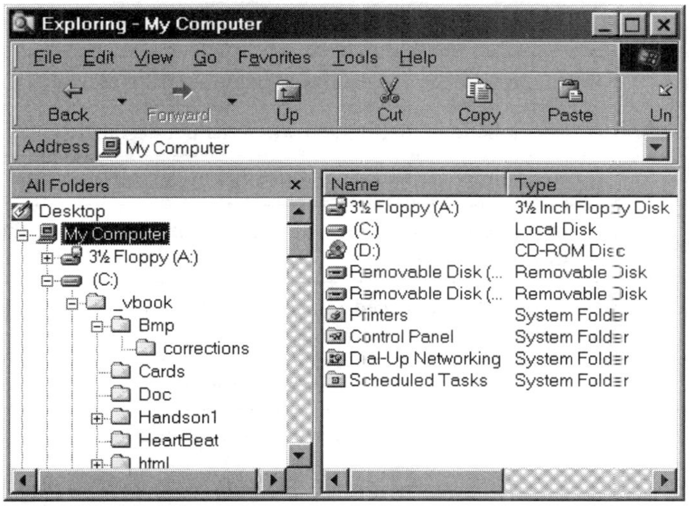

we're going to provide examples that begin in a simple way and add on extra features only when necessary. The reward for learning how to use the TreeView is that it can give programs a decidedly professional appearance and can hold a great deal of information in a small package.

The Nodes Collection. A TreeView control's basic structure revolves around its Nodes Collection, a Collection of Node objects. Each node can have a one *parent* (or no parent), zero or more *siblings* (nodes on the same level), and zero or more *children* (nodes under them). To create a tree, you have to call the Add method in the Nodes Collection (see Table 9), passing it the text you want to place in the node, and indicate where you want to place the node in relation to some other node already in the tree. Table 10 lists the properties and methods for Node objects.

Click Events. When the user clicks on a node, a Click event is generated, and you can use the TreeView's SelectedItem property to identify the node that was selected. You can expand and contract individual nodes, thereby showing or hiding the node's children, and you can force a node to be visible by calling its EnsureVisible method.

Bitmaps and Icons. Using an associated ImageList control, you can assign bitmaps and icons to individual nodes. Each node has an Image property that displays when the node has no visible children, and an ExpandedImage property that displays when the node has visible children.

Adding Nodes to a TreeView. The Add method is called when you add a new node to the tree. Its syntax is:

```
treeview.Nodes.Add( referenceNode, relationship, _
        key, text ) As Node
```

referenceNode is the index or key of an existing node, *key* is a string that produces a unique value for each node in the tree, *text* is a string that is the visible part of the node, and *relationship* is an integer selected from the following list of predefined constants:

Table 6. TreeView Properties.

Property	Description
CheckBoxes	If True, a checkbox is displayed next to each node.
DropHighLight	If True, a node is highlighted when the cursor moves over it.
FullRowSelect	If True, a row can be selected by clicking anywhere in the row.
HideSelection	If False, the selected item will remain highlighted when the TreeView control loses focus.
ImageList	The name of an attached ImageList control, which supplies icons and bitmaps for the TreeView nodes.
Indentation	Amount of indentation (in Twips) between parent and child nodes.
LabelEdit	If set to lvwAutomatic, allows the user to interactively edit a node's text.
LineStyle	Sets/returns the style of lines connecting TreeView nodes. Possible values are tvwTreeLines and tvwRootLines.
Nodes	A collection of Node objects that represents the tree structure.
PathSeparator	Sets/returns the delimiter string used in the path returned by the FullPath property.
SelectedItem	Returns a reference to a Node that has been selected by the user.
Sorted	If True, nodes are sorted alphabetically by their Text property.
Style	Sets/returns or sets the type of graphics and text that appear for each Node object in a TreeView control. Possible values are: Text only; Image and text; Plus/minus and text; Plus/minus, image, and text; Lines and text; Lines, image, and text; Lines, plus/minus, and text; Lines, plus/minus, image, and text.

tvwChild, tvwFirst, tvwLast, tvwPrevious, and tvwNext. The key string cannot begin with a digit.

Examples. The following statement adds a node called "Root Node" to an empty tree. Its key value is "K001":

```
treSample.Nodes.Add(,,"K001",  "Root  Node")
```

The following adds a new node that is a child of an existing node called mnodCurrent, assigning a key value of "K002" and text equal to "Sample Text":

```
treSample.Nodes.Add(mnodCurrent.Key, _
        tvwChild, "K002", "Sample Text")
```

3.4.2 Example: Interactively Building a Tree

(samples: TreeView1)

Table 7. TreeView Methods.

Method	Description
GetVisibleCount	Returns the number of nodes that fit in the internal area of the TreeView.
HitTest	Returns a reference to the node located at given x, y coordinates. Syntax: HitTest (x As Single, y As Single) As Node.
StartLabelEdit	Enables a user to edit a label. (Only used when the LabelEdit property is set to manual.)
EnsureVisible	Make sure a ListItem is visible, scrolling the ListView control if necessary.
Remove	Remove a ListItem from the ListItems collection.
Clear	Removes all objects from the ListItems collection.

Table 8. TreeView Events.

Event	Description
AfterLabelEdit	Occurs immediately after the user has edited the label of a ListItem.
BeforeLabelEdit	Occurs when the user attempts to edit the label of a ListItem.
Expand	Occurs when any node is expanded.
Collapse	Occurs when any node is collapsed.
NodeClick	Occurs when a node is clicked.
NodeCheck	Occurs when a node is checked or unchecked (the CheckBoxes property must be True).

Table 9. Nodes Collection Properties and Methods.

Method	Description
Add	Add a new Node object to the collection.
Clear	Removes all objects from the Nodes collection.
CreateDragImage	Creates a drag image using a dithered version of an object's associated image.
Remove	Remove a Node from the Nodes collection.

Let's take a look at a simple program that lets the user interactively insert nodes in a TreeView control. Run the sample program in the TreeView1 directory of the sample CD-ROM supplied with this book. Type the word *Library* into the Text control and press the Enter key (or click the Add button) to copy this word into the tree. *Library* represents the

Table 10. Node Object Properties and Methods.

Event	Description
Checked	True if this node is currently checked.
Child	Sets/returns a reference to the child node attached to this node.
Children	Returns the number of child nodes attached to this node.
EnsureVisible	Make sure a node is visible by expanding its parent node. (method)
Expand	Expand this node, showing its child nodes. (method)
ExpandedImage	Sets/returns the index or key value of the ListImage object attached to this node when it is expanded to reveal its child nodes.
FirstSibling	Returns a reference to the node stored in the first position of the same level as this node.
FullPath	Returns a string containing the path from the root to this node.
Image	Sets/returns index/key of the ListImage object attached to this node.
LastSibling	Returns a reference to the node stored in the last position of the same level as this node.
Next	Returns a reference to the next node at the same level as this node.
Parent	Returns a reference to the parent node of this node.
Previous	Returns a reference to the previous node at the same level as this node.
Root	Returns a reference to the root node of this node.

root node of the tree. Now type the word *History* into the Text control and add it to the tree. *History* should appear as a child node of *Library*, as in Figure 7.

Figure 7. Adding a Child Node.

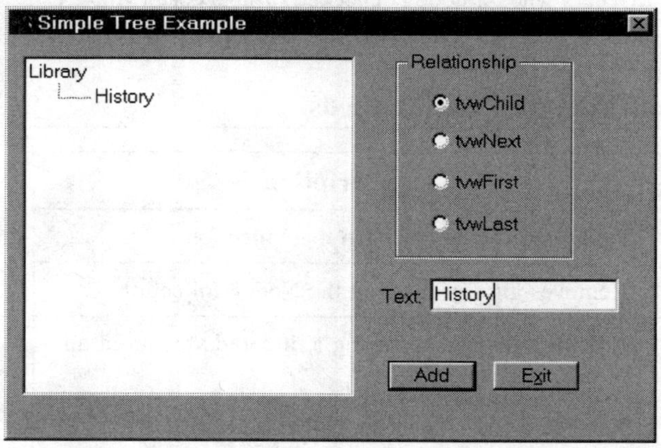

Repeat the same procedure to add the following child nodes: *Art*, *Music*, *Science*, and *Philosophy*. Figure 8 shows the TreeView containing the list of book categories, stored at the second hierarchical level. All are child nodes of the root node.

Figure 8. TreeView with Second-Level Headings.

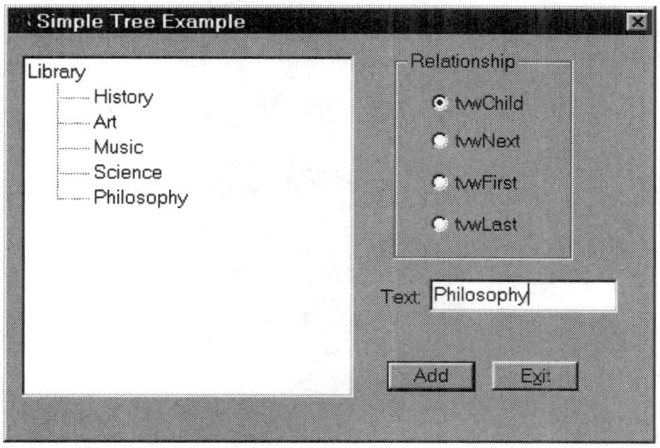

Select the Music node and insert two children, called *Classical* and *Romantic*. The *Music* node remains highlighted even when the focus shifts to the Text control, because the TreeView's HideSelection property was set to False (see Figure 9). Click on the "+" symbol next to *Music* and notice that the node expands and collapses automatically.

Figure 9. Expanded Music Node.

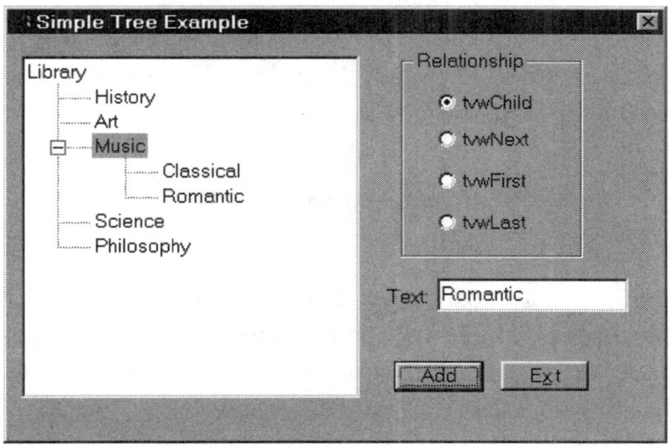

Click on the *Classical* node, select the tvwFirst OptionButton, and type *Baroque*. Notice that the new node is inserted before the current node, at the same hierarchical level. Now click on *Romantic*, select the tvwNext OptionButton, and type *Impressionist*. You should see the sequence of nodes shown in Figure 10.

How Does it Work? Three variables are declared at the module level in frmMain: mnodCurrent identifies the currently selected node, if any. The currently selected type of relationship is contained in mintRelationship. The mintCurrentKey variable contains an integer that is automatically incremented as we add each node.

```
Private mnodCurrent As Node
Private mintRelationship As Integer
Private mintCurrentKey As Integer
```

Figure 10. Using tvwFirst and tvwNext Relationships.

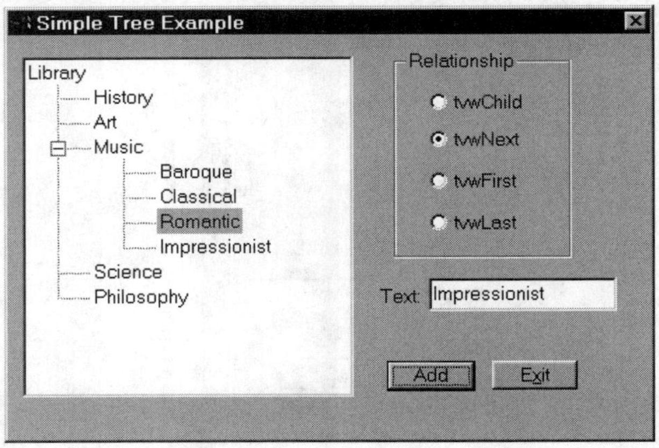

In Form_Load, we set HideSelection to False so nodes will remain highlighted when the user moves the focus to the Text control. We set the default node relationship to tvwChild:

```
Private Sub Form_Load()
   treSample.HideSelection = False
   mintRelationship = tvwChild
End Sub
```

When the user clicks on a node, we assign the SelectedItem property (a Node reference) to the mnodCurrent variable:

```
Private Sub treSample_Click()
   Set mnodCurrent = treSample.SelectedItem
End Sub
```

Adding nodes to the tree is the most complicated part of the program. When the root node is inserted, the mnodCurrent variable will be Nothing, so an if statement calls the Add method without specifying a parent node, a runtime error will occur. We also increment mintCurrentKey to be sure each node has a unique key value:

```
Private Sub cmdAdd_Click()
   Dim nodTemp As Node
   mintCurrentKey = mintCurrentKey + 1

   If mnodCurrent Is Nothing Then
      Set nodTemp = treSample.Nodes.Add(, mintRelationship, _
          "K" & mintCurrentKey, txtValue.Text)
      Set mnodCurrent = nodTemp
   Else
      Set nodTemp = treSample.Nodes.Add(mnodCurrent.Key, _
          mintRelationship, "K" & mintCurrentKey, txtValue.Text)
   End If
   nodTemp.EnsureVisible
End Sub
```

Each OptionButton has a click event handler that assigns a different value to the mintRelationship variable:

```
Private Sub optChild_Click()
  mintRelationship = tvwChild
End Sub

Private Sub optFirst_Click()
  mintRelationship = tvwFirst
End Sub

Private Sub optLast_Click()
  mintRelationship = tvwLast
End Sub

Private Sub optNext_Click()
  mintRelationship = tvwNext
End Sub
```

3.4.3 Traversing and Saving the Tree

(samples: TreeView2)

Occasionally, you might need to save the contents of a TreeView in a file so it can be loaded back into a TreeView at a later time. To do this, you need to *traverse* (visit each node of) the tree. The traditional method is to use a recursive procedure, one that calls itself.

Using the previous TreeView program as a starting point, let's add a new button called Save (See Figure 11). Given the information displayed in the figure, when the user clicks on Save, the following data is saved in a text file. Each record contains a level number, node key, and node text:

```
0,"K1","Root"
1,"K2","Child1"
2,"K5","GrandChild1"
2,"K6","GrandChild2"
2,"K7","GrandChild3"
```

Figure 11. TreeView Version 2.

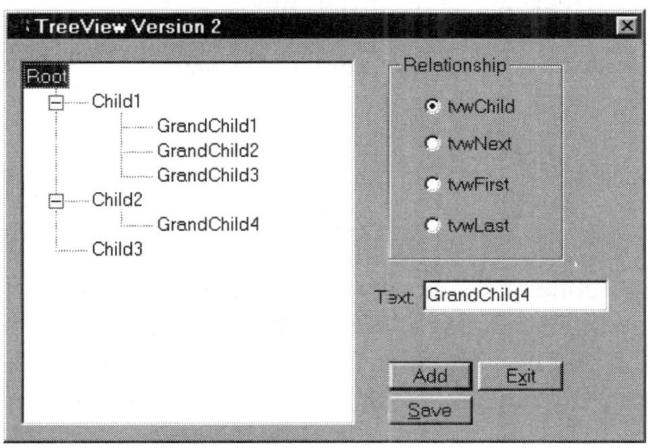

```
1,"K3","Child2"
2,"K8","GrandChild4"
1,"K4","Child3"
```

From the ordering of the data, we can tell that the program has performed a *depth-first inorder traversal*. This means that we add the root node, visit and add its first child (Child1), visiting all the descendants of Child1, back up to Child2, add it, visit its descendants, and so on. This continues until all of the root node's children have been visited.

Program Code. First we code the event handler for the Save button. The call to SaveTree passes the TreeView's root node, the file number, and a number that identifies the nesting level:

```
Private Sub cmdSave_Click()
'Save the tree into a text file.
   Dim intFileNum As Integer
   intFileNum = FreeFile
   On Error GoTo SaveErr
   Open mstrFileName For Output As intFileNum
   'Begin the recursion, starting with the root node.
   Call SaveTree(treSample.Nodes(1).Root, intFileNum, 0)
   Close intFileNum
   Exit Sub
SaveErr:
   MsgBox Error$, vbCritical, "Save Error"
End Sub
```

The **SaveTree** procedure is where things really get interesting. We write the current nesting level (intDepth), the node key, and the node text to the output file. Then, if the node has any children, we loop through the Nodes Collection, looking for any nodes that have the current node as their parent:

```
Private Sub SaveTree(ByVal nodCurrent As Node, _
        ByVal intFileNum As Integer, ByVal intDepth As Integer)
    Dim nodChild As Node
    Write #intFileNum, intDepth, nodCurrent.Key, nodCurrent.Text
    If nodCurrent.Children > 0 Then
       'Look for the children of this node, and save each.
       For Each nodChild In treSample.Nodes
          If Not nodChild.Parent Is Nothing Then
             If nodChild.Parent = nodCurrent Then
                SaveTree nodChild, intFileNum, (intDepth + 1)
             End If
          End If
       Next nodChild
    End If
End Sub
```

For any node that is a child of this node, we call **SaveTree**, passing the child node, the file number, and the nesting level plus 1. We use the term *recursion* to express the idea that a procedure calls itself, exactly what **SaveTree** does in the example. The **SaveTree** procedure can save a tree of virtually any depth, depending on how long one is willing to let the program run. Unfortunately, because each node has no direct link to its children, the procedure must repeatedly loop over the nodes Collection to find the current node's children. This is decidedly inefficient, but still practical for trees having fewer than a few hundred nodes.

3.4.4 Attaching Icons to a TreeView Control

(samples: TreeView3)

Most TreeView controls use graphic images, such as file folders, to augment the tree's appearance. There are two basic steps involved: first you must fill an ImageList control with all bitmaps you plan to use in the tree. Second, set the ImageList property in the TreeView control to the name of your ImageList control. Third, write code in the ImageList Collapse and Expand events that assigns the appropriate graphic to the current TreeView node.

We're going to modify the second version of the sample TreeView program and call it Version 3. This program will attach bitmaps to nodes in the tree, as in the running program shown in Figure 12. First, we need to add an ImageList control to the Form and name it ilsList. To find the bitmaps used in this example, go to the Microsoft Visual Studio installed directory and look for the following path: ..\Common\Graphics\Bitmaps\Outline. Insert the following bitmaps in the ImageList: Open, Closed, Leaf, Minus, and Plus. Assign key

Figure 12. TreeView with Bitmaps.

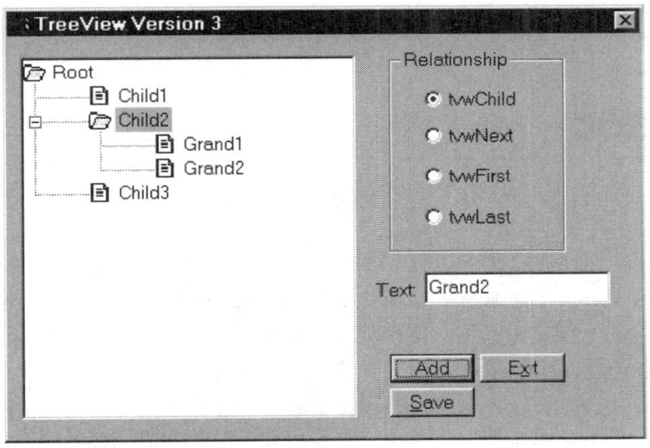

values to the icons, using the same names as their bitmap files, without the .bmp extensions.

If you want to add or remove any images from the ImageList control after it has been attached to a ToolBar, TreeView or ListView, you must break the connection by clearing the latter's ImageList property, modify the ImageList, and reconnect the ImageList.

Next, we need to add code to the program that attaches appropriate icons. First, a single line is added to the end of the cmdAdd_Click event handler. As each node is inserted, its Image property is set to "leaf," which looks like a piece of paper:

```
Private Sub cmdAdd_Click()
   'snip, snip...
```

```
  nodTemp.Image = "leaf"
End Sub
```

Then we add statements to the Expand and Collapse event handlers for the TreeView, assigning either the "open" or "closed" bitmap from the ImageList:

```
Private Sub treSample_Collapse(ByVal Node As _
  MSComctlLib.Node)
  Node.Image = "closed"
End Sub

Private Sub treSample_Expand(ByVal Node As _
  MSComctlLib.Node)
  Node.Image = "open"
End Sub
```

These are the only required modifications, When a new node is inserted, if it is the child of an existing node, the parent node automatically expands, triggering the Expand event. If you prefer, you can use the "plus" and "minus" icons from the ImageList rather than the file folders. You can use any bitmaps you want, for that matter.

Editing Node Text. You may want to let the user edit the nodes in a ListView. An easy way to do this is to display an InputBox when the user double-clicks on a tree node. The following code, for example, does this in the current version of our sample program:

```
Private Sub treSample_DblClick()
'Let the user edit a node's text.
  treSample.SelectedItem.Text = InputBox("Enter new text")
End Sub
```

3.5 COOLBAR CONTROL

3.5.1 Properties

In the previous chapter we introduced you to the ToolBar control, which has been a standard control in Visual Basic for some time. In this chapter, we show how to use the CoolBar, a new ActiveX control introduced by Visual Basic 6 that extends the power of the ToolBar. The CoolBar control allows you to create user-configured toolbars similar to those in Microsoft Internet Explorer. It consists of containers called *bands*. Each band can host one child control, such as a ToolBar, ComboBox, or Text control. Because the CoolBar is only a container, you should use it only to host other controls. At runtime, you can let the user rearrange the order of individual bands by dragging them with the mouse. Table 11 lists the most common CoolBar properties, and Table 12 lists properties of Band objects, the various segments of a CoolBar.

3.5.2 Example: CoolBar, ToolBar, ImageCombo, and Combo

(samples: CoolBar)

Let's create a simple step-by-step example that shows how to create a CoolBar with three bands containing a Toolbar, an ImageCombo, and a Combo box. Its interface is similar to that of the Microsoft Internet Explorer. Later, you might want to extend and improve this

Table 11. CoolBar Properties.

Property	Description
Bands	Collection of Band objects, representing each of the containers in the CoolBar control.
BandBorders	If True, narrow lines appear at the borders of the bands.
FixedOrder	If False, the user can reorder the bands at runtime by dragging bands with the mouse.
ImageList	A reference to an ImageList control that can supply images to the CoolBar bands.
Orientation	Display the CoolBar with either a horizontal or vertical orientation.
Picture	A graphic that is displayed in the CoolBar control's background.
VariantHeight	If True, the bands in the CoolBar control can be displayed with varying heights.

program by adding Internet-enabled controls discussed in Chapter 12, turning it into a simple but useful Web browser. The example is organized in sequential steps:

Table 12. CoolBar Band Object Properties.

Property	Description
AllowVertical	Determines whether the band will be displayed if the CoolBar's orientation is changed to vertical.
Caption	Text that appears between the move handle and the child control in a band.
Child	A reference to a control that is displayed within the band's borders.
FixedBackground	If set to True, the same background picture is displayed across all bands in the CoolBar control. If set to False, each band has its own copy of the picture.
Image	A specific image from the attached ImageList control, which is to appear in the band.
Index	Determined by the order of creating of bands in the control.
NewRow	Determines whether the band will be displayed on a separate row.
Position	Read-only property that returns the position of the band within the CoolBar control, starting with 1 and continuing to the number of bands. When the user rearranges a band at runtime, its Index property remains constant, but its Position property changes.

1. Begin by loading the Coolbar, ToolBar, ImageList and ImageCombo controls into the ToolBox window. Select Components from the Project menu, select both Microsoft Windows Common Controls and Microsoft Windows Common Controls-3.
2. Next, drag a CoolBar Control onto a Form. The default CoolBar has three bands, but you can insert or remove bands in the Coolbar property Window.

Figure 13. Placing Child Controls in the CoolBar

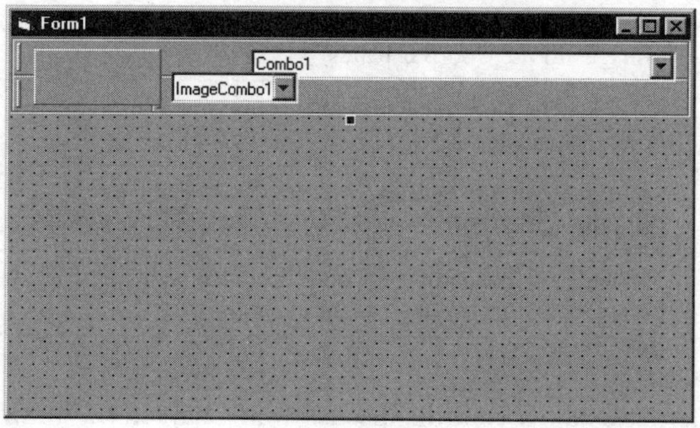

3. Insert a ToolBar, ImageCombo and Combo control into the Coolbar by selecting the CoolBar and dragging the other controls inside the CoolBar's boundaries (see Figure 13).
4. On the Property Page, select the **Bands** tab. The index box now has a value of 1, indicating that you are modifying the properties of the first band (see Figure 14). In the **Child** dropdown list, select **Toolbar1**. Click the right arrow to move to Index 2, select **ImageCombo1** as its child control, move to index 3, and select **Combo1** as its child control. Now Band1 hosts Toolbar1, Band2 hosts ImageCombo1, and Band3

Figure 14. Attaching a Child control to Each Band.

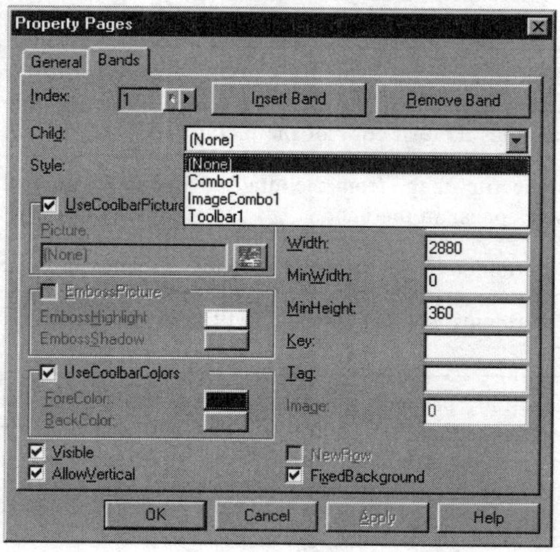

hosts Combo1. (These properties can also be set at runtime, so this step is optional.) Now all the child controls fit in the corresponding bands.

5. Next, place three ImageList controls on the Form. Insert nine color icons into ImageList1. For ImageList2, insert the same nine icons, selecting their black and white counterparts. For ImageList3, insert eight flag icons.
6. Twelve buttons are placed on the Toolbar, representing Band 1 of the CoolBar control (see Figure 15). Some of these buttons will be separators.
7. From the Properties window, we set the appearance of the ToolBar to *ccFlat* and its style to *tbrFlat*.
8. Right click the Toolbar on the first band, selecting the *General* Tab. In the **ImageList** and **DisableImageList** dropdown boxes, select **ImageList2**, containing black and white icons. In the **HotImageList** dropdown list, select **ImageList1**. The latter contains the same icons as ImageList2, but with colors. The HotImageList property becomes active when the user moves the mouse over the ToolBar button at run time.
9. Next, click the **Buttons** Tab. For the Index 1 button, set the **Caption** and **Key** properties to "Back". For the **Style** property, select **tbrDropdown** and assign a value of 1 to the Image property, representing the first icon in the ImageList2 control. Repeat the

Figure 15. Placing Twelve Buttons on the Toolbar

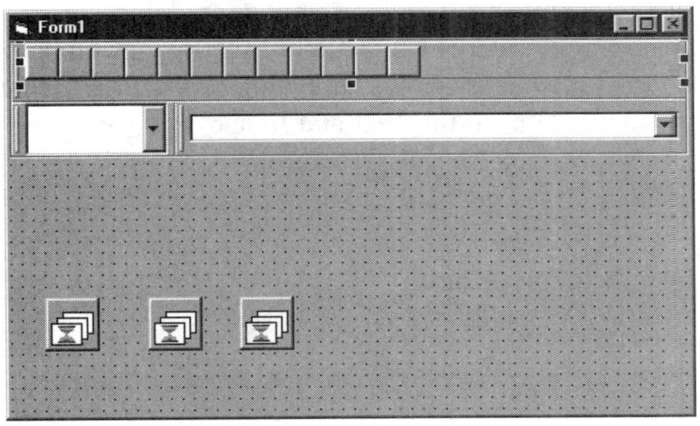

> ***Programming Tip: Uncovering Hidden Controls.***
>
> If you've ever accidentally hidden a label or text box behind a CoolBar or ToolBar, you know it can be an exasperating experience trying to find it. For example, in the program we just looked at, if you copy a Label control to the clipboard and paste a copy of it onto the form, it is hidden behind the CoolBar in the upper left corner of the form. You can usually expose a hidden control by selecting the covering control with the mouse and selecting Order from the Format menu and clicking on Send to Back. But this doesn't work with the CoolBar. Instead, set the CoolBar's Align property to vbAlignNone. You can then drag the CoolBar to the middle of the form, expose the hidden Label control, and move it to an appropriate position. Then, of course, set the Align property of the CoolBar back to its previous value.

same process for the second button, entering "Forward" as the values of the Caption and Key properties, and assign a value of 2 to the *Image* property.

10. For the third button, set its **Style** property to **tbrSeparator** and repeat the process to assign all buttons their corresponding captions and icons. Figure 16 shows the icons in their positions on the ToolBar.

Figure 16 . Binding Icons and Buttons.

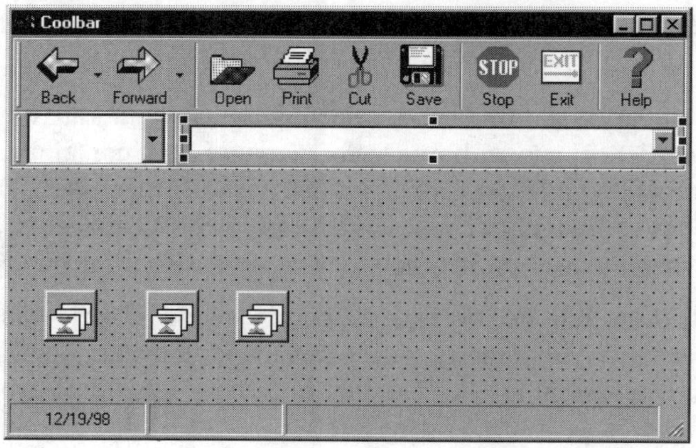

Program Code. There is a relatively small amount of code in this program. Form_Load calls the **Add** method for the ComboItems Collection of the ImageCombo box. The arguments passed to the Add function are in the following order: Index, Key, Text, and Image. At the very least, we would need the Text and Image arguments, the latter being the image's index position in the attached ImageList control:

```
.Add ,,"USA",1
```

Here is the complete Form_Load procedure:

```
Private Sub Form_Load()
'Add the flag icons and country names to the
'ImageCombo box.
   With ImageCombo1.ComboItems
      .Add 1, "USA", "USA", 1
      .Add 2, "AUSTRIA", "AUSTRIA", 2
      .Add 3, "BELGIUM", "BELGIUM", 3
      .Add 4, "BRAZIL", "BRAZIL", 4
      .Add 5, "CANADA", "CANADA", 5
      .Add 6, "DENMARK", "DENMARK", 6
      .Add 7, "FINLAND", "FINLAND", 7
      .Add 8, "FRANCE", "FRANCE", 8
   End With

'Attach the controls to the Bands, showing that we
'can set the order at runtime.
   With CoolBar1
      Set .Bands(1).Child = Toolbar1
      Set .Bands(2).Child = ImageCombo1
      Set .Bands(3).Child = Combo1
```

```
    End With
  End Sub
```

We have also programmed the Exit button. A real program would provide cases for all of the other ToolBar button key values:

```
Private Sub Toolbar1_ButtonClick(ByVal Button As MSComctlLib.Button)
  Select Case Button.Key
    Case "Exit"
      Unload Me
  End Select
End Sub
```

11. Run the finished program as shown in Figure 17.

Figure 17. Finished CoolBar Program.

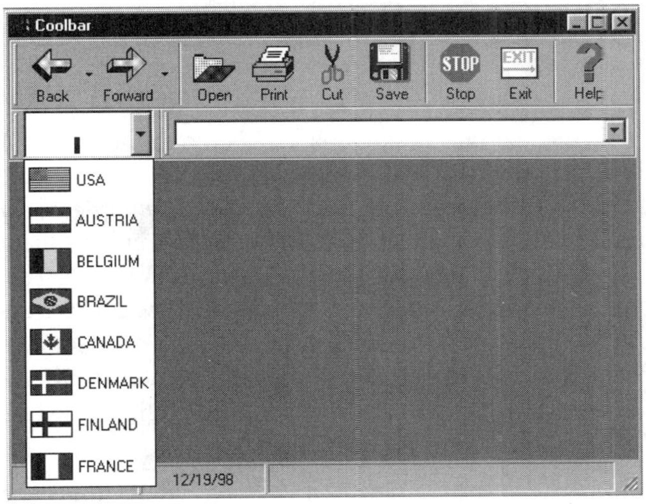

Moving the Bands at Runtime. The FixedOrder property is False by default, allowing the user to drag individual bands to new locations within the CoolBar group (see Figure 18). In our example, the user can drag the bands containing the combo boxes to the top level.

Manipulating Bands using Code. In our sample program, the bands revert to their original positions when the program ends. But in the Form_Load procedure, we showed that you can attach individual controls to the Bands Collection of the CoolBar control at runtime. Just for fun, you might want to experiment with saving the CoolBar band settings in the system registry using the SaveSetting procedure shown in Chapter 2. Then use the GetSetting function to retrieve the information when the program loads.

Figure 18. Moving the CoolBar Bands at Runtime.

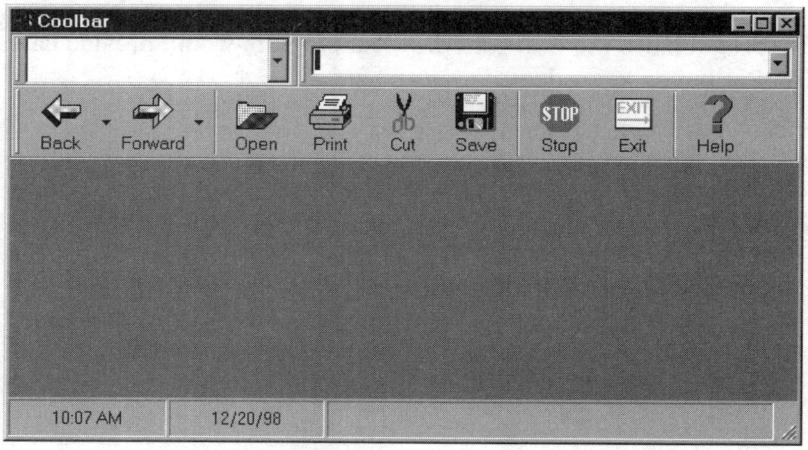

3.6 CREATING MDI APPLICATIONS

3.6.1 Overview

All of the programs we've seen so far in this book use a type of interface called SDI (single document interface), in which all windows displayed by the program are equal and independent. There is another popular type of interface called the *multiple-document interface* (MDI), in which a parent window contains one or more child windows that always remain within the parent's window frame (called its *client area*, or *workspace*). The MDI parent, as it is called, acts as a container for the various MDI child windows. There are many examples of such applications: Microsoft Word, Excel, and Access are some of the more common ones. The Visual Basic development environment defaults to MDI, but it can be configured as SDI by selecting Options from the Tools menu, clicking on the Advanced tab, and selecting the *SDI Development Environment* checkbox.

Why use an MDI interface? Usually it's best suited to applications where you have multiple windows containing similar data. For example, in Visual Basic, it is common to open multiple code windows and switch back and forth between the open windows. When you minimize or close the parent window, all child windows are automatically hidden. At the root of MDI is efficient window management by the application. References to the windows may be stored in a Collection, making it easy to activate individual windows, search for text, and interact with individual window controls.

Also, MDI makes it easy to create multiple instances of the same form at runtime. Imagine that you wish to create a vehicle reservation program, in which the reservation clerk needs to fill in a form with customer data. The clerk might be working on more than one reservation form at the same time, but each of the forms contains the same controls and executable code. In database applications, each MDI Form can display a different table from the database, helping the user to see relationships between tables.

For example, if the MDI parent form has a menu containing the Window/New command, the following procedure creates and displays a new copy of frmChild:

```
Private Sub mnuWindowNew_Click()
  Dim newdoc As New frmChild
  newdoc.Show vbModeless
End Sub
```

MDI child forms can only be shown modelessly, by the way.

Creating an MDI Project. Visual Basic restricts you to only one MDI Form per program, but there can be a virtually unlimited number of child forms. To create an MDI window, select **Add MDI Form** from the Project menu. Any other Form can be an MDI child window, as long as its MDIChild property is set to True. You can also have non-child forms in the same project as MDI child forms.

Properties, Methods, and Events. A list of MDI properties and methods is shown in Table 13.

Table 13. MDI Properties and Methods.

Property/Method	Description
ActiveForm	Returns a reference to the child window that currently has the focus.
ActiveControl	Returns a reference to the control on the active child form that has the focus.
MDIChild	If set to True, the form will remain within the MDI parent's workspace and will be hidden when the parent is closed or resized.
Arrange	Arrange the child windows by cascading from left to right, tiling horizontally or vertically, or arranging all child icons.

ActiveForm property. The ActiveForm property returns a reference to the child window that currently has the focus. For example, we call the SaveFile method on the MDI child Form that is currently active:

```
mdiMain.ActiveForm.SaveFile
```

This is particularly useful when a menu command or ToolBar button is clicked on the MDI main Form and you must carry out the command on the appropriate child Form.

ActiveControl Property. The ActiveControl property returns a reference to the control on the currently active MDI child Form. If you have a ToolBar or menu on the MDI parent Form, you can execute a command that carries out some action on the active control of the active child Form. Copying text to the Windows clipboard, for example, can be done without having to know the specific name of the control. In the following code from an MDI parent Form, we assume the control is a Text control:

```
Clipboard.SetText ActiveForm.ActiveControl.SelText
```

Window List. When you create a menu for an MDI application, you can place a check next to the WindowList property in the menu editor. This causes Visual Basic to automatically display a list of all the currently open child windows. The user can click on any window caption in the list and that window will immediately become the active window. (You can see an example of this in Microsoft Word, for example, in its Window menu.)

Menu Replacement. If any child window has a menu, its menu replaces the MDI parent's menu as soon as the child window is activated. If your program requires the MDI main menu to be visible at all times, you can duplicate the menu on each child widow. Or, you can avoid menus on child windows altogether, so the MDI main menu will always remain visible. If your program uses a ToolBar, the ToolBar should be placed on the MDI main window where it remains visible throughout the program without being affected by child window menus.

Updating Information on Multiple Child Forms. Perhaps the biggest challenge relating to MDI applications is keeping the information in the windows up to date. Figure 19, for example, shows an MDI program that displays membership information and dues payments for a Karate school. If the user clicks on a different name in the Membership window, we must be sure that the Collected Dues Payments window automatically updates itself. This updating is normally done in the Form_Activate event handler, where we write code that tells the program to search for the person who was just selected in the other window. In the Dues Payments Window, for example, we would write:

```
Sub Form_Activate()
   Dim strMemberID As String
   strMemberID = frmMembership.MemberId
   'Now search for the member ID, and display
   'all dues payments made by that person.
   adoPayments.Filter "MemberID = '" & strMemberId "'"
End Sub
```

Figure 19. Multiple Child Forms.

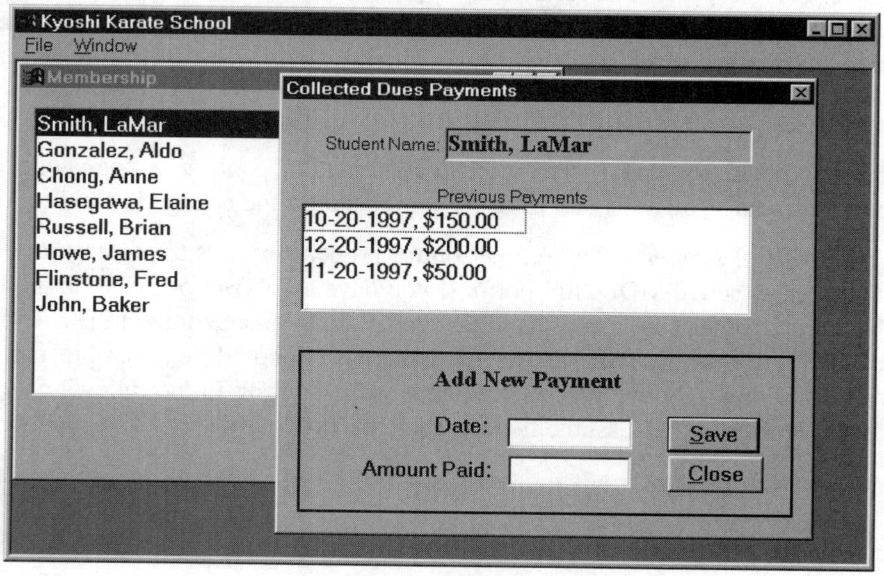

We haven't used database filters yet, of course, but we can assume that the Filter property allows only records containing the selected Member ID to be displayed.

Arranging Child Windows. MDI child windows can be tiled, cascaded (overlapped), or the icons arranged by calling the Arrange method and passing it one of the following Visual Basic constants:

```
frmMDI.Arrange  vbCascade
frmMDI.Arrange  vbTileHorizontal
frmMDI.Arrange  vbTileVertical
frmMDI.Arrange  vbArrangeIcons
```

When a child window is minimized, it appears as a button along the bottom of the MDI parent.

Storing Windows in a Collection. It is often useful to store references to child windows in a Collection, to allow processing them as a group. For example, we create a new window and add it to the mcolChildWin Collection:

```
Dim frmTemp As New frmChild
mcolChildWin.Add frmTemp
frmTemp.Show vbModeless
```

Placing MDI child window references in a Collection makes it easy to perform the same operation on all the windows, using a loop. For example, the following code unloads each window and removes it from the Collection:

```
Dim frm As Form
For Each frm in mcolChildWin
  Unload frm
  mcolChildwin.Remove 1
Next frm
```

You might also want to save key values in the Collection to allow programs to search for a particular window at runtime. The Tag or Caption property could be the key, for example:

```
mcolChildWin.Add frmTemp, frmTemp.Caption
```

3.6.2 Example: MDI Vehicle Reservations

(samples: MDIWin)

In this section, we will create a short program with an MDI interface that displays reservation forms for an imaginary car rental company. The MDI parent Form is shown at design time in Figure 20. The program also has ToolBar buttons that copy and paste text to the Windows clipboard, and a Cascade button that rearranges all of the child windows in an overlapped pattern.

When the user clicks on the New ToolBar button or selects New from the File menu, a Reservation Form (child window) appears within the MDI Form. In Figure 21, an invoice number (00001) has automatically been generated.

Figure 20. MDI Form, in Design Mode.

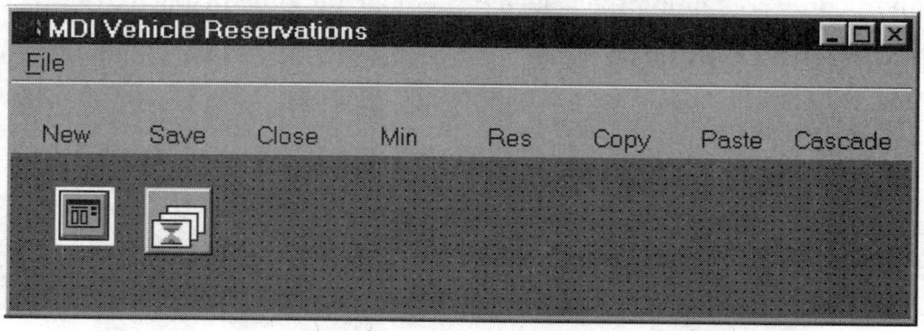

Figure 21. MDI Form with One Reservation form.

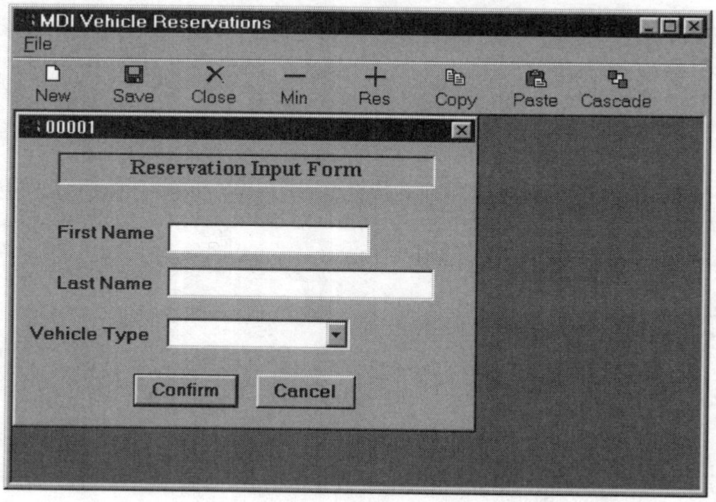

Figure 22. MDI Form with Two Child Windows.

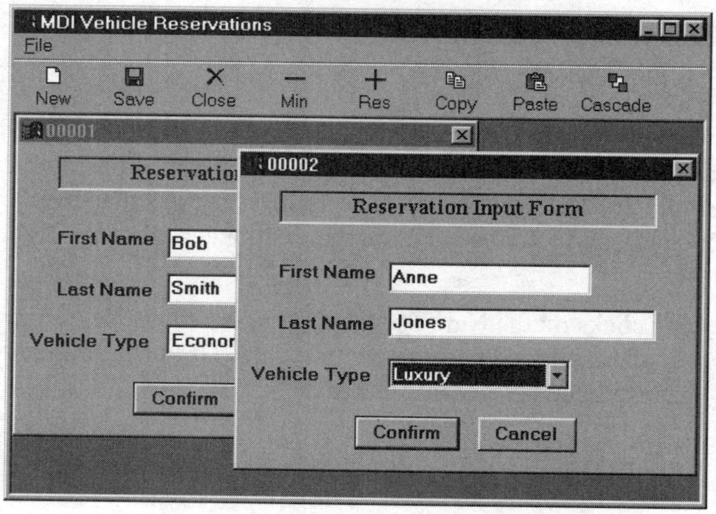

In Figure 22 the user has created a second reservation Form and has filled in various input fields. Notice that the information entered in each MDI child window is different from that in other child windows.

3.6.3 Program Implementation

Let's take a look at the program source code, first in the MDI child window, then in the reservation Form. It is convenient to store a separate reservation ID in each child window. The two click event handlers call procedures located in the MDI main window:

```
Private Sub cmdCancel_Click()
   frmMDIMain.CloseWindow
End Sub

Private Sub cmdConfirm_Click()
   frmMDIMain.SaveReservation
End Sub
```

MDI Main Window. Now let's look at the more extensive code in the MDI main window. We declare a Collection to hold references to the child windows, and an integer called mintResNumber that keeps track of the most recent reservation number:

```
Private mcollChildWin As Collection
Private mintResNumber As Integer
```

During the **Form_Load** event, we resize the main window and connect the ImageList to the ToolBar so the images will show in the ToolBar buttons:

```
Private Sub MDIForm_Load()
   Set mcollChildWin = New Collection
   Width = Screen.Width * 0.7
   Height = Screen.Height * 0.7
   tlbMain.ImageList = ilsMain
   Dim j As Integer, strKey As String
   For j = 1 To ilsMain.ListImages.Count
      strKey = ilsMain.ListImages(j).Key
      tlbMain.Buttons(strKey).Image = strKey
   Next j
End Sub
```

The **SetAllWindowState** procedure lets us loop through the child window Collection and minimize or restore the windows:

```
Public Sub SetAllWindowState(intState As Integer)
   Dim frm As Form
   For Each frm In mcollChildWin
      frm.WindowState = intState
   Next frm
End Sub
```

The ToolBar's **ButtonClick** event handler provides a branch to each of the program's main functions, such as NewReservation, SaveReservation, SetAllWindowState, and CloseWindow. Form here, we can also cut and paste text to the Windows clipboard:

```
Private Sub tlbMain_ButtonClick(ByVal Button As MSComctlLib.Button)
  Select Case Button.Key
    Case "new"
      NewReservation
    Case "save"
      SaveReservation
    Case "minimize"
      SetAllWindowState vbMinimized
    Case "restore"
      SetAllWindowState vbNormal
    Case "close"
      If Not (ActiveForm Is Nothing) Then CloseWindow
    Case "copy"
      If Not (ActiveForm Is Nothing) Then
        Clipboard.SetText ActiveForm.ActiveControl.SelText
      End If
    Case "paste"
      If Not (ActiveForm Is Nothing) Then
        ActiveForm.ActiveControl.Text = Clipboard.GetText
      End If
    Case "cascade"
      Arrange vbCascade
    Case Else
      MsgBox "Unknown button command: " & Button.Key
  End Select
End Sub
```

The **NewReservation** procedure creates a new reservation number and and places it in a new child window. The window is also added to a Collection:

```
Public Sub NewReservation()
  Dim frmTemp As New frmChild, strResNumber As String
  mintResNumber = mintResNumber + 1
  strResNumber = Format(mintResNumber, "00000")
  frmTemp.ReservationId = strResNumber
  mcollChildWin.Add frmTemp, strResNumber  'window,key
  frmTemp.Caption = strResNumber
  frmTemp.Show vbModeless
End Sub
```

When the user decides to close the currently active child window, designated by the ActiveForm property, the **CloseWindow** procedure removes its reference from the Collection:

```
Public Sub CloseWindow()
  mcollChildWin.Remove ActiveForm.ReservationId
  Unload ActiveForm
End Sub
```

This program is, of course, very simple. It demonstrates basic MDI window operation, and best of all, can be customized and enhanced to suit a variety of applications.

3.7 REVIEW QUESTIONS

1. What advantages would there be to creating a TextBox control array over creating several explicitly named TextBox controls?
2. How may a control array be created at design time?
3. How may a control array be created at runtime?
4. What are Visual Basic's object type names for check boxes, Command buttons, and OptionButtons?
5. Assuming that **frmAuthor** was a Form in the current project, write a statement that assigns a reference to the Form to an object variable called **aForm**.
6. How can enumerated constants help to make a control array of TextBox controls more self-documenting? Assume that the TextBox controls correspond to fields in a file.
7. Show an example of creating a new instance of a Form and assigning it to an object variable.
8. Show an example of a procedure that has a Form variable as a parameter.
9. Write a loop that creates a control array of ten Command buttons, assigns values to their captions, and makes all of the buttons visible.
10. What is the purpose of the built-in **Forms** Collection?
11. What assumption does the following loop make about the controls on the current Form? Might this loop cause a runtime error?

```
Dim j As Integer
For j = 0 To Controls.Count - 1
  Controls(j).Text = ""
Next j
```

12. Write a For-Each statement that iterates through all of the controls on the current Form.
13. Can the key value in a Collection be a String, Long, or a Single?
14. In a Collection containing social security numbers and names of people, which value (SSN or name) is likely to be the Collection key? Why?
15. What problem might there be with a Collection that uses last names of cities as keys?
16. Can members of a Collection be accessed randomly? How about sequentially?
17. Can a Collection contain objects of different types?
18. Describe the meaning of each parameter in the Collection.Add method.
19. In the Collection.Add method, which parameter is required?
20. Describe the Collection.Item property and show an example.
21. What is the lowest index value in a user-defined Collection?
22. When resizing the controls on a Form, why is it important to calculate the ratio between the old Form width and the new Form width?

23. Why is a MDI parent window called a *container*?
24. In the sample MDI Car Rental program what was placed in each instance of the MDI child window?
25. What happens to the menu on an MDI parent window when an MDI child window is activated and the child has a menu?
26. Why is it often useful to create a Collection of references to MDI child windows?

3.8 CHAPTER EXERCISES

3.8.1 Jumping Button Program

Write a program that displays a Command button that says "Click Here". When the user tries to click on the button, the button should immediately move to a random location on the same Form:

Hint: The button's MouseMove event executes when the mouse is moved over the button. You can write code that moves the button before it can be pressed by the user:

```
Private Sub cmdTest_MouseMove(Button As Integer, _
     Shift As Integer, X As Single, Y As Single)
End Sub
```

You can have a lot of fun trying this program out on unsuspecting people! Feel free to add some variations of your own to this program, including sound, additional buttons, graphics, and so on.

3.8.2 The Buttons Control Array

Make some improvements to the program in section 3.1.4 that created an array of Command buttons:

- Shuffle the order of the button captions.
- Resize the buttons when the user uses the mouse to resize the Form.
- Ask the user to decide how many buttons are to be displayed. Then arrange the buttons in separate rows, ten to a row.
- Let the user unload the buttons from the Form before the program ends.

3.8.3 Sorted Collection

Write a program that contains a sorted Collection of Employee records. Sort the Collection on the IdNumber field, which is the key for each item. The data value to be inserted is the employee's last name:

```
Dim IdNumber As String * 9
Dim LastName As String * 30
```

Creating a sorted Collection is not as difficult as it sounds. The trick is to write an Insert procedure that places each new item in the proper position in the Collection. To get you started in the right direction, the following program creates a sorted Collection of names. Of course, there are no key fields in this example, so it will have to be modified before it can be applied to Employee records:

```
Dim coll As Collection

Public Sub Main()
  Set coll = New Collection
  Insert "Jones"
  Insert "Smith"
  Insert "Baker"
  Insert "Adams"

  'Display the Collection:
  Dim obj As Variant
  For Each obj In coll
    Debug.Print obj
  Next obj
End Sub

Public Sub Insert(st As String)
'Insert a string in alphabetical order.
  Dim j As Integer
  For j = 1 To coll.Count
    If st < coll.item(j) Then
      coll.Add st, , j    'insert before pos j
      Exit Sub
    End If
  Next j
  coll.Add st     'insert at end
End Sub
```

3.8.4 Mozart MDI, Version 1

Create a music store invoice program, that is loosely modeled after the Mozart Music program from Chapter 2. In this version of the program, let the user add multiple purchases to a ListBox. The program should accumulate the total purchase as each new item is added. Create an MDI main window and make the invoice window an MDI child. Allow the user to edit and create two or three invoices at the same time, each in a separate window. Wait until each invoice is saved before assigning it an invoice number. At that time, display a message box showing the invoice number to the user. If an invoice is canceled, do not assign it an invoice number. Figure 23 shows a sample snapshot of the program at run time.

Figure 23. Mozart MDI, Version 1.

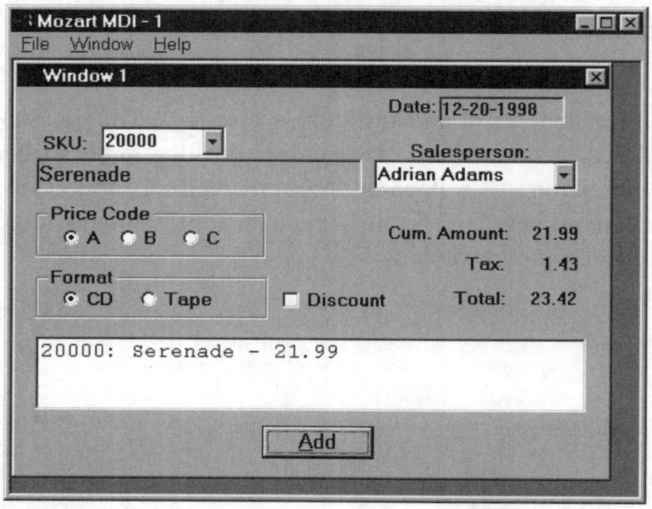

3.8.5 Mozart MDI, Version 2

Continue the previous exercise by allowing the user to remove items from the current invoice. When the user clicks on the Remove button, the currently selected item in the ListBox is removed, and its price is subtracted from the total invoice amount. A sample is shown in Figure 24.

Figure 24. Mozart MDI, Version 2.

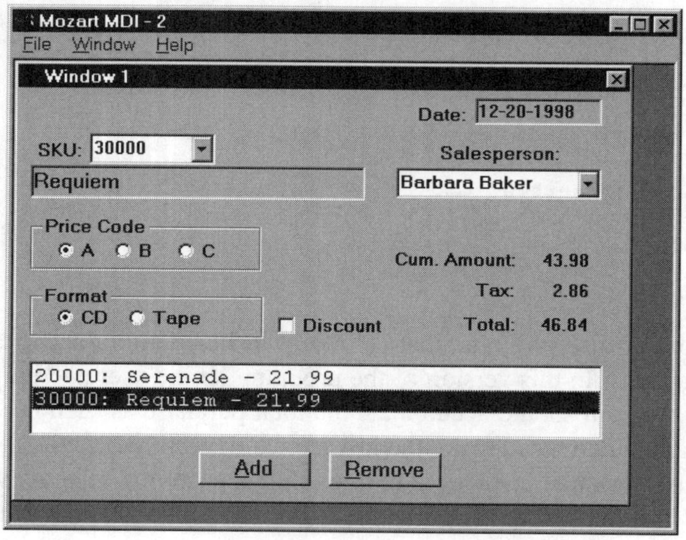

3.8.6 Mozart MDI with a ListView

Continue the previous exercise by converting the ListBox to a ListView control. The ListView should display the SKU number, album title, and price. Allow the user to double-click on a list item and edit its contents.

3.8.7 Mozart Music Using a CoolBar

Add a CoolBar control to the Mozart Music Store program from Chapter 2. Let the CoolBar hold the main menu ToolBar, the button group that selects the discount rate, and the ComboBox that selects the album SKU number. A sample is shown here. Notice that the Caption property is used in the second and third bands to label the SKU ComboBox and the discount buttons (see Figure 25).

Figure 25. Adding a CoolBar to Mozart Music.

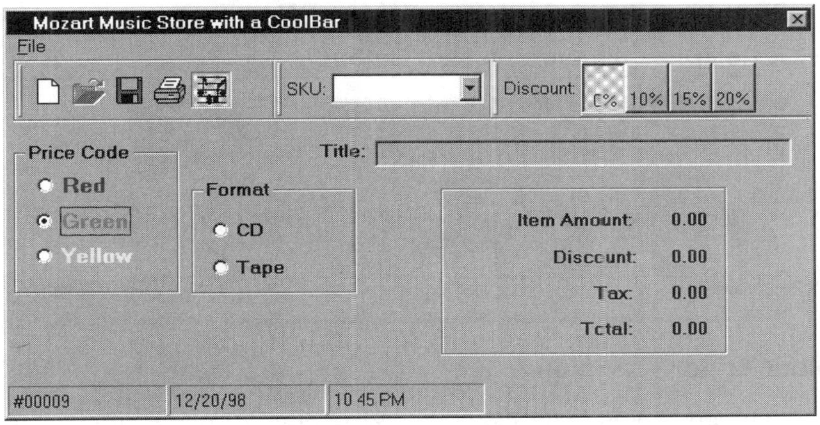

3.8.8 Coolbar Editor - Version 1

Use the Coolbar control to create a text editor similar to the Windows Notepad program (see Figure 26). Use two bands. The top band should contain buttons for the New, Open, Save, Print, Exit and Help commands. The second band should include the Cut, Copy, Paste, Find and Find Next commands. If you would like to use our icons, look in the \Icons directory of the sample program disk for this book. Use two sets of icons, Monochrome and Color, so you can activate the color icon when the user passes the mouse over each button.

3.8.9 Coolbar Editor - Version 2

Modify the program written for the previous exercise: Disable the Cut, Copy and Paste button until the user has selected a block of text.

3.8.10 Coolbar Editor - Version 3

Modify the program written for the previous exercise: Add a third band containing a button labeled "Font". When the user clicks on the Font button, the program lets the user select the current font style and size (See Figure 27).

Figure 26. CoolBar Editor, Version 1

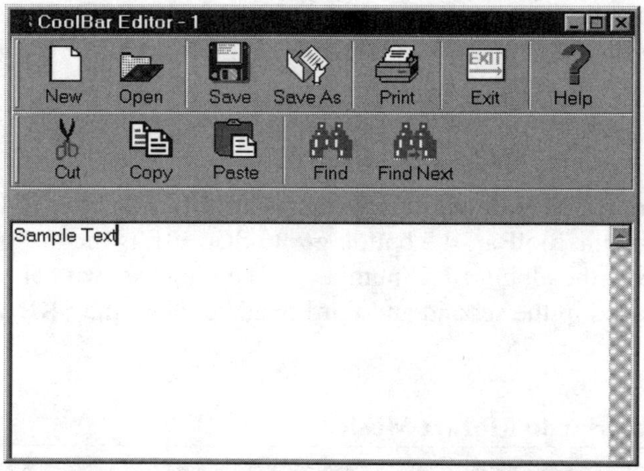

Figure 27. CoolBar Editor with a Font Button.

3.8.11 Coolbar Editor – Version 4

Modify the program written for the previous exercise: Make the program an MDI application. The user should be able to open multiple documents at the same time. Add a Window menu that includes a window list and commands to cascade, minimize, restore, and tile the windows (see Figure 28).

3.8.12 Glossary Program - Version 1

Create a program called Glossary that uses a Collection to hold terms (words) and definitions. The terms will be the Collection keys, and the definitions of the words will be the Collection members. For example, you can store the term **variable** in the glossary along with its definition:

term:	variable
definition:	A named storage area in a program.

The program should load the glossary from a prepared text file on the student disk called **ComputerTerms.gls**, in which each term is on a single line followed by its definition on the following line. Here are several sample lines from the file:

```
variable
A named storage area in a program.
constant
An identifier that is assigned a value that never changes.
```

Figure 28. MDI CoolBar Editor.

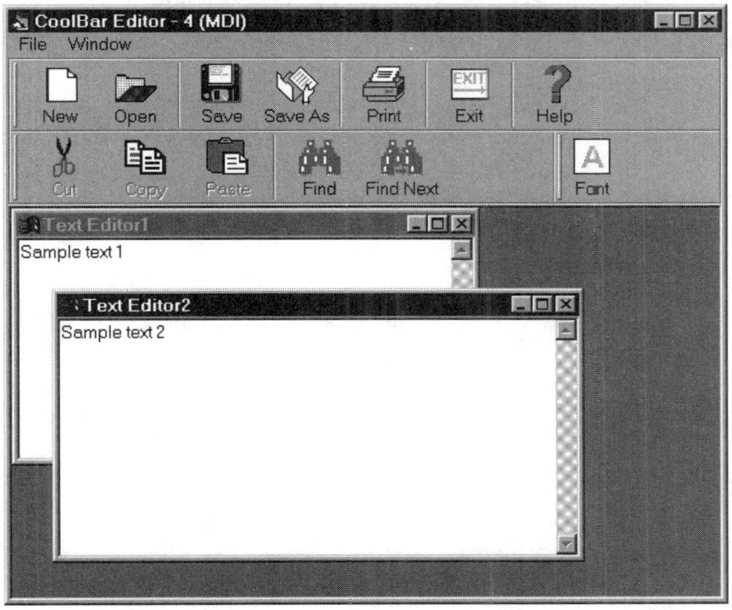


```
object
A program entity that has properties and methods that help it to interact
with other objects.
```

Use a common dialog control to let the user select the file to be loaded into the glossary. After clicking on the File/New command, a File/Open dialog lets the user select a glossary file. Once a file has been loaded, the user can select a term from the ComboBox. When a term is chosen, its definition appears in the Definition, as shown in Figure 29.

Figure 29. Glossary Program, at Startup.

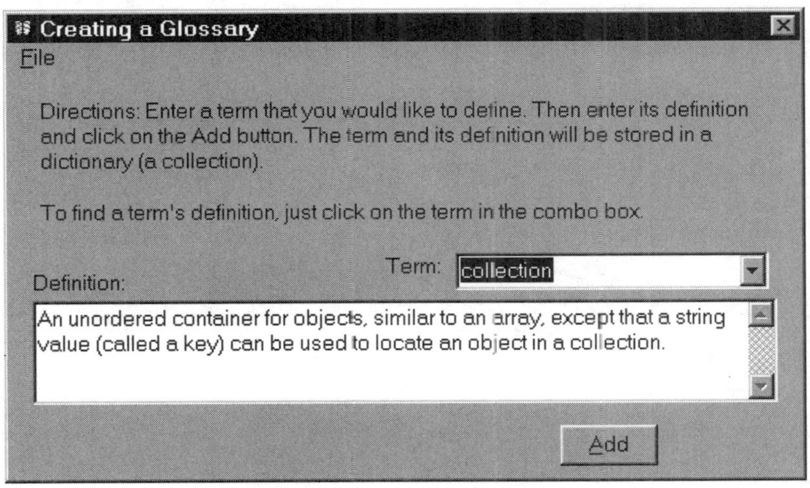

3.8.13 Glossary Program - Version 2

Using the program written for the previous exercise as a starting point, let the user add new terms and definitions to the glossary. Your program should append the new terms to the end of the existing glossary file.

4 Data-Bound Controls

Chapter Contents

Tables and Databases
- Relational Databases
- ActiveX Data Objects (ADO)
- Using the ADO Data Control
- Using Data-Bound Controls
- ADODB Recordsets

Sales Staff Examples
- Displaying Records
- Moving the Recordset Pointer
- Adding, Deleting, and Updating Records
- Sorting Records
- Filtering Records
- Using SQL to Create a Recordset
- Using the Find Method
- Displaying Images
- ADO Control Events (optional)

DataGrid, DataCombo, and DataList
- Properties and Events
- Example: Linking a DataList to a DataGrid
- Example: DataCombo and DataGrid Controls.

Review Questions

Chapter Exercises

4.1 TABLES AND DATABASES

Companies looking for Visual Basic programmers usually expect the applicants to know how to connect their application programs to databases. Experience with one or more database products such as Microsoft Access, Microsoft SQL Server, and Oracle are highly sought after. For this reason, it is critically important for you to integrate database skills into nearly all of your Visual Basic applications.

In this chapter, we begin to address the need to use databases by showing how to display, move through, update, and search for records in databases. Upcoming chapters will explore databases in more depth, building on what you have learned here.

4.1.1 Relational Databases

A *database* may be thought of as a collection of tables containing related information. Microsoft more thoroughly defines it in the MSDN reference library as:

> "(1) A collection of data with a given structure for accepting, storing, and providing on demand, data for multiple users. (2) A collection of interrelated data organized according to a database schema to serve one or more

applications. (3) A collection of data fundamental to a system. (4) A collection of data fundamental to an enterprise."

In fact, a specific type of database that contains relationships between its tables, records, and fields is called a *relational database*. Microsoft Access, for example, is a tool for creating relational databases.

There are other types of databases, such as hierarchical databases, that describe data relationships in a hierarchical, or tree-like fashion. A good example is the Microsoft Windows Explorer, which displays drives, directories, and files in a hierarchical fashion.

A *database table* is a sequence of rows from a database, each containing related information in a consistent format. For example, a table called **SalesStaff** might contain a list of ID numbers and names identifying sales staff personnel in a company:

StaffId	LastName	FirstName
101	Adams	Bill
120	Baker	Anne
330	Colson	Jerry
404	Del Terzo	Daniel
551	Easterbrook	Erin

Each row in a table is also called a *record*. Each column is also called a *field*. In our sample table, the columns are called **StaffId, LastName, and FirstName**. In addition to the SalesStaff table, the same company database might contain a table called **Sales** containing information about sales invoices:

InvoiceID	Date	StaffId	NetAmount
00001	01/02/99	330	55.25
00240	01/03/99	120	36.92
00301	01/05/99	101	14.05
00322	01/07/99	404	89.34
00329	01/07/99	120	128.26
00335	01/10/99	551	4.50

You may have noticed that a relationship exists between the SalesStaff and Sales tables. Each StaffId value in the Sales table matches a corresponding StaffId value in the SalesStaff table, indicating that they refer to the same person. This "joining" of two tables is a powerful feature, which we exploit throughout the next few chapters when displaying information from more than one table at a time.

Cursor. In a database, a *cursor* is a subroutine that returns rows of data to an application program. The rows of data are called the *result set*.

Microsoft Access. It is usually convenient to create database files in Microsoft Access for use on a single desktop machine in Visual Basic. In fact, Visual Basic install directory contains two relational databases supplied by Microsoft: the **Biblio** database (biblio.mdb), and the **NorthWind Traders** database (nwind.mdb). The Biblio database contains sample book titles, publishers, and authors. The NorthWind database contains sales data for a ficticious retail company.

In this book, we will create all our sample databases using Microsoft Access. Table 1 lists the available field types in Access, and Table 2 compares the Access data types to the Visual Basic types.

4.1.2 ActiveX Data Objects (ADO)

In previous versions of Visual Basic, there were two basic ways to read and write data using databases: *Data Access Objects* (DAO) *and Remote Data Objects* (RDO). The former manipulates desktop databases, and the latter manipulates remote databases. The DAO and RDO controls limited Visual Basic programs to using ODBC and Microsoft Jet-compliant data providers. With the release of Visual Basic 6, Microsoft began promoting a new standard, called *ActiveX Data Objects* (ADO). They provided a number of sophisticated data-bound controls that only work with ADO, including the DataList, DataCombo, DataGrid, and Hierarchical FlexGrid.

Table 1. Microsoft Access Field Types.

Field Type	Description
Text	Text and numbers, such as names and addresses, phone numbers and postal codes. A Text field can contain from 0 to 255 characters.
Memo	Lengthy text and numbers, such as comments or explanations. A Memo field can contain up to 1.2 billion characters.
Number	Numerical data on which you intend to perform mathematical calculations, except calculations involving money. The Number data types are: Byte, Integer, Long Integer, Single, and Double.
Date/Time	Dates and times. The same field can store both a date and a time. All dates are stored in U.S. format. Internally, a floating-point number stores the date in the whole number portion, and the fractional portion stores the number of minutes since midnight.
Currency	Used where a field contains monetary values. Don't use the Number data type for currency values, because numbers to the right of the decimal are rounded off during calculations. The Currency data type maintains a fixed number of digits to the right of the decimal.
AutoNumber	Sequential numbers automatically inserted by the database engine. Numbering begins at 1.
Yes/No	Holds values of Yes/No, True/False, On/Off. Corresponds to Visual Basic's Boolean type.
OLE Object	Objects created in other programs using the OLE protocol. Managed by OLE, Image or PictureBox controls.

Table 2. Comparison of MS-Access and Visual Basic Types.

Access Field Type	Visual Basic Type
Yes/No	Boolean
Number(Byte)	Byte
AutoNumber	Long
Currency	Currency
Date/Time	Date
Number (Double)	Double
Number (Long Integer)	Long
OLE Object	String
Memo	String
Number (Single)	Single
Number (Integer)	Integer
Text	String
Hyperlink	String

Microsoft also defined a flexible set of database interfaces called OLE DB. (OLE stands *for Object Linking and Embedding.*) A variety of data sources are supported, including text files, web pages, local, and remote databases. At the time of this writing, there are four OLE DB providers:

- OLE DB Provider for Oracle®
- OLE DB Provider for ODBC
- OLE DB Provider for Microsoft® Jet
- OLE DB provider for Microsoft® SQL Server™

You can still use DAO objects in VB6 programs, as well as the controls that support them, including the intrinsic Data Control, DBGrid, DBList, and DBCombo controls. But the Microsoft documentation that supports them already labels them "obsolete." To avoid the confusion that would result from trying to learn two different sets of interfaces, we will focus exclusively on ADO in this book.

4.1.3 Using the ADO Data Control

The *ADO Data control* uses ActiveX Data Objects (ADO) to quickly create connections between data-bound controls and data providers.

Properties. There are certain properties that must be set in an ADO control before it can use a data source: ConnectionString, RecordSource, and CommandType. The **ConnectionString** property identifies the data source connected to the ADO control. When you select the ConnectionString property on the ADO controls property page, a wizard

> *Tip:* Before using the ADO control in a program, select *Components* from the Project menu and place a check next to *Microsoft ADO Data Control 6.0.*

guides you through the steps in creating this string. Here, for example, is a sample connection string for an Access database called staff.mdb:

```
"Provider=Microsoft.Jet.OLEDB.3.51;Persist " _
  & "Security Info=False;Data Source=C:\VBProgs\staff.mdb"
```

Notice that the connection string includes the full path of the database, which causes a problem when you move your program to a different directory. One remedy is to remove the path from the filename, and place the database file in the same directory as the program. Another solution is to save the database path in the system registry (see Section 2.6), and initialize the Connection property at run time.

The **RecordSource** property identifies a table or query that produces data from the data source. For example, in the database shown earlier in this chapter, we would set RecordSource to "SalesStaff."

The **CommandType** property identifies the type of information that will be placed in the RecordSource property. The three most common choices are:

adCmdText	An SQL command
adCmdTable	The name of a database table
adCmdUnknown	An unknown type of command

All three properties, ConnectionString, RecordSource, and CommandType, may be assigned at design time through the Properties window, or at runtime using program code.

4.1.4 Using Data-Bound Controls

If it were only used by itself, the ADO control would not be very useful. But other controls, called *data-bound controls,* or *data consumers*, can be attached to an ADO control. At runtime, the data control opens the Recordset (usually a database table) and fills all data-

> ***Tip*: Working around an ADO control bug.**
>
> Program statements that access properties and methods of the Recordset object in an ADO control often cause a runtime error such as "Object variable or With block variable not set." This usually happens when the ADO control is not explicitly bound to a text box or label. Fortunately, there is an easy workaround: Call the ADO.Refresh method in the Form_Load or Form_Activate procedure. For example:

```
Sub Form_Load()
  adoMembers.Refresh
End Sub
```

bound controls with data from the first record of the Recordset. When the user clicks on the data control to move forward and backward through the Recordset, the data-bound controls are updated automatically.

According to the Microsoft documentation, any of the following intrinsic Visual Basic controls can be bound to an ADO control: CheckBox, ComboBox, Image, Label, ListBox, PictureBox, and TextBox. Any of the following ActiveX controls may be bound to an ADO control: DataList, DataCombo, DataGrid, Microsoft Hierarchical FlexGrid, RichTextBox, Microsoft Chart, DateTimePicker, ImageCombo, and MonthView.

Linking an ADO Control. In a data-bound control such as a Text control, the **DataSource** property holds the name of an ADO control on the current form. The **DataField** property holds the name of the field in the Recordset attached to this control.

It might be helpful to think of an ADO control as a communication link between a database table and one or more fields on a Visual Basic form. The ADO control knows where to find the data; it makes the data available at run time to any other controls that request the data. As shown in Figure 1, these controls use the DataSource property to connect to the data control, and the DataField property to name the field from the database table supplying the data.

Working with Option Buttons. OptionButton controls, used so often in programs, cannot be directly bound to an ADO control (or a Data Control), so they present a special challenge. Suppose, for example, that a program uses OptionButtons to display a field called Gender from a database table:

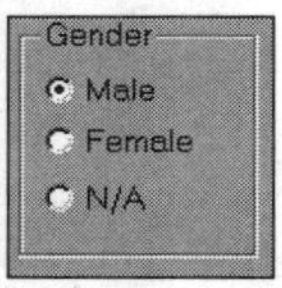

We can create a hidden Text control called txtGender that is bound to the ADO control through the former's DataSource and DataField properties. Whenever the contents of txtGender change, code in the Change event handler updates the appropriate OptionButton:

Figure 1. Connecting a Data Control to a Database and Text control.

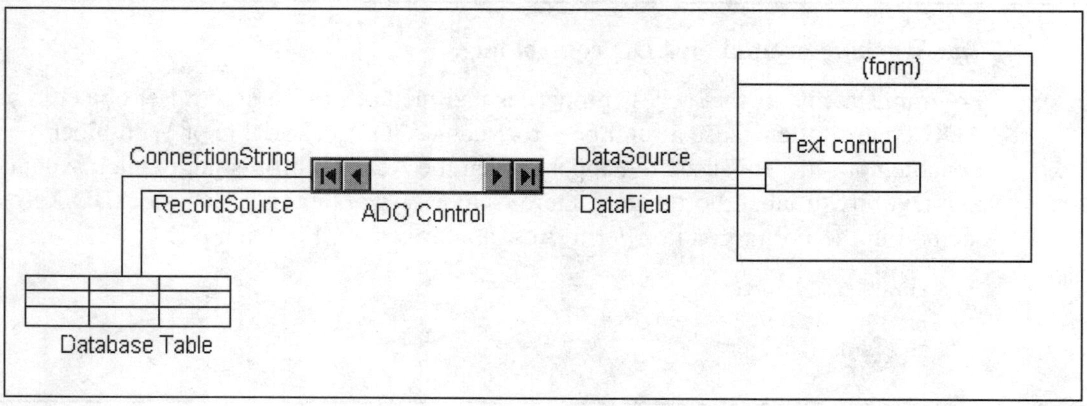

```
Private Sub txtGender_Change()
  If txtGender.Text = "M" Then
    optMale.Value = True
  ElseIf txtGender.Text = "F" Then
    optFemale.Value = True
  Else
    optNoGender.Value = True
  End If
End Sub
```

Conversely, when the user clicks on an OptionButton, the following code assigns a matching string to the Gender field of the current Recordset:

```
Private Sub optFemale_Click()
  adoMembers.Recordset!Gender = "F"
End Sub

Private Sub optMale_Click()
  adoMembers.Recordset!Gender = "M"
End Sub

Private Sub optNoGender_Click()
  adoMembers.Recordset!Gender = "N"
End Sub
```

Another possibility might have been to let each OptionButton assign a string to the txtGender field. Here, for example, is the optFemale_Click procedure code:

```
Private Sub optFemale_Click()
  txtGender.Text = "F"
End Sub
```

But this sets up a recursive loop when the txtGender_Change procedure calls optFemale_Click, which calls txtGender_Change, which calls opt_Female_Click, and so on.

4.1.5 ADODB Recordsets

A Recordset object is a Visual Basic object that defines methods and properties relating to database tables and queries. Under previous versions of Visual Basic, Recordsets were defined under DAO (Data Access Objects), which, as we have explained, has been superseded by ADO. ADO defines a new type of Recordset called an ADODB.Recordset, that has many of the same properties and methods as the older DAO Recordset. Every ADO control has a property called **Recordset**, which is a reference to its underlying Recordset object. Table 3 lists selected properties, and Table 4 lists selected methods. Of these, we will concentrate on all of the Move-related methods first, followed by the AddNew, Update, and Delete methods in the next section of this chapter.

4.2 SALES STAFF EXAMPLES

In this section, we will create a number of short programs that display data from the SalesStaff table of the database shown earlier in this chapter. We will set the ADO control properties as follows:

Table 3. Selected Recordset Properties.

Property	Description
BOF	True when cursor is before the first record in the Recordset.
Bookmark	Returns a variant value that uniquely identifies the current record position. If set, moves the current position to the location identified by a valid bookmark.
EOF	True when cursor is after the last record in the Recordset.
Fields	Collection of Field objects, which hold the Recordset data.
Filter	Selects only certain rows in a Recordset.
RecordCount	Indicates the current number of records.
Sort	List of fields on which to sort the Recordset.

Table 4. Selected Recordset Methods.

Method	Description
AddNew	Adds a new empty record to the Recordset.
Delete	Deletes the current record.
Find	Searches for a matching record, starting from the current position.
Move	Moves the Recordset pointer.
MoveFirst	Moves to the first record.
MoveLast	Moves to the last record.
MoveNext	Moves to the next record.
MovePrevious	Moves to the previous record.
Requery	Refreshes the contents of a Recordset from its data source by reissuing the original command and retrieving the data again.
Resync	Refreshes data in the current Recordset from the underlying database. Does not reissue the original command.
Update	Saves changes made to the current Recordset object in its corresponding database.

Name	adoSalesStaff
ConnectionString	Provider=Microsoft.Jet.OLEDB.3.51;Persist Security Info=False;Data Source=staff.mdb
CommandType	adCmdTable

4.2.1 Displaying Records

(samples: SalesStaff1)

In the first version of this program, the main form contains controls called **txtStaffID**, **txtFirstName**, **txtLastName, txtSalary, chkIsFullTime,** and **txtHireDate.** The

DataSource property for each of these fields contains the name of the ADO control, **adoSalesStaff**. Figure 2 contains a snapshot of the form taken at run time, and Table 5 lists each control along with its DataField property value and database field type.

Figure 2. Sales Staff Program. (Staff1.vbp)

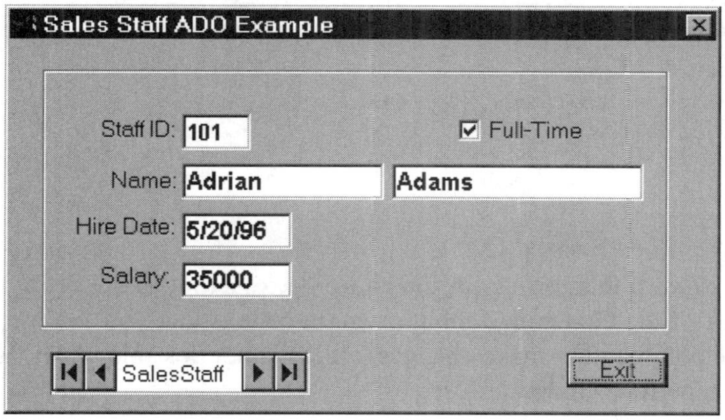

Table 5. Bound Controls, SalesStaff Program.

Control	DataField	Field Type
txtStaffId	StaffID	Text
txtFirstName	FirstName	Text
txtLastName	LastName	Text
txtSalary	Salary	Currency
chkIsFullTime	IsFullTime	Yes/No
txtHireDate	HireDate	Date/Time

When you run this program, use the left and right arrow buttons on the ADO control to move forward and backward through the records. If you modify a field and move to a different record, the changes you make are permanently saved. The following diagram shows the use of each of the buttons on the ADO control:

Program Code. In the code for this program, we set the ADO control properties at runtime. This helps to make the program more self-documenting, and makes it easier to change the database name or location in the future. We assume that the database is in the current project directory:

```
Private Sub Form_Load()
'Establish the database connection, command type,
'and record source.
  With adoSalesStaff
     .ConnectionString = "Provider=Microsoft.Jet.OLEDB.3.51;" _
      & "Persist Security Info=False;Data Source=" _
      & App.Path & "\staff.mdb"
     .CommandType = adCmdTable
     .RecordSource = "SalesStaff"
     .Refresh
  End With
End Sub
```

We're going to stick with this format for the entire book, setting ADO control properties in program code. One of the nice things about program code is that you can use the editor's search and replace command to make changes, which is not possible when values are entered into the Properties window.

4.2.2 Moving the Recordset Pointer

(examples: SalesStaff2)

A Recordset always maintains an internal pointer to the current record, which we also call the *cursor.* When a Recordset is opened, refreshed, or created, the cursor is at the first record. Each of the following examples uses the Recordset attached to an ADO control named **adoSalesStaff**:

```
With adoSalesStaff.Recordset
  .MoveNext                   'next record
  .MovePrevious               'previous record
  .MoveFirst                  'first record
  .MoveLast                   'last record
  .Move 2                     'two records forward
  .Move -2                    'two records backward
End With
```

In some cases, these methods may move the position to a nonexistent record. For example, if you follow MoveLast with MoveNext. This will generate a *trappable error*, meaning that it can be handled with an On Error GoTo statement.

Adding Navigation Buttons to the SalesStaff Program. Let's improve the user interface of the SalesStaff program, shown in Figure 3. First, we will add CommandButtons that make it easier for the user to navigate forward and backward through the Recordset. A menu and a StatusBar have been added, and the ADO control is no longer visible. In this new version of the program, we add program code to each of the new CommandButton click events.

Open and run this program. Use the First, Prev, Next, and Last buttons to move around in the Recordset. Use the Mark button to mark the current location, and use the Return button to return to a marked location. Insert a new record (select Insert from the Edit menu). Remove a record (select Remove from the Edit menu). Modify a record and update it by selecting Update from the Edit menu.

Figure 3. SalesStaff Program, Version 2.

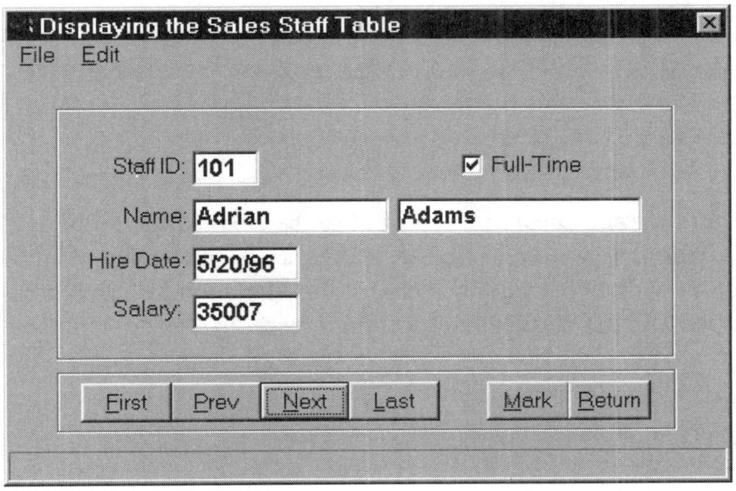

Program Code. When the user clicks on the **cmdFirst** button, we simply call the Recordset.MoveFirst method of the ADO control and post a message on the form's status bar:

```
Private Sub cmdFirst_Click()
  adoSalesStaff.Recordset.MoveFirst
  staMain.SimpleText = "Beginning of File"
End Sub
```

Similarly, the Recordset.MoveLast method moves to the last record:

```
Private Sub cmdLast_Click()
  adoSalesStaff.Recordset.MoveLast
  staMain.SimpleText = "End of File"
End Sub
```

The **cmdNext** button event handler has a little more work to do. It empties the status line, calls the Recordset.MoveNext method on the ADO control to move to the next record, and if the end of file has been reached, backs up to the previous record and updates the status line:

```
Private Sub cmdNext_Click()
  staMain.SimpleText = ""
  adoSalesStaff.Recordset.MoveNext
  If adoSalesStaff.Recordset.EOF Then
    staMain.SimpleText = "End of File"
    adoSalesStaff.Recordset.MovePrevious
  End If
End Sub
```

The **cmdPrev** button empties the status line, calls the Recordset.MoveFirst method, and if the beginning of file (BOF) is reached, moves forward to the first record and updates the status line:

```
Private Sub cmdPrev_Click()
  staMain.SimpleText = ""
  adoSalesStaff.Recordset.MovePrevious
  If adoSalesStaff.Recordset.BOF Then
    staMain.SimpleText = "Beginning of File"
    adoSalesStaff.Recordset.MoveNext
  End If
End Sub
```

BookMarking the Current Location. You can use the **BookMark** property to mark the current cursor location, save it in a variable, and return to the bookmarked location at a later time. The following two event handlers for the Mark and Return buttons set a bookmark and return to the bookmarked location, respectively:

```
Private Sub cmdMark_Click()
'Bookmark the current location.
  mvMark = adoSalesStaff.Recordset.Bookmark
  staMain.SimpleText = "Location marked"
End Sub

Private Sub cmdReturn_Click()
'Return to the bookmarked location.
  adoSalesStaff.Recordset.Bookmark = mvMark
  staMain.SimpleText = "Returned to marked location"
End Sub
```

The mvMark variable is declared at the module level, as a Variant.

4.2.3 Adding, Deleting, and Updating Records

Every ADO control has a Recordset property, which refers to the Recordset currently connected to the database. We will use several Recordset methods in this version of the SalesStaff program for adding, removing, and updating records:

AddNew	Creates a new, blank record
CancelUpdate	Cancels an AddNew operation in progress
Delete	Removes the current record
Update	Saves the current record in the database

Inserting a Record. When the user selects Insert from the Edit menu, the mnuInsert_Click procedure creates a new blank record, disables all CommandButtons within the frame control, and updates the status line to show the operation in progress. Notice that On Error GoTo is used here to trap potential runtime errors:

```
Private Sub mnuEditInsert_Click()
  On Error GoTo InsertErr
  adoSalesStaff.Recordset.AddNew
  fraMoveButtons.Enabled = False
  staMain.SimpleText = "Adding new record"
  txtID.SetFocus
  Exit Sub
InsertErr:
  MsgBox Error$, vbCritical, "Error"
End Sub
```

Update Method. When the user selects Update from the Edit menu, we call the Update method and then the Move method to force the Recordset to update the record:

```
Private Sub mnuEditUpdate_Click()
  On Error GoTo UpdateErr
  adoSalesStaff.Recordset.Update
  adoSalesStaff.Recordset.Move 0      'force the update
  fraMoveButtons.Enabled = True
  staMain.SimpleText = "Record updated"
  Exit Sub
UpdateErr:
  MsgBox Error$, vbCritical, "Error"
End Sub
```

Delete Method. When the user wants to remove a record, we post a message on the status line, call the Delete method and refresh the ADO control. This is necessary to prevent the cursor from pointing to a nonexistent record:

```
Private Sub mnuEditRemove_Click()
  On Error GoTo RemoveErr
  staMain.SimpleText = "Removing: " & txtLastName.Text _
      & ", " & txtFirstName.Text
  adoSalesStaff.Recordset.Delete
  adoSalesStaff.Refresh
  Exit Sub
RemoveErr:
  MsgBox Error$, vbCritical, "Error"
End Sub
```

Sometimes the Refresh method does not update the data displayed in data-bound controls after a record has been deleted. If you experience this problem, the easiest workaround is to reassign the RecordSource property of the ADO control:

```
adoSalesStaff.Recordset.Delete
adoSalesStaff.Recordsource = "SalesStaff'
```

This solution can be used in the Karate School program in the chapter exercises, for example, when the ADO control is bound to a DataGrid control and you want to delete a member from the Recordset.

4.2.4 Sorting Records

(samples: SalesStaff3)

Next, we would like to let the user sort the Recordset attached to an ADO control on various fields. A ComboBox called cboSort has been added to the program, containing the following entries:

StaffId
LastName,FirstName
HireDate
HireDate Desc
Salary

Salary Desc
IsFullTime,LastName,FirstName

When the user selects one of these ComboBox entries, we assign the combo's Text property to the **Sort** property of the ADO Recordset, and the records immediately rearrange themselves. For a snapshot of the main form, see Figure 4. When the program starts up, records are automatically sorted by StaffId. For sorts involving multiple fields such as "LastName,FirstName", the primary sort is on the first field name and the secondary sort is on the second field name. *Note:* The Visual Basic documentation incorrectly says to use DESCENDING rather than DESC, and ASCENDING rather than ASC. Finally, capitalization is not important.

Figure 4. SalesStaff Program.

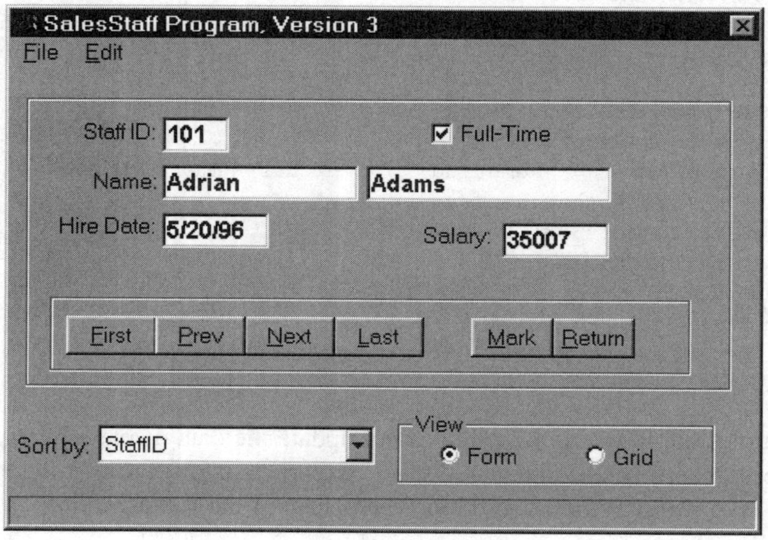

We have added one more feature to this program. A Frame containing two OptionButtons gives the user the opportunity to display the data as a form (the current view) or in a grid, using the DataGrid control. Figure 5 shows the program's appearance when the Grid view has been selected. The user has modified the column widths to display all table fields.

The Sort Property. The Recordset attached to an ADO control has a Sort property that can be set to a string containing the name of one or more Recordset fields. Table 6 contains examples.

We placed the DataGrid control below the viewable area of the form. There are only three properties that must be set for the DataGrid control:

Name	dgdSalesStaff
DataSource	adoSalesStaff
Visible	False

Figure 5. SalesStaff Program Showing a DataGrid.

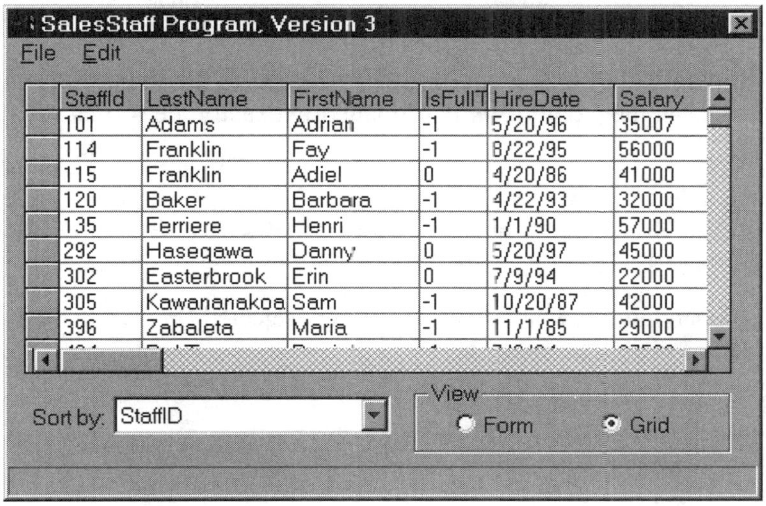

Table 6. Sort String Values for SalesStaff.

Sort String	Description
StaffId	Sort in ascending order by StaffId.
LastName	Sort in ascending order by LastName.
LastName, FirstName	Primary sort by LastName, secondary sort by FirstName, both in ascending order.
HireDate Desc	Sort in descending order by HireDate.
HireDate Asc	Sort in ascending order by HireDate
HireDate Desc, StaffId Asc	Primary sort by HireDate descending, secondary sort by StaffId ascending.

The DataSource property links the DataGrid to the ADO control so we can view the SalesStaff table. To place the DataGrid control in the ToolBox window, select Components from the Project menu and place a check next to "Microsoft DataGrid Control 6.0."

Program Code. The following code has been added to the program. In the Form_Load() procedure, we set the ListIndex property of cboSort, automatically generating a Click event:

```
cboSort.ListIndex = 0     'sort by StaffId
```

Also in Form_Load, we reposition the DataGrid at the same location as the Frame surrounding the TextBoxes, and bring it to the top level by calling the **ZOrder** method. The grid remains invisible until requested by the user:

```
With dgdSalesStaff
   .Top = Frame1.Top + 100
   .Left = Frame1.Left
   .Width = Frame1.Width
```

```
    .Height = Frame1.Height - 100
    .ZOrder 0
  End With
```

In the ComboBox's Click event, we assign its text to the Recordset's Sort property. By design, the text in the ComboBox is formatted in exactly the format recognized by the Sort property:

```
Private Sub cboSort_Click()
  adoSalesStaff.Recordset.Sort = cboSort.Text
End Sub
```

Finally, depending on which OptionButton is selected (Form or Grid), we either make the DataGrid visible or invisible:

```
Private Sub optViewForm_Click()
  dgdSalesStaff.Visible = False
End Sub

Private Sub optViewGrid_Click()
  dgdSalesStaff.Visible = True
End Sub
```

As you can imagine, there is much more that may be done with a DataGrid control. There are so many options, in fact, that an entire section is devoted to the DataGrid later in this chapter.

4.2.5 Filtering Records

(samples: SalesStaff4)

In the English language, to *filter* something means to exclude certain values, as one would place a filter over a camera lens to exclude a range of light frequencies. Similarly, an ADO Recordset uses its Filter property to limit the scope of records included in the current Recordset. The Filter property holds a string containing one or more boolean expressions that compare individual fields with values. Some examples of valid expressions using the SalesStaff table are shown in Table 7. Valid operators are <, >, <=, >=, <>, =, and LIKE. The LIKE operator allows the use of wildcard characters (* and %) for partial string matching. A wildcard character, if used, must be the first and/or last character in the string.

From these examples, it is clear that compound boolean expressions are permitted, and you can use parentheses to clarify the order of operations. Always remember to use the correct delimiters with each field type: single quotes surround values compared to Text fields, #..# surround values compared to Date/Time fields, and no delimiters surround values compared to numeric fields.

There is a limitation regarding combinations of AND and OR: You cannot use parentheses to evaluate an OR condition followed by AND:

```
(LastName = 'Franklin' OR LastName = 'Jones') AND FirstName = 'John'
```

But you can work around this by reworking the expression:

```
(LastName = 'Franklin' AND FirstName = 'John') OR (LastName = 'Jones' AND
FirstName = 'John')
```

Table 7. Sample Filter Property Values.

Filter	Sample Values Found
`StaffId = '821'`	Finds 821
`StaffId LIKE '_01'`	Finds values such as 801, 901, 601
`LastName = 'Gomez'`	Finds 'GOMEZ', 'Gomez', 'gomez'
`HireDate < #01/01/1990#`	Finds 12/6/85, 06/05/89
`Salary > 30000`	Finds 30001, 40000, 99000
`LastName LIKE 'J%'`	Finds 'Jones', 'Johnson', 'jackson'
`FirstName LIKE '%B%'`	Finds 'Barbara', 'Robert', 'Bill'
`HireDate > #01/01/1990# AND HireDate < #01/01/1995#`	Finds 1/5/92, 12/30/1994
`Salary > 30000 Or HireDate < #01/01/1990#`	Finds 31000, 12/31/1989, 42000, 6/10/85

Adding a Filter to the SalesStaff Program. We can easily modify the SalesStaff program to include controls that let the user select a field, an operator, and a value that filters the Recordset. The revised user interface shown in Figure 6 lets the user click next to the "Use Filter" CheckBox, select a field name from the ComboBox on the left, select an operator from the middle combo, and type a value into the textbox (currently containing 30000). The program shows the generated filter string in a label just below the ComboBoxes, and immediately filters the Recordset.

Figure 6. SalesStaff Program with Filter.

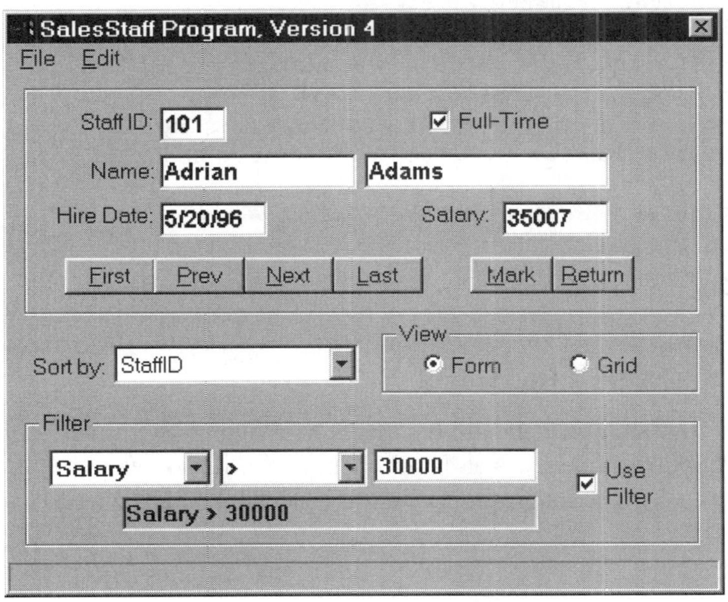

If the user removes the check from "Use Filter", the program displays all records without any filtering.

The LIKE operator allows for partial string matches. For example, the user could search for all LastName values beginning with the letter J:

```
LastName LIKE 'J%'
```

Note: Microsoft Access allows both the % and * characters to be used as wildcards, but only the % symbol works when querying ADODB Recordsets.

Program code. Here is the code written to handle the new controls. The ComboBoxes, the new TextBox, and the CheckBox all call the **RefreshFilterText** procedure:

```
Private Sub cboFieldName_Click()
  RefreshFilterText
End Sub

Private Sub cboOperator_Click()
  RefreshFilterText
End Sub

Private Sub chkUseFilter_Click()
  RefreshFilterText
End Sub

Private Sub txtFilterValue_Change()
  RefreshFilterText
End Sub
```

The **RefreshFilterText** procedure builds a filter string and assigns it to the Filter property of the ADO control's Recordset. If the user does not want to use a filter, the predefined constant **adFilterNone** is assigned instead:

```
Private Sub RefreshFilterText()
'Update the filter property of the Recordset.
  On Error Resume Next
  If chkUseFilter.Value = vbChecked Then
    lblFilter.Caption = cboFieldName.Text & " " & _
        cboOperator.Text & " " & txtFilterValue.Text
    adoSalesStaff.Recordset.Filter = lblFilter.Caption
  Else
    adoSalesStaff.Recordset.Filter = adFilterNone
    lblFilter.Caption = ""
  End If
End Sub
```

4.2.6 Using SQL to Create a Recordset

A powerful way to search for database records is to assign an SQL query string to an ADO control's RecordSource property. Nearly all client-server databases use SQL queries to create Recordsets, so in the long run, it's best to learn to use SQL queries even in desktop applications.

The SQL language in its entirety is a complex language, but you can learn the basics of selecting and sorting records fairly easily. There are three basic parts, or clauses in a SELECT statement in SQL:

```
From <field-list>
Order By <field-list>
Where <boolean-expression>
```

A *field-list* contains one or more field names separated by commas. For example:

```
StaffId,LastName,FirstName
```

A *boolean-expression* may involve just a single comparison, or it may contain multiple comparisons joined by AND and OR operators:

```
Salary > 30000
Salary > 30000 And HireDate < #1/1/1990#
Salary > 30000 Or HireDate < #1/1/1990#
```

The following examples have been prepared to demonstrate some of the more common operations:

1. Display the StaffId, LastName, FirstName, and Salary fields from the SalesStaff table:

```
Select StaffId,LastName,FirstName,Salary
  From SalesStaff
```

2. Display all fields and sort by LastName:

```
Select * From SalesStaff
  Order By LastName
```

3. Display LastName and HireDate, and sort by HireDate in descending order:

```
Select LastName,HireDate From SalesStaff
  Order By HireDate DESC
```

4. Display all fields, but show only employees hired before 1/1/1990. (Don't forget the # delimiters on dates):

```
Select * From SalesStaff
  Where HireDate < #1/1/1990#
```

5. Display all fields, but show only last names starting with the letter J: (Don't forget single quotes around Text fields):

```
Select * From SalesStaff
  Where LastName Like 'J%'
```

6. Display the last names and first names of only full-time employees:

```
Select LastName,FirstName From SalesStaff
  Where IsFullTime = True
```

7. Show only full-time employees hired after 1/1/1990 who have salaries greater than $30,000:

```
Select * From SalesStaff
   Where IsFullTime = True
   And HireDate > #1/1/1990#
   And Salary > 30000
```

SalesStaff Program with SQL. Let's create a new version of the SalesStaff program, this time with a DataGrid control, ADO control, TextBox, and CommandButton. The user types a query string, clicks on the **Go!** button, and the grid displays all records returned by the query. Figure 7 shows the user interface.

(samples: SalesStaff5)

Figure 7. SalesStaff Program with SQL Query.

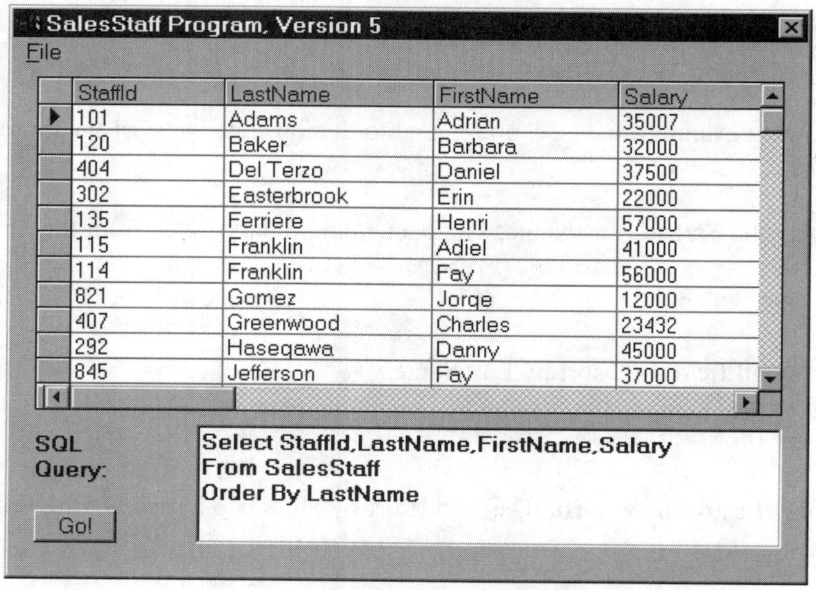

Program Code. Very little code is required in this program. First, the ComandType property for the ADO control is changed within Form_Load:

```
With adoSalesStaff
  ...
  .CommandType = adCmdText          'accept SQL text
  ...
End Sub
```

When the user clicks on the **Go!** Button, the following code executes the query. After assigning a new string to the RecordSource property, we call the Refresh method to show the updated data in the grid:

```
Private Sub cmdGo_Click()
   On Error GoTo BadQueryErr
   With adoSalesStaff
      .RecordSource = txtQuery.Text
      .Refresh
   End With
```

```
  Exit Sub
BadQueryErr:
  MsgBox txtQuery.Text, vbInformation, "Syntax Error in Query"
End Sub
```

4.2.7 Using the Find Method

(samples: SalesStaff6)

The **Find** method provides an easy way to search for a single matching record, using a criteria expression. The Find method uses a comparison expression to find the first matching record. It stops after finding a single match. By default, it searches in a forward direction from the current cursor position. The syntax is:

```
object.Find (Criteria As String, [SkipRecords As Long],_
   [SearchDirection As SearchDirectionEnum], [Start])
```

The only required parameter is *Criteria*. *SkipRecords* lets you skip over a selected number of records, *SearchDirection* lets you set a direction of either forward or backward, and *Start* is a bookmark indicating where the search should start. If you want to search in a backward direction, include the SearchDirection := adSearchBackward argument when calling the Find method.

The following predefined bookmarks can be assigned to the **Start** parameter to set the starting positions: adBookmarkFirst and adBookmarkLast. The following constants can be passed to the SearchDirection parameter (defined by SearchDirectionEnum): adSearchForward and adSearchBackward.

Examples. Let's look at a few examples from the SalesStaff database. We can move to the next record containing a StaffId of 813:

```
adoSalesStaff.Recordset.Find "StaffId = 813"
```

Or, we can move to the beginning of the Recordset and find the first person hired before June 1, 1989:

```
With adoSalesStaff.Recordset
  .MoveFirst
  .Find "HireDate < #6/1/1989#"
  If .EOF Then
    MsgBox "Matching record not found", vbInformation, ""
  End If
End With
```

We can start searching at the end of the Recordset and search in a backward direction, as the following statements demonstrate:

```
With adoSalesStaff.Recordset
  .MoveLast
  .Find txtFind.Text, SearchDirection:=adSearchBackward
  If .BOF Then
    MsgBox "Matching record not found", vbInformation, ""
  End If
End With
```

Always check the EOF (end of file) property after performing a forward search, and check the BOF (beginning of file) property after performing a backward search.

Single Expression Limitation. The ADO's Find method replaces the older DAO FindFirst and FindNext methods, with one serious drawback: The Find method does not accept compound expressions. The following, for example, is not permitted:

```
.Find "HireDate > #1/1/1990# And HireDate < #12/31/1998#"
```

This means, in other words, if you want to search using compound criteria, you must either place the criteria expression in the Filter property, or you must use an SQL query to build a temporary Recordset. Both methods were shown earlier in this chapter.

SalesStaff Program using the Find Method. Figure 8 shows the user interface for Version 6 of the SalesStaff program, which uses the Find method to search for records. The user types an expression into the TextBox, clicks on the **Go!** button, and the record pointer in the DataGrid control identifies the first matching record. If the program cannot find a matching record, it displays a message box notifying the user. The following program code executes the Find method. By querying the EOF property, we know whether or not a matching record was found:

```
With adoSalesStaff.Recordset
   If chkSearchForward.Value = vbChecked Then
      .MoveFirst
      .Find txtFind.Text
      If .EOF Then
         MsgBox "Matching record not found", vbInformation, ""
      End If
   Else
      .MoveLast
      .Find txtFind.Text, SearchDirection:=adSearchBackward
      If .BOF Then
         MsgBox "Matching record not found", vbInformation, ""
      End If
```

Figure 8. SalesStaff Program using the Find Method.

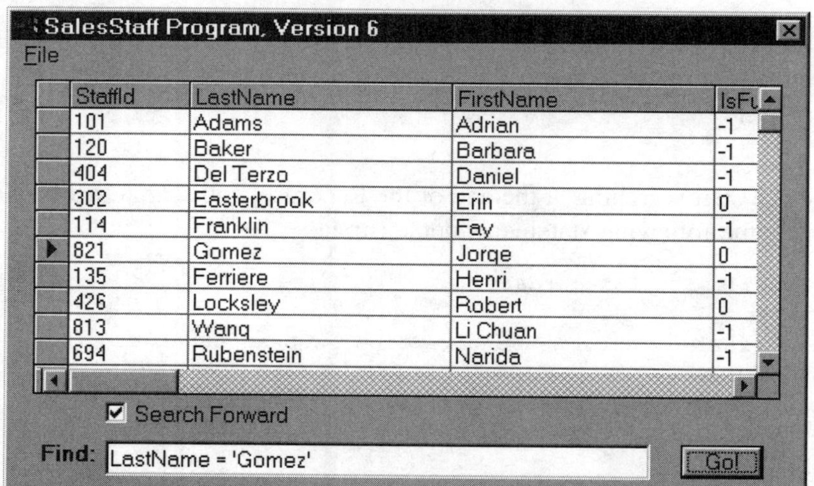

```
  End If
End With
```

4.2.8 Displaying Images

(samples: SalesStaff7)

If you want to display a graphic image stored in a Microsoft Access database, the graphic must be stored in an OLE type field. In Visual Basic, the OLE control can display such a field, but it cannot be bound to an ADO control. Instead, the OLE control must be bound to the intrinsic Data Control. Let's add another table to the SalesStaff database called **Pictures**, containing two fields: StaffId and Picture:

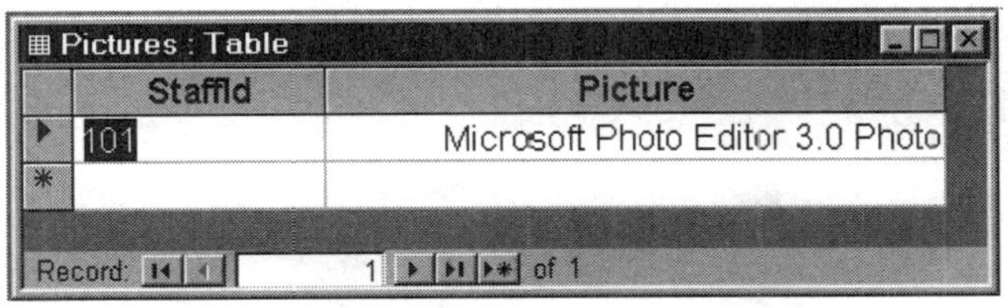

The table just contains one picture for now, but more could easily be added. The following steps are used in this version of the SalesStaff program to display a person's name and picture:

1. Place an ADO control on the form and call it **adoSalesStaff**. Initialize its ConnectionString to the **staff.mdb** database (in the SalesStaff7 directory on the student disk) and set its RecordSource property to **SalesStaff**.
2. Place a Data Control on the form and call it **datPictures**. Set its DatabaseName property to **staff.mdb** and its RecordSource property to **Pictures**.
3. Place an OLE control on the form and call it OLE1. The OLE control is always available in the Visual Basic ToolBox window. When you drag it onto a form, Visual Basic prompts you for a filename to be inserted. Click on the Cancel button. Set its DataSource property to **datPictures** and set its dataField property to **Picture**.
4. Place two TextBox controls on the form and bind them to the ADO control, using DataField values of **FirstName** and **LastName**.
5. Place a CommandButton on the form and label it OK (optional). Figure 9 shows the program at design time.
6. Write program statements that synchronize the Data Control to the ADO control. When the user repositions the ADO control, the **MoveComplete** event triggers. In this procedure, we call the Data Control's **FindFirst** method to search for the staff member's ID number in the Pictures table. If the ID is found, we make the OLE control visible (see Figure 10); otherwise, the OLE control is hidden:

```
Private Sub adoSalesStaff_MoveComplete(ByVal adReason As _
  ADODB.EventReasonEnum, ByVal pError As ADODB.Error, _
  adStatus As ADODB.EventStatusEnum, _
  ByVal pRecordset As ADODB.Recordset)
```

```
    If mblnLoadFinished Then
      datPictures.Recordset.FindFirst "StaffId = '" _
        & adoSalesStaff.Recordset!StaffId & "'"
      If datPictures.Recordset.NoMatch Then
        OLE1.Visible = False
      Else
        OLE1.Visible = True
      End If
    End If
  End Sub
```

Figure 9. SalesStaff with Picture (design mode).

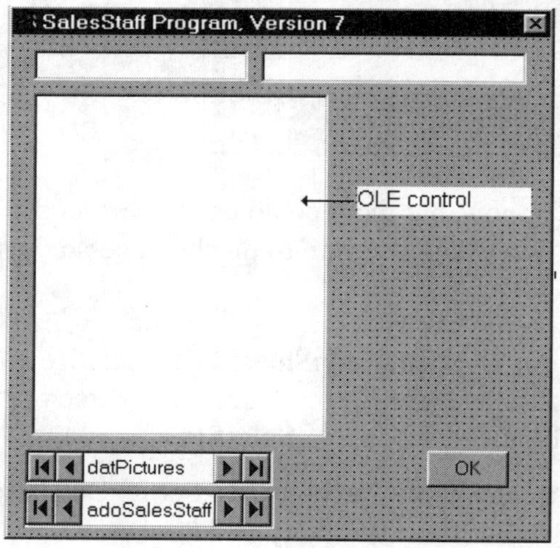

Figure 10. SalesStaff with Picture (run mode).

Notice the reference to the StaffId field in the SalesStaff table made by the following statement:

```
adoSalesStaff.Recordset!StaffId
```

This is actually a shorthand way to refer to the **Value** property of a member of the **Fields** collection belonging to a Recordset object. The "long" form would also have been less efficient in terms of runtime speed:

```
adoSalesStaff.Recordset.Fields("StaffId").Value
```

The Boolean variable, **mblnLoadFinished**, is set to False during the Form initialize event and set to True after the Form_Load procedure finishes. This switch is necessary because the MoveComplete event fires too early – even before Form_Load, before the Data Control has been properly initialized. The following code tracks changes to mblnLoadFinished:

```
Private mblnLoadFinished As Boolean

Private Sub Form_Initialize()
  mblnLoadFinished = False
End Sub

Private Sub Form_Load()
  mblnLoadFinished = True
End Sub
```

4.2.9 ADO Control Events (optional)

(samples: SalesStaff8)

A number of important events are generated by the ADO control. For the purposes of data validation, you may want to write code for the corresponding event handlers. This is a fairly advanced technique, because you often have to deal with a series of events and errors that occur in quick succession. For each event, we will describe the event and show the event handler procedure generated by Visual Basic.

The **WillMove** event occurs just before a pending operation changes the current position in the Recordset:

```
Private Sub adoSalesStaff_WillMove( _
  ByVal adReason As ADODB.EventReasonEnum, _
  adStatus As ADODB.EventStatusEnum, _
  ByVal pRecordset As ADODB.Recordset)
  '(your code here...)
End Sub
```

The **EventReasonEnum** parameter can be one of the following values: adRsnMoveFirst, adRsnMoveLast, adRsnMoveNext, adRsnMovePrevious, adRsnMove or adRsnRequery. The **pRecordset** parameter is a reference to the Recordset for which this event occurred. The **adStatus** parameter is automatically set to the predefined constant adStatusOK if the operation that caused this event was successful. If you set adStatus to adStatusCancel when exiting this procedure, the move operation is cancelled.

The **MoveComplete** event occurs just after the current position in the Recordset has changed. The **adReason** parameter can have any of the values listed under the WillMove event. The **adStatus** parameter is automatically set to adStatusOK if the operation that caused the event was successful, or adStatusErrorsOccurred if the operation failed. The **pError** parameter is a reference to an Error object that was generated if the operation was unsuccessful. You can write code such as the following, that checks adStatus and displays pError information:

```
Private Sub adoSalesStaff_MoveComplete( _
  ByVal adReason As ADODB.EventReasonEnum, _
  ByVal pError As ADODB.Error, _
  adStatus As ADODB.EventStatusEnum, _
  ByVal pRecordset As ADODB.Recordset)

  If adStatus = adStatusErrorsOccurred Then
    MsgBox pError.Description, , "Error " & pError.Number
  End If
End Sub
```

Here is the error message generated when the user tries to move beyond the last record:

Writing code in the MoveComplete procedure does not prevent a runtime error from occurring, so you still need to use error-trapping statements (On Error GoTo) to handle errors.

The **WillChangeRecord** event occurs when the current record is about to be changed. The **adReason** parameter values are the same as those in the WillMove event.

```
Private Sub adoSalesStaff_WillChangeRecord( _
  ByVal adReason As ADODB.EventReasonEnum, _
  ByVal cRecords As Long, _
  adStatus As ADODB.EventStatusEnum, _
  ByVal pRecordset As ADODB.Recordset)
  '(your code here...)
End Sub
```

Similarly, the **RecordChangeComplete** event occurs after a record has changed.

The **WillChangeField** event occurs as soon as a data-bound field loses focus after the user has modified its contents. You can confirm the change with the user before allowing the change to happen. It is very important to call the **Refresh** method if you decide to cancel the update by setting **adStatus** to **adStatusCancel**. Otherwise, a runtime error occurs. In the following example, we also set a bookmark before the Refresh, and use the bookmark to return to the same record:

```
Private Sub adoSalesStaff_WillChangeField( _
```

```
    ByVal cFields As Long, Fields As Variant, _
    adStatus As ADODB.EventStatusEnum, _
    ByVal pRecordset As ADODB.Recordset)
  If MsgBox("Are you sure you want to update the " _
   & "following field? " & vbCrLf & Fields(0).Name, _
     vbQuestion + vbYesNo, "") = vbNo Then
     adStatus = adStatusCancel
     'Set a bookmark, refresh, and return to bookmark.
     mvMark = adoSalesStaff.Recordset.Bookmark
     adoSalesStaff.Refresh
     adoSalesStaff.Recordset.Bookmark = mvMark
  End If
End Sub
```

The **cFields** parameter counts the number of fields being changed. The Fields parameter is an array of Field objects that are about to be changed, as we have done in the sample procedure. The following is a sample snapshot of a message generated by the WillChangeField procedure:

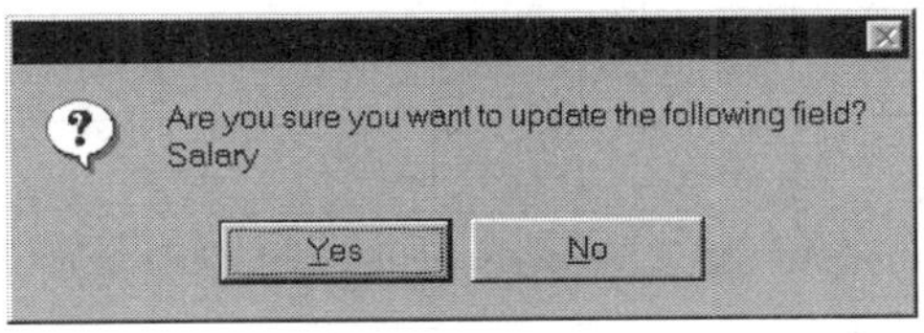

The ADO control will not move to the next record unless the user answers Yes, because moving to the next record would update the field.

There are also the **WillChangeRecordset** and **RecordsetChangeComplete** events, which occur before and after a change to the ADO control's Recordset. The **FieldChangeComplete** event occurs after a field's contents have changed.

4.3 DATAGRID, DATACOMBO AND DATALIST

4.3.1 Properties and Events

The DataGrid, DataCombo, and DataList controls are the ADO counterparts to the DBGrid, DBList, and DBCombo controls used with older DAO recordsets. They are automatically filled from a Recordset attached to an ADO data control. The DataCombo and DataList controls are similar to the standard ComboBox and List controls, but there are some important differences that give them great flexibility and usefulness in database applications. To fill a ComboBox control, for example, requires the use of a loop. But the DataCombo and DataList controls can be filled automatically from an ADO control's Recordset just by setting a few properties.

DataGrid Properties. Some of the more basic DataGrid properties are shown in Table 8. Of these, the most important is the DataSource property, which must be set before any data can appear in the grid.

DataGrid Events. The **Click** event handler for the DataGrid can be used to retrieve the current row and column. The first time the event happens, the Row and Col properties

Table 8. Important DataGrid Properties.

Property	Description
AllowAddNew	Determines whether the user can add new records.
AllowArrows	Enables user to use of keyboard arrow keys to navigate the grid.
AllowDelete	Determines whether the user can delete records.
AllowUpdate	Determines whether the user can modify and update records.
Col	The column number of the currently selected cell. First cell is column 0.
ColumHeaders	Determines whether headers (with field names) will appear above the columns.
CurrentCellModified	Set to True if the user has just modified the currently selected cell.
DataSource	Name of the ADO control providing a recordset to populate the DataGrid.
DefColWidth	Specifies width for auto-created columns.
Row	The row number of the currently selected cell. First cell is row 0.

return the location of the cell that was selected prior to the current one. The following code responds to the user's first mouse click:

```
Private Sub dbgSample_Click()
  With dbgSample
    Debug.Print "Row = " & .Row & ", Col = " & .Col
  End With
End Sub
```

When the user clicks a second time, the Click event handler returns the coordinates of the current cell. We can also trap the **DblClick** event, which returns the currently selected cell (not the previous one):

```
Private Sub dbgSchedule_DblClick()
  With dbgSchedule
    Debug.Print "Row = " & .Row & ", Col = " & .Col
  End With
End Sub
```

DataList Properties. The DataList properties listed in Table 9 provide the necessary attachments to Recordsets that display a list of items and update a bound field. If you only wish to display a list of items, just the **RowSource** and **ListField** properties are required. If a separate Recordset is to be updated, you must also set the DataSource, DataMember, and BoundColumn properties.

Table 9. Important DataList and DataCombo Properties.

Property	Description
BoundColumn	Name of database field that connnects the ListField value to the recordset identified by the DataSource and DataMember properties.
BoundText	Contents of the BoundColumn field, available only at runtime.
DataFormat	Formats the topmost item in a DataCombo, or all items in a DataList. Uses the same formatting characters as the Format() function.
DataMember	Field name bound to the ADO control identified by the DataSource property.
DataSource	ADO control attached to the recordset that is bound to this DataList control.
ListField	Name of field in the recordset that supplies the list items displayed by the control.
MatchEntry	Sets or returns a value indicating how the DataCombo or DataList control performs searches based on user input. Possible values are: dblBasicMatching and dblExtendedMatching.
RowSource	Identifies the data source for list items displayed by the control.
SelectedItem	Returns a value containing a bookmark for the selected record.
Text	Sets or returns the text contained in the selected item.
VisibleCount	Returns a count of the number of visible items.
VisibleItems	Returns an array of bookmarks, one for each visible item in the list.

The **MatchEntry** property is useful when searching for matching entries based on keystroke input. The **dblBasicMatching** option matches only the first keystroke entered. The **dblExtendedMatching** option continues to refine the search as each additional character is entered.

DataCombo Events. The Click event for a DataCombo has a parameter called **Area** that specifies exactly where the user clicked the mouse. There are three possible values:

dbcAreaButton	0	The user clicked the arrow button on the DBCombo control.
dbcAreaEdit	1	The user clicked in the TextBox part of the DBCombo control.
dbcAreaList	2	The user clicked in the drop-down list part of the DBCombo control.

This parameter is important, because you might only be interested in events generated when an item is selected from the drop-down list. The following Click handler uses a Select Case statement to identify the Area:

```
Private Sub dbcSample_Click(Area As Integer)
  Select Case Area
    Case dbcAreaButton
```

```
            Debug.Print "clicked on button"
        Case dbcAreaEdit
            Debug.Print "clicked in TextBox"
        Case dbcAreaList
            Debug.Print "clicked in drop-down list"
    End Select
End Sub
```

4.3.2 Example: Linking a DataList to a DataGrid

(samples: DataList)

To show how the DataList, DataGrid, and DataCombo controls are used, we're going to look at two programs in this section. We will use the Biblio database provided by Microsoft in the Visual Basic install directory and update two tables, **Publishers** and **Titles**:

Publishers:	PubID, Name, Company Name, Address, City, State, Zip, Telephone, Fax, Comments
Titles:	Title, Year Published, ISBN, PubID, Description, Notes, Subjects, Comments

There is a common field, **PubID** (publisher ID) that links the two tables. Every publisher ID found in the Titles table matches a single publisher in the Publishers table.

In the first program, we let the user select a publisher name from a DataList control. The program retrieves and display a list of all books produced by the selected publisher. In Figure 11, the user has selected a publisher name ("M & T"). The DataGrid control displays only books published by M & T.

Control Properties. To see how the connections between the ADO controls and the other data-bound controls work, we need to take a careful look at their property values. First, there are two ADO controls, **adoTitles** and **adoPublishers**, each connected to a different table:

adoTitles:

ConnectionString	Provider=Microsoft.Jet.OLEDB.3.51;Persist Security Info=False;Data Source=C:\Program Files\Microsoft Visual Studio\VB98\Biblio.mdb
CommandType	2-adCmdTable
RecordSource	Titles

adoPublishers:

ConnectionString	Provider=Microsoft.Jet.OLEDB.3.51;Persist Security Info=False;Data Source=C:\Program Files\Microsoft Visual Studio\VB98\Biblio.mdb
CommandType	2-adCmdTable
RecordSource	Publishers

(Depending on where your copy of Visual Basic was installed, you might have to change the database path stored in the ConnectionString properties of the two ADO controls.)

Figure 11. Using Publishers to Display Titles.

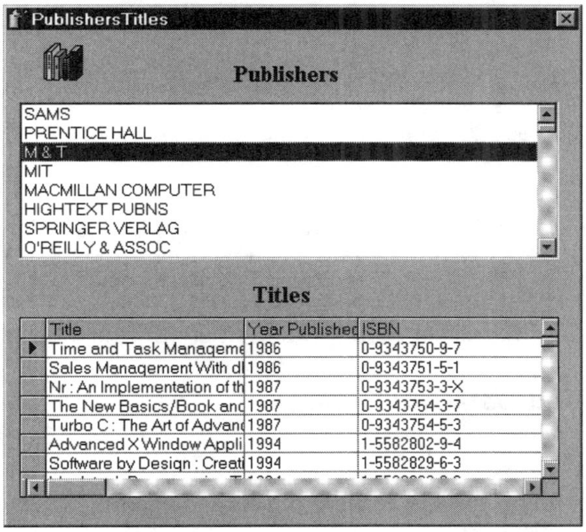

The DataGrid properties in this program are quite simple. The DataSource property identifies the ADO control that will fill the grid:

Name	dgdTitles
DataSource	adoTitles

In the DataList control, the **RowSource** property should be set first, because it connects the DataList to its corresponding ADO control. Next, the **ListField** property identifies the field that will appear in the list at runtime. Finally, the **BoundColumn** property identifies the field that connects the Publishers table to the Titles table:

Name	dblPublishrs
RowSource	adoPublishers
ListField	Name
BoundColumn	PubID

Program Code. We still must write program code to handle the **Click** event for the DataList control. When the user clicks on a publisher name, we fill the grid with books

> ***Tip*: Filter and Sort Properties**
>
> The DataCombo and DataList controls are both unaffected by the ADO Recordset Filter and Sort properties. To demonstrate this, place either a DataList or DataCombo control in the SalesStaff4 program shown earlier in this chapter. Set its RowSource property to adoSalesStaff and set its ListField property to Salary. When you run the program, note that all salaries appear, not just the salaries affected by the Filter property in adoSalesStaff. Calling the ADO control's Refresh or Requery method has no effect. The DataGrid control, on the other hand, shows the results of the Filter and Sort properties.

produced by the selected publisher. The following code handles the dblPublishers_Click event:

```
Private Sub dblPublishers_Click()
   lblPublisherTitle.Caption = dblPublishers.Text
   adoTitles.Recordset.Filter = "PubID =" _
     & dblPublishers.BoundText
End Sub
```

In this procedure, we copied the publisher name (Text property) to a label above the DataGrid. We set the Filter property of the ADO Recordset to the publisher ID number, saved in the BoundText property of the DataList control. The BoundText property is not visible in the Properties window, but is set by the DataList control itself at runtime.

4.3.3 Example: DataCombo and DataGrid Controls

(samples: DataCombo)

Let's write a new program in which the DataGrid control displays the Titles table and the DataCombo displays the Name field from the Publishers table. At run time, when the user selects a title from from the DataGrid, the ADO control moves the Recordset cursor to the selected record in the Titles table (see Figure 12). Using the publisher ID from this record, the DataCombo control displays the name of the publisher corresponding to the publisher ID. If the user selects a different publisher name from the Publishers DataCombo, the corresponding publisher ID in the Titles table is permanently updated. Figure 13 shows the same controls at design time.

Control Properties. This program uses the same two ADO controls as our previous example program:

adoTitles:

ConnectionString	Provider=Microsoft.Jet.OLEDB.3.51;Persist Security Info=False;Data Source=C:\Program Files\Microsoft Visual Studio\VB98\Biblio.mdb
CommandType	2-adCmdTable
RecordSource	Titles

Figure 12. Using Titles to Display Publishers.

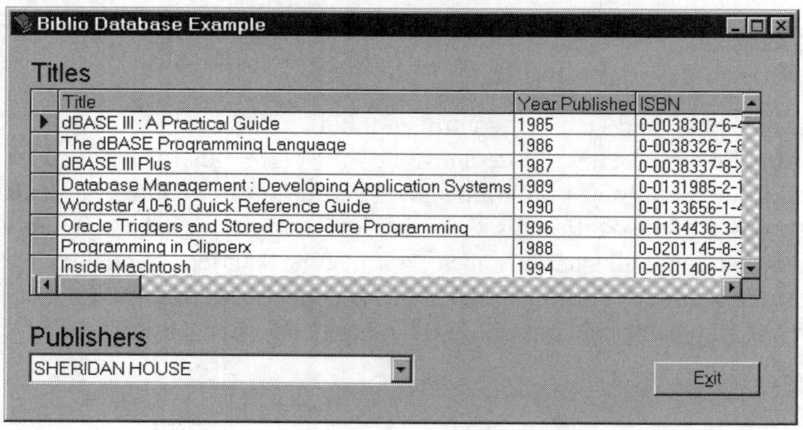

Figure 13. DataGrid and DataCombo (design mode).

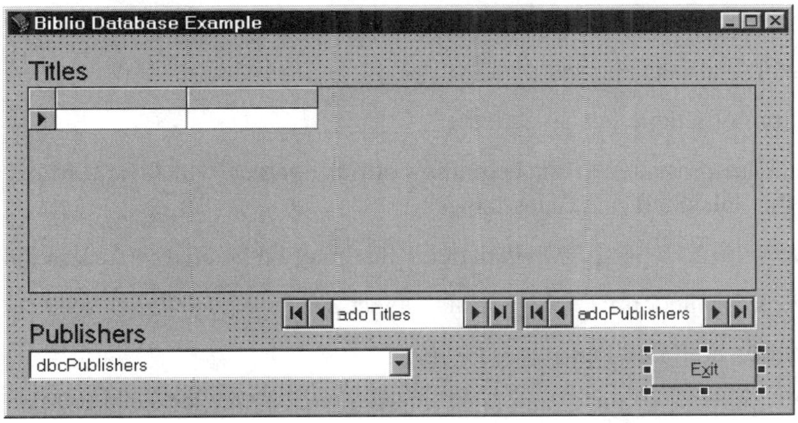

adoPublishers:

ConnectionString	Provider=Microsoft.Jet.OLEDB.3.51;Persist Security Info=False;Data Source=C:\Program Files\Microsoft Visual Studio\VB98\Biblio.mdb
CommandType	2-adCmdTable
RecordSource	Publishers

DataGrid Properties. In the DataGrid control, the DataSource property links the grid to an ADO control's Recordset:

Name	dgdTitles
DataSource	adoTitles

DataCombo Properties. The **RowSource** property of the DataCombo control binds it to the adoPublishers ADO control. The **ListField** property identifies the Name field of the Publishers table as the field that we wish to display:

Name	dbcPublishers
RowSource	adoPublishers
ListField	Name

The **DataField** and **DataSource** properties identify a Recordset and field attached to another data control, adoTitles. When the user selects a new publisher name from the DataCombo, the publisher ID is automatically updated in the Titles table:

DataField	PubID
DataSource	adoTitles

The **BoundColumn** property sets the name of the source field in the Publishers table that supplies a data value to the corresponding record in the Titles table:

BoundColumn	PubID

4.4 REVIEW QUESTIONS

1. Define the term *database*.
2. Each row of a table is also called a ____________.
3. Each column of a table is also called a ____________.
4. In the database presented at the beginning of this chapter, which field forms a relation between the SalesStaff and Sales tables?
5. Name five specific types of *Number* fields that may be created in Access databases.
6. ADO stands for the term: ______ Data Objects.
7. ADO replaces both DAO and ____.
8. What is the purpose of the CommandType property of an ADO control?
9. In Microsoft Access databases, how is the Text field type different from the Memo field type?
10. What type of field is used when you want new values for this field to be automatically generated when records are added to a table?
11. What is the main restriction on the RecordCount property when used with Access databases?
12. Which database field type is best for storing graphic images?
13. Which two properties of an ADO data control must be set before it is connected to a database?
14. How many database tables can be attached to the same ADO control at the same time?
15. What is the recommended name prefix for an ADO control?
16. Describe the Recordsource property of the ADO control.
17. Describe the ConnectionString property of the ADO control.
18. Which standard Visual Basic controls can be bound to an ADO control?
19. Name at least one type of standard control that cannot be bound to an ADO control.
20. Which two properties must be set in a TextBox before it can be automatically updated by an ADO control?
21. Can a CheckBox be bound to an ADO control? If so, what type of database field does it usually represent?
22. When using an ADO control with bound TextBoxes, how are changes saved when the user enters new values?
23. Which Recordset method must be called before the user can begin entering data into a new database record?
24. Which Recordset method saves the contents of the current record?
25. What are the variations on the Move method for Recordsets?

26. Write an SQL filter that dislays only records for full-time employees.
27. When BOF is True, does the cursor point to the first record in a Recordset?
28. Does the MoveLast method move to the same position as EOF?
29. Write a statement that moves the Recordset pointer five rows forward from the current position.
30. If MoveNext is called and the Recordset is empty, how can you prevent a runtime error?
31. What are the two properties of a DataList control that must be set before the list can be filled with the data from an ADO control?
32. Which command halts a Recordset Add or Edit operation in progress?
33. In the DataList control example, how could we display the publisher names in alphabetical order?
34. Which property of a DataList control must be set before the user can enter a multi-character string from the keyboard that repositions the list pointer?
35. Which ADO control method should be called immediately after modifying the RecordSource property?
36. Which properties of a DataCombo control must be set to fill the list with values from a Recordset?
37. Which properties must be set before a DataCombo control can update the fields in a Recordset?
38. What property must be set in a DataGrid control before the names of the Recordset fields can be displayed as column headers?
39. Which property of a DataGrid allows the user to edit individual cells?
40. Which property of a DataGrid allows the user to append new rows to the Recordset?

4.5 CHAPTER EXERCISES

4.5.1 Mozart Music – 1

Titles Table. Revise the Mozart Music 2 program from Chapter 2 in the following ways: Create an Access database called mozart.mdb and create a table called **Titles**. It should have the following fields: SkuNumber (Text, 5), and AlbumTitle (Text, 50). Add an ADO control to the form and attach it to the Titles table. Display the SKU numbers in a DataCombo control.

When the user selects a SKU number, the title of the album should appear in a label, just as it did in the original version of the program. *Hint:* Use the ADO data control's Find method to retrieve the record containing the album title.

4.5.2 Mozart Music – 2

SalesStaff Table. Add a SalesStaff table to the database from the previous exercise, containing the first and last names of salespeople. Allow the user to select a salesperson's name from a DataCombo control, or enter a new salesperson's name into the combo if the correct one cannot be found in the list. Save the salesperson's name along with the rest of the invoice information.

4.5.3 Mozart Music – 3

Invoices Table. Add a table called **Invoices** to the database from the previous exercise, containing the following fields:

```
InvoiceId, Salesperson, Title, Amount, SalesTax, TotalAmount
```

When the user saves the current invoice, write the information to your new database table rather than a text file. You will also need to get the most recent invoice number from the Invoices table. (Be sure to call the ADO control's Refresh method in the Form_Load procedure.)

4.5.4 Mozart Music – 4

Prices Table. The Mozart Music program currently stores the prices of albums within the program code. This method is quite inflexible, in that we would have to modify the program whenever the store decided to change its prices. For this new current version of the program, you need to add a table called **Prices** to the database, containing the following fields and values (PriceCode and MediaType are integers, and Price is type Currency):

PriceCode	MediaType	Price
0	0	21.99
0	1	10.99
1	0	15.99
1	1	8.99
2	0	6.99
2	1	5.99

Modify the program accordingly. In the **CalcPrice** procedure, you will have to search the Prices table, using values for the Pricecode and MediaType. *Hint:* The Find method does not permit compound expressions, but you can use the Filter property instead.

4.5.5 Mozart Music – 5

Sales Wizard. Write a Wizard program that guides the user through the steps of preparing the Mozart Music Sales invoice. Here are some suggested steps:

1. Let the user select an existing salesperson name or enter a new person's name.
2. The user starts to input the first item by selecting a SKU number from a ComboBox.
3. The user selects the price code and format. Explain the meanings of price codes A, B, and C to the user on this panel. The user clicks the Add button to continue.
4. Ask the user if there are any more items. If the answer is yes, return to Step 2; otherwise, proceed to step 5.
5. Display the cumulative invoice amount, tax, and total amount. Ask the user to either save the invoice or cancel.

6. Ask the user if they want to create another invoice. If the answer is yes, return to step 1; if the answer is no, end the program.

Each step should be a separate panel (form), similar to the one shown in Figure 14.

4.5.6 Mail-Order Computer Sales

Write a program that lets the user interactively configure a computer system by selecting a base computer model and adding on various options. On the diskette accompanying this book, there is a database file named **computer.mdb** containing the following tables: Models, CDROM, Displays, Drives, and VideoCards. Sample database data are shown in Figure 15. If your instructor permits, you can update this information to reflect current prices and configurations, which seem to change almost weekly.

As each option is added, show both the individual option price and the total system price (see Figure 16). Each option is represented by a DataCombo control that is linked to an ADO control for the appropriate database table. As the user selects an option, the price shows alongside the DataCombo. *Hint:* Use the MoveFirst and Find methods to accomplish this. The program should also recalculate the total configured price whenever the user selects a new option.

4.5.7 Kyoshi Karate School - 1

Write a simple membership tracking system for a martial arts school called Kyoshi Karate School. Kyoshi *Sensei* (*teacher*) has determined that he wants the program to manage a list of students containing their personal data and dues payments. There will be four windows: Main, Membership, Edit/Add Members, and Dues Collection. Create an Access database named karate.mdb with two tables: Members and Payments.

Payments Table. Each member ID matches a member ID in the Members table. From the sample records, note that the member ID values are not unique in the payments table:

Figure 14. Sample Wizard Panel.

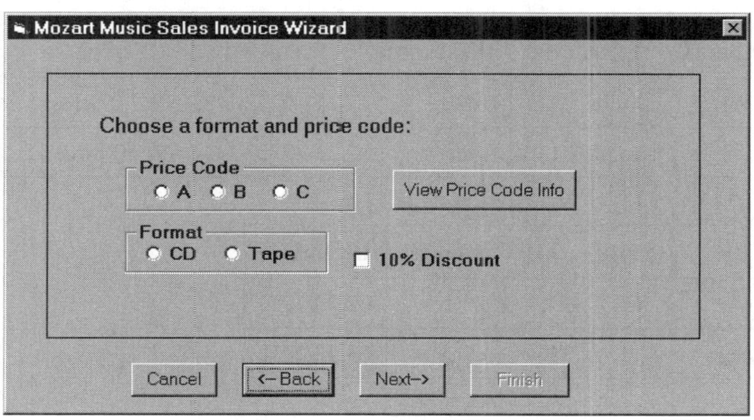

Figure 15. The Models, CDROM, Displays, Drives, and VideoCards Tables.

Models : Table

ModelID	Processor	Price	RAM
MP-133	Pentium 133	$800.00	32
MP-200	Pentium Pro 200	$900.00	32
MP-350	Pentium II 350	$1,200.00	64
MP-400	Pentium II 400	$1,400.00	64
MP-450	Pentium II 450	$1,600.00	128
MP-500	Pentium II 500	$2,000.00	128

Displays : Table

DisplayId	Description	Price
1	15-Inch SVGA Display	200
2	15-Inch XVGA Display	250
3	17-Inch, 1024 X 768 Display	400
4	17-Inch, 1280 X 1024 Display	450
5	19-Inch, 1600 X 1200 Display	600
6	21-Inch, 1600 X 1200 Display	800

Drives : Table

DriveID	Description	Price
1	5.6 GB EIDE	150
3	8.6 GB ATAPI	175
4	6.4 GB SCSI-3	300
5	10.2 GB EIDE	275
6	15.1 GB EIDE	325

CDROM : Table

CDROMId	Description	Price
1	24x CD-ROM	50
2	4x RW CD Recorder	200
3	6x RW CD Recorder	400
4	DVD CD-ROM	150

VideoCards : Table

CardId	Description	Price
1	2D Basic, 4 MB RAM	50
2	2D Ultra, 8 MB RAM	100
3	3D GameMaster, 8 MB	140
4	3D Ultra GameMaster, 16 MB	200

MemberID	PaymentDate	Amount
001	10/01/1997	50.00
004	10/02/1997	75.00
003	10/15/1997	50.00
002	10/15/1997	150.00
004	10/31/1997	75.00

Members Table. Each member ID is a unique long integer, and serves as the record key field. All fields are Text fields, except the birth date, which is of type Date. For all non-required fields, be sure to set the "Allow zero length" option to *Yes*. Otherwise, Visual Basic will report an error when appending a record with blank fields to the file. Add at least five records to the Members table. Here are two sample records:

MemberID	Lastname	Firstname	Phone	Street
001	Smith	LaMar	111-2222	33 NW 10 Street
002	Gonzalez	Aldo	222-3333	44 SW 50 Street

City	State	ZIP	Gender	Birthdate
Miami	FL	33333	M	02/20/1972
Hialeah	FL	34444	M	03/10/1978

Figure 16. Configuring a Computer Purchase.

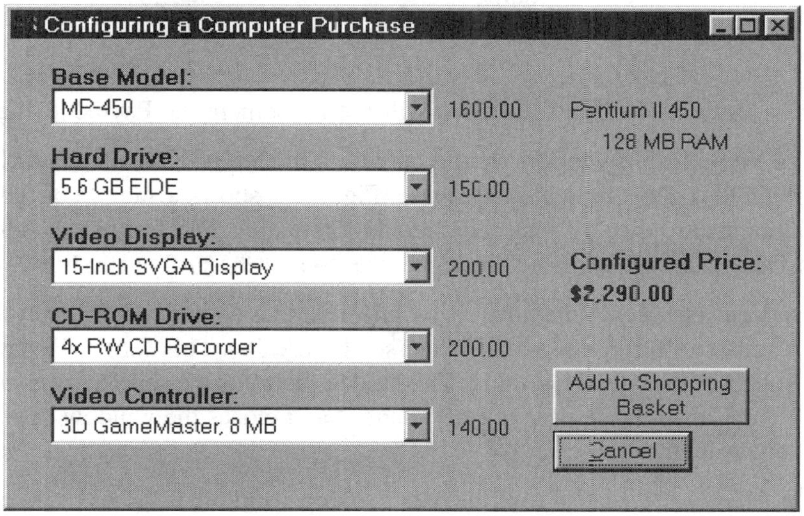

Main Window. The program starts with a main window that has a menu. Display the school name, program name and version, revision date, and so on. Figure 17 shows one possible design. The menu commands are as follows:

```
&File
  E&xit
&Window
  &Membership
```

Membership Window. The menu in the Membership window contains commands to edit and add members, delete a member, display/edit the member's dues payments, and close the window:

```
&Member
  &New
  &Edit
```

Figure 17. Kyoshi Karate Program, Main Window.

```
&Delete
&Payments
(separator)
&Close
```

In this first version of the program, we will not implement the Payments menu choice.

The Membership window should contain a hidden ADO control attached to the Members table in the karate.mdb database. Figure 18 shows a sample of the window. Use a DataGrid control to display each member ID, first name, and last name. Assign specific fields to DataGrid columns, and allow the user to edit the grid at run time.

Adding a New Member. When the user wants to add a new member (from the menu), display a separate form with blank fields (see Figure 19). This form will have its own ADO control linked to the Members table. The Update button saves all changes and closes the window. The Cancel button cancels all changes and closes the window (use the CancelUpdate method).

Editing a Member Record. From the Membership window, if the user selects Edit from the Member menu, display a form containing the current Member record. This can be the same form used when adding a new member. Use the Find method to position the ADO control on the correct record when this window opens. Notice that OptionButtons are used for the member's gender. (Earlier in this chapter, we showed how to update OptionButtons from a Recordset.) When you return to the Membership window, be sure to refresh the ADO control, because some of the member fields may have been modified. You can also use the BookMark property to restore the current position of the record pointer in the DataGrid control.

4.5.8 Kyoshi Karate School - 2

Implement the Payments portion of the Karate School program. When the user selects Payments from the Member menu in the Membership Window, display the Payments window. This window, shown in Figure 20, displays the member name and a list of all previous payments in a DataGrid control. The ADO recordset's Filter property provides the easiest way to select only payments by a particular member, using the MemberId field.

Figure 18. Karate School Membership Window.

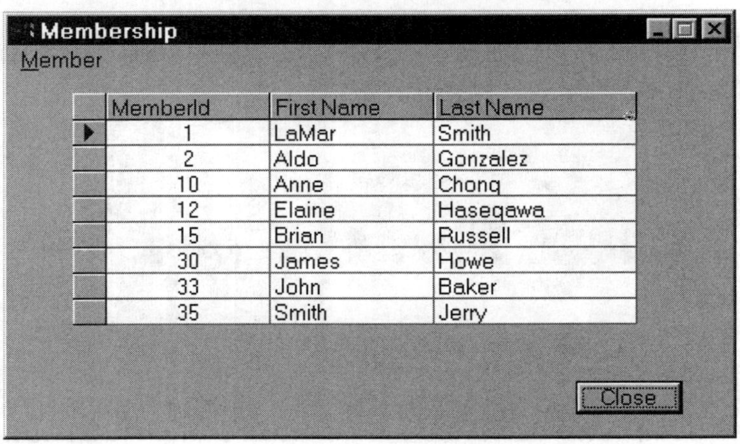

Figure 19. Adding a New Member.

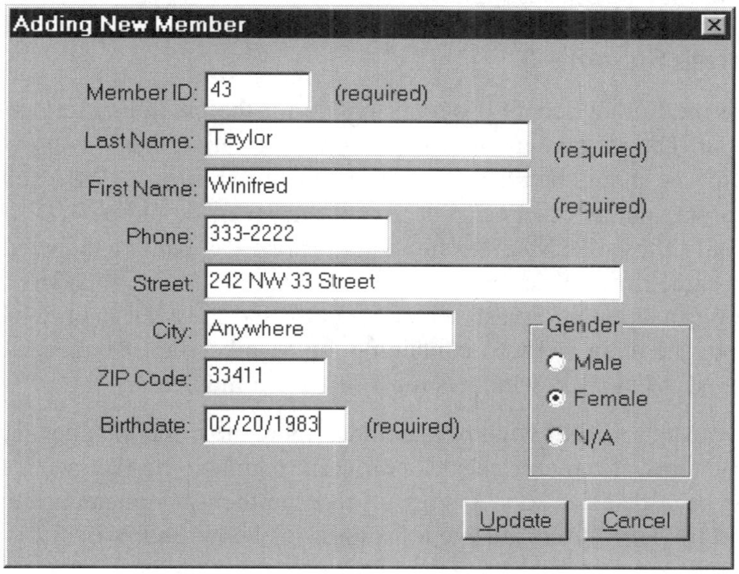

Figure 20. Payments Window.

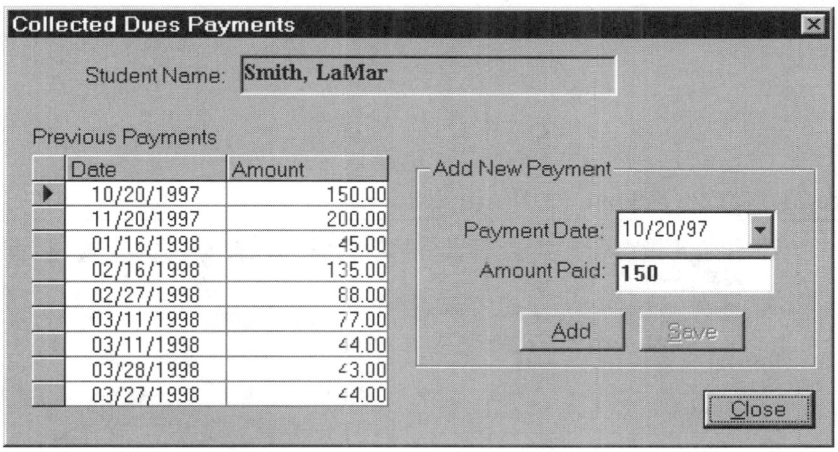

When setting up the DataGrid control's appearance, assign specific Recordset fields to individual DataGrid columns and set the Alignment and Format properties for individual columns. The user must be able to add a new payment to the DataGrid by filling in the date and amount paid and clicking on the **Save** button.

The PaymentDate field should be a **DateTimePicker** control, whose **Value** property yields the date selected by the user. Bind it to the ADO control through the DataSource and DataField properties. If the payment amount is blank, display an error message and let the user try again. Optionally, you can allow the user to modify individual payments and dates directly in the DataGrid. (The DateTimePicker, incidentally, is in the *Microsoft Windows Common Controls-2* group of components.) When the user clicks on the **Add** button, call the Recordset's **AddNew** method. When the user clicks on the **Save** button, call the **Update** method and close the Payments window.

4.5.9 Kyoshi Karate School – 3

MDI. Enhance the Karate School program written for the previous exercise by making it an MDI application. The program name and related information that was previously displayed in the main window should be placed on a separate splash screen. The Main window will be the MDI parent, and all others except the splash screen should be MDI child windows. The user can only show one Membership window, one Payments window, and one Edit window at the same time. Have the program start with the Main procedure inside a code module, so you can show the splash screen modally and the MDI main window modelessly. Figure 21 shows the main window, containing the Membership, Payments, and Member Edit windows. All MDI child windows must be shown modelessly.

The Payments and Edit windows should display the same member record as the Membership window. If the user selects a different member, the Payments and Edit windows must be udpated as soon as they receive the focus. (You can accomplish this by writing code in the Form_Activate event handlers of these windows.)

You might want to revise the menu structure so the user can select Members from the File menu to open up the membership window:

```
File
   Members
   Exit
```

Figure 21. Karate School, MDI Application.

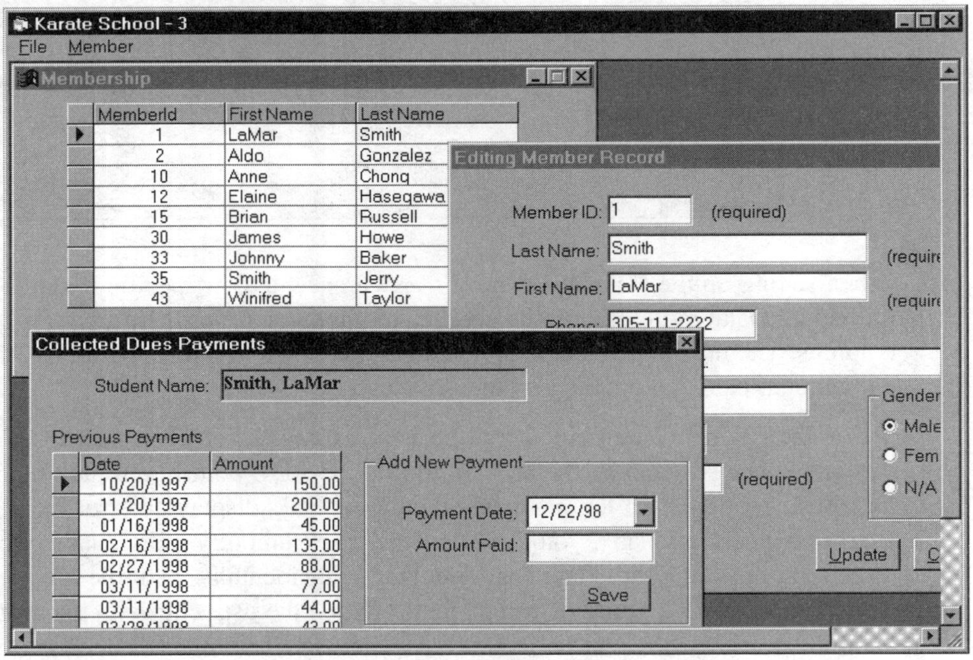

Create a separate Member menu (either on the MDI parent form or on the child form) that is disabled or invisible until the user opens the Membership window:

```
Member
  New
  Edit
  Delete
  Payments
  Close
```

4.5.10 Kyoshi Karate School – 4

Class Schedule. Enhance the Kyoshi Karate School program written for the previous exercise. This version of the program should allow the user to view and edit a class schedule. Add a table called **Schedule** to the existing database containing the following fields:

Name	**Type**	**Description**
ClassId	Long	Identifies the class (unique)
DayNum	Integer	0 = Saturday, 1 = Sunday, etc.
StartTime	Date/Time	Class starting time
StopTime	Date/Time	Class ending time
InstructorId	Long	Identifies the instructor

All fields are required, and the **classId** field must be unique. Fill the table with at least ten records, taking care not to create any classes that would overlap on the same day (see Figure 22). Create another database table named **Instructors** with the following fields:

Name	**Type**	**Description**
InstructorId	Long	Identifies the instructor (unique)
LastName	Text	30 character last name

For each InstructorId found in the Schedule table, provide a corresponding entry in the Instructors table. Use the following data, or substitute other names if you prefer:

```
101     Kyoshi Sensei
115     Jackson
104     Gonzalez
```

Figure 22. Karate Schedule Database Table.

classId	dayNum	startTime	stopTime	instructorId
1	0	4:00:00 PM	4:59:00 PM	104
2	2	5:00:00 PM	6:29:00 PM	151
3	2	6:30:00 PM	7:59:00 PM	126
4	3	9:30:00 AM	11:15:00 AM	151
5	5	9:30:00 AM	11:29:00 AM	104
6	4	4:30:00 PM	4:59:00 PM	151
7	4	5:00:00 PM	6:29:00 PM	104
8	4	6:30:00 PM	7:59:00 PM	126
9	5	5:00:00 PM	6:59:00 PM	101
10	6	5:00:00 PM	7:29:00 PM	142
0	0			0

```
126     Kowalski
142     La Ferriere
151     Davies
```

Schedule Window. Display the class schedule in an MDI child window, using a DataGrid. Sort by DayNum and StartTime (see Figure 23). Allow the user to modify individual entries in the DataGrid.

The DataCombo control shown at the bottom of the Schedule window should display the name of the instructor for the class currently selected in the DataGrid. If the user selects a new instructor name, the instructor ID should update immediately. This can be tricky, so here's the suggested code that handles the Click event in the DataCombo:

```
Private Sub dbcInstructor_Click(Area As Integer)
  If Area = dbcAreaList Then
    adoSchedule.Recordset.Sort = "DayNum, StartTime"
    adoSchedule.Recordset.Requery
  End If
End Sub
```

Figure 23. Kyoshi Karate Class Schedule.

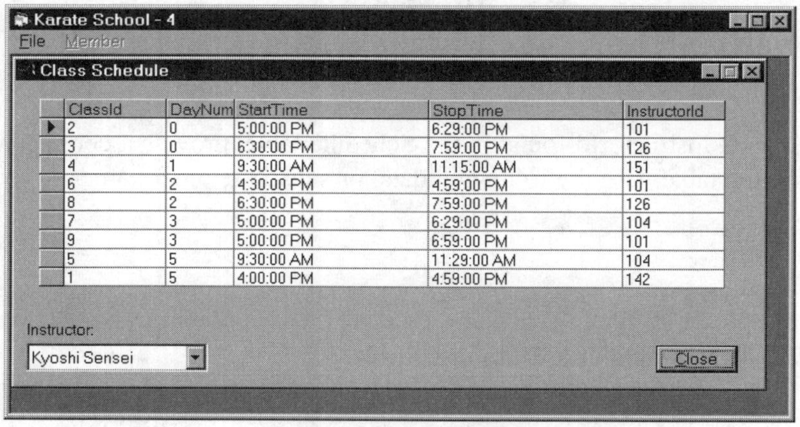

5 ActiveX Data Objects (ADO)

Chapter Contents

Using the Data Environment Designer
- Hands-on Example

Using ActiveX Data Objects
- Connections
- Recordsets
- Adding New Records
- Modifying Existing Records
- Deleting Records
- Troubleshooting ActiveX Error Messages
- SalesStaff Program Example
- Loading SalesStaff into a ListView
- Loading a ComboBox from a Recordset
- Loading a TreeView from a Database
- Creating Command Objects
- Using Query Parameters

Transaction Processing
- Example: Raising Employee Salaries

Multi-user Database Processing (optional)
Review Questions
Chapter Exercises

5.1 USING THE DATA ENVIRONMENT DESIGNER

A *Data Environment* is a description of a Connection between a program and a data source, such as a database file or remote database server. The *Data Environment Designer* is a powerful tool introduced in Visual Basic 6.0 that lets you interactively create Connection and Command objects, and attach Commands to Connections. It also includes the SQL Builder, which simplifies the creating of SQL queries. Here are some basic definitions:

- A DataEnvironment object contains one or more *Connection* objects, each of which describes the location and type of a data source, optional logon information such as a user name and password, and permissions information such as *read-only* or *read-write*.
- A Connection object contains one or more Command objects. A *Command* object contains specific information about which data is retrieved from its associated Connection. The Command can specify a table or SQL query.

- A *cursor* is a procedure that acts like a pointer to a row in a Recordset. There are two types of cursors: *client-side* and *server-side,* depending on where the cursor is being manipulated.

Some Command objects return recordsets, and are therefore called *Recordset returning*. You can write statements that manipulate these returned recordsets at runtime. Other Command objects are *non-Recordset returning*, because they execute action queries or stored procedures. Command objects can also have hierarchical relationships, groupings, and aggregates.

Important: Before you can use the Data Environment designer, you must make it known to Visual Basic. Select **Components** from the **Project** menu, select the **Designers** tab, and place a check next to **Data Environment.**

5.1.1 Hands-On Example

(samples: Medical)

In this section, we will lead you through a simple example that creates a Data Environment, a Connection, and several Commands. You can follow along at the keyboard if you wish, but it should also be possible just to look at the screen snapshots and read the explanations to understand what is being done.

1. To create a data environment project, select **New Project** from the **File** menu, and select **Data Project**. You can also add a data environment to an existing project by selecting **Add Data Environment** from the **Project** menu.
2. A folder called **Designers** appears in the Project window, and inside the folder, a module called **DataEnvironment1** appears. Double click on the latter, displaying a designer window.
3. In the designer window, select **DataEnvironment1**, press F4 to display the Properties window and change its Name property to **deMedical.**
4. Select **Connection1**, press F4, and change its name to **cnAppointments.** This is how the designer window should look:

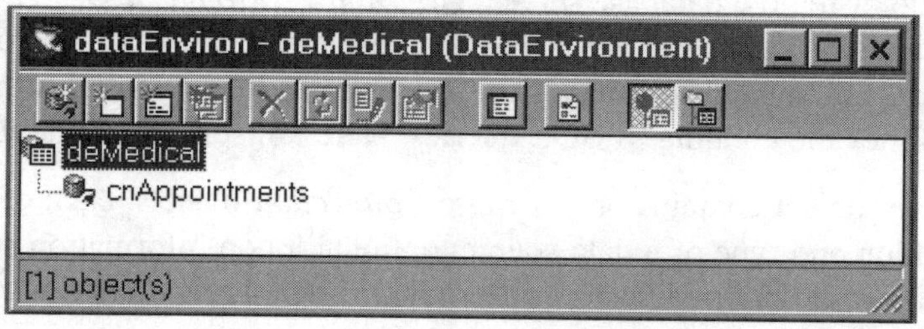

Next, we're going to set properties in the cnAppointments Connection:

5. Right click on **cnAppointments** and select **Properties**. For the Connection type, select "Microsoft JET 3.51 OLE DB Provider" and click on the **Next** button. Click on the

"..." button to browse the disk directory and select **medical.mdb** (provided on the student disk).

6. Click on the **Test Connection** button. A message "Test Connection Succeeded" should appear. (If it doesn't, check to make sure that no other program is currently using the database, and that the database file's property settings do not have "Read-only" checked.)
7. Click the OK button to close the Properties dialog.

Creating a Command Object. Next, we're going to create a Command object and attach it to the cnAppointments Connection. The Command will contain a statement written in SQL that selects all fields and records from the Appointments table.

1. Right click on **cnAppointments** and select **Add Command.** Right click on **Command1** and rename it to **cmShowAll.**
2. Right click on cmShowAll and select Properties to display its Properties page.
3. Click on the **SQL Statement** OptionButton control. In the TextBox control below the OptionButton control, type an SQL statement that displays all fields and records in the Appointments table:

```
SELECT * FROM Appointments
```

4. Click the **Apply** button to check the statement's syntax, fix any errors that appear, and click OK to close the Properties page.

Binding a Command Object to a Form. Next, we will bind the cmShowAll Command to fields on a Form.

1. Open the frmMain window and drag the **cmShowAll** Command name from the Data Environment window to the frmMain window. When you release the mouse button, a number of labels and fields should appear, shown in Figure 1.

Figure 1. Dragging a Command onto a Form.

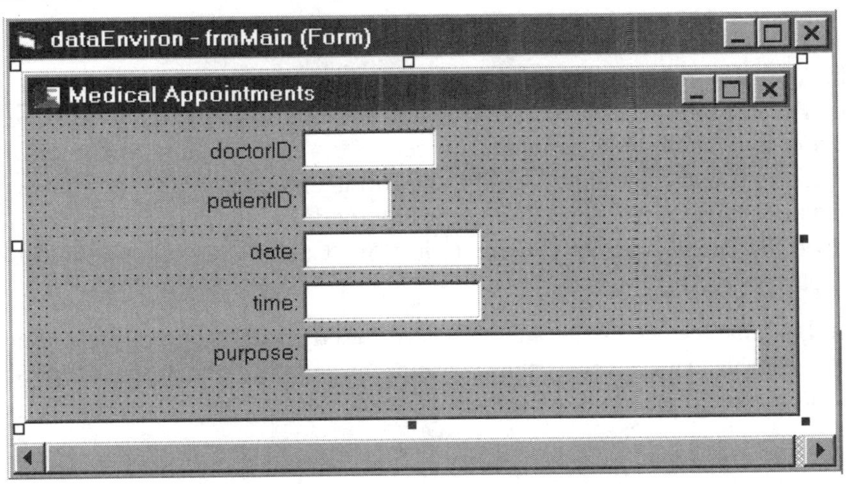

2. From the Project / Properties menu, verify that the project's start up Form is frmMain. Save and run the program. The Form should contain the first record from the Appointments table.

Accessing a Command Object in Program Code. It is fairly easy to create a Recordset from a Command object. For example, declare the following variable in a Form:

```
Private mrsAppointments As Recordset
```

Place a single statement inside Form_Load that assigns the cmShowAll Command object to the Recordset variable.

```
Private Sub Form_Load()
   Set mrsAppointments = deMedical.Recordsets("cmShowAll")
End Sub
```

This example shows that the **Recordsets** Collection is a property belonging to the deMedical DataEnvironment object, and **cmShowAll** is the key of the Command object we wish to use.

Conclusion. This example program duplicates the types of Recordset operations we used in Chapter 4 with data-bound controls. There is an important advantage to using data connections, in that they work for large sets of users and more powerful data sources. All that would have to be changed in the current program is to modify the Provider and Connection properties of the cnAppointments Connection, if a more powerful data provider were used, such as Microsoft SQL Server.

Scalability is the concept used when evaluating how easy it is to increase a program's capacity, size, and scope. You might write a program for only one or two users, only to find that word of your application has spread to everyone in your company. You may be in the position of having to reengineer the program so it can work for hundreds of people. If your program's data source must change from a simple Access database to the more powerful SQL server, for example, extensive modifications should not have to be made to the program's source code.

5.2 USING ACTIVEX DATA OBJECTS

In the previous chapter, we used ADO controls to manipulate databases. As you may have noticed, ADO controls operate on the principle that "one size fits all," meaning that we give up some flexibility in return for convenience. For example, an ADO control establishes a Connection to a database as soon as its parent Form is loaded into memory. The Connection is usually not closed until the Form is unloaded. Some programs require many ADO data controls on the same Form, causing the Form to be a resource hog. ActiveX data objects, on the other hand, let you create just one Connection that manipulates multiple Recordsets.

In this chapter, we create ADO objects directly with program code, without the need for ADO controls. This gives us the flexibility to create Connections, open tables, close tables, and close Connections whenever we want. Each ADO Recordset can be left open only as long as it is required. This helps to save on memory and resources, especially if accessing data from a server.

Before you can use ActiveX data objects in a program, you must add a reference to the project settings. Select **References** from the **Project** menu, and place a check next to *Microsoft ActiveX Data Objects 2.0 Library.*

A Note on DB Providers. We only tested the code in this book with the **Microsoft Jet OLE DB 3.5.1** provider, because that's the software that most Visual Basic students are likely to have. Of course, the Microsoft SQL server is more powerful and robust for multi-user applications than the Jet OLE provider, but it's also more complicated to learn. It's important to remember that every OLE DB provider is slightly different in terms of features and performance.

At the time of this writing, early 1999, the ADO library is new and there are still a number of bugs and workarounds documented on the Microsoft MSDN Web site. An important part of being a professional software developer is to keep up with all of the latest features and bug workarounds in the software you are using. It's not easy, but that's why good programmers get paid good money.

5.2.1 Connections

An *ADODB Connection object* represents a unique session with a data source (from now on, we will simply refer to this as a *Connection*). In the case of a client/server database system, it may be equivalent to an actual network connection to the server. Using the collections, methods, and properties of a Connection, you can configure a Connection, specify an OLE DB provider, open and close the Connection, execute commands, and manage multiple transactions.

Opening a Connection. The first thing a program using ADO Recordsets has to do is create and open a Connection. It must assign a string to its ConnectionString property that identifies the type of data provider and the data source, and call the Open method. This is done in the following example for the **staff.mdb** database that we introduced in the previous chapter:

```
Private cnSalesStaff As ADODB.Connection

Private Sub Form_Load()
  Set cnSalesStaff = New ADODB.Connection
  cnSalesStaff.ConnectionString = "Provider = " _
    & "Microsoft.Jet.OLEDB.3.51; " _
    & "Data Source =" & App.Path & "\staff.mdb"
  cnSalesStaff.CursorLocation = adUseClient
  cnSalesStaff.Open
End Sub
```

You can copy this Connection string value from the Data Environment Designer, or from the ConnectionString property of an ADO data control. You can also cut and paste it from other programs into the current one.

The **CursorLocation** property of a Connection is important if you plan to assign a value to the **Sort** property of one of its recordsets. Include a statement such as the following in your code just before opening the Connection:

```
cnSalesStaff.CursorLocation = adUseClient
```

The default value of CursorLocation is **adUseServer**, which does not allow assignments to the Sort property of any Recordset using the Connection. The only time you have to use adUseServer is when performing batch transactions, explained later in this chapter.

Connection.Execute Method. After an ADODB Connection has been opened, you can quickly create and open a Recordset based on data from the data source by calling the **Execute** method. It has the following syntax when returning rows from a data source:

```
Connection.Execute CommandText, RecordsAffected, Options
```

CommandText can be either the name of a database table or an SQL query. *RecordsAffected* is an output parameter whose value is optionally set by the database provider. *Options* is a long integer that indicates how the CommandText property of the Command object should be interpreted. The values that we are likely to use for *Options* are shown in Table 1. The default is adCmdUnknown.

Examples. The following code uses the ADO connection's Execute method to create a Recordset from a database table called **SalesStaff** and assigns it to the variable **rsSalesStaff**:

```
Dim rsSalesStaff As ADODB.Recordset
Set rsSalesStaff = cnSalesStaff.Execute("SalesStaff", , adCmdTable)
```

The following statements create an ADO Recordset from an SQL query:

```
Dim strSQL As String
strSQL = "SELECT * FROM SalesStaff ORDER BY LastName"
Set rsSalesStaff = cddnSalesStaff.Execute(strSQL,,adCmdText)
```

A Recordset returned by the Execute method always uses a read-only, forward-only cursor. This means that you cannot update the Recordset or call the MoveFirst, MoveLast, or MovePrevious methods. A more flexible way to open a Recordset is to call its **Open** method, which we show in the next section.

Table 1. Options Parameter.

Parameter	Description
adCmdUnknown	(default) Unknown contents of CommandText property.
adCmdText	Indicates that the provider should evaluate the CommandText property as a textual definition of a command, such as an SQL statement.
adCmdTable	Indicates that CommandText contains a table name.
adCmdTableDirect	Indicates that the provider should return all rows from the table named in CommandText.

Mode Property. A Connection has a property called **Mode** that can be assigned any of the values in Table 2. This has to do with whether or not your program allows other programs to simultaneously view and/or update records in the same database. We will discuss multi-user access to databases in Section 5.4.

5.2.2 Recordsets

A number of Recordset properties that were not shown in Chapter 4, appear in this chapter in Table 3. Also, Table 4 contains Recordset methods that were not shown in Chapter 4.

Open Method. You can create a Recordset object and call its **Open** method with a set of parameters that permit a variety of Recordset types and modes. The format of the Open method is:

Table 2. Connection.Mode Property.

Value	Description
adModeUnknown	Indicates that the permissions have not yet been set or cannot be determined (default).
adModeRead	Indicates read-only permissions.
adModeWrite	Indicates write-only permissions.
adModeReadWrite	Indicates read/write permissions.
adModeShareDenyRead	Prevents others from opening connection with read permissions.
adModeShareDenyWrite	Prevents others from opening connection with write permissions.
adModeShareExclusive	Prevents others from opening connection.
adModeShareDenyNone	Prevents others from opening connection with any permissions.

Table 3. Additional Recordset Properties.

Property	Description
AbsolutePosition	Sets or gets the ordinal position of the current record in the Recordset, if the ADODB provider supports it.
CursorType	Sets or gets the type of cursor used in the current Recordset. The choices are: adOpenForwardOnly, adOpenKeyset, adOpenDynamic, and adOpenStatic.
EditMode	Returns the editing status of the current record.Values are adEditNone, adEditInProgress, adEditAdd, adEditDelete.
LockEdits	Indicates the type of locks placed on records during editing. Possible values are: adLockReadOnly, adLockPessimistic, adLockOptimistic, adLockBatchOptimistic
Source	Indicates the source for the data in the Recordset. May be a Command object, an SQL statement, a table name, or a stored procedure.

Table 4. Additional Recordset Methods.

Method	Description
Cancel	Cancels execution of an Execute or Open method call.
CancelBatch	Cancels a pending batch update (UpdateBatch method call).
CancelUpdate	Cancels any changes made to the current record or to a new record prior to calling the Update method.
Clone	Creates a duplicate recordset from the current Recordset.
NextRecordset	Clears the current Recordset and returns the next Recordset by advancing through a series of Commands. (This applies to SQL queries that return more than one Recordset.)
Open (Connection)	Opens a Connection to a data source.
Open (Recordset)	Opens a Recordset.
Save	Saves (persists) the Recordset in a file on the local machine. (Useful for client-server applications, to improve overall efficiency.)
Supports	Determines whether a specified Recordset supports a particular type of functionality. Returns True or False.
UpdateBatch	Writes all pending batch updates to disk.

```
Recordset.Open Source, ActiveConnection, CursorType, LockType, Options
```

Source can be the name of a Command object, an SQL statement, or a table name. Here are brief descriptions of the other parameters:

- *ActiveConnection* may be either a Connection object or a Connection string (same as the ADO control's ConnectionString property).
- *CursorType* equals **adOpenForwardOnly** by default, which only allows the user to scroll through records in a forward direction. To move in both directions and update records, set CursorType to **adOpenStatic**.
- *LockType* equals **adLockReadOnly** by default, which creates a read-only Recordset. To allow the user to update records, use either the **adLockPessimistic** or **adLockOptimistic** option. (Later in this chapter, we will discuss record locking in multi-user databases.)
- *Options* can be one of the values shown previously in Table 1.

If the Connection identified by the ActiveConnection property uses a client-side cursor (adUseClient), then Microsoft says to set the CursorType property of the Recordset to adOpenStatic.

Examples. Let's look at a few examples of calls to the Open method to get a feel for what it can do. We will use the staff.mdb database from the previous chapter as a sample. Each example is assumed to be preceded by a block of statements that creates and opens a Connection:

```
Set cnSalesStaff = New ADODB.Connection
cnSalesStaff.ConnectionString = "Provider = " _
    & "Microsoft.Jet.OLEDB.3.51; " _
    & "Data Source =" & App.Path & "\staff.mdb"
cnSalesStaff.CursorLocation = adUseClient
cnSalesStaff.Open
Set rsSalesStaff = New ADODB.Recordset
```

(We assume that cnSalesStaff and rsSalesStaff were declared at the module level.)

Example 1: Open the SalesStaff table as a forward-only, read-only Recordset:

```
rsSalesStaff.Open "SalesStaff", cnSalesStaff
```

Example 2: Open the SalesStaff table as a static cursor and allow updates:

```
rsSalesStaff.Open "SalesStaff", cnSalesStaff, _
    adOpenStatic, adLockPessimistic, adCmdTable
```

Example 3: Use a query to select only people whose salaries are greater than $30,000 and make it a read-only Recordset:

```
rsSalesStaff.Open "Select * From SalesStaff Where " _
   & "Salary > 30000", cnSalesStaff, _
     adOpenStatic, adLockReadOnly, adCmdText
```

Example 4: Use a query to sort the records in descending order by salary and allow updates:

```
rsSalesStaff.Open "Select * From SalesStaff " _
   & "Order by Salary Desc", cnSalesStaff, _
     adOpenStatic, adLockOptimistic, adCmdText
```

From these examples, you can see that several combinations are possible. A good rule of thumb to follow is this: Use a read-only Recordset if the user will not be updating records. This permits more efficient use of memory than an updateable Recordset. Use **adOpenStatic** if no other users will be accessing the database. Use **adOpenForwardOnly** if records will only be displayed in forward sequence.

5.2.3 Adding New Records

In Chapter 4 we introduced the AddNew and Update methods for ADO Recordsets. We called these methods using the Recordset property of ADO controls:

```
adoSalesStaff.Recordset.AddNew
...
adoSalesStaff.Recordset.Update
```

Now that we have begun to use Recordset objects, we can still call these methods. The following lines add a new SalesStaff record, fill in its fields, and save (update) the record:

```
With rsSalesStaff
   .AddNew
   !StaffId = "1234"
   !FirstName = "Sam"
```

```
      !LastName = "Jones"
      !HireDate = #5/10/1996#
      !IsFullTime = True
      !Salary = 48000
      .Update
   End With
```

To cancel an AddNew operation that has already begun, call the **CancelUpdate** method. This usually happens in two cases: A runtime error might have been caught. Or, the AddNew method was called from one procedure, and the Update or CancelUpdate method is called from somewhere else. If you call AddNew and then try to move to different record before calling Update or CancelUpdate first, a runtime error will result.

5.2.4 Modifying Existing Records

If you used DAO Recordset objects in earlier versions of Visual Basic, you probably expect to call the Edit method before modifying individual Recordset fields. This is not the case with ADO. Just position the cursor on the record you wish to edit, modify the fields, and call the Update method. In the following example, we call the Find method to search for the Staff ID from a TextBox. If the record is found, we assign a value to each field and call the Update method:

```
With rsSalesStaff
   .MoveFirst
   .Find "StaffId = '" & txtStaffId.Text & "'"
   If Not .Eof Then
      !FirstName = txtFirstName.Text
      !LastName = txtLastname.Text
      !HireDate = txtHireDate.Text
      !IsFullTime = (chkFullTime.Value = vbChecked)
      !Salary = txtSalary.Text
      .Update
   Else
      MsgBox "Cannot locate Staff ID " & txtStaffId.Text
   End If
End With
```

EditMode Property. As soon as your program assigns a value to a field in the current Recordset, ADO knows that an edit operation is in progress. You can check the EditMode property (see Table 5) to confirm this, as its value will be equal to the predefined constant **adEditInProgress**. The following example demonstrates this:

```
rsSalesStaff!LastName = "Smith"
If rsSalesStaff.EditMode = adEditInProgress Then
   MsgBox "Edit in progress!"
End If
```

One reason this might be useful information is, if you try to close a Recordset whose EditMode is equal to either **adEditInProgress** or **adEditAdd**, runtime error 3219 occurs, with the message: “The operation requested by the application is not allowed in this context.” In fact, you can only close a Recordset whose EditMode is equal to **adEditNone**. The following user-defined function could be called when closing a Recordset:

Table 5. EditMode Property Values.

Value	Description
adEditNone	No editing operation is in progress.
adEditInProgress	Data in the current record has been modified but not yet saved.
adEditAdd	Indicates that the AddNew method has been invoked, and the current record in the copy buffer is a new record that hasn't been saved in the database.
adEditDelete	Indicates that the current record has been deleted.

```
Public Function CloseRecordset(rsAny As _
       ADODB.Recordset) As Boolean
  If rsAny.EditMode = adEditNone Then
    rsAny.Close
    CloseRecordset = True
  Else
    CloseRecordset = False
  End If
End Function
```

If the CloseRecordset function returns False, the caller knows the Recordset was not closed and can display an appropriate error message. Here, for example, we try to close the Recordset and its Connection during the Form_Unload event:

```
Private Sub Form_Unload(Cancel As Integer)
  If CloseRecordset(mrsSalesStaff) Then
    cnSalesStaff.Close
  Else
    MsgBox "You must cancel the current Add or Edit " _
     & "operation first.", vbInformation, ""
    Cancel = True
  End If
End Sub
```

Be sure the Recordset cursor points to a valid record before your program references the EditMode property. Otherwise, runtime error 3021 occurs:

```
Run-time error '3021':

Either BOF or EOF is True, or the current record has been deleted;
the operation requested by the application requires a current record.
```

If you're in doubt about the cursor position, just call MoveFirst or MoveLast before accessing EditMode.

5.2.5 Deleting Records

To remove a record from an ADO Recordset, call the Delete method. It is important, however, to reposition the cursor to a valid record. Otherwise, Visual Basic will generate a runtime error if you subsequently try to access the current record. You may recall from Chapter 4 that when working with ADO controls, you must call the ADO's Refresh method after deleting a record. When working with Recordset objects, on the other hand, you might want to call Requery, MoveFirst, or MoveLast after deleting a record. Here, for example, we do that with the rsSalesStaff Recordset:

```
rsSalesStaff.Delete
rsSalesStaff.Requery
'(refresh screen controls...)
```

It's important to realize that when you're not using bound controls, you must execute program statements that refresh any controls on the screen that display Recordset fields.

5.2.6 Troubleshooting ActiveX Error Messages

The runtime error messages generated by Visual Basic relating to ActiveX data objects can be tricky to interpret, particularly because they do not explain exactly what went wrong. To help you interpret these messages, we have listed here a number of common runtime errors that occur when writing database programs and their solutions.

Recordset Object Not Created. If you try to open a Recordset before creating a new instance of a Recordset object, you get the following message: *Run-time error '91': Object variable or With block variable not set.* Solution: execute a statement such as the following before the Open statement:

```
Set rsSalesStaff = New ADODB.Recordset
```

Recordset Already Open. If you try to open a Recordset object that has already been opened, you get the following message: *Run-time error '3705': The operation requested by the application is not allowed if the object is open.* Solution: close the Recordset first.

Attempt to Update a Read-Only Recordset. If you call the Update method on a Recordset that was opened with the **adLockReadOnly** option, you get the following message: *Run-time error '3251': The option requested by the application is not supported by the provider.* Solution: change the LockType parameter of the Open statement to **adLockPessimistic** or **adLockOptimistic**.

Attempt to Modify the Sort Property. If you modify the Sort property of a Recordset, you might get the following message: *Run-time error '3251': The option requested by the application is not supported by the provider.* Solution: set the CursorLocation property of the related Connection to **adUseClient**.

Closing a Recordset. If you attempt to close a Recordset whose EditMode is equal to either **adEditInProgress** or **adEditAdd,** you get the following message: *Run-time error '3219': The operation requested by the application is not allowed in this context.* Solution: call the Update or CancelUpdate method to return the EditMode to **adEditNone**.

5.2.7 SalesStaff Program Example

(samples: SalesStaff)

Let's create a variant of the SalesStaff program from Chapter 4, in which we remove the ADO control and use only ActiveX data objects. Users can add new records, delete records, and update existing records. The user interface is shown in Figure 2.

Figure 2. SalesStaff Interface.

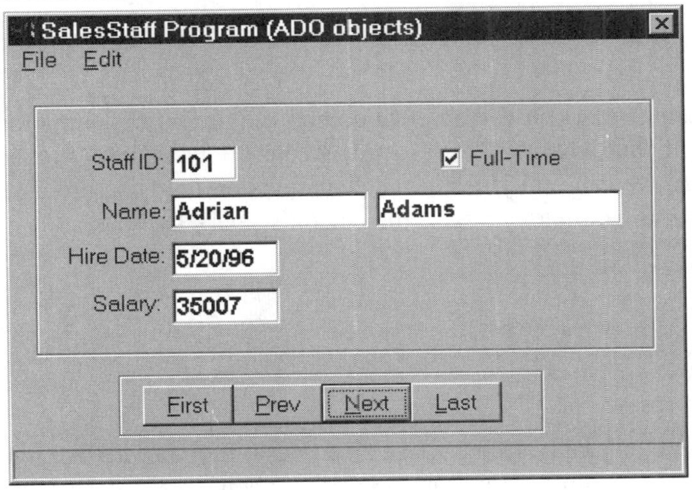

Program Code. The following module level variables are used:

```
Private cnSalesStaff As ADODB.Connection
Private rsSalesStaff As ADODB.Recordset
```

In the **Form_Load** procedure we create and open the database Connection, open the Recordset object, and call LoadControlValues:

```
Private Sub Form_Load()
   Set cnSalesStaff = New ADODB.Connection
   cnSalesStaff.ConnectionString = "Provider = " _
     & "Microsoft.Jet.OLEDB.3.51; " _
     & "Data Source =" & App.Path & "\staff.mdb"
   cnSalesStaff.CursorLocation = adUseClient
   cnSalesStaff.Open
   Set rsSalesStaff = New ADODB.Recordset
   rsSalesStaff.Open "SalesStaff", cnSalesStaff, _
     adOpenStatic, adLockPessimistic, adCmdTable
   LoadControlValues    'fill the text boxes from the Recordset
End Sub
```

The **LoadControlValues** procedure copies Recordset fields into Text controls and a CheckBox. When we used an ADO control, this was not necessary because the controls were bound to the ADO control:

```
Public Sub LoadControlValues()
   With rsSalesStaff
     txtStaffId.Text = "" & !StaffId
     txtFirstName.Text = "" & !FirstName
     txtLastName.Text = "" & !LastName
     txtSalary.Text = "" & !Salary
     txtHireDate.Text = "" & !HireDate
     If !IsFullTime Then
       chkFullTime.Value = vbChecked
     Else
```

```
      chkFullTime.Value = vbUnchecked
    End If
  End With
End Sub
```

If your immediate reaction is that ADO objects require more coding than ADO controls, you're right. But what we give up in convenience, we gain in flexibility. With objects, for example, we can easily perform calculations on fields before assigning them to Text controls. Here, for example, we raise the person's salary by 10%:

```
With rsSalesStaff
  '...
  txtSalary.Text = "" & (!Salary * 1.10)
  '...
End With
```

Notice that we append an empty string to each Recordset field before assigning it to a Text control. This prevents a runtime error from occurring when a Recordset field is null. A field is null when a value has never been assigned to it.

To update the current record, we call SaveControlValues, followed by the Recordset's Update method:

```
SaveControlValues
rsSalesStaff.Update
```

The **SaveControlValues** procedure copies the value from each on-screen control into its appropriate Recordset field. The **IsDate** function is great for validating dates:

```
Public Sub SaveControlValues()
  With rsSalesStaff
    !StaffId = txtStaffId.Text
    !FirstName = txtFirstName.Text
    !LastName = txtLastName.Text
    !Salary = Val(txtSalary.Text)
    If IsDate(txtHireDate.Text) Then
      !HireDate = txtHireDate.Text
    Else
      MsgBox "Invalid date", , "Error"
    End If
    !IsFullTime = (chkFullTime.Value = vbChecked)
  End With
End Sub
```

Adding a new record to the Recordset is as simple as calling the AddNew method and clearing the onscreen controls:

```
rsSalesStaff.AddNew
ClearFields
```

Here is the **ClearFields** procedure:

```
Public Sub ClearFields()
  txtStaffId.Text = ""
  txtFirstName.Text = ""
```

```
    txtLastName.Text = ""
    txtSalary.Text = ""
    txtHireDate.Text = ""
    chkFullTime.Value = vbUnchecked
End Sub
```

Removing a record requires calling the Recordset's **Delete** method. We then have to call **Requery** and fill the current screen controls with a new record. Otherwise, the removed record will still be displayed:

```
Private Sub mnuEditRemove_Click()
    On Error GoTo RemoveErr
    rsSalesStaff.Delete
    rsSalesStaff.Requery
    LoadControlValues
    Exit Sub
RemoveErr:
    MsgBox Error$, vbCritical, "Error"
End Sub
```

Moving the Recordset pointer is the same as with the ADO control, except that we must call the LoadControlValues procedure to update the form's controls. Here is a sample from the button handler that moves to the last record:

```
Private Sub cmdLast_Click()
    rsSalesStaff.MoveLast
    LoadControlValues
End Sub
```

5.2.8 Loading SalesStaff into a ListView

(samples: ListView)

You may have noticed that the TreeView and ListView controls were never mentioned in Chapter 4 when the ADO control was introduced. This was not a coincidence, because neither of these controls can be data bound. There will be times, however, when you want to fill these controls with information from databases. Clearly, this is a situation where direct programming of Recordset objects is needed. Let's demonstrate this by writing a short program that fills a ListView control from the SalesStaff database.

The user interface, shown in Figure 3, contains a ListView with four columns: StaffId, Name, HireDate, and Salary. The Name column is a concatenation of the FirstName and LastName fields from the SalesStaff table. The HireDate and Salary columns have both been formatted using programming statements.

Program Code. Let's take a look at the program code that loads the ListView control. First, the Form_Load procedure creates the Connection and Recordset, exactly the same as in the previous SalesStaff program. The only difference is the last line, where we call the LoadList procedure:

```
Private Sub Form_Load()
    '...(same as previous program)...
    LoadList   'fill the ListView control
End Sub
```

Figure 3. SalesStaff Program with ListView Control.

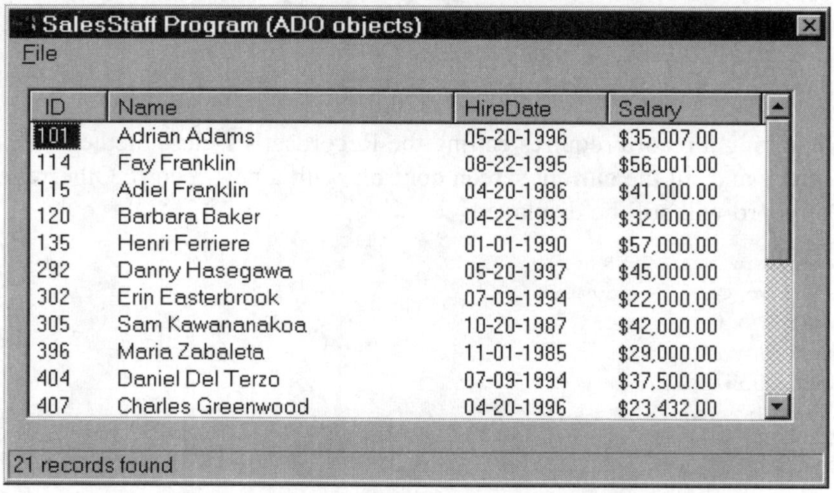

The **LoadList** procedure is the most interesting part of the program, with two steps: first, it builds the four column headers:

```
Public Sub LoadList()
'Build the column headers.
  With lvwStaff
    .ColumnHeaders.Clear
    .ListItems.Clear
    .ColumnHeaders.Add , , "ID", (.Width * 0.15)
    .ColumnHeaders.Add , , "Name", (.Width * 0.4)
    .ColumnHeaders.Add , , "HireDate", (.Width * 0.2)
    .ColumnHeaders.Add , , "Salary", (.Width * 0.2)
    .View = lvwReport
  End With
```

Clearing the ColumHeaders and ListItems collections may not seem necessary right now. But when we re-sort the list, we have to clear the ListView before filling it with the sorted Recordset.

Let's look at the remainder of the LoadList method. It loops through the SalesStaff Recordset and appends each record to the ListView control:

```
'Fill the ListView from the SalesStaff table.
  With rsSalesStaff
    .MoveFirst
    Do Until .EOF
      AddListItem !StaffId, !FirstName & " " & _
        !LastName, Format(!HireDate, "mm-dd-yyyy"), _
         Format(!Salary, "Currency")
      .MoveNext
    Loop
     staMain.SimpleText = rsSalesStaff.RecordCount & _
       " records found"
  End With
End Sub     '(end of LoadList)
```

Sorting Records. By default, the ListView sorts rows on the values in the first column. When the user clicks on another column, the list is resorted, using the values in the new column as a string. The following statement in our program does this by assigning the current column header's index to the SortKey property of the ListView:

```
Private Sub lvwStaff_ColumnClick(ByVal ColumnHeader As _
    MSComctlLib.ColumnHeader)
   lvwStaff.SortKey = ColumnHeader.Index - 1
End Sub
```

But this may not have the intended effect. For example, in Figure 4, the user clicked on the HireDate column, but the dates are clearly not in chronological order. A better approach is to use the Sort property of the rsSalesStaff Recordset to sort the data, and then reload the ListView with the new data. Using this method, the program correctly sorts by HireDate, as you can see in Figure 5. First, we make sure the Sorted property of the ListView is set to

Figure 4. ListView, Incorrectly Sorted by HireDate.

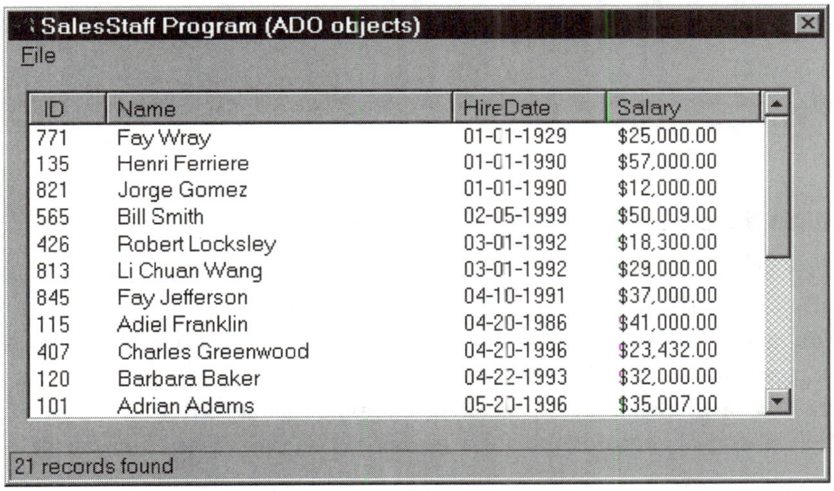

Figure 5. ListView, Correctly Sorted by HireDate.

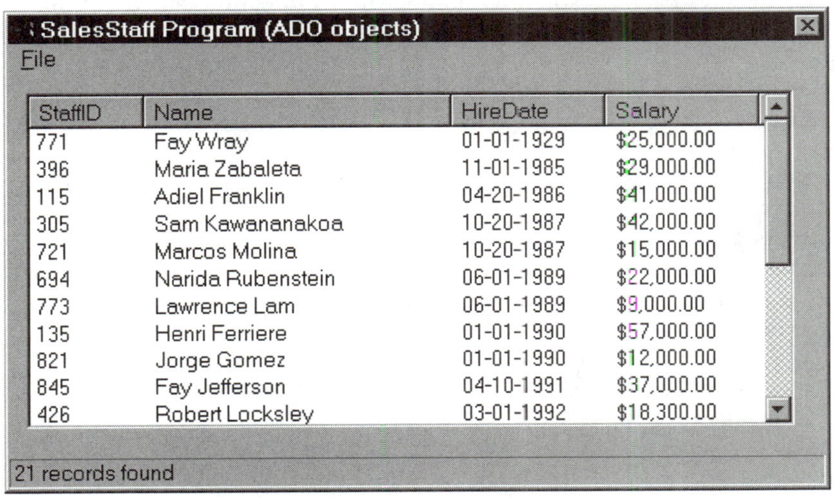

False, so it will not continue to sort the list according to the first column (StaffId). In Form_Load, we have to set the Connection's CursorLocation property to adUseClient; this will allow us to assign values to the Recordset's Sort property later on:

```
cnSalesStaff.CursorLocation = adUseClient
cnSalesStaff.Open
```

In the **ColumnClick** event handler for the ListView, we use a Select Case statement to assign various values to the rsSalesStaff.Sort property. Then the LoadList procedure refills the ListView:

```
Private Sub lvwStaff_ColumnClick(ByVal ColumnHeader As _
    MSComctlLib.ColumnHeader)
   Select Case ColumnHeader.Index
     Case 1
        rsSalesStaff.Sort = "StaffId"
     Case 2
        rsSalesStaff.Sort = "LastName,FirstName"
     Case 3
        rsSalesStaff.Sort = "HireDate"
     Case 4
        rsSalesStaff.Sort = "Salary"
  End Select
  LoadList
End Sub
```

5.2.9 Loading a ComboBox from a Recordset

When you work with ADO objects without using the ADO control, you often have to fill a ComboBox or ListBox using program code. This is fairly easy, using a loop and the MoveFirst and MoveNext statements. One advantage you gain over the DataCombo and DataList controls is flexibility: you can concatenate multiple fields before inserting them in a ComboBox or ListBox, and you can save supplementary information in a Collection variable. You can also calculate values and display them in the ComboBox.

SalesStaff ComboBox. In the following example, we have a ComboBox named cboSalesStaff, into which we want to load the first and last names of each person. At the same time, we save each person's ID number in a Collection called collStaffIDs, using the current list entry as the Collection key:

```
Private collStaffIDs As New Collection

Private Sub FillStaffCombo()
  Dim strTemp As String
  With rsSalesStaff
     .MoveFirst
     Do Until .EOF
        cboSalesStaff.AddItem !LastName & ", " & !FirstName
        strTemp = !StaffId
        collStaffIDs.Add strTemp, _
            cboSalesStaff.List(cboSalesStaff.NewIndex)
        .MoveNext
     Loop
  End With
```

```
End Sub
```

Notice an interesting problem: If we directly pass the StaffId field as an argument to the collection's Add method, a problem occurs later when we try to retrieve the ID from the Collection—it turns up as a null value. The workaround for this is to assign the field to a string variable, and then add the string variable to the Collection, as we have done here.

When the user clicks on the ComboBox control, we can use its Text property to retrieve the person's Id number from the Collection, using the Text as a Collection key:

```
Dim strStaffId As String
strStaffId = collStaffIDs.Item(cboSalesStaff.Text)
```

This will work even if we set the Sorted property of the ComboBox to True, because the order of items in the Collection does not have to match the order in the ComboBox.

5.2.10 Loading a TreeView from a Database

(samples: BiblioTree)

A TreeView control gives you the opportunity to view data from a relational database in a hierarchical format. Let's use two tables from the Biblio database (shipped with Visual Basic) as an example: The **Publishers** table lists the names of book publishers. The **Titles** table is a list of books in which each book has a publisher ID number. An effective use of the TreeView control is to display a list of publishers at the topmost level of the tree. When the user clicks on a publisher name, we can add a list of books produced by the publisher to the current tree node. As the user selects various publishers, the tree is gradually filled in with lists of books. Figure 6 shows the TreeView's list of publishers when the program loads. When the user clicks on the first publisher, AK PETERS, the program takes a moment to load all matching book titles. Figure 7 shows the list of books after the user has expanded the AK PETERS node.

Program Implementation. First, we declare several module-level variables for the Connection, Recordsets, and a tree Node:

```
Private mrsPublishers As ADODB.Recordset
```

Figure 6. Publishers Added to TreeView.

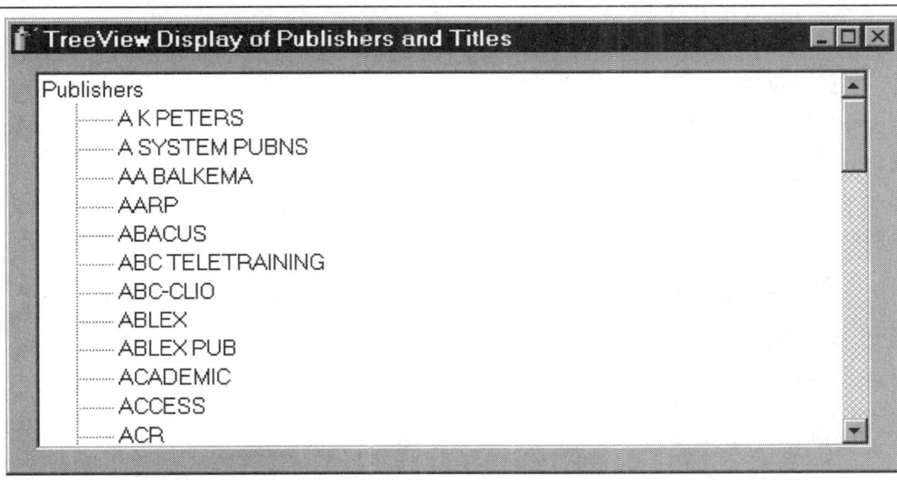

Figure 7. Expanded List of Books by One Publisher.

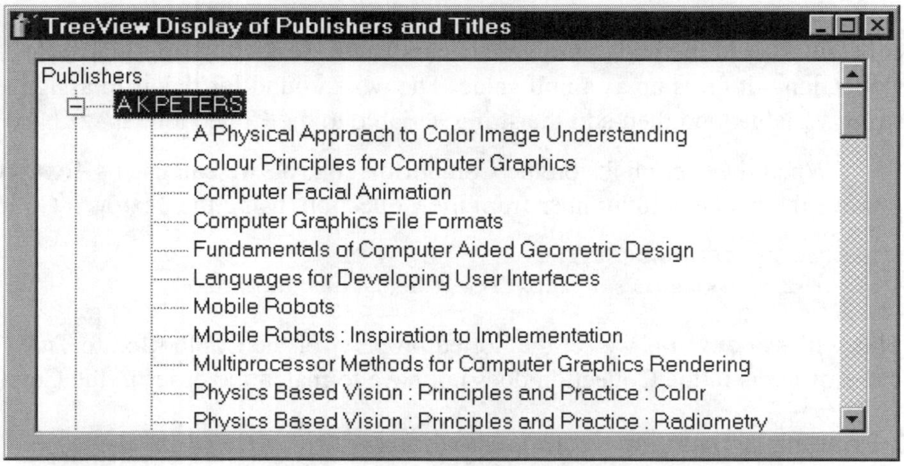


```
Private mrsTitles As ADODB.Recordset
Private cnBiblio As ADODB.Connection
Private mnodCurrent As Node
```

In **Form_Load**, we set up the cnBiblio Connection, open the mrsPublishers Recordset, move to the last record, get the RecordCount property and use it to initialize a ProgressBar control:

```
Private Sub Form_Load()
'Establish the database Connection, Command type,
'and record source.
  Set cnBiblio = New ADODB.Connection
  cnBiblio.ConnectionString = "Provider = " _
    & "Microsoft.Jet.OLEDB.3.51; " _
    & "Data Source =C:\Program Files\Microsoft Visual " _
    & "Studio\VB98\biblio.mdb"
  cnBiblio.CursorLocation = adUseClient
  cnBiblio.Open
  Set mrsPublishers = New ADODB.Recordset
  With mrsPublishers
    .Sort = "Name"
    .Open "Publishers", cnBiblio, adOpenForwardOnly, _
          adLockReadOnly, adCmdTable
    .MoveLast
    prgLoading.Max = .RecordCount
    prgLoading.Value = 0
    .MoveFirst
  End With
End Sub
```

Form_Activate calls DoEvents to refresh the Form's display, and call AddPublishersToTree to begin loading the tree with all publisher names:

```
Private Sub Form_Activate()
  DoEvents              'refresh the screen
  AddPublishersToTree   'load the publisher names
```

```
End Sub
```

The **AddPublishersToTree** procedure creates a root node called "Publishers" and loops through all records in the Publishers table, adding each name to the tree. The ProgressBar is updated as the loop repeats:

```
Private Sub AddPublishersToTree()
  Dim nodTemp As Node, nCount As Integer
  treBiblio.Nodes.Clear
  mrsPublishers.MoveFirst
  Set mnodCurrent = treBiblio.Nodes.Add(, , _
        "root", "Publishers")
  With mrsPublishers
    Do Until .EOF
       Set nodTemp = treBiblio.Nodes.Add(mnodCurrent.Key, _
           tvwChild, "K" & CStr(!pubId), !Name)
      nCount = nCount + 1
      prgLoading.Value = nCount   'update the ProgressBar
      .MoveNext
    Loop
  End With
End Sub
prgLoading.Visible = False    'remove the ProgressBar
lblLoading.Visible = False    'and its Label
nodTemp.EnsureVisible    'expand the tree
mnodCurrent.EnsureVisible    'scroll back to root node
```

At the end of AddPublishersToTree, the ProgressBar is hidden, the tree is expanded to make all nodes visible, and the tree is scrolled back to the top.

The **DblClick** event handler executes when the user double clicks on a Publisher name. The procedure extracts the publisher ID number (an integer) from the key of the selected node, identified by the **SelectedItem** property. The AddTitlesToTree procedure is called from here:

```
Private Sub treBiblio_DblClick()
  Dim pubId As Integer
  Set mnodCurrent = treBiblio.SelectedItem
   'Only expand Publisher nodes.
  If mnodCurrent.Key = "" or mnodCurrent.Key = "root" Then Exit Sub
  pubId = CInt(Mid(mnodCurrent.Key, 2, Len(mnodCurrent.Key) - 1))
  If mnodCurrent.Children = 0 Then       'not expanded yet?
    AddTitlesToTree pubId                'expand it now
  End If
End Sub
```

It is important to check the **Children** property of the selected node, in case the user double clicks on a publisher whose book titles we have already retrieved. Otherwise, we would load a duplicate set of titles.

The **AddTitlesToTree** procedure attaches all titles produced by the publisher to the current tree node. We use the Filter property to select only records having a particular publisher ID. It is necessary to open and close the Recordset here, because this procedure will be called again when the user clicks on a different publisher name:

```
Private Sub AddTitlesToTree(intPublisherId As Integer)
  Screen.MousePointer = vbHourglass
  mrsTitles.Sort = "Title"
  mrsTitles.Filter = "PubId = " & intPublisherId
  mrsTitles.Open "Titles", cnBiblio, _
     adOpenForwardOnly, adLockReadOnly, adCmdTable
  cnBiblio.CursorLocation = adUseClient
  With mrsTitles
    .MoveFirst
    Do Until .EOF
       treBiblio.Nodes.Add mnodCurrent.Key, _
                tvwChild, , !Title
      .MoveNext
    Loop
  End With
  mrsTitles.Close
  Screen.MousePointer = vbDefault
End Sub
```

SQL is Faster! It should be noted that when the previous example was run on a Pentium II/350 computer, it took four seconds to open the mrsTitles Recordset and locate twelve book titles, using the Filter and Sort properties. This shows that the Filter property is unacceptably slow except for small Recordsets. When the following code was substituted, using an SQL statement to create the Recordset, there was no perceptible delay at all:

```
Dim strSql As String
strSql = "Select PubId, Title From Titles Where PubId = " _
    & intPublisherId & " Order By Title"
mrsTitles.Open strSql, cnBiblio, adOpenForwardOnly, _
    adLockReadOnly, adCmdText
```

Clearly SQL queries should be used whenever possible because of their superior performance, and because SQL is the universal language for databases, both big and small.

5.2.11 Creating Command Objects

Microsoft defines an ADO Command object as "a specific Command that you can execute against a data source." You can create one or more ADO Command objects, each of which is associated with a Connection, contains Command text (such as a table name or SQL statement). Command objects are particularly useful if the same Command is to be executed more than once. Among other things, you can do the following with a Command object:

- Define the executable text of the Command (for example, an SQL statement) with the CommandText property.
- Define a parameterized query and store it in the Command.
- Execute the Command and return a Recordset object.
- Execute the Command and perform an update operation on the database, without actually returning a Recordset object.

- Ask the database provider to save a compiled version of the Command, to improve runtime performance.
- Set the Name property of the Command, which makes the Command appear as a method belonging to the associated Connection.
- Pass a Command object to the Source property of a Recordset in order to obtain data.

Executing a Command Object. When calling a Command object's Execute method, the SQL query text is not visible because it is already contained in the CommandText property. The Command.Execute method returns a Recordset reference. The syntax is:

```
Command.Execute RecordsAffected, Parameters, Options
```

RecordsAffected is an optional long integer output parameter returned by the ADODB provider that indicates the number of records affected by the operation. *Parameters* is an optional Variant array of parameter values passed with an SQL statement. The *Options* parameter is an optional long integer indicating how the provider should evaluate the CommandText property of the Command object. *Options* can be any of the values listed earlier for the Connection.Execute method, such as adCmdText, adCmdTable, and adCmdTableDirect.

The following example uses an existing Connection called **cnSalesStaff**. It creates a Command object, sets the CommandText property to an SQL query string, and executes the Command. The Execute method returns a read-only, forward-only Recordset:

```
With cmdSalesStaff
   .ActiveConnection = cnSalesStaff
   .CommandText = "Select * From SalesStaff " _
         & "Where Salary >= 30000"
   .Prepared = True     'compile the query
   Set rsSalesStaff = .Execute(, , adCmdText)
End With
```

5.2.12 Using Query Parameters

(samples: CommandObj)

You can create a query in the CommandText property of a Command that allows different values to be passed to the Command at runtime. In the following example, **pSalary** is the query parameter:

```
Dim cmdSalesStaff As New ADODB.Command
cmdSalesStaff.CommandText = "Select * From SalesStaff " _
   & "Where Salary >= [pSalary]"
```

Before passing values to a query, you must create a Parameter object. Call the **CreateParameter** method, passing it the name of the parameter and the parameter's type:

```
Dim parm As ADODB.Parameter
Set parm = cmdSalesStaff.CreateParameter("pSalary", adSingle)
```

The predefined constant **adSingle** is one of the **ADODB.DataTypeEnum** constants. They are listed in Visual Basic's Object Browser window, including adBoolean, adByte, adChar, adCurrency, adDate, adEmpty, adError, adLong, adSingle, adVarChar, adVariant, and adUnknown.

After creating the Parameter object, append it to the Parameters Collection in the Command object. You can append multiple Parameters to the Collection, as long as each has a different name:

```
cmdSalesStaff.Parameters.Append parm
```

Optionally, you can set the **Prepared** property to True to tell the data provider to compile the query before it is executed the first time. This results in much more efficient execution if a program uses the same query multiple times:

```
cmdSalesStaff.Prepared = True
```

Assign a value to the parameter, possibly from a TextBox control on your program's Form:

```
cmdSalesStaff("pSalary") = Val(txtSelectSalary.Text)
```

Execute the Command and return a Recordset:

```
Set rsSalesStaff = .Execute(, , adCmdText)
```

Sample SalesStaff Program. Let's adapt the SalesStaff program presented earlier in this chapter. We will let the user enter a Salary value, and use a query to display only records having a salary greater than or equal to the selected one. In Figure 8, the user has just typed in a salary of 35008 and clicked on the **Select** button. Only records having Salaries greater than or equal to $35,008 are displayed.

Program Implementation. Three variables are declared at the module level, the Connection, the Recordset, and the Command object:

```
Private cnSalesStaff As ADODB.Connection
Private rsSalesStaff As ADODB.Recordset
Private cmdSalesStaff As ADODB.Command
```

Figure 8. Parameterized Query Example.

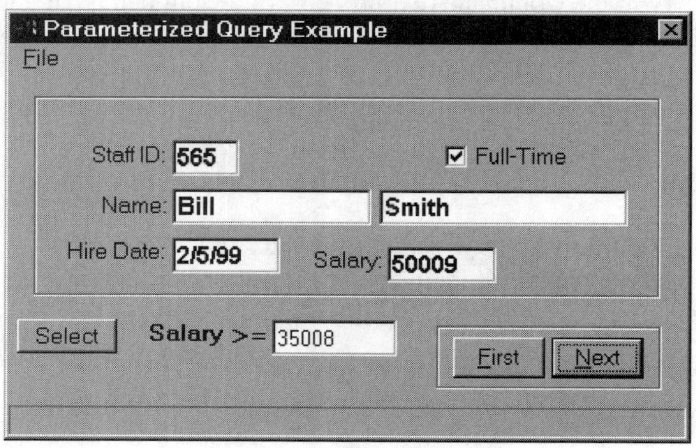

In Form_Load, we create the Connection and Command objects and assign the name **pSalary** to the Parameter object. The Parameter is appended to the Parameters Collection:

```
Private Sub Form_Load()
   Set cnSalesStaff = New ADODB.Connection
   cnSalesStaff.ConnectionString = "Provider = " _
     & "Microsoft.Jet.OLEDB.3.51; " _
     & "Data Source =" & App.Path & "\staff.mdb"
   cnSalesStaff.CursorLocation = adUseClient
   cnSalesStaff.Open
   Set cmdSalesStaff = New ADODB.Command
   Dim parm As ADODB.Parameter

   With cmdSalesStaff
     .Name = "FilterSalaries"          'optional
     .ActiveConnection = cnSalesStaff
     .CommandText = "Select * From SalesStaff " _
                  & "Where Salary >= [minSalary]"
     Set parm = .CreateParameter("minSalary", adSingle)
     .Parameters.Append parm
     .Prepared = True     'optional: precompile the query
   End With
End Sub
```

When the user clicks on a Command button after entering a desired minimum salary, we assign the TextBox value to the parameter, execute the Command that returns a new Recordset, and move to the first record:

```
Private Sub cmdSelect_Click()
  cmdSalesStaff("minSalary") = Val(txtMinSalary.Text)
  Set rsSalesStaff = cmdSalesStaff.Execute(, , adCmdText)
  fraMoveButtons.Enabled = True
  If rsSalesStaff.EOF = False Then
    cmdFirst_Click
    fraMoveButtons.Enabled = True
  Else
    fraMoveButtons.Enabled = False
    ClearFields
  End If
End Sub
```

In one of the chapter exercises, we ask you to create a second Parameter object and call it maxSalary. Then the program can search for salaries within a given range.

5.3 TRANSACTION PROCESSING

A *transaction* is defined as a series of changes made to all databases in a workspace, where the changes are treated as a single unit. Three methods may be used:

- **BeginTrans** begins a new transaction.
- **CommitTrans** ends the current transaction and saves the changes.

- **RollbackTrans** ends the current transaction and restores the database to its state before the transaction began.

Transaction processing is useful when you update two or more interdependent tables. If an error occurs, you need to be able to roll back the changes and restore the database to its original state. For example, theVisual Basic help documentation points out that when transferring financial amounts between accounts, if an error occurs in one table and not the other, the entire transaction can be rolled back. Here is a simulation of such a transaction:

```
Private Sub TransferFunds( rsFrom As ADODB.Recordset,
         rsTo As ADODB.Recordset, amt As Currency )
   On Error GoTo AccountTransferErr
    cnAccountsPayable.BeginTrans
   With rsFrom
      !Balance = !Balance - amt
      .Update
   End With
   With rsTo
      !Balance = !Balance + amt
      .Update
   End With
    cnAccountsPayable.CommitTrans
   Exit Sub
AccountTransferErr:
   MsgBox Error$,vbCritical,"TransferFunds Error"
    cnAccountsPayable.RollbackTrans
End Sub
```

Important: The BeginTrans, CommitTrans, and RollbackTrans methods cannot be called from a client-side Connection, so you must set the CursorLocation property to **adUseServer**.

5.3.1 Example: Raising Employee Salaries

(samples: BatchUpdate)

Using the SalesStaff database, suppose we are considering giving each employee hired before a given cutoff date a 10-percent raise. This would be an ideal use for transaction processing, because we could give the user the option to either save or cancel the changes. Figure 9 shows the program at startup. The user can modify the cutoff date and click on the **Raise Salaries** button to begin the batch transaction.

Form_Load. We will leave out the Form_Load procedure in the current program listing, because it is nearly identical to the ListView example shown earlier in this chapter. There is one exception: the CursorLocation property must be set to **adUseServer**:

```
cnSalesStaff.CursorLocation = adUseServer
```

We also omit all references to the Sort property in this program, because the Sort property requires the use of a client-side Connection.

The cmdRaiseSalaries_Click Procedure. In the event handler for the Command button, the first step is to invoke the BeginTrans method on the Connection. The call to the Requery

Figure 9. ADO Batch Update Example.

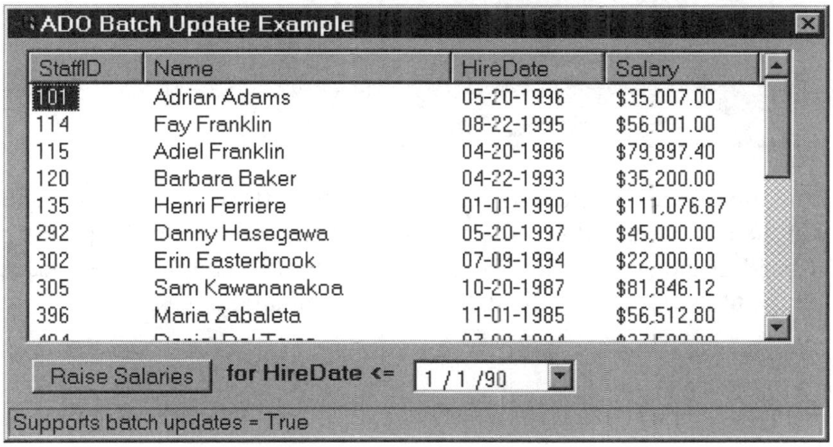

method is necessary after the first time the user clicks on the Raise Salaries button. The Requery method refreshes the data in the internal buffer and prevents a runtime error:

```
On Error GoTo RaiseSalariesErr
rsSalesStaff.Requery           'get original data
cnSalesStaff.BeginTrans
```

Next, using a loop, we compare each hire date to the cutoff date (in a DateTimePicker control), and if it is selected, add 10% to its salary. We also keep a running count and total of the salary raises:

```
With rsSalesStaff
  .MoveFirst
  intCount = 0
  Do Until .EOF
    If !HireDate <= dtpCutoffDate.Value Then
      currAmt = !Salary * 0.1
      !Salary = !Salary + currAmt
      .Update
      intCount = intCount + 1
      currTotal = currTotal - currAmt
    End If
    .MoveNext
  Loop
End With
```

But these changes are not permanent. When the loop ends, a message box displays the number of salaries affected, the total dollar amount of the raises, and asks the user to confirm the changes:

```
intChoice = MsgBox(intCount & " salaries will be increased, " _
  & "for a total cost to the company of " & vbCrLf _
  & Format(currTotal, "currency") _
  & ". Do you want to keep these changes? ", vbYesNo, _
    "Proposed Salary Raise")
```

Here is the message box:

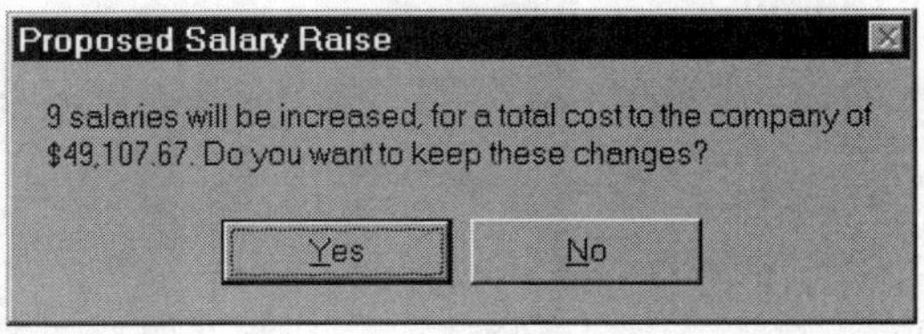

If the user agrees by clicking on the **Yes** button, the CommitTrans method saves the changes in the database, and LoadList reloads the ListView control with the new data. On the other hand, if the user declines by clicking on the **No** button, the RollbackTrans method rolls back the transactions and the database is not modified:

```
If intChoice = vbYes Then
    cnSalesStaff.CommitTrans
   LoadList
Else
    cnSalesStaff.RollbackTrans
End If
Exit Sub
```

If an error should occur during the loop, an error handler informs the user that the transaction will be rolled back:

```
RaiseSalariesErr:
   MsgBox Error$ & ". Batch transaction will be rolled back.", _
             vbInformation, "Error"
    cnSalesStaff.RollbackTrans
```

5.4 MULTI-USER DATABASE PROCESSING (OPTIONAL)

Authors' Note: *In this section we will briefly survey the options provided by the Microsoft Jet ADODB. The section is marked optional because this book is oriented toward desktop applications. The other reason is that the methods that worked consistently under DAO in the previous edition of this book do not seem to work consistently with the Jet ADODB provider. It may just be our inexperience, or it may be that the Jet provider is not set up too well for multi-user applications. In the meantime, we will defer to more powerful products such as Microsoft SQL server and Oracle.*

Each user can easily run a copy of the program because it loads into memory on the user's workstation. The main issue that affects programs with multiple users is their shared access to data. When one user is in the process of modifying a record, the record is automatically locked; this prevents other users from simultaneously updating the same record and overwriting each other's changes. The record might be locked for only a fraction of a second, or it might be locked for several minutes, depending on how the application program is designed.

Record updates in a multi-user environment can follow several different scenarios. In this discussion, we interpret an *update* as an AddNew, Edit, or Delete operation:

1. Two or more users access the same record simultaneously, but only one user modifies the record.

2. Two or more users update different records within the same table.
3. Two or more users try to update the same record simultaneously.

Scenario 1 does not involve record locking, but creates a situation in which the actual record has been modified and the other users are viewing an obsolete copy of the record. Scenario 2 may create a conflict if the database locks a memory block containing the record being updated and surrounding records in the same block. Scenario 3, where multiple users try to simultaneously update the same record, will always cause the record to be locked by the first user who starts to update the record.

Optimistic and Pessimistic Record Locking. There are two general methods of record locking. *Pessimistic locking* prevents other users from updating a record from the time an AddNew or Edit operation executed, until the Update method is executed. *Optimistic locking*, on the other hand, allows other users to update a record even while an AddNew or Edit operation is under way. The only locking that occurs is from the time the Update method begins to execute until the database driver is able to free the locked record.

Recordset.Open Method. Let's return to the Open method used by Recordset objects that we introduced at the beginning of this chapter. As we showed earlier, the syntax of the Open method is:

```
Recordset.Open Source, ActiveConnection, CursorType, _
          LockType, Options
```

The *LockType* parameter allows us to employ optimistic and pessimistic record locking (see Table 6). The *CursorType* parameter controls whether or not updates to records by other users are reflected immediately in the current user's Recordset (see Table 7). The CursorType and LockType properties of Recordsets are read-only when the Recordset is open, and read-write when the Recordset is closed.

Shared Database Processing. Many database applications involve the operation where a user will open a record for viewing and editing, modify the record in some way, and save the modified record. In any application involving a shared database, record updates require some strategic decisions on the part of the designer.

Table 6. LockType Parameter Options.

LockType	Description
adLockReadOnly	(Default) Read-only. You cannot alter the data.
adLockPessimistic	Pessimistic locking, record by record. The provider does what is necessary to ensure successful editing of the records, usually by locking records at the data source immediately upon editing.
adLockOptimistic	Optimistic locking, record by record. The provider briefly locks records only when you call the Update method.
adLockBatchOptimistic	Optimistic batch updates. Required for batch update mode as opposed to immediate update mode.

Table 7. CursorType Options.

CursorType	Description
adOpenStatic	Static cursor. A static copy of the Recordset that is ideal for searching or generating reports. Updates by other users are not visible.
adOpenForwardOnly	Forward-only cursor (default CursorType). This is identical to a static cursor except it only allows the user to scroll in a forward direction.
adOpenDynamic	Dynamic cursor. Additions, changes, and deletions by other users are visible, and all types of movement through the Recordset are allowed.
adOpenKeyset	Keyset cursor. Like a dynamic cursor, but records added by other users are not visible.

Suppose, for instance, two users are viewing/editing hotel reservation records, and both happen to notice that room 2120 is available. User 1 makes a reservation for room number 2120 and confirms. User 2, believing the room to be available, reserves the same room and confirms. User 2 is issued an error message stating that room 2120 is no longer available. In this scenario, the first user to begin viewing and editing the record for room 2120 could be given exclusive use of the record. Otherwise, a customer on the phone with a reservations agent might be told that a particular room is available, only to find out seconds later that the room in question had just been given to another customer.

Example 1: Open the SalesStaff table as a static cursor and prevent other users from simultaneously editing the same records:

```
rsSalesStaff.Open "SalesStaff", cnSalesStaff, _
   adOpenStatic, adLockPessimistic, adCmdTable
```

Example 2: Open the SalesStaff table as a static cursor so the current user cannot see updates made by other users. Set the LockType parameter so other users can simultaneously edit the same records:

```
rsSalesStaff.Open "SalesStaff", cnSalesStaff, _
    adOpenStatic, adLockOptimistic, adCmdTable
```

Example 3: Open the SalesStaff table as a dynamic cursor so the current user can see all updates made by other users. Set the LockType parameter so other users can simultaneously edit the same records:

```
Call rsSalesStaff.Open "SalesStaff", cnSalesStaff, _
    adOpenDynamic, adLockOptimistic, adCmdTable
```

5.5 REVIEW QUESTIONS

1. Which menu command is used to create a Data Environment Designer object?
2. *True or False:* A Data Environment may only contain a single Connection object.

3. *True or False:* A Command object may contain the name of a database file.
4. *True or False:* A Connection object may contain the name of a database file.
5. What are the two types of cursors used by Connection objects?
6. What is the name of the property that controls the type of cursor in a Connection object?
7. When a Command object is executed, does it always return a Recordset?
8. If Visual Basic does not seem to recognize the **ADODB.Recordset** data type, what is the most likely cause of the problem?
9. When you try to select **Add Data Environment** from the **Project** menu but the selection is not available, what should you do?
10. When you drag the name of a Command object from the Data Environment window onto a Form, what do you expect to happen?
11. Show an example of using the Recordsets property of a DataEnvironment object to retrieve a Command object named **cmMyCommand**.
12. Briefly explain why *Scalability* is important in database applications.
13. In the Connection.Execute method, which values may be assigned to the CommandText parameter?
14. Can a Recordset returned by the Connection.Execute method be updated by the program?
15. Give a few examples of values that may be assigned to the Connection.Mode property.
16. In the Recordset.Open method, what types of values are assigned to the *Options* parameter?
17. Describe the Recordset.EditMode property.
18. Show an example of calling the Recordset.Open method and creating a Recordset with a static cursor. Can this Recordset be updated by the program?
19. Which Recordset method is used to cancel a pending batch update operation?
20. Write a few lines of code that add a new record to a Recordset called rsStudents, assign values to the StudentId and LastName fields, and save the new record.
21. How does an ADODB database signal that an *edit* operation is in progress?
22. Why is it necessary to either move the cursor position or call the Requery method after deleting a record?
23. What runtime error message is generated if you try to close a Recordset that has a pending edit operation in progress?
24. In the sample ListView program in this chapter, we assigned a column number to the ListView's SortKey property. What happened?
25. In the TreeView example in this chapter, what did we learn about the Recordset.Filter property, relating to runtime performance?
26. Show an example of creating a Parameter object for a query that will be stored in a Command.

27. Which three methods did we present in the section on transaction processing?
28. Which Recordset method is used to undo the effects of a transaction?
29. What is meant by *pessimistic record locking*?
30. What is meant by *optimistic record locking?*
31. Explain the CommitTrans method.
32. How would a transaction be useful when transferring data from one table to another?
33. In the batch transaction example in Section 5.3.1, what type of batch transaction was carried out on the SalesStaff table?

5.6 CHAPTER EXERCISES

5.6.1 Products Table in a ListView

The Nwind.mdb database located in the Visual Basic install directory contains a number of tables, including the **Products** table. Display the Products table in a ListView control, and allow the user to sort on any column. (In the ListView example shown earlier in this chapters, we showed that the built-in sort function of the ListView does not work with numeric and date fields. Use the same techniques shown in the example to sort the fields correctly.)

5.6.2 Products and Categories in a TreeView

The Nwind.mdb database located in the Visual Basic install directory contains a number of related tables, including the **Products** and **Categories** tables. The ProductID field occurs in both tables and serves as the link between them. Write a program that loads a list of Categories into the top level of a TreeView control. When the user double clicks on a category name, search the Products table for all products matching the same category and attach them to the current tree node.

5.6.3 Query Parameters

In this chapter, we showed how to create a Command object and a Parameter called **minSalary**. We showed how to assign a value to the Parameter at runtime. This was done in one of the SalesStaff program examples. Using this program as a guide, make the following changes: Add a second Parameter object named **maxSalary** to the command's Parameters Collection. Place another TextBox on the Form so the user can input both minimum and maximum salary values. The program should display only salaries falling within the requested range.

5.6.4 Doctors Office Scheduling – 1

(samples: schedule.mdb)

Create a program that schedules medical appointments, called the **Doctors Office Scheduling** program. Here are the general requirements:

- A patient may request an appointment with a specific doctor at a specific date and time.

- When an appointment is scheduled, the program stores the appointment in a database.
- Do not use any ADO controls in this project—do everything with program code that creates and opens ADO recordsets.
- Use an MDI interface with a CoolBar, ToolBar, and StatusBar on the main window. Create four buttons for the New, Save, Exit, and Reports commands. (The Reports button is inactive at present, but will be used in later exercises.)

An appointment consists of a date, time, patient ID, doctor ID, and the purpose of the appointment. Figure 10 shows the MDI parent and MDI child windows as the user is scheduling a new appointment. For now, the user can open only one appointment window at a time.

In the **Schedule New Appointment** window, ComboBox controls are used for the Doctor and Patient selections. Two DateTimePicker controls are used, one for the appointment date, and one for the time. When the user clicks on the **Save** button, the appointment is saved in the database and a message is printed on the status line. *Hint:* When adding the values of the two DateTimePicker controls, use an expression that adds only the Time portion of dtpApptTime, using Visual Basic's **TimeValue** function:

```
dtpApptDate + TimeValue(dtpApptTime)
```

Load the Doctor and Patient combo boxes using program code (these are *not* DataCombo controls). Notice that the Patient ComboBox control includes both the FirstName and LastName fields. Create a Recordset for each and use a loop with MoveFirst and MoveNext to load all of the names. As you load each ComboBox control, you might want to store the ID numbers in a Collection. Do not use the ItemData array of the ComboBox, because it holds long integers, not strings.

Figure 10. Scheduling an Appointment.

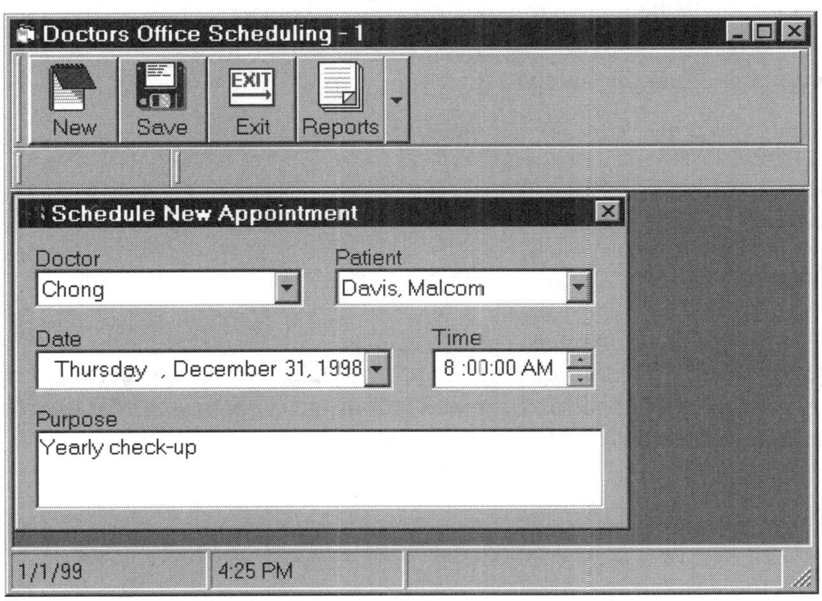

When an appointment is saved, write program statements that look up the Doctor ID and Patient ID, using the names that were selected by the user in the ComboBoxes. The collections containing the doctor and patient ID numbers should help in this regard. When saving the appointment, call the AddNew method and the Update method.

Schedule Database. A Microsoft Access database (schedule.mdb) has been prepared for you containing three tables, Doctors, Patients, and Appointments. Here are their schema:

Doctors:
DoctorId, Text, 4
LastName, Text, 30

Patients:
PatientId, Text, 4
LastName, Text, 30
FirstName, Text, 20
HomePhone, Text, 15

Appointments:
DoctorId, Text, 4
PatientId, Text, 4
ApptDateTime, Date/Time
Purpose, Text, 128

Every Doctor ID in the Appointments table occurs exactly once in the Doctors table. Every Patient ID in the Appointments table occurs exactly once in the Patients table. (This type of Connection is called a *relation*, or *relationship* between the tables.)

5.6.5 Doctors Office Scheduling - 2

Continue the program written for the previous exercise. For this version, the program must allow the user to view all scheduled appointments in various sort orders: (1) by date and time, (2) by doctor ID, and (3) by patient ID. On the main MDI Form set the **Reports** button's style to tbrDropdown, and create a submenu containing one item labeled "All Appointments". Write an event handler that gets the user's click on the button submenu and displays the frmAllAppointments Form. Here, for example, the key value for the drop-down choice is "AllAppointments":

```
Private Sub Toolbar1_ButtonMenuClick(ByVal ButtonMenu _
   As MSComctlLib.ButtonMenu)
   Select Case ButtonMenu.Key
     Case "AllAppointments"
        frmAllAppointments.Show
   End Select
End Sub
```

Create a new Form to display the appointments (frmAllAppointments), using a DataGrid and an ADO control. Provide OptionButton controls so the user can select the sort method. An example is shown in Figure 11.

Figure 11. Listing of All Appointments.

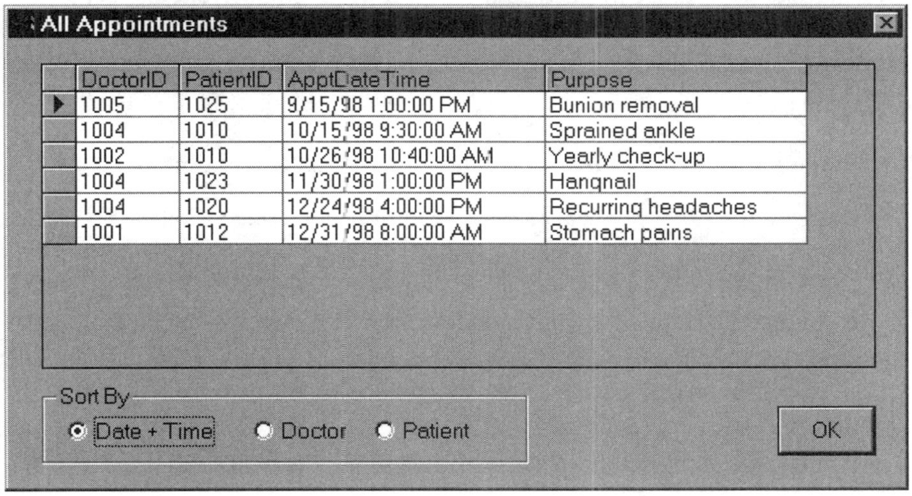

5.6.6 Doctors Office Scheduling - 3

Continue the program written for the previous exercise. Create a new Form that displays all appointments for a selected doctor. Let the user select the doctor's name from a ComboBox control. Use a ListView control to display the appointments.

5.6.7 Doctors Office Appointments - 4

Continue the program written for the previous exercise. In the current program, do not permit two appointments to be scheduled with the same doctor at the same date and time. Display a message box notifying the user of the conflict, and let them try again. To detect a conflict, you will need to search the Appointments table for specific matching values in the DoctorId and ApptDateTime fields.

5.6.8 Concert Hall Ticketing - 1

Specifications. Write a program that could be used in the box office of a concert hall. The easiest way to describe the program's operations is to construct a scenario, or sequence of events:

- When a customer calls in and requests a particular concert, the box office attendant (the user of our program) verifies the concert's date and time.
- The customer asks for the ticket prices in each section of the hall.
- The customer asks for a certain number of tickets, in a particular section of the hall. The attendant verifies that the requested seats are available, and notifies the customer of the total price including tax.
- The customer pays for the tickets and the box office attendant issues the tickets.
- The program updates a database containing counts of the number of available tickets in each section of the concert hall. When tickets are sold, the appropriate count must be reduced.

Assumptions. Tickets purchased for a particular seating section can be used anywhere within that section. Customers cannot return tickets. Only one concert is scheduled per date. There will always be four sections in the concert hall: Orchestra1, Orchestra2, Balcony1, and Balcony2.

Other Specifications. Your program must do the following:

- Provide a way of looking up a concert's title, date, and time.
- Retrieve the price per seat in each section of the concert hall for a particular concert.
- Retrieve the number of available seats in a given section, for a given concert.

Figure 12 shows the main window after the user has selected a concert and section and has entered the customer name and number of tickets. The program automatically recalculates the price, tax, and total when the number of tickets is changed or a different section is chosen.

Figure 12. Selecting a Concert and Section.

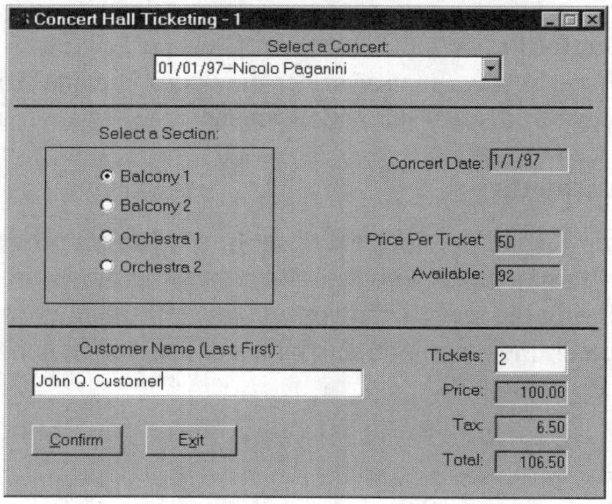

Database Schema. There are three tables in a database file named concert.mdb on the student disk:

Concerts

ConcertDate - date of the concert
Title - description of the concert

Seats

ConcertDate
B1Price - price per seat in the Balcony 1 section
B1Avail - Number of seats that are still available in the section
B2Price - price per seat in the Balcony 2 section
B2Avail - Number of seats that are still available in the section
O1Price - price per seat in the Orchestra 1 section

O1Avail - Number of seats that are still available in the section
O2Price - price per seat in the Orchestra 2 section
O2Avail - Number of seats that are still available in the section

Reservations

ConcertDate - date of the concert
CustomerName (Text, 50)
SectionNumber (Integer, 0 - 3)
NumberOfTickets
AmountPaid (Currency)
TypeOfPayment (cash, check, or credit card), (Text, 5)
CreditCardNumber (Text, 20)
ExpirationDate (Text, 7)

The Reservations table contains a record of all reservations made by all customers. This is a useful reference for both printing tickets and confirming reservations. The SectionNumber field contains a value between 0 and 3, implying 0 = Balcony 1, 1 = Balcony 2, 2 = Orchestra 1, and 3 = Orchestra 2. *Hint:* When using a Find statement to search for a specific concert date, remember to surround the date with date delimiter (#) characters. For example:

```
rsConcerts.Find "ConcertDate = #" & txtDate.Text & "#"
```

5.6.9 Concert Hall Ticketing - 2

Continue the program from the previous exercise. Collect payment information from the customer, which is assembled into an invoice and printed on the screen. The required payment information is:

- Customer name, address, phone, payment method.
- Amount paid.
- Type of payment (cash, check, or credit card).
- For credit card payments, the credit card type, number and expiration date are required.

5.6.10 Concert Hall Ticketing - 3

Use any of the previous Concert Hall Ticketing programs as a starting point for this exercise. Produce a Reservations report on a separate Form that shows the concert date, customer name, number of tickets ordered, and amount paid. Use a ListView control and allow the user to sort on any column. When the user clicks a second time on the same column, sort in descending order.

5.6.11 Concert Hall Ticketing - 4

Use any of the previous Concert Hall Ticketing programs as a starting point for this exercise. Allow the user to select a concert from a ComboBox control. Produce a report in a ListView control that lists, by section, the number of seats sold and the revenue (in dollars) produced by the section. At the end of the report, show the total revenue for the concert.

5.6.12 Biblio TreeView

Modify the **BiblioTree** program from Section 5.2.10: When the user clicks on a book title, let the program display a pop-up window with details about the currently selected book.

5.6.13 Computer Mail-Order Customer Data

The Mail-Order Computer Sales program was introduced in the previous chapter. Make the following improvement: When the configuration is complete, display a separate window and let the salesperson input the customer's name, phone, address, and credit card number. Create a database table called **Customer** that holds all of the customer information. Assign a unique ID number to each customer.

5.6.14 Computer Mail-Order Invoice

The Mail-Order Computer Sales program was introduced in the previous chapter. For the current exercise, make the following improvements to the program

- Add a TextBox control into which the user can enter a customer ID.
- Create a table called **Invoice** with the following fields: CustomerId, InvoiceDate, InvoiceId, ConfiguredPrice, ModelId, and Options. The options field can be type Text, containing a comma-delimited list of option ID numbers.
- When the user confirms the computer configuration by clicking on the OK button, save the current information in a new Invoice record.
- Add a Command button called "Invoices" to a ToolBar in the main window. When the user clicks on the button, a separate window should display all data in the Invoice table. Use a DataGrid control to display the table.

6 Relational Databases and SQL

Chapter Contents

Database Design
    Terminology
    Designing a Database
Using the SQL Language
    Structure of SQL Statements
    A Sample Database
    SELECT Statement
    WHERE Clause
    ORDER BY Clause
    GROUP BY Clause
    HAVING Clause
    TOP Predicate
    Calculated Columns
    Logical Operators
    Selecting from Multiple Tables
    JOIN Clause
    Creating Queries Using SQL Builder
    Creating Queries in Microsoft Access
SQL Data Definition Language (DDL)
    CREATE TABLE
    DROP TABLE/INDEX
    ALTER TABLE
    UPDATE
    DELETE
    INSERT INTO
    CREATE INDEX
DDL Program Example
    Program Code
Designing a Car Rental Database
    Specifications
    Vehicle Inventory
    Models, Categories, and Status
    Rental Prices
    Customers, Reservations, and Invoices
Validation Rules
    Creating Validation Rules
Table Relations
    Creating Table Relations
Designing the Interface
    Running the Program

Review Questions
Chapter Exercises

6.1 DATABASE DESIGN

6.1.1 Terminology

A *relational database management system* (RDMS) is a Collection of data that is organized so that you can look at it in different ways. It contains tables, indexes, queries, filters, views, and validation capabilities. RDMSs are able to maintain links, or relationships, between tables and to ensure that the links are consistent.

As we have already seen, a *table* is a Collection of data that pertains to a single topic, organized into rows and columns. Each row is called a *record,* and each column is called a *field.*

An *index* is a tool that orders a table according to one or more of the table's fields, called *keys*. The index contains all the values of the key field(s). For each key value, the index stores a pointer to the table row in which the key value was found.

A *query* is a command written in the SQL language that either retrieves a set of records according to some criteria, or performs some action on the table. In past chapters, we used queries to build Recordsets. In one case, we assigned a query string to the Recordsource property of an ADO control, and in another, we passed a query as an argument to the Open method of a Recordset object.

A *filter* is a tool that lets you limit the number of records displayed by a query or Recordset. The filter represents a condition that must be true before a record can be displayed. In SQL, a filter is expressed by a WHERE statement, such as: "WHERE Salary > 12000".

A *view* of a database is usually a subset of the entire Collection of data, determined by filters and indexes. A particular view might be limited to only certain fields from a table, or it might combine fields from different tables. We might create a view of an employee table, for instance, that excludes the social security number and salary fields so that unauthorized users cannot see this information.

Database validation can take several forms: Automatic checks can be made for missing field values, values whose type is inconsistent with their declared field types, values that are out of range, and values that do not correlate correctly with other field values. We create *validation rules* to perform some of these checks, and the database system can perform checks between tables to make sure that table relationships are preserved correctly. These *relationships*, called *one-to-one* and *one-to-many*, are described later in this chapter.

6.1.2 Designing a Database

There are two general approaches to designing a database: one is *application-driven*, and the other is *application-independent*. In the first case, a database is designed around a single application program; the input/output needs of the program determine the way tables and relations are set up. In the second case, a database is designed in a more general way, with the intent that multiple application programs will share the data. This type of database is harder to design because one has to anticipate the data needs of programs that have not yet been written.

We will use the application-driven approach to database design in this chapter because it enables us to rapidly build an application program that uses the database. This book focuses on programmming applications and design.

There are a number of steps involved in designing an application-driven database:

1. *Create a model* of the application. Decide which operations will be most critical. Try to determine what data the program will need for input and output. Some data that you thought you needed may later prove to be unnecessary. In a more general design, you might keep the data just in case it might be needed by other programs. But in an application-driven design, you eliminate extra data.
2. *Determine the data sources.* Once you know what the program's inputs and outputs are, you need to know the sources and destinations of specific data. Will some data be from user input, from a shared database, or from other programs? Will the program's output be placed on a Form, transmitted to another program, or sent to a database table for further processing or printing?
3. *Organize the data into tables* so that it can be easily retrieved. Data relating to a single entity should probably be kept in the same table. For example, in a Student Records program, we might have a table called Transcript that contains all courses and grades completed by students. On the other hand, mixing information about this semester's courses with information about room scheduling would not be appropriate. There is a process called *normalization* which is used when building tables in a way that reduces the amount of redundant or hard-to-reach data.
4. *Establish relationships between tables* to allow for automatic checking and updating of records. If a college course registration table contains a studentId number, for example, that Id number can be used to look up information about the student.
5. *Create indexes and establish validation rul*es for the data in your tables. Indexes greatly speed up access to data and provide an easy way to order the data in tables. Validation rules help to ensure that table data is consistent within certain restraints. Bounds checking, set membership, data type checking, and referential integrity checking are some of the more common types of data validation.

6.2 USING THE SQL LANGUAGE

The name SQL stands for *Structured Query Language*, the most widely used language for defining and manipulating relational databases. Nearly all databases produced in recent years support SQL, which greatly helps anyone learning to use a new database program. Generally, SQL statements can be used to create new databases, add and modify tables, search for data, build new tables from existing ones, and to remove tables and data. SQL statements can also be used by programs that select and retrieve data from databases. SQL statements can be used by end users to perform interactive *ad-hoc queries* that retrieve database data.

The ADO database driver passes SQL statements to the database engine itself. Some database operations are more efficient when written in SQL than if explicitly coded using Recordset methods or stepping through a table. If you need to delete all the records in a dataset, for example, a single statement in SQL can do the job. Without SQL, you would have to set up a loop that iterates through all records and removes them one by one.

Microsft ADO uses a standardized version of SQL called **ANSI SQL**, designed by the American National Standards Institute (ANSI). Previously, Visual Basic used a version of SQL called **JET SQL**, the same one used in Microsoft Access. The name JET is taken from the Microsoft JET Database Engine developed for Visual Basic Versions 3, 4, and 5. (If you use the Data Access Objects (DAO) library, you can still use JET SQL in Visual Basic 6.) The two versions of SQL are nearly compatible, with some minor exceptions that we will point out later.

There are actually two languages within SQL: The *data definition language* (DDL) is used for defining databases, tables, and indexes. The *data manipulation language* (DML) is for searching, retrieving, modifying, inserting, deleting, and updating table data.

Terminology. Because SQL queries often refer to Recordsets in memory rather than in a physical database file, records are usually called *rows,* and fields are called *columns*. We will use these terms interchangeably.

Queries. The most common type of SQL statement is called a *query*. It defines the fields to be used when retrieving data, the tables that contain the fields, selection criteria for the records, and the ordering of the retrieved data. Queries can be processed interactively, or they can be stored in the database for later use.

6.2.1 Structure of SQL Statements

An SQL statement consists of the following:

- Manipulative statement: Indicates what type of action will be taken, such as INSERT, DELETE, SELECT, or UPDATE (see Table 1).
- Clauses: Select and sort records, control the grouping and totaling of records. Some keywords used here are WHERE, ORDER BY, and SUM (see Table 2).
- Aggregate functions that process multiple records, possibly a subset of the entire table (see Table 3).

Table 1. Data Manipulation Statements.

Statement	Operation
DELETE	Deletes rows from a table.
INSERT	Inserts rows into a table.
SELECT	Retrieves a group of records from a table and places them in a separate recordset.
UPDATE	Modifies the values of table fields.

Table 2. SQL Clauses.

Clause	Description
FROM	Names the table(s) from which fields are selected.
WHERE	Conditions for selecting records.
GROUP BY	Groups records together and provides summary information.
HAVING	Conditition to be satisfied by each group.
ORDER BY	Sorts records on one or more fields, in a selected order.

Table 3. Aggregate Functions.

Function	Description
AVG	Calculates the average of values in a field.
COUNT	Counts the number of selected records.
SUM	Sums, or totals the selected records.
MAX	Returns the highest value in a certain field.
MIN	Returns the lowest value in a certain field.

6.2.2 A Sample Database

(samples: CompanyData)

The best way to learn SQL is by example, so we will use a small database called **Company** containing two tables, **Employee** and **Payroll**. Each social security number in the Payroll table matches a social security number in the Employee table:

```
Employee (SSN, LastName, FirstName, Phone)
Payroll (SSN, PaymentDate, HoursWorked, HourlyRate )
```

Figure 1 displays a few sample records from the Employee table. Notice that each social security number is unique—it occurs only once in the table. We call the SSN field a *primary key*.

In the Payroll table, social security numbers can appear more than once because the same employee receives paychecks on different dates (see Figure 2). Therefore, the **SSN** field cannot be a primary key. All social security numbers in the Payroll table match records in the Employee table (except for SSN = 425-55-4444, the reason for which will be shown later). The **SSN** field is called a *foreign key*.

6.2.3 SELECT Statement

SELECT is by far the most commonly used SQL statement because it provides a way to obtain certain columns and rows from a table and build a new Recordset. The basic syntax

Figure 1. Sample Records, Employee Table.

SSN	LastName	FirstName	Phone
111-22-3333	Jones	Sam	222-3333
111-30-3000	Baker	Bob	333-2222
111-44-3232	Davidson	Anne	444-3232
200-10-5000	Gonzalez	Arturo	543-1234
222-32-4444	Chong	Helen	522-5678
300-56-9999	Franklin	Bill	677-5432
333-22-5555	Jackson	Deke	877-2424
400-33-2555	Robinson	Diane	888-4444

Figure 2. Sample Records, Payroll Table.

SSN	PaymentDate	HoursWorked	HourlyRate
111-22-3333	1/15/98	40	$13.13
111-44-3232	1/15/98	38.5	$14.70
111-44-3232	2/15/98	38.5	$14.70
222-32-4444	1/15/98	42	$13.13
222-32-4444	2/15/98	42	$13.13
300-56-9999	1/15/98	45	$15.23
300-56-9999	2/15/98	45	$15.23
425-55-4444	1/15/98	37.5	$18.90

for SELECT appears here. Keywords are capitalized, and italicized names are definitions of programmer-supplied information:

```
SELECT fieldlist
  FROM tablelist
  IN databasename
  WHERE search-conditions
  GROUP BY fieldlist
  HAVING group-criteria
  ORDER BY fieldlist
```

SQL is not case-sensitive, so capitalization is unimportant when writing actual statements. Only the SELECT and FROM clauses are required. *fieldlist* is a list of field names, separated by commas. *tablelist* is a list of table names from the current database, separated by commas. Field names may optionally be qualified by their table names. Examples are: Employee.SSN, Payroll.HourlyRate, and Student.Credits.

The following SELECT statement creates a Recordset containing a single column (LastName) from the Employee table:

```
SELECT LastName FROM Employee
```

If you use a wildcard character (*) for the field list, all fields are selected:

```
SELECT * FROM Employee
```

In general, runtime processing is faster if you specify only fields that are needed.

If a field or table name contains embedded spaces or punctuation characters, the name must be enclosed in brackets:

```
SELECT [pay rate] FROM [January Payroll]
```

Queries in Visual Basic. In Visual Basic, we often use SQL queries to create Recordsets. For example, assuming that cnEmployees is a valid open Connection object, we can create the rsEmployees Recordset with a query:

```
rsEmployees.Open "SELECT LastName, FirstName FROM _
   Employee", cnEmployees,,,adCmdText
```

Now **rsEmployees** can be used to fill a ListBox:

```
With rsEmployees
   Do Until .EOF
      List1.AddItem !LastName
      .MoveNext
   Loop
   .Close
End With
```

6.2.4 WHERE Clause

The WHERE clause uses selection criteria to determine which rows of a table are selected. Table 4 shows a list of the comparison operators that may be used. In the following query, only rows from the Payroll table in which the hours worked are greater than 40 are selected:

```
SELECT SSN, PaymentDate, HoursWorked
   FROM Payroll
   WHERE HoursWorked > 40
```

Table 4. Comparison Operators in SQL.

Operator	Description
<	Less than
>	Greater than
<=	Less than or equal to
>=	Greater than or equal to
=	Equal to
<>	Not equal to
BETWEEN	Compares a range of values
LIKE	String pattern matching
IN	Specify records in a database

If this query were used in a Visual Basic program, we would probably not use the constant 40, but would obtain it from a variable (msngFullTime) and append it to the query string (strSQL):

```
strSQL = "SELECT SSN, PaymentDate, HoursWorked " _
  & "FROM Payroll WHERE HoursWorked > " _
  & msngFullTime
```

The SQL query could then be passed to a Connection's Execute method and the resulting Recordset returned into a Recordset variable (rsTemp):

```
Set rsTemp = cnCompany.Execute(strSQL,,adCmdText)
```

You can also assign a query string to the RecordSource property of an ADO control and link the ADO control to a DataGrid. In the next example, rsTemp contains a Recordset:

```
adoPayroll.CommandType = adCmdText
adoPayroll.Recordsource = rsTemp
adoPayroll.Refresh
```

Notice that the CommandType property of the ADO control must be set to adCmdText if the Recordsource contains a SQL query. You must also call the Refresh method to force the ADO control to execute the query.

Range of Values. The following query selects rows in which the hourly pay rate of each employee falls within a certain range:

```
SELECT SSN, HourlyRate FROM Payroll
  WHERE HourlyRate BETWEEN 14 AND 30
```

Implementing this in Visual Basic, we would take care to insert variables for the minimum and maximum values into the query string:

```
strSQL = "SELECT SSN, HourlyRate FROM Payroll " _
 & " WHERE HourlyRate BETWEEN " _
 & msngMinRate & " AND " & msngMaxRate
```

Wildcard Search. You can use the % as a wildcard character, permitting partial string matches. The following query selects all rows in which the **SSN** field begins with the digits '111':

```
SELECT SSN, LastName, FirstName FROM Employee
  WHERE SSN LIKE '111%'
```

The same query in a Visual Basic program would have to include the single quotation marks as part of the query string:

```
strSQL = "SELECT SSN, LastName, FirstName FROM Employee " _
  & "WHERE SSN LIKE '" & strFindSSN & "%'"
```

Single-Character Wildcard. The underscore (_) placeholder allows a single character to be a wildcard. For example, the following query finds all SSN values ending with "23-45-6789":

```
SELECT SSN, LastName, FirstName FROM Employee
```

```
WHERE SSN LIKE '_23-45-6789'
```

Note: JEQ SQL permits the use of * and ? as wildcard characters, but ANSI SQL requires the use of % and underscore (_). The Visual Basic Query Builder (in the Data Environment Designer window) appears to accept the use of * and ?, but it does not return the expected Recordset rows.

Dates and Times. If a date or time literal is compared to a date/time field, the literal must be enclosed in # delimiters:

```
SELECT SSN, HourlyRate FROM Payroll
  WHERE PaymentDate < #02/01/98#
```

In Visual Basic, the same query requires the enclosing string to include # delimiters. In the next example, the date in question is in a TextBox control called txtLastDate:

```
strSQL = "SELECT SSN, HourlyRate FROM Payroll " _
  & "WHERE PaymentDate < #" _
  & txtLastDate.Text _
  & "#"
```

International Dates. The date in a SQL statement must be in standard U.S. format, even when Windows has been set up for another country's date representation. For example, many South American countries represent February 1, 1998 as 01/02/1998. The simplest workaround to this problem is to use the **DateValue** function to convert a date from a country-specific format to the one recognized by SQL:

```
SELECT SSN, HourlyRate FROM Payroll
  WHERE PaymentDate < DateValue('01/02/1998')
```

6.2.5 ORDER BY Clause

The ORDER BY clause makes it possible to sort the Recordset returned by a query on one or more fields, in ascending or descending order. The following query based on the Payroll table, for example, orders the rows by social security number (SSN):

```
SELECT SSN, PaymentDate, HoursWorked
  FROM Payroll
  WHERE HoursWorked > 40
  ORDER BY SSN
```

Or, we can order the records first by payment date and then by social security number, both in ascending order:

```
SELECT SSN, PaymentDate, HoursWorked
  FROM Payroll
  WHERE HoursWorked > 40
  ORDER BY PaymentDate, SSN
```

The following query places the payment dates in descending order and the social security numbers in ascending order:

```
SELECT SSN, PaymentDate, HoursWorked
  FROM Payroll
```

```
WHERE HoursWorked > 40
ORDER BY PaymentDate DESC, SSN
```

6.2.6 GROUP BY Clause

The GROUP BY clause combines records with identical values in a given field list into a single record. The syntax of a SELECT statement using GROUP BY is:

```
SELECT fieldlist
  FROM table
  WHERE criteria
  GROUP BY groupfieldlist
  HAVING groupcriteria
```

Groupfieldlist contains the names of up to ten fields that can be used to group records. The order of field names determines the grouping levels from highest to lowest.

The following query groups records in the Payroll table according to the SSN field and prints the total hours worked by each employee:

```
SELECT SSN, Sum(HoursWorked)
  AS [Total Hours]
  FROM Payroll
  GROUP BY SSN
```

This is the output produced by the query. No duplicate values are displayed in the SSN column:

SSN	Total Hours
111-22-3333	40
111-44-3232	77
222-32-4444	84
300-56-9999	90
425-55-4444	37.5

Multiple grouping levels are possible also. Let's use a modified version of the Payroll table called **DeptPayroll** that includes an additional field identifying each employee's department. Notice that the records are not currently ordered by department:

SSN	Dept	PaymentDate	HoursWorked	HourlyRate
111-22-3333	2	1/15/98	40	$13.13
111-44-3232	1	2/15/98	38.5	$14.70
111-44-3232	1	1/15/98	32	$14.70
222-32-4444	2	1/15/98	48	$13.13
222-32-4444	2	2/15/98	37	$13.13
300-56-9999	1	2/15/98	45	$15.23
300-56-9999	1	1/15/98	40	$15.23
425-55-4444	2	1/15/98	37.5	$18.90

The following query groups the records first by department, then by social security number, and calculates the average hours worked by each person:

```
SELECT Dept, SSN,
  Avg(HoursWorked) AS [Avg Hours]
```

```
FROM DeptPayroll
GROUP BY Dept, SSN
```

The resulting Recordset is automatically sorted on the Dept and SSN columns. Here is the output produced by the query:

Dept	SSN	Avg Hours
1	111-44-3232	35.25
1	300-56-9999	42.5
2	111-22-3333	40
2	222-32-4444	42.5
2	425-55-4444	37.5

6.2.7 HAVING Clause

The HAVING clause can be appended to a SELECT..GROUP BY query to select only certain groups. Suppose we want to display the average hours worked only for employees whose average is greater than 40 hours. We group by both department and social security number:

```
SELECT Dept, SSN, Avg(HoursWorked)
  AS [Avg Hours]
  FROM DeptPayroll
  GROUP BY Dept, SSN
  HAVING (Avg(HoursWorked) > 40)
```

Here is the output from the query:

Dept	SSN	Avg Hours
1	300-56-9999	42.5
2	222-32-4444	42.5

6.2.8 TOP Predicate

The TOP predicate can be added to the SELECT statement, returning a certain number of records that fall at the top or the bottom of a range specified by an ORDER BY clause. Here is the syntax:

```
SELECT TOP n [PERCENT] fieldlist
  FROM tablelist
  WHERE search-conditions
  ORDER BY fieldlist
```

The value that follows TOP must be an unsigned integer. PERCENT is optional. In the DeptPayroll table, for example, the following query returns the social security numbers and pay rates of the top two employees based on their pay rate:

```
SELECT TOP 2
  SSN, HourlyRate
  FROM DeptPayroll
  ORDER BY HourlyRate DESC
```

If we did not include the ORDER BY clause, the query would return an arbitrary set of two rows from the DeptPayroll table that satisfy the WHERE clause. Also, the TOP predicate does not choose between equal values. In the preceding example, if the second and third highest pay rates were the same, the query would return three rows.

You can also use the PERCENT reserved word to return a certain percentage of rows falling at the top or the bottom of a range specified by an ORDER BY clause. The following query returns the 10% of employees with the lowest hourly pay rates:

```
SELECT TOP 10 PERCENT
 SSN, HourlyRate
  FROM DeptPayroll
  WHERE Dept = 2
  ORDER BY HourlyRate ASC
```

6.2.9 Calculated Columns

It is often useful to add a new column to the Recordset created by a SQL statement, using calculated values. Suppose we want to calculate the amount of pay for each employee, using the HoursWorked and HourlyRate fields. This creates a new column:

```
SELECT SSN, HoursWorked * HourlyRate
  FROM Payroll
```

Here is the data generated by the query:

SSN	Expr1001
111-22-3333	525
111-44-3232	565.95
111-44-3232	565.95
222-32-4444	551.25
222-32-4444	551.25
300-56-9999	685.125
300-56-9999	685.125
425-55-4444	708.75

Calculated fields can also be used as criteria for selecting records:

```
SELECT SSN, HoursWorked * HourlyRate
  FROM Payroll
  WHERE HoursWorked * HourlyRate > 500
```

The SQL processor assigns a default name to the calculated field, such as "EXPR1001". We can optionally assign an alias such as **PayAmount** to the calculated field, using the AS clause:

```
SELECT SSN, HoursWorked * HourlyRate AS PayAmount
  FROM Payroll
```

Here is the data generated by the query:

SSN	PayAmount
111-22-3333	525
111-44-3232	565.95
111-44-3232	565.95
222-32-4444	551.25
222-32-4444	551.25
300-56-9999	685.125
300-56-9999	685.125
425-55-4444	708.75

The + operator can be used to create a string expression. In the following query, we display the combined first and last names of all employees:

```
SELECT LastName + ', ' + FirstName AS [Employee Name]
  FROM Employee
```

Here is the data generated by the query:

Employee Name
Jones, Sam
Baker, Bob
Davidson, Anne
Gonzalez, Arturo
Chong, Helen
Franklin, Bill
Jackson, Deke
Robinson, Diane

6.2.10 Logical Operators

The AND and OR logical operators can be used to combine expressions, and the NOT operator reverses an expression's meaning. Usually, the operators appear in the WHERE clause. The following statement selects rows in which the hourly pay rate is between 14 and 30, and the payment date is less than February 1, 1998:

```
SELECT SSN, HourlyRate, PaymentDate FROM Payroll
  WHERE HourlyRate Between 14 AND 30
  AND PaymentDate < #02/01/98#
```

SSN	HourlyRate	PaymentDate
111-44-3232	$14.70	1/15/98
300-56-9999	$15.23	1/15/98
425-55-4444	$18.90	1/15/98

The following query selects all rows in which the calculated pay amount is greater than 500, as well as all rows in which the hourly pay rate is greater than 20. The output from this query is shown in Figure 3:

```
SELECT SSN, HourlyRate, HoursWorked,
  HoursWorked * HourlyRate AS GrossPay
```

```
FROM Payroll
WHERE HoursWorked * HourlyRate > 500
OR HourlyRate > 20
```

Figure 3. Multiple Conditions in the WHERE Clause.

SSN	HourlyRate	HoursWorked	GrossPay
111-22-3333	$13.13	40	525
111-44-3232	$14.70	38.5	565.95
111-44-3232	$14.70	38.5	565.95
222-32-4444	$13.13	42	551.25
222-32-4444	$13.13	42	551.25
300-56-9999	$15.23	45	685.125
300-56-9999	$15.23	45	685.125
425-55-4444	$18.90	37.5	708.75

6.2.11 Selecting from Multiple Tables

Most databases consist of more than one table with relationships between the tables. SQL statements can select individual fields from more than one table at a time. Here, again, is the structure of the Employee and Payroll tables that we have used in examples so far:

```
Employee (SSN, LastName, FirstName, Phone)
Payroll (SSN, PaymentDate,  HoursWorked, HourlyRate )
```

Notice that the field **SSN** occurs in both tables: It is the *primary key* in the Employee table, and it is called a *foreign key* in the Payroll table. There is a *one-to-many* relationship between Employee and Payroll: For every *one* social security number in the Employee table, there can be *many* instances of the same number in the Payroll table.

When writing a SELECT statement using the **SSN** field, we have to use the notation table.field to clarify which table's **SSN** value is being referenced. The following statement pulls data from the Employee and Payroll tables:

```
SELECT Employee.SSN, LastName, PaymentDate
  FROM Employee, Payroll
  WHERE Employee.SSN = Payroll.SSN
```

For readability, it is often a good idea to supply table names for all fields, whether they are required or not:

```
SELECT Employee.SSN,Employee.LastName,Payroll.PaymentDate
  FROM Employee, Payroll
  WHERE Employee.SSN = Payroll.SSN
```

The DISTINCTROW option eliminates any duplicate rows in the resulting data set:

```
SELECT DISTINCTROW Employee.SSN,Employee.LastName,
  Payroll.PaymentDate
  FROM Employee, Payroll
  WHERE Employee.SSN = Payroll.SSN
```

When you create a Recordset from two or more tables, matching the records with the WHERE clause, there is one drawback: the Recordset cannot be updated. If updates are required, you must use the JOIN clause to combine two or more tables.

Avoiding Redundant Queries. A common mistake made when learning SQL is to select records from two or more tables without using the WHERE or JOIN clauses. The database will create a *Cartesian product* of the tables. Suppose, for example, that one table contained three members (10,20,30) and another table contained three members (A,B,C). Then the Cartesian product would consist of all possible member pairs:

(10,A), (10,B), (10,C), (20,A), (20,B), (20,C), (30,A), (30,B), (30,C)

If we produce a Cartesian product between two tables having 1000 records each, the resulting data set contains one million records! In a network environment, most database administrators are reluctant to let general users run ad-hoc SQL queries on multi-user databases because queries of this type can bring the system to a standstill. The following query would create a Cartesian product with the Employee and Payroll tables:

```
SELECT LastName, FirstName, HoursWorked
  FROM Employee, Payroll
```

6.2.12 JOIN Clause

The JOIN clause indicates how the rows from two or more tables are to be related together. There are three types of joins: *inner, left,* and *right.* Imagine joining two tables, called **Table1** and **Table2:**

- INNER JOIN: Only include rows where the joined fields from Table1 and Table2 are equal.
- LEFT JOIN: All rows from Table1 and only rows from Table2 where the joined fields are equal.
- RIGHT JOIN: All rows from Table2 and only rows from Table1 where the joined fields are equal.

To illustrate the three types of join methods, we will start with the Employee table in Figure 4 and the Payroll table in Figure 5.

Inner Join. The following INNER JOIN includes only records having the same social security numbers in both tables:

Figure 4. Employee Table.

SSN	LastName	FirstName	Phone
111-22-3333	Jones	Sam	222-3333
111-30-3000	Baker	Bob	333-2222
111-44-3232	Davidson	Anne	444-3232
200-10-5000	Gonzalez	Arturo	543-1234
222-32-4444	Chong	Helen	522-5678
300-56-9999	Franklin	Bil	677-5432
333-22-5555	Jackson	Deke	877-2424
400-33-2555	Robinson	Diane	883-4444

Figure 5. Payroll Table.

SSN	PaymentDate	HoursWorked	HourlyRate
111-22-3333	1/15/98	40	$13.13
111-44-3232	1/15/98	38.5	$14.70
111-44-3232	2/15/98	38.5	$14.70
222-32-4444	1/15/98	42	$13.13
222-32-4444	2/15/98	42	$13.13
300-56-9999	1/15/98	45	$15.23
300-56-9999	2/15/98	45	$15.23
425-55-4444	1/15/98	37.5	$18.90

```
SELECT DISTINCTROW Employee.SSN, LastName,
   PaymentDate, HoursWorked
   FROM Employee
   INNER JOIN Payroll
   ON Employee.SSN = Payroll.SSN
```

The Recordset created by this query appears in Figure 6. At first it appears that duplicate records have been created, but note that the PaymentDate values for the same employees are different.

Inner Join with Sort. The following query sorts the resulting Recordset in order by last name and payment date, as shown in Figure 7:

```
SELECT DISTINCTROW Employee.SSN, LastName,
   PaymentDate, HoursWorked
   FROM Employee
   INNER JOIN Payroll
   ON Employee.SSN = Payroll.SSN
   ORDER BY LastName, PaymentDate
```

Figure 6. Inner Join Example.

SSN	LastName	PaymentDate	HoursWorked
111-22-3333	Jones	1/15/98	40
111-44-3232	Davidson	1/15/98	38.5
111-44-3232	Davidson	2/15/98	38.5
222-32-4444	Chong	1/15/98	42
222-32-4444	Chong	2/15/98	42
300-56-9999	Franklin	1/15/98	45
300-56-9999	Franklin	2/15/98	45

Figure 7. Inner Join with Multiple Sorts.

SSN	LastName	PaymentDate	HoursWorked
222-32-4444	Chong	1/15/98	42
222-32-4444	Chong	2/15/98	42
111-44-3232	Davidson	1/15/98	38.5
111-44-3232	Davidson	2/15/98	38.5
300-56-9999	Franklin	1/15/98	45
300-56-9999	Franklin	2/15/98	45
111-22-3333	Jones	1/15/98	40

Left Join. The following LEFT JOIN includes all rows from Employee, and only rows in Payroll that match the social security numbers of rows in Employee:

```
SELECT DISTINCTROW Employee.SSN, LastName,
  PaymentDate, HoursWorked
  FROM Employee
  LEFT JOIN Payroll
  ON Employee.SSN = Payroll.SSN
```

The resulting data set (Figure 8) contains four rows from the Employee table that have no matching rows in the Payroll table. This type of query can be useful when you want to look for potential missing records; in this case, missing Payroll records.

Right Join. The following RIGHT JOIN includes all rows from Payroll, and only the rows from Employee where the social security numbers are equal. Notice that the first field in the SELECT list is now Payroll.SSN:

```
SELECT DISTINCTROW Payroll.SSN, LastName,
  PaymentDate, HoursWorked
  FROM Employee
  RIGHT JOIN Payroll
  ON Employee.SSN = Payroll.SSN
```

The resulting data set (Figure 9) contains one row from the Payroll table that did not have a matching row in the Employee table. That would normally indicate an error, because every Payroll record should contain a social security number for an existing company employee.

Figure 8. Left Join Example.

SSN	LastName	PaymentDate	HoursWorked
111-22-3333	Jones	1/15/98	40
111-30-3000	Baker		
111-44-3232	Davidson	1/15/98	38.5
111-44-3232	Davidson	2/15/98	38.5
200-10-5000	Gonzalez		
222-32-4444	Chong	1/15/98	42
222-32-4444	Chong	2/15/98	42
300-56-9999	Franklin	1/15/98	45
300-56-9999	Franklin	2/15/98	45
333-22-5555	Jackson		
400-33-2555	Robinson		

6.2.13 Creating Queries Using SQL Builder

(samples: SQLBuilder)

The easiest way to create a SQL query in Visual Basic is to use the **SQL Builder** (also called the **Query builder**), which is accessed through the Data Environment Designer. You can also execute the resulting query directly from your program code, and you can use the query to generate data for a report. Particularly when multiple table joins are involved, it's nice to let the Query Builder do the coding for you.

Figure 9. Right Join Example.

SSN	LastName	PaymentDate	HoursWorked
111-22-3333	Jones	1/15/98	40
111-44-3232	Davidson	1/15/98	38.5
111-44-3232	Davidson	2/15/98	38.5
222-32-4444	Chong	1/15/98	42
222-32-4444	Chong	2/15/98	42
300-56-9999	Franklin	1/15/98	45
300-56-9999	Franklin	2/15/98	45
425-55-4444		1/15/98	37.5

First, we create a DataEnvironment named deCompanyData, a Connection named cnCompany, and a Command named PayrollSales. The techniques for doing this were shown in the previous chapter:

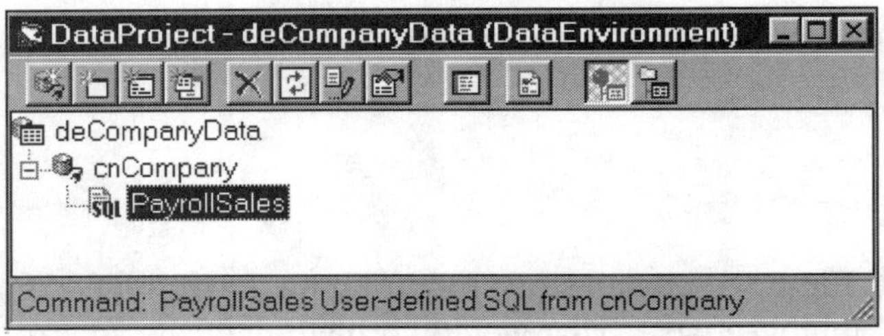

When setting the Command properties, we click on a button called **SQL Builder**. A new window called **Data View** appears, showing all of the available tables in the Company database, as in Figure 10. We can then drag the Employee, Sales, and Payroll tables into the upper pane of the SQL Designer. The same figure shows the Query Builder window after adding the three tables. The SSN fields in each of the tables are automatically connected by a line because the fields have the same name. The Query Builder assumes that a relation exists between the three tables, using the SSN field as the common link.

The Query Builder has already started to create a SQL query, but no fields have been selected yet, so the query will not run. The next step is to place checkmarks next to the

Figure 10. Data View and Query Builder Windows.

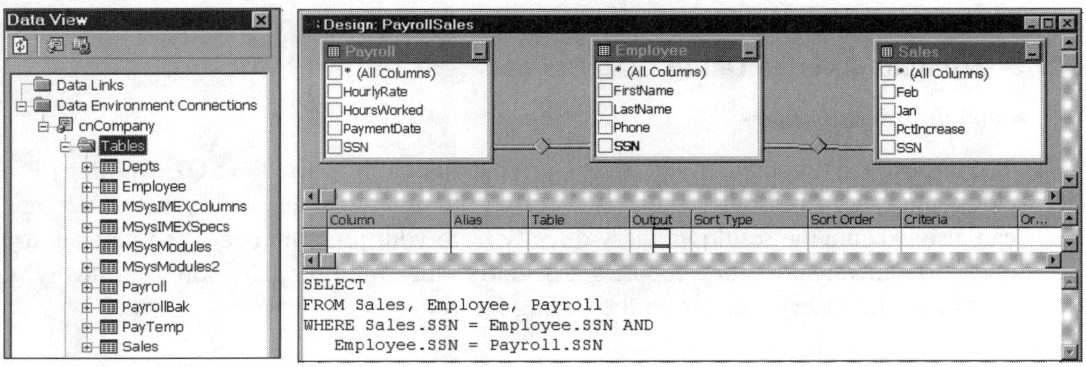

following field names: LastName, HourlyRate, HoursWorked, PaymentDate, Jan, and Feb. The names appear in the middle panel of the Builder:

Column
LastName
HourlyRate
HoursWorked
PaymentDate
Jan
Feb

The following SQL code is generated. Notice that the tables are joined using a WHERE clause that compares the SSN field in each table:

```
SELECT Employee.LastName, Payroll.HourlyRate,
   Payroll.HoursWorked, Payroll.PaymentDate, Sales.Jan,
   Sales.Feb
FROM Sales, Employee, Payroll
WHERE Sales.SSN = Employee.SSN AND
   Employee.SSN = Payroll.SSN
```

Now, let's add some filtering criteria. We type "> 40" in the same row as **HoursWorked**, in the column marked **Criteria**. The following clause is automatically added to the end of the query:

```
AND (Payroll.HoursWorked > 40)
```

When you right-click the mouse on the Query Builder window, a popup menu appears. Select **Run** to view the Recordset produced by the query. Here is a sample:

LastName	HourlyRate	HoursWorked	PaymentDate	Jan	Feb
Chong	13.125	42	1/15/98	250	55
Chong	13.125	42	2/15/98	250	55
Franklin	15.225	45	1/15/98	400	350
Franklin	15.225	45	2/15/98	400	350

Finally, we can type the expression LastName+', '+FirstName into the column currently containing the LastName field. Edit the SQL code by inserting "Name" as the alias for the combined field:

```
SELECT Employee.LastName + ', ' + Employee.FirstName AS Name,
   Payroll.HourlyRate, Payroll.HoursWorked, Payroll.PaymentDate,
   Sales.Jan, Sales.Feb
FROM Sales, Employee, Payroll
WHERE Sales.SSN = Employee.SSN AND
   Sales.SSN = Payroll.SSN AND (Payroll.HoursWorked > 40)
```

This is the output from our final version of the query after selecting **Run** from the popup menu:

Name	HourlyRate	HoursWorked	PaymentDate	Jan	Feb
Chong, Helen	13.125	42	1/15/98	250	55
Chong, Helen	13.125	42	2/15/98	250	55
Franklin, Bill	15.225	45	1/15/98	400	350
Franklin, Bill	15.225	45	2/15/98	400	350

Displaying in a DataGrid. Let's show how to connect the Command object we just created to a DataGrid control on the program's main Form. All we have to do is put a DataGrid on the Form, set its DataSource to the **deCompanyData** DataEnvironment, and set its DataMember property to the name of the **PayrollSales** Command object in design mode:

DataSource: deCompanyData
DataMember: PayrollSales

The DataGrid displays the same Recordset we saw just now in the Query Builder:

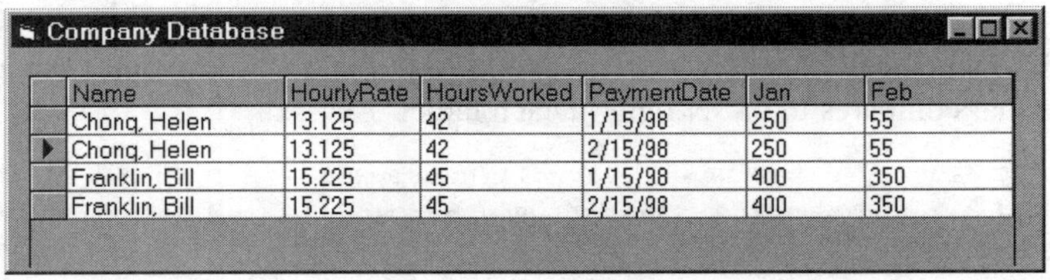

Name	HourlyRate	HoursWorked	PaymentDate	Jan	Feb
Chong, Helen	13.125	42	1/15/98	250	55
Chong, Helen	13.125	42	2/15/98	250	55
Franklin, Bill	15.225	45	1/15/98	400	350
Franklin, Bill	15.225	45	2/15/98	400	350

One of the advantages to using a DataEnvironment to create queries is that you can create a number of different Command objects within the same Connection. Each Command can be displayed in a different DataGrid. If we were still using ADO controls, each DataGrid would require its own ADO control, a decidedly wasteful approach.

6.2.14 Creating Queries in Microsoft Access

Microsoft Access has a Query Wizard that greatly simplifies the writing of SQL queries. From the database window, you can select the Queries tab and click the New button. Select the Simple Query Wizard, which displays the following window. In this window (Figure 11), you select the tables and fields that you want to be displayed in the data set produced by the query.

For example, we could select SSN, LastName, and FirstName from the Employee table, along with PaymentDate and HoursWorked from the Payroll table. After the wizard has finished, click the View/SQL menu to see the query's SQL source code. This query was generated when we selected the SSN, LastName, FirstName, PaymentDate, and HoursWorked fields from the two tables:

```
SELECT DISTINCTROW [Employee].[SSN], [Employee].[LastName],
   [Employee].[FirstName], [Payroll].[PaymentDate],
   [Payroll].[HoursWorked]
  FROM Employee
  INNER JOIN Payroll
  ON [Employee].[SSN] =[Payroll].[SSN]
```

By default, Access places brackets around the field names, which is only necessary when field names contain embedded spaces or punctuation. This query can be pasted directly into a Visual Basic program, or the query can be given a name and saved in the database itself.

Microsoft Access will not let you use the Query Wizard to create a query that involves two tables unless you set table relationships first (one-to-one, or one-to-many). Later in this chapter, we show you how to create these relationships.

Figure 11. Query Wizard, Microsoft Access.

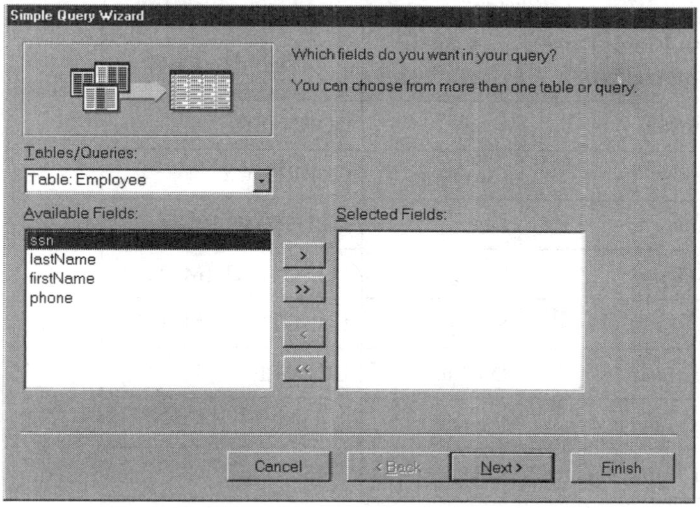

6.3 SQL DATA DEFINITION LANGUAGE (DDL)

SQL is also a powerful data definition language (DDL), that can create and delete tables, indexes, and views. SQL action queries, as they are called, carry out immediate actions on a database. They are: DELETE, INSERT INTO, UPDATE, and MAKE-TABLE. Such queries are said to be *non-Recordset returning*. You may recall that queries using the SELECT statement, on the other hand, are *Recordset returning*.

6.3.1 CREATE TABLE

The CREATE TABLE statement creates a new database table. You have to supply field descriptions. Leaving out constraints and indexes, the basic syntax is:

```
CREATE TABLE tablename
   (field1 type [(size)] [NOT NULL]
   [, field2 type [(size)] [NOT NULL]
   [, ...]]
   )
```

where *tablename* is the name of a table that does not already exist, *type* is the field type, and *size* is only relevant for Text and Binary fields. The NOT NULL field option specifies that new records must have valid data in the field—in Access, the *required* option is set to True. A comparison of Access, Visual Basic, and SQL type descriptors is shown in Table 5.

The following SQL statement creates a table called **Depts** that contains a variety of field types. The table and field names are in bold type:

```
CREATE TABLE Depts
  (ID Long NOT NULL,
   Name Text(20) NOT NULL ,
   Active YesNo NOT NULL,
   NumMembers Short,
```

Table 5. Comparison of Access, Visual Basic, and SQL Types.

Access Field Type (numeric type)	VBasic Data Type	Jet SQL Type
AutoNumber	Long	COUNTER
Currency	Currency	CURRENCY
Date/Time	Date	DATETIME
Hyperlink	String	LONGTEXT (MEMO)
Memo	String	LONGTEXT (MEMO)
Number (Double)	Double	DOUBLE
Number (Integer)	Integer	SHORT
Number (Long Integer)	Long	LONG
Number (Single)	Single	SINGLE
Number (Byte)	Byte	BYTE
OLE Object	String	LONGBINARY
Text	String	TEXT (CHAR)
Yes/No	Boolean	BOOLEAN (YESNO)

```
    Sales Currency,
    Created DateTime,
    Comments Memo)
```

Note that a **Short** field type in SQL is the same as an **Integer** type in Access.

6.3.2 DROP TABLE/INDEX

The **DROP** statement removes either a table or an index. There are two variations:

```
DROP TABLE tablename
DROP INDEX indexname ON tablename
```

For example, we can drop the PayTemp table:

```
DROP TABLE PayTemp
```

Or, we can drop the salesNdx index from the Depts table:

```
DROP INDEX salesNdx ON Depts
```

DROP INDEX does not affect any data in the table. Of course, a table must be closed before it can be dropped, or before any of its indexes can be dropped.

6.3.3 ALTER TABLE

The ALTER TABLE command adds a column to a table and optionally assigns a default value to each row, or it drops a column. There are two basic formats:

```
ALTER TABLE tablename
   ADD fieldname fieldtype[(size)]
   [NOT NULL]

ALTER TABLE tablename
   DROP fieldname
```

Examples:

```
ALTER TABLE Payroll
   ADD HireDate DATETIME NULL

ALTER TABLE Payroll
   ADD Department SHORT NULL

ALTER TABLE Payroll
   Drop HireDate

ALTER TABLE Payroll
   DROP Department
```

6.3.4 UPDATE

The UPDATE statement is used to create what is called an *update* query. This type of query modifies values in one or more fields in one or more tables. The syntax is:

```
UPDATE table
   SET fieldname = newvalue
   WHERE criteria
```

You can update many records at the same time, modifying one or more fields. The updated records can also be in different tables. The following statement, for example, increases the pay rate in all rows of the Payroll table by 5%:

```
UPDATE Payroll
   SET HourlyRate = HourlyRate * 1.05
```

The following query increases the hourly pay rate for all employees paid after a given payment date:

```
UPDATE Payroll
   SET HourlyRate = HourlyRate * 1.05
   WHERE PaymentDate > #05/01/1999#
```

Sales Table Examples. We will introduce a new table called **Sales**, shown in Figure 12. The Jan and Feb columns list the amount of goods sold by the employee, in thousands of dollars. The PctIncrease column represents the percent of increase in sales between January and February. Initially, the field is blank, so we can write an update query that calculates the percent increase:

Figure 12. The Sales Table.

SSN	Jan	Feb	PctIncrease
111-22-3333	50	65	30.00%
111-30-3000	75	95	26.67%
111-44-3232	550	620	12.73%
200-10-5000	22	48	118.18%
222-32-4444	250	55	-78.00%
300-56-9999	400	350	-12.50%
333-22-5555	475	425	-10.53%
400-33-2555	827	890	7.62%

```
UPDATE Sales
   SET PctIncrease = (Feb - Jan) / Jan
```

6.3.5 DELETE

The DELETE statement removes one or more rows from a Recordset. The WHERE clause can be used to select the rows. The syntax is:

```
DELETE [table.*]
   FROM tablelist
   WHERE criteria
```

The *table* argument is only required when deleting from multiple tables. Be careful: Once a row has been deleted, it cannot be recovered. If you specify more than one table, none of the tables can contain the primary key of a one-to-many relationship. You can, however, remove rows from the *many* side of a one-to-many relationship.

The following command deletes all rows from the Payroll table in which the payment date is before January 1, 1998:

```
DELETE FROM Payroll
   WHERE PaymentDate < #1/1/1998#
```

The following command deletes all rows from the Payroll table and retains the empty table in the database:

```
DELETE FROM Payroll
```

In a Visual Basic program, use a Connection object's Execute method to execute SQL action queries. If cnEmployees is an open database object, for example, the following statement deletes all the rows from the Payroll table:

```
cnCompany.Execute "DELETE FROM Payroll"
```

6.3.6 INSERT INTO

The INSERT INTO statement adds new records to a table. This is also called an *append* query. You can add a single record by supplying all of its field data, or records can be appended from another table, using an append query.

Single-Record Append. A single-record append query has the following syntax:

```
INSERT INTO target
   [(field1[,field2[,...]])]
   VALUES(value1,[,value2[,...])
```

You have to specify all of the field values. If you omit the field names, you must specify the field values in the order defined by the table structure.

For example, the following appends a new record to the Payroll table:

```
INSERT INTO Payroll (SSN, PaymentDate, HoursWorked, HourlyRate)
  VALUES('400-33-2555', #1/15/1998#, 47.5, 17.50)
```

In Visual Basic, each of these values is usually stored in TextBox controls, so the corresponding program statement concatenates TextBox names into the SQL command.

```
strSQL = "INSERT INTO Payroll (SSN, PaymentDate, HoursWorked, " _
 & "HourlyRate) VALUES ('" _
 & txtSSN.Text _
 & "', #" _
 & txtPaymentDate.Text _
 & "#, " _
 ...etc...
```

We execute the query, using the Connection object:

```
cnCompany.Execute(strSQL,,adCmdText)
```

The following is an alternate syntax for the same operation:

```
INSERT INTO Payroll (SSN, PaymentDate, HoursWorked, HourlyRate)
  SELECT '400-33-2555', #1/15/1998#, 47.5, 17.50
```

Multiple-Record Append. A multiple-record append query has the following syntax:

```
INSERT INTO target
   SELECT [source.]field1[,field2[,...]
   FROM tablename
```

The following statement copies all records from the Payroll table to the PayTemp table, since all field names are identical:

```
INSERT INTO PayTemp
  SELECT *
  FROM Payroll
```

The following statement selects and appends only full-time employees from the Payroll table to the PayTemp table:

```
INSERT INTO PayTemp
  SELECT *
  FROM Payroll
  WHERE HoursWorked >= 40
```

6.3.7 CREATE INDEX

The CREATE INDEX statement creates a new index for an existing table. The syntax is:

```
CREATE [ UNIQUE ] INDEX indexname
   ON tablename (field1 [ASC|DESC][, field2 [ASC|DESC], ...])
   [WITH { PRIMARY | DISALLOW NULL | IGNORE NULL }]
```

The following creates a non-unique index called **ssnNdx**, on the **SSN** field in the **PayTemp** table (there are duplicate social security numbers in this table):

```
CREATE INDEX ssnNdx
   ON PayTemp(SSN)
```

The following creates a unique index called **pKey** on the **ID** field in the **Depts** table, and makes it the primary key:

```
CREATE UNIQUE INDEX pKey
   ON Depts(ID)
   WITH PRIMARY
```

The default order for indexes is ascending, but you can specify descending order by following the field name with DESC. The following creates an index called **salesNdx** on the **Sales** field of the **Depts** table, arranging the values in descending order:

```
CREATE INDEX salesNdx
   ON Depts(Sales DESC)
```

6.4 DDL PROGRAM EXAMPLE

(samples: DDL_Updates)

In this section, we're going to show a short program that uses SQL to modify the Company database. It creates and removes tables and inserts and deletes records. The program's opening screen (not shown) presents the following choices:

- Add/Remove/Select Table
- Insert/Delete Records
- Add New Field

If the user selects the first option, the Add/Remove/Select Table window appears. The user can add a new table to the database, remove an existing table, or select an existing table for further updates:

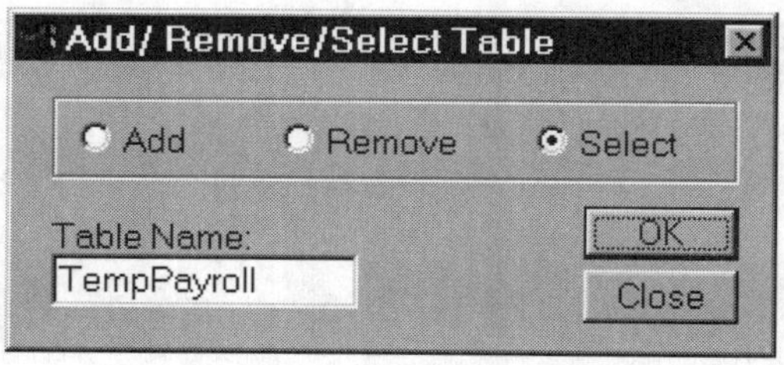

From the main window, if the user wants to Insert and Delete records from a table that was just added or selected, the Insert/Delete window appears (Figure 13). The user can enter values into the textboxes for the four fields at the bottom of the Form and click on Insert to create a new record. Or, the user can select a record from the DataGrid and click on Delete to remove the record. We are careful to refresh the DataGrid after each of these operations.

If the user selects the Add New Field command from the main window, the following Form appears. After selecting a default value for the Department field, the user clicks on Go to complete the operation and close the window:

If the Department field already exists, the program automatically deletes it and adds the field again. By returning to the Insert/Delete window, you can verify that the Department field was added and that all records contain the default value.

Figure 13. Insert/Delete Window (DDL Example).

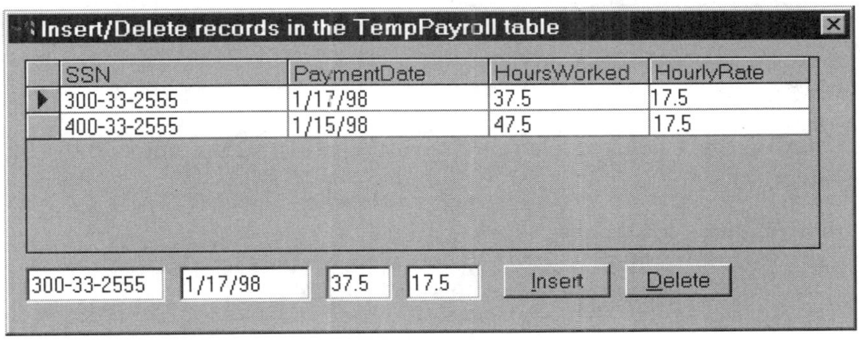

6.4.1 Program Code

Let's take a look at the source code for this program. The program has two global variables, stored in a code module: cnCompany, the Connection object, is our reference to the Company database. The other variable, strTableName, is the name of the currently selected table:

```
Public cnCompany As ADODB.Connection
Public strTableName As String
```

Add/Remove/Select Table Form. In the Add/Remove/Select Table Form, if the user decides to add a new table, the following statements are executed:

```
Dim strSQL As String
On Error GoTo AddRemoveErr
strSQL = "CREATE TABLE " & txtTableName.Text _
    & "(SSN TEXT(15) NOT NULL, " _
    & "PaymentDate DATETIME, " _
    & "HoursWorked SINGLE, " _
```

```
      & "HourlyRate SINGLE)"
   cnCompany.Execute (strSQL)
```

If the user wants to remove an existing table, the following statements are executed:

```
strSQL = "DROP TABLE " & txtTableName.Text
cnCompany.Execute  (strSQL)
```

If the user simply wants to select an existing table, we assign the table name to a global variable:

```
strTableName = txtTableName.Text
```

Insert/Delete Records Form. In the Form_Load procedure of the Insert/Delete Records Form, we establish a Connection for the ADO control and set the DataSource property of the DataGrid control:

```
Private Sub Form_Load()
   adoPayroll.ConnectionString = cnCompany.ConnectionString
   adoPayroll.CommandType = adCmdText
   adoPayroll.RecordSource = "Select * from " & strTableName _
      & " order by SSN"
   Set dgdPayroll.DataSource = adoPayroll
   adoPayroll.Refresh
   Caption = "Insert/Delete records in the " _
      & strTableName & " table"
End Sub
```

The **cmdInsert_Click** procedure uses the INSERT INTO command to add a new record to the table:

```
Private Sub cmdInsert_Click()
   mstrSQL = "INSERT INTO " & strTableName & " " _
    & "(SSN, PaymentDate, HoursWorked, " _
    & "HourlyRate) VALUES ('" _
    & txtSSN.Text _
    & "', #" _
    & txtPaymentDate.Text _
    & "#, " _
    & Val(txtHoursWorked.Text) _
    & ", " _
    & Val(txtHourlyRate.Text) & ")"
```

Also in this procedure, we have to close and reopen the Connection to see the new record. Simply calling Requery or Refresh does not accomplish this:

```
   cnCompany.Execute mstrSQL
   cnCompany.Close
   cnCompany.Open
   adoPayroll.Refresh
End Sub
```

The **cmdDelete_Click** procedure uses the DELETE FROM command to delete a record from the table. It requires a WHERE condition to uniquely identify the record. Otherwise, all records would be deleted:

```
Private Sub cmdDelete_Click()
  mstrSQL = "DELETE FROM " & strTableName & " " _
       & "WHERE SSN = '" & txtSSN.Text & "'"
  cnCompany.Execute (mstrSQL)
  cnCompany.Close
  cnCompany.Open
  adoPayroll.Refresh
End Sub
```

Finally, when the user selects a record in the DataGrid, we copy the current record values into the TextBox controls at the bottom of the Form:

```
Private Sub dgdPayroll_Click()
  With adoPayroll.Recordset
    txtSSN.Text = "" & !SSN
    txtPaymentDate.Text = "" & !PaymentDate
    txtHoursWorked.Text = "" & !HoursWorked
    txtHourlyRate.Text = "" & !HourlyRate
  End With
End Sub
```

Adding a New Field. The code that lets the user add a new Department field to the current table is shown here. The ALTER TABLE statement inserts the new field. If the field already exists, a runtime error is generated; the error handler drops the field and attempts to add the table again:

```
Private Sub cmdAddColumn_Click()
  On Error GoTo AddColumnErr
  cnCompany.Execute "ALTER TABLE " & strTableName _
    & " " & "ADD Department SHORT NULL"

  cnCompany.Execute "UPDATE " & strTableName & " " _
     & "Set Department = " & txtDefaultDept.Text
  Unload Me
  Exit Sub
AddColumnErr:
  If Err.Number = -2147217865 Then       'Table doesn't exist
    MsgBox Err.Description, vbInformation, "Error"
  Else
    MsgBox "This field already exists, so it will be " _
      & "replaced", vbInformation, ""
    cnCompany.Execute "ALTER TABLE " & strTableName _
      & " " & "DROP Department"
    Resume
  End If
End Sub
```

After the new column is added, the UPDATE command sets each department value to the default value input by the user.

This program should help give you an alternative way to perform database maintenance. In addition to using Recordset methods such as AddNew and Update, you can use SQL to do the same operations. The trend in Visual Basic program is definitely toward using SQL as much as possible, for reasons of scalability and efficiency.

6.5 DESIGNING A CAR RENTAL DATABASE

6.5.1 Specifications

(samples: Stellar)

Let's create a database and design the user interface for an application program for an imaginary Car Rental Company called **Stellar Car Rentals**. We will call this the **Rentals** database. The general types of service that such a program should offer are:

- Make advance reservations for car rentals.
- Create and store an invoice when a car is rented.
- Keep track of all cars in the company inventory.
- Update an invoice when a car is returned by the customer.

The database will contain a number of tables, each related to a topic or grouping in the application. The best way to design the tables is to think about what information will be required for each step in the rental process: Reservations, Rentals, Returns, and Inventory.

Reservations. When a customer calls to reserve a Stellar vehicle, the reservations clerk collects and stores the following information:

- A reservation confirmation number.
- The customer's name, phone, address, and credit card information.
- The date the vehicle will be rented, and the date when it was returned.
- The requested vehicle category (economy, midsize, etc.).
- The daily and weekly rental rate quoted to the customer.
- Miscellaneous notes or comments.

We can create a database table with all of the above information and add a record to the table when the reservation is made. But we also see that rental rates require information from another source, most likely a table containing daily and weekly rental rates for each type of vehicle. Further, we can assume that rental rates change all the time for competitive reasons—this means that the reservations clerk will have to lock in a price for the customer that is unaffected by rate changes that might occur before the actual rental takes place.

Rentals. When a Stellar vehicle is rented by a customer, an invoice must be prepared and saved in the database. The invoice should contain the following information:

- An invoice number.
- The date and time the car was rented.
- The expected return date.
- The vehicle ID number.
- The customer's name, phone, address, and credit card information.
- The total amount due.

- The amount paid.
- Notes or comments.

We can already see the potential for duplication of data. The customer's name, phone, and address are needed for both reservations and invoices. This will be a factor in our database design, causing us to separate the customer information and make it available to both invoices and reservations.

Returns. When a vehicle is returned, the return date is filled in and the invoice is completed. At that time, the invoice could be moved to a history file and kept for future reference.

Inventory. At the time a vehicle is rented, the clerk will have to search for an available vehicle that matches the size stated on the reservation. Rental agencies rarely reserve specific vehicles for customers, but they do try to guarantee a certain size or style when a reservation is made. We want to store the following information about each vehicle:

- The vehicle ID number
- The vehicle Model, such as "Mercury Sable, 4-door".
- The vehicle Category, such as "Luxury", "Midsize", or "Economy".
- The vehicle Status, such as "Available", "Rented", or "Maintenance".

At this point, there is enough available information to begin designing the tables for a database. In nearly every table, there will be a record key that makes it possible to locate individual records.

Table Descriptions. The Rentals database contains the following tables:

- **Customer**: Information about each customer who has either made a reservation or rented a vehicle.
- **Invoice**: The rental invoice that is created at the time a vehicle is rented.
- **Price**: Daily and weekly rental rates for each type of vehicle, based on the date of the rental.
- **Reservation**: Information that is saved when each customer calls to reserve a vehicle for an upcoming rental.
- **Vehicle**: Information about each vehicle in the company's inventory.
- **Model**: A lookup table containing standard vehicle models and their descriptions.
- **VehicleStatus**: A lookup table containing standard vehicle status codes and their descriptions.
- **Category**: A lookup table containing standard vehicle categories their descriptions.

6.5.2 Vehicle Inventory

To keep track of Stellar's inventory, let's create a table called **Vehicle.** We need to know the vehicle's category (Economy, Compact, etc.) and its status (available or not). Each record contains a unique vehicle ID number, called a *record key*. Table 6 shows a preliminary version of the Vehicle table, with a few sample records that have intentionally misspelled text values. It is clear from this sample that there would be a lot of duplicate data. Most disturbing is the fact that a data entry clerk might misspell the text fields, making it very difficult to perform a reliable search for specific values. What if we wanted to locate all "Minivan" vehicles? Only one of the vehicles in Table 6 would be found.

A preferred design for the Vehicle table would be to convert all text fields into short codes (Table 7). This design greatly reduces the possibility of misspelling, and minimizes the amount of redundant data. If a customer wants to rent a Lincoln Town Car, we can just search for ModelId = 3. Or, if the customer wants a luxury car, we can search for CategoryId = LX. Alphanumeric codes such as these can usually be understood by employees who are familiar with the company's operations.

Table 6. Preliminary Design for Vehicle Table.

VehicleId	Model	Category	Status
100	Chevy Geo	Economy	Available
101	VB Rabbit	Economi	Rentd
102	Plymouth Voyager	Minivan	Availabl
103	Ford Aerostar	Mnivan	Rented
104	Lincoln Town Car	Luxury	Available
105	Ford Aeorostar	Minvian	Maintenence

6.5.3 Models, Categories, and Status

When printing reports or when asking for input from inexperienced users, we need to make the full descriptions of the codes available in separate tables. The best way to do this is to create *lookup tables,* each of which contains a list of codes and their matching descriptions. The table of vehicle models is called **Model** (Table 8), the table of vehicle categories is called **Category** (Table 9), and the table of status values is called **VehicleStatus** (Table 10). These lookup tables display easily in DataCombo and ComboBox controls.

6.5.4 Rental Prices

When a reservation is made or a rental invoice is processed, the clerk and the customer need to know how much it costs to rent the vehicle. Rental rates are typically determined by types of vehicles and seasonal changes in prices. Each record in the **Price** table (see Table 11) holds a vehicle category, a date range, and the applicable daily and weekly rental rates. Table 12 displays sample records for the Price table, with rental rates for economy and compact vehicles. The date ranges for each type of vehicle do not have to be the same, giving us some degree of flexibility. If it were possible to calculate the weekly rate directly from the daily rate, we would not have to place the weekly rate in this table. But at Stellar Rentals, the weekly rate is assumed to be independent of the daily rate. Both rates would ordinarily be determined by external factors such as marketing and competition.

Table 7. The Vehicle Table.

VehicleId	ModelId	CategoryId	StatusId
100	1	EC	A
101	4	EC	R
102	5	MV	A
103	6	MV	R
104	3	LX	A
105	6	MV	M

Table 8. The Model Table.

ModelId	Description
1	Chevy Geo
2	Toyota Tercel
3	Lincoln Town Car
4	VW Rabbit
5	Plymouth Voyager
6	Ford AeroStar

Table 9. The Category Table.

CategoryId	Description
EC	Economy
CM	Compact
MS	Midsize
LX	Luxury
MV	Minivan

Table 10. The VehicleStatus Table.

StatusId	Description
M	Maintenance
A	Available
R	Rented

Table 11. Price Table Fields.

Name	Type	Comments
CategoryId	Text (2)	Foreign key (Category)
StartDate	Date	Date the price takes effect.
EndDate	Date	Date the price ends.
DailyRate	Currency	Rental rate, per day.
WeeklyRate	Currency	Rental rate, per week.

Table 12. Sample Records in the Price Table.

CategoryId	StartDate	EndDate	DailyRate	WeeklyRate
EC	01-01-1999	03-31-1999	19.95	110.00
EC	04-01-1999	07-31-1999	24.95	125.00
EC	08-01-1999	12-31-1999	18.95	105.00
CM	01-01-1999	03-31-1999	24.95	125.00
CM	04-01-1999	07-31-1999	30.95	155.00
CM	08-01-1999	11-30-1999	26.95	131.00
CM	12-01-1999	01-15-2000	28.95	131.00

6.5.5 Customers, Reservations, and Invoices

Customer information must be accessible to both reservations and rentals. We might want to keep track of customers past and present, send out sales literature, or collect on unpaid rentals. This information is in the **Customer** table (Table 13). The **Reservation** table, shown in Table 14, contains data collected by a clerk when a customer reserves a car. The **Invoice** table, shown in Table 15, contains data collected by a clerk first when the vehicle is rented: the date and time in the RentalDate field. Later, when the vehicle is returned, the clerk saves the date and time in the ActReturnDate field.

6.6 VALIDATION RULES

An Access database is able to store and evaluate *validation rules* for tables and fields. If you violate a rule when inserting data into a field or record, a trappable runtime error is generated. This is a great convenience, because it means that programs sharing the same database do not have to employ nearly as much validation code as they would for databases that have no validation rules.

Both tables and fields can have validation rules, but there are fundamental differences between the two:

- A *field-level* validation rule can only make references to built-in functions and itself.

Table 13. The Customer Table.

Name	Type	Comments
CustomerId	Long	Record key
LastName	Text (30)	
FirstName	Text (20)	
Street1	Text (40)	
Street2	Text (40)	Not required
City	Text (20)	
State	Text (15)	
ZipCode	Text (10)	
Country	Text (20)	Not required
HomePhone	Text (20)	

Table 14. The Reservation Table.

Name	Type	Comments
ReservationId	Long	Record key
CustomerId	Long	Foreign key (Customer table)
RentalDate	Date/Time	
ReturnDate	Date/Time	
ModelId	Long	Foreign key (Model table)
DailyRate	Currency	
WeeklyRate	Currency	
CreditCardNum	Text (30)	
Notes	Memo	Not required

- A *record-level* (or *table-level*) validation rule can call built-in functions, and it can also make references to various fields within the same record.

Each validation rule is accompanied by a corresponding *validation text* property. It contains a message that is automatically displayed when a validation error is triggered.

Field-Level Validation Rules. Table 16 contains a list of field-level validation rules that have been placed in the Rentals database. This is provided as a sample, but no doubt there are many other validation rules that would be useful.

Table 15. The Invoice Table.

Name	Type	Comments
InvoiceId	Long	Record key
VehicleId	Long	Foreign key
CustomerId	Long	Foreign key
RentalDate	Date/Time	Date/time rented
ExpReturnDate	Date/Time	Expected return date/time
ActReturnDate	Date/Time	Actual return date/time
AmountDue	Currency	Amount to be paid
AmountPaid	Currency	Amount paid so far
CreditCardInfo	Text (30)	Card number, expiration date
Notes	Memo	Not required

Record-Level Validation Rules. You can create a validation rule that applies to an entire record. For example, in the Price table, we have a rule that makes sure the starting date of each record is less than or equal to its ending date:

Validation rule: `[StartDate]<=[EndDate]`
Validation text: `StartDate must be less than or equal to EndDate`

In a validation rule, field names must be enclosed in square brackets. Table 17 contains several record-level validation rules for the Rentals database. Each rule compares two fields in the same record for reasonable and consistent values.

6.6.1 Creating Validation Rules

To create validation rules in Microsoft Access, open the database, select a particular table, and click the **Design** button. To create a field-level rule, click on the field name and look at the listing of field properties at the bottom of the window. Enter the validation rule here, and add the corresponding validation text in the box just below it. For example, in the Price table, the properties of the DailyRate field are shown in Figure 14.

Microsoft Access provides an *expression builder* tool that activates when you enter a validation rule for a field or record. This tool provides a list of all available built-in functions, which are also explained in the Functions Reference help topic. The built-in functions are grouped into five categories: Conversion, Date/Time, General, Math, and Text.

To create a record-level validation rule, select **Properties** from the **View** menu. Figure 15 shows a validation rule for the Price table that compares the StartDate and EndDate fields when a record is inserted or modified. You can also enter a table description in this window.

Table 16. Field-Level Validation Rules for the Rentals Database.

Field Name	Validation Rule
Vehicle.VehicleId	Between 1 And 9999
Customer.CustomerId	Between 1 And 9999
Reservation.ReservationId	Between 1 And 9999
Invoice.InvoiceId	Between 1 And 9999
Price.DailyRate	Between 1 And 200
Price.WeeklyRate	Between 1 And 1000
Reservation.DailyRate	Between 1 And 200
Reservation.WeeklyRate	Between 1 And 1000
Invoice.AmountDue	> 0

Table 17. Record-Level Validation Rules.

Table	Validation Rule
Reservation	[ReturnDate] >= [RentalDate]
Invoice	[ExpReturnDate] >= [RentalDate]
Price	[StartDate] <= [EndDate]

6.7 TABLE RELATIONS

The Invoice and Reservation tables both contain ID numbers that relate to other tables. For example, the Reservation table contains a CustomerId and a VehicleId. These are called *foreign keys* because they match the primary key fields of other tables. In the Invoice table, shown in Figure 16, the VehicleId field connects to the same field in the Vehicle table. In the latter table, VehicleId is the primary key. We say that a *relation* (or *relationship*) exists between the Vehicle table and Reservation table.

Figure 14. Validation Rule for DailyRate Field.

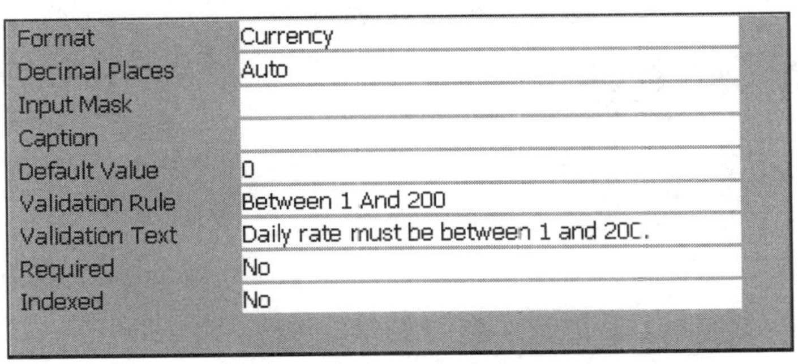

Figure 15. Record-Level Validation Rule.

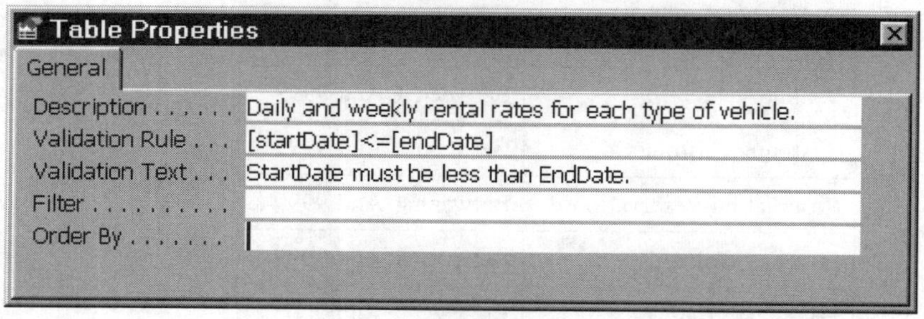

There are two common types of *relations* between database tables, determined by the fields that link the tables together. Let's call the tables *table-x* and *table-y:*

- **One-to-one relation:** Each record in table-x matches only one record in table-y. This relation might be created when part of an existing table is split away and assigned a more restrictive security level.
- **One-to-many relation:** Each record in table-x can match one or more records in table-y. This is probably the most common type of table relation. In the Rentals database, for example, in the Vehicle table, each vehicle ID is unique; but in the Invoice table, the same vehicle ID may appear many times.

Table 18 lists the various relations we have created in this database. In the Primary Table column, the record key field is always the link. For example, each customer ID in the Invoice table matches only one customer ID in the Customer table. When a new reservation is created, we create a corresponding customer record. When an invoice is created, we use the same customer ID from the reservation, which has to match a record in the Customer table.

Joining Tables. Table relations also make it easy to display reports and forms containing joined information from different tables. Suppose we were to create a report based on information from the Invoice table. The **Rental Date** column is from the Invoice table, **LastName, FirstName**, and **phone** are from the Customer table:

Figure 16. Relation Between Invoice and Vehicle Tables.

Invoice Table

InvoiceId	VehicleId
1001	105
1002	101
1003	104
1004	102
1005	103

Vehicle Table

VehicleId	ModelId	CategoryId
100	1	EC
101	4	EC
102	5	MV
103	6	MV
104	3	LX
105	6	MV
106	5	MV
107	5	MV
108	3	LX
109	1	EC

Rental Date	Customer Name	Customer Phone	Vehicle Description
02/01/98	Jackson,Robert	(305)233-4444	Ford Taurus
02/05/98	Chong,Anson	(202)333-1234	Toyota Camry

Retrieving the **Vehicle Description** involves a two-step process: First, the VehicleId from the Invoice table forms a link to the Vehicle table. Then, the ModelId in the Vehicle table forms a link to the Model table.

Referential Integrity Rules. Microsoft Access can enforce referential integrity rules that check for consistency between related tables. Checks of this type happen when a record in a table is added, modified, or deleted. For example, there is a one to many relation between Customer.CustomerId and Invoice.CustomerId. This means that for every value of Invoice.CustomerId, there must be a matching value in the Customer table.

The one-to-many relation between Vehicle and Invoice requires that every VehicleId in the Invoice table must also exist in the Vehicle table. If this rule is not enforced, a record could be inserted into the Invoice table having an unknown or erroneous vehicle ID. This problem would show itself as soon as we tried to print reports, search the database, or join two tables.

6.7.1 Creating Table Relations

In Microsoft Access, select **Relationships** from the **Tools** menu to set a relation between any two tables in the current database. For example, let's create a relation between the Vehicle table and the Invoice table using VehicleId as the linking field. Select the Vehicle table first because VehicleId is its primary key, and click on the Add button. Select the Invoice table the same way. Now the two tables appear in the Relationships window.

- To create a connection between the two tables, drag the mouse from the Vehicle.VehicleId field to the Invoice.VehicleId field. A dialog box immediately appears; place a check next to "Enforce Referential Integrity", as in Figure 17.
- Click on OK, then on Create. Access will shown a line between the tables shows that a one-to-many relationship exists between the two tables (the ***inifinity*** symbol indicates "many"). The Vehicle table has VehicleId as its *primary key,* and the Invoice table has VehicleId as a *foreign key*. Similarly, we would create all of the relationships listed earlier in Table 18.

6.8 DESIGNING THE INTERFACE

Now that we have a reasonably good database design and some sample data for the Stellar Car Rental application, it's time to begin working on the visual interface. Designing a good visual interface is a tricky business, because software users have widely varying opinions about how they want a program to look and behave. Users will have different levels of expertise. Making the software easy to use for beginners should not prevent expert users from working efficiently. The software should be easy to use at all levels.

When we create the user interface for the rental reservation system, we will stick to a fairly standard Windows interface and attempt to make the program easy to use. The

Table 18. Relations in the rentals.mdb Database.

Primary Table.Field	Secondary Table.Field
Category.CategoryId	Vehicle.CategoryId
Category.CategoryId	Reservation.CategoryId
Customer.CustomerId	Invoice.CustomerId
Customer.CustomerId	Reservation.CustomerId
Model.ModelId	Vehicle.ModelId
Vehicle.VehicleId	Invoice.VehicleId
VehicleStatus.VehicleStatusId	Vehicle.VehicleStatusId

reservations agents who use this program will be on the phone with customers, so we will keep in mind the following design goals:

- Keep the amount of typing to a minimum. Because they will be using the software almost continuously, we will try to provide keystrokes that provide command shortcuts.
- They will need to be able to look up information quickly when a customer asks questions about rental rates and availability of vehicles.
- The user might want to display and manage multiple reservation windows at the same time. In that case, we should try to create a reservation class that keeps track of the current state of individual Reservation objects.

6.8.1 Running the Program

When the program starts up, it displays an MDI window with a ToolBar and StatusBar, shown in Figure 18. Only the Open, Exit, and Help buttons are enabled. When the user clicks on **Open** to open a database file, a common dialog control window provides a way to find the file. When the database is open, the remaining buttons on the ToolBar are enabled:

Programming Tip: When creating a relation between two tables in Microsoft Access, you may receive an error message saying that the data in your tables violates the database's referential integrity. For example, in the Vehicle-Invoice relation, some of the VehicleId values in the Invoice table might not have matching values in the Vehicle table. To fix the problem, open both tables, inspect the values, and correct the vehicleId fields until they match. After doing this, try to save the table relation again.

Figure 17. Choosing the Type of Relation.

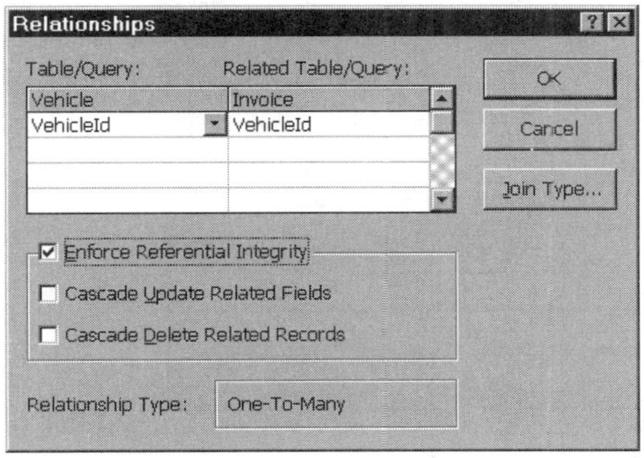

Customer Information Window. If the user clicks on the **Customers** button, a Customer Information window appears, allowing individual customers to be located via their phone numbers (see Figure 19). The user types in an area code and phone number in the box at the top of the window, which the program uses to search for a matching customer record. The user can also create, modify, and save a new customer record in this window.

Reservations Window. When the user clicks on the **Reservations** button in the Main window, the Reservations window appears, shown in Figure 20. If the user clicks on the **New** button to create a new reservation, a new reservation ID is created and inserted into the Reservation ID ComboBox. The **Edit** button lets us modify a reservation. The **Save** button saves the current reservation. The **Find** button searches for a reservation by reservation ID. The **Notes** button displays a TextBox with extra comments about the reservation. We use a CoolBar control to hold both a ToolBar and a ComboBox with the reservation ID numbers.

When the user enters the rental date and selects the type of vehicle to be rented, the daily and weekly rental rates are immediately displayed. If the user enters a rental date that is not listed in the Price table, a message appears in the main window's status bar indicating that rental rates are not available for the requested date.

Rental Rates. The main MDI window also has a ToolBar button labeled **Rates** that provides a quick way for the reservation agent to view a table of rental prices for each type

Figure 18. Stellar Car Rentals, Main Window.

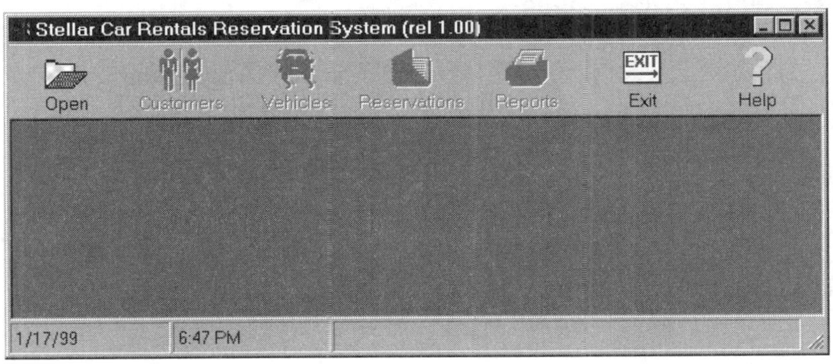

Figure 19. The Customer Information Window.

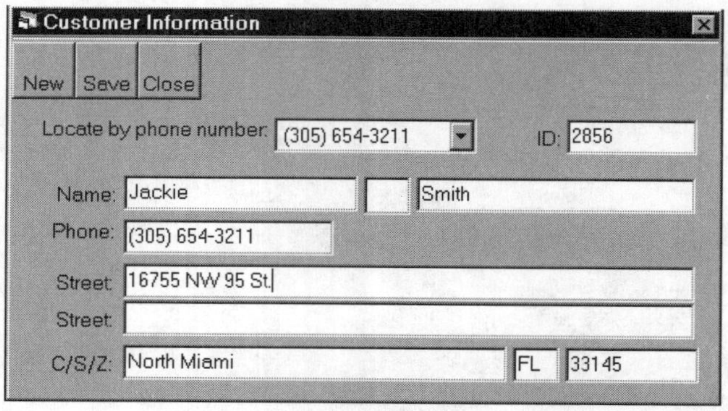

Figure 20. The Reservations Window.

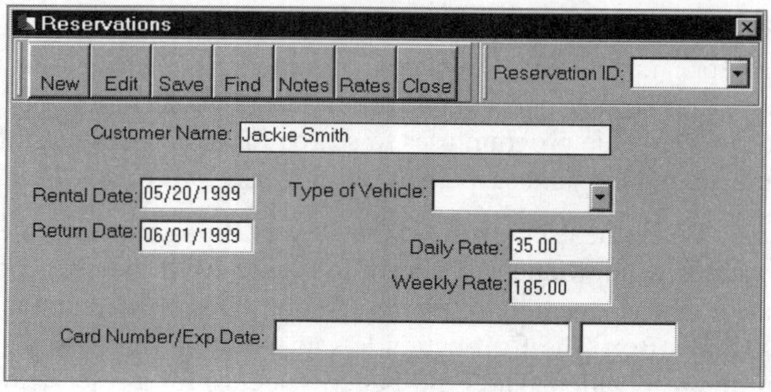

of car and date range. The Rental Prices window in Figure 21 contains an ADO control linked to the Price table, and a DataGrid control to display the data.

Summary. What we've done here is to sketch out an interesting, yet practical database application. Nearly every type of business that deals with customers has either a purchasing or reservation system, where a database must be built from transactions and information retrieved on demand. In the Chapter exercises, you will be asked to write the code for this application, and to expand it further.

Figure 21. Rental Prices Window.

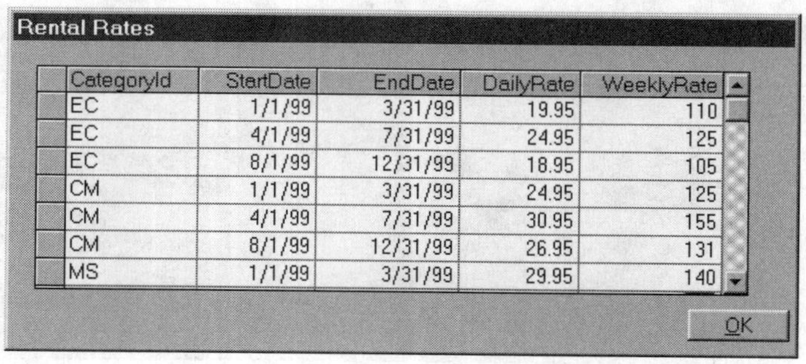

6.9 REVIEW QUESTIONS

1. Describe a relational database management system, including the names of its various components.
2. What is the relationship between a table and a row?
3. What is the relationship between a column and a field?
4. An *index* orders a table according to one or more of the table's fields; these fields are called ______.
5. Can a query be used to update the Recordsource property of an ADO control? Why or why not?
6. Why would a programmer want to create a *view* of a database?
7. What types of rules can be created and saved with a database to help ensure that its data is consistent?
8. What does *one-to-many* mean in relation to a database structure?
9. What advantages does an application-independent design have over an application-driven design?
10. Which database design step suggests that you try to determine which operations will be most critical?
11. Once you have determined the data sources, which database design step follows?
12. What is the name of the process used when creating tables to eliminate redundant data?
13. What do the letters "SQL" stand for, in terms of database languages?
14. What is an *ad-hoc query*?
15. Which two languages make up SQL? Which one is Recordset-returning?
16. What is the purpose of the WHERE clause?
17. What is the purpose of the ORDER BY clause?
18. Name at least two *aggregate* functions.
19. Which part of a SELECT statement is considered the *filter*?
20. In the Employee and Payroll tables that appeared at the beginning of this chapter, which field was common to both tables?
21. Write a SELECT statement that displays all last and first names from the Employee table.
22. Write a SELECT statement that displays fields called **SSN** and **hourlyPay** from a table called **EmployeeData**.
23. Show an example of using a SQL query to create a Recordset in Visual Basic, using a Connection object.
24. Write a SELECT statement that displays only rows of the Payroll table in which the **HourlyRate** field contains a value between 20 and 30.

25. Write a SELECT statement that displays only rows of the Payroll table in which the **HourlyRate** field contains a value between 20 and 30, and **HoursWorked** field is greater than 40.

26. Write a SELECT statement that displays only rows of the Employee table in which the **phone** field contains the digits "2222".

27. Write a SELECT statement that calculates and displays a student's social security number and grade point average (GPA) using the data in the table called **Transcript.** Divide the totalPoints by credits to get the overall GPA:

```
Transcript(SSN,TotalPoints,Credits)
   ("111-44-3232",80,25)
   ("222-32-4444",120,42)
```

28. Write a SELECT statement that displays the SSN and LastName from the Employee table, along with the PaymentDate and HourlyRate from the Payroll table. Use the WHERE clause.

29. Which option in the SELECT statement guarantees that all resulting rows will be different from each other?

30. What is the purpose of the JOIN clause?

31. What is a *Cartesian product* in relation to joins between database tables?

32. What are the three types of *joins* between pairs of tables?

33. Which type of join only includes rows where the joined fields from both tables are equal?

34. What is the general syntax of the UPDATE statement?

35. Write an UPDATE statement for the Payroll table that increases each employee's pay rate by 10%.

36. For the following Department table, write a statement that calculates the percent increase in the credits field between Fall (earlier) and Spring (later):

```
Department(FallCredits,  SpringCredits,  percentChange)
( 480,  560,  0)
( 840,  720,  0)
( 670,  710,  0)
(etc.)
```

37. Write a statement that deletes the Payroll table.

38. Write a statement that deletes an index called ssnNdx from the Payroll table.

39. Write a statement that copies all records from a table called Transcript to a table called Temp.

40. Write a statement that creates an index for the Transcript table that orders records in descending order by the student last names.

41. Write a statement that creates a new table with the following structure: (StudentID - Long, LastName – Char(30), totalCredits - Integer)

6.10 CHAPTER EXERCISES

6.10.1 Stellar Car Rental - 1

MDI with Customer Information. Use the design for the Stellar Car Rental application presented in this chapter as a guide when completing this exercise. Create the main MDI window, with the ToolBar and StatusBar. Implement the Customer Information window, shown earlier in Figure 19. A list of customer phone numbers is loaded into the ComboBox control, and the user can use it to search for a customer. The user can create new customer records, and update changes to existing customers.

6.10.2 Stellar Car Rental - 2

Reservation Window. Continue the program written for the previous exercise. Implement the Reservation window, shown earlier in Figure 20. When the user selects a reservation ID from the ComboBox located on the right side of the CoolBar control, display the reservation in the various Text controls on the Form.

6.10.3 Stellar Car Rental - 3

Vehicle Inventory. Continue the program written for the previous exercise. Implement the **Vehicles** button in the MDI main window. The Stellar Car Rental branch manager needs a list of the complete vehicle inventory, showing the following fields: Vehicle ID, Model, Category, Status. Use a ListView control and display the complete descriptions, shown in Figure 22. Let the user sort on any column, and filter the records by selecting one of three vehicle status values: available, rented, and maintenance.

6.10.4 Stellar Car Rental - 4

Rental Rates. Continue the program written for the previous exercise. Implement the Rental Rates window, which was shown earlier in Figure 21. The window should be displayed when the user clicks on the **Rates** button in the Reservations window.

6.10.5 Stellar Car Rental – 5

SQL Queries. Create SQL queries for each of the following, and activate the queries from a Visual Basic program:

- List all customers who have rented a vehicle between two given dates. Let the user enter the two dates.
- List all invoices where the return date is less than today's date.
- List all reservations where the rental date is equal to today's date.

6.10.6 Stellar Car Rental – 6

SQL Queries. Create SQL queries for each of the following, and activate the queries from a Visual Basic program:

- List all customers who rent luxury cars.
- Count all reservations for a given type of vehicle.

Figure 22. Vehicle Table Query.

VehicleId	Model	Status	Category
100	Chevy Geo	Available	Economy
101	Toyota Tercel	Rented	Compact
102	Plymouth Voyager	Available	Minivan
103	Ford Aerostar	Rented	Minivan
104	Mitsubishi Galant	Available	Luxury
105	Plymouth Voyager	Maintenance	Minivan
106	Ford Aerostar	Rented	Minivan
107	Toyota Previa	Available	Minivan
108	Acura Legend	Available	Luxury
109	Chevy Geo	Maintenance	Economy
110	Lincoln Town Car	Available	Luxury
111	Ford Taurus	Available	Midsize

- List all vehicles whose status is *maintenance*.

6.10.7 Doctors Office Scheduling - 1

Appointment Listing. This exercise is based on the Doctors Office Scheduling programs from the previous chapter's exercises. In the grid that displays all appointments, display the name of each doctor rather than the Doctor ID. Also, display the full name of each patient, rather than the Patient ID. Create a SQL query that joins the Doctors, Patients, and Appointments tables, and assign the query to the RecordSource property of the ADO control. The user must be able to sort by ApptDateTime, Doctor, or Patient.

6.10.8 Searching for Books with SQL

Search for Book Titles. Using the Biblio database supplied with Visual Basic, write a program that lets the user search for book titles using a date range and a partial title string match. Use a DataGrid control to display the matching rows from the table. A sample of the program is shown in Figure 23. In this example, the user has selected all book titles containing "Oracle" published between 1995 and 1999. The program should also display the following text representation of the query just before it executes:

6.10.9 Yachting Regatta Program - 1

MDI Application. The SeaWind Yacht Club keeps track of the results of multiple sailboat races that together make up a single regatta. Write an MDI application that lets the user display and modify information for several races and several sailboats. Create separate MDI child windows for the **RaceInfo** and **BoatInfo** tables. The RaceInfo table's structure is described in Table 19. For now, the Handicap Minutes and Adjusted Time fields should

Table 19. Description of the RaceInfo Table.

Field	Data Type	Description
BoatNumber	Text(3)	Identifies the boat. Matches one of the boat numbers in the BoatInfo file.
RaceNumber	Text(2)	Unique for each race (1..10).
StartingTime	Date/Time	Time when the race started.
FinishingTime	Date/Time	Time when the boat finished the race.
HandicapMinutes	Integer	Number of minutes to be added to the boat's actual completion time.
AdjustedTime	Integer	Length of time taken to complete the race, adjusted by the boat's handicap.
Comments	Memo	Notes concerning special race conditions or pending protests involving this boat.

be set to zero. Create a database table called **BoatInfo** that contains the fields shown in Table 20.

6.10.10 Yachting Regatta Program - 2

Quick Reference to Boat Information. Continue the Yachting Regatta program from the previous exercise. Provide the following additional features:

- When displaying the window containing the race information (RaceInfo records), let the user quickly display information about a single boat by double-clicking on the boat number.

Figure 23. Querying the Biblio Database.

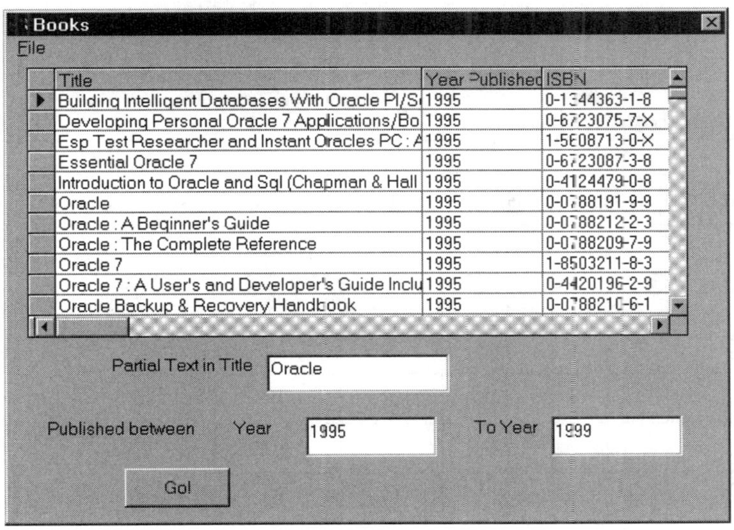

Table 20. BoatInfo Table Description.

Field	Data Type	Description
BoatNumber	Text(3)	Matches boat numbers in the RaceInfo file.
BoatName	Text(20)	The boat's name.
OwnerName	Text(30)	Last name, first initial.
HandicapFactor	Single	0.0 to 2.00, used when calculating the Handicap Minutes in the RaceInfo table.

- Calculate the *handicap minutes* and *adjusted time* for each boat in each race, using the formula described in the next paragraph. Display these values in the *RaceInfo* window (these two fields were originally left empty.)

Handicap. In sailboat races involving boats of different sizes and configurations, boats vary greatly in their speed. Therefore, a handicapping system is used that will give each boat a more or less equal chance of winning the race. In this program, you will calculate the handicap minutes (HCM) for a boat in a particular race by multiplying the scratch boat time (SBT) by the boat's handicap factor (HCF). A fast sailboat would have a large handicap factor, and a slow boat would have a small one. Table 21 contains some examples of calculations. For the same boat, more handicap minutes are applied to a longer race than a shorter one.

6.10.11 Yachting Regatta - 3

Boat Ranking for Each Race. Using the Yachting Regatta programs from the previous exercises, calculate and display the ranking of each boat for each race. For each race, the boat in first place will have the lowest adjusted time. The adjusted time (AT) is calculated from the starting time (ST), finishing time (FT) and handicap minutes (HCM) as follows: AT = (FT - ST) + HCM. For each race, produce a database table such as the one shown in Table 22.

Table 21. Sample Handicaps.

Race #	Boat #	SBT	HCF	HCM
1	1	180	.8	144
1	2	180	.5	90
1	3	180	.1	18
2	1	60	.8	48
2	2	60	.5	30
2	3	60	.1	6

Table 22. Yachting Regatta Boat Ranking.

Boat Name	Rank	Adjusted Time
Blue Star	1	220
Windward Passage	2	270
Ticonderoga	3	275
Kialoa II	4	280
Queen Mab	5	310
Novia del Mar	6	400

7 DataReport, MSHFlexGrid, and MSChart

Chapter Contents

Data Report Designer
- DataReport Objects
- Building a Report Using SQL
- Author Table Example
- Joining the Titles and Publishers Tables
- Reports with Groups
- Grouping by Creating Summary Fields
- Showing Reports from ADO Connections using Program Code
- One Record per Page

Hierarchical FlexGrid Control
- Binding to a DataEnvironment
- Displaying Hierarchical Data in a Report

MSChart Control
- Simple MSChart Example
- MSChart with Labels
- Interactively Filling a Chart at Run Time
- Binding a Chart to an ADO Control

Review Questions
Programming Exercises

7.1 DATA REPORT DESIGNER

(All of the examples in Section 7.1 are from the same Visual Basic project stored in the DataReport directory.)

In this section, we show how to create reports in Visual Basic 6. The Data Report Designer utility is a new feature that first appeared in Visual Basic 6.0, drawing on many of the report design features of Microsoft Access. Crystal Reports, which was shipped with Visual Basic Versions 4 and 5, is no longer bundled with Visual Basic (you can download a copy from their web site).

Before creating a report, you must create a Data Environment, a Connection, and a Command object. If you need help using the Data Environment Designer tool, refer to Section 5.1 in Chapter 5. You also need to add the necessary designer components to your Visual Basic setup. To do this, select **Components** from the **Project** menu and click on the **Designers** tab. Make sure the Data Environment and Data Report items are checked.

The ReportDesigner Toolbox. The report designer toolbox contains six controls that may be placed directly on a report. The specific report design controls appear when you are designing a report, if you click on the **DataReport** Command button at the bottom of the ToolBox window.

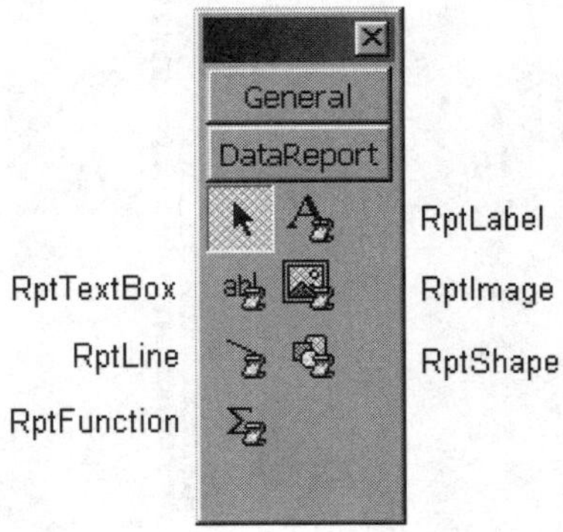

A **Label** (RptLabel) control may contain any characters and is designed to display a field name or title. A **TextBox** (RptTextBox) control must be linked to a field in a Command object, typically a database or query field. It works much the same way as a Label bound to an ADO control on a Visual Basic Form. An **Image** (RptImage) control can hold a graphic such as an icon or bitmap. The **Line** (RptLine) and **Shape** (RptShape) controls display lines and a variety of shapes on the report. A **Function** (RptFunction) control can be configured to automatically calculate a sum, average, count, minimum value, or maximum value.

7.1.1 DataReport Objects

To understand how reports are created in Visual Basic, you have to become familiar with the properties, methods, and events of DataReport objects. Table 1 describes the set of properties that are unique to DataReports. The DataMember and DataSource properties must be initialized at design time unless you plan to create an ADO object at run time and attach it to the report.

Avoiding Errors. At design time, if you set a report's DataMember property to the name of a Command object, and later rename the Command, the report will not run. You must set the report's DataMember property to the new Command name. Similarly, if you alter the attached Command object by renaming columns or changing the selection of columns, any attached reports will not work until the individual report TextBoxes are updated. Some of the more common run time error messages associated with reports are shown in Table 2.

Viewing and Printing Reports. A number of different methods are available for DataReport objects, shown in Table 3.

When a data report is shown, printed, or exported, there are at least two separate steps that Visual Basic goes through:

- **Query:** A SQL query is sent to the data provider. In our examples, the provider is a Jet ADO Database.

Table 1. DataReport Properties.

Property	Description
Caption	Text that appears in the report window title bar.
DataMember	The name of the Command object providing data to the report. If the Command object contains child commands, those commands also provide data.
DataSource	The name of the DataEnvironment object containing the Connection object that generates this report.
GridX, GridY	Specify the horizontal divisions of the alignment grid in design mode. Controls will automatically snap to these grid lines. Larger values for GridX and GridY give you more precise control over the positions of controls.
Margins: TopMargin, BottomMargin, LeftMargin, RightMargin	Sizes of report margins, measured in Twips. For reports displayed on the screen, left and top margins of 600 Twips seem to work well. For output to a printer, the default value of 1440 Twips is appropriate.
ReportWidth	The width of all sections of the report, in Twips.
Title	The title of the report, which shows up when exporting to HTML and when using the Insert Control Command to place a report title in the report heading or page heading area.

Table 2. Data Report Runtime Error Messages.

Error Message	Explanation
"DataField <Command>.<field> not found."	Either the DataMember property or the DataField property of an RptTextBox object in the report is incorrect. The DataMember property must contain the name of a Command object, and the DataField property must contain the name of a field within a Command object.
"Failed getting rowset(s) from current data source."	The report's DataMember property does not contain the name of a Command object in the DataEnvironment named by the report's DataSource property.
"Invalid data source."	The report's DataSource property does not contain the name of a DataEnvironment object.

- **Processing:** The data retrieved by the query is processed by Visual Basic, creating the report in a temporary file. You can monitor the progress of this step by writing code in the report form's **ProcessingTimeout** event handler procedure.

A third step is also required if the report is either printed or exported to a file:

- **Printing/Exporting:** The report is printed on the printer or exported to either a plain text or HTML file. This step is asynchronous, allowing the Visual Basic program to continue doing other event processing. The report is generated as a background process.

Table 3. DataReport Methods.

Method	Description
ExportReport	Export the report to either HTML (for Web pages) or plain text.
Hide	Hide a report window.
PrintReport	Print the report on the default printer.
Refresh	Immediately update a report window.
Show	Display the report in a modeless window. If this Command is issued from a form, the form must also be shown modelessly. This Command requires at least one printer to have been installed on the computer.

You can write code in the report form's **AsyncProgress** event handler procedure to monitor the progress of this step.

Event Sequences. The following events occur, in order, when a report is generated:

- **Initialize**: Occurs after the query has completed.
- **Resize**: Occurs when the report window is displayed and when the window is resized or moved.
- **Activate**: Occurs when the report window becomes the active window.
- **ProcessingTimeout**: Occurs approximately once per second, beginning when the query has completed, and ending when the report has been completely generated.
- **Deactivate**: Occurs if another window has become the active window.
- **QueryClose**: Occurs just before the report window is closed.
- **Terminate**: Occurs when all references to the DataReport have been released.

A DataReport has a code window that can be accessed by double clicking on the report at design time. Any of the seven events just listed can be automatically given an event handler procedure. We can use this to our advantage, for instance, when a report takes a long time to create by showing its progress and allowing the user to cancel the remaining part of the report.

7.1.2 Building a Report Application

In this section, we will build a Visual Basic application that demonstrates a number of different types of reports. Before creating each of the reports, we will build the startup form that launches the reports. There are six Command buttons, one for each report type, plus an Exit button:

1. Authors (all)
2. Titles and ISBN Numbers
3. Titles and their Publishers

4. Titles Grouped by Publisher
5. Books, Listed One per Page
6. User-Selected Books

The following event handler procedures are needed:

```
Private Sub cmdAuthors_Click()
   rptAuthors.Show
End Sub

Private Sub cmdTitles_Click()
   rptTitles.Show
End Sub

Private Sub cmdTitlesAndPublishers_Click()
   rptTitlesAndPublishers.Show
End Sub

Private Sub cmdPublisherGrp_Click()
   rptPublisherGrp.Show
End Sub

Private Sub cmdBooks_Click()
   rptBooks.Show
End Sub

Private Sub cmdUserSelected_Click()
'The frmSelectBooks form must be shown modelessly
'because it will in turn show the data report
'window modelessly.
   frmSelectBooks.Show vbModeless
End Sub

Private Sub cmdExit_Click()
   Unload Me
End Sub
```

Displaying the Report's Progress. If you write code in the report's **ProcessingTimeout** event handler procedure, you can display progress information for the user, and you can cancel a Show, PrintReport, or ExportReport operation in progress. In the following example, we display a ProgressBar control on the program's main form that provides a visual cue to the user that the report is being generated, as in Figure 1.

Of course, we don't know how many pages the report will contain, so if the progress bar fills up, we can clear it and begin filling it again. We also provide a Cancel button so the user can stop generating the report and see only the pages generated so far. The following code, placed in the ProcessingTimeout event handler of the report window, updates the progress bar and checks to see if the user has clicked on the Cancel button:

```
Private Sub DataReport_ProcessingTimeout(ByVal Seconds As Long, _
      Cancel As Boolean, ByVal JobType As _
      MSDataReportLib.AsyncTypeConstants, _
```

Figure 1. Showing a Progress Bar.

```
     ByVal Cookie As Long)

' Update the progress bar on frmMain.
  With frmMain.prgShow
    .Value = (.Value + (.Max / 20)) Mod .Max
  End With
  frmMain.SetFocus      'bring frmMain to the front
  DoEvents              'allow frmMain to be repainted

' Check to see if the user has cancelled the report.
  Cancel = frmMain.CancelReport
End Sub
```

Setting the Cancel property to True automatically stops further report generation. The techniques shown here for canceling the report can be applied to any program that uses the report designer. We must call the DoEvents method when switching focus to another Form within a procedure. Without DoEvents, the Form getting the focus in our example is not repainted until the report is completely finished.

In the **Initialize** event handler of the report Form, we make the progress bar and Cancel button visible on frmMain, and initialize its public CancelReport variable to False:

```
Private Sub DataReport_Initialize()
  With frmMain
    .CancelReport = False
    .cmdCancel.Visible = True
    .prgShow.Visible = True      'enable progress bar
    .prgShow.Value = 0
  End With
End Sub
```

In the **QueryClose** event handler of the DataReport, we hide both the progress bar and Cancel button on frmMain:

```
Private Sub DataReport_QueryClose(Cancel As Integer, _
    CloseMode As Integer)
  With frmMain
    .prgShow.Visible = False
    .cmdCancel.Visible = False
```

```
  End With
End Sub
```

In frmMain, when the user clicks on the Cancel button, we set the public CancelReport variable to True:

```
Public CancelReport As Boolean
Private Sub cmdCancel_Click()
  CancelReport = True
End Sub
```

7.1.3 Author Table Example

In the first few examples in this section of the chapter, we will use the Biblio.mdb database supplied with Visual Basic. Biblio contains several tables relating to books and publishers:

- Authors: ID numbers, names, and birth dates of book authors.
- Publishers: Names and addresses of publishers.
- Titles: Detailed information about individual books, including their ISBN number, title, publisher ID, and year published.
- TitleAuthor: A table that binds ISBN numbers to author ID numbers.

Creating a Data Environment. Let's create a data environment and a Connection to the Biblio database. We carry out the following steps:

1. Create a new project, select the project type as **Data Project**, and rename the form to **frmMain**.
2. Double click on **DataEnvronment1** to open the Data Environment window. Right click on **Connection1**, rename it to Biblio, right click again, and select **Properties**. Click on the **Provider** tab and select "Microsoft Jet 3.51 OLE DB Provider."
3. Click on the **Connection** tab, and locate the Biblio.mdb database. By default, this file is installed in the C:\Program Files\Microsoft Visual Studio\VB98\Biblio.mdb, but the file might be located somewhere else on your computer. Test the connection and close the Properties page.
4. Right click on the **Biblio** Connection and select **Add Command**. Rename the Command to **Authors**.
5. Right click on the **Authors** Command and select **Properties**. Under the **General** tab, set the database object to **Table** and the object name to **Authors**. Click OK to close the Properties window.

Creating a Data Report. After creating a DataEnvironment, a Connection, and a Command object, we can create a new Data Report and attach it to the DataEnvironment. If you create a data project when Visual Basic first starts up, you already have a single empty report object called DataReport1. Otherwise, right click in the Project window, select **Add**, and select **Data Report.** Once a DataReport has been created, the following steps are required:

1. From the Project window, double click on DataReport1 to open the Report Designer window. Bring up its Properties window and set the following values:

Name	rptAuthors
Caption	All Authors
DataSource	DataEnvironment1
DataMember	Authors
Title	Listing of the Author Table

2. Using the mouse, drag the Authors Command object into the Detail area of the report. Click the mouse in the report area to un-select the fields that were just pasted in.
3. Rearrange the text boxes and their labels with the mouse, placing the field labels in the Page Header area, and moving the report text boxes into a horizontal line in the Detail area. (Label controls have dashed-line boxes around them, and TextBox controls have solid line boxes.)
4. Select all of the field labels in the heading area, display the Properties window, and set the Font to Bold.
5. Add a title, date, and page number to the page header area: In the ToolBox window, click on the tab labeled **DataReport** to expose the data report tools. Select the Label tool and place it in the page header area, and set its Caption property to "Complete Listing of the Authors Table". Set its font to 10 point bold.
6. Right click inside the page header area, and select **Insert Control**, and select **Current Page Number**. The symbol **%p** should appear in the header area. Insert another control into the header area, this time a Label. Set its caption to "Page". Insert another control, called "Current Date (Short Format)". It will appear as **%d** in the header area. The report now appears as in Figure 2.
7. Bring up frmMain, insert a new Command button, set its Caption to "AllAuthors Report" and place the following code in its click event hander:

```
rptAuthors.Show    'display the report on the screen
```

8. Make sure frmMain is the Project startup form, and run the program. Click on the Command button, and wait about 10 seconds (on a 350MHz Pentium) for the report to generate itself. Figure 3 shows a sample of the output.

Figure 2. Editing the Report Page Header.

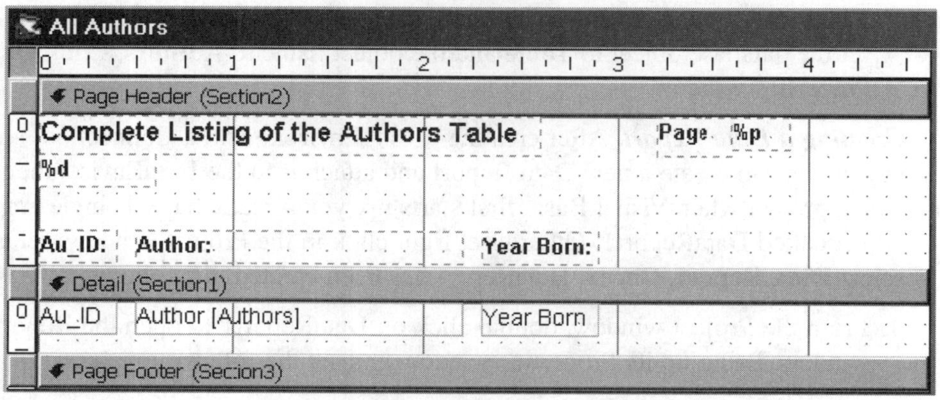

Figure 3. Report Listing All Authors.

Complete Listing of the Authors Table Page 1
11/8/98

Au_ID:	Author:	Year Born:
1	Jacobs, Russell	
2	Metzger, Philip W.	
3	Boddie, John	
4	Sydow, Dan Parks	
6	Lloyd, John	
8	Thiel, James R.	

7.1.4 Building a Report Using SQL

Next, adding to the same program, let's build a report using the Titles table and the SQL Builder. A primary advantage to using SQL is that it gives you the ability to sort and select rows from one or more tables. Each detail line of the report will contain a book title, the year it was published, and the book's ISBN number. The report will be sorted by the book title. We will build this report step-by-step:

1. Create a new Command object: In the Data Environment1 window, right click on **Biblio** (a Connection object), and select **Add Command**. Rename the Command to **Titles**.
2. Attach the Titles table to the new Command object: Right click on the **Titles** Command and select **Properties**. In the General tab of the Properties window, select **SQL Statement** and click on the **SQL Builder** button.
3. When the SQL Builder window opens, look for another window that just appeared, called the **Data View** window. In this window, expand the tree until the **Titles** table name appears.
4. Drag the Titles table from the Data View window into the upper portion of the SQL Builder window. Place checks next to the Title, Year Published, and ISBN fields. These field names appear in the grid area.
5. In the grid area of the SQL Builder, find the **Sort Order** column and click in the row corresponding to the **Title** field. Select '1' for this field, indicating that the primary sort field is **Title**. The following SQL statement should immediately appear in the SQL builder window:

```
SELECT Title, 'Year Published', ISBN
FROM Titles
ORDER BY Title
```

6. Run and test the query by right clicking in the upper pane of the SQL Builder and selecting **Run**. The query data appears in the lower portion of the SQL Builder window. (This gives us a chance to experiment with different queries.)

7. Close the SQL Builder window and answer **Yes** when asked to save. Close the Data View window.
8. In the Project window, right click the **Designers** folder, and select **DataReport** from the **Add** submenu. Set the following report properties:

Name	rptTitles
Caption	rptTitles
DataSource	DataEnvironment1
DataMember	Titles
Title	Listing of Book Titles

9. From the Data Environment window, drag the **Titles** Command object into the detail area of the report. Move the field labels into the page header and align the labels with the fields. Place a Line control on the report in the page header area.
10. To add a heading to the report, right click inside the page header area, and select **Insert Control** and select **Report Title**. Drag the dotted rectangle to the right, making it larger. Set its font to 10 points bold. Set its alignment to centered.
11. Select the report Image control from the ToolBox and place a copy in the report's page heading area. Select the Image and set its Picture property to an icon file of your choice.
12. Place another Command button on frmMain, double click on it, and add a program code statement that will show the report called rptTitles. Run and test the program.

A sample of the report output appears in Figure 4. You can always customize this report by adding a date and time, a page footing, page number, and so on. You can also place shapes such as circles and rectangles on the report.

7.1.5 Joining the Titles and Publishers Tables

Let's join the Titles and Publishers tables so we can view each book title and its publisher name. First, we create a Command object with the following properties:

Property	***Value***
Name	TitlesAndPublishers
Connection	Biblio

Then we use the Query Builder tool to create the following query in the Command object:

```
SELECT Titles.Title, Publishers.Name
  FROM Titles, Publishers
  WHERE Titles.PubID = Publishers.PubID
  AND (Titles.Title < 'C')
  ORDER BY Titles.Title
```

> ***Tip:*** Sometimes, after having selected specific areas of a report, you may want to display the Properties window for the report itself. To do this, click on the report window's caption bar and press F4 to display its properties.

Figure 4. Book Titles Report.

Listing of Book Titles

Title	Year	ISBN
1-2-3 Database Techniques	1990	0-8802234-6-4
1-2-3 For Windows Hyperguide/Book and Disk	1993	1-5676127-1-7
1-2-3 Power MacRos/Book and Disk	1992	0-8802230-4-0
1-2-3 Power Tools (Bantam Power Tools Series	1991	0-5533436-6-X
1-2-3 Release 2.2 PC Tutor/Book and Disk	1990	0-8802262-5-0
1-2-3 Secrets/Book and Disk	1993	1-8780587-3-8
10 Minute Guide to Access	1994	1-5676123-0-X
10 Minute Guide to Access (Best Selling)	1994	1-5676145-0-7
10 Minute Guide to Access for Windows 95	1995	0-7897055-5-9
10 Minute Guide to Act! for Windows	1995	1-5676153-9-2
10 Minute Guide to Lotus Approach	1994	1-5676140-7-8
10 Minute Guide to Lotus Notes for Windows	1993	1-5676117-6-1
10 Minute Guide to Paradox 4	1992	1-5676102-7-7
10 Minute Guide to Paradox for Windows	1994	1-5676149-4-9

We have limited the book titles to the first three letters of the alphabet (plus numbers) to speed up the query. This SQL code was created using Query Builder.

Each book title is joined to its publisher name, the titles are sorted alphabetically, and only titles starting with an ASCII character lower than 'C' are displayed. Figure 5 shows a sample of the Query Builder window with our query.

Let's create a new report called **rptTitlesAndPublishers**, connect it to the TitlesAndPublishers Command, and drag the Title and Publisher fields into the report, and add a nice title. Here are the report properties:

Figure 5. Query Builder, Joining theTitles and Publishers Tables.

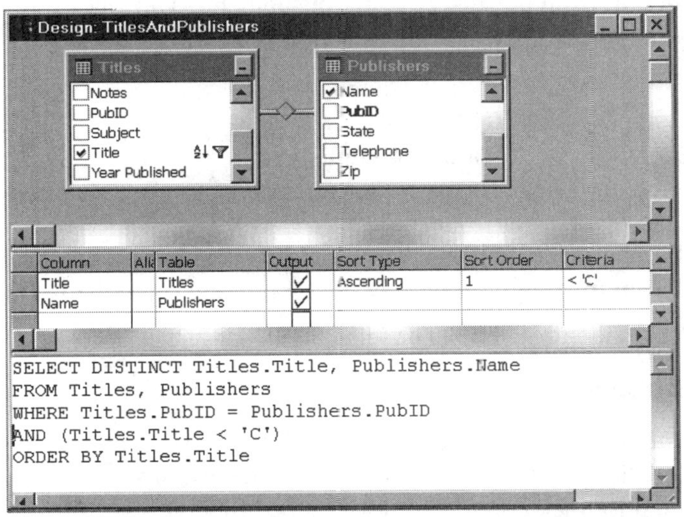

Name	rptTitlesAndPublishers
Caption	rptTitlesAndPublishers
DataSource	DataEnvironment1
DataMember	TitlesAndPublishers
Title	Titles and Publishers

Figure 6 shows a sample of the report output.

Figure 6. Titles and Publishers Report.

Titles and Publishers

Book Title	Publisher
1-2-3 Database	QUE CORP
1-2-3 For Windows	ALPHA BOOKS
1-2-3 Power	QUE CORP
1-2-3 Power Tools	BANTAM
1-2-3 Release 2.2 PC	QUE CORP
1-2-3 Secrets/Book	IDG
10 Minute Guide to	ALPHA BOOKS
10 Minute Guide to	ALPHA BOOKS
10 Minute Guide to	QUE CORP
10 Minute Guide to	ALPHA BOOKS
10 Minute Guide to	ALPHA BOOKS
10 Minute Guide to	ALPHA BOOKS
10 Minute Guide to	ALPHA BOOKS
10 Minute Guide to	ALPHA BOOKS
10 Minute Guide to Q	Sams

Adding a Footer with a Counter. Let's add one more feature to this report, a footer containing a count of the number of books in the table. Right click anywhere in the report designer window and select "Show Report Header/Footer". Right click in the report footer area, and select **Function** from the **Insert Control** submenu. This places a Function in the footer area. Display its properties window and set the following values:

Name	rfnTitleCount
DataField	Title
DataMember	TitlesAndPublishers
Functiontype	rptFuncRCnt (counter)

Place a Label in the report footer just to the right of the counter and set its caption to "Titles were found." Run the program, display the report, and go to the last page where the counter is displayed.

7.1.6 Reports with Groups

The DataEnvironment designer allows Command objects to be combined in hierarchical relationships. Such relationships make it easy to create record groups in reports. For example, if you wanted to track company sales grouped by cities within counties, County would be the parent Command and City would be the child Command:

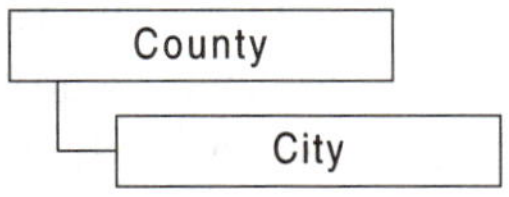

What is needed, then, is a way of relating a Command hierarchy to sections of reports. The lowest level Command (in this case, City) corresponds to the report detail line. The parent Command (County) corresponds to the report's group header and footer sections. Here is a sample report structure, showing levels 1 and 2:

Group Header (County) - 1
Detail (City) - 2
Group Footer (County) - 1

Rules for Placing TextBox Controls. When a Command object corresponds to a report section, any field from the Command may be placed in the report (as a TextBox) in its corresponding section on the report. The field may also be placed at a lower level. A field from the County table, for example, can be placed at level 1 in the group header or footer, or at level 2 in the detail (City) area of the same report.

Carrying the idea of groups a little farther, let's also include Region and State groups at the highest levels. In other words, for every Region, for every State, for every County, there are sales within a City:

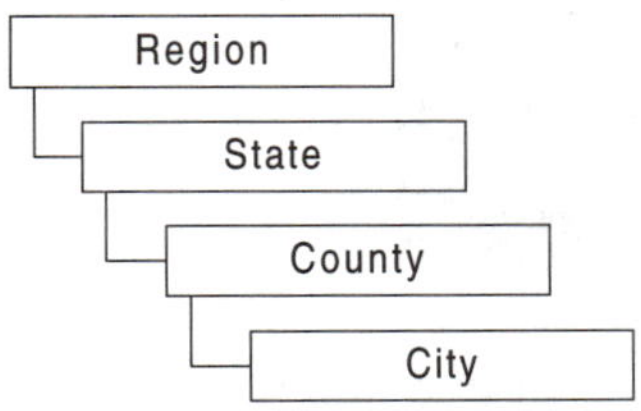

The corresponding report must now have separate group headers and footers for Region (level 1), State (level 2), and County (level 3). Meanwhile, City (level 4) is still in the detail area. Using the rules stated earlier, the Region command can be inserted into any of the areas shown here:

Group Header (Region) - 1
Group Header (State) - 2
Group Header (County) - 3
Detail (City) - 4
Group Footer (County) - 3
Group Footer (State) - 2
Group Footer (Region) - 1

Similarly, the State Command can be inserted into levels 2, 3, and 4. The County Command can be inserted into levels 3 and 4. The City Command can only be inserted into level 4.

Example: Creating a Publishers – Titles Hierarchy. Let's use the techniques shown in this section to create a simple Command hierarchy that involves the Publishers and Titles tables from the Biblio database. To try this, first insert a Command called **Publishers** and attach it to the Publishers table in the database. Then right click on the Publishers Command and add a child Command. Rename the child Command to **Titles** and attach it to the Titles table in the database. If you already have a Command called Titles, an error message will display. Just delete the old Command and try to rename the new Command again. Before closing the Properties window for the Titles Command, click on the **Relation** tab. Click on the **Add** button to relate the Titles Command to its parent Command, Publishers. This is shown in Figure 7. Click OK to close the Properties window.

Figure 7. Relating a Command to its Parent.

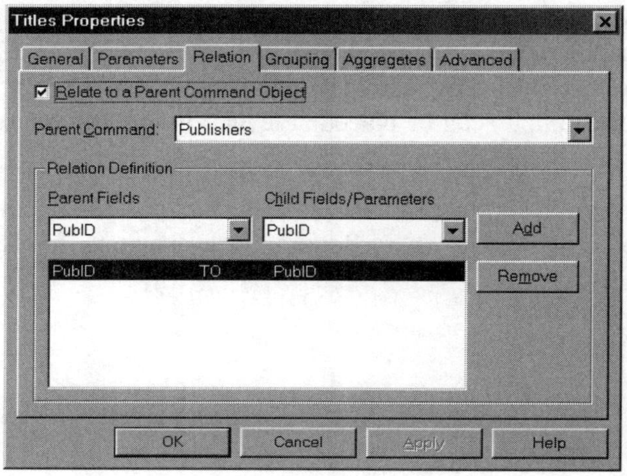

By default, the properties window tries to connect two tables using a field by the same name. If no two such fields exist, you can still select specific field names before clicking on the **Add** button. Notice also that the "Relate to a Parent Command Object" checkbox must be checked. After closing the Properties window for Titles, Figure 8 shows the Data Environment window with the parent-child relationship of **Publishers** and **Titles**. Here is how to create the report, in steps:

1. Create a new DataReport and set the following properties:

Name	rptTitlesWithinPublishers
DataSource	DataEnvironment1
DataMember	Publishers *(the parent Command)*

2. Right click on the report and select "Insert Group Header/Footer." For the moment, we will omit the report header and page header sections of the report. In Figure 9, notice that the Publisher fields have been placed in the group header and footer, and the Title fields have been placed in the detail section. The report's output is also displayed in the figure. As an experiment, try to place a Title field in the group header section. The mouse pointer changes to a *not-permitted* icon (circle with diagonal line), and you cannot insert the field.

Figure 8. Data Environment Showing Publishers, Titles.

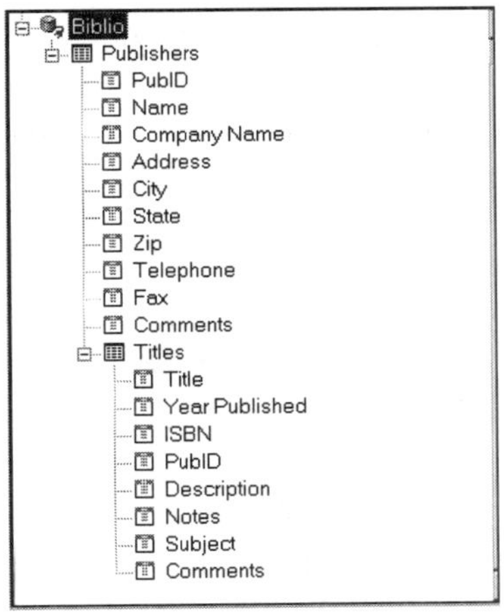

Figure 9. Titles Within Publishers (design and output).

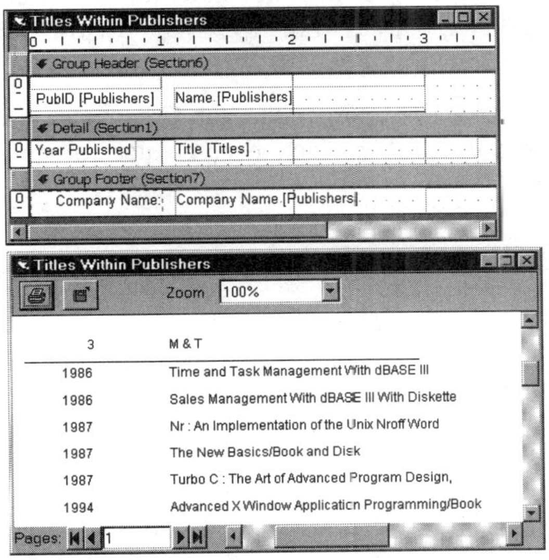

3. Finally, to display this report, add a Command button to the form and place the following code in its Click event:

```
rptTitlesWithinPublishers.Show
```

Note: Always set the DataSource and DataMember properties before adding fields to a report. Otherwise, the report designer will not prevent you from inserting fields in the wrong report sections. This causes a run time error later when you try to show the report.

7.1.7 Grouping by Creating Summary Fields

In addition to grouping using hierarchical Command objects, it is also possible to use the properties in a single Command object to create summaries. Using the Biblio database, for example, let's create a report that groups book titles by publisher and shows the total number of books published in each group. This is done using a Command property called **Grouping**. Again, we will do this in five steps:

1. Delete the existing Publishers command, and create a new Command object by the same name. Insert an SQL query that joins the Publishers and Titles tables using the Publisher ID, selects only book titles beginning with a value less than "C", and sorts the result by both publisher and book title:

```
SELECT DISTINCT Publishers.Name AS 'Publisher Name',
  Titles.Title AS 'Book Title'
  FROM Titles, Publishers
  WHERE Titles.PubID = Publishers.PubID
  AND (Titles.Title < 'C')
  ORDER BY Publishers.Name, Titles.Title
```

Notice that we created an alias name for Titles.Tile called "Book Title", and an alias for Publishers.Name called "Publisher Name".

2. Also in the Properties window, select the **Grouping** tab, place a check next to "Group Command Object", and set the Grouping Command Name to **PublisherGrp.** Select **Publisher Name** in the left ListBox, copy it to the right-hand ListBox. The Grouping properties panel should now apear as in Figure 10.
3. Click OK to close the Properties window. Notice that the Command object has automatically been renamed, and separate folders have been created for summary fields and detail fields:

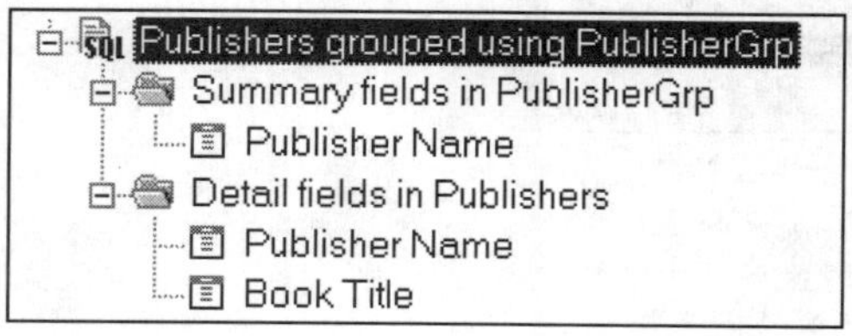

Figure 10. Grouping Properties Panel.

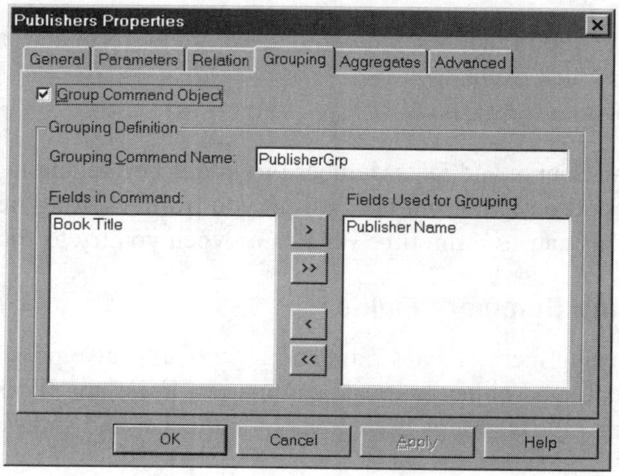

4. Create a new data report and set the following properties:

Name	rptPublisherGrp
Caption	Group Titles by Publisher
DataSource	DataEnvironment1
DataMember	PublisherGrp
Title	Grouping Titles by Publisher

5. Open the report designer window and make sure the Group Header/Footer is visible. If it is not, right click on the report and select **Insert Group Header/Footer**. In the Data Environment, drag **Publisher Name** from the **Summary Fields** folder to the group header area of the report. Drag the **Book Title** field from your Command object to the detail area of the report. Rearrange the labels, draw a horizontal line, and your report should look like the one in Figure 11. The report is launched from the "Titles Grouped by Publisher" button on the main form, using the following Click event handler:

```
Private Sub cmdPublisherGrp_Click()
   rptPublisherGrp.Show
End Sub
```

Figure 11. Grouping Titles by Publisher.

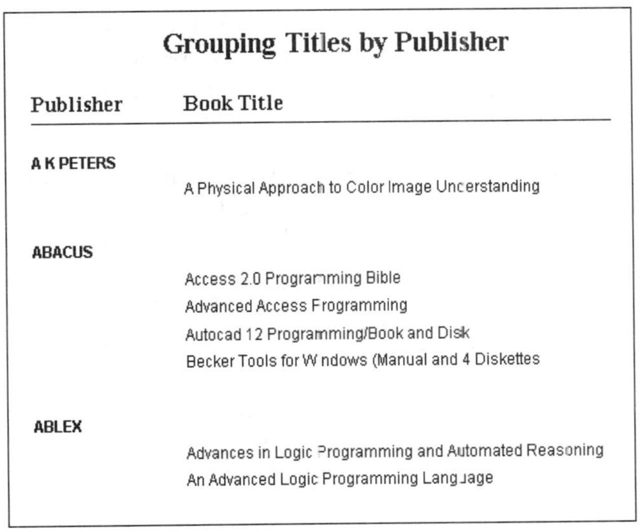

Grouping Titles by Publisher

Publisher	Book Title
A K PETERS	
	A Physical Approach to Color Image Understanding
ABACUS	
	Access 2.0 Programming Bible
	Advanced Access Programming
	Autocad 12 Programming/Book and Disk
	Becker Tools for Windows (Manual and 4 Diskettes
ABLEX	
	Advances in Logic Programming and Automated Reasoning
	An Advanced Logic Programming Language

7.1.8 Showing Reports from ADO Connections in Program Code

It often happens that you need to use SQL to select and order records, but part of the query depends on user input. The input might be stored in Text controls and Option buttons, for example. This means that we have to pass the SQL string to a Connection object and use the Connection to display a report.

You can create an ADO data Connection object at run time, pass it a Connection string containing the database type and file path, and open the Connection. This approach gives you the flexibility to modify queries at run time based on user input. For example, using the Biblio database, the user might want to print only titles published after 1995. The following selection screen could be used:

Designing the Report. The DataReport designer lets you insert TextBoxes in a report without binding them to specific Command objects. You must, however, assign a value to the **DataField** property of each TextBox. In our sample report, the DataField values are BookTitle, Year, and Publisher:

There is also a report field (shown here as "%i") that displays the contents of the **Title** property at run time. When the report is shown, we have to match up fields from the SQL query with the DataField values we have just described. Figure 12 shows a sample report using the user's criteria.

Program Code. In the program code, we have a number of tasks to take care of: Create the Connection, open a Recordset using a query, assign the Recordset to the DataSource property of the report, and show the report:

```
Private mstrSQL As String          'SQL query
Private mstrOp As String           'operator
Private cnBiblio As ADODB.Connection
```

In Form_Load, we create and open the Connection, using a filename from frmMain:

Figure 12. Report Using Selection Criteria.

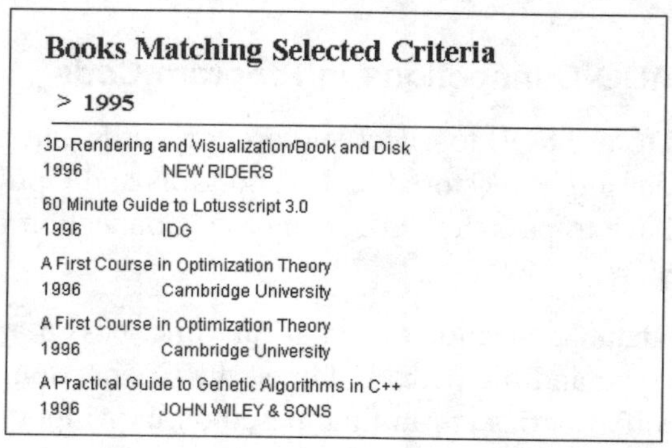

```
Private Sub Form_Load()
  Set cnBiblio = New ADODB.Connection
  cnBiblio.ConnectionString = "Provider = " _
    & "Microsoft.Jet.OLEDB.3.51; " _
    & "Data Source =" & frmMain.DbaseFileName
  cnBiblio.Open
  mstrOp = " < "
End Sub
```

When the user selects one of the three relational operators with an OptionButton control array, we assign an appropriate value to the mstrOp variable:

```
Private Sub optOperator_Click(Index As Integer)
  Select Case Index
    Case 0:
      mstrOp = " < "
    Case 1:
      mstrOp = " = "
    Case 2:
      mstrOp = " > "
  End Select
End Sub
```

When the user clicks on the **Search** button, its Click event handler creates an SQL query that incorporates the relational operator (mstrOp) and the year (txtYear.Text) selected by the user. Notice that alias names were created that exactly match the DataField properties we assigned to the rptTextBox controls on the report (Year, BookTitle, Publisher):

```
Private Sub cmdSearchYear_Click()
  mstrSQL = "SELECT DISTINCTROW Titles.[Year Published] " _
    & "AS Year, Titles.Title AS BookTitle, " _
    & "Publishers.Name AS Publisher " _
    & "From Publishers INNER JOIN Titles " _
    & "ON Publishers.PubID = Titles.PubID " _
    & "WHERE [Year Published] " _
    & mstrOp & txtYear.Text _
    & " ORDER BY Title"
```

Still in the same procedure, we execute the query using the Connection object, assign the resulting Recordset to the DataSource property of the report (rptSelectBooks), and show the report:

```
  With rptSelectBooks
    Set .DataSource = cnBiblio.Execute(mstrSQL)
    .Title = mstrOp & " " & txtYear.Text
    .Show
  End With
End Sub     '(end of cmdSearchYear_Click)
```

It turns out that if you try to use actual table field names such as **Titles.Title** in the DataField properties of rptTextBox controls, the DataReport generates a run time error. This is probably because we have not initialized the DataMember property of each control to an existing Command object. In any event, that is why we created an alias for each field displayed by the query in this example.

7.1.9 One Record Per Page

Sometimes it is useful to display a single record on each page of a report. Let's try this, using the Titles table from the Biblio database. Create a Command called **Books** and attach the following SQL query that selects books published after 1998 with a price less than $30:

```
SELECT * FROM Titles
   WHERE (Val(Description) < 30.00)
   AND (Val(Description) > 0)
   AND 'Year Published' > 1998
   ORDER BY Title
```

Create a report, call it **rptBooks**, and attach it to the Books query. Drag the Command object into the detail line area. Assign a large font to the book's Title property. In the Detail area of the report, set the **ForcePageBreak** property to **rptPageBreakAfter**. This tells the report to insert a page break after each book. Figure 13 show a sample of the first page of the output.

Figure 13. Sample First Page, Books Report.

Harvard Graphics Tips and Tricks

Year Published:	1999
ISBN:	0-7821102-1-5
PubID:	722
Description:	25
Notes:	
Subject:	
Comments:	{}

7.2 HIERARCHICAL FLEXGRID CONTROL

The Hierarchical FlexGrid control, an MSHFlexGrid object, displays Recordset data in a grid-like format. Similar to the DataGrid control, it has one important advantage: it can display hierarchical relationships between database tables. For example, we will show how to display a list of publishers from the Biblio database in the first column of an MSHFlexGrid. Then, for each publisher, we will show a list of books produced by each publisher in subsequent columns.

The parallel between this control and the TreeView control is readily apparent. The TreeView works alongside the ListView to display detailed information in a hierarchy. The Hierarchical FlexGrid, on the other hand, incorporates the detail view directly into its structure.

Unlike the DataGrid control, the Hierarchical FlexGrid does not allow users to interactively edit its contents. We will show how you can work around this restriction, by displaying a TextBox control exactly on top of a selected grid cell. The cell contents can be saved in the underlying Recordset, fooling users into believing they are interactively editing grid cells.

7.2.1 Binding to a Data Environment

(samples: MSHFlexGrid)

In this section, we will take you through a series of steps that create a Data Environment, a Connection, and two Command objects. We will attach the Command objects to a Hierarchical FlexGrid using the following steps:

1. Open a new project, and select **Data Project** from Project Type dialog box. Double click **DataEnvironment1**, shown in Figure 14.
2. Select **Connection1** and press F4 to display the Properties window. Change its Name property to **cnBiblio**. Right click cnBiblio and select **Properties**. In the Data Link Properties dialog box, click on the **Provider** tab and select the Microsoft Jet 3.51 OLE DB Provider and click the **Next** button. Navigate to the Biblio.mdb file's location. Click the **Test Connection** button, wait for the confirmation message, and click the **OK** button.
3. Right click **cnBiblio** and select **Add Command**. Rename Command1 to **cmPublishers**. Right click cmPublishers and click **Properties**, as in Figure 15. In the **Database Object** entry, select **Table** from the dropdown list. In the **Object Name** entry, select **Publishers** from the dropdown list. Click the **OK** button to save your changes.
4. Right click on **cmPublishers** to display a shortcut menu and select **Add Child Command**. Rename the new Command object to **cmTitles**. Display the cmTitles Properties window. In the **Database Object** entry, select **Table** from the dropdown list. In the **Object Name** entry, select **Titles** from the dropdown list. Click the **Apply** button to save your changes and leave the window open. Select the **Relation** tab and click the **Add** button to add PubID, which is called the *relation definition*, or common field. Click the **Apply** button (see Figure 16).

We have just created a hierarchical relationship between the Publishers and Titles tables, using the PubID field. The Publishers table is the parent of the Titles table, shown in

Figure 14. Building the DataEnvironment.

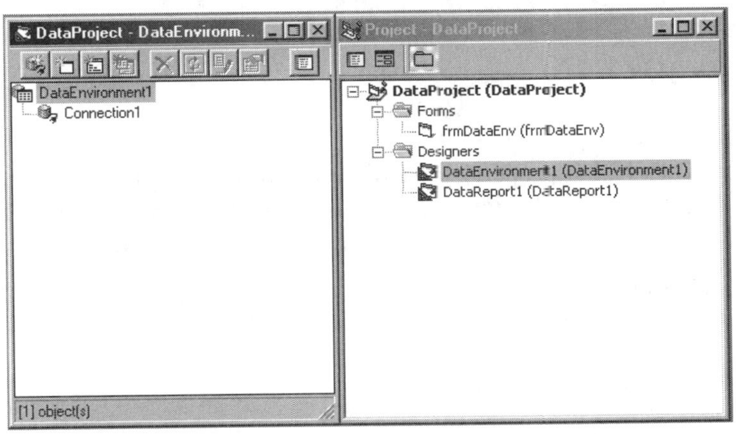

Figure 15. Modifying cmPublishers Properties.

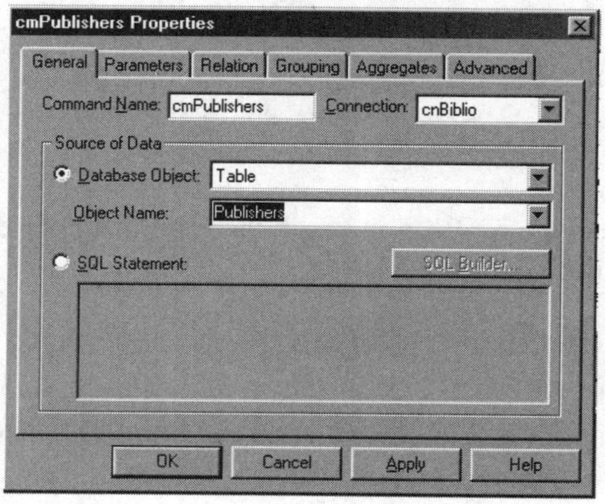

Figure 16. Setting the Relation between Publishers and Titles.

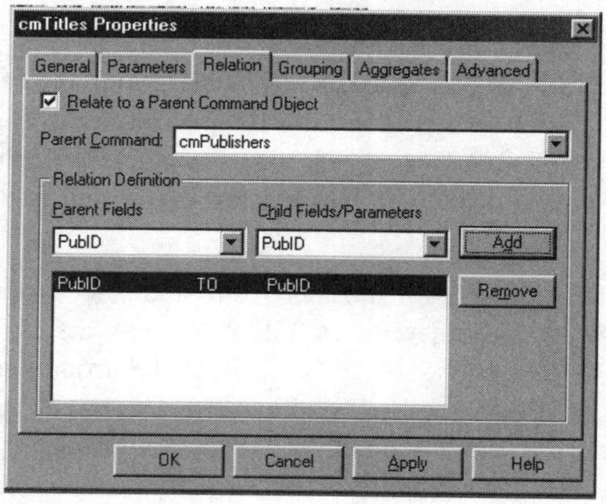

Figure 17. At the same time, for each publisher, there are multiple titles, creating a *one-to-many* relation. Let's create a column that shows the number of books produced by each publisher. Display the Properties window for cmPublishers. Select the **Aggregates** tab, click the **Add** button, as in Figure 18. Input the following properties:

Name	TotalBooks
Function	Count
Aggregates On	cmTitles
Field	Title

Set the form's Name property to **frmMain**. Select Components from the Properties window and select **Microsoft Hierarchical FlexGrid Control 6.0 (OLE DB)**. Place an MSHFlexGrid control on the Form and set the following properties:

DataEnvironment:

Name	deHFlexGrid

MSHFlexGrid:

Name	MSHFlexGrid1
DataSource	deHFlexGrid
DataMember	cmPublishers
AllowUserResizing	flexResizeColumn

DataReport:

Name	drHFlexGrid

Figure 17. Command Hierarchy, Publishers and Titles.

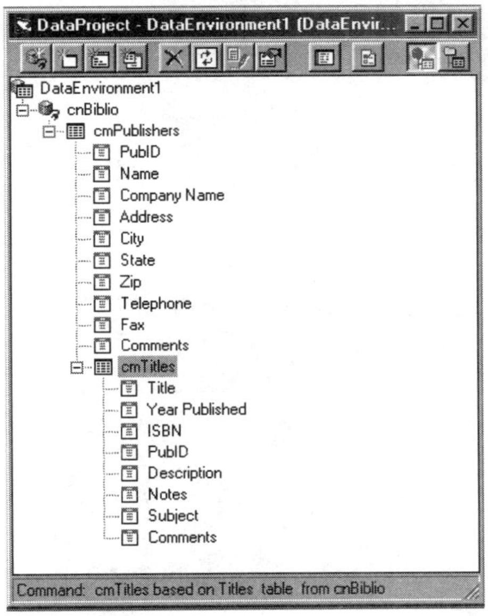

Display the MSHFlexGrid Properties window, click on **Custom**, and select the **Bands** tab (*bands* are grid report columns). Select **Company Name** and **TotalBooks** fields for Band 0, as in Figure 19. Select the **Title, Year Published, ISBN,** and **Subject** fields for Band 1.

Run the program, as in Figure 20. Alongside each publisher appears the aggregate column we created called **TotalBooks**. If you click on the small plus sign (+) next to any publisher name, a list of books produced by the publisher appears in the Title column. If you click on the same icon, the list of books disappears.

7.2.2 Properties and Methods

Now that you have used the MSHFlexGrid control, this would be a good time to become familiar with its more important properties:

- **AllowBigSelection**: Sets or returns a value that specifies whether or not clicking on a column or row header should cause the entire column or row to be selected.

Figure 18. Creating an Aggregates Function.

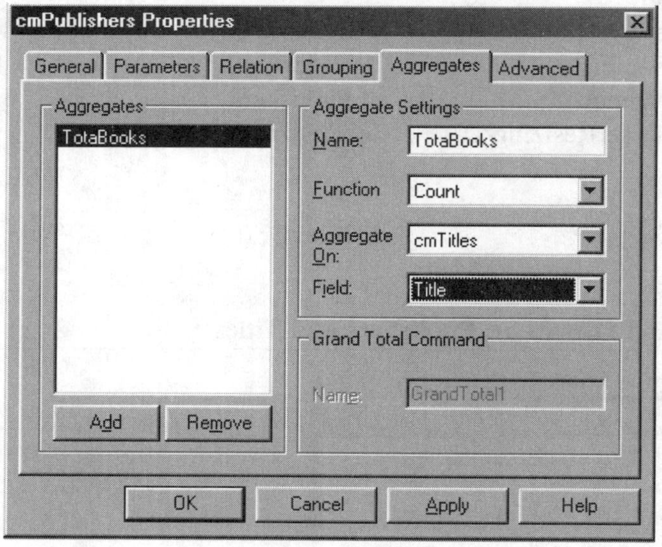

Figure 19. Configuring Band 0.

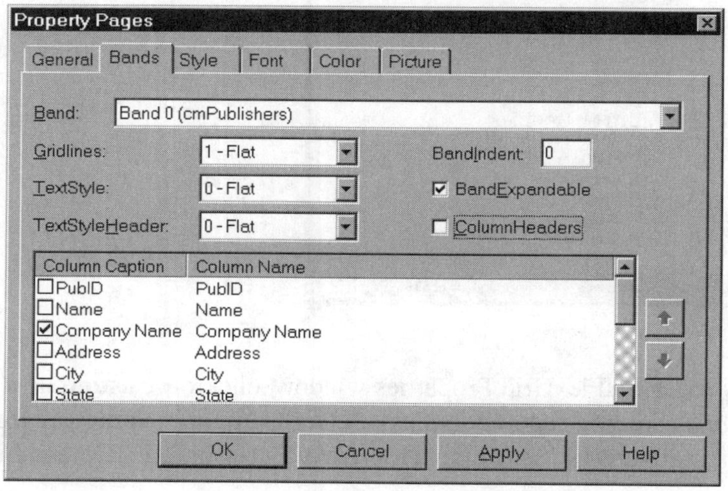

- **AllowUserResizing**: Sets or returns a value that specifies whether or not the user can use the mouse to resize rows and columns in the grid.
- **BackColor**: Sets or returns the background color of all non-fixed cells in the grid.
- **BandDisplay**: Specifies whether the bands display horizontally or vertically within the grid.
- **BandExpandable**: Sets or returns a value that determines whether the current band can be expanded and collapsed.
- **BandIndent**: Specifies the number of columns to indent a band.

Figure 20. Sample MSHGrid Output.

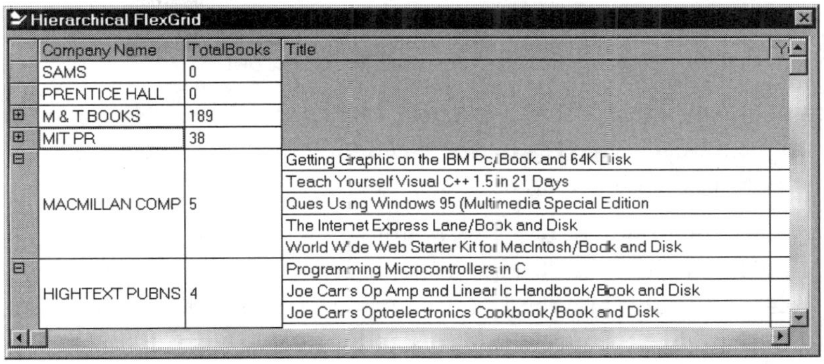

- **CellBackColor**: Sets or returns the background color of individual non-fixed cells in the grid.
- **CellPicture**: Sets or returns an image to be displayed in the current cell. Not available at design time.
- **FixedCols**: Sets or returns the total number of fixed columns in the grid.
- **ColWidth**: Sets or returns the width of a column, in twips, in the specified band.
- **DataField**: Sets or returns the name of the field bound to the specified column in the specified band.
- **FillStyle**: Sets or returns a value that determines whether setting the Text property or one of the cell formatting properties applies the change to all selected cells, or just to the active cell in the grid.
- **RowHeight**: Sets or returns the height of the specified rows, in twips.
- **Text**: Sets or returns the text in a cell or range of cells.

Here is a list of the MSHFlexGrid's more important methods:

- **AddItem**: Adds a row to the HFlexGrid
- **Clear**: Clears the contents (all text, pictures, and cell formatting) of the grid. Does not affect the number of rows and columns within the grid.
- **ClearStructure**: Clears any structure (mapping information) from the grid.
- **CollapseAll**: Collapses all rows of the specified band within the grid.
- **ExpandAll**: Expands all rows of the specified band within the grid.
- **RemoveItem**: Removes a row from a grid at run time.

7.2.3 Displaying Hierarchical Data in a Report

In this section, we will create a DataReport from the MSHFlexGrid data created in the previous section. Here's what we need to do, in five steps:

1. In the Project Explorer window, double click drHFlexGrid (a Data Designer object).

2. Click the title bar of DataReport1 and press F4 to display its Properties window. Set the DataSource property to deHFlexGrid, set the DataMember property to cmPublishers (the parent Command), set the Name property to drHFlexGrid, and set the Caption property to "Publishers and Titles Report".

3. Right click anywhere inside the report window and select **Retrieve Structure** from the pop-up menu. Click the **Yes** button when the message "Replacing existing report layout with new data hierarchy?" appears.

4. In the Data Environment window, double click deHFlexGrid and drag **CompanyName** and **TotalBooks** into the Group Header section of the report window. Drag **Title, ISBN** and **Year Published** into the Detail section. Using the tools in the Data Report Toolbox window, rearrange the report controls and create a report title. The report design is shown in Figure 21.

5. Add an ImageList, a ToolBar, and two CommandButtons to the program's main Form. The Form_Load procedure sets the widths of the columns in the MSHFlexGrid, and the ButtonClick procedure shows the DataReport when the user clicks on the **Reports** button. Insert the following code:

```
Private Sub Form_Load()
  MSHFlexGrid1.ColWidth(0) = 300
  MSHFlexGrid1.ColWidth(1) = 1500
  MSHFlexGrid1.ColWidth(2) = 1000
End Sub

Private Sub Toolbar1_ButtonClick(ByVal Button _
            As MSComctlLib.Button)
  Select Case Button.Key
    Case "Reports"
      drHFlexGrid.Show
    Case "Exit"
      Unload Me
  End Select
End Sub
```

The program is now ready to run and display the report.

Figure 21. Publishers and Titles Report.

7.3 MSCHART CONTROL

Perhaps the most impressive-looking ActiveX control available in Visual Basic is the Microsoft Chart (MSChart) control. It takes nearly all the work out of displaying line charts, two- and three-dimensional bar charts, area graphcs, pie charts, and so on. You can use it to display charts both at design time and at run time. The most important enhancement is that it can be bound to an ADO data source.

7.3.1 Simple MSChart Example

(Samples: ChartSimple)

In this section, we will show how to assign data to the MSChart control at run time, using Arrays and the ChartData Property. First, we create a standard EXE Project, and place a check next to **Microsoft Chart Control 6.0** in the **Project > Components** menu. Add an MSChart control named MSChart1 to the Form. Insert the following code into the Form_Load procedure:

```
Private Sub Form_Load()
'Use a one-dimensional Variant array to
'hold the chart data.
  Dim arrProfit(1 To 12) As Variant
  Dim i As Integer
  For i = 1 To 12
    arrProfit(i) = i * 2
  Next i
  MSChart1.ChartData = arrProfit
End Sub
```

Run the program and view the data shown in Figure 22. The chart displays a simulated 12 months of profit in millions of dollars for a ficticious Internet startup company. The labels for each month are missing from the chart, but we will add them during the next step.

Figure 22. MSChart, Simple Example.

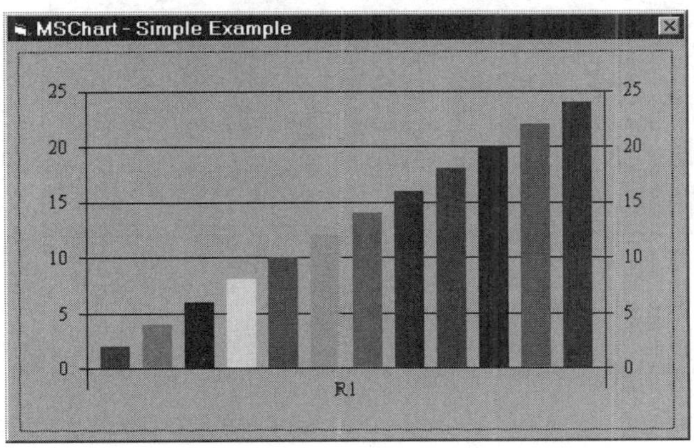

7.3.2 MSChart with Labels

(Samples: ChartLabels)

Let's add labels to the X-Axis of our chart. First, we create a multidimensional array. The first series is assigned strings that become labels on the chart's X-Axis. Insert the following code on the Form_Load procedure:

```
Private Sub Form_Load()
'Use a two-dimensional Variant array to hold the generated MSChart
'data. The first array series holds the labels for the X-Axis.
    Dim arrProfit(1 To 12, 1 To 2) As Variant
    Dim i As Integer
    arrProfit(1, 1) = "Jan"
    arrProfit(2, 1) = "Feb"
    arrProfit(3, 1) = "Mar"
    arrProfit(4, 1) = "Apr"
    arrProfit(5, 1) = "May"
    arrProfit(6, 1) = "Jun"
    arrProfit(7, 1) = "Jul"
    arrProfit(8, 1) = "Aug"
    arrProfit(9, 1) = "Sep"
    arrProfit(10, 1) = "Oct"
    arrProfit(11, 1) = "Nov"
    arrProfit(12, 1) = "Dec"
    For i = 1 To 12
     arrProfit(i, 2) = i * 2
    Next i
    MSChart1.ChartData = arrProfit
End Sub
```

When you run the program, you should see the chart shown in Figure 23.

Figure 23. MSChart with X-Axis Labels.

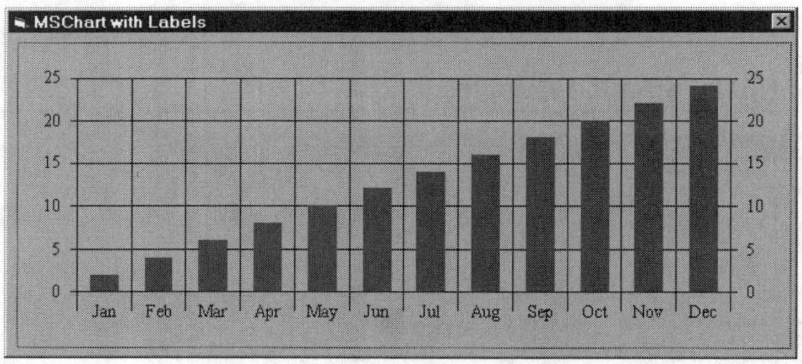

7.3.3 Interactively Filling a Chart at Run Time

(samples: ChartInteractive)

Let's create a program that fills an MSChart control at run time, using interactive input from the user. Figure 24 shows the main window at design time. We display TextBox arrays at the top of the window to get input from the user, in the form of profits for each quarter of the year, for Divisions A, B, and C. The form contains an MSChart control at the bottom that displays the data entered by the user. OptionButtons and a ComboBox let the user select the type of graph to display.

Properties. The following are various properties that must be set at design time:

Label1 (Label)

- Index 0
- Caption ""
- Index 3
- Caption Third Quarter
- Index 4
- Caption Fourth Quarter
- Index 5
- Caption Division A
- Index 6
- Caption Division B
- Index 7
- Caption Division C
- Index 8
- Caption Total

lblTotal (Label)

- Index 0
- Index 1
- Index 2
- Index 3

txtDivisionA (TextBox)

- Index 0
- Index 1
- Index 2
- Index 3

Figure 24. MSChart RunTime Project Interface.

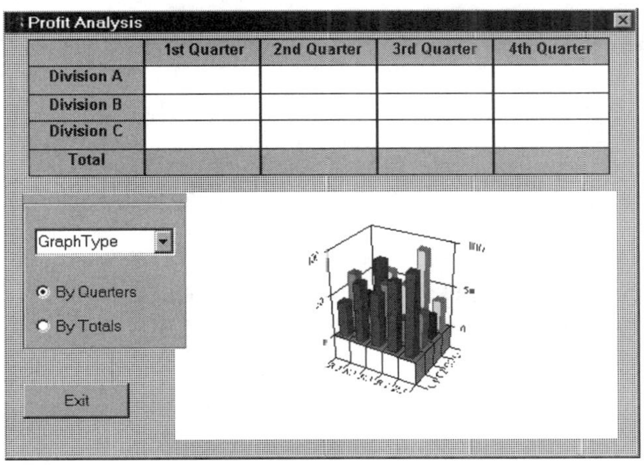

txtDivisionB (TextBox)
  Index 0
  Index 1
  Index 2
  Index 3
txtDivisionC (TextBox)
  Index 0
  Index 1
  Index 2
  Index 3

cboGraphType (ComboBox)

optByQuarters (OptionButton)

optByTotal (OptionButton)

MSChart1 (MSChart)

Program Code. The following is a complete listing of the program's source code. First, we declare the arrays needed to hold the data that will be displayed by the chart:

```
Option Explicit
'Four series of data are required for the chart:
'Series 0 for labels, Series 1 for Division A,
'Series 2 for Division B, and Series 3 for Division C.
Private arrProfit(0 To 3, 0 To 3) As Variant

'Two series of data are required for the totals:
'Series 0 for the labels, and Series 1 for the totals.
Private arrTotal(0 To 3, 0 To 1) As Variant
```

The **cboGraphType_Click** procedure modifies the ChartType property, based on the user's ComboBox selection. The ListIndex property of the ComboBox happens to match the constants used by the MSChart's ChartType property, except for the 10th entry, which must be matched to a ChartType value of 14:

```
Private Sub cboGraphType_Click()
  Dim intGraphType As Integer

  If cboGraphType.ListIndex = 10 Then
    intGraphType = 14
  Else
    intGraphType = cboGraphType.ListIndex
  End If

  MSChart.ChartType = intGraphType
  If optByQuarters.Value = True Then
    ByQuarters
  Else
```

```
    ByTotals
  End If
End Sub
```

Form_Load sets the default ChartType to a 2D Bar chart:

```
Private Sub Form_Load()
  cboGraphType.ListIndex = 1
End Sub
```

When the user clicks on one of the OptionButtons, we call the appropriate graphics procedures. You can see samples of both in Figures 25 and 26.

In the **Change** event handler for the txtDivisionA TextBox, we verify that a numeric value was entered, assign the value to the corresponding position in the arrProfit array, and calculate the total for the current quarter. The graph is replotted:

```
Private Sub txtDivisionA_Change(Index As Integer)
  If Not (txtDivisionA(Index).Text = "" _
  Or txtDivisionA(Index).Text = "-") Then
    If IsNumeric(txtDivisionA(Index)) = False Then
      MsgBox "You must enter a numeric value"
      txtDivisionA(Index).Text = ""
      Exit Sub
    End If
  End If

  'Assign array with the entered value from txtDivisionA:
  arrProfit(Index, 1) = Val(txtDivisionA(Index).Text)

  'Calculate the total for the Current quarter.
  CalculateTotal

  'Plot the input data.
  cboGraphType_Click
End Sub
```

The same types of operations are performed when the user changes the amounts for Divisions B and C:

```
Private Sub txtDivisionB_Change(Index As Integer)
  If Not (txtDivisionB(Index).Text = "" _
  Or txtDivisionB(Index).Text = "-") Then
    If IsNumeric(txtDivisionB(Index)) = False Then
      MsgBox "You must enter a numeric value"
      txtDivisionB(Index).Text = ""
      Exit Sub
    End If
  End If
  arrProfit(Index, 2) = Val(txtDivisionB(Index).Text)
  CalculateTotal
  cboGraphType_Click
End Sub
```

Figure 25. Displaying a 2D Bar Chart by Quarter.

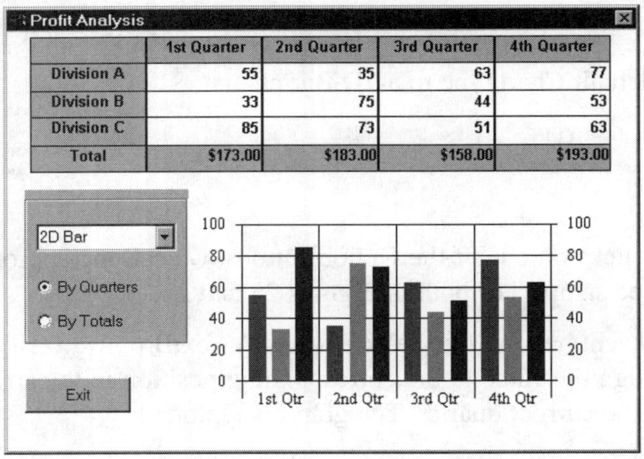

Figure 26. Displaying a 2D Bar Chart Totals.

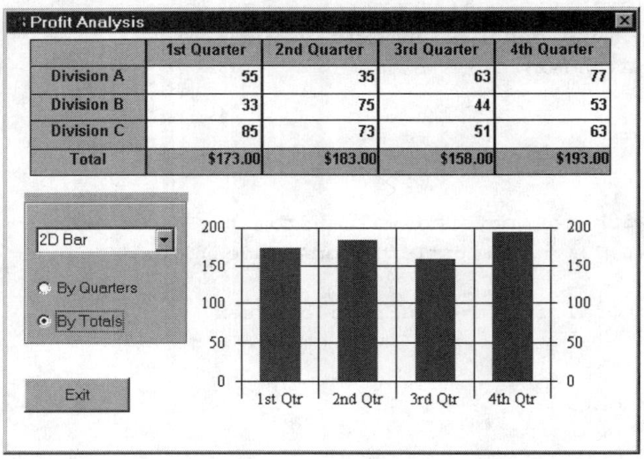


```
Private Sub txtDivisionC_Change(Index As Integer)
  If Not (txtDivisionC(Index).Text = "" _
  Or txtDivisionC(Index).Text = "-") Then
    If IsNumeric(txtDivisionC(Index)) = False Then
      MsgBox "You must enter a numeric value"
      txtDivisionC(Index).Text = ""
      Exit Sub
    End If
  End If
  arrProfit(Index, 3) = Val(txtDivisionC(Index).Text)
  CalculateTotal
  cboGraphType_Click
End Sub
```

The **CalculateTotal** procedure uses a loop to sum the profits for the divisions, within the four quarters of the year. It then displays the totals in labels:

```
Public Sub CalculateTotal()
  Dim i As Integer, j As Integer, sngTemp As Single
  For j = 0 To 3          '1-4 quarters
    sngTemp = 0
    'Sum of each quarter
    For i = 1 To 3 'DivisionA - DivisionC
      sngTemp = sngTemp + arrProfit(j, i)
    Next i
    arrTotal(j, 1) = sngTemp
  Next j
  'Display the total by quarters
  For j = 0 To 3
    lblTotal(j).Caption = Format(arrTotal(j, 1), "Currency")
  Next j
End Sub
```

The **ByQuarters** and **ByTotals** procedures modify the arrProfit and arrTotal arrays, respectively. These values are placed in chart labels:

```
Public Sub ByQuarters()
     arrProfit(0, 0) = "1st Qtr"
     arrProfit(1, 0) = "2nd Qtr"
     arrProfit(2, 0) = "3rd Qtr"
     arrProfit(3, 0) = "4th Qtr"
     'Plot the data by quarters
     MSChart.ChartData = arrProfit
End Sub

Public Sub ByTotals()
     arrTotal(0, 0) = "1st Qtr"
     arrTotal(1, 0) = "2nd Qtr"
     arrTotal(2, 0) = "3rd Qtr"
     arrTotal(3, 0) = "4th Qtr"
     'Plot the data by Totals
     MSChart.ChartData = arrTotal
End Sub

Private Sub cmdExit_Click()
  Unload Me
End Sub
```

7.3.4 Binding a Chart to an ADO Control

(samples: ChartADO)

The MSChart control can be an ADO bound control, allowing you to plot numeric data from an ADO data provider. It cannot, however, be used with a standard Data Control, which is based on DAO. You can also bind an MSChart to an ADO Recordset created at run time, or to a Command object created by the Data Environment Designer. In this section, we will create a program that shows how to bind an ADO control to an MSChart.

First, we create a database called CompanyChart.mdb containing three tables called Profits, Expenses, and Projection. Each Recordset object has four fields: the first contains labels for the X-axis, and the remaining fields are be displayed as chart series data. Here, for example, is the Profit table:

Profit : Table

Division	First Quarter	Second Quarter	Third Quarter	Fourth Quarter
(blank)	$0.00	$0.00	$0.00	$0.00
DivisionA	$46.00	$23.00	$60.00	$72.00
DivisionB	$45.00	$67.00	$32.00	$36.00
DivisionC	$52.00	$43.00	$35.00	$68.00
	$0.00	$0.00	$0.00	$0.00

Record: 5 of 5

Notice that we intentionally filled the first record of each table with zeros. Our copy of the MSChart control appears to ignore the first record in the attached Recordset (We haven't figured out why, but we're sure Microsoft must have a very good reason for this) .

Let's create a new Visual Basic project. Because we are using ADO, we have to add a reference to the Microsoft ActiveX Data Objects2.0 Library from the **Project > References** menu.

Place an MSChart control and a ComboBox control on the same form, as in Figure 27. (Your chart will appear in color, whereas the printed page here shows only shades of gray.)

Program Code. The following source code is added to the form:

```
Option Explicit
Private rsProducts As New ADODB.Recordset
Private cnCompany As New ADODB.Connection
```

Form_Load initializes the ComboBox to the names of the database tables that can be selected by the user:

```
Private Sub Form_Load()
  With cboDataSelection
    .AddItem "Profit"
    .AddItem "Expenses"
    .AddItem "Projection"
    .ListIndex = 0
  End With
End Sub
```

When the user clicks in the **cboDataSelection** ComboBox, the Click event handler opens an ADO Connection, uses an SQL query to open a Recordset called **rsProducts**, and sets the chart's DataSource property to the new Recordset:

```
Private Sub cboDataSelection_Click()
  Dim strQuery As String, strSelectedData As String
  MSChart1.TitleText = cboDataSelection.Text
  cnCompany.ConnectionString = _
    "Provider=Microsoft.Jet.OLEDB.3.51; Data Source =" & _
    App.Path & "\CompanyChart.mdb"
  cnCompany.Open
  strSelectedData = cboDataSelection.Text
  strQuery = "SELECT * FROM " & strSelectedData
```

Figure 27. MSChart / ADO Example, Main Form.

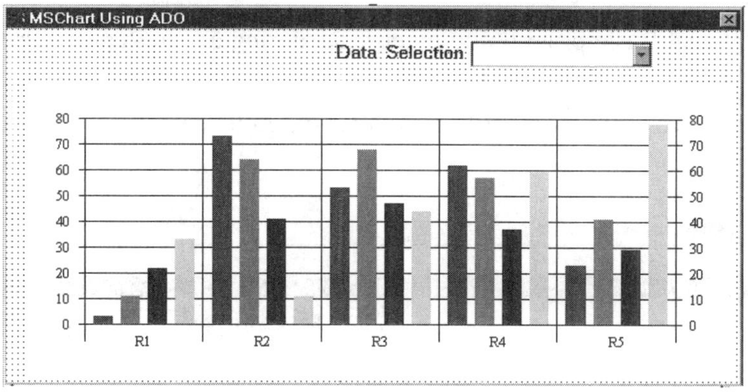


```
    rsProducts.Open strQuery, cnCompany, adOpenStatic
    With MSChart1
      .ShowLegend = True
      Set .DataSource = rsProducts
    End With
    cnCompany.Close
End Sub
```

Run the Program. When running the program, we can select any one of three charts, Profit, Expenses, or Projection, from the ComboBox. The Profit and Expenses charts, for example, appear in Figures 28 and 29, and the Projection chart appears in Figure 30. Because this book is printed in black and white, the bar colors do not show. But they colors will appear if you run the program from sample program disk. You can modify these colors by bringing up the Properties window, clicking on **Custom**, and selecting the **Series Color** tab.

7.4 REVIEW QUESTIONS

1. What is the menu Command sequence that adds both a Data Environment and a DataReport to your Visual Basic project?
2. What are the names of the six controls in the Report Designer Toolbox window?
3. Which control in the Report Designer Toolbox does calculations?
4. Which control in the Report Designer Toolbox displays the contents of a database field?
5. What is the purpose of the DataMember property of a DataReport?
6. What is the purpose of the DataSource property of a DataReport?
7. How can you make the contents of the Title property of a DataReport appear on the report itself?
8. If the message "Failed getting rowset(s) from current data source" appears when you invoke the Show method of a DataReport, what is the likely source of the problem?
9. Which DataReport method produces an HTML file?

10. What are the two run time steps a DataReport must go through when the Show method is invoked?
11. *(y/n)*: Can a Visual Basic program do other tasks during a DataReport's Printing/Exporting step?
12. Which run time event occurs every second after the Activate event when a DataReport is generated?

Figure 28. Profit Chart.

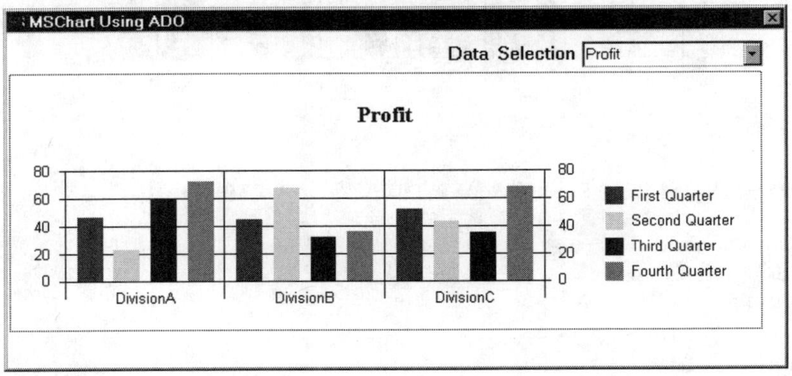

Figure 29. Expenses Chart

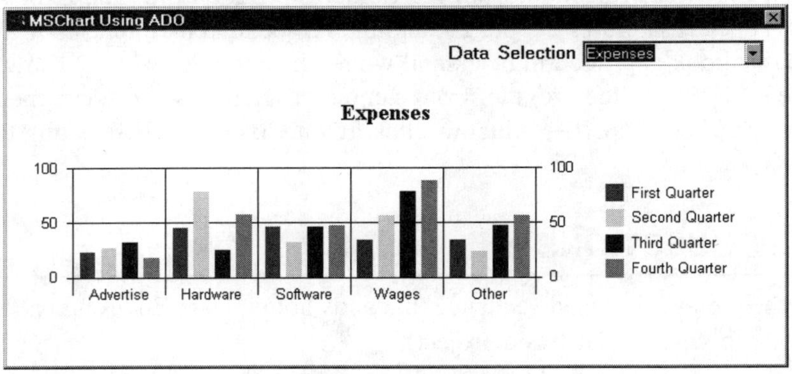

Figure 30. Projection Chart

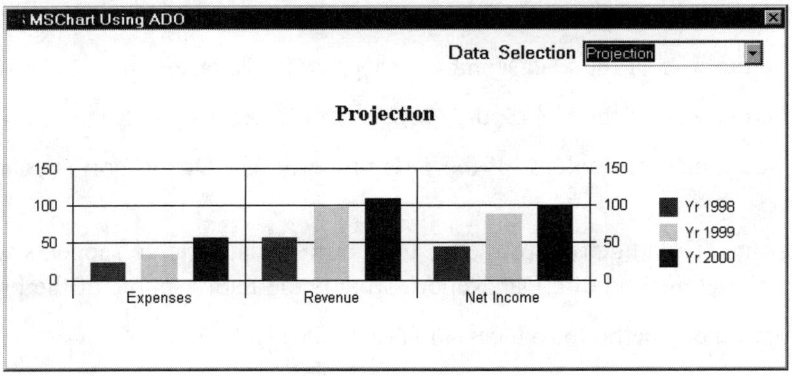

13. Which run time event occurs just before the DataReport window is closed?
14. What is the Command to create a new DataReport object at design time?
15. How do you add a page number to a DataReport?
16. How do you activate the SQL Builder tool in the DataEnvironment window?
17. How do you add a counter to the end of a DataReport?
18. Suppose a parent Command named cmStates has a child Command named cmCities. Which Command name should be assigned to the DataMember property of a DataReport?
19. Suppose a parent Command named cmStates has a child Command named cmCities. Which Command name should be copied into the Group Header area of a DataReport?
20. If a report shows Cities within States within Regions, which of these groups can appear in any Group Heading or Detail area of the report? Explain.
21. If a report shows Cities within States within Regions, which of these groups can appear only in the Detail area of the report?
22. What are the steps in the Command Properties window to create summary fields?
23. What advantage is there to showing a DataReport from an ADO Connection object that you create in program code?
24. What is the primary difference between the MSHFlexGrid control and the DataGrid control?
25. (y/n): Does the MSHFlexGrid allow the user to edit its contents?
26. Which properties must be set before an MSHFlexGrid can display data?
27. Which MSHFlexGrid property allows bands to be displayed horizontally?
28. Which MSHFlexGrid property allows an image to be loaded into a cell at run time?
29. Which MSHFlexGrid method expands all rows of a specified band within the grid?
30. Which MSChart property contains a two-dimensional array of labels and cell data?
31. How are the X-Axis labels initialized in an MSChart control?
32. Which MSChart property determines whether a two-dimensional bar chart or a line chart is displayed?

7.5 PROGRAMMING EXERCISES

7.5.1 NorthWind - 1

This group of exercises uses the NorthWind database (nwind.mdb) installed in the Visual Basic home directory.

Orders by Customer. Use the NorthWind database to create a report that shows a list of orders placed by each customer. Create two Command objects, in which the **Customers** Command is based on the Customers table and the **Orders** Command is based on the Orders table. The Orders Command should be a child Command of the Customers Command. In the latter, create an aggregate field that counts the number of orders for the current customer. Display the count in the group header area. Figure 31 shows a sample of the output.

7.5.2 NorthWind - 2

Orders by Customer, SQL Version. As in the previous exercise, use the NorthWind database to create a report that shows a list of orders placed by each customer. In this version, use SQL queries to sort the Customers Command by customer ID, and sort the Orders query in descending order by order date.

Figure 31. NorthWind Orders by Customer.

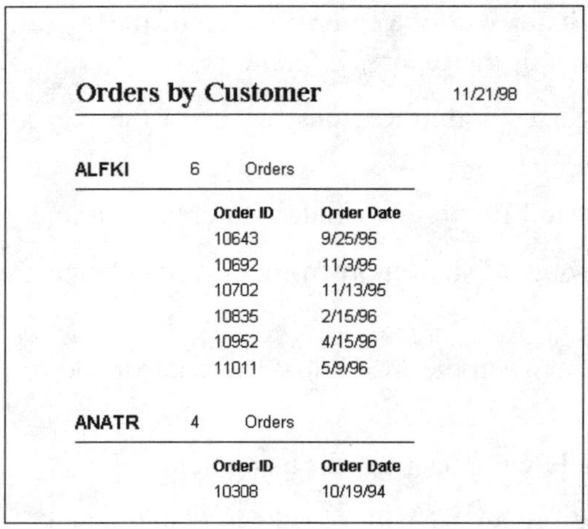

7.5.3 NorthWind - 3

Orders with Customer Selection. Create an SQL query for the Customers/Orders grouping that only shows orders for a single customer. At run time, let the user input a customer ID. Your program should generate the appropriate query string, pass it to the Execute method of an ADO object, and link the object to a report.

7.5.4 NorthWind - 4

Orders by Customer with Grand Total. Choose one of the previous two exercises as a starting point for this exercise. Add a grand total that shows the total number of customers.

7.5.5 NorthWind - 5

Customer Orders, MSHFlexGrid. Create a program that uses an MSHFlexGrid to display a list of customers. For each customer, show the company name, country, phone number, total number of orders, and the total order amount. Also, for each order, show the Order ID, order date, and the order total. Figure 32 shows a sample.

7.5.6 NorthWind – 6

Customer Orders, DataReport. Create a DataReport that shows approximately the same information as the MSHFlexGrid in the previous exercise. Figure 33 shows a sample report.

7.5.7 Mail-Order Computer Sales

Invoice DataReport. In Chapter 5, in Exercise 5.6.14, we asked you to create an Invoice table containing information about the current sales transaction. At that time, the Invoice table was shown in a DataGrid control. For the current exercise, create a DataReport showing all computer sales from the Invoice table.

Figure 32. Customer Orders, MSHFlexGrid.

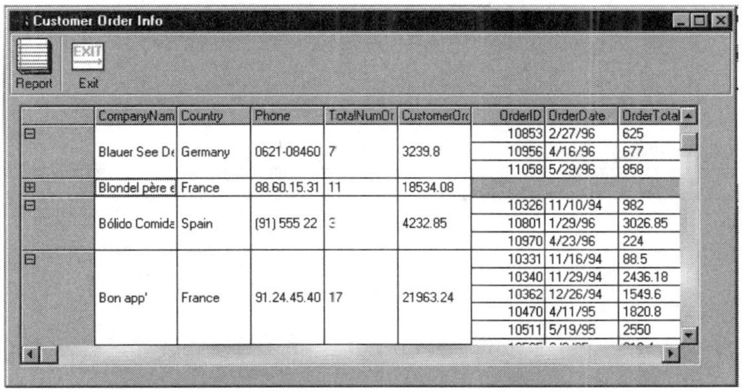

7.5.8 Kyoshi Karate School - 1

Membership Report. The Kyoshi Karate School (from the Chapter 4 exercises) needs to have a membership report that lists the ID numbers, last and first names, birth dates, and phone numbers of its members. The records should be sorted in ascending order by last name (see a sample in Figure 34). Once you have designed this report, allow the user to launch the report from the main window's ToolBar. Let the user select the mode of output: file, screen, or printer.

7.5.9 Kyoshi Karate School - 2

Enhanced Member Report. Improve the Membership Report completed in the previous exercise: Concatenate the first and last names into a single string. Capitalize all of the column titles. Display the current date on the report. Display a count of the total number of members in the report footer.

7.5.10 Kyoshi Karate School - 3

Dues Payments Report. The Kyoshi Karate School has been collecting dues payments from members for some time. The Payments table consists of three columns: member name, payment date, and payment amount. Create a report that summarizes the dues payments for each member.

Figure 33. Customer Orders, DataReport.

Customer Order Information Page 1

Customer Order Information

Company Name	**Alfreds Futterkistesss**
Country:	Germany
Phone:	030-0074321
Fax:	030-0076545

Number of Orders: 6 **Order Amount:** $4,273.00

OrderID:	**OrderTotal:**
10643	$814.50
10692	$878.00
10702	$330.00
10835	$845.80
10952	$471.20
11011	$933.50

Company Name	**Ana Trujillo Emparedados**
Country:	Mexico
Phone:	(5) 555-4729
Fax:	(5) 555-3745

Figure 34. Membership Listing, Alphabetical.

Membership Listing

ID	lastName	firstName	phone	birthDate
10	Chong	Anne	232-2323	
32	Flinstone	Fred	809-8837	2/20/04
2	Gonzalez	Aldo	123-2345	6/ 6/76
12	Hasegawa	Elaine	313-34554	2/20/75
30	Howe	James	414-2345	
33	John	Baker		5/20/81
15	Russell	Brian	646-93873	5/20/74
1	Smith	LaMar	111-2222	2/20/72

7.5.11 Kyoshi Karate School - 4

Class Schedule Report. Create a report listing the class schedule table from the Karate School Exercises in Chapter 4. The primary sort should be on the day number and the secondary sort should be on the class starting time. Give the user the option of printing the report in a window, on the printer, or to a file.

7.5.12 MSChart Interactive

Using the Interactive MSChart example shown earlier in this chapter, add another OptionButton that lets the user display profits by *Division*. Figure 35 shows an example.

Figure 35. Profits by Division (MSChart).

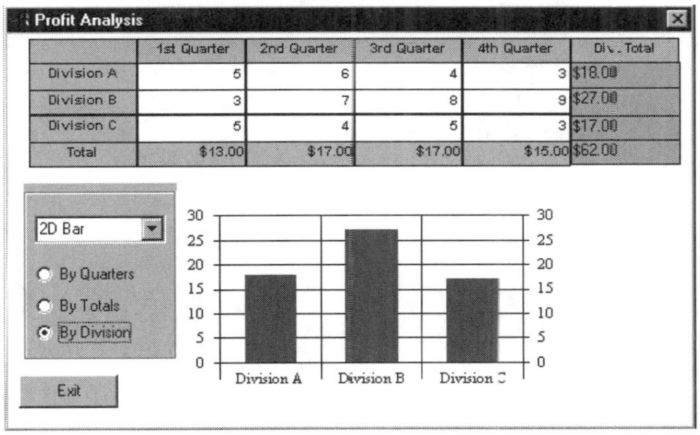

8 Creating Class Modules

Chapter Contents

Classes and Objects
- Object-Oriented Design
- Class Modules
- Creating Instances of a Class
- Properties
- Event Handlers
- Methods

Student Class Example
- Program Design
- Program Implementation

Student Collection Class
- Program Design
- The Main Form
- The CStudent Class
- The CStudentCollection Class

Client-Server Example: Rental Rates
- Client-Server Design
- Client Program
- CRentalPrices Class
- Creating an ActiveX Server
- Registering and Unregistering Components

Doctors Office Scheduling
- Program Specifications
- User Interface Design
- Class Interfaces
- Class Relationships
- Program Code

Review Questions

Chapter Exercises

8.1 CLASSES AND OBJECTS

One of the most exciting developments in computer software over the last twenty years has been *object-oriented programming*, nicknamed "OOP". It is a way of designing and coding applications that has led to using interchangeable software components to build larger programs. Object-oriented programming languages first appeared in the early 1980s, with ALGOL, SmallTalk, and C++. The legacy from these languages is the gradual development of object-like visual tools for building programs. In Visual Basic, for example, Forms, CommandButtons, CheckBoxes, ListBoxes, and other controls are ideal examples of objects. Object-oriented designs help to produce programs that are well-suited to ongoing development and expansion.

Classes. A *class* is a program structure defining a distinguishing set of characteristics. In effect, a class identifies a specific data type. To use an analogy from nature, mammals in the cat family (*Felidae*) have similar characteristics: sharp claws, whiskers, paws, and a carnivorous diet. We could speak of the *Felidae* class, and individual instances of cats would be called *objects,* or *instances*. Similarly, in a computer program, all class instances share common characteristics. Visual Basic controls and forms, for example, are classes. In the Toolbox window, each icon represents a class. When you select the CommandButton control from the ToolBox and place it on a Form, as in Figure 1, you are creating an *instance* of the CommandButton class. An instance is also called an *object*.

Figure 1. CommandButton Class and CommandButton Object.

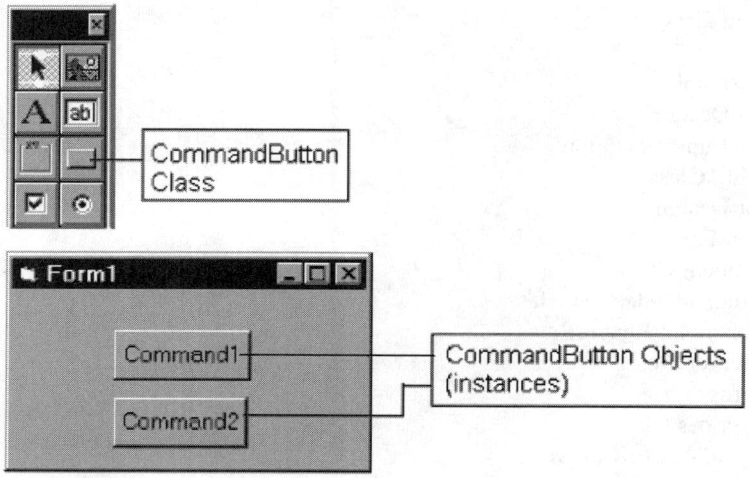

Properties, Methods, and Event Handlers. The way a program communicates with each object is determined by the properties and methods defined in the object's class. The CommandButton class, for example, has properties such as **Left**, **Top**, **Caption**, and **Name**. Each CommandButton object contains its own unique set of property values. In the example shown in Figure 1, the two CommandButtons have different values in their Top and Caption properties.

Methods are shared by all instances of a class; the Move method in the CommandButton class is the same for all CommandButton objects.

Event Handlers are also methods, but they are specific to individual objects. For example, a Form with several CommandButtons will almost always have different code written each each button's Click event handler.

8.1.1 Object-Oriented Design

Object-oriented programming is not just a matter of randomly dropping classes into a program. The real challenge is to design classes in such a way that the resulting objects will effectively cooperate and communicate. The primary goal is to address the needs of the application, or problem being solved. A secondary goal is to design classes that can outlive the current application and possibly be useful in future programs.

The first step after creating the program specifications is to analyze the application requirements. *Object-oriented analysis*, as it is called, often starts with a detailed specifications of the problem to be solved. A term often applied to this process is called *finding the classes.* In every problem and every application, there are classes waiting to be found. It is the designer's job to discover just what those classes are. A famous sculptor once said that inside every block of marble, there is a work of art waiting to be discovered.

Finding the Classes. Classes are the fundamental building blocks of object-oriented applications. When designing object-oriented programs, we first select classes that reflect physical entities in the application domain. For example, the user of a record-keeping program for a college might describe some of the application's requirements as follows:

> We need to keep a **list of students** that lets us track the courses they have completed. Each student has a **transcript** that contains all information about completed courses. At the end of each semester, we will calculate the grade point average of each **student**. At times, users will search for a particular **course** taken by a student.

Notice the highlighted nouns and noun phrases in this description: list of students, transcript, student, and course. These would ordinarily become classes in the program's design.

Looking for Control Structures. Classes can also be discovered in the description of processing done by an application, or in the description of control structures. For example, what if the application involved scheduling of college classes for students? Here is another possible description from the program specifications:

> We also want to schedule classes for students, using the college's master schedule to determine the times and room numbers for each student's class. When the optimal arrangement of classes for each student has been determined, each student's class schedule will be printed and distributed.

In this description, we anticipate a need for a controlling agent that could be implemented as a class. We might call it **Scheduler**, a class that matches up each student's schedule with the college master schedule.

Describing the Classes. The next step, after finding the classes in an application, is to describe the classes in terms of attributes and operations. *Attributes* are characteristics of each object that will be implemented as properties. Attributes describe the properties that all objects of the same class have in common. Classes also have *operations*, which are actions the class objects may perform, or messages to which they can respond. Operations are implemented as class methods. Based on the record-keeping application that we described earlier, Table 1 describes some of its important attributes and operations.

The complete set of attributes and operations is often incomplete during the early stages of design, because it is difficult to anticipate all the application requirements. As a design develops, the need often arises for additional properties and methods that improve communication between objects. Rather that being seen as a weakness, however, one of the strengths of the object-oriented design process is that it accommodates ongoing modifications.

Interface and Implementation. The *class interface* is the portion that is visible to the Application programmer who uses the class. The program written by such a person is also

Table 1. Sample Attributes and Operations.

Class	Attributes (properties)	Operations (methods)
Student	ID, LastName, FirstName, Transcript	Print, Input
StudentList	AllStudents, Count	Add, Remove, FindStudent
Course	Semester, Name, Grade, Credits	Print, Input
Transcript	CourseList, Count	Print, Search, CalcGradeAvg

called the *client program*, in reference to the client-server relationship between a class and the programs that use it. The class interface provides a way for clients to communicate (send messages) to class objects. In Visual Basic, a class interface is created by declaring public properties, methods, and events.

The class *implementation* is the portion of a class that is hidden from client programs; it is created from private instance variables, private properties, and private methods. The hiding of data and procedures inside a class is achieved through a process called *encapsulation*. In this, it might be helpful to visualize the class as a "capsule" around its data and procedures.

Inheritance. In passing, we should note that Visual Basic is not completely object-oriented, primarily because it leaves out an essential feature: inheritance. *Inheritance* lets programmers create new classes that inherit, or derive characteristics of existing classes. For example, you might want to start with a Student class that has only general information for all types of students. But special types of students might require the creation of classes such as GraduateStudent, ExchangeStudent, StudentEmployee, and so on. These new classes would share all the characteristics of the Student class, and they would each add new characteristics that made them specialized. Languages such as C++, Java, and SmallTalk support inheritance.

8.1.2 Class Modules

In Visual Basic, you define a class by creating a Form, an ActiveX control, or a class module. A *class module* is a special type of code module that contains variables, properties,

Application Programmers vs. Class Programmers

Here's an analogy proposed by *E.W.*: Imagine a virtual car (automobile). Application Programmers can tell a car to go by calling the **PushGasPedal** method and stop the car by calling the **PushBrakePedal** method. An Application Programmer doesn't need to know how the PushGasPedal method works, just that it does. The Programmer who builds the car (called the *Class programmer*) does all the detail work to make the car methods work. If the PushBrakePedal method is called, the gas pedal has to be cleared, pressure has to be placed on the master brake cylinder, brake fluid transfers pressure on the brake pads against the wheel, and the car slows down.

events, and methods. Properties are implemented as public procedures, and variables are generally private. Methods may be either public or private. Events will be explained later in this chapter, in Section 8.1.5.

Up to this point in the book, we have presented Forms as user interfaces for programs. It is important to realize, however, that Forms are also classes. They do have one important drawback: they cannot be accessed by procedures outside their own program. Class modules, on the other hand, can be shared by procedures in other programs.

To add a class module to a project in Visual Basic, select **Add Class Module** from the **Project** menu. After adding a class module, bring up the Properties window and set the Name property of the class to a descriptive name, such as **CStudent**. Your class module will be saved as part of the current project.

Once a class module has been created, program statements can be used to create instances of the class. Subject to memory limitations, you can create as many instances of the same class as you wish. The same program may also contain multiple class modules, each defining a different type of object.

Naming Conventions. When naming classes, we suggest using the naming convention used by Microsoft's C++ *Foundation Classes*, by prepending a capital "C" to class names. That is why a class of students is called **CStudent**. In the Visual Basic doumentation, Microsoft suggests using the prefix "cls" with object variables created in client programs. For example, a CStudent object declared inside a procedure could be called **clsStudent**:

```
Dim clsStudent As CStudent
```

Similarly, a CStudent object declared at the module level could be called **mclsStudent**:

```
Private mclsStudent As CStudent
```

Having said this, the authors admit to not being 100% consistent, as sometimes CStudent objects are declared in our programs with names such as **aStudent**, **mStudent**, **tempStudent**, **objStudent**, and so on. (At least the word *Student* appears in the name!)

8.1.3 Creating Instances of a Class

To create an instance of a class, declare a variable of the class type. At runtime, use the **New** statement to create a class instance and the **Set** statement to assign the instance to a variable. For example, we create instances of the **CStudent** class called clsStudent1 and clsStudent2:

```
Dim clsStudent1 As CStudent, clsStudent2 As CStudent
Set clsStudent1 = New CStudent
Set clsStudent2 = New CStudent
```

Each instance of a class has its own unique copy of the variables inside the class module. At the same time, all instances of the same class share the same set of procedures.

It is a good habit to remove objects that are no longer needed, to allow the program to free memory for other purposes. An object is removed by setting its reference variable to **Nothing** (a Visual Basic keyword). This releases all memory used by the object:

```
Set clsStudent1 = Nothing
```

Creating an Array. You can use a loop to create an array of class objects:

```
Dim clsStudents(1 To 10) As CStudent
Dim j As Integer
For j = 1 To 10
   Set clsStudents(j) = New CStudent
Next j
```

You can use another loop to release the memory used by the array:

```
Dim j As Integer
For j = 1 To 10
   Set clsStudents(j) = Nothing
Next j
```

Going Out of Scope. If an object is created inside a procedure, it is automatically removed from memory when the procedure ends. This is called *going out of scope*. An object declared at the Form level is automatically released when all references to the Form are set to Nothing. There is one exception to the above rule: An object variable is retained in memory if at least one reference to the variable still exists. Suppose that a module-level variable named mclsStudent is assigned a reference to a local variable named clsTempStudent:

```
Private mclsStudent As CStudent

Private Sub cmdShow_Click()
   Dim clsTempStudent As New CStudent
   Set mclsStudent = clsTempStudent
End Sub
```

When this procedure ends, mclsStudent retains a reference to the CStudent object created in the cmdShow_Click procedure, and the object continues to exist in memory.

8.1.4 Properties

(samples: Employee)

To the user of a class object, a *property* acts like a variable belonging to the object. For example, when we set the Caption property of a Form, we are really calling a property procedure:

```
frmMain.Caption = "Main Form"
```

A property consists of one or two procedures that control access to private variables inside the object's class definition. The private variables are also called *instance variables*.

To create a property, select **Add Procedure** from the **Tools** menu. When the **Insert Procedure** dialog box appears, type in the property name and select the **Property** OptionButton, shown in Figure 2.

Properties nearly always have Public scope so they can be accessed from outside their enclosing class module. If we created a property called **IdNumber**, for example, the following procedures would be automatically inserted into the current class module. They are incomplete, but they provide a framework:

Figure 2. Add Procedure Dialog.

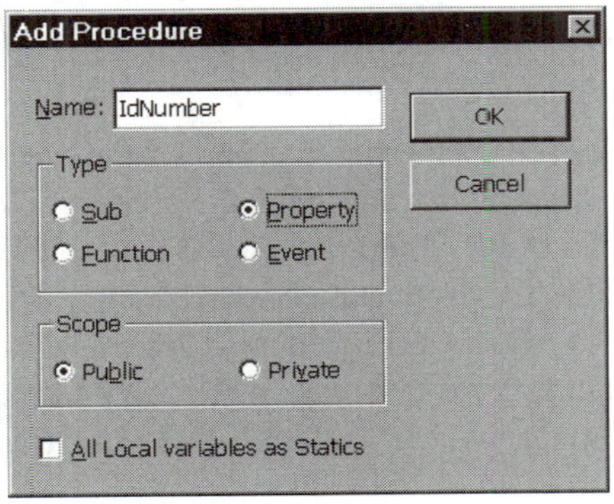


```
Public Property Get IdNumber() As Variant
End Property

Public Property Let IdNumber(vNewValue As Variant)
End Property
```

Get is a keyword that indicates that the procedure returns the value of the property. It is a function, so we specify the return type and place an assignment statement in the procedure body that returns the value of the instance variable **mstrIdNumber:**

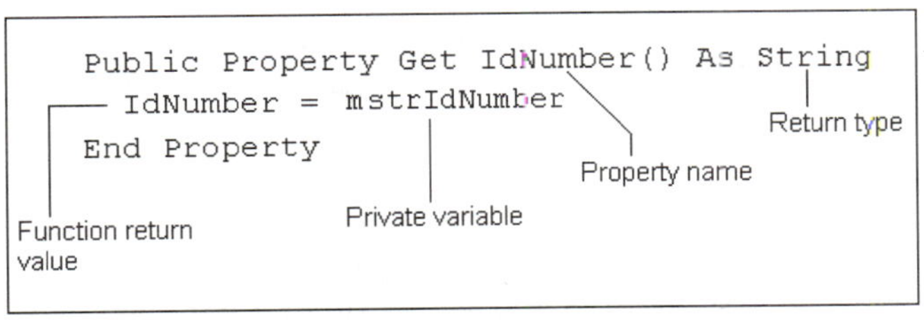

Let is a keyword that indicates that the caller is assigning a value to the property. This is how we might implement the procedure, which assigns the **strId** parameter to a private instance variable named **mstrIdNumber**:

```
Private mstrIdNumber As String
Public Property Let IdNumber(strId As String)
  mstrIdNumber = strId
End Property
```

It is very important to make the data type of the **strId** parameter the same as the type of **mstrIdNumber**, to avoid a syntax error.

A **Property Set** procedure is the same as **Property Let**, except that the former is used when assigning an object reference to private instance variable. For example, the **Set Payroll** property does this:

```
Private mcolPayroll As Collection
Public Property Set Payroll(colPayroll as Collection)
  Set mcolPayroll = colPayroll
End Property
```

Read-Only Properties. Sometimes it is useful to make a property read-only. Client programs can query the property to get its value, but they cannot modify it. If you want a property to be read-only, omit its **Let** or **Set** property procedure.

Public Properties, Private Instance Variables. Properties are part of the class interface and instance variables are not. The last thing we would want is for the user of an object to directly modify an instance variable, because we would have no ability to prevent invalid values from being placed in the object. This is why instance variables are declared *private*, making them hidden inside the object. It is much easier to debug programs in which we enforce this hiding, because we often include error trapping in Property Let and Set procedures. In the IdNumber Property, for example, we can include some error trapping to make sure **strId** is not blank:

```
Public Property Let IdNumber(strId as String)
   strId = Trim$(strId)
   If Len(strId) > 0 Then
     m_strIdNumber = strId
   Else
     MsgBox "Error: Employee ID cannot be blank "
   End If
End Property
```

Examples. The following statements in a client program create a CEmployee object and set its properties:

```
Set mclsEmployee = New CEmployee
With mclsEmployee
   .IdNumber = txtIDNumber.Text
   .LastName = txtLastName.Text
End With
```

The following statements copy the property values of a CEmployee into TextBox controls on the client program's Form:

```
With mclsEmployee
   txtIDNumber.Text = .IdNumber
   txtLastName.Text = .LastName
End With
```

CEmployee Class Example. Let's create a simple class that holds the ID numbers and last names of employees. From the Project menu, we select **Add Class Module**, and set its Name property to **CEmployee**. The class contains two private instance variables, two public properties named **IdNumber** and **LastName**, and a public method called **PrintOn:**

```
'Private instance variables
Private mstrIdNumber As String
Private mstrLastName As String
```

Each instance variable has corresponding **Get** and **Let** property procedures:

```
Public Property Get IdNumber() As String
  IdNumber = mstrIdNumber
End Property
```

```
Public Property Let IdNumber(strIdNum As String)
  mstrIdNumber = strIdNum
End Property

Public Property Get LastName() As String
  LastName = mstrLastName
End Property

Public Property Let LastName(strName As String)
  mstrLastName = strName
End Property
```

8.1.5 Event Handlers

There are two standard event handlers associated with each class object. **Class_Initialize** is automatically invoked by Visual Basic whenever an object is created, and **Class_Terminate** is automatically invoked when an object is destroyed. Neither handler may contain any parameters or return type. Here, for example, we set class properties to default values when an object is created:

```
Private Sub Class_Initialize()
  mstrIdNumber = "000-00-0000"
  mstrLastName = "(unknown)"
End Sub
```

In the following **Terminate** event handler, we print a message to the immediate window. When tracing a program, this can help us track the lifetime of CEmployee class objects:

```
Private Sub Class_Terminate()
  Debug.Print "Student object terminated"
End Sub
```

Automatic Cleanup. If a class object contains another class object, Visual Basic terminates both objects if the first object is set to Nothing. Suppose, for example, that a CStudent object contained a private variable of type CTranscript:

```
' CStudent class definition
Private mTranscript As CTranscript
```

If a particular instance of CStudent is terminated, VB automatically calls the Terminate event handler for the student's transcript. (The only exception to this rule is, if the same CTranscript object is referenced by another variable, the object is not destroyed.)

Custom Event Names. In addition to standard events such as Initialize and Terminate, a class can declare its own events and raise them at run time. First, the event is declared in the declarations area of the class module. Here is one called BlankId:

```
Public Event BlankId()
```

Notice that the event declaration resembles that of a procedure. In fact, Events can have parameters:

```
Public Event InvalidPayRate(curPayRate As Currency)
```

The class can then raise Events in its methods or property procedures at run time with the RaiseEvent statement:

```
RaiseEvent BlankId
RaiseEvent InvalidPayRate( curPayRate )
```

In the Student Class Example program comping up in Section 8.2, we will show how a client program can respond to Events raised by a class.

8.1.6 Methods

In addition to properties, class modules can contain methods. A *method* is a procedure that acts upon an object. Public methods and properties together form what we call the *class interface.* For example, VB's Debug object has a method called Print; when we pass a Print message to the Debug object, it prints a string into the Immediate window:

```
Debug.Print "The value of N is ";N
```

You can create other useful methods that enhance a class. For example, the following **AsString** method concatenates the CEmployee properties into a single string with an end-of-line character after each:

```
Public Function AsString() As String
  AsString = "ID Number: " & mstrIdNumber & vbCrLf & _
     "Last Name: " & mstrLastName & vbCrLf
End Function
```

The **PrintOn** method prints the CEmployee property values on the Form passed to the method as **aForm**:

```
Public Sub PrintOn(aForm As Form)
  aForm.Print "ID Number = "; mstrIdNumber & vbCrLf _
  & "---Last Name = "; mstrLastName
End Sub
```

A class method can be either a Sub procedure or a Function procedure. A method called by statements outside the class are always Public. Methods called only from within a class are Private.

8.2 STUDENT CLASS EXAMPLE

8.2.1 Program Design

(samples: Student)

Let's write a short program that inputs the ID, first name, and last name of a student, using a class called **CStudent**. The program will create an object, fill it with data, retrieve the same data, and display the values.

The user interface is in **frmMain**, where the user can enter the ID, first name, and last name of a student, as in Figure 3. When the **Get** button is clicked, the TextBoxes are copied to the properties of a CStudent object. The **Clear** button clears the text boxes.

Figure 3. Student Class Demonstration, Main Form.

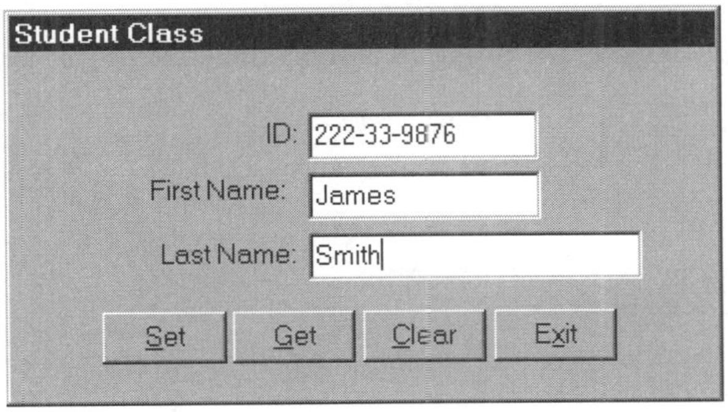

Error Trapping. If the user tries to assign a blank ID number, the following message appears when the **Set** button is clicked. The error is detected by the CStudent class IdNumber property procedure, and the error message is displayed by an event handler in frmMain:

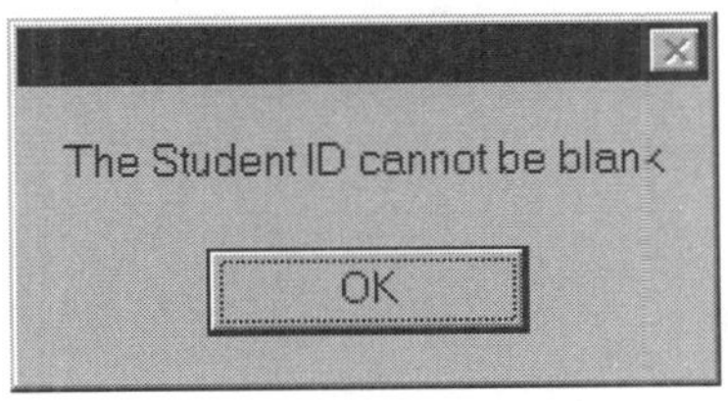

8.2.2 Program Implementation

The program's startup Form, frmMain, creates an instance of CStudent in Form_Load:

```
Private WithEvents mclsStudent As CStudent

Private Sub Form_Load()
  Set mclsStudent = New CStudent
End Sub
```

The cmdClear button clears the TextBoxes:

```
Private Sub cmdClear_Click()
  txtID.Text = ""
  txtLastName.Text = ""
  txtFirstName.Text = ""
End Sub
```

When the **Get** button is clicked, the program retrieves the ID number, FirstName, and LastName from mclsStudent, the CStudent object:

```
Private Sub cmdGet_Click()
  With mclsStudent
    txtID.Text = .IdNumber
    txtFirstName.Text = .FirstName
    txtLastName.Text = .LastName
```

```
    End With
End Sub
```

When the **Set** button is clicked, the program assigns the contents of the text boxes to the CStudent properties:

```
Private Sub cmdSet_Click()
  With mclsStudent
    .IdNumber = txtID.Text
    .FirstName = txtFirstName.Text
    .LastName = txtLastName.Text
  End With
End Sub
```

The CStudent Class. Here is a listing of the CStudent class source code. It begins with the declaration of three private variables and a public event procedure:

```
Private mstrIdNumber As String
Private mstrLastName As String
Private mstrFirstName As String
Public Event BlankId()

Private Sub Class_Initialize()
  mstrIdNumber = "000-00-0000"
End Sub
```

Each property has a Get and Let procedure:

```
Public Property Get IdNumber() As String
  IdNumber = mstrIdNumber
End Property

Public Property Let IdNumber(strId As String)
  strId = Trim$(strId)
  If Len(strId) > 0 Then 'cannot be blank
    mstrIdNumber = strId
  Else
    RaiseEvent BlankId
  End If
End Property

Public Property Get FirstName() As String
  FirstName = mstrFirstName
End Property

Public Property Let FirstName(strName As String)
  mstrFirstName = strName
End Property

Public Property Get LastName() As String
  LastName = mstrLastName
End Property

Public Property Let LastName(strName As String)
  mstrLastName = strName
```

```
End Property
```

Event Handling Code. This program handles the blank student ID error in an interesting way that tells us something about the way classes and their clients communicate. The CStudent class declares public event name called **BlankId:**

```
Public Event BlankId()
```

In the **Let IdNumber** property procedure, the **BlankId** event is raised if the strId parameter is an empty string:

```
Public Property Let IdNumber(strId As String)
  strId = Trim$(strId)
  If Len(strId) > 0 Then        'cannot be blank
    mstrIdNumber = strId
  Else
    RaiseEvent BlankId          'raise an event
  End If
End Property
```

In frmMain, the CStudent object is declared using the **WithEvents** qualifier:

```
Private WithEvents mclsStudent As CStudent
```

Also in frmMain, the **BlankId** event handler procedure is automatically called when CStudent calls RaiseEvent. This is where the message box is displayed:

```
Private Sub mStudent_BlankId()
  MsgBox "Attempt to assign an empty string to IdNumber.", _
    vbInformation, "Error"
End Sub
```

When a class method detects an error condition, it is generally better to raise an event rather than immediately display a message box. The client program can either ignore the event or respond via its own event handler procedure. The client can often determine the context in which the error occurred, and is probably more qualified to decide how to handle the error than the class method.

Using the Err.Raise Method. As an alternative, the class method can call the standard **Err.Raise** method when an error is detected, passing a custom error number and description that will be detected and displayed by the client. The following version of the **Let IdNumber** procedure uses Err.Raise:

```
Public Property Let IdNumber(strId As String)
  strId = Trim$(strId)
  If Len(strId) > 0 Then        'cannot be blank
    mstrIdNumber = strId
  Else
    Err.Raise vbObjectError + 513, "Attempt to " _
    & "assign an empty string to IdNumber."
  End If
End Property
```

The client program can use On Error GoTo to trap the error without having to code a separate event handler. When passing an error number to the Err.Raise method, Microsoft suggests adding a value greater than 512 to the predefined constant vbObjectError to avoid clashes with existing error codes.

8.3 STUDENT COLLECTION CLASS

(samples: StudentColl)

Most object-oriented applications do not have just a single class; instead, they are implemented as the interaction between two or more classes. A component is a group of classes that work closely together. Component classes belong together and are mutually dependent on each other.

It is often useful to use diagrams to express class relationships. In the program we are about to show, the CStudentCollection class and CStudent class exhibit a *containing* relationship. That is, a collection of students *contains* one or more student objects, shown by the following diagram:

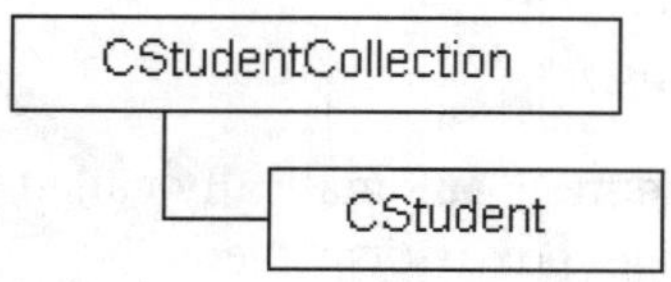

8.3.1 Program Design

We want the user to input information for a student and have the resulting CStudent object added to a collection. The collection is represented by the CStudentCollection class. The class also allows the user to search for a student either by ID number or by last name. The main window is shown in Figure 4. First, the user enters the data for several students, clicking the **Add** button each time. Next, by clicking on **Show All Students**, the listing appears in Figure 5.

The user can enter an ID number and ask the program to locate a matching student. The **Find ID** button activates the search. The user can also enter a last name and click on **Find Name**, and the program will display the student's ID number.

8.3.2 The Main Form

The code in frmMain, the startup Form for this program, is listed here. Notice that we use the **WithEvents** qualifier for both the CStudentCollection and CStudent objects, so Visual Basic will generate event handler procedures for them:

```
Private WithEvents mAllStudents As CStudentCollection
Private WithEvents mclsStudent As CStudent

Private Sub Form_Load()
   Set mAllStudents = New CStudentCollection
   Set mclsStudent = New CStudent
End Sub
```

Figure 4. Student Collection, Main Window.

Figure 5. Displaying All Students.

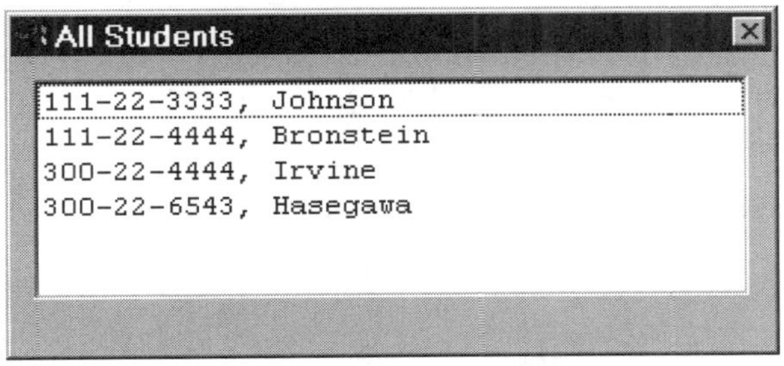

To create an event handler for mAllStudents or mclsStudent, you just select the object's name from the ComboBox in the upper-left corner of the main Form's code window.

Adding a Student. To add a new student to the collection, the program creates an instance of CStudent, sets its properties with data from TextBoxes, and calls the **Add** method in the CStudentCollection class:

```
Private Sub cmdAddStudent_Click()
  If Len(Trim$(txtID.Text)) = 0 Or _
    Len(Trim$(txtLastName.Text)) = 0 Then
    Exit Sub
  End If
  Set mclsStudent = New CStudent
  With mclsStudent
    .IdNumber = txtID.Text
    .LastName = txtLastName.Text
  End With
  mAllStudents.Add mclsStudent
End Sub
```

Finding an ID. To find a student's ID number, the program creates a CStudent object, sets its ID number, and calls the **FindByID** method in the CStudentCollection class. If a value of True is returned, a TextBox is filled with the student's last name:

```
Private Sub cmdFindID_Click()
  mclsStudent.IdNumber = txtID.Text
  If mAllStudents.FindByID(mclsStudent) Then
    txtLastName.Text = mclsStudent.LastName
```

```
  Else
    txtLastName.Text = "(not found)"
  End If
End Sub
```

Displaying All Students. When the user clicks on the **Show All Students** button, the Click event handler uses a For-Each statement to fill a ListBox on the frmDisplay Form with the student names and ID numbers in the collection:

```
Private Sub cmdShowAll_Click()
  Dim aStudent As CStudent
  For Each aStudent In mcollStudents.Students
    frmDisplay.lstAllStudents.AddItem aStudent.AsString
  Next aStudent
  frmDisplay.Show vbModal
End Sub
```

The mcollStudents collection is cleared simply by creating a new instance of the CStudentCollection class and assigning it to mcollStudents:

```
Private Sub cmdClear_Click()
  Set mcollStudents = New CStudentCollection
  txtID.Text = ""
  txtLastName.Text = ""
End Sub

Private Sub cmdExit_Click()
  Unload Me
End Sub
```

A **DuplicateKey** event is raised by the CStudentCollection class when its Add method is called and passed a duplicate key value:

```
Private Sub mcollStudents_DuplicateKey()
  MsgBox "Duplicate ID Numbers are not allowed", , ""
End Sub
```

A **BlankId** event is raised by the CStudent class when the client program assigns a blank string to the IdNumber property:

```
Private Sub mStudent_BlankId()
  MsgBox "The ID number cannot be blank", , ""
End Sub
```

8.3.3 The CStudent Class

The CStudent class is identical to the CStudent class shown earlier in Section 8.2.2, so we need not discuss it here.

8.3.4 The CStudentCollection Class

The CStudentCollection class encapsulates a collection and provides methods and properties that make the collection easier to use. The collection holds only references to CStudent objects. The class also declares a Public event named DuplicateKey:

```
Public Event DuplicateKey()
Private mcolStudents As Collection
```

The **Class_Initialize** event handler creates a new Collection object and assigns it to mcolStudents, a private variable:

```
Private Sub Class_Initialize()
  Set mcolStudents = New Collection
End Sub
```

The **Add** method attempts to add a CStudent object to the collection, using the ID number as the collection key. If a duplicate ID is encountered, a **DuplicateKey** event is raised:

```
Public Function Add(clsStudent As CStudent) As Boolean
  On Error GoTo AddError
  mcolStudents.Add clsStudent, clsStudent.IdNumber
  Add = True
  Exit Function
AddError:
  RaiseEvent DuplicateKey
  Add = False
End Function
```

The **Count** property is read-only, returning the number of students in the collection:

```
Public Property Get Count() As Integer
'Return the number of students in the Collection.
  Count = mcolStudents.Count
End Property
```

The **Students** property returns a reference to the collection of students, which makes it possible for the caller to have full read-write access to the collection:

```
Public Property Get Students() As Collection
'Return a reference to the student Collection.
  Set Students = mcolStudents
End Property
```

You may want to disallow such references to private instance variables, on the grounds that it circumvents the principle of data encapsulation. On the other hand, Visual Basic ActiveX controls such as ListView and TreeView permit this type of direct access to their collections.

The **FindByID** method searches the collection for a matching ID, using the Collection's key field. Recall that Set must be used when assigning a value to clsStudent:

```
Public Function FindByID(clsStudent As CStudent) As Boolean
'Search for a student in the Collection, using his/her ID number.
'Return True if found, False if not found. The Item method
'raises a runtime error 5 if the ID is not found, but we do not
'report this to the client.
  On Error GoTo NotFound
  Set clsStudent = mcolStudents.Item(clsStudent.IdNumber)
  FindByID = True
```

```
    Exit Function
NotFound:
    FindByID = False
End Function
```

8.4 CLIENT-SERVER EXAMPLE: RENTAL RATES

Now that we have seen an actual class module, let's take a look at another class that acts as a *database server*. Many applications, Visual Basic and otherwise, are designed in layers, providing a clear separation of tasks. The *data provider* layer is already implemented by the ADODB database provider. We're going to implement the next layer up, which we will call the *data server* layer. Specifically, this is a class called **CRentalPrices** that provides, on request, the daily and weekly car rental prices from the Stellar Car Rentals database in Chapter 6.

8.4.1 Client-Server Design

(samples: RentalRates)

In earlier chapters, our programs simply opened database Connections and Recordsets and did their own data retrieval. Consider what might happen in a company having numerous programs that require access to the same database. Each would require its own Connection, and each would have to be tailored to the exact table and field names in the database. A change to a single database field name would require all such programs to be updated, compiled, and tested. Our **CRentalPrices** class, on the other hand, provides a convenient way for client programs to get the data they need without having to know anything about the internal structure or location of the database. This approach is called *client-server* programming.

The interface for the CRentalPrices class consists of only a single function called **GetRentalRates**. It has two input parameters, strCategoryId and dtmRentalDate. It has two output parameters, curDailyRate and curWeeklyRate, and returns a Boolean result determining its success.

```
Public Function GetRentalRates(ByVal strCategoryId As String, _
    ByVal dtmRentalDate As Date, ByRef curDailyRate As Currency, _
    ByRef curWeeklyRate As Currency) As Boolean
```

The procedure searches for a particular category of vehicle and for a range of dates. If the vehicle category and rental date are found in the database, the function returns True and sets the values of curDailyRate and curWeeklyRate to the appropriate prices. If the function cannot find a matching category and rental date, it returns False and sets both rental rates to zero.

Price Table. The Price table contains, for each category of vehicle in the Stellar Car Rental company, the daily and weekly rental rates for various ranges of dates. To refresh your memory, Table 2 shows the table design and Table 3 contains a few sample records from the database.

Table 2. Price Table Fields.

Name	Type	Comments
CategoryId	Text	Identifies the vehicle category.
StartDate	Date	Date the price takes effect.
EndDate	Date	Date the price ends.
DailyRate	Currency	Rental rate, per day.
WeeklyRate	Currency	Rental rate, per week.

Table 3. Sample Records in the Price Table.

CategoryId	StartDate	EndDate	DailyRate	WeeklyRate
EC	01-01-1999	03-31-1999	19.95	110.00
EC	04-01-1999	07-31-1999	24.95	125.00
EC	08-01-1999	12-31-1999	18.95	105.00
CM	01-01-1999	03-31-1999	24.95	125.00
CM	04-01-1999	07-31-1999	30.95	155.00

8.4.2 Client Program

Our client program, created for the purpose of testing the CRentalPrices class, is very simple. It consists of a single Form with input fields for the vehicle category and rental date.

The Rental Date is selected by a DateTime Picker control. When the user clicks on the **Get Prices** button, the database search begins. The resulting prices (or a message saying that prices could not be found) appear in a Label.

Program Listing. The client program, **frmMain**, contains a CRentalRates object called mclsRentalRates:

```
Private mRentalRates As CRentalRates

Private Sub Form_Load()
  Set mclsRentalRates = New CRentalRates
End Sub
```

The **cmdGetRate_Click** procedure calls the GetRentalRates method, passing it the vehicle category from a TextBox, and the rental date from a DateTimePicker control. If the method returns True, the daily and weekly rates are formatted and placed in a Label:

```
Private Sub cmdGetRate_Click()
  Dim curDailyRate As Currency, curWeeklyRate As Currency
  If mclsRentalRates.GetRentalRates(txtCategoryId.Text, _
    dtpRentalDate.Value, curDailyRate, curWeeklyRate) Then
```

```
    lblResult.Caption = "Daily rate = " _
      & Format(curDailyRate, "Currency") _
      & ", Weekly rate = " _
      & Format(curWeeklyRate, "Currency")
  Else
    lblResult.Caption = "Rental rates not found"
  End If
End Sub
```

Clearly, obtaining the vehicle rental rates is easy for the client program, because all of the details are buried in the CRentalRates server class. This allows the client program to concentrate on its own processing requirements without being burdened by database details.

8.4.3 CRentalPrices Class

Implementation Code. The CRentalPrices implementation contains two private variables, one to hold the open database Connection, and another to hold the Recordset. Both are opened in the Class_Initialize event handler. This uses ADO object programming methods shown in Chapter 5:

```
Private mcnRentals As ADODB.Connection
Private mrsPrices As ADODB.Recordset

Private Sub Class_Initialize()
  Set mcnRentals = New ADODB.Connection
  mcnRentals.ConnectionString = "Provider = " _
    & "Microsoft.Jet.OLEDB.3.51; " _
    & "Data Source =" & App.Path & "\rentals.mdb"
  mcnRentals.Open
  Set mrsPrices = New ADODB.Recordset
  Call mrsPrices.Open("Price", mcnRentals, _
    adOpenStatic, adLockPessimistic, adCmdTable)
End Sub
```

The **Class_Terminate** event handler closes both the Connection and the Recordset:

```
Private Sub Class_Terminate()
  mrsPrices.Close
  mcnRentals.Close
End Sub
```

The **GetRentalRates** method performs a search for a matching vehicle category and a rental date. If the rental date, stored in dtmRentalDate, falls between the values of StartDate and EndDate in any row of the Recordset, the method immediately returns True and fills in the values of curDailyRate and curWeeklyRate:

```
Public Function GetRentalRates(ByVal strCategoryId As String, _
  ByVal dtmRentalDate As Date, ByRef curDailyRate As Currency, _
  ByRef curWeeklyRate As Currency) As Boolean
  Dim strQuery As String
  strQuery = "CategoryId = '" _
    & strCategoryId & "' AND StartDate <= #" _
    & dtmRentalDate & "# AND EndDate >= #" _
```

```
      & dtmRentalDate & "#"
    With mrsPrices
      .Filter = strQuery
      If .EOF Then
        GetRentalRates = False
        curDailyRate = 0
        curWeeklyRate = 0
      Else
        GetRentalRates = True
        curDailyRate = !DailyRate
        curWeeklyRate = !WeeklyRate
      End If
    End With
  End Function
```

We might also have chosen to close the existing Recordset and create a new one with a full SQL query. In this implementation, however, we simply assigned a conditional expression to the Filter property of the already opened mrsPrices Recordset.

Summary. There are a number of ways to improve the CRentalPrices server class, of course. Methods could be added that would allow client programs to retrieve all prices for a particular vehicle category, regardless of the rental date. Client programs, with the proper security clearance, could be allowed to update records in the Price table. The class can, in other words, expand to fit almost any future needs. It is both simple and modular.

You have probably noticed that the client program (frmMain) and the CRentalPrices class are both inside the same Visual Basic project. If CRentalPrices is to be truly useful to other programs, it must be compiled into its own separate program, as either a DLL (dynamic link library) or EXE (executable) program. This is actually a simple conversion, first by removing frmMain, and second by altering some of the project and class properties.

8.4.4 Creating an ActiveX Server

(samples: RentalRatesDLL)

In this section, we're going to modify a few properties of the CRentalPrices class and compile it into an **in-process ActiveX server**, having a filename extension of DLL. The advantage of doing this is that the new DLL can be loaded and run by any client program. The client will no longer have to be within the same project as CRentalPrices. We can do this in a series of steps:

- From the **Project > Properties** menu, select the **General** tab. Under **Project Type,** select **ActiveX DLL.** Under **Startup Object**, select **(None)**.
- Set **Project Name** to **RentalRates**. Click OK to close the Properties window.

> ***Tip:*** If you are running Visual Basic under Windows/NT with a security setup, you probably will not be able to register components. Only a user with Adminstrator access to the machine can do that. But you should be able to register components on your home computer.

- Bring up the CRentalPrices code window, press F4, and set the **Instancing** property to **MultiUse**. This will make the class visible to other programs.
- From the File menu, select **Make RentalRates.dll.** This will compile your server.

Create a Test Program. Now we need to create a new project that contains a test program. Let's add another project to the existing one:

- Select **Add Projec**t... from the **File** menu, and select **Standard EXE** as the project type. The project window caption should immediately change to **Project Group – Group1**, and the DLL server and the client program should both appear.
- Rename the new project to **TestProgram**, remove Form1, and add **frmMain** from the previous version of the program (see Figure 6) to the project. The Project Group window should now appear like this:

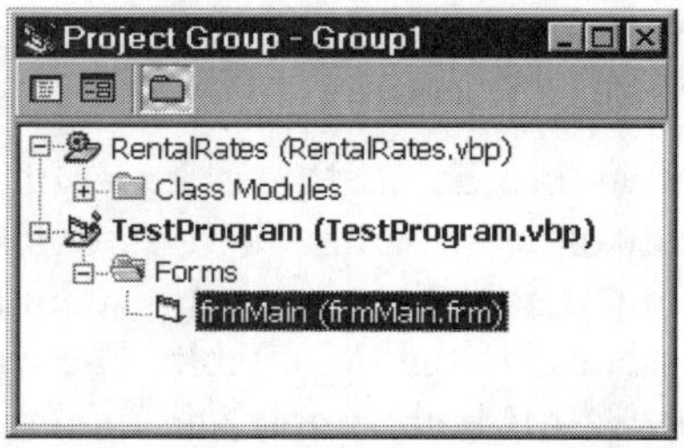

- Right-click the **TestProgram** project name in the Project Group window and select **Set as Start Up** from the popup menu.
- Select **References** from the Project menu, and place a check next to **RentalRates**:

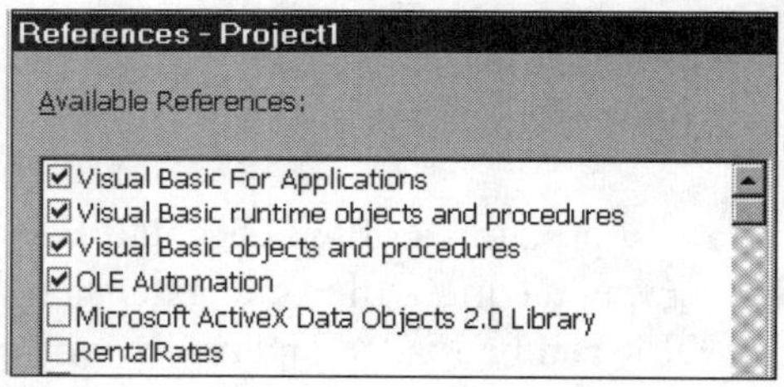

(When we compiled RentalRates DLL, Visual Basic automatically created an entry for it in the System Registry.)

Figure 6. Test Program for the RentalPrices Server.

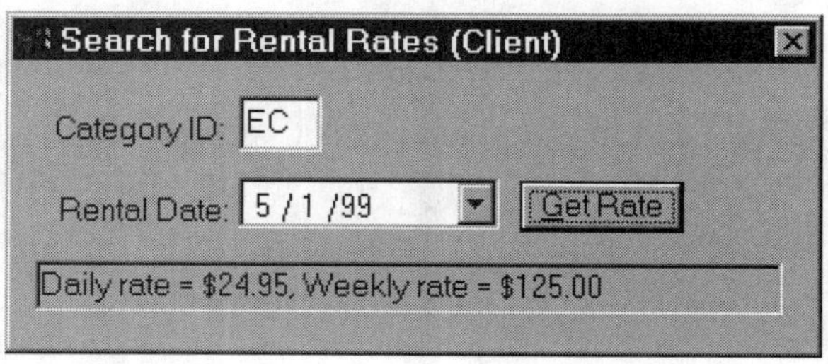

- Run the test program.

How does the test program know that the CRentalRates class exists, now that CRentalRates is in a separate project? This is accomplished by Microsoft's COM (*Component Object Model*) architecture. The CRentalRates class has been given an entry in the Windows System Registry, allowing any program that uses COM to create instances of the class. Along with the class name, all of its Public procedures (in this case, GetRentalRates) are visible to other applications. Take a moment, for example, to open the Object Browser and look for the CRentalRates class:

- Select **Object Browser** from the View menu.
- From the **<All Libraries>** ComboBox, select **RentalRates**. This name, incidentally, was the name of our DLL project. An ActiveX server can contain multiple classes.
- In the **Classes** pane in the lower left part of the window, double click on **CRentalRates**. In the right-hand pane, when you click on GetRentalRates, a list of function parameters appears at the bottom of the Object Browser window.

Isn't that cool? Now your ActiveX server can be seen by all COM-aware applications on your computer.

A Stand-Alone Test Program. But aren't we really doing the same thing as before, running the test program from the same project as the ActiveX server? Not exactly, because we currently have two projects belonging to the same program group. This is the ideal mode for testing a new server. Now, however, we're ready to take the final step, that of creating a completely separate, stand-alone test program:

- From the File menu, select **New Project**. Make it a Standard EXE project.
- Remove Form1 from the project.
- Select **Add File...** from the Project menu and select the frmMain.frm filename that we created earlier (see Figure 6).
- Add a reference to RentalRates in the **Project > References** menu.
- Run the program and see that it works.

Summary. Imagine the world of possibilities open to you, now that you know how to create ActiveX servers. Entire applications can be divided into classes, with some of them acting as servers. You can mix and match servers between different applications. As long as each server encapsulates database tables and queries, client programs do not have to get involved with low-level database details. ActiveX servers can also run across a network, so you can provide just one copy of each that is shared by programs running on multiple computers attached to a network server.

8.4.5 Registering and Unregistering Components

(samples: RegisterDLL)

When creating ActiveX servers it often becomes necessary to manually register and unregister servers. If, for example, you wanted to remove the RentalRates server from the Windows Registry, you could use the **RegEdit** program that we demonstrated in Chapter 2. But RegEdit can let you accidentally damage other valid Registry entries, and it requires some effort to find and remove all references to a particular server. A much easier way exists. At the Windows **Start** menu, choose **Run**, and enter the following command line, where **RentalRates.dll** is the name of the DLL you wish to register, in the c:\vbprogs directory:

```
regsvr32  c:\vbprogs\RentalRates.dll
```

Or, if you want to un-register the same DLL, type the following command line:

```
regsvr32  /U  c:\vbprogs\RentalRates.dll
```

The only disadvantage to running the REGSVR32 program is that you have to know the complete pathname of the DLL. If you have to move the DLL to another directory after registering it, be sure to un-register it before moving it, and re-register it in its new location. If you want to find out whether a certain DLL is registered, select **References** from the **Project** menu in Visual Basic, and look for the DLL's descriptive name. If it appears, the DLL is registered.

A Simple VB Program. There is an even easier way to register components. A simple program, written in Visual Basic by the authors, automates the process of registering and unregistering components (see Figure 7). You can use it to get rid of old Visual Basic 5 controls left behind after uninstalling Visual Basic 5.0. The **Browse** button lets you navigate from the current directory to anywhere on the computer, and the **System Directory** button takes you directly to the directory where most Windows applications store their components. In general, registered components have file extensions of DLL, OCX, EXE, and AX.

This is a handy program to compile and keep around on your Windows desktop. It only takes a second to run, and really helps when you are creating new versions of an ActiveX component. Be careful, of course, because this program can also remove components required by other applications. If you do so, you either have to re-register these components, or you have to reinstall their host applications.

Program Code. This program simply acts as a *wrapper* around the REGSVR32 program. At the root of it is the Shell command that executes another program and lets you pass parameters:

```
Private Sub cmdOK_Click()
   mstrCmdOption = ""
   If optUnRegister Then mstrCmdOption = "/U "
   Shell WindowsDirectory() + "\system\regsvr32.exe " _
        & mstrCmdOption & txtFileName.Text, 1
End Sub
```

Figure 7. Component Registration Utility.

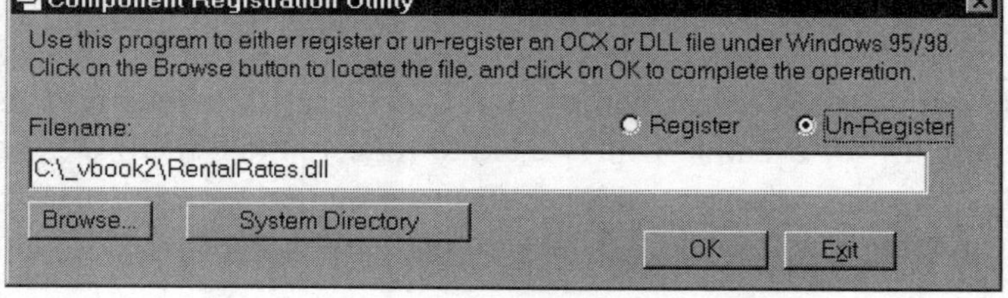

The cmdOK_Click procedure checks the value of the optUnRegister Option button, and if it is True, adds the **/u** parameter to the command line. WindowsDirectory is a function we wrote that returns the path to the Windows directory. It will be explained in detail in Chapter 10.

8.5 DOCTORS OFFICE SCHEDULING

(samples: DoctorSchedule)

It is now time to create a more complete program involving multiple classes and forms. The program, called **Doctors Office Scheduling**, sets and displays appointments made by patients at a medical office. We assume that several doctors work at the office, and that all current patient names are on file. The program displays past appointments for record-keeping purposes, and schedules upcoming appointments. An essential element in this program's design is that we show how different classes can interact, forming useful relationships.

8.5.1 Program Specifications

Here are the program's major functions:

- A patient can request an appointment with a specific doctor at a specific date and time.
- When an appointment is scheduled, the program stores the appointment data in a database. For each appointment, we identify the patient, the doctor, the date and time, and the purpose of the appointment.
- The user can view all appointments currently scheduled, and all appointments scheduled for a particular patient.

8.5.2 User Interface Design

The user interface for this program consists of the following windows:

- Splash screen
- Main MDI window with a ToolBar
- Input Appointment form
- Appointment Display form containing a DataGrid
- Patient Selection form

Program Startup. The program begins with a Splash screen, shown in Figure 8. The main MDI window appears soon after, shown in Figure 9. It uses a ToolBar button for each of the program's main functions: **NewAppt**, **ShowAll**, **Patient**, and **Exit**. The NewAppt button displays a form into which the user can enter all of the information about a new appointment. The ShowAll button displays a list of all scheduled appointments, sorted by date and time. The Patient button displays a list of all appointments scheduled for a single patient.

New Appointment. When the user clicks on the **NewAppt** button, the Input Appointment form appears, in Figure 10. The user selects a doctor ID and patient name from ComboBox controls, selects the date and time from DateTimePicker controls, and enters the purpose of the visit into a TextBox.

If the user clicks on **OK**, the appointment is saved; if the user clicks on **Cancel**, the appointment is discarded. If the appointment time is before 8:30 a.m. or after 4:45 pm, the following message displays:

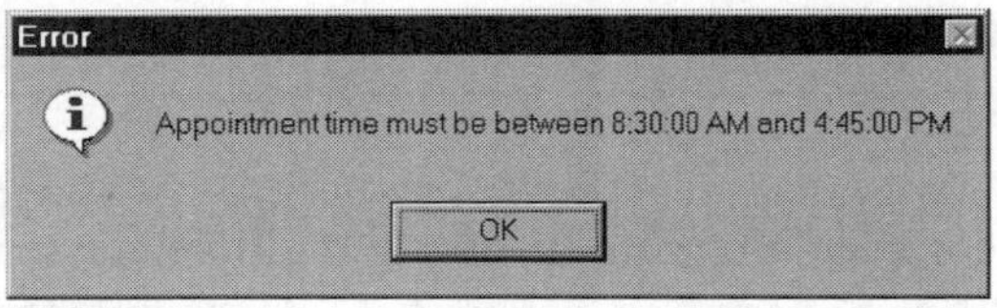

Figure 8. Splash Screen.

Figure 9. Doctors Office Scheduling, Main MDI Window.

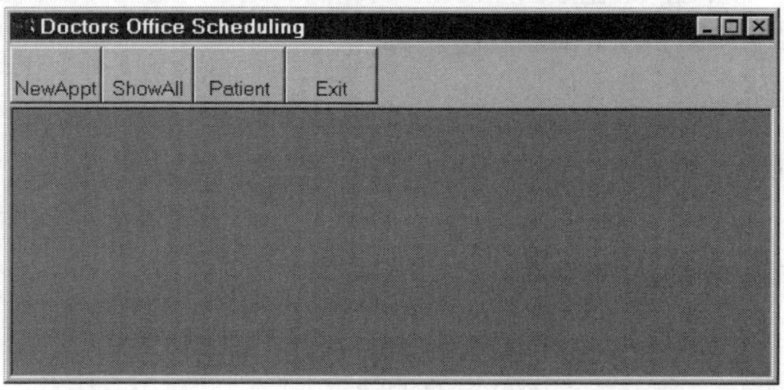

Figure 10. Adding a New Appointment.

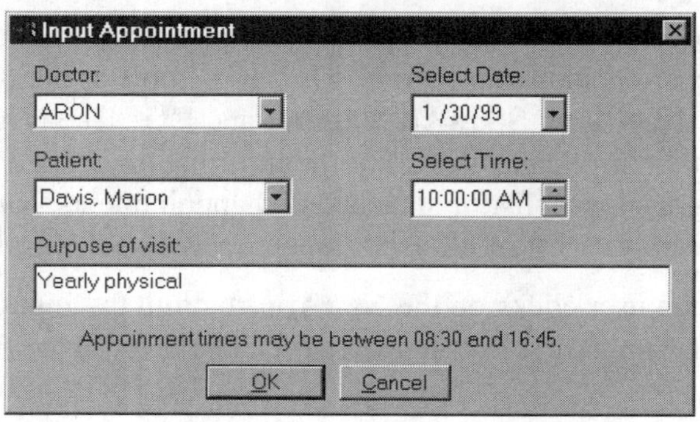

Back in the main window, the user can also view a list of all appointments in the calendar by clicking the **Show All** button (Figure 11). A DataGrid control is used.

The user can also view all appointments made by a single patient. A ComboBox lists the patient names. Once a name has been selected, a window displays the appointments (Figure 12).

Our program allows the user to create multiple instances of the Appointment display window, both for all patients, and for individual patients. Figure 13 shows an example with three open windows.

8.5.3 Class Interfaces

The CPatient class represents a single patient. The CAppointment class represents a single appointment. The CApptCalendar class represents the appointment calendar that contains CAppointment objects. The various forms in the program are also classes. Table 4 describes the properties and public methods of the CAppointment class. Table 5 describes the CPatient class, and Table 6 describes the CApptCalendar class.

Figure 14 shows the complete list of forms, code modules, and class modules in the Project window of this program.

Figure 11. Viewing All Appointments.

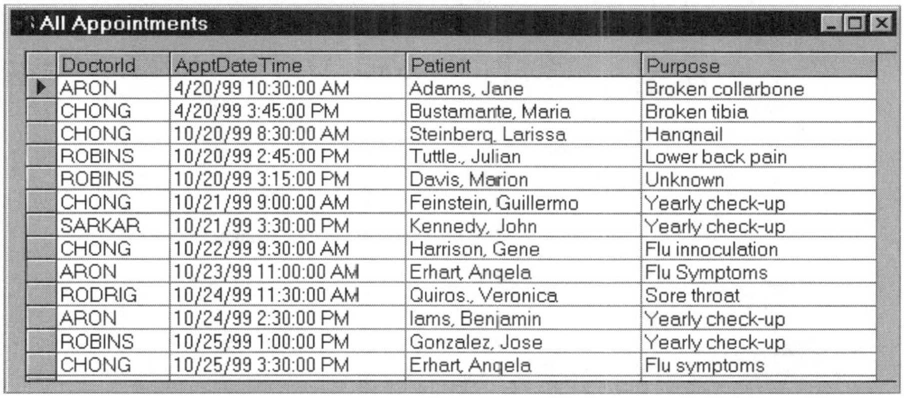

All Appointments

DoctorId	ApptDateTime	Patient	Purpose
ARON	4/20/99 10:30:00 AM	Adams, Jane	Broken collarbone
CHONG	4/20/99 3:45:00 PM	Bustamante, Maria	Broken tibia
CHONG	10/20/99 8:30:00 AM	Steinberg, Larissa	Hangnail
ROBINS	10/20/99 2:45:00 PM	Tuttle., Julian	Lower back pain
ROBINS	10/20/99 3:15:00 PM	Davis, Marion	Unknown
CHONG	10/21/99 9:00:00 AM	Feinstein, Guillermo	Yearly check-up
SARKAR	10/21/99 3:30:00 PM	Kennedy, John	Yearly check-up
CHONG	10/22/99 9:30:00 AM	Harrison, Gene	Flu innoculation
ARON	10/23/99 11:00:00 AM	Erhart, Angela	Flu Symptoms
RODRIG	10/24/99 11:30:00 AM	Quiros., Veronica	Sore throat
ARON	10/24/99 2:30:00 PM	Iams, Benjamin	Yearly check-up
ROBINS	10/25/99 1:00:00 PM	Gonzalez, Jose	Yearly check-up
CHONG	10/25/99 3:30:00 PM	Erhart, Angela	Flu symptoms

Figure 12. Appointments for a Single Patient.

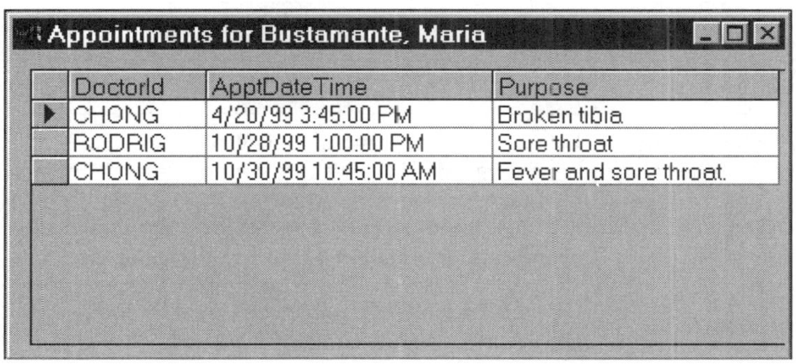

Appointments for Bustamante, Maria

DoctorId	ApptDateTime	Purpose
CHONG	4/20/99 3:45:00 PM	Broken tibia
RODRIG	10/28/99 1:00:00 PM	Sore throat
CHONG	10/30/99 10:45:00 AM	Fever and sore throat

8.5.4 Class Relationships

Before we look at the detailed program code for this application, it is helpful to study the relationships between classes. At runtime, certain objects contain instances of other objects, thereby controlling them. In Figure 15, each relationship has been numbered (1-5). Rela-

Figure 13. Viewing Several Display Windows.

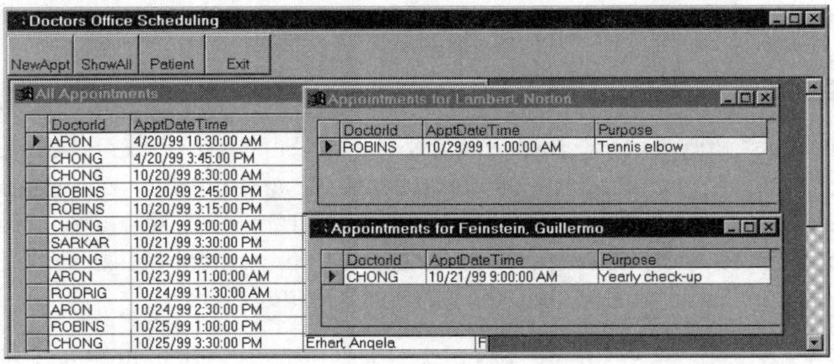

Table 4. Public Properties and Methods of the CAppointment Class.

Properties	Description (Data Type)
DoctorId property	Doctor ID (String)
PatientId property	Patient ID (String)
ApptDate property	Date of the appointment (Date)
ApptTime property	Time of the appointment (Date)
Purpose property	Describes the purpose of the appointment (String)
InputFromUser	Interactively inputs an appointment from the user by displaying a dialog box. Returns True if the user confirms the appointment, or False, if the user cancels.
AsString	Returns a string representation of the appointment.
AsRecordset	Stores the appointment data into a Recordset object that matches the Appointment table in the Rentals database.
ReadRecord	Reads a record from an open Recordset into the current appointment.

Table 5. Public Properties and Methods of the CPatient Class.

Name	Description (Data Type)
PatientId property	Patient ID (String)
PatientName property	Last name, first name of the current patient.
SelectByName	Displays a list of patient names in a ComboBox and lets the user select a name. Sets the PatientId property to the patient's ID from the database.
LookupPatientName	Given a Patient ID number, this method looks up and returns the full name of a patient.

tionship #1 shows that modMain displays both frmSplash and frmMain. In #2, frmMain creates an instance of CApptCalendar. In #3, the CApptCalendar creates instances of CAppointment, CPatient, and frmDisplay. In #4, the CAppointment class creates instances of frmApptInput and CPatient. And in #5, the CPatient class creates an instance of frmSelectPatient.

How do these class relationships work in actual practice? We can use an example to illustrate: When the user clicks on the AddAppt button on the ToolBar in frmMain, the following sequence of events takes place:

Table 6. Public Methods of the CApptCalendar Class.

Methods	Description
AddAppointment	Shows an input form, gets appointment data from the user, and adds the appointment to the calendar.
ShowPatientAppointments	Shows all appointments for a particular patient.
ShowAllAppointments	Shows all appointments for all patients and doctors.

Figure 14. Doctors Project Window.

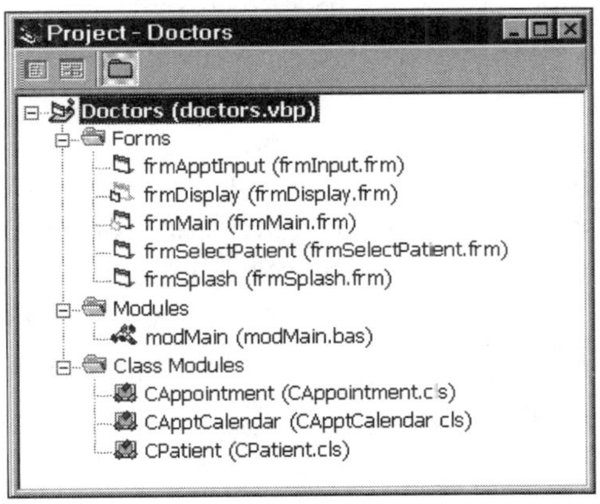

Figure 15. Class Relationship Diagram.

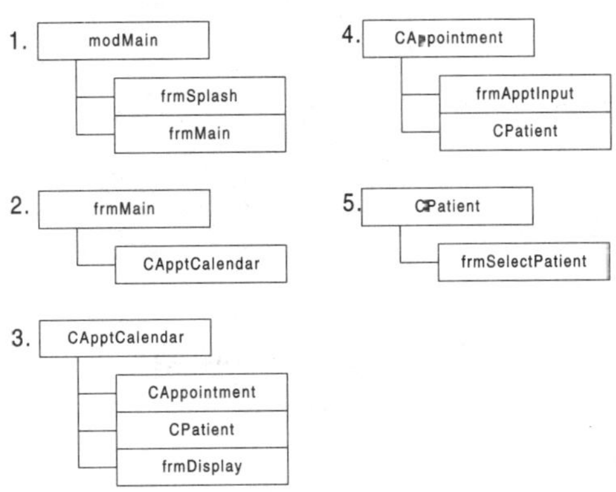

1. frmMain calls the CApptCalendar.AddAppointment method.
2. In the AddAppointment method, CApptCalendar creates a CAppointment object and calls the CAppointment.InputFromUser method.
3. In the InputFromUser method, CAppointment sets several properties of the frmApptInput form, and then displays it.
4. The user enters all necessary input into the frmApptInput Form and clicks the OK button.
5. Back in the InputFromUser method, CAppointment calls its private SaveAppointment method to copy data from frmApptInput into the CAppointment instance variables.
6. Back in the AddAppointment method, CApptCalendar adds a new record to the database and calls the AsRecordset method in the CAppointment class, passing it an empty Recordset object.
7. The AsRecordset method copies the class instance variables into a Recordset object
8. The AddAppointment method (in CApptCalendar) updates the database record, and now the appointment has been saved.

Of course, that sequence of events was not easy to follow if you haven't seen the program's source code. In the next section we do just that, and that will give you a chance to trace through the eight steps we just described, when the user creates a new appointment.

8.5.5 Program Code

Some readers like to see all the source code for an example program, while others don't. Most of the time, we present only the most important code from programs used in this book. In this section, however, we show the complete source code for the Doctors Office Scheduling program, with all its gory details. You can browse through it quickly and get a general impression, read it thoroughly and inspect every detail, or you can just skip it completely and go on to the next chapter.

frmSplash Form. Here is the code for the splash screen:

```
Private Sub cmdOk_Click()
  Unload Me
End Sub

Private Sub Form_Load()
  lblVersionInfo.Caption = "Version " & App.Major & "." & App.Minor
  Timer1.Enabled = True
End Sub

Private Sub Timer1_Timer()
  Unload Me
End Sub
```

frmMain Form. This is the code for the MDI Parent window with a ToolBar control named tlbMain. It contains an instance of the appointment calendar, called mclsCalendar:

```
Dim mclsCalendar As CApptCalendar
```

```
Private Sub MDIForm_Load()
  Set mclsCalendar = New CApptCalendar
  Me.Width = Screen.Width * 0.8
  Me.Height = Screen.Height * 0.8
End Sub

Private Sub tlbMain_ButtonClick(ByVal Button _
        As MSComctlLib.Button)
  On Error GoTo ButtonClickErr
  Select Case Button.Key
    Case "NewAppt"
      mclsCalendar.AddAppointment
    Case "ShowAll"
      mclsCalendar.ShowAllAppointments
    Case "Patient"
      mclsCalendar.ShowPatientAppointments
    Case "Exit"
      Unload Me
  End Select
  Exit Sub
ButtonClickErr:
  MsgBox Err.Description, vbCritical, Err.Number
End Sub
```

frmApptInput Form. The frmApptInput Form is displayed by the CAppointment class when the user wants to input an appointment:

```
Private mblnSaveAppt As Boolean        'SaveAppt property
Private mdtmEarlyTime As Date          'EarliestApptTime property
Private mdtmLateTime As Date           'LatestApptTime property
Private mstrDoctorID As String         'DoctorId property
Private mstrPatientID As String        'PatientId property
Private mrsDoctors As ADODB.Recordset
Private mrsPatients As ADODB.Recordset
Private mcollPatientIDS As Collection

'************* PUBLIC INTERFACE ***************

Public Property Let EarliestApptTime(early As Date)
  mdtmEarlyTime = early
End Property

Public Property Let LatestApptTime(late As Date)
  mdtmLateTime = late
End Property

Public Property Get DoctorID() As String      'read-only
  DoctorID = mstrDoctorID
End Property

Public Property Get PatientID() As String     'read-only
  PatientID = mstrPatientID
End Property
```

```
Public Property Get ShouldSave() As Boolean  'read-only
' True indicates that the user wants to
' save this appointment.
  ShouldSave = mblnSaveAppt
End Property

'************* PRIVATE IMPLEMENTATION ***************

Private Sub Form_Activate()
  lblTimeRange = "Appoinment times may be between " _
    & Format$(mdtmEarlyTime, "hh:mm") & " and " _
    & Format$(mdtmLateTime, "hh:mm") & "."
End Sub

Private Sub cboDoctors_Click()
  mstrDoctorID = cboDoctors.Text
End Sub

Private Sub cboPatients_Click()
'Use the ListIndex to get the appropriate Patient ID from
'the mcollPatientIDS Collection.
  mstrPatientID = mcollPatientIDS(cboPatients.ListIndex + 1)
End Sub

Private Sub cmdCancel_Click()
  mblnSaveAppt = False
  Me.Hide
End Sub

Private Sub cmdOk_Click()
  If ValidateFields Then
    mblnSaveAppt = True
    Me.Hide
  End If
End Sub

Public Sub FillComboBoxes()
  Set mrsDoctors = New ADODB.Recordset
  Set mrsPatients = New ADODB.Recordset
  Set mcollPatientIDS = New Collection
  Dim strTemp As String

  With mrsDoctors
    Call .Open("Doctors", gcnDoctors, _
        adOpenStatic, adLockPessimistic, adCmdTable)
    Do Until .EOF
      cboDoctors.AddItem !DoctorID
      .MoveNext
    Loop
    .Close
  End With

  With mrsPatients
```

```
      Call mrsPatients.Open("select * from Patients " _
        & "order by " & "LastName, FirstName", _
        gcnDoctors, adOpenStatic, adLockPessimistic, _
        adCmdText)
      Do Until .EOF
        cboPatients.AddItem !LastName & ", " & !FirstName
        strTemp = !PatientID
        mcollPatientIDS.Add strTemp
        .MoveNext
      Loop
      .Close
    End With
  End Sub

  Private Function ValidateFields() As Boolean
    ValidateFields = False
    'Check for a doctor ID.
    If cboDoctors.ListIndex = -1 Then
      MsgBox "A doctor must be selected", _
       vbInformation, "Error"
      Exit Function
    End If

    'Check for a patient name.
    If cboPatients.ListIndex = -1 Then
      MsgBox "A patient must be selected", _
       vbInformation, "Error"
      Exit Function
    End If

    'Check for valid time range.
    With dtpApptTime
      Dim tm As Date
      tm = TimeValue(.Value)
      If tm < mdtmEarlyTime Or tm > mdtmLateTime Then
        MsgBox "Appointment time must be between " _
          & mdtmEarlyTime & " and " & mdtmLateTime, _
            vbInformation, "Error"
        Exit Function
      End If
    End With

    MsgBox "Appointment confirmed.", vbInformation, ""
    ValidateFields = True
  End Function
```

frmDisplay Form. This Form displays appointments in a DataGrid control named dgdAppts:

```
Private Sub Form_Resize()
  dgdAppts.Width = Width + 400
  dgdAppts.Height = Height - 500
End Sub
```

frmSelectPatient Form. This Form displays a ComboBox named cboPatient containing the names of all patients:

```
Private Sub cboPatient_Click()
  Me.Hide
End Sub
```

modMain Code Module. The modMain module contains the global connection variable, gcnDoctors, and it opens the Connection and shows the frmMain and frmSplash windows. It is the startup module for the program itself:

```
Public gcnDoctors As ADODB.Connection

Public Sub Main()
  Set gcnDoctors = New ADODB.Connection
  gcnDoctors.ConnectionString = "Provider = " _
    & "Microsoft.Jet.OLEDB.3.51; " _
    & "Data Source =" & App.Path & "\doctors.mdb"
  gcnDoctors.Open
  frmMain.Show vbModeless
  frmSplash.Show vbModal
End Sub
```

CAppointment Class. Here is the complete source code for the CAppointment class:

```
Const mdtmEarliestApptTime As Date = #8:30:00 AM#
Const mdtmLatestApptTime As Date = #4:45:00 PM#
Private mstrDoctorID As String
Private mstrPatientID As String
Private mdtmApptDate As Date
Private mdtmApptTime As Date
Private mstrPurpose As String

'************** PUBLIC INTERFACE ***************

Public Property Get DoctorID() As String
  DoctorID = mstrDoctorID
End Property

Public Property Let DoctorID(newValue As String)
  mstrDoctorID = newValue
End Property

Public Static Property Get PatientID() As String
  PatientID = mstrPatientID
End Property

Public Static Property Let PatientID(newValue As String)
  mstrPatientID = newValue
End Property

Public Property Get ApptDate() As Date
  ApptDate = mdtmApptDate
End Property
```

```
Public Property Let ApptDate(newValue As Date)
  mdtmApptDate = newValue
End Property

Public Property Get ApptTime() As Date
  ApptTime = mdtmApptTime
End Property

Public Property Let ApptTime(newValue As Date)
  mdtmApptTime = newValue
End Property

Public Property Get Purpose() As String
  Purpose = mstrPurpose
End Property

Public Property Let Purpose(newValue As String)
  mstrPurpose = newValue
End Property

Public Function InputFromUser() As Boolean
'Uses a separate Form (frmApptInput) to get
'information from the user.

  With frmApptInput
    .FillComboBoxes
    .EarliestApptTime = mdtmEarliestApptTime
    .LatestApptTime = mdtmLatestApptTime
    .Show vbModal
    If .ShouldSave Then
      SaveAppointment
      InputFromUser = True
    End If
  End With
End Function

Public Function AsString() As String
'Return a string representation of an
'appointment.

  Dim aPatient As New CPatient
  Dim strPatientName As String
  strPatientName = aPatient.LookupPatientName(PatientID)
  AsString = DoctorID & aPatient & _
    Format$(ApptDate, "Medium Date") & "  " & _
    Format$(ApptTime, "Medium Time") & "  " & _
    Purpose
End Function

Public Sub AsRecordset(R As Recordset)
'Store this CAppoinment object into a Recordset
'that matches the Appointment table in the
'Rentals database.
```

```
    On Error Resume Next
    R!DoctorID = DoctorID
    R!PatientID = PatientID
    R!ApptDateTime = ApptDate + ApptTime
    R!Purpose = Purpose
End Sub

Public Sub ReadRecord(rsAppt As Recordset)
'Transfer data from current database record to
'this object.

   With rsAppt
      DoctorID = "" & !DoctorID
      PatientID = "" & !PatientID
      ApptDate = "" & !Date
      ApptTime = "" & !Time
      Purpose = "" & !Purpose
   End With
End Sub

'************* PRIVATE IMPLEMENTATION ***************

Private Sub SaveAppointment()
'Called when the OK button in frmApptInput
'is clicked.

   With frmApptInput
      DoctorID = .DoctorID
      PatientID = .PatientID
      ApptDate = DateValue(.dtpApptDate.Value)
      ApptTime = TimeValue(.dtpApptTime.Value)
      Purpose = .txtPurpose.Text
   End With
   Unload frmApptInput
End Sub
```

CPatient Class. The following is the complete source code for the CPatient class:

```
Dim mstrPatientID As String
Dim mstrPatientName As String
Dim mstrTableName As String
Dim mrsPatients As Recordset

'************* PUBLIC INTERFACE *****************

Public Sub SelectByName()
'Let the user select a patient name from a list. The name and
'ID are placed in the PatientId and PatientName Properties.

   On Error GoTo SelectByNameErr
   Dim mcollPatientIDS As New Collection
   Dim strTemp As String
```

```
  With mrsPatients
    .MoveFirst
    Do Until .EOF
      frmSelectPatient.cboPatient.AddItem !LastName & ", " _
        & !FirstName
      strTemp = !PatientID
      mcollPatientIDS.Add strTemp
      .MoveNext
    Loop
  End With

  With frmSelectPatient
    .Show vbModal
    mstrPatientID = mcollPatientIDS(.cboPatient.ListIndex + 1)
    mstrPatientName = .cboPatient.Text
  End With
  Exit Sub

SelectByNameErr:
  MsgBox Error$, vbInformation, "Error"
End Sub

Public Property Get PatientID() As String
  PatientID = mstrPatientID
End Property

Public Property Get PatientName() As String
  PatientName = mstrPatientName
End Property

Public Function LookupPatientName(strId As String)
'Given a Patient ID, return the person's full name.

  With mrsPatients
    .MoveFirst
    .Find "PatientId = " & strId
    If .EOF Then
      LookupPatientName = ""
    Else
      LookupPatientName = !LastName & ", " & !FirstName
    End If
  End With
End Function

'************* PRIVATE MEMBERS *****************

Private Sub OpenTable()
  Set mrsPatients = New ADODB.Recordset
  Call mrsPatients.Open(mstrTableName, gcnDoctors, _
     adOpenStatic, adLockPessimistic, adCmdTable)
End Sub

Private Sub Class_Initialize()
```

```
    mstrTableName = "Patients"
    OpenTable
  End Sub

  Private Sub Class_Terminate()
    mrsPatients.Close
  End Sub
```

CApptCalendar Class. The following is the complete listing of the code in the CApptCalendar class:

```
Private mrsAppointments As ADODB.Recordset
Private mstrTableName As String
Private mblnTableOpen As Boolean

'************* PUBLIC INTERFACE ***************

Public Sub AddAppointment()
'Show an input Form, get appointment
'data from the user, add to calendar.
  If Not mblnTableOpen Then Exit Sub
  On Error GoTo AddApptErr
  Dim anAppt As New CAppointment
  If anAppt.InputFromUser Then
    mrsAppointments.AddNew
    anAppt.AsRecordset mrsAppointments
    mrsAppointments.Update
    Exit Sub
  End If
  Exit Sub
AddApptErr:
  Err.Raise vbObjectError + 513, vbCritical, _
      "Cannot Add Appointment"
End Sub

Public Sub ShowAllAppointments()
'Show all appointments in a DataGrid.
 If Not mblnTableOpen Then Exit Sub
 Dim frmTemp As New frmDisplay          'new MDI child Form
 On Error GoTo ShowAllApptsErr
 With frmTemp
   .Caption = "All Appointments"
   .Show vbModeless
   .adoAppts.ConnectionString = gcnDoctors.ConnectionString
   .adoAppts.RecordSource = _
     "select DoctorId, ApptDateTime, Patients.LastName " _
       & "+ ', ' + Patients.firstName As Patient, Purpose " _
       & "From Appointments Inner Join Patients " _
       & "On Appointments.PatientId = Patients.PatientId " _
       & "Order by ApptDateTime"

     .adoAppts.Refresh
 End With
 Exit Sub
```

```
ShowAllApptsErr:
  Err.Raise vbObjectError + 514, vbCritical, _
      "Error in ShowAllAppointments"
End Sub

Public Sub ShowPatientAppointments()
'Show appointments for a single patient.
'First, let user select a patient.
  If Not mblnTableOpen Then Exit Sub
  Dim aPatient As New CPatient
  aPatient.SelectByName
  If aPatient.PatientID = 0 Then Exit Sub 'cancelled

'Use an SQL query to create a temporary Recordset
'containing appointments for the selected patient,
'ordered by date and time.
  Dim frmTemp As New frmDisplay  'new MDI child Form
  Dim strQuery As String
  On Error GoTo ShowPatientApptsErr
  strQuery = _
      "select DoctorId, ApptDateTime, Purpose " _
      & "From Appointments Inner Join Patients " _
      & "On Appointments.PatientId = Patients.PatientId " _
      & "Where Patients.PatientId = '" & aPatient.PatientID _
      & "' " _
      & "Order by ApptDateTime"
   With frmTemp
     .Show vbModeless
     .Caption = "Appointments for " + _
         aPatient.PatientName
     .adoAppts.ConnectionString = gcnDoctors.ConnectionString
     .adoAppts.RecordSource = strQuery
     .adoAppts.Refresh
   End With
   Exit Sub
ShowPatientApptsErr:
  Err.Raise vbObjectError + 515, vbCritical, _
      "Error in ShowPatientAppts"
End Sub

'************* PRIVATE IMPLEMENTATION ***************

Private Sub OpenTable()
'Open the Appointments table.
  On Error GoTo OpenTableErr
  Set mrsAppointments = New ADODB.Recordset
  Call mrsAppointments.Open(mstrTableName, gcnDoctors, _
    adOpenStatic, adLockPessimistic, adCmdTable)
  mblnTableOpen = True
  Exit Sub
OpenTableErr:
  MsgBox Error$, vbCritical, "OpenTable Method"
  mblnTableOpen = False
End Sub
```

```
Private Sub Class_Initialize()
   mstrTableName = "Appointments"
   mblnTableOpen = False
   OpenTable
End Sub

Private Sub Class_Terminate()
   If mblnTableOpen Then mrsAppointments.Close
End Sub
```

8.6 REVIEW QUESTIONS

1. What are the names of three object-oriented programming languages that first appeared in the early 1980s?
2. What is the most obvious influence on Visual Basic produced by more traditional object-oriented programming languages?
3. How do you define *class* in object-oriented terms?
4. How is an object different from a class?
5. Do the icons in the Visual Basic ToolBox represent classes, or objects?
6. How are properties different from methods?
7. Is there a separate copy of the **SetFocus** method in every CommandButton on the same Form?
8. Does each CommandButton on the same Form have its own copy of the **Visible** property?
9. Do all OptionButtons on the same Form share the same event handler?
10. How do classes relate to physical entities in real-world programming applications?
11. In a student record-keeping program, what attributes might be assigned to a college transcript class?
12. What is *encapsulation*?
13. Which essential feature of object-oriented programming was left out of Visual Basic?
14. Does every instance of a class have to be assigned its own class module?
15. Code a Dim statement that declares a variable of type CTranscript.
16. Code a statement that creates a CTranscript object and assigns it to the variable from the previous question.
17. Code a statement that releases the memory used by the object variable used in the previous two questions.
18. Code a single statement that both declares an object variable and creates a new instance of the CTranscript class.
19. What happens to an object that is created inside a procedure when the procedure finishes?

20. What is an *instance variable*?
21. Can the name of an instance variable be the same as the name of a property within the same class?
22. What three procedures are used to retrieve and assign the value of a property?
23. Can two different classes have a property by the same name? If so, can you think of an example?
24. Code an example of a property named **LastName** that assigns a string value to an instance variable named **mstrLastName**.
25. Why are instance variables usually declared private in classes?
26. How might a class prevent an out-of-range value from being assigned to one of its properties?
27. How does one create a read-only property?
28. Which event fires when a class object is created?
29. Which event fires when a class object is destroyed?
30. Fill in the missing word: A class interface is composed of properties and ____________.
31. How does a class transmit error information to clients?
32. In the CAppointment class in the Doctors Office Appointments program, what does the **AsString** method accomplish?
33. How might a *private* method be used?
34. At the end of the following example, how many CStudent objects exist?

```
Dim st1 As New CStudent
Dim st2 As CStudent
Set st2 = st1
```

35. At the end of the following example, how many CStudent objects exist?

```
Dim st1 As New CStudent
Dim st2 As CStudent
Set st2 = st1
Set st1 = Nothing
```

The following questions refer to the Student Class program shown in Section 8.2:

36. Does the CStudent class load and display frmMain, or is it the other way around?
37. What error checking is performed by the StudentId property?
38. What error checking is performed by the LastName property?

The following questions refer to the Student Collection Class program shown in Section 8.3:

39. How does a *containing* relationship exist between the classes in this program?

40. How is the standard Collection class used in this program?
41. In this program, do any of the classes load and display forms?
42. In the CStudentCollection class, how does the Add method prevent the user from inserting two students with the same ID number?
43. What operation is carried out by the Initialize event handler in the CStudentCollection class?
44. What does the **FindByID** method accomplish in CStudentCollection class?
45. What happens when the **Item** method of a Collection fails to find a matching key value?

8.7 CHAPTER EXERCISES

8.7.1 Student Collection: Searching for Names

In the CStudentCollection class in Section 8.3, the FindByLastName method locates only the first student in the collection matching the requested name. Revise this method so that it returns a collection containing all students having the same name. Run and test the revised program.

8.7.2 Saving the Student Collection

Modify the Student Collection program in Section 8.3 so that it saves the collection in a database before the program exits. When the program starts up, load the collection from the database.

8.7.3 Student Collection: Completed Courses

In the Student Collection program, Add a collection of college courses to the CStudent class. When the program starts, read the course data for each student from a database. When the user searches for a student by either ID or name, display a list of all courses completed by the student. The members of the course collection should be objects containing the following data:

```
'CCourse Class:
Private mstrCourseNumber As String
Private mstrYearSem As String
Private mintCredits As Integer
Private mstrGrade As String
```

Table 7 displays eight sample records.

8.7.4 Student Collection: The CCourse Class

Using the program written for the previous exercise, add the following methods and call each from your program:

- AsString: Return a string representation of the course.
- SetFields(crsNum, yearSem, cred, grd): Assign values to all four class properties.

Table 7. Sample Courses, Student Collection.

Student ID	Course Number	Year/Sem (yyss format)	Credits	Grade (A=4, F=0)
111-22-3333	ENG 1001	9601	3	4
111-22-3333	BIO 1050	9601	4	3
111-22-3333	MTH 1022	9602	3	4
111-22-3333	FRE 2051	9602	3	2
111-22-4444	PHY 1010	9601	3	4
111-22-4444	GEO 1702	9602	4	3
111-22-4444	GER 1051	9602	3	4
111-22-4444	CHM 1021	9602	4	3

- Input: Let user input a new course, and add the course to the current student's course Collection.

8.7.5 Object-Oriented Glossary Program

Use the Glossary program from Exercise 3.8.12 in Chapter 3 as a starting point for this exercise. Create class modules called CDefinition and CGlossary. Provide methods that load the glossary from a database table, save it in a table, search for keywords, and so on. Write a test program that creates two instances of the CGlossary class and displays each one in a separate MDI child window.

8.7.6 CMotor Class

Create a program that tracks electric motors for a manufacturing plant. The CMotor class should have the following properties:

MotorId	5-digit string, such as "02340"
Description	String, up to 80 characters long
RPM	Single, values in the range 10 to 10000
Voltage	Single, values in the range 1 to 500
Status	String, 3 characters.

The Status values are:

ON	Motor is online and running
OFF	Motor is online but not running
MNT	Undergoing maintenance and cleaning
NA	Motor is not available

Create a database table whose fields correspond to the CMotor class properties. Insert at least 10 records into the table. Create an input Form in your Visual Basic program that lets users input new motor records. Create another Form that displays all motors in a DataGrid control.

8.7.7 CMotorCollection Class

Continuing the previous exercise, create a second class called CMotorCollection. This class represents the entire collection of motors owned by the company. It opens and closes the database, reads the motors from the database, and displays motors according to various criteria, sorting on different fields. Use a ListView control to display the collection of motors. Provide methods such as AddMotor, RemoveMotor, and FindMotor.

8.7.8 Mozart Music: CInvoice Class

In Exercise 3.8.4 in Chapter 3, you were asked to create an MDI version of the Mozart Music program. For the current exercise, create a class called CInvoice and use it to encapsulate properties and methods appropriate to a sales invoice. Here are suggested properties: InvoiceID, InvoiceDate, CumAmount, Tax, and Total.

8.7.9 Object-Oriented Time Clock

Using the Time Clock program from Exercise 2.8.9 in Chapter 2 as a guide, create a class called **CTimeClock** that encapsulates the various calculations used in the program. Here is a suggested list:

- Read-Only properties: StartTime, StopTime, ElapsedMinutes
- Read-Write property: ClientName
- Public Methods: StartClock, StopClock

The StartTime and StopTime properties contain Date/Time values. The ElapsedMinutes property contains a long integer representing the number of minutes between the starting and ending times. The StartClock and StopClock methods begin and end the timing sequence, respectively.

In the program's main Form, declare a variable of type CTimeClock; in Form_Load, create an instance of the class:

```
Private mClock As CTimeClock
Private Sub Form_Load()
   Set mClock = New CTimeClock
End Sub
```

When the user clicks on the Start button, call the StartClock method and pass it the current time:

```
mClock.StartClock Now
```

Similarly, when the use clicks on Stop, call the StopClock and ElapsedMinutes methods:

```
mClock.StopClock Now
lblElapsed.Caption = mClock.ElapsedMinutes
```

8.7.10 E-Mail Address Book

Write a program that lets the user display and modify an address book containing names, e-mail addresses, and phone numbers. The program should contain at least two classes: CAddress, and CAddressList. The CAddress class contains the following information about one person: name, email address, phone, and comments. The CAddressList class encapsulates a collection of CAddress objects. It contains operations that let the user add, remove, display, and edit individual address entries.

The main window, shown in Figure 16, displays the names from the address book in a ListBox, loaded from a database table. The user should be able to input new names and addresses, using a Form similar to the one shown in Figure 17.

8.7.11 Yachting Regatta – 1

MDI RaceInfo and BoatInfo. The SeaWind Yacht Club keeps track of the results of multiple sailboat races that together make up a single regatta. Write an MDI application that lets the user display information for several races and several sailboats. Create separate MDI child windows that display properties from the CRaceInfo and CBoatInfo classes. At any time, one race and one boat can be displayed at the same time. The **CRaceInfo** class has the properties shown in Table 8. For now, the Handicap Minutes and Adjusted Time properties should be set to zero. Store each CRaceInfo object in a database table. Create a second class called **CBoatInfo** that contains the following properties, shown in Table 9.

8.7.12 Yachting Regatta - 2

Calculate Boat Handicaps. Continue the Yachting Regatta program from the previous exercise. Provide the following additional features:

Figure 16. E-Mail Address Book, Main Window.

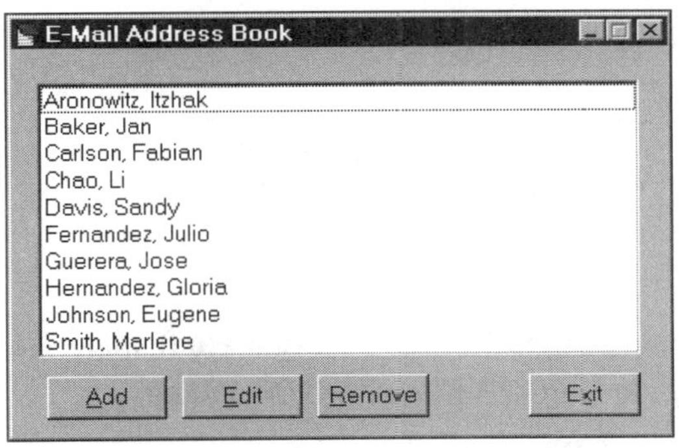

Figure 17. Adding a New Name and Address.

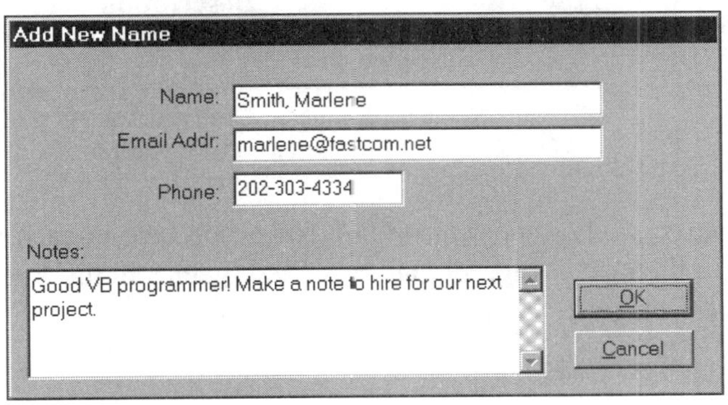

Table 8. CRaceInfo Properties.

Property	Description
Boat Number	Three-digit number that identifies the boat. Matches one of the numbers in the BoatInfo table.
Race Number	Unique three-digit number that identifies each race.
Starting Time	Time when the race started.
Finishing Time	Time when the boat finished the race.
Handicap Minutes	Number of minutes to be added to the boat's actual completion time.
Adjusted Time	Length of time taken to complete the race, adjusted by the boat's handicap.
Comments	Notes concerning special race conditions or pending protests involving this boat.

Table 9. CBoatInfo Properties.

Property	Description
BoatNumber	Matches boat numbers in the RaceInfo file.
BoatName	The boat's name.
OwnerName	Last name, first initial.
HandicapFactor	0.0 to 2.00, used when calculating the Handicap Minutes in the RaceInfo table.

- When displaying the RaceInfo window, let the user quickly display information about the current boat by selecting *BoatInfo Window* from the menu.
- Add the following fields to the **CRaceInfo** class:

Field	Data Type	Description
Race date	Date	Date of the race.
Scratch Boat Time	Long	Number of minutes estimated for completion of the race by a pre-selected boat, called the "scratch boat".

- Calculate the *handicap minutes* and *adjusted time* for each boat in each race, using the formula described in the next paragraph. Display these values in the *RaceInfo* window (these two fields were originally left empty.)

Handicap. In sailboat races involving boats of different sizes and configurations, boats vary greatly in their speed. Therefore, a handicapping system is used that will give each boat a more or less equal chance of winning the race. In this program, we will calculate the handicap minutes (HCM) for a boat in a particular race by multiplying the scratch boat time (SBT) by the boat's handicap factor (HCF). A fast sailboat would have a large handicap factor, and a slow boat would have a small one. Table 10 shows some examples of calculations. For the same boat, more handicap minutes are applied to a longer race than a shorter one.

8.7.13 Yachting Regatta - 3

Boat Rankings per Race. Using the Yachting Regatta programs from the previous exercises, calculate and display the ranking of each boat for each race. For each race, the boat in first place will have the lowest adjusted time. The adjusted time (AT) is calculated from the starting time (ST), finishing time (FT) and handicap minutes (HCM) as follows: AT = (FT - ST) + HCM. For each race, produce a table such as the one shown in Table 11.

8.7.14 Yachting Regatta - 4

Overall Boat Rankings. Using the Yachting Regatta programs from the previous exercises, calculate the overall ranking of each boat, inclusive of all races. The boat's rank in a particular race determines the number of points counted against the boat. The boat with the highest overall ranking is the one with the lowest overall points. For example, if boat X's rank in four races is 1, 1, 4, 5, it has 11 overall points. If boat Y's rank in four races is 2, 3, 3, 4, it has 12 overall points. Therefore, boat X is awarded a higher overall ranking than boat Y.

8.7.15 Doctors Office Scheduling

Raising CApptCalendar Events. The CApptCalendar class in the Doctors Office Scheduling program uses the Err.Raise statement notify the client program about runtime errors. For the current exercise, use the RaiseEvent statement to raise events that can be trapped by the client program. In the ShowPatientAppointments and ShowAllAppointments methods, for example, raise an event such as CannotQueryDatabase. In the OpenTable method, raise an event such as CannotOpenTable.

Table 10. Sample Race Handicap Calculations.

Race #	Boat #	SBT	HCF	HCM
001	001	180	.8	144
001	002	180	.5	90
001	003	180	.1	18
002	001	60	.8	48
002	002	60	.5	30
002	003	60	.1	6

Table 11. Sample Results for Race Number 1.

Boat Name	Rank	Adjusted Time
Blue Star	1	220
Windward Passage	2	270
Ticonderoga	3	275
Kialoa II	4	280
Queen Mab	5	310
Novia del Mar	6	400

9 Creating ActiveX Components

Chapter Contents

ActiveX Components
- Types of Objects Provided by Components
- ActiveX Controls

StudentIdText ActiveX Control
- Creating a Test Program
- Adding Events to the Control
- Resizing the Control
- Making the Control Data-Bound
- Using a DataRepeater Control

AddAppointment ActiveX Control
- Program Specifications
- User Interface
- Client Program
- Saving and Restoring Properties
- Raising Events
- Implementing Property Procedures
- AddAppointment Source Code
- Client Program Listing

Using the ActiveX Control Wizard
- Running the Wizard
- Wizard-Generated Source Code
- Customizing the SourceCode
- Test Program

Using the ActiveX Property Wizard
- Property Pages for the OptionGroup Control

Creating an ActiveX DLL
- The DoctorSchedule DLL
- Client Program Implementation
- Instancing Property
- DoctorSchedule Implementation
- CSchedule Class
- CAppointment Class
- CPatient Class
- Testing the Compiled Component

Creating an Out-Of-Process Component
- Converting DoctorSchedule to an ActiveX EXE Server
- Where To Go From Here

Review Questions

Chapter Exercises

9.1 ACTIVEX COMPONENTS

Component software development is the assembling of programs from tested, standardized components. Microsoft has created an open standard called the *component object model* (COM) that permits software components to interact with each other. *ActiveX* is a specific implementation of COM, that provides a set of interfaces that components can use to export classes, properties, methods, and events.

Programs can be assembled from components that you create, components that are part of standard libraries, and existing programs that support ActiveX. Before ActiveX was created, programs could expose objects, methods, and properties using a technique known as *OLE automation*. Programs that provided objects were called *OLE servers*. ActiveX is an extension and refinement of OLE that also supports object distribution and usage over the Internet.

An *ActiveX component* is a unit of executable code such as an .exe, .dll, or .ocx file, that follows the ActiveX specification for providing objects. ActiveX components use object-oriented programming techniques to define the classes, methods, and properties that make up the component source code. But ActiveX is more than just object-oriented programming—it provides the mechanism so that unrelated objects can work together. For example, when building ActiveX controls, it is a natural process to assemble them from a group of existing controls. When contained in an ActiveX control, the existing controls are called *constituent controls.*

Microsoft has promoted ActiveX components as a way of enabling cross-platform program development. This means the same programs will work in Windows 95/98, Windows NT, or on Internet browser pages. ActiveX components can also be used with Microsoft applications such as Word, Excel, and Access. One area that is particularly exciting is using ActiveX components as connections to database servers on the Internet. This allows an ActiveX component running on a Web page to communicate with a database and pass data back to the user's Web browser.

9.1.1 Types of Objects Provided by Components

Components can provide three general types of objects: ActiveX Controls, ActiveX Documents, and Code Components.

- ***ActiveX Controls.*** ActiveX controls are user interface components that can be assembled onto a Visual Basic Form. These controls can be created and tested within the VB development environment, then exported to OCX files for other applications to use, including Web browsers. The term *UserControl* is another name for an ActiveX control. Literally thousands of ActiveX controls are available, some included with Visual Basic, and others through both shareware and commercial sources. It is usually easier and faster to obtain existing controls and add them to your programs than to code similar routines yourself.
- ***ActiveX Documents.*** ActiveX documents are applications designed to be launched by Microsoft Internet Explorer. Close relatives of ActiveX documents are Dynamic HTML programs, which we demonstrate in Chapter 12.

- ***Code Components.*** A code component is a library, or cluster, of related classes. Client programs can create object instances at runtime, using the classes provided by the component. The objects often do not have a visual component, but they provide some functionality used by other applications. A good example of a code component is Microsoft Excel, which can export objects such as worksheets and charts. Similarly, the Microsoft ADO library exports objects such as Recordsets and Connections.

9.1.2 ActiveX Controls

An ActiveX control, or *UserControl object*, is a component that can be placed in a Visual Basic toolbox window and used by developers. When saved as an OCX file, an ActiveX control can be used in development environments such as C++, Microsoft Access, and Borland Delphi. Throughout this book, we have been using ActiveX controls such as MSHFlexGrid, ListView, and TreeView.

A class module, as shown in Chapter 8, contains properties and methods and is exportable to external programs, but it has no visible user interface. The only way to produce a user interface for a class module is to have it show a Form. As we found in the Doctors Office Scheduling program, there is an awkward relationship between a class module and the forms it displays. The class can pass information to a form, but the form has no way to set class properties or call class methods unless the class sets a property in the form that is a backward reference to the class. The following diagram reflects this relationship:

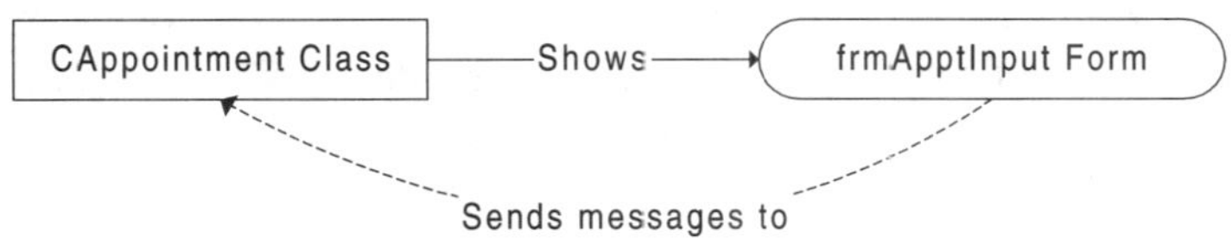

An ActiveX control, on the other hand, combines a class module with a built-in user interface. It can contain public properties and methods, raise events, display visual controls, and still encapsulate instance variables, properties, and methods. Most importantly an ActiveX control may act as a container for other ActiveX controls.

Design Time, Run Time. When discussing any of the ActiveX controls in this chapter, we distinguish between what happens at design time and what happens at run time. A *designer* places an instance of a *UserControl* on a form in design mode. We call the program created by this person the *client* program. When the client program runs, there is a *user* who interacts with the program.

Methods. We created class modules with properties and methods, so the conceptual groundwork has already been laid for using ActiveX. Methods in ActiveX controls may be either public or private.d

Properties. The user of an ActiveX control can read and write its properties in either design mode or at run time. When you place a TextBox on a Form, for example, properties can be set in design mode that are saved in the Form's file. When the file is loaded into memory at a later time, the property values are retained. If an ActiveX control's creator permits it, properties can also be modified at run time.

Delegating. A UserControl control often contains constituent controls. The UserControl can have public properties and methods designed to pass data and messages to the constitutent controls. The constituent controls themselves are hidden from client programs. This process is called *delegating*. For example, a UserControl might contain a TextBox control, and it might have a public Text property. When a client program assigns a value to the Text property, the UserControl delegates the value to the internal TextBox.

Events. When creating an ActiveX control, you define specific named events that the control can generate. A client program containing your ActiveX control may contain specific event handlers to respond to events generated by your control. The response to a message is achieved by writing code in a message handler procedure. An ActiveX control can also respond to events generated by its constituent controls and pass those events on to the client program.

Before a UserControl can raise a specific event, it must declare, or define the event's name. An event declaration looks a lot like the first line of a procedure declaration. Its syntax is:

```
[Public] Event eventName [(arglist)]
```

eventName is the name of the event that will be raised by the control. An event cannot return a value. Events can have the same types of arguments as ordinary procedures, except named arguments, optional arguments, and ParamArray arguments.

Setting Debugging Options. In the **Tools > Options** menu, you can control the way runtime errors are handled. The *Break on All Errors* option, for example, enters break mode and displays a Debug window when any runtime error is encountered. This is useful for finding out *exactly* which source code line caused the runtime error. On the other hand, when testing Classes and ActiveX controls, you can set the option to *Break in Class Module*, which means that any unhandled error produced in a class causes the project to enter break mode at the line of code in the class that produced the error.

Now it's time to be practical. The best way to understand ActiveX components is to create them yourself. In the coming sections of this chapter, we will create two different ActiveX controls. We will also create a code component that acts as a database server.

9.2 STUDENTIDTEXT ACTIVEX CONTROL

(samples: StudentIdX)

Let's use a simple sequence of steps to create an ActiveX control containing a TextBox into which the user can enter a Student ID number. We will make some assumptions about the length and format of the number. It is suggested that you try the following seven steps at the computer:

1. Run Visual Basic, select the *New Project* command, and choose **ActiveX Control** as the project type.
2. The *User Control Form* is the rectangular gray window containing a grid in the middle of the screen. This is where controls are designed. Bring up the Properties window (F4) and change the name of the form to **StudentIdText.** Set the **BorderStyle** property

to None. This prevents a border from being drawn around the control when it is placed on a client Form.

3. Place a label on the UserControl, as in Figure 1. Set its caption to **Student ID** and set its alignment to right-justified. Place a TextBox control on the Form just to the right of the Label control, set its Text property to blank, and set its Name to **txtID**.

Figure 1. Designing the StudentIdText Control.

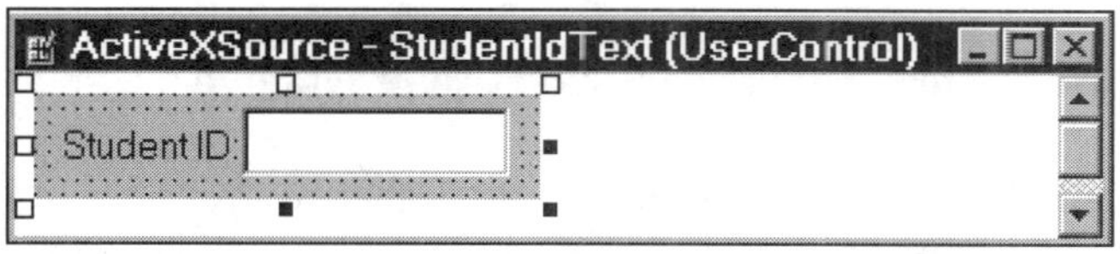

4. In the Project Explorer window, right-click the project name and bring up its Project Properties window, shown in Figure 2. Set the project name to **ActiveXSource** and type a short project description: "Text box containing Student ID number". Click OK to close this window.

Figure 2. Project Properties Window.

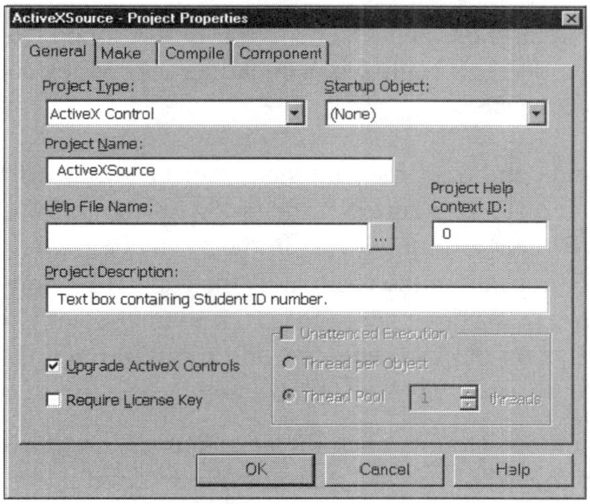

5. Double click the TextBox to bring up its **Change** event handler. Write the following code:

```
Private Sub txtID_Change()
  If Not IsNumeric(txtID.Text) Then
    txtID.SelStart = 0
    txtID.SelLength = Len(txtID.Text)
  End If
End Sub
```

(If a nonnumeric character is typed into the TextBox, all text in the box is highlighted as if someone had dragged a mouse over it.)

5. Create Property Get and Property Let procedures to handle the IdNumber property:

```
Public Property Get IdNumber() As String
  IdNumber = txtID.Text
End Property

Public Property Let IdNumber(strNewId As String)
  txtID.Text = strNewId
End Property
```

6. Save the project. We are ready to create a short test program that displays the control we just created.

Constituent Controls. Both the txtID Textbox and the Label control next to it are called *constituent controls*. Much of our focus in this chapter will be on how properties and messages are passed from a UserControl to its constituent controls.

Delegating. The technique for exposing the properties and methods of constituent controls is called *delegating*. The IdNumber property exposed by the UserControl, for example, passes on values it receives to the Text property of the txtId TextBox. There is no need to create a separate instance variable in the UserControl to hold the IdNumber.

9.2.1 Creating a Test Program

Let's create a short program that tests our new UserControl. In this mode, we are the *developer*, the programmer who places a control in a container and writes code to interact with the control. Here are the three steps:

1. Select the **Add Project** command from the File menu; select **Standard EXE** as the project type. Rename the Form to **frmTest**. Set the project name to **IdTest**. Figure 3 shows the contents of the Project Group, viewed in the *Project Explorer* window. Notice that the new control appears in the toolbox as the following icon: The control has also been registered as a new component type. To see this, select **Components** from the **Project** menu, click on the **Controls** tab, and scroll through the list until you find the description *Text box containing Student ID number* (see Figure 4).

2. Close the **Components** window. Double click the new ActiveX control's icon in the Toolbox window, causing an instance of the control to be inserted in the test program's form. Notice that the control is the same size as when we saved it, shown in Figure 5.

Figure 3. Project Group for the StudentIdText Control.

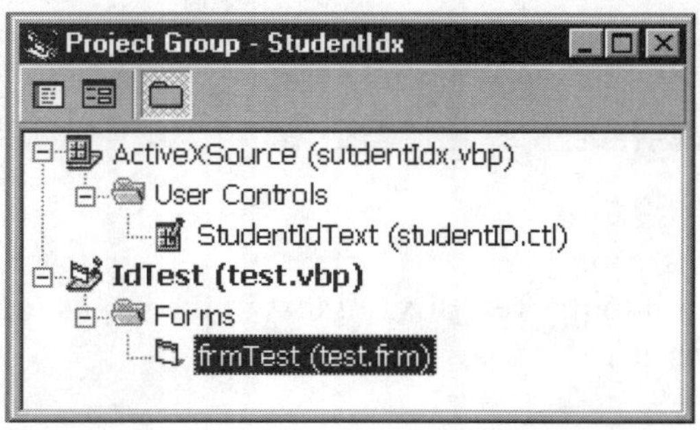

3. Run the test program and type in a numeric student number. If you try to enter any more digits, they will be refused. Backspace over one of the digits and enter a letter. Oops! The input text is selected as in Figure 6, signaling to the user that a nonnumeric character was entered.

The **ForeColor**, **BackColor**, **Font**, and **TextAlign** properties allow a UserControl to make its appearance match that of its container. For example, in the InitProperties event, which each instance of a UserControl receives when it is first placed on a container, it's a good idea to set the control's ForeColor, BackColor, Font, and TextAlign properties to the values provided by the ambient properties.

The **AmbientChanged** event is triggered when one of the ambient properties was changed by the container holding a UserControl. You can optionally write code in this event handler that updates corresponding properties in the UserControl.

Figure 4. The Visual Basic Components Window.

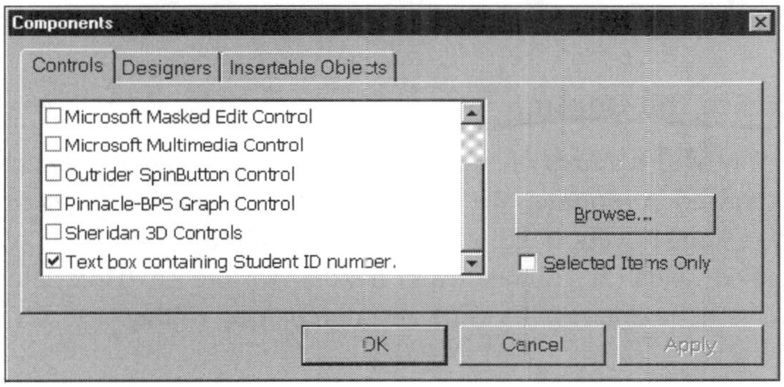

Figure 5. The Test Program.

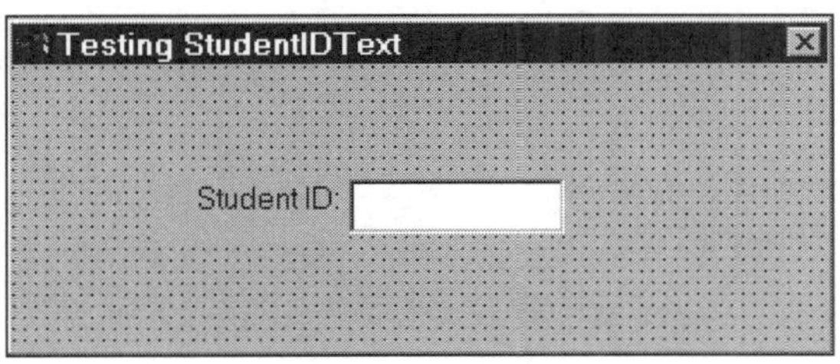

Figure 6. Running the Test Program.

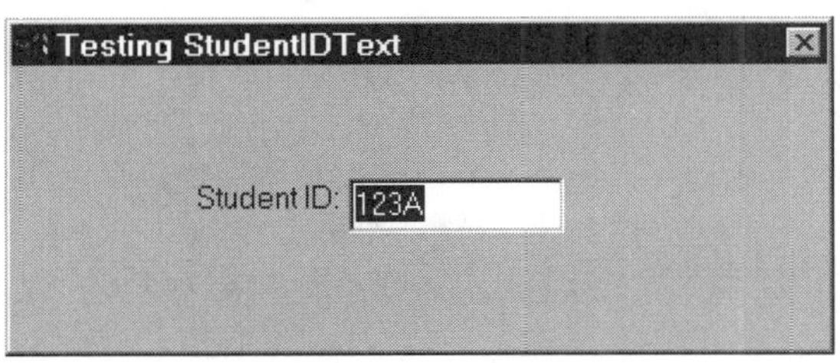

AmbientProperties Object

The variable called **Ambient** is a reference to an AmbientProperties object, which makes available what are called *ambient properties* of the container that holds a UserControl. (In our test program, the container was a Form.) The complete set of properties belonging to an AmbientProperties object is: BackColor, DisplayAsDefault, DisplayName, Font, ForeColor, LocaleID, MessageReflect, Palette, RightToLeft, ScaleUnits, ShowGrabHandles, ShowHatching, SupportsMnemonics, TextAlign, UIDead, and UserMode. You can safely access any ambient properties of this object that are visible in the Object Browser window. Always use an error handler when working with Ambient properties, in case the container does not support a particular property.

The most important of these properties is **UserMode**, which allows an instance of your control to determine whether it's executing at design time (UserMode = False) or at run time. Some properties, for example, can only be set in design mode or at run time.

9.2.2 Adding Events to the Control

One of the most powerful features of ActiveX controls is their ability to define specific events that can be raised at runtime. We will define two events for this control: **IdChanged** is raised when the Change event handler detects a change to the contents of the TextBox. **InvalidData** is raised when the Change event handler for the TextBox determines that non-digit characters have been entered. Modify the source code so that it looks like the following:

```
Public Event InvalidData()
Public Event IdChanged()

Public Property Get IdNumber() As String
  IdNumber = txtID.Text
End Property

Public Property Let IdNumber(strNewId As String)
  txtID.Text = strNewId
End Property

Private Sub txtID_Change()
  RaiseEvent IdChanged
  If Not IsNumeric(txtID.Text) Then
    txtID.SelStart = 0
    txtID.SelLength = Len(txtID.Text)
    RaiseEvent InvalidData
  End If
End Sub
```

Let's perform the modifications in four steps:

1. Let's switch to the **IdTest** project and double-click on the frmTest module name. The main Form still contains the StudentIdText control; double-click on it. Notice that if you select the control name from the ComboBox on the left, an InvalidData event handler is automatically created, as in Figure 7.

Figure 7. The InvalidData Event Handler.

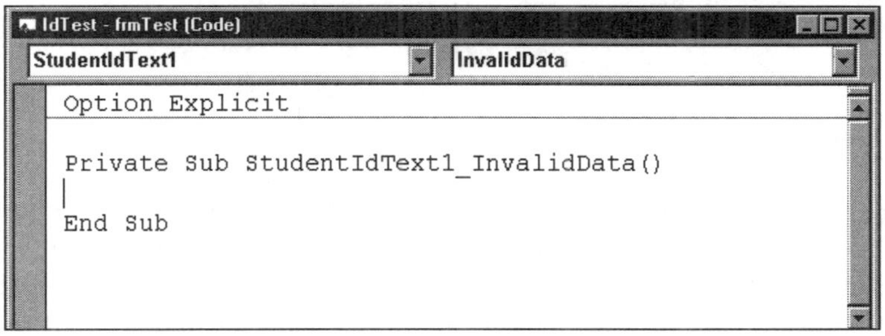

2. Write statements in this event handler that display a message box:

```
Private Sub StudentIdText1_InvalidData()
  MsgBox "A student number may contain only digits.", _
    vbExclamation, "Error"
End Sub
```

3. Write a statement in Form_Load that assigns a value to the IdNumber property:

```
Private Sub Form_Load()
  StudentIdText1.IdNumber = "0000000"
End Sub
```

4. Run the test program again. Enter a non-digit character and view the new message box. The program is complete, so save it one more time.

9.2.3 Resizing the Control

If an Application programmer resizes a UserControl, it is usually expected that it will automatically adjust the sizes and positions of its constituent controls. This can get complicated, particularly when controls must be a minimum size to display their contents in a meaningful way. We can provide a simple way, however, for the Text control holding the ID number to expand and contract horizontally when the UserControl is resized. The following **Resize** event handler in the StudentIdText control's source code does the trick:

```
Private Sub UserControl_Resize()
  txtID.Width = UserControl.ScaleWidth - txtID.Left - 50
End Sub
```

9.2.4 Making the Control Data-Bound

(samples: StudentId_DB)

It is often useful to make a UserControl data-bound. It must have both Get and Let property procedures, and one of its properties must be selected to bind to a Recordset field. In this section, we're going to make the IdNumber property of the StudentIdText control data-bound.

In our new version of the StudentIdX UserControl, the Property Let procedure for IdNumber calls **CanPropertyChange** to verify that the Id number can be updated. It also calls **PropertyChanged** to signal that the update actually took place:

```
Public Property Let IdNumber(strNewId As String)
  If CanPropertyChange("IdNumber") Then
    txtID.Text = strNewId
    PropertyChanged "IdNumber"
  End If
End Property
```

Calling PropertyChanged is essential if you want a data-bound control's value to be saved in a Recordset. The Visual Basic doumentation recommends calling CanPropertyChange. Interestingly, the function always returns True, even if the underlying Recordset is read-only. According to the *Component Tools Guide*, not calling CanPropertyChange could cause errors in some control containers.

The **Change** event handler for the txtID TextBox has also been improved. As before, we still raise the IdChanged and InvalidData events. Now, we also use PropertyChanged to signal that the IdNumber property has been modified, for data-binding purposes:

```
Private Sub txtID_Change()
  RaiseEvent IdChanged
  If IsNumeric(txtID.Text) Then
    PropertyChanged "IdNumber"
  ElseIf Len(txtID.Text) > 0 Then
    txtID.SelStart = 0
    txtID.SelLength = Len(txtID.Text)
    RaiseEvent InvalidData
  End If
End Sub
```

Notice that we do allow the StudentId number to be blank. This is necessary because the ADO Recordset's **AddNew** method always clears data-bound fields.

To select the IdNumber property to be data bound, we open the code window for the control and select **Procedure Attributes...** from the **Tools** menu. Figure 8 shows this dialog. We do the following:

- Select IdNumber in the **Name** ComboBox.
- Type in a description of the property.
- Click on the **Advanced** button.
- Click on the CheckBoxes shown in Figure 8.

The most important CheckBox, of course, is the one labeled **Property is data-bound.** This causes the DataField and DataSource properties to appear in the Properties window when the developer selects our control. The **Show in DataBindings collection** CheckBox is optional here, and is only required when you have more than one property that

Figure 8. Procedure Attributes Dialog.

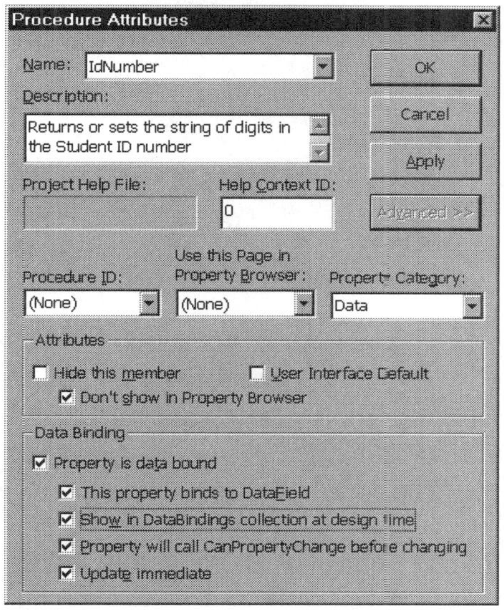

will be data-bound. In one of the Chapter exercises we ask you to bind multiple properties. Click the OK button to save the selections.

Test Program. Let's return to the test program that we developed earlier for the StudentIdText control. If we select the control and display the Properties window, the DataField, DataFormat, DataSource, and DataMember properties appear. Their values can be set either in design mode or at run time. Here are a few more tasks we have to complete:

- Add an ADO control to the form and name it **adoStudents**. Set its Connection property to the database on the sample disk named **students.mdb.** Set the Recordsource property to Students, and set the CommandType property to adCmdTable.
- Add a Command button to the form, set its **Caption** to **New**, and its Name property to **cmdNew**. This button will be clicked when the user wants to add a new student record.
- Add a second Command button to the form, set its Caption to **View List**, and its Name property to **cmdViewList**. This button will not be used yet.

Figure 9 shows the startup form in this new version of the Test program. The user can scroll through the Recordset with the arrows on the ADO control, and can add new students to the database by clicking on the **New** button.

Figure 9. Test Program Startup Form.

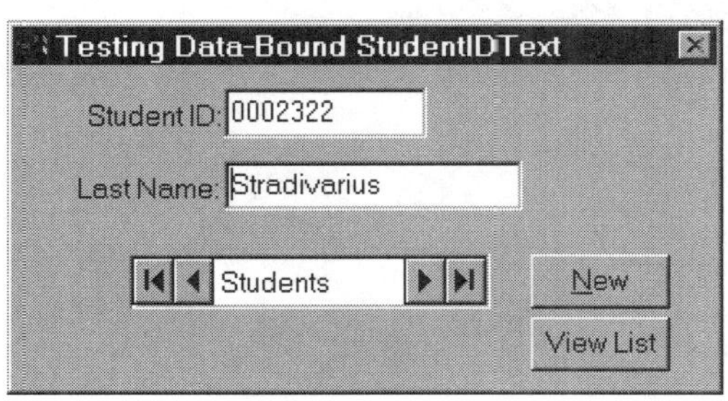

Source Code. Here is the complete source code for the test program:

```
Private Sub cmdNew_Click()
   adoStudents.Recordset.AddNew
End Sub

Private Sub StudentIdText1_InvalidData()
  MsgBox "A student number may contain only digits.", _
    vbInformation, "Error"
End Sub
```

9.2.5 Using a DataRepeater Control

Let's take the Test program one step further by adding a new Form and placing both an ADO control and a DataRepeater control on it. The **DataRepeater** control displays multiple instances of any ActiveX control in a scrolling list. Figure 10 shows the finished program we are in the process of building. The following seven steps are necessary:

1. First, we must compile the StudentIdText control to an OCX file. Select the ActiveXSource project in the Project window. From the **File** menu, choose **Make StudentID.ocx**, and click OK to compile the control.
2. Select the Test program in the Project window, add a new Form to the project, name it **frmDataRepeater**, and set its Caption to **DataRepeater Control**.
3. Place an ADO control on the Form, set its ConnectionString, CommandType, and RecordSource properties exactly the same as the ADO control on the program's startup form.
4. Select **Components** from the **Project** menu, place a check next to **Microsoft DataRepeater Control 6.0 (OLEDB)** and click the OK button. Place a DataRepeater control on the new Form. Set its DataSource property to **adoStudents** and its Caption property to **Students**.
5. Click on the DataRepeater's **RepeatedControlName** property and drop down a list of registered ActiveX controls. Select the one named **ActiveXSource.StudentIdText** (it will only appear if you remembered to compile it into an OCX file).
6. Bring up the DataRepeater's property page and select the **RepeaterBindings** tab, as in Figure 11. Select **IdNumber** as the PropertyName and **IdNumber** as the DataField, and click on the **Add** button. Click the **OK** button to close the window.

Figure 10. DataRepeater Control Demonstration.

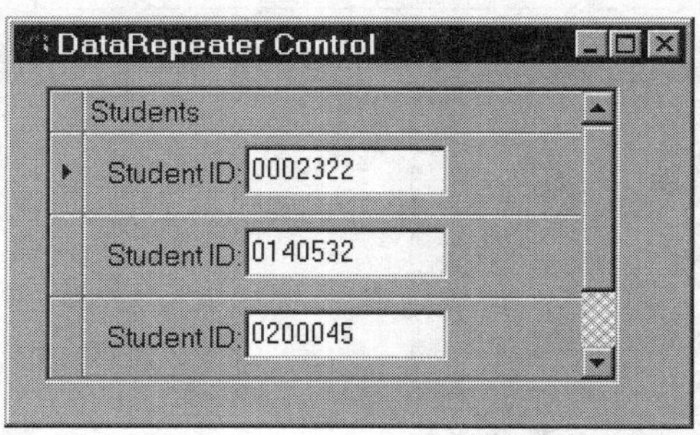

7. On the startup form for the Test program, double click on the **ViewList** button, and insert the following code that shows the new form:

```
Private Sub cmdViewList_Click()
   frmDataRepeater.Show vbModeless
End Sub
```

Run the program and scroll up and down through the student ID numbers. Of course, it's not too exciting just looking at ID numbers, but the techniques shown here could easily be applied to ActiveX controls with multiple data-bound fields. The combined power of the DataRepeater and the wide selection of ActiveX controls provides a rich set of possibilities.

The **RepeaterBindings** collection is probably the most powerful property of the DataRepeater control. It allows you to connect a data-bound property in an ActiveX control with any field in the database attached to the ADO control specified in the DataSource property. The DataBindings collection in the UserControl helps make this possible.

Figure 11. Setting the RepeaterBindings Property.

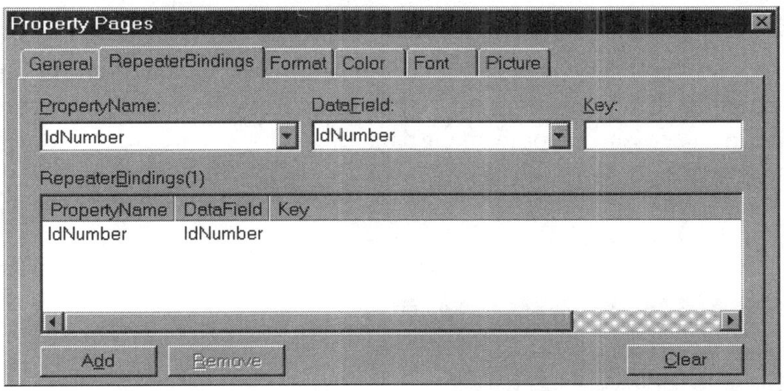

9.3 ADDAPPOINTMENT ACTIVEX CONTROL

9.3.1 Program Specifications

(samples: AddApptX)

In Chapter 8, the Doctors Office Scheduling program contained several classes, including CAppointment. This class encapsulated methods, objects, and a Form called frmApptInput relating to individual appointments. Let's re-create the visual component of that class and adapt it into an ActiveX control called **AddAppointment**. The AddAppointment control will input all information from the user regarding a single appointment.

Design Mode Properties. In our sample control, when the control is placed on a form, the designer can set the **BackColor** property, which affects the background color of the control. The programmer can also set the control's **Caption** property. When the container form is saved, the controls' properties will automatically be saved in the form.

Run Time Properties. The AddAppointment control contains the following read-only properties that can only be accessed at run time: DoctorName, PatientName, ApptDate, ApptTime, and Purpose.

Events. At run time, the user selects a doctor and patient from ComboBoxes, and enters the date, time, and purpose of the appointment. When the OK button is clicked, the field contents are validated and the control raises a **Save** event. If the Cancel button is clicked, the control raises a **Cancel** event.

If the user forgets to fill in an input field and clicks on the Save button, the UserControl generates a **MissingField** event. The client program responds to this in an event handler procedure that displays a Message box.

Project Group Window. The Project Group window (Figure 12) shows the UserControl's project (AddAppointmentX), and the client program (TestProject). The client program contains a single form called frmMain.

9.3.2 User Interface

The AddAppointment control contains Labels, CommandButtons, DateTimePickers, a TextBox, and ComboBoxes (see Figure 13). Any properties set for these controls in design mode will be in effect when instances of the control are created.

9.3.3 Client Program

When our ActiveX control has been placed on a Form in the client program and all supporting code written in the client program, the program may be tested. In Figure 13, the user has just input all necessary appointment data.

Figure 12. The Visual Basic Project Group Window.

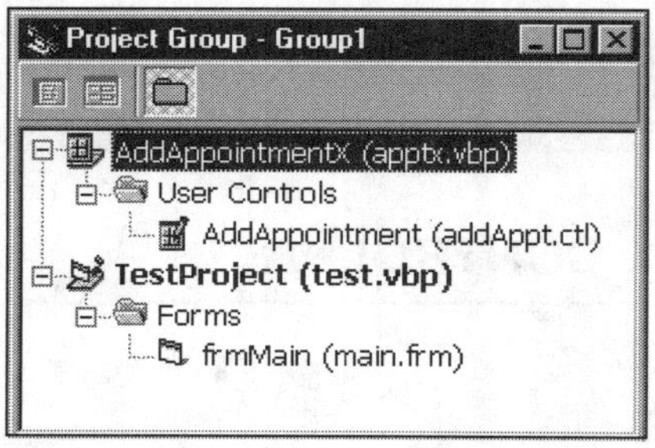

Figure 13. Entering Appointment Data.

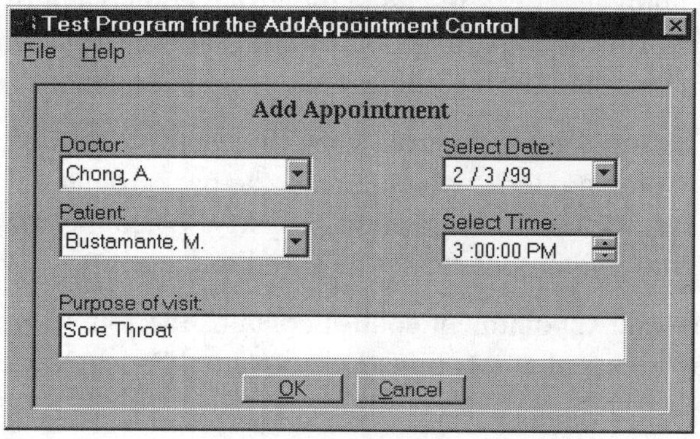

In Figure 14, the client program displays a confirmation message after receiving a **Save** event from the AddAppointment control. The program displays a confirmation message box when the user clicks on **OK.** The names of the patient and doctor are obtained from the control's properties.

Client Menu. The following menu exists in the client program's Form:

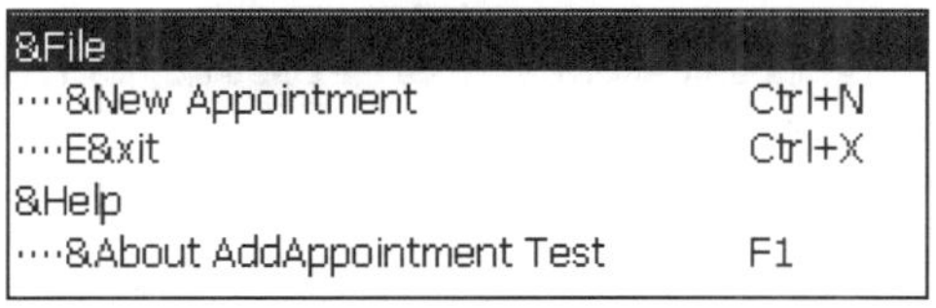

When the user selects **New Appointment** from the **File** menu, the Clear method is called in the AddAppointment control:

```
Private Sub mnuFileNew_Click()
   aptAdd.Clear
End Sub
```

Figure 14. Confirmation Message Displayed by Client Program.

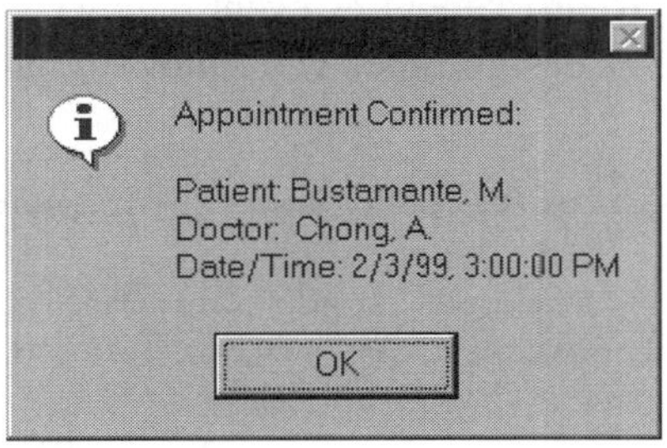

9.3.4 Saving and Restoring Properties

When a UserControl is placed on a form by an Application programmer, an **InitProperties** event is automatically generated. The event handler assigns default values to properties. For example, the following handler initializes the Caption and BackColor properties that belong to this control

```
Private Sub UserControl_InitProperties()
   Set UserControl.Font = Ambient.Font
   Caption = m_def_Caption
   BackColor = m_def_Backcolor
End Sub
```

Ambient Object. The Form, or *container* in the client program that contains a UserControl is referenced in code with the name **Ambient**. In the **InitProperties** event handler, for example, it is common to set the ActiveX control's Font property to the same value in Ambient.Font. You may have noticed this behavior with Visual Basic's intrinsic controls: when a Label or TextBox is placed on a Form, for example, it is always assigned the same

Font properties as the Form itself. If the designer subsequently alters the Form's Font property, however, the individual controls are not automatically updated.

WriteProperties Event. The **UserControl_WriteProperties** event handler makes it possible to write the UserControl's property values to the container file, a .FRM file at design time. The properties are stored in a specialized type of collection called a **PropertyBag**. The following procedure saves the control's Caption and BackColor properties:

```
Private Sub UserControl_WriteProperties(PropBag As PropertyBag)
   PropBag.WriteProperty "Caption", Caption, caption_default
   PropBag.WriteProperty "BackColor", BackColor, backColor_default
End Sub
```

The syntax of the **WriteProperty** method is

```
object.WriteProperty(dataName, value[, defaultVal])
```

object is a PropertyBag object, *dataName* is a string that identifies the property to be placed in the bag, *value* is the data value to be saved, and *defaultVal* is the default value for this property. The last parameter is optional, but highly recommended because it reduces the size of the container file. Visual Basic only writes a property value to the container file if the property's value is different from the default value.

ReadProperties Event. The **UserControl_ReadProperties** event handler gets the saved property values stored in the container file at design time. The following procedure restores the Caption and BackColor properties:

```
Private Sub UserControl_ReadProperties(PropBag As PropertyBag)
   On Error Resume Next
   Caption = PropBag.ReadProperty("Caption", m_def_Caption)
   BackColor = PropBag.ReadProperty("BackColor", m_def_BackColor )
End Sub
```

Notice that default property values are still used. Also, the **On Error Resume** statement is there to prevent the program from halting if the designer assigns an invalid property value while editing the form file with a text editor.

Properties Window. Figure 15 shows the properties window that appears when the AddAppointment control has been placed on the client program's main window.

AddAppointment Events. Coming back to our AddAppointment control example, we want it to support several user-defined events, shown in the declarations section of the UserControl:

```
Public Event MissingField(fieldName As String)
Public Event Save()
Public Event Cancel()
```

In the client program we have written, the control instance is called **aptAdd**. This means that an empty event handler is generated in frmMain whose name is a combination of the control name and the event name: aptAdd_MissingField

The following is the implementation of the **MissingField** event handler in the test program. It displays a message box with the name of the missing field:

```
Private Sub aptAdd_MissingField(fieldName As String)
  MsgBox "The following field is missing: " & fieldName, _
    vbInformation, "Error"
End Sub
```

Figure 16 shows an example of a message box displayed at run time by the MissingField event handler.

Figure 15. AddAppointment Properties Window.

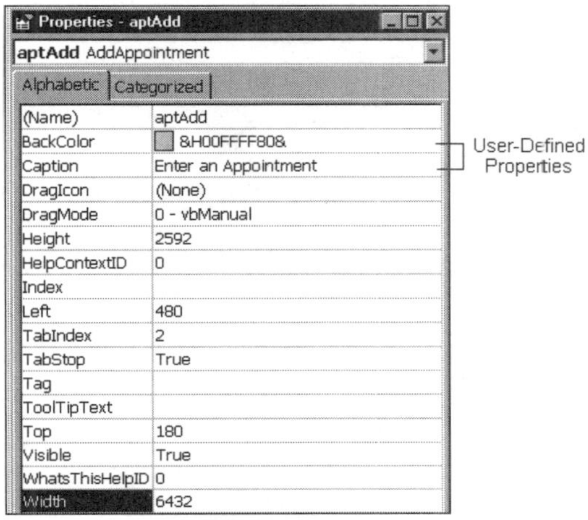

Figure 16. MissingField Event Message.

9.3.6 Implementing Property Procedures

You may recall that we created property procedures for class modules in Chapter 8. Property procedures in UserControls are nearly identical, except that the Let property should always include a call to **PropertyChanged**, which notifies Visual Basic that a property has been changed. The following is an example from the AddAppointment control:

```
Public Property Let Caption(strNew As String)
  lblCaption.Caption = strNew
  PropertyChanged "Caption"
End Property
```

Unless PropertyChanged is called, Visual Basic will not generate a WriteProperties event, and the control instance's properties are not saved. A programmer using this ActiveX control would lose any changes that were made to the control's properties the next time the project was loaded from disk.

9.3.7 AddAppointment Source Code

Let's take a look at the source code for the AddAppointment UserControl. This control inputs information from the user that can be used to schedule an appointment:

```
'Default design property values:
Const m_def_BackColor As Integer = vbButtonFace
Const m_def_Caption As String = "Add Appointment"

'Custom Events raised by this control:
Public Event MissingField(fieldName As String)
Public Event Save()
Public Event Cancel()

'*********** Public Properties *************
'The following properties may be set at design
'time and/or run time.

Public Property Get Caption() As String
  Caption = lblCaption.Caption
End Property

Public Property Let Caption(strNew As String)
  lblCaption.Caption = strNew
  PropertyChanged "Caption"
End Property

Public Property Get BackColor() As OLE_COLOR
  BackColor = UserControl.BackColor
End Property

Public Property Let BackColor(ByVal color As OLE_COLOR)
'Copy the same background color to the constituent
'Label controls.
  UserControl.BackColor = color
  lblCaption.BackColor = color
  Dim j As Integer
  For j = 0 To 4
    lblField(j).BackColor = color
  Next j
  PropertyChanged "BackColor"
End Property

'*********** Runtime Properties *****************
'All of the following properties are read-only.

Public Property Get PatientName() As String
  PatientName = cboPatients.Text
End Property

Public Property Get DoctorName() As String
  DoctorName = cboDoctors.Text
End Property
```

```
Public Property Get ApptDate() As String
  ApptDate = DateValue(dtpApptDate.Value)
End Property

Public Property Get ApptTime() As String
  ApptTime = TimeValue(dtpApptTime.Value)
End Property

Public Property Get Purpose() As String
  Purpose = txtPurpose.Text
End Property

'************ Public Methods ********************

Public Sub Clear()
  cboPatients.ListIndex = -1
  cboDoctors.ListIndex = -1
  txtPurpose.Text = ""
End Sub

'*********** Private Event Handlers ********

Private Sub cmdCancel_Click()
  RaiseEvent Cancel
End Sub

Private Sub cmdOk_Click()
  If ValidateFields Then
    RaiseEvent Save
  End If
End Sub

'************* Private Methods *************

Private Function ValidateFields() As Boolean
  ValidateFields = True
  'Check for a doctor.
  If cboDoctors.ListIndex = -1 Then
    RaiseEvent MissingField("Doctor Name")
    ValidateFields = False
  End If

  'Check for a patient.
  If cboPatients.ListIndex = -1 Then
    RaiseEvent MissingField("Patient Name")
    ValidateFields = False
  End If

  'Check for purpose of visit.
  If Trim$(txtPurpose.Text) = "" Then
    RaiseEvent MissingField("Purpose of Visit")
    ValidateFields = False
  End If
End Function
```

```
Private Sub UserControl_WriteProperties(PropBag As PropertyBag)
'Save the properties in the container form. Always use defaults,
'because this reduces the size of the container file (usually
'a .FRM file). Visual Basic only writes the property value to
'the container file if the property's value is different from
'the default value.

   PropBag.WriteProperty "Caption", Caption, m_def_Caption
   PropBag.WriteProperty "BackColor", BackColor, m_def_BackColor
End Sub

Private Sub UserControl_ReadProperties(PropBag As PropertyBag)
'Read the properties from the container form.
'It is important to assign values to the properties,
'not the instance variables, so the constituent controls
'can be updated.
   On Error Resume Next
   Caption = PropBag.ReadProperty("Caption", m_def_Caption)
   BackColor = PropBag.ReadProperty("BackColor", m_def_BackColor)
End Sub

Private Sub UserControl_InitProperties()
'This procedure is activated by the InitProperties event, which
'occurs only when a control instance is first placed on a form.
   Set UserControl.Font = Ambient.Font
   Caption = m_def_Caption
   BackColor = m_def_BackColor
End Sub
```

9.3.8 Client Program Listing

The following code listing is from the client program that holds an instance of the AddAppointment ActiveX control as aptAdd:

```
Private Sub aptAdd_Cancel()
   MsgBox "Appointment Cancelled", vbInformation, ""
   aptAdd.Clear
End Sub

Private Sub aptAdd_MissingField(fieldName As String)
   MsgBox "The following field is missing: " & fieldName, _
     vbInformation, "Error"
End Sub

Private Sub aptAdd_Save()
'A Save event was raised by the AddAppointment control.
  With aptAdd
     MsgBox "Appointment Confirmed: " & vbCrLf & vbCrLf _
       & "Patient: " & .PatientName & vbCrLf _
       & "Doctor:  " & .DoctorName & vbCrLf _
       & "Date/Time: " & .ApptDate & ", " & .ApptTime, _
          vbInformation, ""
  End With
```

```
    'At this point, the client program should save
    '  the appointment in a database.
End Sub

Private Sub mnuFileExit_Click()
   Unload Me
End Sub

Private Sub mnuFileNew_Click()
   aptAdd.Clear
End Sub

Private Sub mnuHelpAbout_Click()
   frmAbout.Show vbModal
End Sub
```

9.4 USING THE ACTIVEX CONTROL WIZARD

(samples: OptionGroup)

One of the best tools supplied with Visual Basic is the **ActiveX Control Wizard**. You can use it to generate most of the code required for assigning, retrieving, and saving a UserControl's properties. It also generates code for events and class methods. As you have probably noticed, it can be tedious to code all of this code by hand.

9.4.1 Running the Wizard

To enable the ActiveX Control Wizard, select **Add-In Manager** from the **Add-Ins** menu. Locate the entry for **VB6 ActiveX Ctrl Interface Wizard**. In the **Load Behavior** frame in the lower right corner of the window, place checks next to **Loaded/Unloaded** and **Load on Startup**. While you're at it, do the same thing for the **Property Page Wizard**, which we will use in Section 9.5. Click on **OK** to close the dialog.

OptionGroup Control. In this section, we're going to create a simple ActiveX control called **OptionGroup** that encapsulates as many as four OptionButton controls inside a Frame. The motivation for creating this control comes from often having to write code that identifies which button in a group as been selected and returns a single value.

OptionButton controls have no data binding capabilities, so additional code must be written to read and write them from databases. Section 4.1.4 of Chapter 4, you may recall, showed how to simulate the binding of OptionButtons to an ADO control through an invisible data-bound TextBox control. In the chapter exercises, we ask you to make the OptionGroup control data-bound. Here are the necessary steps for creating the UserControl:

Step 1: Create the Visual Interface. Place a frame on the new UserControl and place an array of four OptionButtons inside the frame, as shown in Figure 17. Set the frame's Caption to an empty string. Increase the width of each OptionButton so it extends nearly to the right side of the frame.

Step 2: Run the Control Interface Wizard. Run the ActiveX Control Interface Wizard, which we will just refer to as the *Wizard* from now on. Figure 18 shows the opening message displayed by the Wizard, explaining what it can do. Click the **Next** button to continue.

Figure 17. The OptionGroup Visual Interface.

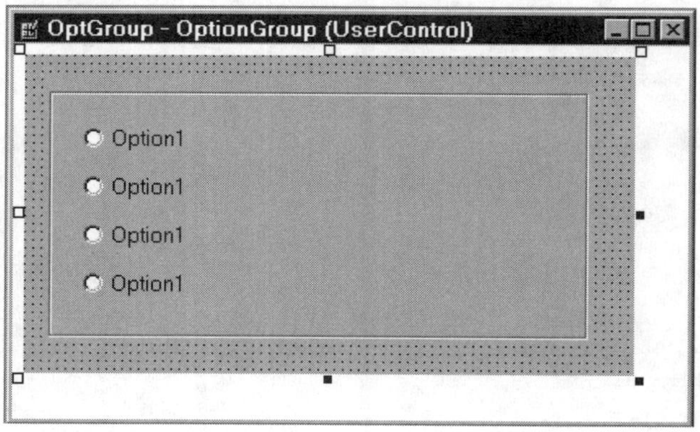

Figure 18. Opening Message, ActiveX Control Wizard.

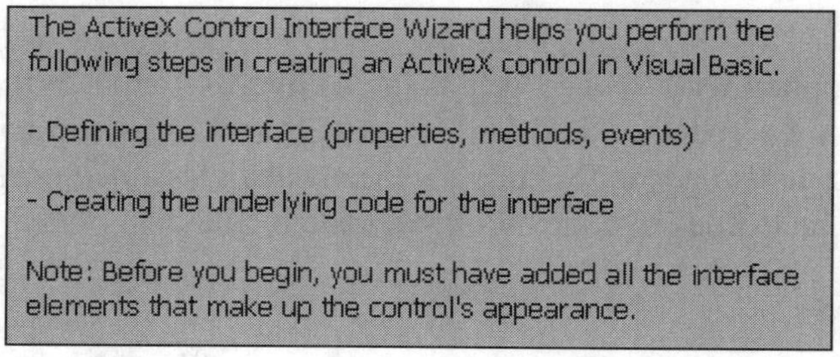

Step 3: Selecting Class Members. Select the following properties, methods and events by moving their names to the ListBox on the right side of the window: BackColor, BackStyle, BorderStyle, Caption, Click, Enabled, ForeColor, and Value. Some existing properties, methods, and events will have to be removed from this ListBox. Click the **Next** button to continue.

Step 4: Custom Interface Members. The next panel is labeled **Custom Interface Members.** Create a custom property named **Buttons**, which represents an array of OptionButton objects. Click the **Next** button to continue.

Step 5: Set Mapping for the OptionGroup Control. The next panel, shown in Figure 19, lets you map, or assign, the control's properties, methods, and events to corresponding ones in the constituent controls. In our case, the constituent controls are the Frame and array of OptionButtons. Not all properties and methods can be mapped to controls in this panel. For example, we did not map the **Value** property because it requires custom code. The Value property will be set to the index of the OptionButton clicked by the user, or to –1 if no button is clicked.

Table 1 lists the mapping of propertes chosen for this Wizard session. In addition to these properties, the **Click** event must be mapped to the OptionButton array. When the user clicks on an OptionButton in our ActiveX control, a corresponding Click event is generated in the client program.

Figure 19. Set Mapping for the OptionGroup Control.

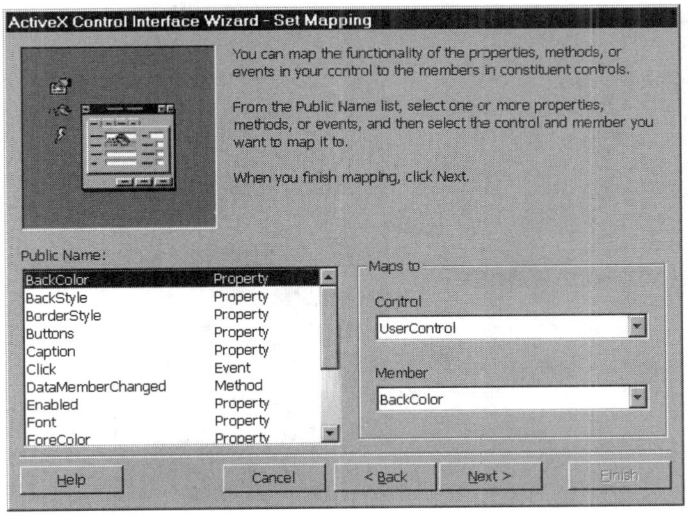

Table 1. Mapping Properties to Constituent Controls.

Property	Maps To Constituent Property
BackColor	UserControl.BackColor
ForeColor	UserControl.ForeColor
Enabled	Frame1.Enabled
BackStyle	UserControl.BackStyle
BorderStyle	UserControl.BorderStyle
Caption	Frame1.Caption

Step 6: Set Attributes. The next panel, called **Set Attributes,** lets you set attributes for any properties that are not mapped to existing controls. In our case, the Buttons and Value properties have not been mapped. In Figure 20, we make the Value property an integer and assign it an initial value of –1.

Notice that this panel allows you to decide whether or not each property can be read or written both at design time and at run time. Set the **Buttons** property to **Read-Only** at run time, and **Not Available** at design time. Click the **Finish** button to close the Wizard and generate source code for the ActiveX control.

9.4.2 Wizard-Generated Source Code

Let's take a look at the source code generated by the Wizard. A number of comment lines have been placed in the file, which the Wizard uses to keep track of properties, methods, and events. These lines make it possible for you to run the Wizard again and modify earlier choices. It's certainly fortunate that we did not have to write all of this code:

Figure 20. Set Attributes for the OptionGroup Control.

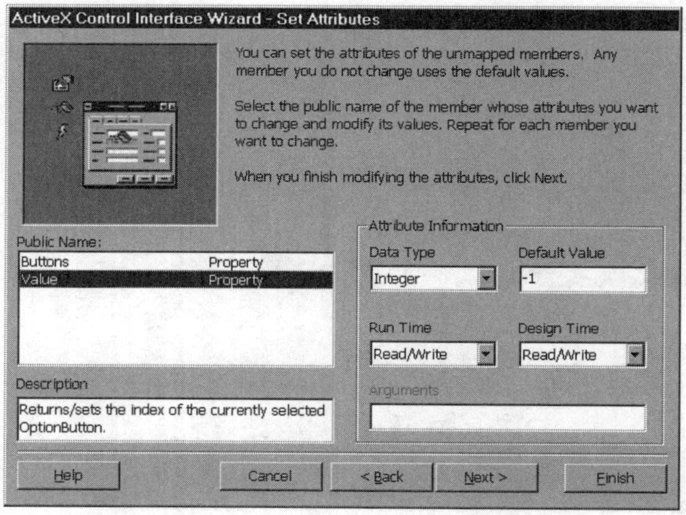


```
Const m_def_Value = -1
Dim m_Value As Integer
Event Click()

'WARNING! DO NOT REMOVE OR MODIFY THE FOLLOWING COMMENTED LINES!
'MappingInfo=UserControl,UserControl,-1,BackColor
Public Property Get BackColor() As OLE_COLOR
  BackColor = UserControl.BackColor
End Property

Public Property Let BackColor(ByVal New_BackColor As OLE_COLOR)
  UserControl.BackColor() = New_BackColor
  PropertyChanged "BackColor"
End Property

'WARNING! DO NOT REMOVE OR MODIFY THE FOLLOWING COMMENTED LINES!
'MappingInfo=UserControl,UserControl,-1,ForeColor
Public Property Get ForeColor() As OLE_COLOR
  ForeColor = UserControl.ForeColor
End Property

Public Property Let ForeColor(ByVal New_ForeColor As OLE_COLOR)
  UserControl.ForeColor() = New_ForeColor
  PropertyChanged "ForeColor"
End Property

'WARNING! DO NOT REMOVE OR MODIFY THE FOLLOWING COMMENTED LINES!
'MappingInfo=Frame1,Frame1,-1,Enabled
Public Property Get Enabled() As Boolean
  Enabled = Frame1.Enabled
End Property

Public Property Let Enabled(ByVal New_Enabled As Boolean)
  Frame1.Enabled() = New_Enabled
```

```
  PropertyChanged "Enabled"
End Property

'WARNING! DO NOT REMOVE OR MODIFY THE FOLLOWING COMMENTED LINES!
'MappingInfo=UserControl,UserControl,-1,BackStyle
Public Property Get BackStyle() As Integer
  BackStyle = UserControl.BackStyle
End Property

Public Property Let BackStyle(ByVal New_BackStyle As Integer)
  UserControl.BackStyle() = New_BackStyle
  PropertyChanged "BackStyle"
End Property

'WARNING! DO NOT REMOVE OR MODIFY THE FOLLOWING COMMENTED LINES!
'MappingInfo=UserControl,UserControl,-1,BorderStyle
Public Property Get BorderStyle() As Integer
  BorderStyle = UserControl.BorderStyle
End Property

Public Property Let BorderStyle(ByVal New_BorderStyle As Integer)
  UserControl.BorderStyle() = New_BorderStyle
  PropertyChanged "BorderStyle"
End Property
'
'WARNING! DO NOT REMOVE OR MODIFY THE FOLLOWING COMMENTED LINES!
'MappingInfo=Frame1,Frame1,-1,Caption
Public Property Get Caption() As String
  Caption = Frame1.Caption
End Property

Public Property Let Caption(ByVal New_Caption As String)
  Frame1.Caption() = New_Caption
  PropertyChanged "Caption"
End Property

Private Sub optButton_Click(Index As Integer)
  RaiseEvent Click
End Sub

Private Sub UserControl_InitProperties()
  m_Value = m_def_Value
End Sub

Private Sub UserControl_ReadProperties(PropBag As PropertyBag)
 UserControl.BackColor = PropBag.ReadProperty("BackColor", &H8000000F)
 UserControl.ForeColor = PropBag.ReadProperty("ForeColor", &H80000012)
 Frame1.Enabled = PropBag.ReadProperty("Enabled", True)
 UserControl.BackStyle = PropBag.ReadProperty("BackStyle", 1)
 UserControl.BorderStyle = PropBag.ReadProperty("BorderStyle", 0)
 Frame1.Caption = PropBag.ReadProperty("Caption", "")
 m_Value = PropBag.ReadProperty("Value", m_def_Value)
End Sub
```

```
Private Sub UserControl_WriteProperties(PropBag As PropertyBag)
  Call PropBag.WriteProperty("BackColor", UserControl.BackColor,
    &H8000000F)
  Call PropBag.WriteProperty("ForeColor", UserControl.ForeColor,
    &H80000012)
  Call PropBag.WriteProperty("Enabled", Frame1.Enabled, True)
  Call PropBag.WriteProperty("BackStyle", UserControl.BackStyle, 1)
  Call PropBag.WriteProperty("BorderStyle", UserControl.BorderStyle, 0)
  Call PropBag.WriteProperty("Caption", Frame1.Caption, "")
  Call PropBag.WriteProperty("Value", m_Value, m_def_Value)
End Sub

'WARNING! DO NOT REMOVE OR MODIFY THE FOLLOWING COMMENTED LINES!
'MemberInfo=7,0,0,-1
Public Property Get Value() As Integer
  Value = m_Value
End Property

Public Property Let Value(ByVal New_Value As Integer)
  m_Value = New_Value
  PropertyChanged "Value"
End Property

'WARNING! DO NOT REMOVE OR MODIFY THE FOLLOWING COMMENTED LINES!
'MemberInfo=14,0,0,0
Public Property Get Buttons() As Variant
  Buttons = m_Buttons
End Property

Public Property Let Buttons(ByVal New_Buttons As Variant)
  m_Buttons = New_Buttons
  PropertyChanged "Buttons"
End Property
```

9.4.3 Customizing the Source Code

The code generated by the ActiveX Control Wizard is generally very helpful, but we still have to do some customizing before the control will work correctly. To begin with, we define an extra constant that is used for range checking:

```
Const MAX_BUTTON_INDEX As Integer = 3
```

The **Property Let** procedure for the **Value** property checks the range of the input parameter, and if the value is valid, it is used to select one of the OptionButtons:

```
Public Property Let Value(ByVal New_Value As Integer)
  Dim j As Integer
  m_Value = New_Value
  If m_Value < 0 Or m_Value > MAX_BUTTON_INDEX Then
    For j = 0 To MAX_BUTTON_INDEX
      optButton(j).Value = False
    Next j
  Else
    optButton(m_Value).Value = True
```

```
  End If
  PropertyChanged "Value"
End Property
```

If the new index value is out of range, this procedure automatically clears all the OptionButtons. An Application developer can clear the buttons simply by assigning –1 to the control's Value property.

The **Let BackColor Property** procedure needs some fine tuning because it must delegate the same color to both Frame1 and the optButton() array:

```
Public Property Let BackColor(ByVal New_BackColor As OLE_COLOR)
  UserControl.BackColor() = New_BackColor
  Frame1.BackColor = New_BackColor
  Dim j As Integer
  For j = 0 To MAX_BUTTON_INDEX
    optButton(j).BackColor = New_BackColor
  Next j
  PropertyChanged "BackColor"
End Property
```

The **Get Buttons** property returns a reference to the optButton control array:

```
Public Property Get Buttons() As Object
  Set Buttons = optButton             'custom code
End Property
```

Visual Basic does not allow a property to return a reference to an array, so that is why we had the Buttons property return type Object.

In the **UserControl_ReadProperties** procedure, the saved BackColor and ForeColor values are assigned to the BackColor and ForeColor properties:

```
Private Sub UserControl_ReadProperties(PropBag As PropertyBag)
  BackColor = PropBag.ReadProperty("BackColor", &H8000000F) 'custom code
  ForeColor = PropBag.ReadProperty("ForeColor", &H80000012) 'custom code
```

In the same procedure, we have to modify the statement that reads the Value property at design time and initializes the correct OptionButton. The code-generated line simply assigns a value to the private variable m_Value. Instead, we must assign to the Value property so the OptionButton will be set:

```
m_Value = PropBag.ReadProperty("Value", m_def_Value)   'original
Value = PropBag.ReadProperty("Value", m_def_Value)     'custom code
```

The **Click** event handler for the optButton array has an extra statement added that assigns **Index** to the private **m_Value** variable:

```
Private Sub optButton_Click(Index As Integer)
  m_Value = Index                   'custom code
  RaiseEvent Click
End Sub
```

9.4.4 Test Program

All that remains is to write a short test program for the OptionGroup control. The test program's startup form contains the OptionGroup control and a StatusBar control (see Figure 21).

Figure 21. Testing the OptionGroup Control.

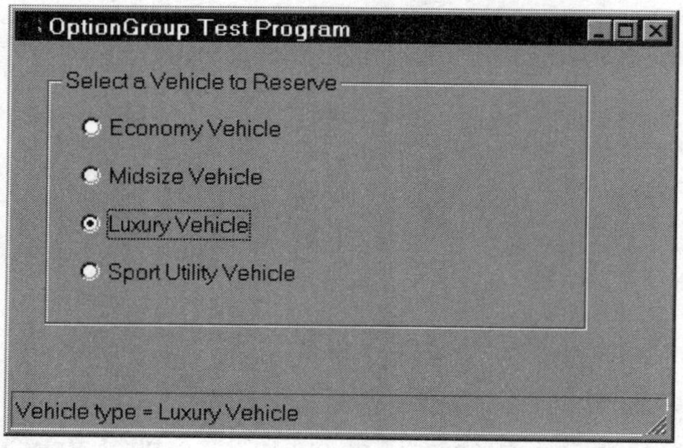

In **Form_Load**, we set the control's Caption property and assign captions to each of the OptionButtons. This is possible because the Buttons property returns a reference to the optButton control array:

```
Private Sub Form_Load()
  With OptionGroup1
    .Caption = "Select a Vehicle to Reserve"
    .Buttons(0).Caption = "Economy Vehicle"
    .Buttons(1).Caption = "Midsize Vehicle"
    .Buttons(2).Caption = "Luxury Vehicle"
    .Buttons(3).Caption = "Sport Utility Vehicle"
  End With
End Sub
```

In **Form_Activate**, we set the Value property to –1, thereby unselecting all buttons. This was necessary because the OptionGroup control is the one and only Tab stop on the containing form, and this causes the first OptionButton to be set automatically:

```
Private Sub Form_Activate()
'Un-select all buttons.
  OptionGroup1.Value = -1
End Sub
```

There is a **Click** event handler that gets the Value property from the control and uses it as an index into the Buttons array. This makes it possible to retrieve the button's caption and display it on the StatusBar:

```
Private Sub OptionGroup1_Click()
  With OptionGroup1
    sbrTest.SimpleText = "Vehicle type = " _
      & .Buttons(.Value).Caption
  End With
End Sub
```

9.5 USING THE ACTIVEX PROPERTY PAGE WIZARD

(samples: PropWizard)

A Property Page provides a convenient way for application developers to set properties in an ActiveX control. Particularly when a property value cannot be simply typed into a TextBox in the standard Properties window, a more sophisticated interface is needed. As the property page creator, you can supply ComboBoxes OptionButtons, CommandButtons, and so on, to make the job easier for a developer using your control.

9.5.1 Property Pages for the OptionGroup Control

At the beginning of Section 9.5 we asked you to install both the ActiveX Control Interface Wizard and the Property Page Wizard. Now we're ready to try the Wizard out on the OptionGroup control from the previous section. These are the required steps:

1. Run the Property Page Wizard. After the greeting panel, which can be disabled in the future, you are asked to select which property pages in the current project will be displayed.
2. Click the **Add** button to add a new page and call it **General**. Your screen should appear as in Figure 22. Remove the check next to **StandardFont**, because we have not implemented a Font property for this control. Click the **Next** button to continue.
3. The next panel (Figure 23) lets you select which properties you want to display on each property page. With the **General** page selected, copy all available properties to the ListBox on the right side.
4. Click the **Next** button to continue, and click the Finish button to end the Wizard. You will see a page of notes, which can optionally be saved to a text file for later reference.
5. With the Test program's startup form displayed, delete the OptionGroup control from the form and paste it again from the ToolBox window.

Figure 22. Property Page Wizard After Adding the General Page.

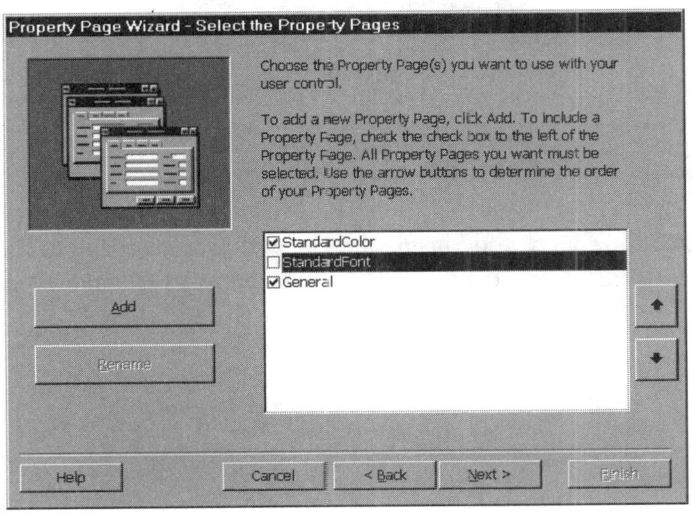

Figure 23. Adding Fields to the General Property Page.

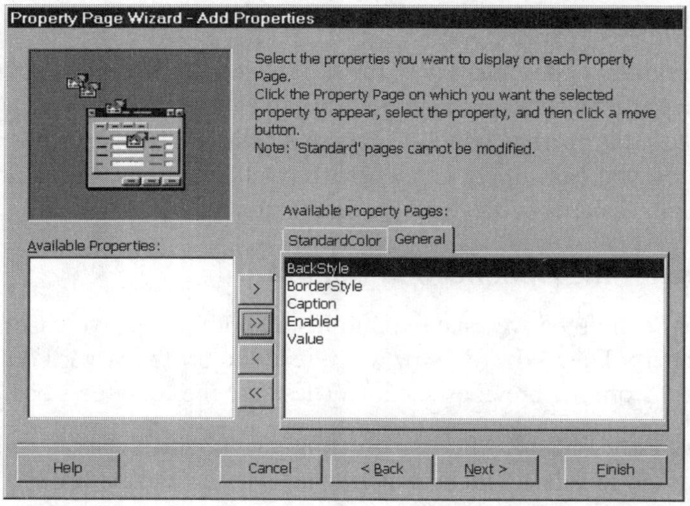

6. Right click the OptionGroup control and select **Properties**. This should bring up the property pages. The Color property page appears in Figure 24. If you click on the General tab, notice that the user interface is somewhat barren, particularly for the BackStyle and BorderStyle properties.

Figure 24. Color Property Page.

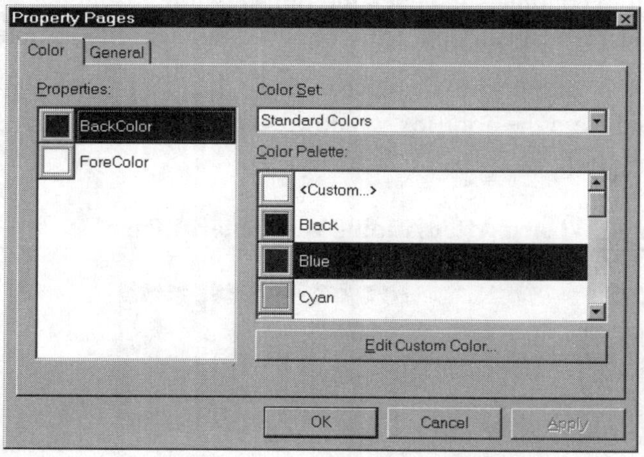

You can inspect the source code inside the General property page to see some of the mechanics. Each TextBox sets a property called **Changed** in its Change event handler:

```
Private Sub txtValue_Change()
    Changed = True
End Sub

Private Sub txtCaption_Change()
    Changed = True
```

```
End Sub

Private Sub txtBorderStyle_Change()
    Changed = True
End Sub

Private Sub txtBackStyle_Change()
    Changed = True
End Sub

Private Sub chkEnabled_Click()
    Changed = True
End Sub
```

The **ApplyChanges** procedure copies values from the controls into a collection called SelectedControls:

```
Private Sub PropertyPage_ApplyChanges()
     SelectedControls(0).Value = txtValue.Text
     SelectedControls(0).Caption = txtCaption.Text
     SelectedControls(0).BorderStyle = txtBorderStyle.Text
     SelectedControls(0).BackStyle = txtBackStyle.Text
     SelectedControls(0).Enabled = (chkEnabled.Value = vbChecked)
End Sub
```

The **SelectionChanged** procedure copies values from the SelectedControls object back into controls:

```
Private Sub PropertyPage_SelectionChanged()
     txtValue.Text = SelectedControls(0).Value
     txtCaption.Text = SelectedControls(0).Caption
     txtBorderStyle.Text = SelectedControls(0).BorderStyle
     txtBackStyle.Text = SelectedControls(0).BackStyle
     chkEnabled.Value = (SelectedControls(0).Enabled And vbChecked)
End Sub
```

Customizing the Property Page. To finish this example, we need to customize the General property page by providing ComboBox controls that make it easier for the user to select appropriate values for the BackStyle and BorderStyle properties. A sample is shown in Figure 25. We insert two ComboBox controls, called cboBackStyle and cboBorderStyle, and enter values into their List properties:

cboBackStyle.List:

0 – Transparent
1 – Opaque

cboBorderStyle.List:

0 – None
1 – Fixed Single

Of course, some revision of the source code is necessary. First, we insert Change event handlers for the ComboBoxes:

Figure 25. General Property Page (Customized).

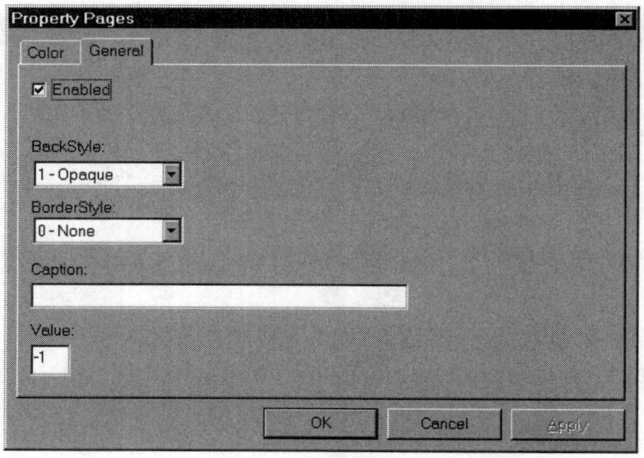


```
Private Sub cboBackStyle_Change()
   Changed = True
End Sub

Private Sub cboBorderStyle_Change()
   Changed = True
End Sub
```

Then we modify the SelectionChanged and ApplyChanges procedures to use the ListIndex properties of the ComboBox controls rather than TextBoxes:

```
Private Sub PropertyPage_ApplyChanges()
   SelectedControls(0).Value = txtValue.Text
   SelectedControls(0).Caption = txtCaption.Text
   SelectedControls(0).BorderStyle = cboBorderStyle.ListIndex
   SelectedControls(0).BackStyle = cboBackStyle.ListIndex
   SelectedControls(0).Enabled = (chkEnabled.Value = vbChecked)
End Sub

Private Sub PropertyPage_SelectionChanged()
   txtValue.Text = SelectedControls(0).Value
   txtCaption.Text = SelectedControls(0).Caption
   cboBorderStyle.ListIndex = SelectedControls(0).BorderStyle
   cboBackStyle.ListIndex = SelectedControls(0).BackStyle
   chkEnabled.Value = (SelectedControls(0).Enabled And vbChecked)
End Sub
```

That's it. We now have a customized property page for the OptionGroup ActiveX control.

9.6 CREATING AN ACTIVEX DLL

An *in-process component*, or *ActiveX DLL component*, shares the same address space with its client program. An *out-of-process component*, or *ActiveX EXE component*, runs in its own address space, as a stand-alone program. In this chapter, we will show how to create both types of components. In-process components tend to run faster than out-of-process components, because the former can easily communicate with its client via the stack and pointer variables. An out-of-process component, on the other hand, requires a different, slower method of communication between component and client called marshaling. The actual mechanics of marshaling are beyond the scope of our chapter, but you can read about it further by looking up "marshaling" in the index of the MSDN Library CD.

9.6.1 The DoctorSchedule DLL

(samples: DoctorDLL)

Let's borrow part of the Doctors Office Scheduling program from Chapter 6, simplify it, and turn it into an ActiveX DLL. The DLL is called **DoctorSchedule** and it contains the CSchedule, CPatient, and CAppointment classes. The DLL does not have a visual element. Instead, it is a database server, providing data to client programs on demand.

Type Library. The **DoctorSchedule** component exposes the **CSchedule** class to other programs. DoctorSchedule is the name of the component's *type library*, which may be seen in the Object Browser window, shown in Figure 26. If the name **CSchedule** exists in more than one library, fully qualified references to the name must be made in program code to include specific library names:

```
DoctorSchedule.CSchedule
CollegeSchedule.CSchedule
```

Project Group. Our project group contains two projects—one for the DLL, and one for a client program that demonstrates and tests the DLL. In Figure 27, the Project Group includes the DoctorSchedule project for the ActiveX component, and **TestProgram**, the client program.

The client program prompts the user for a patient ID number, and when the Search button is clicked, retrieves a list of all appointments for the patient. Figure 28 shows the results of searching for one patient's appointments.

Figure 26. DoctorSchedule Type Library, in Object Browser.

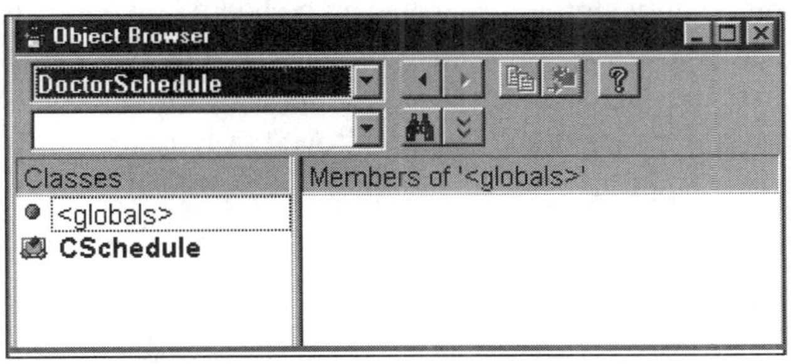

Figure 27. The Project Group for the DoctorSchedule Component.

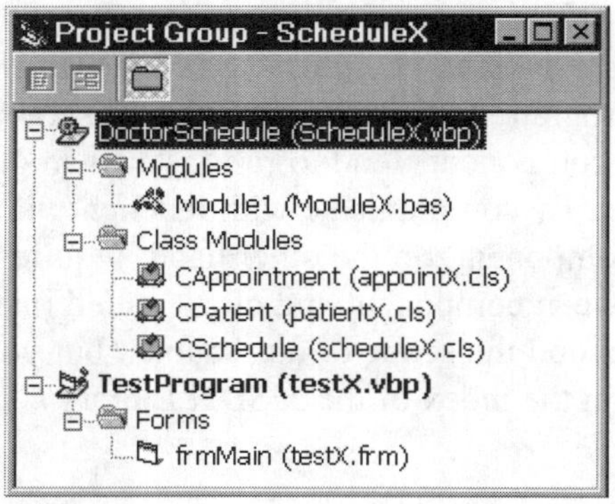

Figure 28. The Client Program, Retrieving Appointments.

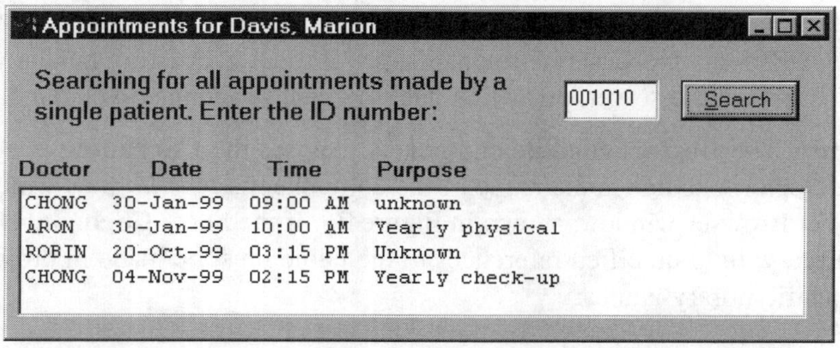

The DoctorSchedule Component. If the client program has no knowledge of the database structure or mechanics of retrieving appointment schedules from the database, clearly these tasks must be handled inside the DoctorSchedule component. Therefore, the CSchedule class searches the database for records containing specific patient ID numbers. It creates instances of the CPatient and CAppointment classes so methods in these classes can act as helpers.

In the DoctorSchedule project properties window, we set the following options:

- Project Type: ActiveX DLL
- Project Name: DoctorSchedule

9.6.2 Client Program Implementation

The client program is remarkably simple. It creates a CSchedule object, calls a method called **GetAppts** that returns a collection of appointments for a single patient, and displays the appointments in a ListBox. The following is the complete source code for this program. Two objects are created in Form_Load and later destroyed in Form_Unload:

```
Private WithEvents mclsSchedule As CSchedule
Private mcolApptList As Collection

Private Sub Form_Load()
  Set mclsSchedule = New CSchedule
```

```
  Set mcolApptList = New Collection
End Sub

Private Sub Form_Unload(Cancel As Integer)
  Set mclsSchedule = Nothing
  Set mcolApptList = Nothing
End Sub
```

When the user clicks on the **Search** button, **cmdSearch_Click** calls **GetAppts**, passing it a patient ID number and an empty collection. The server fills in the **apptList** collection with strings representing appointments, and the strings are inserted into a ListBox:

```
Private Sub cmdSearch_Click()
  Dim j As Integer, appt As CAppointment, strDoctor As String * 5
  On Error GoTo Search1
  lstAppointments.Clear
  ClearCollection mcolApptList

  If mclsSchedule.GetAppts(txtPatientId.Text, mcolApptList) Then
    For j = 1 To mcolApptList.Count
      Set appt = mcolApptList(j)
      strDoctor = appt.DoctorId
      lstAppointments.AddItem strDoctor & "  " & _
        Format(appt.ApptDate, "Medium Date") & "  " & _
        Format(appt.ApptTime, "Medium Time") & "  " & _
        appt.Purpose
    Next j
    Me.Caption = "Appointments for " & mcolApptList(1).PatientName
  Else
    MsgBox "No matching appointments were found."
  End If
  Exit Sub
Search1:
  MsgBox Error$, vbInformation, ""
End Sub
```

If an unhandled error occurs during the call to GetAppts, an event is raised by the CSchedule class and displayed in the following procedure:

```
Private Sub mclsSchedule_ReadError(Err As ErrObject)
  MsgBox "Error occurred while reading the schedule file. " _
    & Err.Description, vbCritical, "ReadError Event"
End Sub
```

ClearCollection is a general-purpose loop that removes all members of a Collection object:

```
Public Sub ClearCollection(coll As Collection)
  Dim obj As Variant
  For Each obj In coll
    coll.Remove 1
  Next obj
End Sub
```

This example shows how the hard work has all been offloaded onto the ActiveX server. In particular, only the server has detailed knowledge about the database structure. This creates a clear separation of tasks. Any number of programs might use this ActiveX server to search for appointments. The component needs to be written and debugged only once.

9.6.3 Instancing Property

The three classes in this component, CSchedule, CAppointment, and CPatient, each have an **Instancing** property. This property controls the way in which client programs outside of the component's project may create instances of the class. There are six possible Instancing values: MultiUse, GlobalMultiUse, Private, PublicNotCreateable, SingleUse, and GlobalSingleUse.

MultiUse. For ActiveX DLL components, the default value for Instancing is *MultiUse*, meaning that one instance of the component can provide any number of objects to client applications. If the Instancing property were *GlobalMutiUse*, client programs could invoke class methods without explicitly declaring an instance of the class. In the DoctorSchedule component, for example, CSchedule is *MultiUse*.

Private. If the Instancing property of a class is *Private*, other applications cannot access type library information about the class, and cannot create class instances. In the DoctorSchedule component, the CPatient class is private. If the instancing property of CSchedule were *Private*, however, the client program would not be able to create an instance of CSchedule. The error message shown in Figure 29 would appear.

Figure 29. Error Message When Instancing = Private.

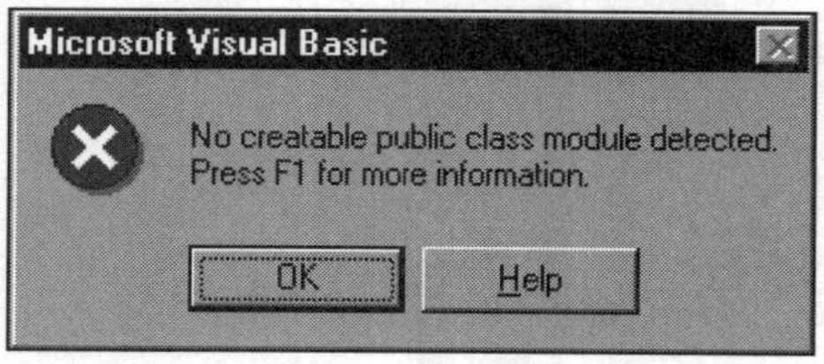

PublicNotCreateable. If the Instancing property is *PublicNotCreateable*, other applications can use instances of the class only if the component creates the objects first. In DoctorSchedule, for example, the CAppointment class is PublicNotCreateable. The client program needs to access certain properties of CAppointment objects.

SingleUse, GlobalSingleUse. If the Instancing property is *SingleUse*, other applications can create objects from the class, but every created object starts a new instance of the component. If the Instancing property is *GlobalSingleUse*, it is similar to SingleUse except that class methods can be called as if they are global procedures. Only out-of-process components (EXE) can be SingleUse or GlobalSingleUse.

Table 2 cross-references the types of components and programs created by Visual Basic, using an X to indicate which Instancing properties are permitted.

If you plan on creating multiple instances of a class, read Chapter 8 of the Visual Basic *Component Tools Guide* manual (available on the MSND CD). It deals with the important issues of scalability and multithreading, which are beyond the scope of the current book. For example, the chapter explains what happens when two or more processes are simultaneously requesting services from the same component. The issues raised are important in any multitasking environment where programs are competing for the same resources.

Table 2. Permitted Values of the Instancing Property.

Instancing Property	ActiveX Exe	ActiveX DLL	ActiveX Contol	Standard Exe
Private	X	X	X	X
PublicNotCreateable	X	X	X	
SingleUse	X			
GlobalSingleUse	X			
MultiUse	X	X		
GlobalMultiUse	X	X		

9.6.4 Global Data

The DoctorSchedule component has a code module (moduleX.bas) with single global variable called **gcnDoctors**. It holds the ADO Connection object that is shared by the three classes in the component:

```
Public gcnDoctors As ADODB.Connection
```

9.6.5 CSchedule Class

The CSchedule class declares three private instance variables: **mrsAppointments** is a reference to the database table containing scheduled appointments:

```
Private mrsAppointments As ADODB.Recordset
Public Event ReadError(Err As ErrObject)
```

The **Class_Intitialize** event handler opens an ADO Connection to the doctors.mdb database, and the **Class_Terminate** event handler closes the Connection:

```
Private Sub Class_Initialize()
  Set gcnDoctors = New ADODB.Connection
  gcnDoctors.ConnectionString = "Provider = " _
    & "Microsoft.Jet.OLEDB.3.51; " _
    & "Data Source =" & App.Path & "\doctors.mdb"
  gcnDoctors.Open
End Sub

Private Sub Class_Terminate()
  gcnDoctors.Close
  set gcnDoctors = Nothing
End Sub
```

The **GetAppts** method is called by a client program to get a list of appointments scheduled by a particular patient. The calling program passes a patient ID along with an empty Collection object to hold all matching appointments. The function returns True if at least one appointment is found:

```
Public Function GetAppts(ByVal strPatientID As String, _
                ByRef apptList As Collection) As Boolean
  GetAppts = False
  Dim strQuery As String
  On Error GoTo GetApptsErr
  strQuery = _
      "Select * From Appointments " _
      & "Where PatientId = '" & strPatientID & "' " _
      & "Order by ApptDateTime"

  Set mrsAppointments = New ADODB.Recordset
  Call mrsAppointments.Open(strQuery, gcnDoctors, _
    adOpenStatic, adLockPessimistic, adCmdText)

  Dim anAppt As CAppointment
  With mrsAppointments
    Do While Not .EOF
      Set anAppt = New CAppointment
      GetAppts = True
      anAppt.ReadRecord mrsAppointments
      apptList.Add anAppt
      .MoveNext
    Loop
    .Close
  End With
  Exit Function
GetApptsErr:
  GetAppts = False
  RaiseEvent ReadError(Err)
End Function
```

Notice also that we raise an Event called **ReadError** if there is problem with processing the query against the database. If, for example, we had misspelled the table name as **Appointment** rather than **Appointments**, the following message would be generated in the client program. Beginning with the second sentence, the **Description** property of the **Err** object is displayed:

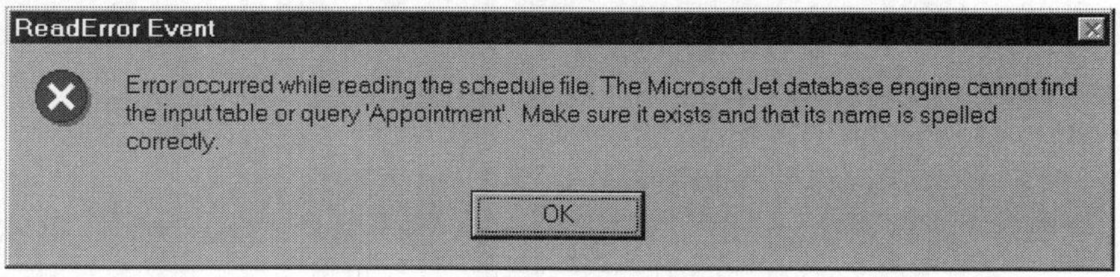

> ***Programming Tip:*** In the CSchedule class, you might be tempted to handle errors inside the GetAppts method by displaying a message box. But this is considered poor style when writing ActiveX components. The Visual Basic manual says in no uncertain terms, "A well behaved component does not intrude on the client application's user interface by displaying message boxes containing error text."

9.6.6 CAppointment Class

If you looked carefully at the code in the GetAppts method, you noticed that it creates an instance of the CAppointent class. This means that we have to include CAppointment in the project. This class is simpler than the original version in Chapter 8 because it includes only the properties and the AsString, AsRecordset, and ReadRecord methods:

```
Private mstrDoctorID As String
Private mstrPatientID As String
Private mdtmApptDate As Date
Private mdtmApptTime As Date
Private mstrPurpose As String
```

Various Property Get procedures return the doctor ID, patient name, appointment date and time, and the purpose of the appointment:

```
Public Property Get DoctorId() As String
  DoctorId = mstrDoctorID
End Property

Public Property Get ApptDate() As Date
  ApptDate = mdtmApptDate
End Property

Public Property Get ApptTime() As Date
  ApptTime = mdtmApptTime
End Property

Public Property Get Purpose() As String
  Purpose = mstrPurpose
End Property

Public Property Get PatientName() As String
  Dim aPatient As New CPatient
  PatientName = aPatient.GetPatientName( mstrPatientID )
End Property
```

The **ReadRecord** method copies data from the current record of an open Recordset into the object's instance variables:

```
Public Sub ReadRecord(rsAppt As Recordset)
  With rsAppt
    mstrDoctorID = "" & !DoctorId
    mstrPatientID = "" & !PatientID
    mdtmApptDate = DateValue("" & !ApptDateTime)
```

```
      mdtmApptTime = TimeValue("" & !ApptDateTime)
      mstrPurpose = "" & !Purpose
    End With
  End Sub
```

9.6.7 CPatient Class

The CPatient class is needed in the DoctorSchedule component because it provides a way to associate a patient ID number with the patient name. Here is its source code listing:

```
Private mrsPatients As ADODB.Recordset

Private Sub Class_Initialize()
  Set mrsPatients = New ADODB.Recordset
  Call mrsPatients.Open("Patients", gcnDoctors, _
     adOpenStatic, adLockPessimistic, adCmdTable)
End Sub

Private Sub Class_Terminate()
  mrsPatients.Close
End Sub
```

The **GetPatientName** method searches the table with a patient ID number, and if successful, returns the patient's name:

```
Public Function GetPatientName(strId As String)
  With mrsPatients
    .MoveFirst
    .Find "PatientId = " & strId
    If .EOF Then
      GetPatientName = ""
    Else
      GetPatientName = !LastName & ", " & !FirstName
    End If
  End With
End Function
```

9.6.8 Testing the Compiled Component

Once you have run and tested an in-process component in the Visual Basic development environment, you can compile the component into a DLL file and test it with the following steps:

1. From the File menu, select the **Make ScheduleX.dll** to create the .dll file.
2. Select the DoctorSchedule in the Project Group window, and select the **Remove Project** command from the **File** menu.
3. A warning message will appear: "The project is referenced from another project. Are you sure you want to remove it?" Click on **Yes** to remove the project.
4. Run the test program. It will load and execute the saved DLL component automatically.

9.7 CREATING AN OUT-OF-PROCESS COMPONENT

Not all applications lend themselves to using in-process components, and it is not always practical to use an ActiveX DLL. The DoctorSchedule component, for example, might be more useful as a stand-alone executable program that could provide services to any number of applications that happen to be running at the same time. Out-of-process components can show both modal and modeless forms, and if designed as such, can be run as stand-alone programs.

Microsoft Word and Excel are good examples of out-of-process components. Any Windows application that supports OLE automation or ActiveX technology can create an instance of a Word document or Excel worksheet.

Client programs can also run *asynchronously* in relation to out-of-process ActiveX components. This means, for example, that a client program can make a request for data or services from a component, and then continue its own processing until notified by the ActiveX component that the requested data is ready or the service is completed. This involves the use of asnynchronous call backs and events, which is thoroughly explained in Chapter 8 of the Visual Basic *Component Tools Guide*, Part 2.

9.7.1 Converting DoctorSchedule to ActiveX EXE Server

(samples: DoctorEXE)

Converting the DoctorSchedule component into an out-of-process component (an ActiveX EXE) involves the following steps:

1. Load the DoctorSchedule project file created in Section 9.4 (scheduleX.vbp).
2. In the project properties window, change the project type to **ActiveX EXE**.
3. Select the CSchedule class and set its Instancing property to **SingleUse**.
4. Select **Make ScheduleX.exe** from the **File** menu, to create a *reference executable*. This executable file does not have to be created again unless you modify the component.

Testing the Out-of-Process DoctorSchedule Component. When you create an out-of-process ActiveX component, it is a good idea to run and debug it from within the Visual Basic environment. If you want, you can set breakpoints in the component's code and in the code of the client program. The component and the client program must run in two separate instances of Visual Basic. The following steps are required:

1. Load just the DoctorSchedule project file (scheduleX.vbp)
2. Run the DoctorSchedule project from the VB development environment. Minimize Visual Basic while DoctorSchedule is still running.
3. Start a second instance of Visual Basic and load the client program's project (testX.vbp). Select **References** from the **Project** menu. Locate the entry for DoctorSchedule.vbp, and click on its CheckBox. There might be two entries for the Doctor Schedule, one for the .vbp file, and the other for the .exe file. You can tell them apart by looking at the **Location** label at the bottom of the window. You must choose

the .vbp file in order to debug the component in the Visual Basic development environment.

4. Run the client program and search for the appointments for one or more patients. When you halt the program, always do so by closing its window. Do not halt the client program by clicking on Visual Basic's **End** button or by selecting **End** from the **Run** menu. Doing so would abort the program and prevent it from releasing memory used by objects.
5. Activate the original copy of Visual Basic, the one containing the DoctorSchedule component. Ordinarily, the ActiveX component would have halted and unloaded itself as soon as none of its objects were referenced by client programs. Because it is running in the Visual Basic environment, however, it does not halt as expected. The only way to stop it is to click on the **End** button in the Visual Basic toolbar.

You can, if you wish, modify the DoctorSchedule component, but just remember to recompile it and run it again before running the client program. To test DoctorSchedule.exe from outside Visual Basic, run the client program from either the VB Editor or from the Windows Explorer. The DoctorSchedule component will automatically load and execute.

Testing the Stand-Alone EXE Server. There is just one last test to be done with the DoctorSchedule server. We want to find out if a compiled Visual Basic application can interact correctly with the compiled ScheduleX.exe server. We will assume that you have already compiled the server. Try the following steps:

1. Open the TestX project (the client) in Visual Basic and compile it to TextX.exe. Close the project.
2. Run two instances of TestX.exe from the Windows Explorer window. In each, click on the **Search** button to display all appointments for a selected patient ID.
3. Press the Ctrl-Alt-Del keys and look at the Windows Task Manager. Note that two instances of the DoctorSchedule server are running. Recall that we set the Instancing property of the CSchedule class to SingleUse, so each client program created a separate instance of the server.
4. Close both client programs and note that both instances of the DoctorSchedule server are no longer running.

9.7.2 Where to Go from Here

The explanations given about concepts and techniques relating to creating ActiveX components in this chapter are merely a brief introduction. If you would like to dive wholeheartedly into this topic, read Part 2 of the Visual Basic *Component Tools Guide*. Here are the topics in Part 2 of the manual:

- **Chapter 1. ActiveX Components.** A brief discussion of ActiveX concepts and definitions of terms.
- **Chapter 2. Creating an ActiveX DLL.** You get a chance to create a simple ActiveX DLL that reverses the characters in a string.

- **Chapter 3. Creating an ActiveX EXE Component.** This is an interesting program called the Coffee project, where you create an out-of-process ActiveX server that notifies the client program when the coffee is ready.
- **Chapter 4. Creating an ActiveX Control.** This chapter shows you how to create an ActiveX control called ShapeLabel, save and load its properties, raise events, and create a property page.
- **Chapter 5. Creating an ActiveX Document.** You build your first ActiveX document that contains a window and menu; it saves and loads its properties. This requires Internet Explorer 3.0 or later to run.
- **Chapter 6. General Principles of Component Design.** The topics in this chapter and in Chapter 7 contain background information that relate to all ActiveX component types.
- **Chapter 7. Debugging, Testing, and Deploying Components.** Besides debugging and testing, this chapter covers the generating and handling of errors, providing user assistance (Help), deploying ActiveX components.
- **Chapter 8. Building Code Complements.** Really advanced stuff regarding asynchronous call-backs, multithreading, binding, and marshaling.
- **Chapter 9. Building ActiveX Controls.** Continuation of Chapter 2: Adding properties and methods, raising events, named constants, setting up a test project, debugging, distributing, and localizing ActiveX controls.
- **Chapter 10. Creating Property Pages for ActiveX Controls.**
- **Chapter 11. Building ActiveX Documents.** Continuation of Chapter 5, using ActiveX pages on the Internet.
- **Chapter 12. Creating Data Sources.** Building data-aware class modules, such as the ADO Data control.

Of course, look for the many shareware ActiveX controls that are available on the Internet. Start with **www.microsoft.com** and follow their links to Visual Basic Web sites.

Don't forget about the web page devoted to this book! We provide lots of supplemental programs, ActiveX controls, and links to other Visual Basic locations on the Internet:

```
www.pobox.com/~irvinek/books/vb6
```

If you are identified as an instructor who has adopted this book, you can download improved and updated solutions to the programming exercises and new chapter exercises that are designed specifically for use with this book.

9.8 REVIEW QUESTIONS

1. Define *component software development.*
2. What is the name of the model created by Microsoft that permits software components to interact with each other?
3. In what way is ActiveX more than just object-oriented programming?

4. What is the term that applies to a group of controls inside a single ActiveX control?
5. What relationship do OLE servers have with ActiveX components?
6. If an ActiveX component is created in Visual Basic, can it be used in an Excel application?
7. What are the three general types of objects provided by ActiveX components?
8. How are code components different from ActiveX controls?
9. What type of ActiveX component compiles into an OCX file?
10. What type of ActiveX component compiles into a DLL file?
11. Are in-process servers compiled into EXE files?
12. What is the primary difference between a class module and an ActiveX component?
13. Show an example of declaring an event called FileError inside an ActiveX control's source code.
14. Show an example of raising the FileError event in an ActiveX control's source code.
15. In the StudentIdText UserControl demonstrated in Section 9.2, what happens when the user enters a nonnumeric character?
16. What relationship does a client program have to an ActiveX component?

The following questions refer to the AddAppointment ActiveX control:

17. Which design mode properties may be set in the AddAppointment control?
18. Which runtime properties may be accessed in the AddAppointment control? Are they read-write properties, or read-only?
19. How can a property be designated as read-only?
20. What happens when the user forgets to select a doctor from the ComboBox?
21. Which event occurs when an ActiveX control is first placed on a form?
22. Which event occurs if the designer modifies either the Caption or BackColor property of the AddAppointment control?
23. Why is it important to supply default property values when calling the WriteProperty method?
24. What is a PropertyBag object?
25. Which event handler executes when a Form file containing an ActiveX control is opened at design time?
26. What are the three user-defined events declared in the AddAppointment component?
27. Why is it important to call PropertyChanged inside a *Property Let* procedure? In other words, what would happen if it were not called?
28. What is the difference between an *in-process component* and an *out-of-process component*?
29. Why is DoctorSchedule called a *type library?*
30. Is an ActiveX DLL an in-process or out-of-process component?

31. What does PublicNotCreateable mean when applied to the Instancing property?
32. Which Instancing property values are allowed for ActiveX DLLs?
33. Which Instancing property values are allowed for ActiveX Controls?
34. What special operation does CSchedule perform when an instance of the class is first created? What is the name of the event handler where this happens?
35. Why is it important to use the On Error statement inside the Terminate event of an ActiveX component?
36. What special steps must be taken to debug an out-of-process component?
37. Is it possible to run an out-of-process component from the Windows Explorer? If so, how is it done?

9.9 CHAPTER EXERCISES

9.9.1 StudentInfo Control - 1

Add a LastName Property. Use the StudentIdText ActiveX control introduced at the beginning of this chapter as a starting point for this exercise. Add another field for the student's last name, and bind it to the LastName field in the students database. Modify the test program so it works with your new control.

9.9.2 StudentInfo Control - 2

StudentInfo DataRepeater. Continue the previous programming exercise. Add a DataRepeater control to the program and use it to display multiple instances of the StudentInfo control. Be sure to add entries in the RepeaterBindings collection for both the StudentId and LastName fields. Finally, sort the records in ascending order by last name.

9.9.3 AddAppointment Control - 1

Saving the Appointment. The client program for the AddAppointment ActiveX control example presented in this chapter does not save the appointment in a database. For the current exercise, add the necessary code to the aptAdd_Save() procedure in the client program to save the current appointment. Use ADO object methods, demonstrated in Chapter 5.

9.9.4 AddAppointment Control - 2

Data-Bound Properties. Use the AddAppointment ActiveX control shown in this chapter as a starting point for this exercise. Make each of the following properties data-bound: DoctorId, PatientId, ApptDateTime, and Purpose. Write a short test program with an ADO control that displays the Recordset and allows the user to add new appointments.

9.9.5 AddAppointment Control - 3

ForeColor Property. The AddAppointment UserControl presented in this chapter has a BackColor property that affects the UserControl itself, as well as its constituent Label controls. For the current exercise, implement a ForeColor property in the same manner.

9.9.6 Stellar Car Rentals - 1

Select Vehicles by Category. Use the Stellar Car Rentals database introduced in Chapter 6. Create an ActiveX control that lets the user select a vehicle category (Economy, Compact, ...) from a ComboBox. The control should immediately display a list of cars from the Vehicle table matching the selected category.

9.9.7 Stellar Car Rentals - 2

Display Individual Reservations. Use the Stellar Car Rentals database introduced in Chapter 6. Create an ActiveX control that displays a single reservation from the Reservations table. Make the following properties data-bound: ReservationId (read-only), CustomerId, RentalDate, ModelId. Allow the user to scroll through the records with an ADO control and update all fields except the ReservationId.

9.9.8 Stellar Car Rentals - 3

Reservation List. Continue the previous programming exercise. Add a DataRepeater control to the form and allow the user to scroll through reservation records, sorted on the RentalDate field.

9.9.9 Stellar Car Rentals - 4

Rental Rates Grid. In the Stellar Car Rental exercises at the end of Chapter 6, we asked you to display a DataGrid containing daily and weekly vehicle rental rates. For this project, create an ActiveX control that encapsulates an ADO control and DataGrid so the user can display price information (see Figure 30).

Figure 30. Stellar Rental Rates ActiveX Control.

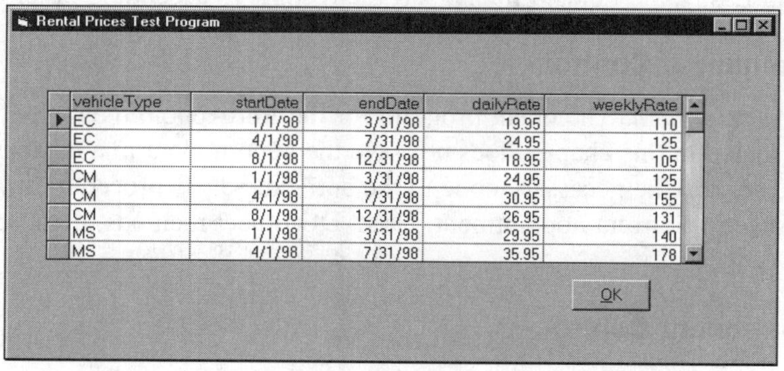

9.9.10 OptionList Control – 1

ButtonCount Property. Use the OptionList ActiveX control shown in this chapter as a starting point for this exercise. Add a property called ButtonCount that lets the designer choose the number of OptionButtons to display. Recall from Chapter 3 that you can use the Load statement to add new elements to a control array at runtime. The frame around the buttons should automatically resize itself to accomodate the selected number of buttons.

9.9.11 OptionList Control – 2

Horizontal Resizing. Continue the previous programming exercise. When the designer resizes the OptionList control, write code in the Resize event handler to resize the OptionButtons. Allow resizing only in the horizontal direction.

9.9.12 OptionList Control – 3

Horizontal and Vertical Resizing. Continue the previous programming exercise. When the designer resizes the OptionList control, write code in the Resize event handler to resize the OptionButtons. Allow resizing in both horizontal and vertical directions.

9.9.13 OptionList Control – 4

Font Property. Add a Font property to the OptionList control presented earlier in this chapter. Your Let Property procedure must delegate the procedure parameter to the constituent controls, namely Frame1 and optButton(). Test the control by setting Font properties at design time.

9.9.14 Publisher ActiveX Control

Use the Biblio database to create an ActiveX control that displays Publisher IDs and names in TextBoxes (see Figure 31). Use a DataRepeater control to display multiple publishers, as in Figure 32.

You will need to add property and field names to the RepeaterBindings collection in the DataRepeater control. A sample is provided in Figure 33. Table 3 contains suggested properties for the ADO control and the DataRepeater control.

Figure 31. Publisher ActiveX Control.

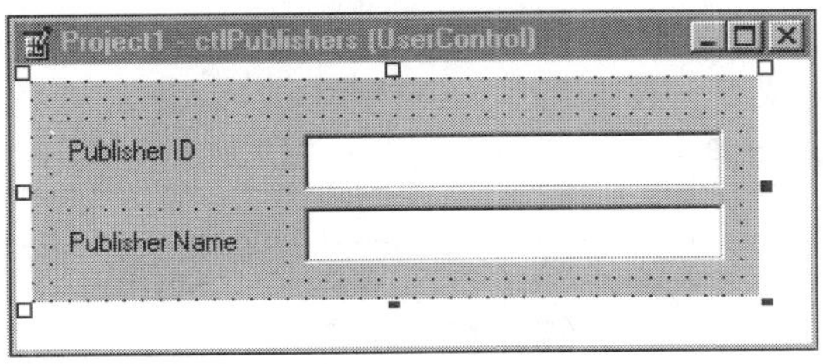

Figure 32. Data Repeater with Publisher Control.

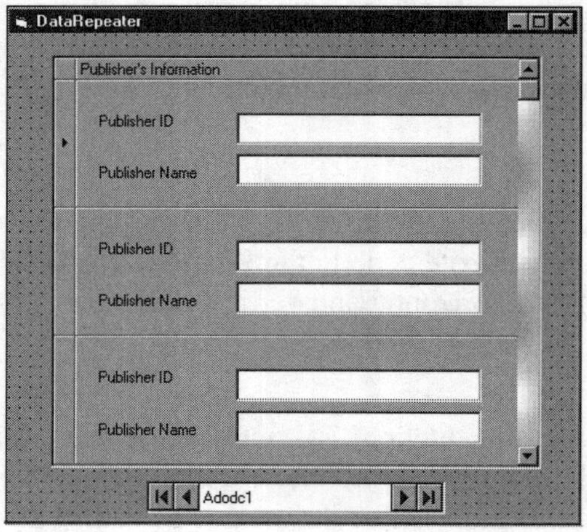

Figure 33. RepeaterBindings Collection Settings.

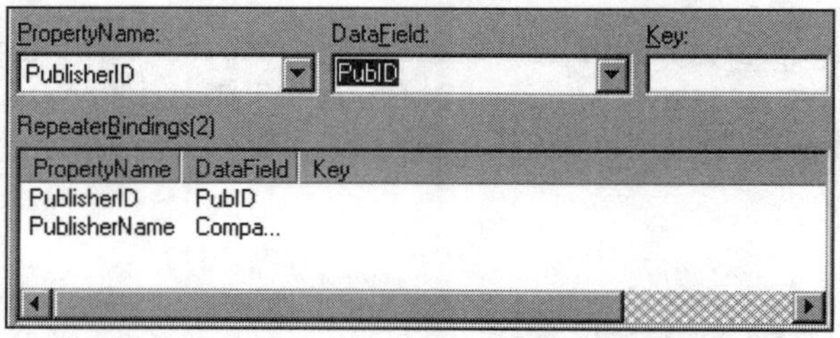

Table 3. ADO and DataRepeater Properties.

Object	Property	Setting
ADO Control	Name	Adodc1
	ConnectionString	Provider=Microsoft.Jet.OLEDB.3.5-1;Persist Security Info=False;Data Source=C:\Program Files\Microsoft Visual Studio\VB98\Biblio.mdb
	RecordSource	Publishers
DataRepeater Control	Name	DataRepeater1
	DataSource	Adodc1
	RepeatedControlName	PublishersCtl.ctlPublishers

10 Using OLE and ActiveX Servers

Chapter Contents

OLE Containers and ActiveX Servers
- Object Linking and Embedding

OLE Container Control
- Example: Creating an Embedded Word Object
- Example: Creating an Embedded Excel Worksheet
- CreateLink Method

OLE Container Program
- Program Specifications
- Creating a New Excel Worksheet
- Creating a New Word Document
- Inserting an Excel Worksheet
- Inserting a Word Document
- Program Implementation

Using MS-Office Code Components
- Visual Basic for Applications
- Example: Creating a Word Document
- Word Classes, Properties, and Methods
- OLE Automation with Excel
- Excel: Statistical Score Analysis

College Admissions Program
- Program Specifications
- Program Design
- Program Implementation
- Conclusion

Review Questions

Chapter Exercises

10.1 OLE CONTAINERS AND ACTIVEX SERVERS

This chapter is all about letting Visual Basic tap into the power of other desktop applications. Foremost among these are the Microsoft Office products, including Word, Excel, Access, and PowerPoint. We will show how to create and open documents, spreadsheets, and charts in two different ways: first, using Visual Basic's **OLE Container** control, and second, using **ActiveX Code Components** (formerly called OLE Automation Servers).

OLE automation was the first technology built on COM, the Microsoft Component Object Model architecture. It gave programs the ability to expose their objects, properties, and methods to other programs. An OLE container program or document could contain both embedded and linked objects created by other programs. Microsoft now uses the term **ActiveX** for this technology, which has been expanded to include networks and the

Internet. At the same time, the **OLE Container** control has retained its name, probably for compatibility with Visual Basic 5 applications.

Applications. Imagine a Visual Basic program that displays a company quarterly sales summary. It might include a spreadsheet containing the sales data, a pie chart that graphically displays the sales, a popup calendar for scheduling the next sales meeting, and a document containing several paragraphs that summarize the sales results. Finally, you might like to let the user click on an icon and attach a short note in response to your sales summary. The text portion of the memo would be created in Word; the spreadsheet and chart would be created by Excel, a technical diagram could be created by Visio, and the short response note could be created by WordPad.

Similarly, when creating a multimedia tutorial, you might like to include text, pictures, music, a video clip, and sound effects. A database could be used to store all these elements as ActiveX objects, and SQL statements could be used to search the database for relevant keywords. All of the objects mentioned in these two examples can be incorporated into Visual Basic programs, using ActiveX objects.

Using External Objects. There are two basic ways to use external objects in a Visual Basic program:

- Select the **OLE container** control from the ToolBox and place a copy of it on a form. This control can hold various types of objects such as documents, drawings, worksheets, sound files, and video clips.
- Using programming statements, create instances of ActiveX objects, and directly call their methods and properties. For example, you can create a Microsoft Excel Application object. Using the methods associated with the Excel code component, you can create a new Workbook and associated WorkSheet.

10.1.1 Object Linking and Embedding

The two basic types of ActiveX objects that can be manipulated by a container application are *embedded objects* and *linked objects*:

- An **embedded object** stores all of its data inside the container application. In other words, if a Visual Basic program is a container for a Word document, the entire document is stored inside the Visual Basic program, along with the name of the program that created the object, Microsoft Word. When the user selects the embedded object, Word is activated and the user can edit the document. Embedded objects can be created in Visual Basic using the **OLE Container** control.
- A **linked object** stores its data outside the container application, in a separate file that was created by the program that supplied the object. For example, a Worksheet file created by Excel can be a linked object. The container application stores only an image of the data, along with link references to the file containing the actual object. Any application containing a link to the same object can display and update the data. The modified file will be displayed in all applications that are linked to it.

One factor to be taken into consideration when using object linking or embedding is that the user of an external object must have a copy of the necessary software on their system. The examples in this chapter require Word 97 and Excel 97; the remaining programs mentioned are already supplied with Windows.

10.2 OLE CONTAINER CONTROL

The OLE container control is a general-purpose tool for inserting any type of registered OLE object. The OLE container comes with an extensive set of properties and methods. Objects can be either linked or embedded, and the OLE container can be bound to a Data control. This means that OLE objects can be stored in databases.

10.2.1 Example: Creating an Embedded Word Object

(samples: Ole_Word)

The easiest way to create an embedded object is to name the object's type at design time when the OLE container is placed on a form. The following steps show how to do this:

Step 1. Create a new form called **frmWord** and add the following menu. Set the **NegotiatePosition** property of mnuFile to 1 (Left):

```
&File     mnuFile
  E&xit   mnuFileExit
```

Drag an OLE container control onto the form so that it fills most of the form. It will resemble a text box, as in Figure 1. Immediately, the **Insert Object** window pops up; select **Microsoft Word Document** and click OK (Figure 2).

The **Create New** option creates an embedded object; the **Create From File** option creates a linked object. When you click OK, Word is immediately activated, and a simplified Word menu is displayed.

Step 2. Write a short note, shown in Figure 3.

Step 3. Set the Name property of the OLE container control to **oleWord**. Run the program and observe in Figure 4 that the Word menu has disappeared, leaving only the OLE container's text on the form. Or, you can make the container a little less obvious by setting the OLE container's BorderStyle to none and BackColor to the same color as the form's background. When the user double clicks on the text, the object is activated and the text can be modified.

NegotiateMenus Property. Notice that the Word menu does not appear when the user edits the document. If you want an embedded object's menu to appear at runtime when the user activates the object, you must set the form's NegotiateMenus property to True.

NegotiatePosition Property. If you create a menu on the enclosing form of an OLE control, you can use the **NegotiatePosition** property of individual submenus to determine whether or not they will be displayed along with the activated object's menu. By default, the NegotiatePosition property equals 0 (none); if you change it to 1 (Left), 2 (Middle), or 3 (Right), the submenu will remain on the menu bar when the OLE object is activated.

Step 4. Set the NegotiateMenus property to True on the main form. Create the following menu on the form and set the NegotiatePosition property of mnuFile to 1 (left):

Figure 1. OLE Container, Word Document.

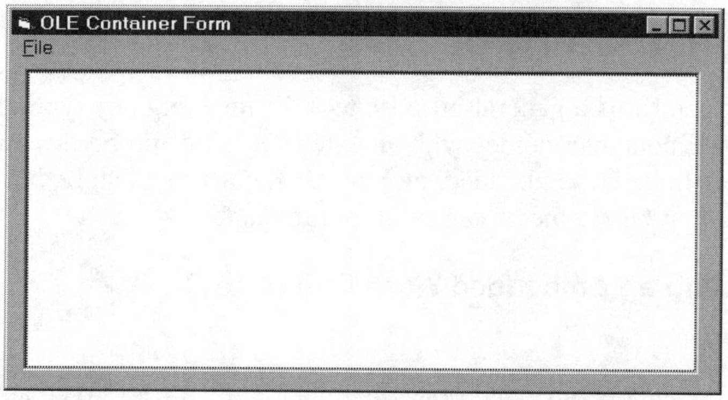

Figure 2. Insert Object Dialog.

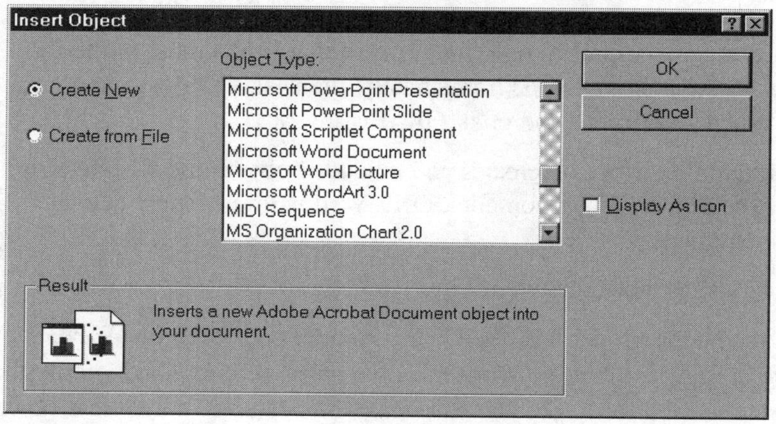

Figure 3. Editing the OLE Word Document.

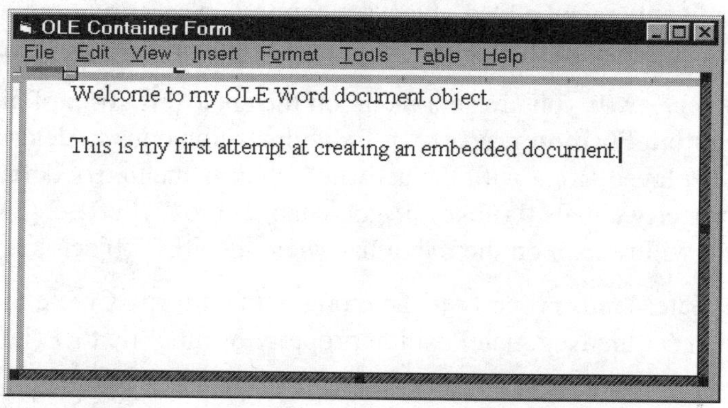

Figure 4. Editing OLE Word Document at Run Time.

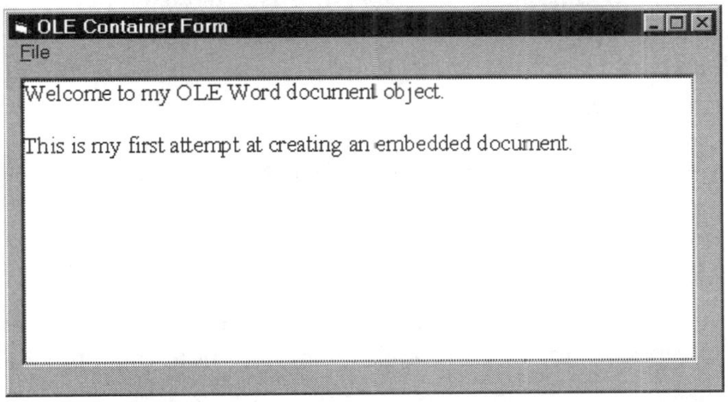


```
&File          mnuFile
  &Save        mnuFileSave
  &Open        mnuFileOpen
  E&xit        mnuFileExit
```

Run the program, activate the OLE object, and notice that the File menu appears at the left side of Word's menu.

NegotiateToolbars Property. The NegotiateToolbars property on an MDI form is useful because it lets you determine whether or not the OLE object's ToolBars will appear on the parent window. The MDI parent form is not required to already have a ToolBar. ToolBars are usually contained in a PictureBox on the parent form. The NegotiateToolbars property of the PictureBox determines whether the existing parent tool bar is completely replaced by the OLE object's toolbar.

Saving an OLE Container Object. The OLE control's **SaveToFile** method saves the embedded object to a binary file in OLE 2.0 format. Here, the object is saved in a file called sample.bin:

```
Private Sub mnuFileSave_Click()
  Dim intFilenum As Integer
  intFilenum = FreeFile
  Open "sample.bin" For Binary As intFileNum
  oleWord.SaveToFile intFilenum
  Close intFilenum
End Sub
```

An OLE container control may also be bound to a Data control, and OLE objects can be stored in databases.

Reading an OLE Container Object. The OLE control's **ReadFromFile** method loads an embedded object from an OLE 2.0 binary file called sample.bin:

```
Dim intFilenum As Integer
intFilenum = FreeFile
Open "sample.bin" For Binary As intFilenum
oleWord.ReadFromFile intFilenum
Close intFilenum
```

Right Clicking the Mouse. At either design time or run time, you can edit an embedded document by right clicking the mouse on the object. This activates a popup menu with at least two choices: **Edit** and **Open**. Select the Open command, and a copy of Word will run with the document displayed in it. Best of all, Word's complete **File** menu will be available, so you can save or print the object.

10.2.2 Example: Creating an Embedded Excel Worksheet

(samples: OLE_Excel)

You can also create an embedded object inside an OLE control at runtime, by using the **CreateEmbed** method. This is a flexible approach because it allows the same OLE container to hold different types of objects, although it can only hold one object at a time.

CreateEmbed Method. There are two basic forms of the CreateEmbed method. You can either specify a filename which will be used as a template for the embedded object, or you can specify a class name:

```
oleControl.CreateEmbed sourceFilename
oleControl.CreateEmbed "",class
```

For example, using a Word document called **memo.doc** as a template, the following statement places a copy of the document inside the OLE control:

```
OLE1.CreateEmbed "memo.doc"
```

The OLE control immediately displays memo.doc.

Using a Class Name. The second form of the **CreateEmbed** method takes a class name as a parameter. Class names are placed in the Windows registry by installation programs for OLE-aware programs. To view a list of available class names, select the OLE control, display the properties window, and click the button next to the **Class** property. A **ListBox** will display a list of all registered class names, shown in Figure 5.

The following statement, for example, creates a new Word document:

```
OLE1.CreateEmbed "", "Word.Document.8"
```

The following statement creates an Excel Chart:

```
OLE1.CreateEmbed "", "Excel.Chart.8"
```

10.2.3 Hands-on Chart Example

Try the following hands-on example: Create a new Form and place two OLE containers on it. When the Insert Document window appears, click on the Cancel button. Place the following statements inside Form_Load:

```
OLE1.CreateEmbed "", "Excel.Chart.8"
OLE2.CreateEmbed "", "Excel.Chart.8"
```

Set the SizeMode property of both controls to **AutoSize**. This will make the controls automatically size themselves to the embedded chart.

Figure 5. Registered Class Names (sample).

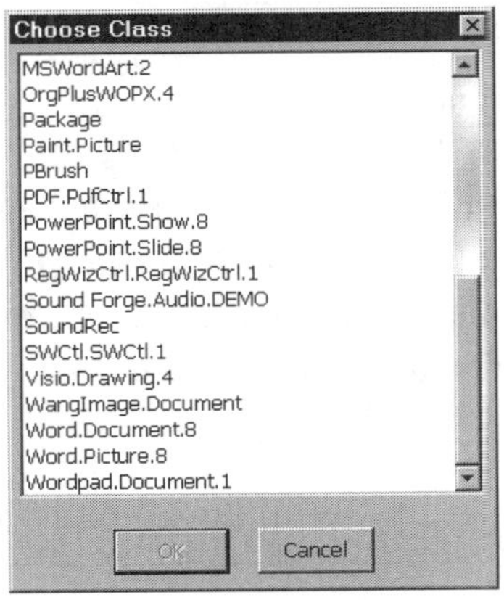

Run the program. The same chart, with sample data, will appear in both OLE containers, as in Figure 6. Activate the container on top and click on the tab labeled "Sheet 1".

Click once on the lower OLE control to deactivate the Worksheet. The form will display the Worksheet and the chart that graphically represents the data.

The Windows clipboard can easily be used to transfer objects between OLE controls and between other Windows applications that support OLE. For example, add a CommandButton to the current Form and write the following statements in the click event: They copy the chart in OLE1 to the Clipboard and paste the Clipboard into OLE2:

```
OLE1.Copy
OLE2.Paste
```

Figure 6. Worksheet and Chart Containers.

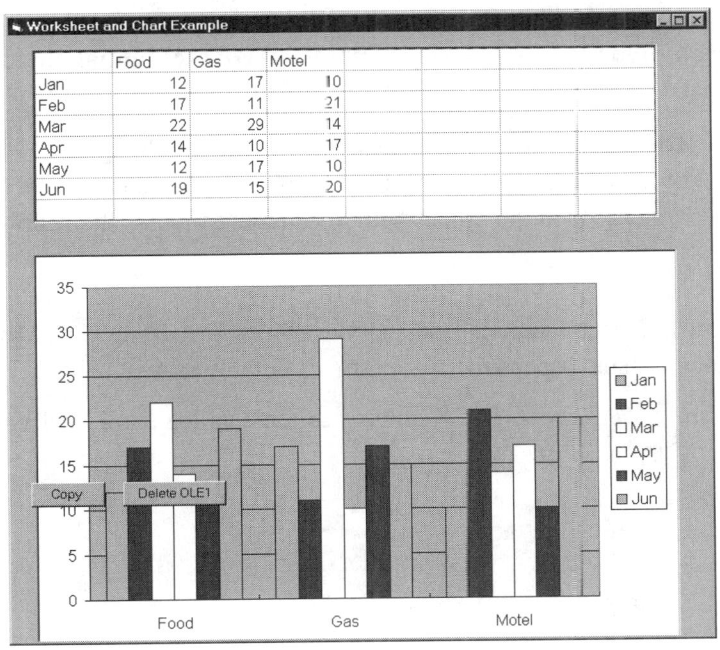

To test this, modify one of the numbers in the Worksheet in OLE1. Click the Command button, and notice that OLE2 now has the same change that you made to OLE1.

SizeMode Property. The SizeMode property contains an integer that determines how the OLE container is sized, or how its image is displayed when it contains an object. In our examples, the SizeMode property was set to AutoSize. The property can be set either at design time or at run time to one of the values shown in Table 1. In general, **Autosize** is best when inserting an existing spreadsheet or document, because the user can expand the form holding the OLE control at runtime. The OLE control expands automatically as far as it needs to, up to the right and bottom borders of the enclosing form.

Table 1. SizeMode Property Values.

SizeMode	Description
Clip	The object, displayed in actual size, is clipped to the control's borders. (vbOLESizeClip)
Stretch	The object is sized to fill the control, which may alter the object's proportions. (vbOLESizeStretch)
Autosize	The control is resized to display the entire object. (vbOLESizeAutoSize)
Zoom	The object is resized to fill the container as much as possible, while still retaining its original proportions. (vbOLESizeStretch)

AutoActivate Property. The AutoActivate property controls the way in which the user can activate an OLE object for editing. It can be set in either design mode or run mode. The default is vbOLEActivateDoubleclick, meaning that the user can double click the mouse to activate the object. If you set the property to **vbOLEActivateManual**, the user cannot activate the object.

DoVerb Method. The DoVerb method can be used to open an OLE object for some action, usually editing. The main reason for using DoVerb is if the AutoActivate property is set to *manual*, the program can open the object with a statement such as the following:

```
OLE1.DoVerb  vbOLEShow
```

The **vbOLEShow** constant specifically opens the object for editing. The **vbOLEPrimary** constant, on the other hand, opens the object for its default action.

Loading an Existing Worksheet. The following statements load an Excel Worksheet and set the SizeMode property to **Clip**:

```
ole1.SizeMode  =  vbOLESizeClip
ole1.CreateEmbed  "budget.xls"
```

When activated by the user, it appears as a spreadsheet that can be modified (Figure 7). The user can change the spreadsheet's size by dragging the handles along the sides. Individual numbers can be changed, causing the total to recalculate.

Figure 7. In-Place Editing of the Expenses Worksheet.

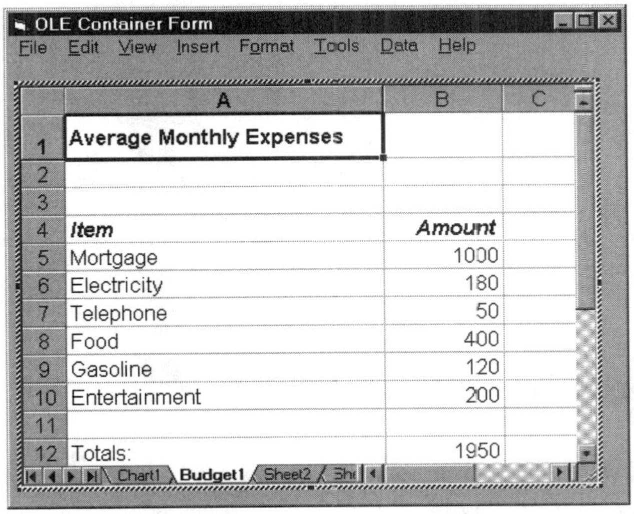

10.2.4 CreateLink Method

The CreateLink method creates a linked object from the contents of a file. The general syntax is:

```
oleControl.CreateLink  sourceDoc  [,sourceItem]
```

where *sourceDoc* is the filename from which the OLE control will be linked, and *sourceItem* names the data within the file that will be linked; *sourceItem* is optional. The values placed in the sourceDoc and sourceItem parameters override the properties by the same names in the OLE control.

When an object is created with this method, the OLE container control displays an image of the file specified by the SourceDoc property. If the OLE object is saved, only the link references are saved, because the original document is saved by its own application. For example, the following statement creates a link to the **budget.xls** Worksheet file:

```
OLE1.CreateLink  "budget.xls"
```

This displays the Worksheet on the OLE control as if it were an embedded object, but the difference becomes clear when the user activates the object. The Excel program itself starts up, allowing the user full access to its menus and toolbars (see Figure 8).

If the user makes any changes to the sheet and saves it in Excel, the link to the Visual Basic program is automatically updated. Any other OLE links that exist between the source document and other containers are also updated.

Figure 8. Linked Worksheet Example.

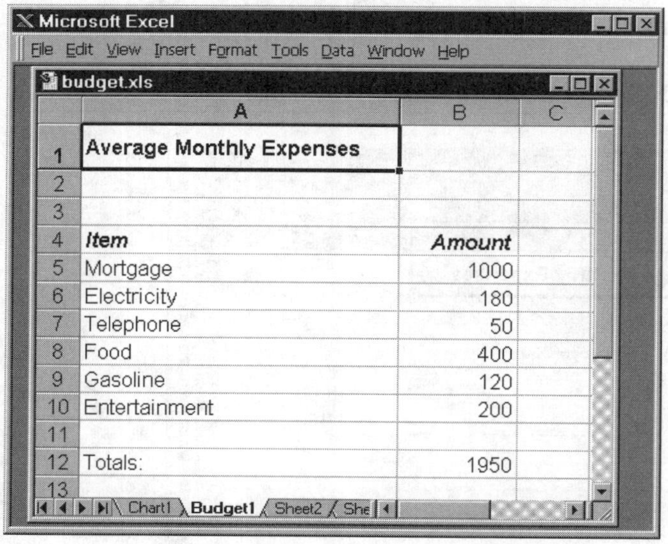

Update, Delete, and Close. If another application should modify the linked object at the same time that our program is displaying it, it would be necessary to call the **Update** method to display the most recent version of the object. For example:

```
OLE1.Update
```

The **Delete** method immediately deletes the object and frees the memory used by it. Otherwise, an OLE object would be deleted automatically when the form was closed or when replaced by another object (using CreateLink or CreateEmbed).

The **Close** method, useful only with embedded objects, terminates the connection to the application that created the object. From the user's point of view, the Close method simply deactivates the OLE control. If the object is inactive already, Close has no effect.

10.3 OLE CONTAINER PROGRAM

(samples: OLEContainer)

Let's write a simple program using the OLE container control that lets the user do the following:

- Create a new Excel Worksheet or Chart.
- Create a new Word Document.
- Open an existing Excel Worksheet.
- Open an existing Word Document.

Each of the objects will be embedded, not linked.

10.3.1 Creating a New Excel Worksheet

The main window contains only an OLE container control and a File menu. To create a Worksheet, the user selects the **File > New > Worksheet** menu command (see Figure 9). After the user clicks on **File > Close,** the embedded Worksheet displays only its data.

Figure 9. Creating a New Worksheet.

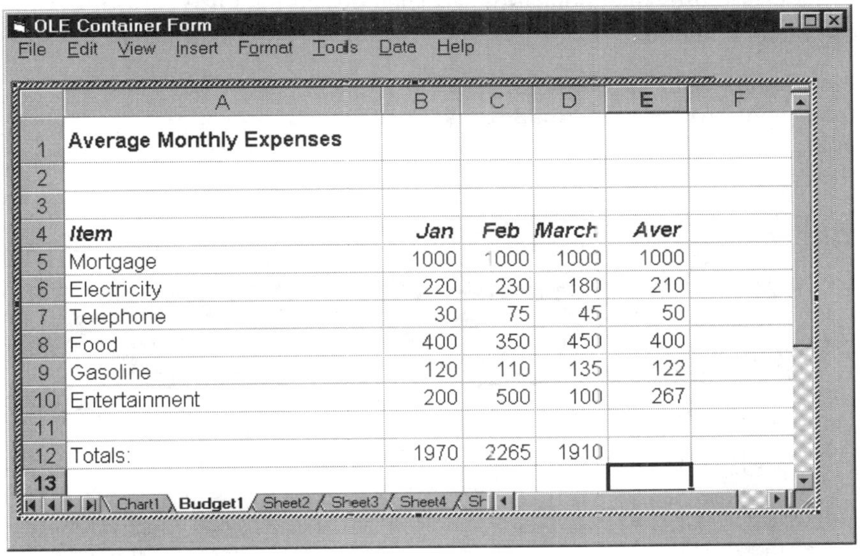

10.3.2 Inserting an Excel Worksheet

To insert an existing Worksheet, the user selects the **File > Insert > Worksheet** menu command. This brings up a **File Open** Common dialog, in which the user selects a Worksheet file to insert. The selected file is embedded in the OLE control, and is not activated until the user double clicks (see Figure 10).

10.3.3 Inserting a Word Document

To insert an existing Word document, the user selects the **File > Insert > Document** menu command. Again, a File Open Common dialog lets the user select a document file, and the file is embedded in the OLE control. Word automatically selects the "Page" view, shown in Figure 11. Because the SizeMode of the OLE control is set to **AutoSize**, the OLE control expands as much as it is able to without going beyond the edge of the form. When the user resizes the form, the OLE control automatically resizes itself. When the user double clicks on the document, the Word menu activates and the document may be edited.

10.3.4 Program Implementation

The project contains one form, called **frmOLE**. The OLE container control is named **OLE1**, and the common dialog control is named **dlgInsert**.

Form_Load initializes the CancelError and Filter properties of dlgInsert, the dialog used for opening files:

```
Private Sub Form_Load()
   ChDrive App.Path
   ChDir App.Path
   dlgInsert.CancelError = True
   dlgInsert.Filter = "Excel file (*.xls)|*.xls|" _
      & "Word Document (*.doc)|*.doc|All files (*.*)|*.*"
End Sub
```

The user closes the application associated with the OLE control by selecting the **File > Close** menu command:

```
Private Sub mnuFileClose_Click()
'Close the OLE object's application.
   OLE1.Close
End Sub
```

Figure 10. The Embedded Budget Worksheet.

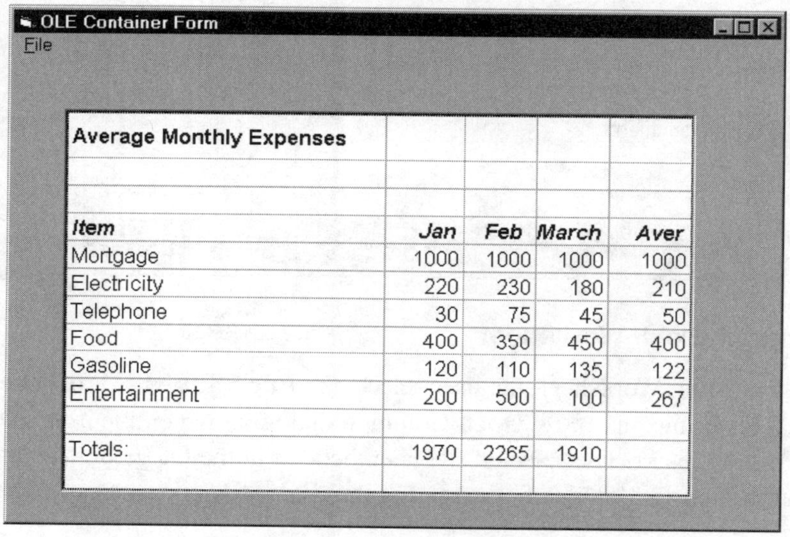

Figure 11. Resizing a Form Containing a Document.

```
Private Sub mnuFileExit_Click()
  Unload Me
End Sub
```

Inserting a Worksheet. When the user wants to insert a Worksheet, a File Open Common dialog is displayed, and the selected filename is passed to the CreateEmbed method of the OLE control:

```
Private Sub mnuInsertWorksheet_Click()
'Let user select a Worksheet to embed.
  On Error GoTo InsertWorksheet1
  dlgInsert.DialogTitle = "Select a Worksheet to Insert"
  dlgInsert.FilterIndex = 1
  dlgInsert.ShowOpen
  OLE1.CreateEmbed dlgInsert.filename
  Exit Sub
InsertWorksheet1:
End Sub
```

Inserting a Word Document. Inserting a Word document is nearly identical to inserting a Worksheet, except that different values are assigned to the DialogTitle and FilterIndex properties:

```
Private Sub mnuInsertDocument_Click()
'Let user select a document to insert.
  On Error GoTo InsertDocument1
  dlgInsert.DialogTitle = "Select a Document To Insert"
  dlgInsert.FilterIndex = 2
  dlgInsert.ShowOpen
  OLE1.CreateEmbed dlgInsert.filename
  Exit Sub
InsertDocument1:
End Sub
```

Creating a New Chart. The user clicks on the **File > New > Chart** menu command to create a new embedded Excel chart. The **DoVerb** method activates Excel automatically:

```
Private Sub mnuNewChart_Click()
'Create and activate a new Excel chart.
  OLE1.CreateEmbed "", "Excel.Chart.8"
  OLE1.DoVerb vbOLEPrimary
End Sub
```

Creating a Word Document. The user selects the **File > New > Document** menu command to create and activate a new Word document:

```
Private Sub mnuNewDocument_Click()
'Create and activate a new Word document.
  OLE1.CreateEmbed "", "Word.Document.8"
  OLE1.DoVerb vbOLEPrimary
End Sub
```

Creating a New Worksheet. The user selects the **File > New > Worksheet** menu command to create a new Excel Worksheet:

```
Private Sub mnuNewWorksheet_Click()
'Create a new Excel Worksheet.
   OLE1.CreateEmbed "", "Excel.Sheet.8"
   OLE1.DoVerb vbOLEPrimary
End Sub
```

10.4 USING MS-OFFICE CODE COMPONENTS

All the Microsoft Office 97 applications support ActiveX, and all can serve as ActiveX code components. This means, for example, that a Visual Basic program can create an invisible Excel Worksheet, modify the Worksheet using program code, call Excel functions, and save the Worksheet in a file. All this can happen in the background, without the user knowing about it. The concept of objects as plug-in components is fundamental to ActiveX, giving an application program the option of constructing applications from a wide range of code components. Before using the Microsoft Word and Excel code components, you must select **References** from the **Project** menu in Visual Basic, and place checks next to both **Microsoft Word 8.0 Object Library** and **Microsoft Excel 8.0 Object Library**.

10.4.1 Visual Basic for Applications

One of the most popular uses of ActiveX in Visual Basic is the use of objects exposed by Office 97 components. Excel, Word, Access, Visual Basic, PowerPoint, and Project all support a common language, called Visual Basic for Applications (VBA). You may have noticed that VBA is one of the object types available in Visual Basic, displayed by the Object Browser. For example, Figure 12 shows a list of methods and properties from the VBA Financial class.

You can call VBA methods and access VBA constants and properties within Visual Basic as if they were part of the native Visual Basic language. For example, the **DateDiff** function returns the number of time intervals between two dates. The following sets n to 151, the number of days between 1/1/99 and 6/1/99:

```
n = DateDiff("d", #1/1/1999#, #6/1/1999#)
```

10.4.2 Example: Creating a Word Document

(samples: WordServer)

There are two ways to create a Word document using ActiveX components: The older, but still useable way to create a document is to call the **CreateObject** function, passing it the class name for a Word application. Then a new Document object is created, using the **Add** method:

```
Private mobjWord As Object
Set mobjWord = CreateObject("Word.Application")
mobjWord.Documents.Add
```

Figure 12. The VBA Financial Class (Object Browser).

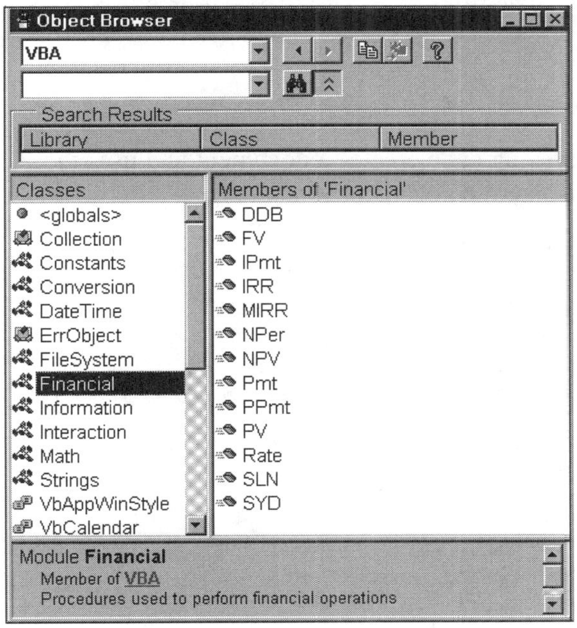

The new, preferred way to create a Word document is to declare an object variable of type Word.Application. Use the the **New** operator to create an instance of Word.Application, and then call **Add** to create the new Document:

```
Private mobjWord As Word.Application
Set mobjWord = New Word.Application
mobjWord.Documents.Add
```

Some non-Microsoft desktop applications are still not ActiveX-compliant, and require calling CreateObject. When you can, try to use the newer syntax. Creating an instance of Word.Application also creates an invisible running instance of Microsoft Word.

When we call the ActiveDocument method, Word returns a reference to the document we just created:

```
Dim objDoc As Word.Document
Set objDoc = Word.ActiveDocument
```

Every document has a **Range** property, which is a portion of a document. Here, the **InsertBefore** method is called, passing it some text to be inserted into the document just before the current position:

```
objDoc.Range.InsertBefore "Insert this text." & vbCrLf
```

The Word application can be displayed with the document in an edit window:

```
mobjWord.Visible = True
```

The user can modify and save the document, and even close Word. In case Word is still running at the end of the program, the **Quit** method terminates it. The single argument, False, indicates that the user will not be prompted to save the document:

```
mobjWord.Quit False
Set mobjWord = Nothing
```

Sample Program. The following code creates a document and uses the Word ActiveX server to insert text and display the document:

```
Private mobjWord As Word.Application

Private Sub cmdCreateDoc_Click()
   Dim sampleText As String
   sampleText = "This text was passed to the " _
      & "Microsoft Word 8.0 ActiveX server." & vbCrLf

      Dim objDoc As Word.Document
      Set mobjWord = New Word.Application
      mobjWord.Documents.Add
      Set objDoc = mobjWord.ActiveDocument
      objDoc.Range.InsertBefore sampleText
      mobjWord.Visible = True
End Sub

Private Sub cmdCloseDoc_Click()
    On Error Resume Next
    mobjWord.Quit False
    Set mobjWord = Nothing
End Sub
```

The program's main window, shown in Figure 13, has two operations: Create Document and Close Document. Figure 14 shows the window displayed by Microsoft Word when the user clicks on Create Document. The user can directly modify the document, save it, and close Word. In case the user does not close Word, clicking on the Close Document button in frmMain will also terminate Word.

Figure 13. OLE Automation Program, Main Window.

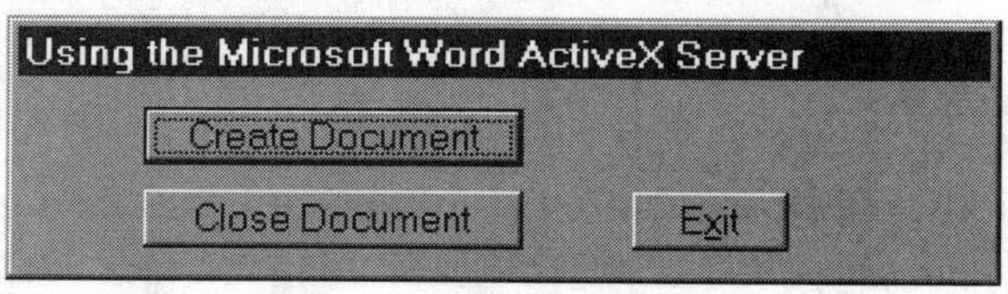

10.4.3 Word Classes, Properties, and Methods

Some useful Microsoft Word 8.0 classes, properties, and methods are listed in Table 2. This is only a minimal list, compared to the complete set of objects listed in the Visual Basic Object Browser.

Using the Macro Recorder. A practical way to learn how to accomplish simple tasks in Word is to run the macro recorder from within Word itself. Use the following steps:

1. Use the mouse to select any text that will be affected by the macro.
2. Choose the **Tools > Macro > Record New Macro** command from the menu.
3. Click on the macro recorder's **Start** button.
4. Carry out the actions you wish to record.
5. Click on the macro recorder's **Stop** button.

The cursor could be placed on a paragraph, for example, the macro recorder started, and the left and right margins indented by 1/2 inch. The following statements would be generated:

Figure 14. Create Document Window.

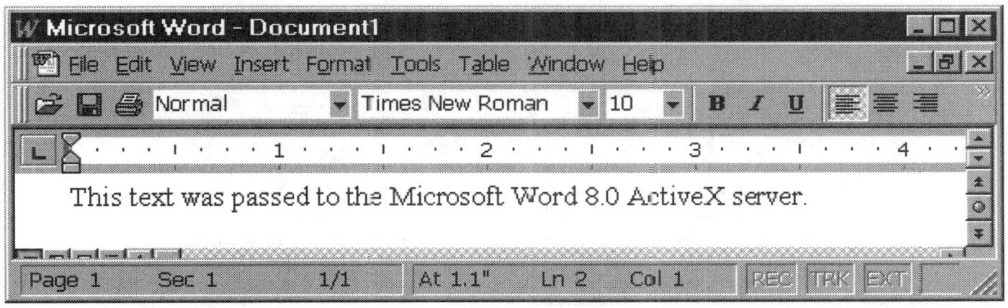

Table 2. Word 8.0 Classes, Properties, and Methods.

Class	Property / Method	Description
Application	Documents	Collection of documents, starting with index 1; index may also be a string containing the document name.
	ActiveDocument	The currently active document.
	Selection	Selected range or insertion point in a document. Useful in search and replace operation
	Visible	If True, Word is displayed on the screen. By default, Visible is False.
Document	PageSetup	A PageSetup object.
	Paragraphs	Collection of paragraphs, starting with index 1.
	Close	Close the document. Optionally, changes may be saved.
	CheckSpelling	Perform a spell-check of this document.
Documents	Add	Add a new document to the collection. A template name may optionally be specified.
	Save	Save the current document.
	SaveAs	Save the current document. May optionally supply a filename and format type.

Table 2 (Cont). Word 8.0 Classes, Properties, and Methods.

Class	Property / Method	Description
PageSetup	TopMargin	Integer, measured in points.
	LeftMargin	Integer, measured in points.
	RightMargin	Integer, measured in points.
	BottomMargin	Integer, measured in points.
	Orientation	wdOrientLandscape or wdOrientPortrait.
Paragraph	Alignment	Can be assigned wdAlignParagraphLeft, wdAlignParagraphCenter, wdAlignParagraphRight, or wdAlignParagraphJustify.
	Format	Returns the ParagraphFormat object associated with the paragraph.
	LeftIndent, RightIndent	Amount of indent on left and right, measured in points.
	Range	The Range object returned by all characters between the beginning and end of the paragraph.
	Style	Set or return the formatting style of the paragraph.
Range	Start	Starting byte offset of a range of bytes (integer).
	End	Ending point of a range.
	Font	The current font (a Font object).
	InsertBefore	Insert text at the beginning of a range.
	InsertAfter	Insert text at the end of a range, causing it to expand.
	MoveStart	Move the starting point of a range.
	SetRange	Modify Start and End values in the range.
Font	Bold	True/False
	Italic	True/False
	Underline	True/False
	Name	A string, such as "Times New Roman".
	Size	Point size, as an integer.

```
Selection.ParagraphFormat.LeftIndent  =  InchesToPoints(0.5)
Selection.ParagraphFormat.RightIndent  =  InchesToPoints(0.5)
```

From this, it is clear that the **ParagraphFormat** property of a paragraph has properties called LeftIndent and RightIndent, measured in points.

The following is an example of a macro recording made when the **File > Page Setup** command was executed:

```
With ActiveDocument.PageSetup
   .LineNumbering.Active = False
   .Orientation = wdOrientPortrait
   .TopMargin = InchesToPoints(1.5)
   .BottomMargin = InchesToPoints(1)
```

```
    .LeftMargin = InchesToPoints(1.5)
    .RightMargin = InchesToPoints(1)
    .Gutter = InchesToPoints(0)
    .HeaderDistance = InchesToPoints(0.5)
    .FooterDistance = InchesToPoints(0.5)
    .PageWidth = InchesToPoints(8.5)
    .PageHeight = InchesToPoints(11)
    .FirstPageTray = wdPrinterDefaultBin
    .OtherPagesTray = wdPrinterDefaultBin
    .SectionStart = wdSectionNewPage
    .OddAndEvenPagesHeaderFooter = False
    .DifferentFirstPageHeaderFooter = False
    .VerticalAlignment = wdAlignVerticalTop
    .SuppressEndnotes = False
    .MirrorMargins = False
End With
```

We would never want to modify all of these properties, of course, but some might be selectively changed. The following example sets the margins in the page setup:

```
With objWord.ActiveDocument.PageSetup
    .TopMargin = InchesToPoints(1.5)
    .BottomMargin = InchesToPoints(1)
    .LeftMargin = InchesToPoints(1.5)
    .RightMargin = InchesToPoints(1)
End With
```

Finding and Replacing Text. It is possible to find and replace text inside a Word document. The following code, recorded by the Macro recorder in Word, can be used by a Visual Basic program to search for "frog" and replace it with "prince":

```
Selection.Find.ClearFormatting
Selection.Find.Replacement.ClearFormatting
With Selection.Find
    .Text = "frog"
    .Replacement.Text = "prince"
    .Forward = True
    .Wrap = wdFindContinue
    .Format = False
    .MatchCase = False
    .MatchWholeWord = False
    .MatchWildcards = False
    .MatchSoundsLike = False
    .MatchAllWordForms = False
End With
Selection.Find.Execute Replace:=wdReplaceAll
```

Because **Selection** is a property in Word's Application class, it must be qualified by the name of the Word application object:

```
Dim objWord As New Word.Application
objWord.Documents.Add
'Create a document, insert some text...
'Search and replace:
```

```
With objWord.Selection.Find
   .ClearFormatting
   .Replacement.ClearFormatting
   .Text = "frog"
   .Replacement.Text = "prince"
   .Forward = True
   .Wrap = wdFindContinue
   .Format = False
   .MatchCase = False
   .MatchWholeWord = False
   .MatchWildcards = False
   .MatchSoundsLike = False
   .MatchAllWordForms = False
   .Execute Replace:=wdReplaceAll
End With
```

10.4.4 Using the Excel ActiveX Server

(samples: ExcelServer)

Excel 5.0 was the first Microsoft product that introduced Visual Basic for Applications, and continues to be an excellent implementation of the language. To use it in Visual Basic, you must select **Microsoft Excel 8.0 Object Library** from the **Tools > References** menu. After doing this, view the rather large set of Excel classes in the Object Browser. Creating an Excel Worksheet involves a few simple steps:

1. Create an Excel Application object.
2. Add a Workbook object to the application.
3. Locate the active Worksheet and assign it to an object variable.
4. Assign formulas and values to specific Worksheet cells.

Tables 3 and 4 list some important methods and properties that you will likely use when running Excel as an ActiveX server.

Retrieving a Budget Amount. We can create a simple Excel example that opens an existing Worksheet in budget.xls, retrieves a single budget amount, and displays it in a Label on the Visual Basic form. First, we declare two module-level variables to hold the Excel Application and the Excel Workbook:

```
Private mobjExcel As Excel.Application
Private mobjWbook As Excel.Workbook
```

When the user clicks on a Command button, we create an instance of Excel and open the budget.xls Worksheet:

```
Private Sub cmdBudget_Click()
  Cn Error GoTo cmdBudgetErr
  Screen.MousePointer = vbHourglass
  Set mobjExcel = New Excel.Application
  mobjExcel.Workbooks.Open FileName:=App.Path & "\budget.xls"
```

Still in the same procedure, we get a reference to the active Worksheet and access the value in cell at row 4, column 2 (also known as cell B4). Cells are referenced in the form (row,col), where the cell in the upper-left corner of the worksheet is (1,1). The value in cell B4 is assigned to the lblBudget Label:

```
Dim objWsheet As Excel.Worksheet
Set objWsheet = mobjExcel.ActiveWorkbook.ActiveSheet
Screen.MousePointer = vbDefault
lblBudget.Caption = "Mortgage item = " & _
  objWsheet.Cells(4, 2).Value
```

Calling the **Quit** method shuts down the instance of Excel running in the background, and setting mobjExcel to Nothing releases the memory used by the object:

```
  mobjExcel.Quit
  Set mobjExcel = Nothing
  Exit Sub
cmdBudgetErr:
  Screen.MousePointer = vbDefault
  MsgBox Error$, , "Error"
End Sub
```

10.4.5 Excel: Statistical Score Analysis

(samples: StatAnalysis)

To demonstrate a more compelling example that uses Excel as an ActiveX server, let's write a client program that performs the following steps, in order:

1. Generates an array of 50 random test scores.
2. Places the scores in a ListBox.
3. Creates a hidden Worksheet object.
4. Inserts the scores into a column of Worksheet cells.
5. Inserts formulas into Worksheet cells that calculate the standard deviation, median score, and arithmetic mean (average) of the column containing the scores.
6. Retrieves the formula results from the Worksheet and displays them in Labels.

Visual Basic does not have built-in functions that compute the mean, median, and standard deviation. These functions are, however, available in Excel, so this provides some motivation to use Excel as an ActiveX server. Figure 15 shows a sample of the program's output, showing the list of scores and the calculated values returned by Excel.

Program Implementation. Let's go through the program's code in some detail. In the declarations section of the main form, the following variables are declared:

Table 3. Some Useful Excel Methods.

Class.Method	Description
Workbook.Close	Close the current Workbook.
Application.Quit	Quit the Excel application.
Workbooks.Add	Add a new Workbook to the Workbooks collection.

Table 4. Some Useful Excel Properties.

Class.Property	Description
Worksheet.Cells(r,c).Value	The value stored in a single cell.
Worksheet.Cells(r,c).Formula	The formula stored in a single cell.
Application.ActiveWorkbook	The currently active Workbook.
Workbook.ActiveSheet	The currently active Worksheet.

Figure 15. Excel ActiveX Server, Statistics Example.

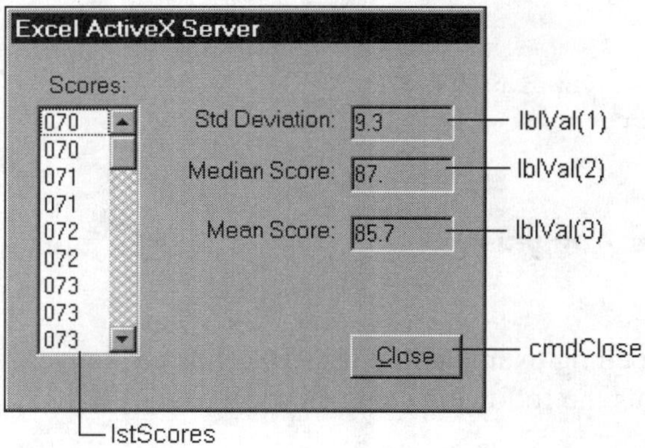


```
Const mintScoreCount As Integer = 50
Private mintScore(0 To mintScoreCount - 1) As Integer
Private mobjExcel As Excel.Application
Private mobjWorkbook As Excel.Workbook
Private mobjWorksheet As Excel.Worksheet
```

CreateScores fills the Score() array with fifty random integers between the values 70 and 100. The scores are also displayed in a ListBox:

```
Private Sub CreateScores()
  Dim j As Integer
  For j = 0 To mintScoreCount - 1
    mintScore(j) = (Rnd() * 30) + 70
    lstScores.AddItem Format$(mintScore(j), "000")
  Next j
End Sub
```

Form_Load calls CreateScores and it creates the necessary Excel objects—Application, Workbook, and WorkSheet:

```
Private Sub Form_Load()
  Randomize            're-seed random number generator
  CreateScores
  Set mobjExcel = New Excel.Application
  Set mobjWorkbook = mobjExcel.Workbooks.Add
  Set mobjWorksheet = mobjExcel.ActiveWorkbook.ActiveSheet
```

```
   FillCells
   CalcStatistics
End Sub
```

The **FillCells** procedure fills a column of Worksheet cells with the array of scores. In case there is a delay loading Excel, an hourglass cursor is temporarily assigned to the mouse:

```
Private Sub FillCells()
   Screen.MousePointer = vbHourglass
   Dim j As Integer
   For j = 0 To mintScoreCount - 1
      mobjWorksheet.Cells(j + 1, 1).Value = mintScore(j)
   Next j
   Screen.MousePointer = vbDefault
End Sub
```

CalcStatistics inserts formulas that calculate the standard deviation, median, and average value of the column containing the scores. To provide some flexibility, the formulas will work with up to 100 scores in column A:

```
Private Sub CalcStatistics()
   Screen.MousePointer = vbHourglass
   mobjWorksheet.Cells(1, 2).Formula = "=STDEV(A1:A100)"
   mobjWorksheet.Cells(2, 2).Formula = "=Median(A1:A100)"
   mobjWorksheet.Cells(3, 2).Formula = "=Average(A1:A100)"
```

CalcStatistics also retrieves the values calculated by the three formulas and inserts them into labels on the current form:

```
   '(continued...)
   Dim row As Integer
   For row = 1 To 3
      lblVal(row).Caption = Format$(mobjWorksheet.Cells _
        (row, 2).Value, "####.#")
   Next row
   Screen.MousePointer = vbDefault
End Sub
```

The **Form_Unload** event handler calls the Close method to close the current workbook, and the Quit method to quit Excel. Failing to do so would leave a copy of Excel in memory:

```
Private Sub Form_Unload(Cancel As Integer)
   Set mobjWorksheet = Nothing
   wbook.Close False
   Set mobjWorkbook = Nothing
   mobjExcel.Quit
   Set mobjExcel = Nothing
End Sub
```

This program example only begins to show the potential for using Excel as an ActiveX server. Aside from creating a Worksheet from scratch, another useful technique is to plug values into an existing Worksheet and perform a series of calculations that would be awkward if done in Visual Basic. This will be suggested in the Chapter exercises.

10.5 COLLEGE ADMISSIONS PROGRAM

10.5.1 Program Specifications

(samples: College)

Let's write a program that simplifies the job of an admissions officer at a fictitious college called the **Better Business College**. An important task given to such a person is to answer inquiries by prospective students. The inquiries might be general, or they might be specific. Some specific questions might be related to the following:

- Business degrees
- Computer degrees
- Courses in computer applications
- Courses in computer programming
- Information about faculty
- Tuition and fees

Naturally, it is a lot of work to generate letters that specifically answer the questions asked by each applicant. But our program can speed up the process by pulling paragraph topics and applicant information from a database and generating the response letters automatically. An important goal of our program is expandability. It must be easy for the admissions officer to add new applicants and topics to the database.

Just a reminder, in case you skipped the previous section of the book: Before Visual Basic can use Microsoft Word as an ActiveX server, a reference to the Microsoft Word 8.0 Library must be added to your project. Select **References** from the Project menu, and place a check in the box next to **Microsoft Word 8.0 Object Library**.

10.5.2 Program Design

The college in our current example is assumed to already have two database tables, one containing response paragraphs relating to each admissions topic, and another containing the names and addresses of students who have contacted the college. Using the database information, we use the Microsoft Word document and fill it with the student's name and response paragraphs. The document is displayed, and the user has the opportunity to modify, print, and save the document.

The program consists of a single form, as in Figure 16, with a Tabbed Dialog control. One of the panels consists of information on applicants, and the other panel contains paragraph topics for the form letters. When the program starts up, no database is open. The user clicks on the **File > Open** menu command, bringing up an **Open Document Database** dialog box. There is one database in the current directory, called **college.mdb**.

Figure 16. Main Window, College Admissions.

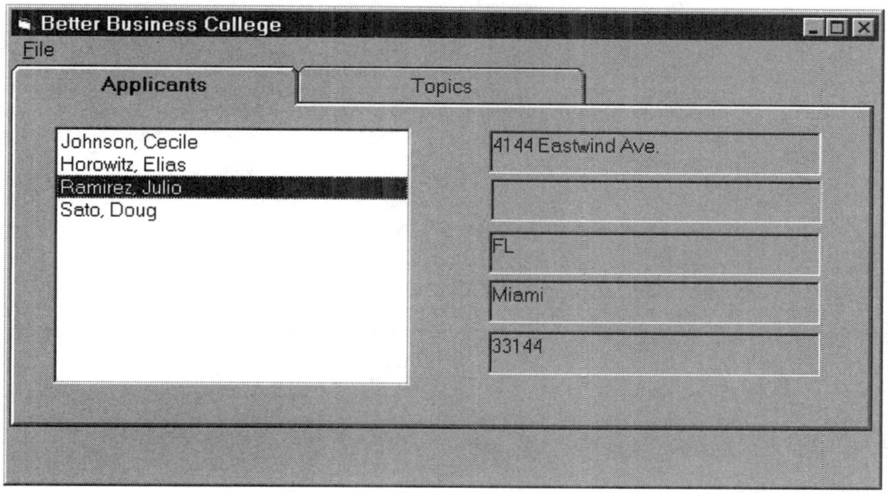

After the database is open, the user uses the mouse to select the name of the applicant who will receive the letter. Upon selecting a name, the person's address appears on the same form.

Select the Topics. After an applicant is selected, the user selects the paragraph topics to insert in the letter. In Figure 17, for example, a letter is generated as a response to an initial inquiry about the college. It includes a discussion of business degrees, an explanation of the tuition plan, and the names of faculty.

The user can also view the text of the topic paragraphs by double clicking on individual topics, as in Figure 18.

When the user selects all relevant topics and clicks the **File > Generate Letter** menu command, the program creates and fills a Word document. Figure 19 shows a sample letter that was generated and displayed by the program. Some fonts were directly modified by the

Figure 17. Select Response Topics.

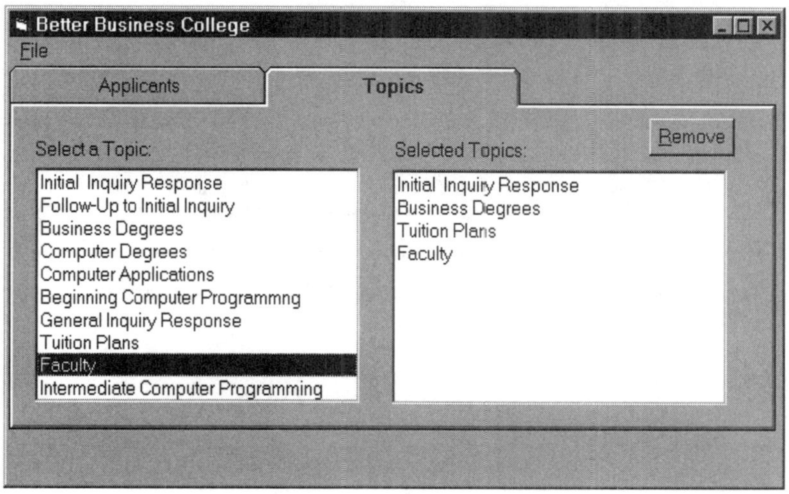

Figure 18. Sample Topic Paragraph.

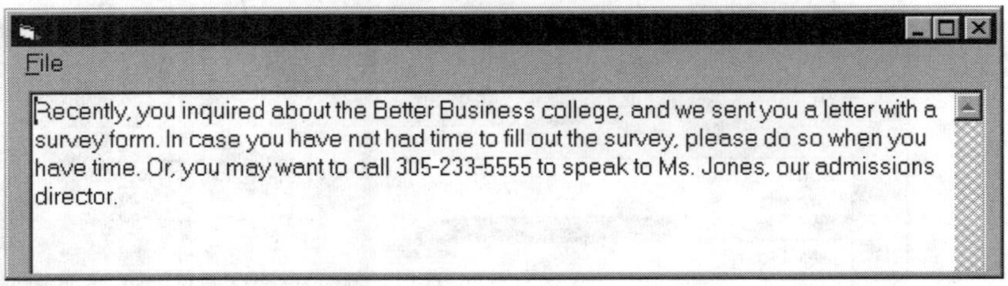

Figure 19. Generated Response Letter.

Better Business College

111 NorthWind Way, Miami, Florida, 33133

Tuesday, March 25, 1997

Dr. Julio Ramirez
4144 Eastwind Ave.
Miami, FL 33144

Dear Julio:

Thank you for your inquiry about the Better Business College. We offer a number of business and computer degrees designed to help you to enter the job market quickly, at a high starting salary. On the survey form accompanying this letter, please indicate your interest areas, and return the survey to us. If you would like to speak to one of our staff, please call our office at 305-233-5555, or visit our web site at www.BetterBus.com.

Our graduates have been placed in many Fortune-500 companies, starting at competitive salaries. The major degree areas for business at our college are: Marketing, Finance, Accounting, and International Banking.

The following faculty serve as department heads at the Better Business College:

Marketing:	John Adams
Finance:	Susan Bennington
Accounting:	Jerry Highsmith
Systems Analysis:	Brenda Brown
Computer Applications:	Itzhak Leibowitz

To better suit your needs, we offer four different tuition plans at the Better Business College:

• By paying the entire year's tuition in advance, you receive a 20% discount off the standard rate.

• By paying the year's tuition in two installments, one at the beginning of the year and another halfway through the year, you receive a 10% discount off the standard rate.

• By paying the year's tuition in four equal installments, you receive the standard rate.

• If you wish to pay tuition in monthly installments, there is a 3% surcharge to cover processing costs.

Sincerely,

Dr. John Q. Smyth, Director

user. Of course, this letter is only one among many that could be generated from list of available response topics.

10.5.3 Program Implementation

The main Form's menu consists of the following items:

```
File                    mnuFile
  Open                  mnuFileOpen
  Create Letter         mnuFileCreate
  Exit                  mnuFileExit
```

Let's take a look at the program's source code. In the general declarations section are the connection variable, two recordset variables for the applicants and the paragraph responses, and a Word object that will be used later:

```
Const mstrDirectorName As String = "Dr. John Q. Smyth"
Private mcnCollege As ADODB.Connection
Private mrsApplicants As ADODB.Recordset
Private mrsResponses As ADODB.Recordset
Private mobjWord As Object
```

The following code displays a File Open dialog box that lets the user select the database name to be loaded. Two procedures fill ListBoxes with response topics and applicant names:

```
Private Sub mnuFileOpen_Click()
  On Error GoTo Open1
  dlgOpen.CancelError = True
  dlgOpen.ShowOpen
  OpenDatabase dlgOpen.fileName
  FillResponseList
  FillApplicantList
  Exit Sub
Open1:
'User cancelled, so no action taken.
End Sub
```

The **OpenDatabase** procedure closes the Applicants and Responses tables, before closing the database. The On Error Resume Next statement lets the program skip any statement that causes a runtime error, because the tables might already be closed:

```
Private Sub OpenDatabase(fileName As String)
  On Error Resume Next
  mrsApplicants.Close
  mrsResponses.Close
  mcnCollege.Close
```

The database, Responses table, and Applicants table are all opened as ADO Recordsets:

```
  On Error GoTo OpenDatabaseErr
  Set mcnCollege = New ADODB.Connection
  mcnCollege.ConnectionString = "Provider = " _
    & "Microsoft.Jet.OLEDB.3.51; " _
    & "Data Source =" & App.Path & "\college.mdb"
```

```
    mcnCollege.Open
    Set mrsResponses = New ADODB.Recordset
    Set mrsApplicants = New ADODB.Recordset
    Call mrsResponses.Open("Responses", mcnCollege, _
         adOpenStatic, adLockPessimistic, adCmdTable)
    Call mrsApplicants.Open("Applicants", mcnCollege, _
         adOpenStatic, adLockPessimistic, adCmdTable)
    Exit Sub
OpenDatabaseErr:
    MsgBox Error$, vbCritical, "OpenDatabase"
End Sub
```

The **FillResponseList** procedure, called from FileOpen_Click, fills the Responses ListBox with all available topics. The topic's ID number is stored in the ItemData array:

```
Private Sub FillResponseList()
    On Error GoTo FillResponseErr
    lstResponses.Clear
    With mrsResponses
       .MoveFirst
       Do Until .EOF
          lstResponses.AddItem !Description
          lstResponses.ItemData(lstResponses.NewIndex) = _
            !ResponseId
          .MoveNext
       Loop
    End With
    Exit Sub
FillResponseErr:
    MsgBox Error$, vbInformation, "FillResponseList"
End Sub
```

Similarly, the **FillApplicantList** procedure fills the applicant ListBox with first and last names:

```
Public Sub FillApplicantList()
    On Error GoTo FillApplicantErr
    lstApplicants.Clear
    With mrsApplicants
       .MoveFirst
       Do Until .EOF
          lstApplicants.AddItem !LastName & ", " & !FirstName
          lstApplicants.ItemData(lstApplicants.NewIndex) = _
             !ApplicantId
          .MoveNext
       Loop
    End With
    Exit Sub
FillApplicantErr:
    MsgBox Error$, vbInformation, "FillApplicantList"
End Sub
```

When the user selects an applicant from the ListBox, the record containing his/her address is located:

```
Private Sub lstApplicants_Click()
  On Error GoTo LoadAddressErr
  Dim id As Long
  id = lstApplicants.ItemData(lstApplicants.ListIndex)
  With mrsApplicants
    .MoveFirst
    .Find "ApplicantId = " & id
    If Not .EOF Then
      lblField(0).Caption = "" & !Street1
      lblField(1).Caption = "" & !Street2
      lblField(2).Caption = "" & !City
      lblField(3).Caption = "" & !State
      lblField(4).Caption = "' & !ZipCode
    End If
  End With
  Exit Sub
LoadAddressErr:
  MsgBox Error$, vbInformation, "Error"
End Sub
```

When one of the response topics is clicked, the topic name is copied to the ListBox on the right side of the form, named **lstSelected**. It is the lstSelected ListBox that will be used when building the form letter:

```
Private Sub lstResponses_Click()
   lstSelected.AddItem lstResponses.Text
   lstSelected.ItemData(lstSelected.NewIndex) = _
      lstResponses.ItemData(lstResponses.ListIndex)
End Sub
```

If the user double clicks on a response topic, the program displays the topic's entire paragraph in a separate form called **frmSample**. This was previously shown in Figure 18:

```
Private Sub lstResponses_DblClick()
  Dim id As Long
  id = lstResponses.ItemData(lstResponses.ListIndex)
  With mrsResponses
    .Find "ResponseId = ", id
    frmSample.txtSample.Text = !Body
  End With
  frmSample.Show vbModal
End Sub
```

The **cmdRemove** button removes a selected topic from the lstSelected ListBox:

```
Private Sub cmdRemove_Click()
  Dim n As Integer
  n = lstSelected.ListIndex
  If n >= 0 Then
    lstSelected.RemoveItem n
  End If
End Sub
```

The **CreateLetter** procedure builds a Word document, using the Word ActiveX server. The student's name and address are pulled from the **Applicants** table:

```
Public Sub CreateLetter()
  Dim j As Integer, st As String, txt As String
  If Not Check_Selections Then Exit Sub
  On Error GoTo CreateDocumentErr
  With mrsApplicants
    st = vbCrLf & Format$(Now, "Long Date") _
       & vbCrLf & vbCrLf _
       & "" & !Title & " " _
       & !FirstName _
       & " " & !LastName & vbCrLf _
       & !Street1 & vbCrLf
      txt = "" & !Street2
      If txt <> "" Then st = st & txt & vbCrLf
      st = st & "" & !City & ", " _
           & !State & " " _
           & !ZipCode & vbCrLf & vbCrLf _
           & "Dear " & !FirstName _
           & ":" & vbCrLf & vbCrLf
  End With  '(mrsApplicants)
```

Continuing the CreateLetter procedure, it loops through the selected topics ListBox, locates the matching database record containing the topic paragraph, and builds a string containing the paragraphs:

```
  With mrsResponses
    .MoveFirst
    For j = 0 To lstSelected.ListCount - 1
      .Find "ResponseId = " & lstSelected.ItemData(j)
      If Not .EOF Then
        st = st & !Body & vbCrLf & vbCrLf
      End If
    Next j
  End With
```

A closing statement is added to the letter:

```
  st = st & vbCrLf & "Please let me know if there is " _
    & "any other way we can help you. " & vbCrLf & vbCrLf _
    & "Sincerely," & vbCrLf & vbCrLf & vbCrLf _
    & mstrDirectorName & ", Director" & vbCrLf
```

Still in the same procedure the string **st** is inserted into a new Word document:

```
  Dim pos As Integer
  Dim objDoc As Word.Document
  Dim objRange As Word.range
  Set mobjWord = New Word.Application
  mobjWord.Documents.Add
  Set objDoc = mobjWord.ActiveDocument
  objDoc.PageSetup.TopMargin = InchesToPoints(2.5)
  Set objRange = objDoc.range(Start:=0, End:=0)
  CreateHeading objRange            'company name, etc.
```

```
    objDoc.Paragraphs(1).Alignment = wdAlignParagraphCenter
    objDoc.Paragraphs(2).Alignment = wdAlignParagraphCenter
    objRange.InsertBefore st        'body of letter
    objDoc.SaveAs App.Path & "\temp.doc", wdFormatDocument
    mobjWord.Visible = True
    Exit Sub
  CreateDocumentErr:
    MsgBox Error$, vbInformation, "CreateDocument"
  End Sub
```

The **CreateHeading** procedure inserts two heading lines containing the company name and address:

```
Public Sub CreateHeading(range As Word.range)
   range.InsertBefore "Better Business College" & vbCrLf
   range.Font.Bold = True
   range.Font.Italic = True
   range.Font.Size = 18
'Move start of range to next paragraph.
   range.MoveStart Unit:=wdParagraph
   range.InsertBefore "111 NorthWind Way, Miami, FL 33133" _
        & vbCrLf
   range.Font.Size = 8
   range.MoveStart Unit:=wdParagraph
End Sub
```

Each range has a **Font** object with properties such as Bold and Italic. After a title line has been inserted, it counts as a paragraph because it ends with a hard return (vbCrLf). The **Range.MoveStart** method moves the input pointer beyond the current paragraph so more text can be added. After all text has been inserted in the letter, Word is shown on the screen, holding the new document. The user can edit, print, and save the document as needed.

A few miscellaneous procedures are also included here. The **Check_Selections** procedure verifies that an applicant name has been selected and that at least one response topic was chosen:

```
Public Function Check_Selections() As Boolean
   Check_Selections = True
   If lstApplicants.ListIndex = -1 Then
      MsgBox "An applicant must be selected before creating the " _
          & "letter. ", vbInformation, "Error"
      lstApplicants.SetFocus
      Check_Selections = False
      Exit Function
   End If
   If lstSelected.ListCount = 0 Then
      If MsgBox("No response topics were selected. Do you " _
        & "still want to create the letter?", vbYesNo, "") _
        = vbNo Then Check_Selections = False
      Exit Function
   End If
End Function

Private Sub mnuFileCreate_Click()
```

```
'Create the form letter.
  CreateLetter
End Sub

Private Sub Form_Unload(Cancel As Integer)
'When the form unloads, we close the Recordsets and the Connection. Then
Word is closed and its reference is set to Nothing:
  On Error Resume Next
  mrsResponses.Close
  mrsApplicants.Close
  mcnCollege.Close
  mobjWord.Quit
  Set mrsReponses = Nothing
  Set mrsApplicants = Nothing
  Set mcnCollege = Nothing
  Set mobjWord = Nothing
End Sub

Private Sub mnuFileExit_Click()
  Unload Me
End Sub
```

10.5.4 Conclusion

There are certainly many other improvements that could be made to this program. For example:

- Use commands to name and save the document.
- Build other databases for this program for other types of businesses.
- Load a Word template file with formatting and fonts, and use it to build applicant letters.
- Allow new paragraphs to be added to the Responses table.
- Allow new applicant records to be added to the Applicants table.
- Allow existing applicant records to be modified.
- When a document is created, keep a copy of the document and assign it a date and applicant ID number for future reference.
- Provide a retrieval system for documents, accessible by applicant ID.

10.6 REVIEW QUESTIONS

1. What is an *ActiveX container program*?
2. What is the new term that replaces *OLE automation*?
3. Would you classify an ADO source such as JET OLEDB as a source of external objects, or as an ActiveX container?
4. Based on what you have read in this chapter, do you think it is likely that an ActiveX component could be created in Visual Basic and placed on an Excel Worksheet?

5. Assuming that an ActiveX server exposes objects to other applications, how does that make it easy to use?
6. If you wanted to integrate text, pictures, and sound into the same Visual Basic Form, which single control from the Toolbox window would be the most useful?
7. What are the two basic ways in which ActiveX objects can be inserted into Visual Basic programs?
8. What is the purpose of the CreateObject procedure?
9. Show an example using the New operator that replaces a call to CreateObject.
10. What type of object does the Windows Paint program expose?
11. What are three types of objects exposed by Excel?
12. What are the differences between *linked* and *embedded* objects?
13. Is it necessary to own a copy of Microsoft Word when using the OLE Container control to edit a Word document?
14. Where can you find a list of available insertable objects?
15. How can the Object Browser help you to locate exposed objects?
16. If OLE and ActiveX did not exist, can you think of some other way programs might pass data and commands to other programs?
17. If a Word document is opened inside an OLE container control, how can changes to this document be saved in a binary file?
18. What is the purpose of the NegotiateMenus property in the Form class?
19. If you want the OLE application menu to share space with the enclosing Form's File menu, which property should be set?

The following questions refer to the OLE container control:

20. Which OLE method allows you to create an embedded object at run time? Show a sample call to this method.
21. How can you locate a list of class names in the properties list of an OLE control?
22. What are the four possible values for the SizeMode property?
23. What is the effect of setting SizeMode = Autosize?
24. What is the purpose of the AutoActivate property?
25. Under which conditions is the DoVerb method useful?
26. Show an example of using the CreateEmbed method to load an existing Excel Worksheet into an OLE control.
27. Which OLE method creates a linked object from an existing Worksheet? Show an example.
28. When a linked object is activated by the user, are the menus and ToolBars of the host application program displayed? (For example, if the linked object is a Worksheet, the host application would be Microsoft Excel.)

29. Which programming language is the native language for Microsoft Excel, Word, Access, PowerPoint, and Project?

The following questions refer to the Word and Excel ActiveX Servers:

30. Name at least three classes exposed by the Word 8.0 object library.
31. Using the Word 8.0 object library, how would you set the top margin of the page setup to 1.5 inches? (Assume that the variable **objDoc** already contains a reference to the active document.)
32. Write statements in Visual Basic that would create a Word application object and add a new document object to the Documents collection.
33. Show an example in Visual Basic that creates an Excel application object, adds a new Worksheet to the Workbooks collection, and obtains a reference to the active Worksheet.
34. Assuming that the variable **currWorksheet** contains a reference to the active Worksheet in an Excel object, write statements that place the number 100 in cell A2 (column A, row 2).

The following questions refer to the College Admissions Program:

35. When the user clicks on an applicant name, how does the program retrieve the applicant's address?
36. When the user clicks on a paragraph topic in the ListBox, how is the matching topic retrieved from the database?
37. How does the program allow the user to browse through specific response topic paragraphs before generating a letter?
38. What is the purpose of the following statement in the CreateHeading procedure?

```
objRange.MoveStart  Unit:=wdParagraph
```

39. Which procedure verifies that an applicant name was selected, and that at least one response topic was selected?

10.7 CHAPTER EXERCISES

10.7.1 Mozart Music Instruments

For the Mozart Music Store, create an Excel spreadsheet detailing quarterly sales and rentals of musical instruments for the current year. Each row should be represented by a different type of instrument; each column will be a different quarter of the year. Use an OLE control to link the spreadsheet shown in Figure 20 to your program. Use the CreateLink method, so the complete Excel menu will be displayed. The user will be able to display, edit, and save the spreadsheet.

10.7.2 Hardbodies Health Club

In Chapter 2, there were a series of exercises relating to the Hardbodies Health Club application. The program managed a membership list, for example. For the current program, create an Excel spreadsheet that lists the dues collections for each member, on a monthly basis. Each row will be a different member, and each column will be a month in

Figure 20. Excel Worksheet, Mozart Music.

	A	B	C	D	E	F	G
1	**Mozart Music Inc., Quarterly Rental Income**						
2							
3			**Rentals by Quarter**				
4	**Instrument**	**Jan-Mar**	**Apr-Jun**	**Jul-Aug**	**Sep-Dec**	**Total**	**Average**
5	Flute	500	350	500	475	1,825	456
6	Alto Saxophone	800	675	640	825	2,940	735
7	Tenor Saxophone	600	500	425	335	1,860	465
8	Bb Clarinet	400	425	450	475	1,750	438
9	Oboe	250	225	175	265	915	229
10	Bassoon	125	100	95	85	405	101
11	Violin	94	190	125	94	503	126
12	Viola	72	72	50	72	266	67
13	Cello	228	200	355	475	1,258	315
14	Electric Guitar	670	620	610	750	2,650	663
15							
16	**Quarterly Totals:**	3,739	3,357	3,425	3,851	**14,372**	

the current year. Then create a new form in the Visual Basic program that contains an OLE container control, and link the control to the Excel spreadsheet. Allow the user to display, edit, and save changes to the spreadsheet.

Extra: Ask the user to enter a user ID and password; look up the ID and password in a database table, determine the person's security level (1, 2, or 3) and restrict their access to the Excel spreadsheet according to the following scheme:

- Level 1 security: Display, edit, and save the spreadsheet.
- Level 2 security: Display the spreadsheet only.
- Level 3 security: Cannot display the spreadsheet.

10.7.3 Depreciation Schedule

In the exercises at the end of Chapter 2, the *Depreciation Schedule* program calculated the depreciation of computer and office equipment over a five-year period. Now that you know how to use ActiveX components, call Excel's *fixed-declining balance* depreciation function, which has the following syntax:

```
DB(cost, salvage, life, period, month)
```

cost is the initial cost of the asset, *salvage* is the value at the end of the depreciation, *life* is the number of periods over which the asset is being depreciated, *period* is the period for which you want to calculate the depreciation, and *month* is the number of months in the first year. If *month* is omitted, it is assumed to be 12. The value for *period* must use the same units as *life*. For example, Table 5 shows the result of using this function with the following values: cost = 10000, salvage = 1000, life = 5, period (1..5), month = 7.

Your job is to rewrite the Depreciation Schedule program using the Excel ActiveX server, and call its fixed-declining balance function.

Table 5. Fixed-Declining Balance Example.

Year	Depreciation
1	$2,152.50
2	$2,895.73
3	$1,827.20
4	$1,152.97
5	$727.52

10.7.4 Family Photo Album

Write a program that stores and displays names and photographs of your friends and family in a database. The photographs can be taken with a digital camera or scanned from snapshots, and can be in GIF, TIFF, JPEG, BMP, or other graphical formats.

Step 1. Create an Access database, and create a table with a Text field that describes each photo, and an OLE field that stores the photo itself.

Step 2. Open the table, insert a description of the first photo, and move to the OLE field. Select **Object** from the **Insert** menu, and click on the **Insert from File** option. Select the graphic file name containing the picture.

Repeat steps 1 and 2 for all pictures that will be stored in the database.

Step 3. Create a Visual Basic program and place the following objects on the main form:

- A label that holds the photo's description.
- A Data control. Set the Databasename and Recordsource properties to the database and table containing the photos. (The Data control uses the older DAO object library, so you might need to check the Visual Basic documentation that shows how to use the Data control.)
- An OLE container control. Set the Datasource property to the data control name, and set the Datafield property to the name of the database field containing the graphic images.
- A Command button that will let the user decide when to display the picture.

Set the following properties for the OLE container:

```
Visible = False
AutoActivate = Manual.
```

In the Command button click event procedure, the following statement activates the OLE control and displays its contents:

```
OLE1.DoVerb vbOLEShow
```

A sample of the main window as the program is running is shown in Figure 21. When the user clicks on the command button, the type of graphic file will determine how the file is displayed. For example, on my system, the *LView Pro* program is associated with files having a GIF, JPG, or TIF extension. This application activates automatically when the OLE control is activated (Figure 22).

Figure 21. Picture Database, Main Window.

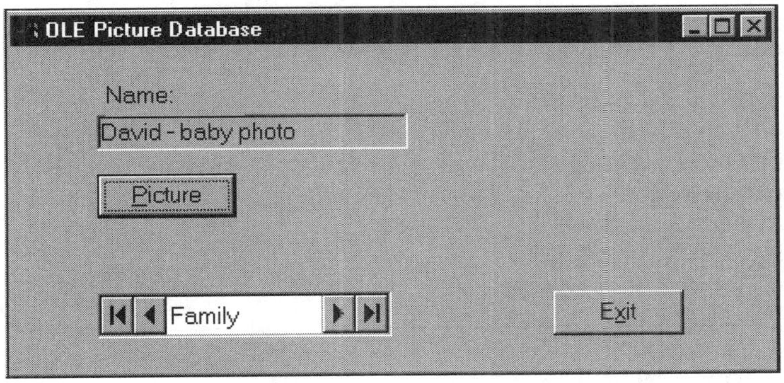

Figure 22. Sample Photo (OLE field).

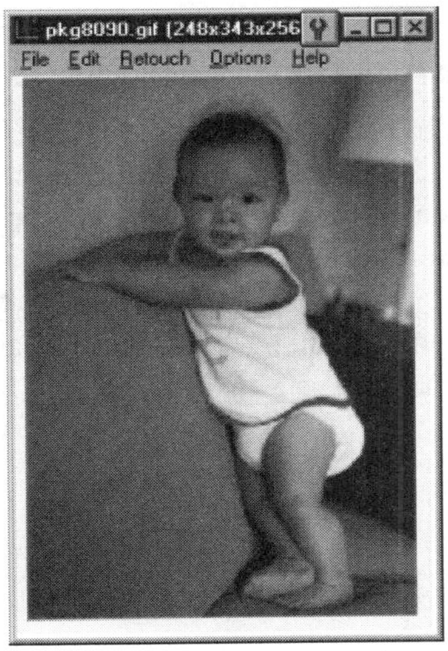

10.7.5 Personal Stock Portfolio - 1

Write a program that helps the user manage a personal stock portfolio. First, create a Worksheet that shows the name of each stock or mutual fund along with its initial purchase information (see Figure 23). Display the purchase date, number of shares, price per share, and amount invested (number of shares * price per share). Right-click on the worksheet's name tab, reame it to **InitialPurch**, and save the Excel file under the name **stock.xls.** Then write a Visual Basic program that uses the Worksheet as an ActiveX server. The user cannot see the Worksheet, but your program should display certain information such as the amount invested for each asset and the total initial investments.

Figure 23. Personal Stock Portfolio (the InitialPurch worksheet).

	A	B	C	D	E	F
1	**Personal Stock Portfolio**					
2	**Initial Purchases**					
3						
4		**Purchase**	**Num**	**Price Per**	**Amount**	
5	**Asset Name**	**Date**	**Shares**	**Share**	**Invested**	
6						
7	Merlin Futures	01/01/94	450	35.72	16,074	
8	Oz Foreign Travel	03/01/94	225	22.50	5,063	
9	Aladdin Technology	05/05/95	1024	75.20	77,005	
10	Narnia Cap. Growth	03/01/93	965	22.40	21,616	
11	Star Fleet Medical	06/20/96	895	62.10	55,580	
12						
13	**Total Initial Investments:**				**175,337**	
14						

10.7.6 Personal Stock Portfolio - 2

Using the Excel Worksheet and program written in the previous exercise, provide some additional features: create a database file called **stocks.mdb** and create a table called **Performance**. This table should contain the name of each stock or fund, the initial purchase price (per share), the number of shares purchased, and the price per share for the first day of each quarter of the year, as well as for the last day of the year (see Table 6).

Write a Visual Basic program that uses Excel as an ActiveX server. Use Excel methods to add a new Worksheet to the stocks.xls file, and fill it with the fields from the Performance table in the database that you created for this project (the Worksheet is displayed in Figure 24). Insert formulas in the Worksheet that calculate the market value of each stock for each quarter. Each formula multiplies the price per share by the number of shares purchased. For example, Aladdin Technology on 4/1/97 is 74.3 dollars per share and we own 1024 shares, so the market value on that date is $76,032 (74.3 * 1024). Finally, display the Worksheet for the user.

Table 6. Performance Table Description.

Field Name	Field Type
stockName	Text, 30
initShares	Number, Single
initPurchPrice	Number, Single
price_Jan	Number, Single
price_Apr	Number, Single
price_Jul	Number, Single
price_Oct	Number, Single
price_Dec	Number, Single

Figure 24. Excel: Personal Stock Portfolio.

	A	B	C	D	E	F	G	H
1	**Personal Stock Portfolio**							
2	**Performance, 1997**							
3				**Price Per Share**				
4	**Asset Name**		**Initial**	**1/1/97**	**4/1/97**	**7/1/97**	**10/1/97**	**12/31/97**
5	Merlin Futures		35.72	34.0	34.8	34.0	36.0	38.0
6	Oz Foreign Travel		22.50	21.2	23.0	24.5	25.7	28.1
7	Aladdin Technology		75.20	75.1	74.3	78.2	82.1	88.4
8	Narnia Cap. Growth		22.40	25.2	22.1	25.1	27.6	29.9
9	Star Fleet Medical		62.10	64.0	67.0	69.0	75.0	82.0
10								
11				**Market Value**				
12			**Shares**	**1/1/97**	**4/1/97**	**7/1/97**	**10/1/97**	**12/31/97**
13	Merlin Futures		450	15,300	15,638	15,300	16,200	17,100
14	Oz Foreign Travel		225	4,770	5,175	5,513	5,787	6,325
15	Aladdin Technology		1,024	76,902	76,032	80,097	84,081	90,522
16	Narnia Cap. Growth		965	24,318	21,355	24,250	26,653	28,854
17	Star Fleet Medical		895	57,280	59,965	61,755	67,125	73,390
18								

11 Tapping Into the Windows API

Chapter Contents

DLL Procedures
- The Need for External Procedures
- Static and Dynamic Linking

Declaring and Calling DLL Procedures
- The Declare Statement
- The API Viewer Utility Program
- Example: Flashing a Window Caption

Parameters in DLL Procedures
- String Parameters
- Numeric Parameters
- User-Defined Types
- Example: GetWindowsDirectory

Getting Disk Drive Information

Blending Color Across a Form

Setting Tab Stops in a ListBox
- User Interface
- Program Source Code

Review Questions

Chapter Exercises

11.1 DLL PROCEDURES

11.1.1 The Need for External Procedures

Visual Basic is optimized for a straightforward, easy to learn approach to Windows application programming. It shields the programmer from most low-level details of Windows programming. It is almost impossible to write a Visual Basic program, for example, that abnormally terminates because of a memory boundary violation. But this "safe" approach creates some limitations to what programs can do, if they are restricted only to the objects, methods, and properties that exist in Visual Basic. If you want to go beyond these and tap into the full power of Windows programming, the way to do it is by calling external procedures, whether the procedures are supplied by Windows, are written by third-party vendors, or are procedures that you write yourself. In short, external procedures are designed to add power and flexibility:

- Many Windows and system-level progamming tasks cannot be accomplished purely by writing Visual Basic code. External procedures provide a way to do this.

- Specific details about hardware devices can be hidden inside external libraries of procedures, allowing only an "interface" or accepted range of messages to be sent to the libraries by application programs.
- Tasks that are performance-critical, such as graphics, calculations, and file I/O, can be coded in languages such as C, C++, and Assembly Language. The code that carries out such tasks can be placed in external procedures and called from Visual Basic.

11.1.1 Static and Dynamic Linking

Nearly all programming languages let you write programs that call *external procedures,* that is, procedures that are not part of the original program. External procedures are often written in another language, sometimes part of a library purchased from a third-party vendor. There are many custom controls and libraries for Visual Basic that enhance its power and range of applications. External procedures must be linked to their calling program. There are two general ways to do this, by either static or dynamic linking.

Static linking is a way of binding external procedures to a program in such a way that the program and the procedures it calls are stored in the same executable file. An advantage to this approach is that all of a program's executable code is in the same place, so it is not necessary to guess which files are required in order for the program to run. On the other hand, there is a major disadvantage: If more than one program has to link to the same procedure, each will contain a separate copy of the procedure. This results in large executable programs and considerable use of memory at run time.

Dynamic linking allows compiled procedures to be stored in a separate file from the calling program; this file is called a *dynamic link library,* or *DLL.* There are distinct advantages to this approach:

- The same DLL procedures can be shared by multiple programs without their needing to have their own copies.
- A DLL procedure is usually not loaded into memory until a program calls it. When the procedure is no longer needed, it can be removed from memory. This results in smaller programs and more efficient use of memory.
- A DLL library can be modified and improved without having to recompile the programs that use it. Windows, for example, undergoes regular upgrades in which internal details of its DLLs are modified.

DLL filenames can have a variety of extensions, such as DLL, VBX, OCX, DRV, AX, and EXE. Visual Basic custom controls and *ActiveX* controls are also DLLs.

Application Programmer's Interface (API). The best examples of DLL procedures are in Windows itself. The complete collection of external procedures supplied by Windows is called the **Windows API library,** where **API** stands for **Application Programmer's Interface.** The API library contains procedures, constants, and data structures that let you hook into the full power of Windows programming. The API library is spread out over a number of different DLL files. The most common ones are kernel32.dll, user32.dll, gdi32.dll, and comdlg32.dll.

Passing parameters and getting return values from the API procedures can be tricky because the API data types are based on the 'C' programming language. Some translation is necessary to pass and return data to Visual Basic programs. In Section 11.3 we will explain many details related to parameter passing.

11.2 DECLARING AND CALLING DLL PROCEDURES

There are two basic steps to calling a DLL: First it must be declared, using the **Declare** statement. Next, it is called in the same way that you call ordinary Visual Basic procedures.

11.2.1 The Declare Statement

The **Declare** statement identifies the procedure's name, DLL filename, and parameter list. The syntax is:

```
[Public | Private ] Declare Sub name Lib "libname"
      [Alias "aliasname" ][([paramlist])]
```

Elements enclosed in brackets [. . .] are optional: *name* is the name of the procedure, *libname* is the name of the DLL file containing the procedure, *aliasname* indicates that the procedure being called has another name inside the DLL, and *paramlist* is the procedure's parameter list, which has the same syntax as all Visual Basic procedures. By default, Declare is Public.

The syntax for declaring a function procedure is almost the same, except that it uses the **Function** keyword and returns a data type:

```
[Public | Private ] Declare Function name Lib "libname" [Alias
    "aliasname" ] [([arglist])][As type]
```

A Declare statement qualified as **Public** can only be placed in a code module (.BAS file). Declare statements in Forms and class modules must be declared **Private**, and must be located outside of any procedure.

Using an Alias. Rarely, the name of a DLL procedure is the same as a Visual Basic keyword, or the name contains characters that would not be allowed in a Visual Basic identifier. In either case, an **alias** is used in the Declare statement. Windows API functions having an alias name ending with the letter "A" are 32-bit functions.

Getting the Right Declaration. Most programmers who use the Windows API to any great extent rely on a reference book detailing the various Windows API procedures. One well-known source is Daniel Appleman's *Visual Basic Programmer's Guide to the Win32 API.* Fortunately, Visual Basic is supplied with text files containing the Declare statements for all API procedures, for both 16-bit and 32-bit platforms. Some of the filenames are Win30api.txt, Win31api.txt, and Win32api.txt.

11.2.2 The API Viewer Utility Program

In the Visual Basic 6.0 Program group accessible from the Start menu in Windows 95/98/NT, you can run the **Text Api Viewer** program. This program, shown in Figure 1, loads a text file containing declarations of data types, constants, and Declare statements for all Microsoft Windows API functions. When you run the program for the first time, select **Load Text File** from the **File** menu, and open the file called Win32api.txt. The program builds a database called Win32api.mdb.

Figure 1. The API Viewer Program.

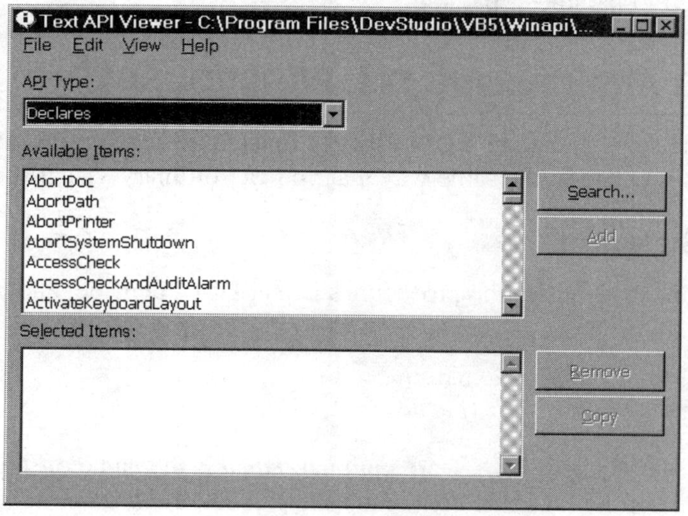

The next time you run the program, select the **Load Database File** command from the **File** menu, and open the **Win32api.mdb** file. Then select either Constants, Declares, or Types from the ComboBox. For example, if we select **Declares**, we then see a list of API procedures. In Figure 2 we have selected the **GetSystemInfo** procedure and clicked the **Add** button to add its name to the list at the bottom.

When the lower box contains all the items you want, click the **Copy** button to place the declarations on the Windows Clipboard. You can then paste the Clipboard contents into the declarations section of a module or Form.

11.2.3 Example: Flashing a Window Caption

(samples: FlashWindow)

For a quick introduction to DLLs, let's write a short program that calls two API functions: **FlashWindow**, a Windows API function procedure that flashes the caption area of a window, and **Sleep**, a procedure that creates a delay in a program's execution. The program flashes a window's caption off and on at regular intervals. Here are the required steps:

Step 1. Create a new program and name its startup Form **frmMain**. Create a code module named **Module1** and place the following in the declarations area:

```
Declare Sub Sleep Lib "kernel32" _
     (ByVal dwMilliseconds As Long)

Declare Function FlashWindow Lib "user32" Alias "FlashWindow" _
      (ByVal hwnd As Long, ByVal bInvert As Long) As Long
```

In **FlashWindow**, the first parameter, **hwnd**, is a handle to the window that will be flashed. The second parameter, **bInvert**, must be non-zero if we want to toggle the window's caption bar, and zero if we want to return the caption bar to its original state.

Figure 2. Selecting API Functions.

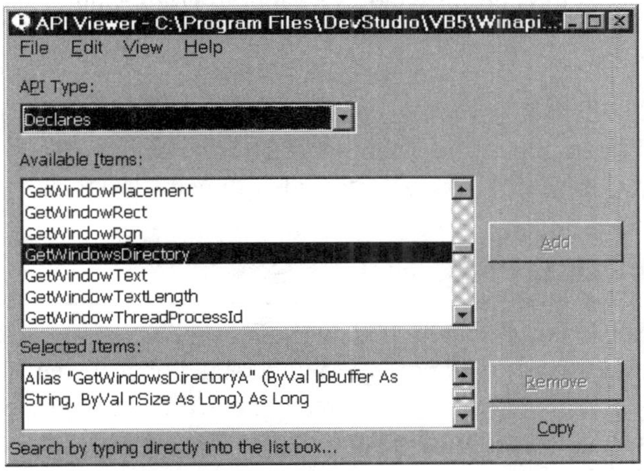

Step 2. Next, create a command button on frmMain, set its caption to "Flash", and place the following code inside its Click event procedure. It toggles the form's caption off and on, with a 100 millisecond delay between calls to FlashWindow:

```
Private Sub Command1_Click()
  Dim j As Integer
  For j = 1 To 4
    FlashWindow Me.hWnd, 1
    Sleep 100
  Next j
End Sub
```

Run the program and observe the flashing caption area of the main window.

The **hWnd** property is only available at run time. It is called a *window handle*, and is a unique long integer that identifies a window or a control. We have used hWnd in any programs in this book before. But hWnd was designed for just this situation, when a window handle is passed to a DLL procedure.

Modular Design. Rather than call a DLL function directly, a better approach is to create a procedure "wrapper" around the DLL function that simplifies its use. In the following example, **FlashCaption** has two parameters: a Form object, and a count of the number of times the caption should be flashed:

```
Public Sub FlashCaption(F As Form, count As Integer)
'Flash the caption bar of a Form, <count> times.
  Dim j As Integer
  For j = 1 To count
    FlashWindow F.hWnd, 1   'DLL call
    Sleep 100               'DLL call
  Next j
End Sub
```

A wrapper like this can provide both simplicity and flexibility to its callers. In this case, we allow the caller to decide how many times the caption should be flashed. It is unnecessary for the calling procedure to worry about using a loop or calling the Sleep procedure. Now we can flash the current window's caption with a single statement:

```
FlashCaption Me, 4
```

FlashWindow has only two parameters, but most Windows API procedures are more complex. Using a Visual Basic procedure as an interface layer surrounding DLL calls can help prevent runtime errors caused by passing invalid arguments to DLLs.

11.3 PARAMETERS IN DLL PROCEDURES

Because DLL procedures have traditionally been written in the C language, DLL declarations ordinarily use C data types. It is important to understand how Visual Basic data types compare to C data types so arguments can be correctly passed to DLL procedures. In Table 1, all Visual Basic parameters require the **ByVal** qualifier. In addition, Table 2 lists a number of Windows API data types that must also be translated to Visual Basic. Fortunately, the hard work of translating the Windows API procedure parameters into Visual Basic has already been done for you, so you can copy and paste them from the from the **Text API Viewer** program into your programs. If you use DLL procedures from another source (your own DLLs or those written by another party), you will have to translate C parameter types to Visual Basic types.

Passing by Value or Reference. By default, Visual Basic passes arguments by reference. DLL procedures, on the other hand, follow the C/C++ default of passing arguments by value. This means that in the Declare statement for DLL functions, Visual Basic programs must explicitly use the **ByVal** qualifier, unless the DLL parameter is a pointer. We use the terminology that refers to *parameters* as the identifiers in a procedure declaration, and *arguments* as the values that are passed to a procedure.

Table 1. C and Visual Basic Parameter Types.

C Parameter Type	VB Parameter Type	Comments
char, unsigned char	Byte	Do not use String * 1, because VB Strings use 16-bit Unicode characters.
short, unsigned short	Integer	VB Integer is always signed.
int, unsigned, long, unsigned long	Long	VB Long is always signed.
float	Single	
double	Double	
NULL	String	Use the vbNullString constant.
char *	String	Always pass ByVal.

Table 2. Windows API and Visual Basic Parameter Types.

Windows API Parameter Type	Visual Basic Parameter Type	Comments
BYTE	Byte	Unsigned in C, signed in VB
WORD	Integer	Unsigned in C, signed in VB
BOOL	Long	Boolean (True <> 0, False = 0)
DWORD	Long	32-bit address, unsigned in C, signed in Visual Basic
HWND, HPEN, HGLOBAL	Long	Handle to a Windows object
LPSTR	ByVal As String	Pointer to a character string
FARPROC	(not supported)	32-bit pointer to a procedure

11.3.1 String Parameters

When passing a String variable to an API function, the ByVal qualifier must be used in the parameter declaration. When ByVal is used, Visual Basic copies the string variable to a null-terminated string and passes the address of the string to the procedure. The procedure can modify the string if necessary. In other words, the usual meaning of ByVal does not apply when passing strings.

If a DLL procedure needs to insert characters into a string parameter, storage space for the characters must be reserved before the procedure is called. A String declaration such as the following, by itself, does not reserve any space, and a runtime error would result if a DLL tried to insert characters into the string:

```
Dim buffer As String
```

On the other hand, the following statement reserves sixty-one bytes of storage for **buffer** and fills it with null bytes. Now a DLL procedure can insert as many as sixty characters into the buffer and follow it with a null byte:

```
buffer = String(61,0)
```

When reserving space for characters, remember that one additional character position must be reserved for the null byte appended to all strings by C/C++ programs.

Passing NULL Rather Than a String Pointer. Some DLL functions allow a string parameter to be either a pointer to a string or the value NULL. The Visual Basic equivalent to NULL is the predefined constant **vbNullString**.

11.3.2 Numeric Parameters

Boolean Values. There is an important difference between the way C/C++ and Visual Basic treat boolean values. In C/C++, **True** equals any nonzero integer value, and **False** equals zero. In Visual Basic, True equals –1 and False equals 0. So if you pass True from Visual Basic to a DLL, everything is fine. But if a DLL returns a nonzero value, the Visual

Basic program will not interpret it as being True unless by coincidence the value happens to be equal to –1.

A Visual Basic program can use a simple boolean expression to convert the long integer returned by a DLL function to a boolean value. For example, if MyDLL returns zero, **result** will equal False; otherwise, **result** will equal True:

```
Dim result As Boolean
result = MyDLL() <> 0
```

Or, a less cryptic way of converting the result would be the following:

```
Dim n as Long, result As Boolean
n = MyDLL()
If n = 0 Then
  result = False
Else
  result = True
End If
```

Unsigned Integers. Windows API procedures and other DLLs often have unsigned integer parameters. All Visual Basic integers are signed, which potentially creates an overflow problem. An unsigned long in C/C++, for example, holds a value between 0 and 4,294,967,295. But the range for a Long in Visual Basic is –2,147,483,648 to +2,147,483,647.

Floating-Point Numbers. The Single and Double data types in Visual Basic are compatible with the single and double types in C/C++, as long as the C/C++ compiler uses the IEEE floating-point standard and the Microsoft calling convention for floating-point numbers.

Handles. Handles are 32-bit integers that identify objects such as forms and controls. Handles are compatible with Visual Basic's **Long** data type. They are never used for calculations, so the difference between a signed value versus an unsigned one is irrelevant.

11.3.3 User-Defined Types

When a DLL procedure parameter is a pointer to a structure, the equivalent in Visual Basic is to create a user-defined type and declare the parameter with the ByRef qualifier. For example, RECT is a user-defined type that is used in many Declare statements for API procedures:

```
Type RECT
  Left As Long
  Top As Long
  Right As Long
  Bottom As Long
End Type
```

For example, the **DrawText** API function names **lpRect** as one of its parameters, where "lp" indicates that the parameter is a long (32-bit) pointer to a RECT structure:

```
Declare Function DrawText Lib "user32" ...
  (..., ByRef lpRect As RECT, ...) As Long
```

By default, Visual Basic passes parameters by reference, so the **ByRef** qualifier can be omitted from the Declare statement.

If a C/C++ structure contains a string (also known as a character array), the Visual Basic program must declare this as an array of bytes.

11.3.4 Example: GetWindowsDirectory

(samples: WindowsDir)

Sometimes it is useful to know the full path of the Windows directory. It is there, for example, that the win.ini file is stored. The GetWindowsDirectory procedure returns the path in **winPath**, along with the length of the string in **count**:

```
Declare Function GetWindowsDirectory Lib "kernel32" Alias _
         "GetWindowsDirectoryA" (ByVal winPath As String, _
         ByVal count As Long) As Long
```

In this section, we can demonstrate a simple program that displays the Windows directory, shown in Figure 3.

Before calling GetWindowsDirectory, we have to prepare the **winPath** parameter by padding the string with null bytes. The following example uses the **String** function to allocate 128 bytes of storage for winPath:

```
Dim winPath As String, count As Long
winPath = String(128, Chr$(0))
count = GetWindowsDirectory(winPath, 128)
WindowsDirectory = Left(winPath, count)
```

After GetWindowsDirectory is called, **count** equals the number of bytes placed inside **winPath**, and the **Left** function extracts only **count** characters from winPath.The following program listing is a simple demonstration of this procedure:

```
Private Declare Function GetWindowsDirectory Lib "kernel32" _
    Alias "GetWindowsDirectoryA" (ByVal winPath As String, _
    ByVal count As Long) As Long

Private Function WindowsDirectory() As String
   Dim winPath As String, count As Long
   winPath = String(128, Chr$(0))
   count = GetWindowsDirectory(winPath, 128)
   WindowsDirectory = Left(winPath, count)
End Function
```

Figure 3. Windows Directory Path.

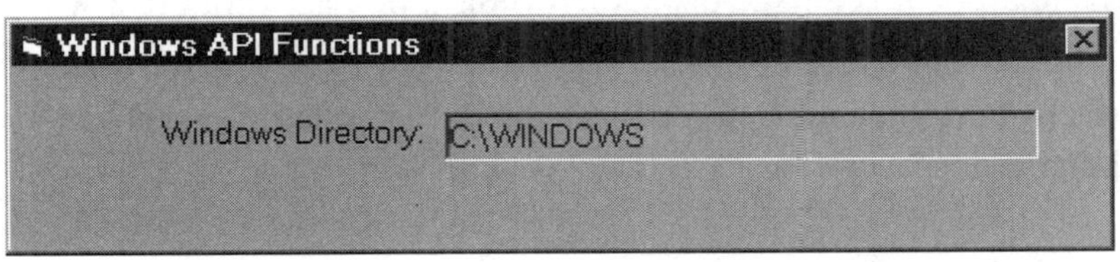

```
Private Sub Form_Load()
   lblWinDir = WindowsDirectory()
End Sub
```

There are many Windows API procedures that can prove useful to Visual Basic programmers. A few of these are listed in Table 3.

Table 3. Some Useful Windows API Procedures.

API Procedure	Description
BitBlt	Copy a bitmap from one device context to another.
BringWindowToTop	Activate a window.
CreateCompatibleBitmap	Create a device-independent bitmap.
ExtractIcon	Find and extract icons from an executable file or DLL.
FindExecutable	Find the executable program that is associated with a specified filename. For example, a filename such as myfile.txt is usually associated with the Notepad editor because of the .txt extension.
GetLogicalDrives	Determine which logical drive letters exist.
GetSystemDirectory	Get the full path name of the Windows system directory.
GetSystemInfo	Get information about the computer's hardware.
GetSystemMetrics	Get information about the Windows environment.
GetWindowsDirectory	Get the full path name of the Windows directory.
SetActiveWindow	Activate a window.
IsWindow	Determines if a window handle is valid. Can be called before using the handle for other operations.
SendMessage	Send a message to a window. The procedure does not return until the message is processed.

11.4 GETTING DISK DRIVE INFORMATION

(Samples: DriveInfo)

In this section, we will call two Windows API functions dealing with disk drives and combine them in a simple program named **DriveInfo**.

The **GetDriveType** function identifies the type of disk drive, indicating whether it uses removable disks, it is a fixed disk, a RAM disk, or a network drive. We can also use it to find out how many logical drives are connected to the computer.

The **GetDriveFreeSpace** function tells us the size of a disk drive as well as the amount of remaining free space.

GetDriveType. The declaration for GetDriveType shows that it receives a single argument, a string containing the path of a root directory of a drive, such as "A:\" or "D:\". The function returns a long integer that identifies the drive type:

```
Private Declare Function GetDriveType Lib "kernel32" Alias _
   "GetDriveTypeA" (ByVal nDrive As String) As Long
```

The function returns 0 if the drive does not exist, or 1 if the requested drive cannot be identified. The other return values are specified by constants:

```
Const DRIVE_REMOVABLE = 2
Const DRIVE_FIXED = 3
Const DRIVE_REMOTE = 4
Const DRIVE_CDROM = 5
Const DRIVE_RAMDISK = 6
```

GetDriveFreeSpace. The documentation for the GetDriveFreeSpace function indicates that the first parameter is a string containing the root path to a drive ending with "\", such as "C:\". The remaining parameters are, in order:

- ***Number of sectors per cluster.*** This varies quite a bit, depending on the file system and the size of the hard disk. For example, on a FAT file system under Windows 95, cluster sizes of 16K or 32K are common. Under Windows/NT using the NTFS file system, clusters often contain only 512 bytes.
- ***Bytes per sector.*** This value is nearly always 512.
- ***Number of free clusters.*** This will vary greatly, depending on the capacity of the disk and the number of sectors ber cluster.
- ***Total number of drive clusters.*** Also varies depending on the disk capacity and number of sectors per cluster.

Here is the **GetDiskFreeSpace** function declaration:

```
Private Declare Function GetDiskFreeSpace Lib "kernel32" Alias _
   "GetDiskFreeSpaceA" ( _
   ByVal lpRootPathName As String, _
   ByRef lpSectorsPerCluster As Long, _
   ByRef lpBytesPerSector As Long, _
   ByRef lpNumberOfFreeClusters As Long, _
   ByRef lpTotalNumberOfClusters _
   As Long) As Long
```

Aside from the first parameter, the remaining names start with the "lp" prefix, indicating that they are pointers to long integers. In Visual Basic, these parameters are passed by referece (ByRef).

Sample Program. Figure 5 shows the program when it starts up. A ListBox is filled with the names and descriptions of all logical drives in the system. When the user clicks on a drive name, the StatusBar control at the bottom of the Form displays the available drive space, in kilobytes.

Program Listing. To find out how the program works, let's take a detailed look at the program listing. We start by declaring the constant values known to be returned by

Figure 5. The DriveInfo Program, after Selecting a Drive.

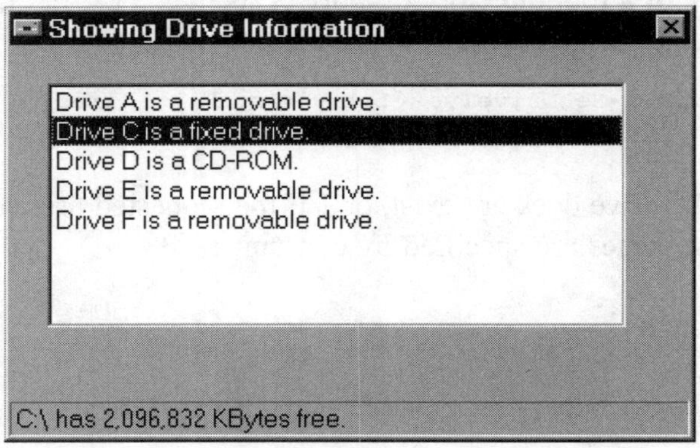

GetDriveType:

```
Private mcolDriveNames As Collection
'GetDriveType return values
Const DRIVE_REMOVABLE = 2
Const DRIVE_FIXED = 3
Const DRIVE_REMOTE = 4
Const DRIVE_CDROM = 5
Const DRIVE_RAMDISK = 6
```

GetDriveType and GetDiskFreeSpace are both declared:

```
Private Declare Function GetDriveType Lib "kernel32" Alias _
   "GetDriveTypeA" (ByVal nDrive As String) As Long

Private Declare Function GetDiskFreeSpace Lib "kernel32" Alias _
  "GetDiskFreeSpaceA" ( _
  ByVal lpRootPathName As String, _
  ByRef lpSectorsPerCluster As Long, _
  ByRef lpBytesPerSector As Long, _
  ByRef lpNumberOfFreeClusters As Long, _
  ByRef lpTotalNumberOfClusters As Long) _
  As Long
```

RemoveSlash is a simple utility program that removes the trailing "\" from a string:

```
Private Function RemoveSlash(st As String) As String
  RemoveSlash = Left(st, Len(st) - 2)
End Function
```

In **Form_Load**, we loop through all 26 letters of the alphabet. For each drive found, we use a Select-Case statement to identify the drive type. Also, if it is an active drive, we add its name to a collection (mcolDriveNames) for later use:

```
Private Sub Form_Load()
  Dim i As Integer
  Dim lngDriveNum As Long
  Dim strDriveName As String
  Set mcolDriveNames = New Collection
```

```
  For i = 0 To 25  'Check 26 possible drives, letters A-Z.
    strDriveName = Chr(i + 65) & ":\"
    lngDriveNum = GetDriveType(strDriveName)
    If lngDriveNum > 1 Then
      mcolDriveNames.Add strDriveName  'add drive name to collection
    End If

    Select Case lngDriveNum
      Case DRIVE_REMOVABLE
        List1.AddItem "Drive " & RemoveSlash(strDriveName) & _
        " is a removable drive."
      Case DRIVE_FIXED
        List1.AddItem "Drive " & RemoveSlash(strDriveName) & _
        " is a fixed drive."
      Case DRIVE_REMOTE
        List1.AddItem "Drive " & RemoveSlash(strDriveName) & _
        " is a remote drive."
      Case DRIVE_CDROM
        List1.AddItem "Drive " & RemoveSlash(strDriveName) & _
        " is a CD-ROM."
      Case DRIVE_RAMDISK
        List1.AddItem "Drive " & RemoveSlash(strDriveName) & _
        " is a RAM disk."
      Case Else
    End Select
  Next i
End Sub
```

The **Click** event handler of the ListBox looks up the drive name in the collection we filled earlier, and passes it to the GetDiskFreeSpace function:

```
Private Sub List1_Click()
'When the user selects a drive, call the GetDiskFreeSpace function
'to get the available space on the drive.

  Dim strDriveName As String, lngSectorsPerCluster As Long, _
      lngBytesPerSector As Long, lngNumFreeClusters As Long, _
      lngTotNumClusters As Long, lngKBytesFree

  strDriveName = mcolDriveNames(List1.ListIndex + 1)

  GetDiskFreeSpace ByVal strDriveName, _
     lngSectorsPerCluster, lngBytesPerSector, _
     lngNumFreeClusters, lngTotNumClusters
```

We use the return values from **GetDiskFreeSpace** to calculate the number of free kilobytes. The number of free clusters is multiplied by the sectors per cluster, and by the bytes per sector. The product is divided by 1024, the size of 1 kilobyte:

```
  lngKBytesFree = (lngNumFreeClusters * lngSectorsPerCluster _
     * lngBytesPerSector) / 1024

  sbrDriveInfo.SimpleText = strDriveName & " has " _
```

```
    & Format(lngKBytesFree, "##,###,##0") & " KBytes free."
End Sub
```

11.5 BLENDING COLOR ACROSS A FORM

(samples: BlendColor)

Windows API functions give the Visual Basic programmer a great deal more control over graphics that is available with build in Visual Basic functions. Even when the same functions exist in Visual Basic, they frequently are not as fast as direct calls to the Windows API. We're going to present an example here of a program that lets the user select two colors, called **colorStart** and **colorEnd**. The program then fills another form's background with a gradual blend between colorStart and colorEnd. The program draws the colors one pixel at a time, which is not nearly as efficient as drawing one line at a time, but it does give you the option of varying the drawing pattern in the future.

The SetPixelV function from the Windows API takes four input values: a handle to the object receiving the pixel (in our case, a Form), the X and Y coordinates of the pixel, and the color of the pixel:

```
Private Declare Function SetPixelV Lib "gdi32" (ByVal hdc As Long, _
    ByVal x As Long, ByVal y As Long, ByVal crColor As Long) As Long
```

The return value, a long integer, returns a nonzero value if it was successful, or zero if it failed.

Color values. Windows uses a 3-part color identifier, called an RGB value. The lowest 8 bits are the Red portion of the color, the next 8 bits are the Green portion of the color, and the next higher 8 bits are the Blue portion of the color. Each 8-bit value can be between 0 and 255. Figure 6, for example, shows a color of pure red would be 0 - 0 - 255. The color purple would be represented as 255 - 0 - 255.

Visual Basic has a function named **RGB** that converts three separate colors (red, green, blue) to a single long integer representing the combined color. For example, pure blue would be represented by the following function call:

```
RGB(0,0,255)
```

Figure 6. RGB Color Mapping.

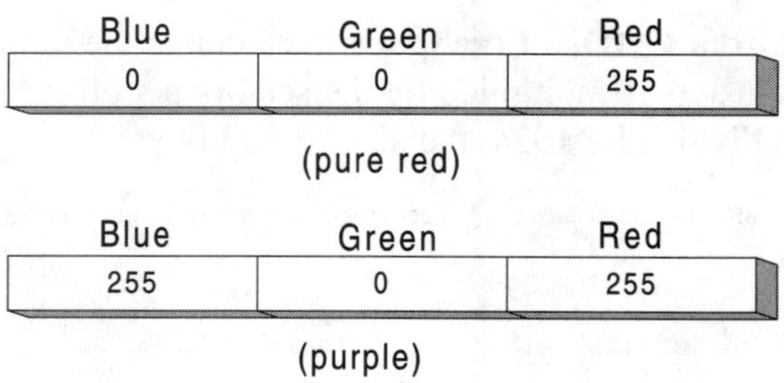

Conversely, three functions written for this program split an RGB color into its component parts. (If you know assembly language, you can see why we perform these operations; otherwise, don't worry about it--they work):

```
Public Function AsRed(clr As Long)
  AsRed = clr Mod 256
End Function

Public Function AsGreen(clr As Long)
  AsGreen = (clr Mod 65536) / 256
End Function

Public Function AsBlue(clr As Long)
  AsBlue = clr / 65536
End Function
```

User Interface. This program first displays a small color selection Form with two Labels and a command button, shown in Figure 7. Each Label displays a color in its BackColor property. When the user clicks on one of the color rectangles, a Color Common Dialog window appears, letting the user select a new color, which is assigned to the Label's BackColor property. When the OK button in this dialog window is clicked, a second, larger Form appears. The colors selected by the user create a gradual blend from one color to another on the new Form.

Figure 7. Color Selection Dialog and Main Window.

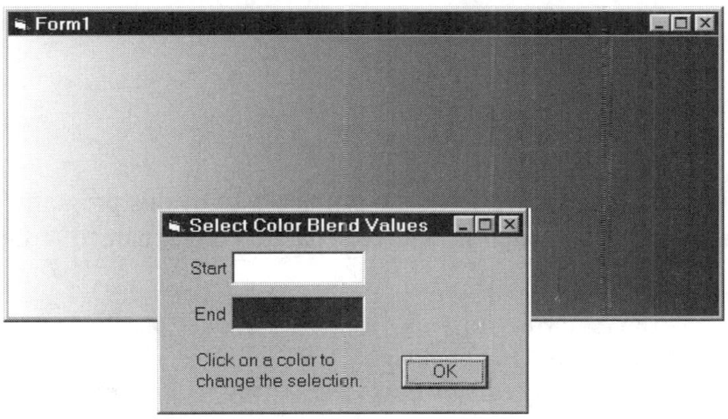

Implementation. First, let's look at the code in the color selection Form. The Click event handler for the OK button sets two properties in frmMain, the Form that will have the blended colors: **ColorStart**, and **ColorStop**. It calls the **FillBlendedColor** method in the other Form, and displays the Form:

```
Private Sub cmdOK_Click()
  With frmMain
     .ColorStart = lblStartColor.BackColor
     .ColorStop = lblEndColor.BackColor
     .FillBlendedColor
     .Show
  End With
End Sub
```

When the user clicks on the two Label controls displaying the current color choices, a Common Dialog control is shown:

```
Private Sub lblEndColor_Click()
   cdlColor.ShowColor    'Common Dialog control
   lblEndColor.BackColor = cdlColor.Color
End Sub

Private Sub lblStartColor_Click()
   cdlColor.ShowColor
   lblStartColor.BackColor = cdlColor.Color
End Sub
```

The frmMain Form. Most of the program code is in frmMain. We have to declare the SetPixelV Windows API function, along with two private variables that will hold the ColorStart and ColorStop properties:

```
Public mclrStart As Long   'starting color for blend
Public mclrStop As Long    'ending color for blend
Private Declare Function SetPixelV Lib "gdi32" (ByVal hdc As Long, _
    ByVal x As Long, ByVal y As Long, ByVal crColor As Long) As Long
```

We provide Property Let functions for ColorStart and ColorStop:

```
Public Property Let ColorStart(ByVal newColor As Long)
   mclrStart = newColor
End Property

Public Property Let ColorStop(ByVal newColor As Long)
   mclrStop = newColor
End Property
```

The **FillBlendedColor** procedure is the primary part of this program. We convert the mclrStart (starting color) RGB value into three separate colors, named redStart, greenStart, and blueStart:

```
Public Sub FillBlendedColor()
'Fill the main Form with the chosen color
   Dim redStart As Integer, greenStart As Integer, blueStart As Integer
   redStart = AsRed(mclrStart)
   greenStart = AsGreen(mclrStart)
   blueStart = AsBlue(mclrStart)
```

Still in the same procedure, we calculate the ratios between the amount of change in each color, compared to the width of the Form. It is very important to set the ScaleMode to Pixels here before using the ScaleWidth property; otherwise, the ScaleWidth will be measured in Twips, a much larger measurement:

```
   Me.ScaleMode = 3                       'Pixel mode required
   Dim redRatio As Single, greenRatio As Single, blueRatio As Single
   redRatio = (AsRed(mclrStop) - redStart) / Me.ScaleWidth
   greenRatio = (AsGreen(mclrStop) - greenStart) / Me.ScaleWidth
   blueRatio = (AsBlue(mclrStop) - blueStart) / Me.ScaleWidth
```

This is a technique called *scaling*, used in nearly all graphics programs to adapt one set of measurements to another. The difference between two color values is *scaled* to the physical distance (in pixels) between the two sides of the window.

When the ratios have been calculated, we can use a nested loop to draw vertical lines across the window, each in a slightly different color. The counter, i, is multiplied by each color ratio, and the resulting value is added to the color's starting value. We reassemble the three separate colors into a single RGB value, and pass that to SetPixelV:

```
    Screen.MousePointer = vbHourglass
    Cls
    Dim i As Long, j As Long, clrValue As Long
    For i = 0 To Me.ScaleWidth - 1
        clrValue = RGB(redStart + Int(i * redRatio), _
        greenStart + Int(i * greenRatio), _
        blueStart + Int(i * blueRatio))
        For j = 0 To Me.ScaleHeight - 1
          SetPixelV Me.hdc, i, j, clrValue
        Next j
    Next i
    Screen.MousePointer = vbDefault
  End Sub
```

Repainting the Window. One last problem to be solved can be noticed when the user covers the main Form with another window. A blank "cutout" is created on the Form because the graphics are not redrawn automatically. An easy solution is to set the Form's **AutoRedraw** property to True, at design time or at run time:

```
Private Sub Form_Load()
  AutoRedraw = True
End Sub
```

Ordinarily, AutoRedraw defaults to False to allow faster repainting of Forms. As an alternative, you can redraw graphics on your Forms in the Form_Paint event handler procedure.

11.6 SETTING TAB STOPS IN A LISTBOX

(samples: Tabstops)

A frequent problem that Visual Basic programmers have when trying to display more than one column in a ListBox is that the columns do not line up when a proportional font is used. This happens because each character has a different width. A solution used earlier in this book was to use a monospace font such as Courier New. But it is still possible to use proportional fonts, given a knowledge of Windows API functions—use the **SendMessage** API function to send an LB_SETTABSTOPS message to the ListBox.

Let's write a program that shows how to set tab stops in a ListBox. Allow the user to interactively move the tab stop positions, using a separate scroll bar to control each tab stop. Add several lines of text to the ListBox, with four columns in each line.

We can start with the declaration of the **SendMessage** function. The first parameter is a handle to the ListBox, the second parameter is the message to be sent, the third parameter counts the number of tab stops to be set, and the fourth parameter is a pointer to the first element of an array of tab stop values:

```
Declare Function SendMessage Lib "user32" Alias "SendMessageA" _
   (ByVal hwnd As Long, ByVal wMsg As Long, ByVal wParam As Long, _
   lParam As Any) As Long
```

The following statements declare and initialize the procedure arguments before calling SendMessage:

```
Const LB_SETTABSTOPS = &H192
Dim numTabs As Long, tabArray(0 to 5) As Long
numTabs = 3
tabArray(0) = 48
tabArray(1) = 96
tabArray(2) = 144
SendMessage List1.hwnd, LB_SETTABSTOPS, numTabs, tabArray(0)
```

When calling SendMessage, the last parameter is **tabArray(0)**. Because Visual Basic passes by reference, this is the same as passing a pointer to the first element of the array. After this message has been sent, it is necessary to call the ListBox's Refresh method to force it to redraw itself:

```
List1.Refresh
```

As in other examples of API procedures shown in this chapter, it is a good idea to create a function that acts as a wrapper around SendMessage. The parameters would be a ListBox, an array of tab positions, and the number of tabs:

```
Sub SetTabStops(lbox As ListBox, tabArray() As Long, numTabs As Long)
   SendMessage lbox.hwnd, LB_SETTABSTOPS, numTabs, tabArray(0)
End Sub
```

11.6.1 User Interface

Figure 8 shows the program's user interface, with lines and labels indicating the names of the labels and scroll bars. The user can click on the three horizontal scroll bars to change each of the three tab stops. A label just below the ListBox displays the Font.Name and Font.Size properties of the ListBox.

Moving the Tab Stops. When the user clicks on a scroll bar, the number just above it (a label) is updated, and the appropriate tab column in the ListBox moves. In Figure 9, for example, the user has scrolled the first tab stop backward from 48 to 29.

The final step in getting this program to work is to implement the **Change** event procedure of the hsbTab array (the horizontal scroll bars). The basic steps are as follows:

- Set the appropriate tabArray element to the current scroll bar value.
- Set the label caption above the scroll bar with the scroll bar's Value property.
- Call SetTabStops to change the tab stops in the ListBox.
- Redraw the ListBox, using the ListBox Refresh method.

Figure 8. Tab Stop Program at Startup.

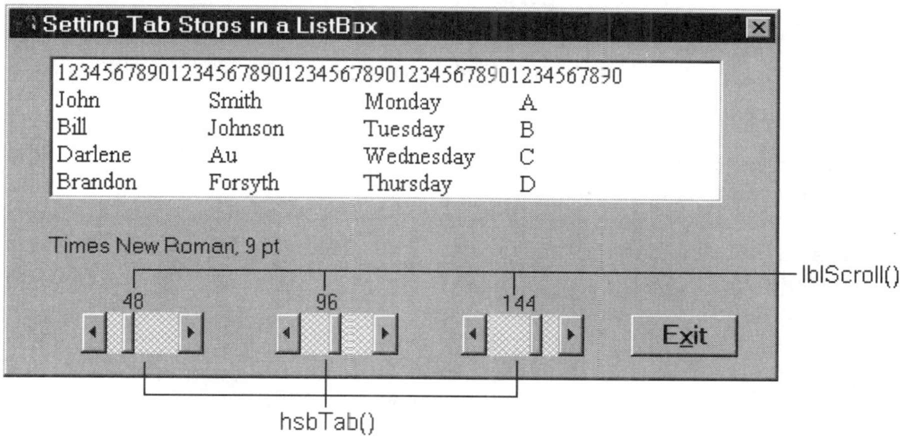

Figure 9. Tab Stop Program after Scrolling First Tab Stop.

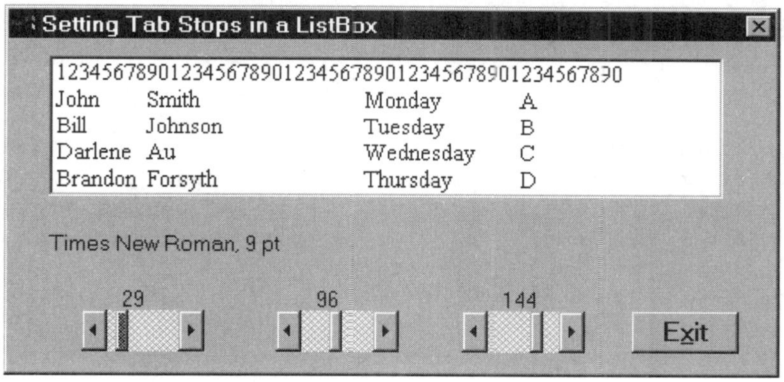

11.6.2 Program Source Code

Let's take a look at the program's source code. In module1.bas, we put the Declare statement for SendMessage, and code the SetTabStops function:

```
Const LB_SETTABSTOPS = &H192

Declare Function SendMessage Lib "user32" Alias "SendMessageA" _
  (ByVal hwnd As Long, ByVal wMsg As Long, ByVal wParam As Long, _
  lParam As Any) As Long

' Set the tab stops for a specified ListBox.
' The tab stops are stored in an array of integers.
' The entries in the array are specified in dialog base units,
' where each base unit represents 1/4 of the average character
' width in the current font.
'
Sub SetTabStops(lbox As ListBox, tabArray() As Long, _
      numTabs As Long)
  Dim returnCode As Long
```

```
  returnCode = SendMessage(lbox.hwnd, LB_SETTABSTOPS, _
     numTabs, tabArray(0))
End Sub
```

frmMain Source Code. In frmMain, the program's startup Form, we declare an array of six tab stop values:

```
Private Tstop(0 To 5) As Long
Private NumStops As Long

Private Sub cmdExit_Click()
  Unload Me
End Sub

'Each dialog base unit represents 1/4 of the average
'character width in the current font.
```

In Form_Load, we place some test data into the ListBox, set the Font properties, and assign a set of default tab stop positions to the ListBox:

```
Private Sub Form_Load()
  Dim tb As String, j As Integer
  tb = Chr$(9)
  lblFont = List1.Font.Name & ", " & List1.Font.Size & " pt"

  List1.AddItem "1234567890123456789012345678901234567890"
  List1.AddItem "John" + tb + "Smith" + tb + "Monday" + tb + "A"
  List1.AddItem "Bill" + tb + "Johnson" + tb + "Tuesday" + tb + "B"
  List1.AddItem "Darlene" + tb + "Au" + tb + "Wednesday" + tb + "C"
  List1.AddItem "Brandon" + tb + "Forsyth" + tb + _
      "Thursday" + tb + "D"

   'Initialize the scroll bars with default tab stops.
  hsbTab(0) = 48
  hsbTab(1) = 96
  hsbTab(2) = 144
  NumStops = 3

  For j = 0 To NumStops - 1
    Tstop(j) = hsbTab(j).Value
  Next j
  SetTabStops List1, Tstop(), NumStops
  List1.Refresh
End Sub
```

The **Change** event handler is called when one of the horizontal scroll bars is moved. It uses the **Index** parameter to assign the appropriate tab stop value to the **Tstop** array, and calls **SetTabStops** to do the actual move:

```
Private Sub hsbTab_Change(Index As Integer)
'Set the tabstop array element to the current scroll bar value.
   Tstop(Index) = hsbTab(Index).Value
'Update the label above the scroll bar.
   lblScroll(Index).Caption = hsbTab(Index).Value
```

```
'Change the tab stops in the ListBox.
  SetTabStops List1, Tstop(), NumStops
  List1.Refresh      'Redraw the ListBox.
End Sub
```

11.7 REVIEW QUESTIONS

1. What are some *low-level* programming tasks? What are some *high-level* tasks?
2. What three letters are the acronym for the Windows DLL procedure library?
3. Name at least two reasons for calling DLL procedures from Visual Basic.
4. What is static linking? What is its primary advantage?
5. What is dynamic linking? In particular, how is it different from static linking?
6. Does an ActiveX control use static linking or dynamic linking?
7. Why is the sharing of a single DLL procedure by several programs useful?
8. Name at least three well-known file extensions for DLL files.
9. How are the C and C++ programming languages related to DLL procedures?
10. Can a DLL be created in Visual Basic?
11. In what way is an ActiveX component like a DLL? How is it different?
12. How is the Declare statement important when calling a DLL from a Visual Basic program?
13. What is the purpose of an alias name in the Declare statement?
14. What does the sample FlashWindow procedure do?
15. How can you make a program pause for one second?
16. Describe the **API Text Viewer** program.
17. What is a window handle?
18. What is the equivalent, in Visual Basic, of the C and C++ languages' pointers to a string?
19. Should a string created by a DLL procedure be assigned directly to a Visual Basic variable, or should it be assigned to an array of characters?
20. What is the Visual Basic equivalent to a LPSTR data type when passed by the Windows API?
21. When passing an integer argument to a DLL procedure, should it be passed by value or by reference?
22. Which API function returns the path to the directory where Windows is installed?
23. When Visual Basic passes an empty string to an API function, why is it important to fill the string first?
24. How can an API function be used to set tab stops in ListBoxes?
25. Show an example of passing a pointer to an array of integers from Visual Basic to a DLL function named FillArray. The array should be named TempArray.

11.8 CHAPTER EXERCISES

11.8.1 BlendColor Program

The BlendColor program presented in Section 11.5 of this Chapter automatically blends the color from left to right. Modify the color selection Form to allow the user to choose either a horizonal direction or a vertical direction (top to bottom) for the color blending.

11.8.2 DriveInfo Program

Modify the DriveInfo program presented in Section 11.4 of this Chapter so that it displays the following information for each drive: Sectors per cluster, Available Clusters, Total number of Clusters, and Total drive capacity (in kilobytes).

11.8.3 Karate School MDI

In Chapter 4, Exercise 4.5.9 was to create an MDI window for the Karate School application. For the current exercise, adapt the BlendColor program in this chapter (Section 11.5) so it can be used in the Karate School program.

11.8.4 Playing WAV Files

Write a simple program that calls the Windows API **sndPlaySound** function that plays a WAV file. Here is the appropriate Declare statement:

```
Declare Function sndPlaySound Lib "winmm.dll" _
    Alias "sndPlaySoundA" (ByVal lpszSoundName As String, _
    ByVal uFlags As Long) As Long
```

The first parameter is a string containing the WAV filename. The second parameter, uFlags, should be one of the following:

```
Private Const SND_ASYNC = &H1
Private Const SND_SYNC = &H0
```

SND_ASYNC indicates that the sound is to be played asynchronously. The function returns immediately after beginning the sound. SND_SYNC indicates that the sound is to be played synchronously and the function does not return until the sound ends. When you write this program, demonstrate both ways of calling the procedure: synchronously and asynchronously.

11.8.5 Selecting and Playing WAV Files

Continue the program you wrote for the previous exercise. In this program, display a list of WAV files in a Common Dialog control. Play the file as soon as the user selects a file and closes the dialog. Use the **GetWindowsDirectory** API function to make the Common Dialog Control automatically show the Windows directory.

11.8.6 Keeping a Window On Top

Write a program that displays a toolbox-like window and keeps it on top, even when another window is activated. The **SetWindowPos** function in the Windows API can be used to keep a window continually on top of all other windows. Many graphics drawing programs, for example, keep a toolbox window on top. It appears to "float" above all other windows. Here is the Declare statement:

```
Declare Function SetWindowPos Lib "user32" (ByVal hwnd As Long, _
    ByVal hWndInsertAfter As Long, ByVal x As Long, _
    ByVal y As Long, ByVal lngWidth As Long, _
    ByVal lngHeight As Long, ByVal wFlags As Long) As Long
```

The first parameter is a handle to the window itself. The second parameter should be the following value:

```
Const HWND_TOPMOST = -1
```

Parameters x and y are the coordinates of the window, lngWidth is the width, and lngHeight is the height. The last parameter is a flag with the following value:

```
Const SWP_SHOWWINDOW = &H40
```

11.8.6 Adjusting ListView Column Widths

The Windows API function **SendMessage** can automatically adjust the widths of columns in a ListView control to match the data appearing in the columns and headers. This prevents column data from being truncated, and avoids wasted space between columns. Using the Music Catalog (ListView) program from Chapter 3 as a starting point, call the SendMessage function and adjust the column widths (see Figure 10). Here is the Declare statement for SendMessage:

```
Public Declare Function SendMessage Lib "user32" _
    Alias "SendMessageA" ( _
    ByVal hwnd As Long, _
    ByVal wMsg As Long, _
    ByVal wParam As Long, _
    lParam As Any) _
    As Long
```

Figure 10. Music Catalog Program with Adjusted Columns.

The first parameter is a handle to a ListView control. The second parameter is a long integer containing &H101E, the Windows message called LVM_SETCOLUMNWIDTH. The third parameter is the column number, starting with 0 for the first column. The fourth parameter is a long integer containing -2 if you want to use the column headers when determining the column widths, and -1 if the headers are not to be considered (try both values, to see which you prefer). Pass the fourth parameter by value.

Create a wrapper procedure called **AdjustLVColumns** that takes two parameters: a ListView, and a Boolean variable indicating whether or not column headers should be used when adjusting the columns. Use a loop inside the procedure that goes through the ColumnHeaders collection of the ListView and calls SendMessage for each column.

12 *Internet Programming*

Chapter Contents

- Internet Transfer Control
  - Properties
  - Methods
  - Events
  - HTML Viewer Example
  - Downloading Files from an FTP Site
  - FTP Browser Program Implementation
- Dynamic HTML
  - Overview
  - Dynamic HTML Events
  - Keyboard Events
  - Mouse Events
  - Focus and Selection Events
  - Other DHTML Events
- Using the DHTML Page Designer
  - Creating the DHTML Pages
  - Coding a Command Button
  - Importing Existing HTML Pages
  - Managing Program State Between DHTML Pages
- ACME Car Rental Example
  - Design
  - Car Rental Program, Page 1
  - Car Rental Program, Page 2
  - Car Rental Program, Page 3
  - Summary
- Winsock Control
  - Comparing TCP and UDP Protocols
  - Winsock Properties
  - Winsock Events
  - Winsock Client-Server Example
  - FrmSwitchboard Implementation
  - FrmClient Implementation
  - FrmServer Implementation
- Creating HTML HELP
  - Introduction
  - Creating HTML files with Microsoft Word
  - Creating the Main Help Window
  - Creating a Table of Contents
  - Creating an Index File
  - Compiling a Help Project
  - Hooking HTML Help to a Visual Basic Program
  - Creating a Frameset
  - Contents HTML File
  - Index HTML File

Visual Basic Host Program
Advantages to Using HTML Help
Review Questions
Programming Exercises

12.1 INTERNET TRANSFER CONTROL

Since the Internet took off a few years ago, it has become more and more involved in people's daily lives, as well as in the business world. There are millions of people surfing the Web every day, there are many business transactions through the Internet, and e-commerce is becoming critical and essential for many businesses to be competitive and survive. Because of the importance of the Internet, learning to make your applications communicate with the Internet has become equally important.

Two years ago, programming an Internet application was a big challenge. Fortunately, Microsoft has created an ActiveX control that makes Internet programming easier, called the **Internet Transfer Control**. You can use *hypertext transfer protocol* (HTTP) to connect to World Wide Web servers to retrieve *hypertext markup language* (HTML) documents. Using *file transfer protocol* (FTP), you can log on to remote servers, download, and upload files.

12.1.1 Properties

Table 1 lists the properties of the Internet Transfer Control.

12.1.2 Methods

Table 2 lists all the methods of the Internet Transfer Control.

12.1.3 Events

There is only one event for the Internet Transfer Control, **StateChanged**, which is triggered whenever there is a state change in the connection. Its syntax is shown here:

```
object_StateChanged(ByVal State As Integer)
```

The **StateChanged** event is important because its argument specifies which state the control has entered. You can write code that responds accordingly. For example, if the control has entered the **icConnected** state (successfully connected to the host computer), you can notify the user. Table 3 lists the various event states.

12.1.4 HTML Viewer Example

(samples: HTMLViewer)

In this section we will demonstrate a program that uses the Internet Transfer Control to download HTML pages from the World Wide Web to a local computer. The following components must be added to the project: **Microsoft Internet Transfer Control 6.0**, **Microsoft Common Dialog Control 6.0**, **Microsoft Windows Common Controls 6.0**, and **Microsoft Windows Common Controls-3 6.0**. In adition, we have to select **References** from the **Project** menu, and select **Microsoft Internet Controls.** This exposes the

Table 1. Internet Transfer Control Properties.

Property Name	Data Type	Description
AccesType	Integer	Sets or returns a value that determines whether the control accesses the Internet directly or through a proxy server.
Document	String	Returns or sets the file name or document name to be used by the Execute method.
Password	String	Returns or sets the password for logging onto remote computers.
Protocol	Integer	Returns or sets a value that specifies the protocol (FTP, HTTP or Secure HTTP) to be used by the Execute method.
Proxy	String	Returns or sets the name of the proxy server used to access the Internet.
RemoteHost	String	Returns or sets the address of the remote computer.
RemotePort	String	Returns or sets the remote computer's port number.
RequestTimeOut	Long	Returns or sets the length, in seconds, to wait before a time-out error occurs.
ResponseCode	Long	Returns the most recent status code from a remote connection.
ResponseInfo	String	Returns the text of the last error that occurred from the remote connection.
StillExecuting	Boolean	Returns a value that specifies if the Internet Transfer control is executing an operation.
URL	String	Returns or sets the URL used with the Execute and OpenURL methods.
Username	String	Returns or sets the user name when logging onto a remote computer.

SHDocVw ActiveX library, containing the **InternetExplorer** application object. It is this object that we use to display Web pages in a browser-like window.

Figure 1 shows the program's user interface, which includes a CoolBar, ToolBar, Status Bar, ComboBox (cboURL), and a TextBox (txtDownload).

Program Implementation. Next, let's take a look at the program's source code. First, we declare a string variable to hold the current URL, and we declare Explorer, an **InternetExplorer** object belonging to the **SHDocVw** library. This object lets the program use Internet Explorer as a Web page browser:

```
Private mstrURL As String
Public Explorer As SHDocVw.InternetExplorer
```

Table 2. Internet Transfer Control Methods.

Method	Description
Cancel	Cancels the current request and closes any currently established connections.
Execute	Executes a request to a remote server.
GetChunk	Retrieves data from a remote server in the StateChanged event. Use this method after invoking the Execute method as a GET operation.
GetHeader	Gets header text from an HTTP file.
OpenURL	Opens and retrieves the document at the specified URL.

Table 3. Event States of the Internet Transfer Control.

Constant	Value	Description
icNone	0	No state to report.
icHostResolvingHost	1	Looking up the IP address of the specified host computer.
icHostResolved	2	Has found the IP address of the specified host computer.
icConnecting	3	Currently connecting to the host computer.
icConnected	4	Successfully connected to the host computer.
icRequesting	5	Currently sending a request to the host computer.
icRequestSent	6	Successfully sent the request to the host computer.
icReceivingResponse	7	Receiving a response from the host computer.
icResponseReceived	8	Successfully received a response from the host computer.
icDisconnecting	9	Disconnecting from the host computer.
icDisconnected	10	Successfully disconnected from the host computer.
icError	11	An error occurred while communicating with the host computer
icResponseCompleted	12	The request has completed and all data has been received from the host computer.

Whenever the contents of the URL ComboBox changes, the program clears all HTML code from the TextBox:

```
Private Sub cboURL_Change()
  txtDownLoad.Text = ""
End Sub
```

Figure 1. HTML Viewer Program, in Design Mode.

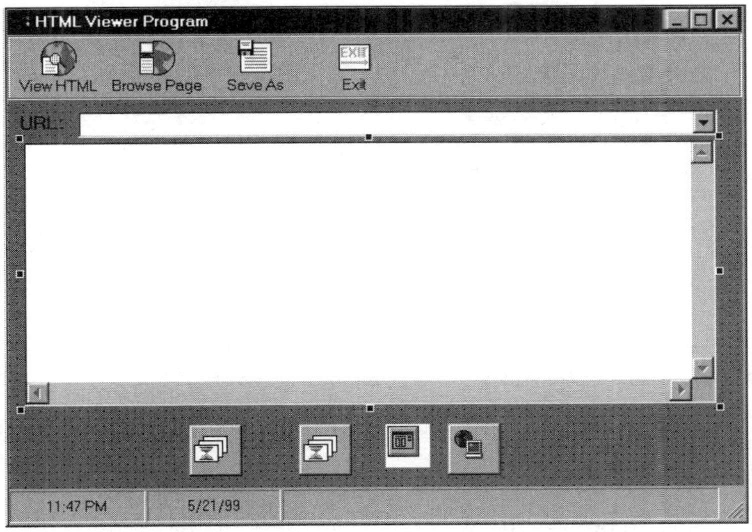


```
Private Sub Form_Load()
  cboURL.ListIndex = 0
End Sub
```

When the user clicks on a ToolBar button, the program selects one of several procedures to execute:

```
Private Sub Toolbar1_ButtonClick(ByVal Button As MSComctlLib.Button)
  Select Case Button.Key
    Case "ViewHTMLSource"
      ViewHTMLSource
    Case "BrowseWebPage"
      BrowseWebPage
    Case "FileSaveAs"
      FileSaveAs
    Case "Exit"
      Unload Me
  End Select
End Sub
```

If the user clicks on the **Save As** button, the program first verifies that HTML source code has already been downloaded into the TextBox. It then shows a **File SaveAs** dialog, and lets the user save the HTML in either a text file or an HTML source file:

```
Public Sub FileSaveAs()
  If txtDownLoad.Text = "" Then
    ViewHTMLSource    'First, display the HTML source
  End If

  On Error GoTo UserCancelled
  Dim intFileNumber As Integer
  With CommonDialog1
    .CancelError = True
    .FileName = ""
```

```
        .DefaultExt = "TXT"
        .Filter = "Text file (*.TXT)|*.TXT|HTML file " _
           & "(*.HTML;*.HTM)|*.HTML;HTM"
        .ShowSave
        On Error GoTo FileIOError
        If .FileName <> "" Then
          intFileNumber = FreeFile
          Open .FileName For Output As intFileNumber
          Print #intFileNumber, txtDownLoad.Text
          Close intFileNumber
        End If
      End With
      Exit Sub
    FileIOError:
      MsgBox Error$, vbExclamation, "File I/O Error"
    UserCancelled:
      'do nothing
    End Sub
```

If the user wants to browse the Web page identified by the current URL, the program activates the InternetExplorer object by calling the **Navigate** method. This causes the Web page to be displayed in a separate window:

```
Public Sub BrowseWebPage()
  On Error GoTo BrowsePage_Error
  Set Explorer = New SHDocVw.InternetExplorer
  Explorer.Visible = True
  Explorer.Navigate cboURL.Text
  Exit Sub
BrowsePage_Error:
  MsgBox Error$, , ""
End Sub
```

If the user wants to display the HTML source code for the Web page identified by the current URL, the program downloads and displays the page, using the InternetTransfer control (Inet1). The **OpenURL** method downloads the page and returns a string containing the Web page's contents:

```
Public Sub ViewHTMLSource()
  On Error GoTo ViewHTML_Error
  StatusBar1.Panels(3).Text = "Downloading the HTML source code..."
  mstrURL = cboURL.Text              'Get the URL from the ComboBox
  'Check the left 11 characters for "http://www."
  'Check the left 4 characters for "www."
  If Left(mstrURL, 11) = "http://www." Or _
    Left(mstrURL, 4) = "www." Then
    'Copy the HTML code into the TextBox.
    txtDownLoad.Text = Inet1.OpenURL(mstrURL)
    StatusBar1.Panels(3).Text = "Done"
  Else
    MsgBox "Please enter a valid URL in the edit box", , ""
    StatusBar1.Panels(3).Text = ""
  End If
  Exit Sub
```

```
ViewHTML_Error:
   StatusBar1.Panels(3).Text = ""
   MsgBox Error$, , ""
End Sub
```

Testing the Program. When you run the program, click the **View HTML** button. In Figure 2 you can see an Internet Web page. Next, click the **Download** button. You should see the HTML source code for the same Web page, as in Figure 3. You can click on the **Save** button

Figure 2. Browsing an HTML Page.

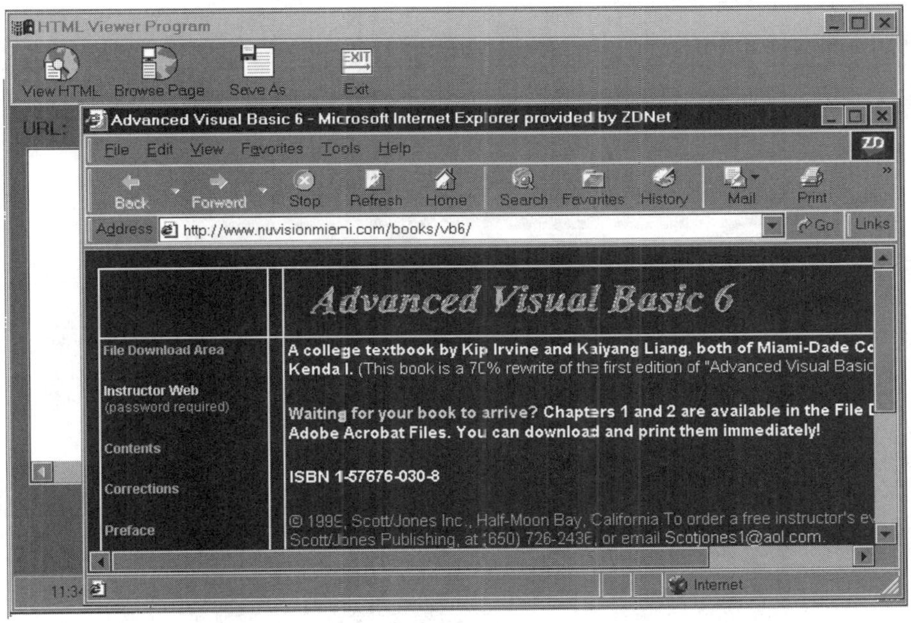

Figure 3. Viewing HTML Source Code.

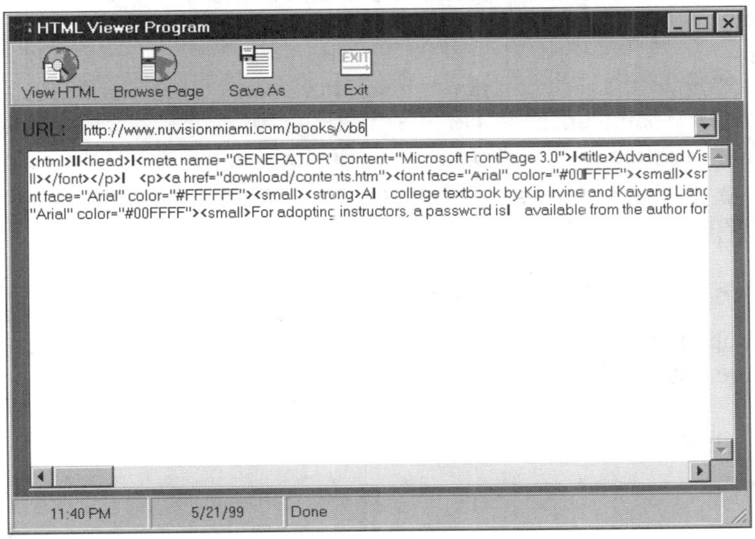

to save the downloaded HTML as Text or in HTML format to a file on your computer's disk drive.

12.1.5 Downloading Files from an FTP Site

(samples: FTPBrowser)

Let's now look at a new program that shows how to download files from an FTP site. The user interface, which is very similar to the previous example program, appears in Figure 4. This program uses the **Execute** method and the **Get** operation to copy files from a specified FTP server, and it uses the **StateChanged** event to check for either the completion of the data transfer, or errors during the transfer. If the data transfer is successful, the file is copied to the local computer's hard drive.

Figure 4. FTP Browser in Design Mode.

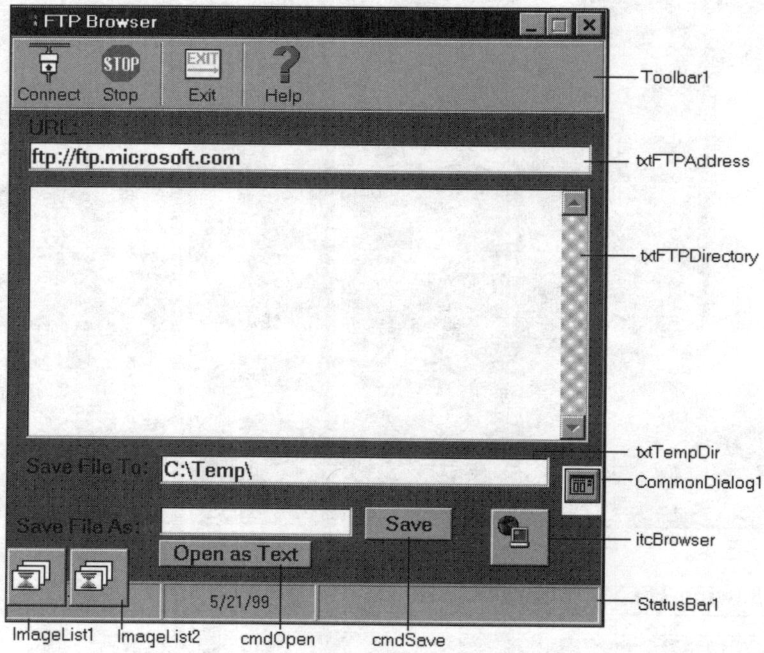

Figure 5 shows the program at runtime, after connecting to an FTP site. Double clicking a directory name opens it. Double clicking a filename selects the file. Clicking on the Save button downloads the selected file to the local computer. If the user tries to save a file that already exists, a warning message displays, giving the user a chance to use a different filename.

12.1.6 FTP Browser Program Implementation

Let's take a look at the source code for the FTP Browser program. First, the module declarations are listed:

```
Private mstrTempDir As String
Private mstrDirectory As String
Private mblnConnected As Boolean
Private mblnCanceled As Boolean
Const BUFFER_SIZE As Integer = 1024
```

Figure 5. Connected FTPBrowser.

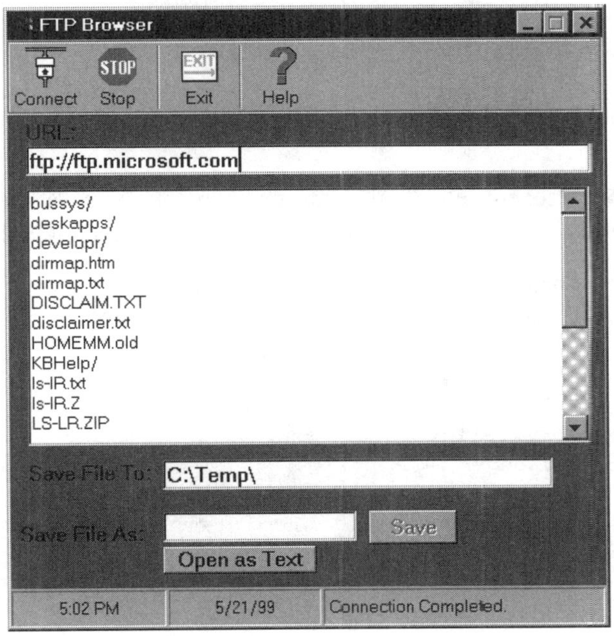

If the user double clicks an entry in the txtFTPDirectory TextBox. The program checks the last character of the entry selected by the user to determine whether it is a filename or directory name. If it is a filename, the GetRemoteFileName procedure is called. If the entry is a directory name, the OpenDirectory procedure is called:

```
Private Sub txtFTPDirectory_DblClick()
  On Error GoTo Browse_Error
  mblnCanceled = False
  txtFTPDirectory.Enabled = False
  mstrTempDir = txtTempDir

 'If the last character is "/", it is a directory name.
 'otherwise, it must be a filename.
  If txtFTPDirectory.SelLength Then
    If Right(txtFTPDirectory.SelText, 1) = "/" Then
      OpenDirectory
    Else 'It is a file.
      GetRemoteFileName
    End If
  End If
  Exit Sub
Browse_Error:
  If Err = icExecuting Then    'operation in progress?
    'Try to cancel the current operation
    itcBrowser.Cancel
    'If Cancel is not working, notify the user
    If itcBrowser.StillExecuting Then
      StatusBar1.Panels(3).Text = _
        "Cannot cancel the current operation."
```

```
        Else
            Resume   'Resubmit the current request
        End If
    Else
        MsgBox Error$,,"Error"
    End If
End Sub
```

The **OpenDirectory** procedure calls the InternetTransfer control's **Execute** method with the **DIR** parameter to change to the new directory. Here is the DblClick event handler:

```
Public Sub OpenDirectory()
'Open and display the selected directory.

    'Add selected item to FTP address text box.
    txtFTPAddress = txtFTPAddress.Text & "/" & _
        Left(txtFTPDirectory.SelText, _
        txtFTPDirectory.SelLength - 1)
    'Display directory
    mstrDirectory = Right(txtFTPAddress, Len(txtFTPAddress) _
        - Len(itcBrowser.URL))
    itcBrowser.Execute , "Dir " & mstrDirectory & "/*"
End Sub
```

The **GetRemoteFileName** procedure reads the complete FTP Address and directory path, separates the path and filename, and copies the filename to another TextBox in preparation for saving the file on the local computer:

```
Public Sub GetRemoteFileName()
    Dim strFilename As String
    cmdSave.Enabled = True

    'Construct the complete remote pathname
    mstrDirectory = Right$(txtFTPAddress.Text, _
        Len(txtFTPAddress.Text) _
        - Len(itcBrowser.URL)) & "/" & txtFTPDirectory.SelText

    'Remove the leading "/"
    mstrDirectory = Right$(mstrDirectory, Len(mstrDirectory) - 1)
    strFilename = mstrDirectory

    'Find the last segment, which is just the filename
    Do
        strFilename = Right$(mstrDirectory, _
            Len(strFilename) - InStr(strFilename, "/"))
    Loop Until InStr(strFilename, "/") = 0
    txtFileName.Text = strFilename
    txtFTPDirectory.Enabled = True
End Sub
```

When the user clicks on the **Save** button, the program calls the Internet Transfer Control's **Execute** method with the **Get** operation to download the file from the remote FTP host to the local computer:

```
Private Sub cmdSave_Click()
  If Len(Trim$(txtFileName.Text)) = 0 Then
    MsgBox "Filename cannot be blank.", vbInformation, _
           "Save Error"
    Exit Sub
  End If
  itcBrowser.Execute , "Get " & mstrDirectory & _
    " " & txtTempDir.Text & txtFileName.Text
End Sub
```

If the user presses the Enter key, the program interprets this as a command to connect to the remote host:

```
Private Sub txtFTPAddress_KeyPress(KeyAscii As Integer)
  If KeyAscii = Asc(vbCr) Then
    KeyAscii = 0        'absorb the keystroke
    ConnectToRemoteHost
  End If
End Sub
```

The **StateChanged** event is triggered automatically by the Internet Transfer control. The event handler determines when to retrieve data using the **GetChunk** method. To do this, we use a Select Case statement and test for **icResponseCompleted**. This informs us that the transfer has completed. The **GetChunk** method retrieves the buffer's contents. It has one parameter, specifying the buffer size:

```
Private Sub itcBrowser_StateChanged(ByVal State As Integer)
  Select Case State
    Case icError
      StatusBar1.Panels(3).Text = Left$(itcBrowser.ResponseInfo, _
        Len(itcBrowser.ResponseInfo) - 2)
      If itcBrowser.ResponseCode = 80 Then
        MsgBox "A file by this name already exists. " _
          & "Please select another name and click Save again.", _
          vbInformation, "Cannot Save File"
        txtFTPDirectory.Enabled = True
      Else
        MsgBox itcBrowser.ResponseInfo, vbInformation, "Error"
        txtFTPDirectory.Enabled = True
      End If
    Case icResolvingHost, icRequesting, icRequestSent
      StatusBar1.Panels(3).Text = "Searching..."
    Case icHostResolved
      StatusBar1.Panels(3).Text = "Found."
    Case icReceivingResponse, icResponseReceived
      StatusBar1.Panels(3).Text = "Receiving data..."
    Case icResponseCompleted
      Dim strBuffer As String
      'Get data from buffer.
      strBuffer = itcBrowser.GetChunk(BUFFER_SIZE)
      'If the data is a directory, display it.
      If strBuffer <> "" Then
        If mblnConnected = False Then
          StatusBar1.Panels(3).Text = "Connection Completed."
```

```
            Else
               StatusBar1.Panels(3).Text = "Data Retrieval Completed."
            End If
            txtFTPDirectory.Text = strBuffer
            txtFTPDirectory.Enabled = True
            mblnConnected = True
            lblInstruction.Caption = _
              "Double Click the file to download in " & txtTempDir
         Else
            StatusBar1.Panels(3).Text = "File saved in " & _
            mstrTempDir & "."
            txtFTPDirectory.Enabled = True
         End If
         mblnCanceled = True
         Exit Sub
      Case icConnecting, icConnected
         StatusBar1.Panels(3).Text = "Connecting..."
      Case icDisconnecting
         StatusBar1.Panels(3).Text = "Disconnecting..."
      Case icDisconnected
         StatusBar1.Panels(3).Text = "Disconnected"
      Case Else
   End Select
End Sub
```

When the user clicks the **Open As Text** button, the program launches the NotePad editor program and displays the file named in the txtTempDir and txtFileName TextBoxes:

```
Private Sub cmdOpen_Click()
'Open the selected file as text
   If txtFileName.Text <> "" Then
      Shell "Notepad.exe " & txtTempDir.Text & txtFileName.Text, 1
   End If
End Sub
```

The event handler for the ToolBar allows the user to connect to a remote host, stop the current operation, exit the program, or display a help window:

```
Private Sub Toolbar1_ButtonClick(ByVal Button As _
   MSComctlLib.Button)
   Select Case Button.Key
      Case "Connect"             'connect to FTP host
         StatusBar1.Panels(3).Text = "Connecting to host..."
         ConnectToRemoteHost
      Case "Stop"                'stop current operation
         itcBrowser.Cancel
         txtFTPDirectory.Enabled = True
         If mblnCanceled = False Then
            StatusBar1.Panels(3).Text = "Operation canceled."
         End If
      Case "Exit"
         Unload Me
      Case "Help"
         ShowHelp
```

```
  End Select
End Sub
```

The **ConnectToRemoteHost** procedure uses the FTP address and directory name to connect to a remote FTP server. It then downloads a list of files and directories from the server and displays them in a TextBox:

```
Public Sub ConnectToRemoteHost()
  On Error GoTo ErrOpenURL
  mblnCanceled = False
  txtFTPAddress.SelStart = 0
  txtFTPAddress.SelLength = Len(txtFTPAddress)
  itcBrowser.URL = txtFTPAddress.Text
  itcBrowser.Execute , "Dir "
  txtFTPAddress.Text = itcBrowser.URL
  Exit Sub

ErrOpenURL:
  Select Case Err.Number
    Case icBadUrl
      MsgBox "Bad address. Please reenter."
    Case icConnectFailed, icConnectionAborted, _
      icCannotConnect
      MsgBox "Unable to connect to network."
    Case icInetTimeout
      MsgBox "Connection timed out."
    Case icExecuting
      'Cancel previous request
      itcBrowser.Cancel
      'Check whether cancel worked
      If itcBrowser.StillExecuting Then
        StatusBar1.Panels(3).Text = _
          "Cannot cancel request."
      Else
        Resume    'Resubmit current request
      End If
    Case Else
      MsgBox Error$,,"Error"
  End Select
End Sub

Private Sub ShowHelp()
  MsgBox "To view an FTP site, click on the Connect button." _
    & vbCrLf _
    & "To change to a new directory, double-click on " _
    & "the directory name." _
    & vbCrLf _
    & "To select a file for downloading, " _
    & "double-click on its filename and click " _
    & "the Save button.", vbInformation, "FTP Browser Help"
End Sub
```

Summary. The Internet Transfer control provides an easy way to get started in building Web-aware Visual Basic applications. You can access files and HTML documents from

Internet servers around the world, using the HTTP and FTP protocols. With a little imagination, you can create a program that automatically searches across Web links for information.

12.2 DYNAMIC HTML

12.2.1 Overview

Dynamic HTML is an extension of traditional HTML (*HyperText Markup Language*). Whereas HTML lets you create static (non-changing) documents, DHTML extends this and allows you to create dynamic documents. Because of the static nature of HTML pages, interactive components are difficult to build and reuse. DHTML allows authors to create interactive Web pages. With it, you can access and manipulate every element on a Web page, dynamically update its content, and interact with users without relying on scripts or server-side processing.

With the **DHTML Page Designer**, a component of the Visual Basic 6 Professional and Enterprise editions, you can integrate DHTML into Visual Basic applications and create Web pages. Here are some important DHTML terms and properties:

- **The InnerText** property changes or retrieves a block of text between the start and end tags of the current element without affecting existing HTML tags. You cannot set the InnerText property while a document is loading: you must wait for the **onload** event before attempting to set it. The syntax is:

```
object.innerText = string
```

- **The SPAN** tag is used within an element to group a part of it that is too small to capture with regular HTML tags. For example, you can use the SPAN tag to group a few sentences within a paragraph, so you can manipulate only those sentences with program code.

- The **BaseWindow object** represents an instance of the browser and is used to display the Document object.

- The **Document object** represents the HTML page viewed in the browser. You use events in the Document object to access the DHTML object model and handle user actions in the browser.

12.2.2 Dynamic HTML Events

Most events in the Dynamic HTML object model are similar to events in the Visual Basic programming model. All event names in Dynamic HTML are preceded by the word "on." You can locate most common events by looking for them under this prefix.

Comparing Visual Basic Events to Dynamic HTML Events. In the following sections, we will compare some of the more commonly used events in Visual Basic to their counterparts in Dynamic HTML. We also note any additional information required for their use.

12.2.3 Keyboard Events

Keyboard events in Dynamic HTML and keyboard events in Visual Basic are almost identical. Table 4 lists the common Visual Basic keyboard events and their Dynamic HTML counterparts.

12.2.4 Mouse Events

Mouse events in Dynamic HTML are similar to mouse events in Visual Basic, but there are a few events in DHTML which are not available in Visual Basic. Table 5 lists the common Visual Basic mouse events and their Dynamic HTML counterparts.

12.2.5 Focus and Selection Events

Table 6 lists the common Visual Basic focus and selection events and their Dynamic HTML counterparts.

Table 4. DHTML Keyboard Events.

Visual Basic Event	DHTML Equivalent	Description
KeyDown	onkeydown	Triggered when a key is pressed.
KeyPress	onkeypress	Triggered when keyboard input is an ASCII character (A-Z, 0-9, but not F1-F12, Page Up etc.).
KeyUp	onkeyup	Triggered when a key is released.

Table 5. DHTML Mouse Events.

Visual Basic Event	DHTML Equivalent	Description
click	onclick	Triggered when a user single clicks on the element. Also triggered when the user presses ENTER on an element that can receive focus.
doubleclick	ondblclick	Triggered when a user double clicks on the element.
mousedown	onmousedown	Triggered when a user presses the mouse button.
mouseup	onmouseup	Triggered when a user releases the mouse button.
mousemove	onmousemove	Triggered when a mouse has moved over an element.
N/A	onmouseover	Triggered to indicate that the mouse has entered the new element.
	onmouseout	Triggered to indicate that the mouse has left the original element.

Table 6. DHTML Focus and Selection Events.

Visual Basic Event	DHTML Equivalent	Description
GotFocus	onfocus	Triggered when the user moves to an element capable of receiving input, such as a button or text box.
LostFocus	onblur	Triggered when you move out of a control that is capable of receiving input.
SelChange	onselectstart onselect	The **onselectstart** event is triggered when a selection is first initiated - for example, when the user clicks on a character or object in the document. The **onselect** event is triggered when the user changes a selection - for example, by moving the mouse over a portion of the document while holding down the mouse button.
DragDrop, DragOver	ondragstart	Triggered when a user first begins to drag the selection.

12.2.6 Other DHTML Events

There are other equivalent events between Visual Basic and DHTML, which are listed in Table 7.

Table 7. Other DHTML Events

Visual Basic Event	DHTML Equivalent	Description
Change	onchange	Triggered when a user presses the Tab key or the Enter key on an element, moving away from it. In Visual Basic, the Change event is triggered as soon as a user performs any action within the control.
Error	onerror	Triggered if an error occurs while loading an image or other element, or when a scripting error occurs.
Initialize	Onready, statechange	Triggered when the page changes state from initializing to interactive and from interactive to loaded. A page is interactive as soon as the user can interact with it by scrolling or clicking on anchors or elements. A page is loaded when all the content has been downloaded.
Load	onload	Triggered after the document is loaded and all the elements on the page have been completely downloaded.
Resize	onresize	You do not need to write code to handle resizing of an HTML page as you do a Visual Basic form. Resize in HTML happens automatically.
Scroll	onscroll	Triggered whenever the scroll bar for the page or any element within it is repositioned.
Unload	onunload	Triggered immediately before the document is unloaded (when navigating to another document).

12.3 USING THE DHTML PAGE DESIGNER

12.3.1 Creating the DHTML Pages

(samples: Lotto)

Let's build a simple application program in DHTML using the Page Designer, that generates random numbers for a state lottery. It will have a single main window with a Command button, plus a hypertext link to a second window that displays an About window. Here are the steps:

1. Start a new project and select **DHTML Application**. In the Project window, click "+ " to open the Designer window, and double click the name **DHTMLPage1**.
2. Click the right-hand pane, type **LOTTERY** and press the **Enter** key three times. Figure 6 shows the Page Designer window.
3. Type 0 [Space] [Space] [Space] [Space] 0 [Space] [Space] [Space] [Space] 0 [Space] [Space] [Space] [Space] 0 [Space] [Space] [Space] [Space] 0 [Space] [Space] [Space] [Space] 0 [Space] [Space] [Space] [Space] 0.
4. Select P(0 0 0 0 0 0) and press F4 to display the Properties window. Set the **ID** property to **LotteryNumber**.
5. One by one, select each 0 in the right-hand window and click on the ToolBar button entitled "**Wrap selection in <SPAN>...</SPAN>**". (You can view a ToolBar button title by holding the mouse over the button for a second or more.) Figure 7 shows the results after expanding the LottoNumber item in the left-hand window. Now select each SPAN tag, press F4, and change its ID property to one of the following: **Number1**, Number2, ..., **Number6**.
6. Create a Command button, set its ID property to **bnGenerateNumber,** and set its Value property to **Generate Number** (see Figure 8).

Figure 6. DHTML Page Designer, Step 1.

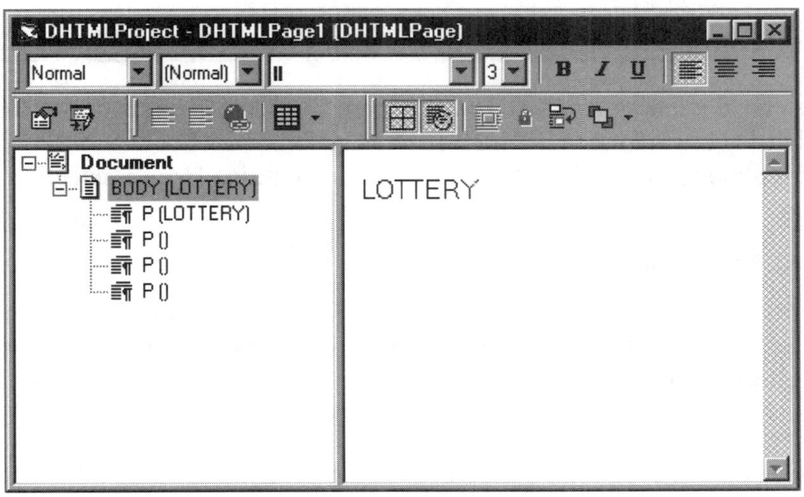

Figure 7. Setting the Wrap Selection.

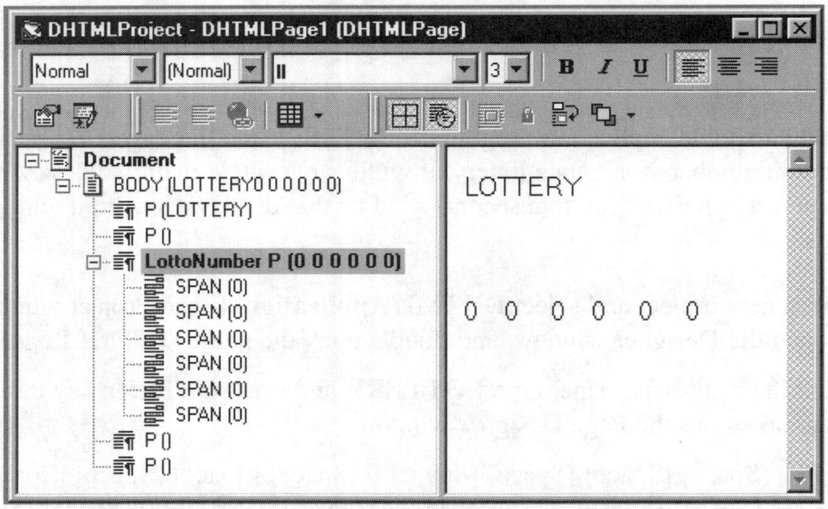

Figure 8. Command Button Inserted.

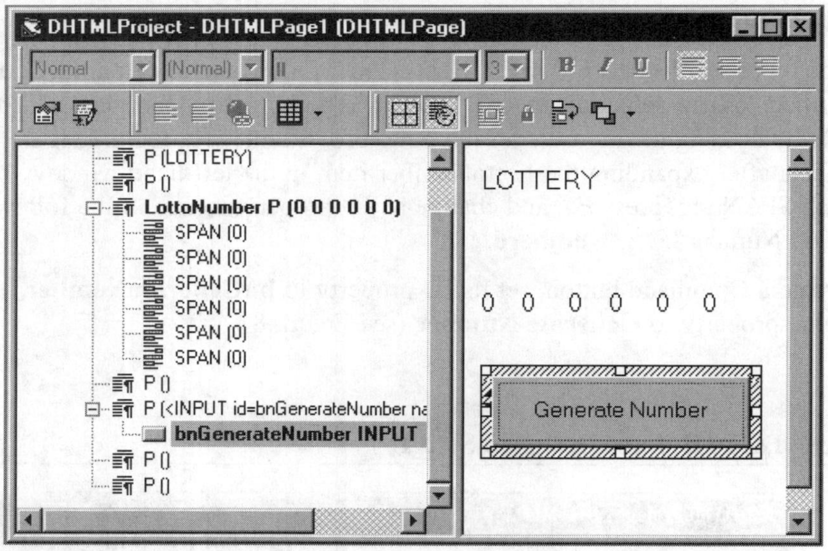

7. Let's create a link to another HTML page. Click the mouse on one of the P() items in the left-hand window. In the right-hand window, type "About Lottery," select the text with the mouse, and select the ToolBar button entitled "**Make selection into link"** (see Figure 9)

12.3.2 Coding a Command Button

The **onclick** event handler for the **bnGenerateNumber** CommandButton works the same way as the **Click** Event handler in Visual basic. In this procedure, we first define an array called **Lotto**, containing 49 integers, because the Lottery number selections are from 1 to 49. We assign values to the 49 entries in the Lotto array, and randomly shuffle the values:

Figure 9. Linking to Another Page.

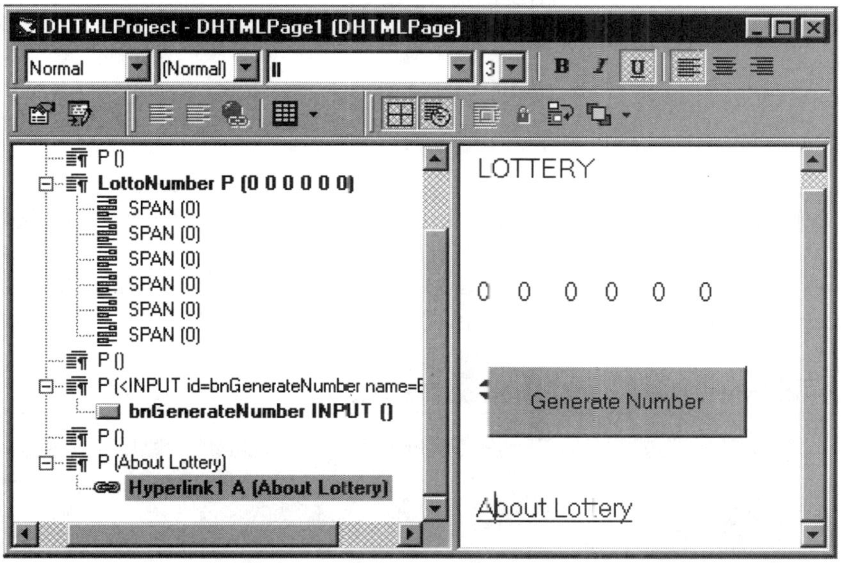


```
Private Function bnGenerateNumber_onclick() As Boolean
'Lotto numbers 1 - 49
  Dim Lotto(1 To 49) As Integer
  Dim temp As Integer
  Dim j As Integer
  Dim n As Integer

'Assign values for the Lotto array
  For j = 1 To 49
      Lotto(j) = j
  Next j

'Randomly shuffle the Array values
  For j = 1 To 49
    n = Int(49 * Rnd + 1)
    temp = Lotto(j)
    Lotto(j) = Lotto(n)
    Lotto(n) = temp
  Next j

'Display the first six Lotto numbers
'for Number1 -- Number6 on the page.
   Number1.innerText = Lotto(1)
   Number2.innerText = Lotto(2)
   Number3.innerText = Lotto(3)
   Number4.innerText = Lotto(4)
   Number5.innerText = Lotto(5)
   Number6.innerText = Lotto(6)
End Function
```

The **Load** event handler sets up the hRef property of Hyperlink1 and calls Visual Basic's Randomize method to re-seed the random number algorithm with a different number each time the program runs:

```
Private Sub DHTMLPage_Load()
   Hyperlink1.hRef = App.Path & "\lotto.htm"
   Randomize
End Sub
```

Let's start to build the program: In Microsoft Word, create a file called Lotto and save it in HTML format (see Figure 10). Next, run the program. Click the **Generate Number** button, as in Figure 11. Finally, click on the hypertext label "About the Lotto" to see the HTML page we created earlier. This is the linked File called **Lotto.html**.

Figure 10. Word Document Saved as HTML.

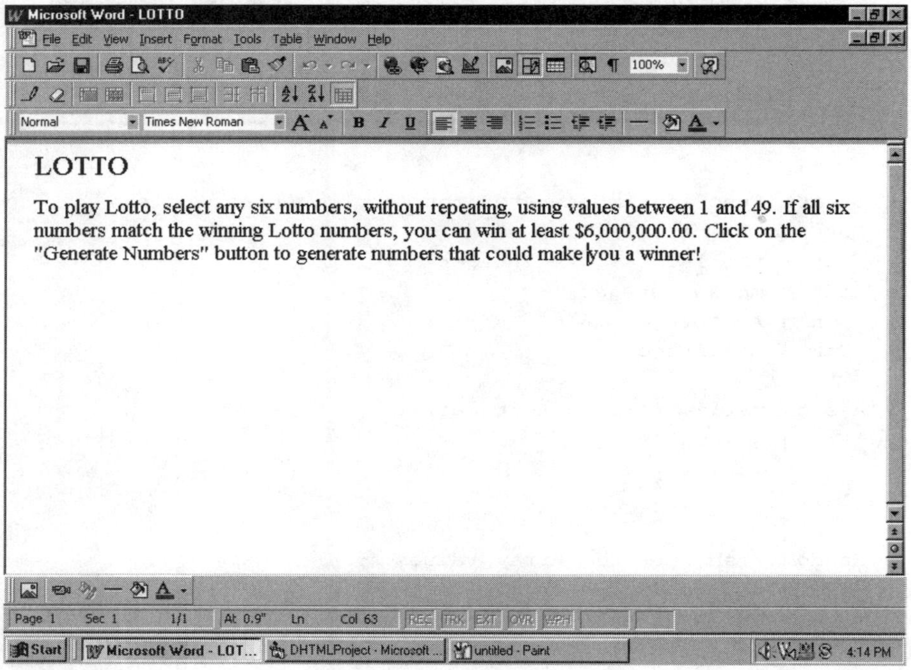

12.3.3 Importing Existing HTML Pages

(samples: LottoImport)

You can import existing HTML pages into the Page Designer, which is easier than designing an HTML page from scratch. You can use different tools to design the interface of the HTML pages, add them to the Page Designer, put some controls on the pages, and then do the programming.

Let's now create the same Lotto project interface we did in the previous example, but this time using Microsoft Word. The file is saved in HTML format. In the Page Designer, we import the HTML page and add a Command button and a hyperlink. Finally, we can copy the source code from the earlier Lotto project. Here are the steps involved in building the interface:

Figure 11. Executing the Program and Generating Numbers.

1. Open MS Word and create a user interface like the one in Figure 12. (The Money and Child are separate images, from clip art in Microsoft Clip Art Gallery 5.0.)
2. Save the file in Word format, using the filename **LottoImport.doc**. Save it again in HTML format as **LottoImport.htm**.
3. Open a New DHTML project, right click **DHTMLPage1**, select **Add**, and select **DHTML Page**.

Figure 12. Designing a DHTML Interface in Microsoft Word.

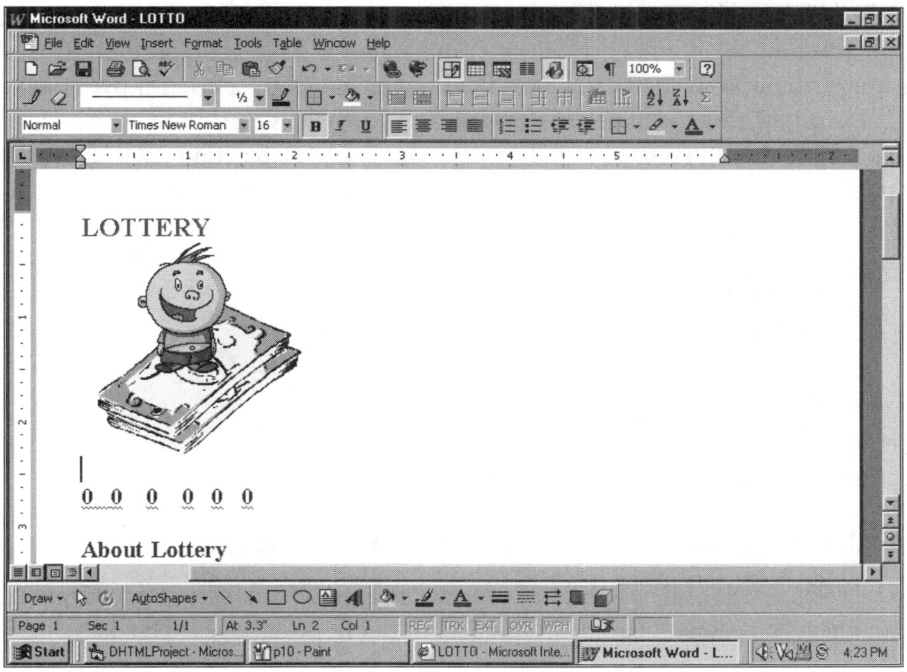

4. Select **Save HTML** and save it into an external file. Click the **Open** (Using existing HTML file) button, as in Figure 13. Select the HTML file called **LottoImport** that we saved in Word.
5. Right click the larger image box, select **Properties** , select **Image Source**, and select **Image1.gif** (the folder containing the saved HTML file). Select **Apply**. Do the same for the smaller Image, loading **Image2.gif.**
6. You can rearrange the images by right clicking the images and selecting **Absolute Position**, and you can rearrange the text. Repeat the process demonstrated in the previous Lotto example: apply **Span** to each "0" and assign an ID to each number (Number1 through Number6). Create the hyperlink for "About Florida Lottery".

Figure 13. Open an Existing HTML Page.

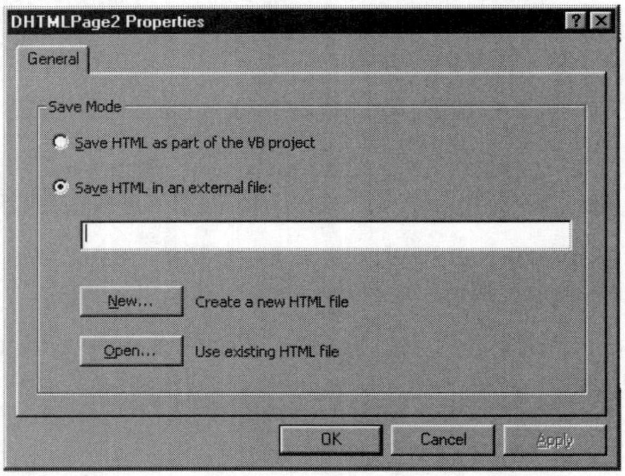

Note: When you design a page, there are two modes: *absolute* and *relative*. In **absolute position** mode, all items you drag or move on the page are placed at the exact location where you release the cursor. Absolute mode allows finer control over the layout of a page, but is not as flexible as relative positioning. In **relative position** mode, each new item you put on the page is placed in the next available cursor position. With relative positioning, the page can easily adjust to the size of the end user's browser window.

7. Add a CommandButton to the form, similar to the one in the previous Lotto project, and copy the attached code from the previous version of the program. Here are the new contents of the DHTMLPage_Load procedure:

```
imgMoney.src = App.Path & "\Image1.gif"
imgChild.src = App.Path & "\Image2.gif"
Hyperlink1.href = App.Path & "\lotto.htm"
```

Run the program, as shown in Figure 14.

12.3.4 Managing Program State Between DHTML Pages

DHTML and HTML pages are *stateless*, meaning that when you navigate from one page to another, you cannot access information stored in prior pages. This is by design, so a Web

Figure 14. Adding the Generate Number Button.

server processing hundreds or thousands of simultaneous requests does not have to save separate information for each user. Once a requested page is sent to a user, the server conveniently "forgets" that the user exists.

When writing useful applications in DHTML, however, we need some way to save state information on the user's computer so this information can be passed between pages. Internet Explorer uses a type of file called a *cookie* for this purpose. In Visual Basic, the **PutProperty** function stores data in a cookie, and the **GetProperty** function retrieves data from a previously created cookie. GetProperty and PutProperty are part of the modDHTML module added to a Visual Basic project that was created using the **DHTML Application** template. The following are the declarations of these two functions:

```
Public Sub PutProperty(objDocument As HTMLDocument,
           strName As String, vntValue As Variant,
           Optional Expires As Date)

Public Function GetProperty(objDocument As HTMLDocument,
                strName As String) As Variant
```

Parameters:

objDocument	An HTML.Document object
strName	A unique property name
vntValue	A value to be stored in the property
Expires	Date on which the cookie is no longer valid

12.4 ACME CAR RENTAL EXAMPLE

(samples: CarRental)

Let's create a simple program for a ficticious company named **ACME Car Rentals.** It lets the user enter some basic information about a car rental, such as the type of car and the number of days the car will be rented. The program determines the rental rate and calculates the total rental amount. By Visual Basic standards, the program is trivial; in DHTML, it requires some careful coding to save state variables.

12.4.1 Design

The program contains three DHTML pages. On the first page, a customer enters his/her first and last name and selects a type of car to rent, as in Figure 15. On the second page, shown in Figure 16, the customer enters the desired number of rental days. On the third page, shown in Figure 17, the program displays the completed invoice indicating the total amount due.

Figure 15. Car Rental Program, Page 1.

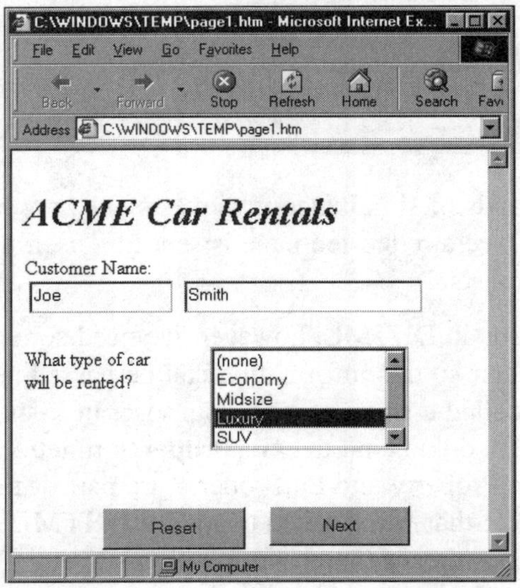

Figure 16. Car Rental Program, Page 2.

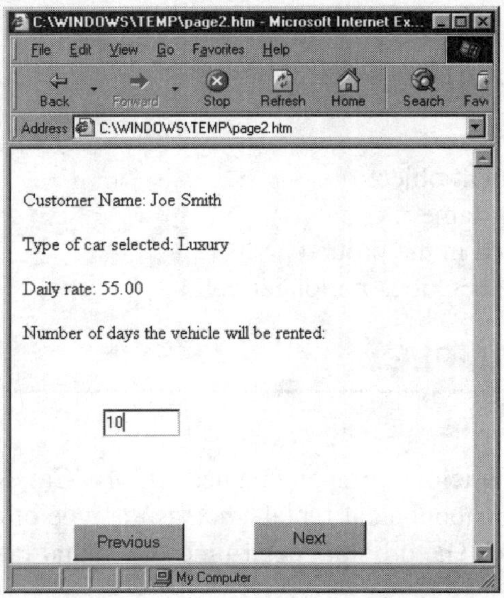

Figure 17. Car Rental Program, Page 3.

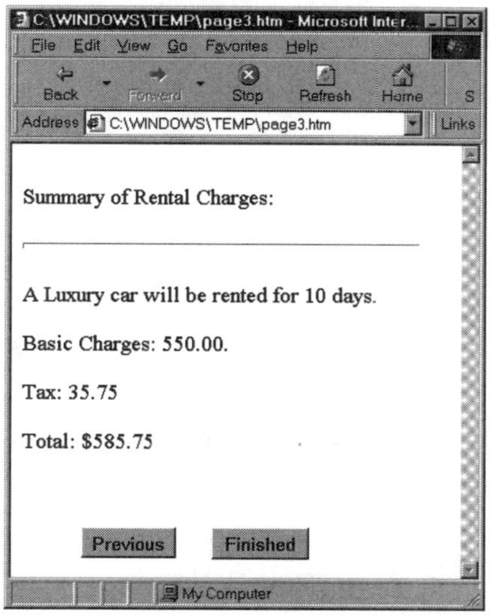

12.4.2 Car Rental Program, Page 1

The first DHTML page inputs the customer name and car selection. When we're ready to move to the second page, we store the information the customer entered. We call **PutProperty** to copy txtLastName to the Property **prLastName**, and copy txtFirstName to the Property **prFirstName**:

```
Private Function cmdNext_onclick() As Boolean
   PutProperty DHTMLPage.Document, _
      "prLastName", txtLastName.Value
   PutProperty DHTMLPage.Document, _
      "prFirstName", txtFirstName.Value
```

Next, the same procedure gets the ListBox value (an integer) and translates it to a string containing the name of an HTML file. The **BaseWindow.Navigate** statement causes a jump to **page2.htm**, the second DHTML page in this program:

```
 Dim strLocation As String, n As Integer
 n = Val(List1.Value)
 If n > 0 Then
    PutProperty DHTMLPage.Document, "prVehicleTypeInt", n
    PutProperty DHTMLPage.Document, "prVehicleType", _
       Choose(n, "Economy", "MidSize", _
       "Luxury", "Sport-Utility", "Minivan")
    PutProperty DHTMLPage.Document, _
      "prDailyRate", Choose(n, 30, 42, 55, 52, 47)
    BaseWindow.navigate "page2.htm"
 End If
End Function
```

The **Choose** function returns a string from an array, indexed by the value of the function's first parameter. The value of n, the first parameter, is from the ListBox containing the types of cars.

The **Load** event handler retrievs state variables and loads them into the two TextBox controls and a ListBox control:

```
Private Sub DHTMLPage_Load()
'Avoid errors caused when trying to get blank properties.
  On Error Resume Next
  txtFirstName.Value = _
    GetProperty(DHTMLPage.Document, "prFirstName")
  txtLastName.Value = _
    GetProperty(DHTMLPage.Document, "prLastName")
  List1.Value = _
    CInt(GetProperty(DHTMLPage.Document, "prVehicleTypeInt"))
End Sub
```

In the **cmdNext_onclick** event procedure, we call **PutProperty** to store information before navigating to the second page (page2.htm):

```
PutProperty DHTMLPage.Document, "prVehicleTypeInt", n
PutProperty DHTMLPage.Document, "prVehicleType", _
  Choose(n, "Economy", "MidSize", _
  "Luxury", "Sport-Utility", "Minivan")
PutProperty DHTMLPage.Document, _
  "prDailyRate", Choose(n, 30, 42, 55, 52, 47)
BaseWindow.navigate "page2.htm"
```

The **onclick** event handler for the Reset button simply clears fields on the form:

```
Private Function ResetButton1_onclick() As Boolean
  txtFirstName.Value = ""
  txtLastName.Value = ""
  List1.Value = 0
End Function
```

12.4.3 Car Rental Program, Page 2

Let's look at the source code for the second DHTML page. This page gets information from the first page and lets the customer enter the number of rental days. We use the **GetProperty** method to retrieve the DailyRate from the Property **prDailyRate** (on Page 1) and display it in **DailyRate.innerText** on Page 2. We also call **GetProperty** to retrieve the first and last name from Page 1:

```
Private Function cmdNext_onclick() As Boolean
  PutProperty DHTMLPage.Document, "prDaysRented", txtDays.Value
  BaseWindow.navigate "page3.htm"
End Function

Private Function cmdPrevious_onclick() As Boolean
  BaseWindow.navigate "page1.htm"
End Function
```

In the **DHTMLPage_Load** event handler, we call GetProperty to retrieve the user input from Page 1:

```
Private Sub DHTMLPage_Load()
```

```
'Get the customer name, days rented, daily rate,
'and Vehicle Type from properties set in the
'first page and display them here.
  txtDays.Value = _
    GetProperty(DHTMLPage.Document, "prDaysRented")
  DailyRate.innerText = _
    Format(GetProperty(DHTMLPage.Document,"prDailyRate"),"Standard")
  CustomerName.innerText = _
     GetProperty(DHTMLPage.Document, "prFirstName") _
     & " " & GetProperty(DHTMLPage.Document, "prLastName")
  VehicleType.innerText = _
    GetProperty(DHTMLPage.Document, "prVehicleType")
End Sub
```

12.4.4 Car Rental Program, Page 3

Let's look at the source code implementation for Page 3. Private variables are declared for all data used in the calculations:

```
Const TAX_RATE As Single = 0.065
Private mDailyRate As Single
Private mDaysRented As Single
Private mCharges As Single
Private mTax As Single
Private mTotal As Single
```

The DHTMLPage_Load event procedure does three things: it loads property values into variables, performs calculations, and displays the calculated values:

```
Private Sub DHTMLPage_Load()
  VehicleType.innerText = GetProperty(DHTMLPage.Document, _
    "prVehicleType")
  mDailyRate = CSng(GetProperty(DHTMLPage.Document, "prDailyRate"))
  mDaysRented = CSng(GetProperty(DHTMLPage.Document, "prDaysRented"))
  daysRented.innerText = mDaysRented

'Calculate the basic charges, tax, and total amount.
    mCharges = mDailyRate * mDaysRented
    mTax = mCharges * TAX_RATE
    mTotal = mCharges + mTax

'Display the calculated values:
  charges.innerText = Format(mCharges, "Standard")
  tax.innerText = Format(mTax, "Standard")
  total.innerText = Format(mTotal, "Currency")
End Sub

Private Function cmdPrevious_onclick() As Boolean
'Return to Page 2.
  BaseWindow.navigate "page2.htm"
End Function

Private Function cmdFinished_onclick() As Boolean
'Clear all property variables and return to Page 1.
```

```
    PutProperty DHTMLPage.Document, "prVehicleType", ""
    PutProperty DHTMLPage.Document, "prDailyRate", 0
    PutProperty DHTMLPage.Document, "prLastName", ""
    PutProperty DHTMLPage.Document, "prFirstName", ""
    PutProperty DHTMLPage.Document, "prDaysRented", 0
    PutProperty DHTMLPage.Document, "prVehicleTypeInt", 0
    BaseWindow.navigate "page1.htm"
End Function
```

12.4.5 Summary

When building DHTML applications in Visual Basic, you have complete access to the richness of DHTML combined with the power of Visual Basic code and controls. A DHTML application reduces traffic on Web servers because each user request can be processed on the client side. It does not have to be routed through the Web server. Of course, it must also be pointed out that DHTML is strictly a client-side tool, so it does not help when your program needs to save information directly on the Web server.

DHTML also gives you dynamic interaction within Web pages. Because Visual Basic code can be used on Web pages, you can directly manipulate any element on a page and create and manage new elements at run time. This gives DHTML documents a truly dynamic user interface.

In DHTML applications, program state management is improved. Ordinary HTML applications are *stateless.* That is, no information about an HTTP request is maintained after a response is received from the server. Visual Basic DHTML applications allow you to save their state between server requests, permitting multipage applications.

12.5 WINSOCK CONTROL

The Microsoft Winsock control lets you connect to a remote computer, and exchange information using either **User Datagram Protocol (UDP)** or **Transmission Control Protocol (TCP)**. Both protocols are useful in client/server applications. The Winsock control itself is invisible at run time. In this section, we will create a "Chat" application that permits interactive communication between two computers across a network, using the Winsock control and TCP protocol.

12.5.1 Comparing TCP and UDP Protocols

It might be useful at this point to compare the TCP and UDP protocols:

- **TCP** is a *connection-based* protocol. That is, the user must establish a connection before exchanging data. If an application requires acknowledgment from the server or client when data is sent or received, use TCP. If a large amount of data is to be transferred, use TCP because it maintains the connection and ensures the integrity of transmitted data.
- **UDP** is a *connectionless* protocol. The user does not have to establish a connection before sending data to other computers. UDP is simpler than TCP and requires less overhead, but there is no way to verify that a message, once sent, has been received. If data is sent intermittently between computers and can be safely ignored, UDP is best.

12.5.2 Winsock Properties

Table 8 displays properties of the Winsock control, Table 9 contains settings for the **State** property, and Table 10 displays a list of Winsock methods.

Table 8. Winsock Control Properties.

Property	Type	Description
LocalHostName	String	Returns the local computer name. Read-only at run time, and unavailable at design time.
LocalIP	String	Returns the IP address of the local computer in the IP address dotted string format (xxx.xxx.xxx.xxx). Read-only at run time, and unavailable at design time.
LocalPort	Long	Returns or sets the local port to use.
Protocol	0 or 1	Returns or sets the protocol, either sckTCPProtocol or sckUDPProtocol.
RemoteHost	String	Returns or sets the remote computer to which a control sends or receives data. Read/Write property, available at both run time and design time. You can provide a host name, for example, "ftp://ftp.microsoft.com," or an IP address string in dotted format, such as "100.0.1.1".
RemoteHostIP	String	Returns the IP address of the remote machine.
RemotePort	Long	Returns or sets the remote port number to which a connection is made. Read/Write property, available at both run time and design time.
State	Integer	Returns the state of the control, expressed as an enumerated type. Read-only and unavailable at design time.

Table 9. State Property Values.

Constant	Value	Description
sckClosed	0	Closed (default value)
sckOpen	1	Open
sckListening	2	Listening
sckConnectionPending	3	Connection pending
sckResolvingHost	4	Resolving host
sckHostResolved	5	Host resolved
sckConnecting	6	Connecting
sckConnected	7	Connected
sckClosing	8	Peer is closing the connection
sckError	9	Error

12.5.3 Winsock Events

Table 11 lists events generated by the Winsock Control.

12.5.4 Winsock Client-Server Example

(samples: Winsock)

Let's create a simple Winsock application that lets two users interactively chat over a network. The program has three forms: the **Switchboard**, the **Client**, and the **Server**. The **SwitchBoard** form lets the user choose to be a client, a server, or both. The **Server** form goes online and waits for an incoming call from a client. The **Client** form initiates a call to a known server, and when the server answers, the client sends a message. Here are the required steps to create the program:

Table 10. Winsock Control Methods.

Method	Description
Accept	For TCP server applications only. This method is used to accept an incoming connection from a client computer when handling a ConnectionRequest event.
Connect	(TCP only) Requests a connection to a remote computer.
Close	Closes a TCP connection from client or server applications.
GetData	Retrieves the current block of data from the input buffer and stores it in a variable of type Variant.
Listen	Invoked by the server. Creates a socket and sets it in listen mode, waiting for a connection request from a client.
SendData	Sends data to a remote computer.

Table 11. Winsock Control Events.

Event	Description
Close	Occurs when the remote computer closes the connection.
Connect	Occurs when a connection operation is completed.
ConnectionRequest	Occurs when a server receives a request for a connection from a remote client.
DataArrival	Occurs when new data arrives.
Error	Occurs when an error occurs in background processing, such as failed to connect, or failed to send or receive in the background.
SendComplete	Occurs when a send operation is completed.
SendProgress	Occurs while data is being sent.

1. Create a new Standard EXE project.
2. Select **Components** from the **Project** menu and place a check next to "Microsoft Winsock Control 6.0".
3. Create a form called **frmSwitchboard** and add all the controls found in Figure 18.
4. Create the **frmClient** form, shown in Figure 19.
5. Create the **frmServer** form, shown in Figure 20.

Figure 18. The SwitchBoard Form.

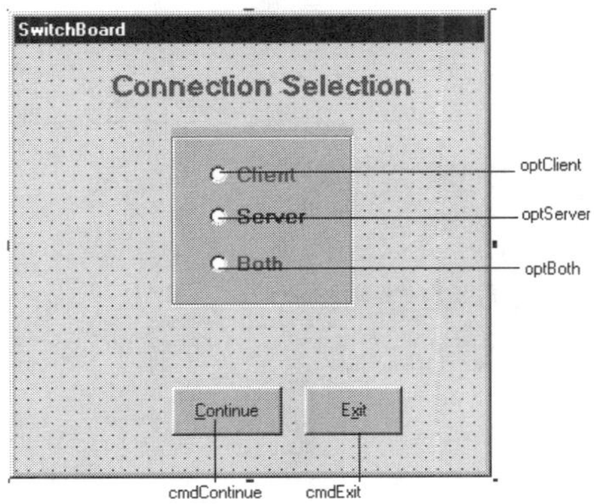

Figure 19. The Client Form.

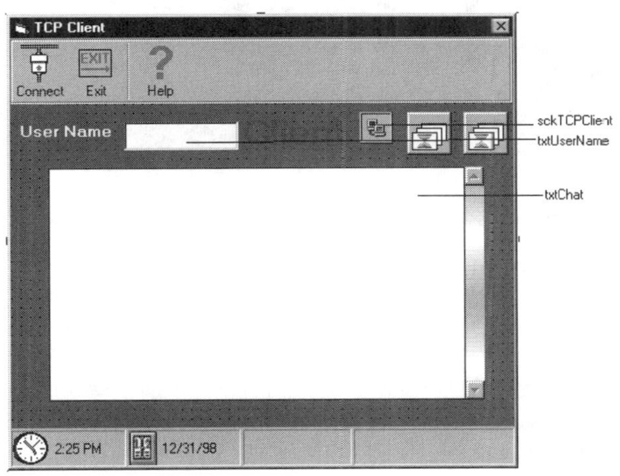

12.5.5 FrmSwitchboard Implementation

Here is the implementation code for the frmSwitchBoard Form:

```
Private Sub cmdContinue_Click()
  If optClient Then
    frmClient.Show
  ElseIf optServer Then
    frmServer.Show
  Else
    frmServer.Show
```

```
      frmServer.Left = 6000
      frmClient.Show
      frmClient.Left = 0
    End If
    Me.Hide
  End Sub

  Private Sub cmdExit_Click()
    Unload Me
    Unload frmClient
    Unload frmServer
  End Sub
```

Figure 20. The Server Form.

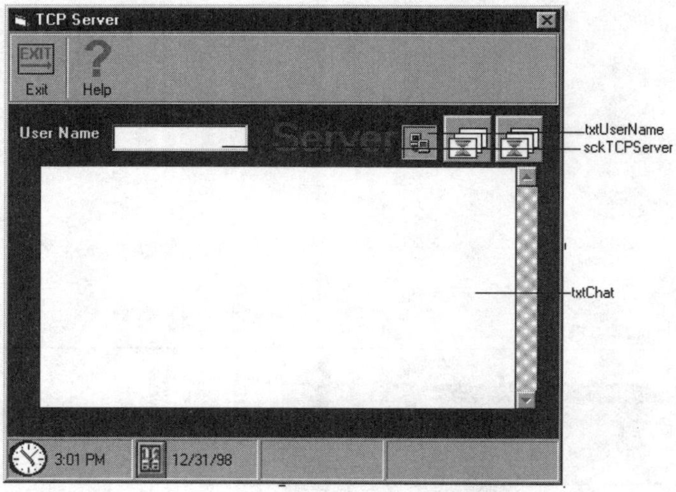

12.5.6 FrmClient Implementation

Here is the implementation code for the frmClient Form:

```
Private Sub Form_Load()
'Set the remote port number.
  sckTCPClient.RemotePort = 1
End Sub

Private Sub sckTCPClient_Connect()
  'After connected, show the nethood icon
  'to display successful connection.
  staStatusbar.Panels(3).Picture _
    = LoadPicture(App.Path & "\nethood.ico")
  'display the message
  staStatusbar.Panels(3).Text = "Connected"
  'display the remote server name.
  staStatusbar.Panels(4).Text _
    = "Remote server: " & sckTCPClient.RemoteHost
End Sub
```

```
Private Sub sckTCPClient_DataArrival(ByVal bytesTotal As Long)
  Dim strData As String
  'get the data
  sckTCPClient.GetData strData
  'display the data
  txtChat.Text = txtChat.Text & strData & vbCrLf
  'set the focus to the next line
  txtChat.SelStart = Len(txtChat)
End Sub

Private Sub Toolbar1_ButtonClick(ByVal Button As _
          MSComctlLib.Button)
  Dim strRemoteHost As String
  Select Case Button.Key
    Case "Connect"
      Connect
    Case "Exit"
      Unload Me
      Unload frmServer
      Unload frmSwitchBoard
  End Select
End Sub

Public Sub Connect()
  Dim strRemoteHost As String
  Dim intChoice As Integer
  'Check if it is already connected
  If sckTCPClient.State = sckConnected Then
    MsgBox "You are already connected", , "Connection"
    Exit Sub ' do not need to connect
  End If
  sckTCPClient.Close
  'Input box for the user to enter remote host IP or name
  strRemoteHost = _
    InputBox("Enter RemoteHost Name (or IP)", "Connection")
  'If blank remote name, exit
  If Len(Trim$(strRemoteHost)) = 0 Then Exit Sub
  sckTCPClient.RemoteHost = strRemoteHost
  'Connect to the server with the remote name
  '  the user just entered.
  sckTCPClient.Connect
End Sub

Private Sub txtChat_KeyPress(KeyAscii As Integer)
  Static strSending As String
  Dim strUserName As String
  'If not connected, data cannot be sent.
  If sckTCPClient.State <> sckConnected Then
    MsgBox "Please click Connect" _
       & " before you send data.", _
      vbInformation, "Client Connect"
    KeyAscii = 0
    Exit Sub
  End If
```

```
  'User can put his/her name in the box
  '  when chatting, so the other party can see
  '  who is talking on the other end.
  'If it is blank, the computer name will be the
  '  default name used.
  If Len(Trim$(txtUserName)) <> 0 Then
    strUserName = txtUserName
  Else
    strUserName = sckTCPClient.LocalHostName
  End If
  'If the Enter key is pressed, the data will sent to
  '  the server. The prefix will be the user name or
  '  the computer name.
  If KeyAscii = Asc(vbCr) Then
    sckTCPClient.SendData _
      ">>" & strUserName & ": " & strSending
      strSending = ""
  Else
    strSending = strSending & Chr(KeyAscii)
  End If
End Sub
```

12.5.7 FrmServer Implementation

The following code listing is taken from the frmServer form:

```
Private Sub Form_Load()
'Set the remoteport number.
   sckTCPServer.LocalPort = 1
'It is in the listening mode
   sckTCPServer.Listen
'Display the status
   staStatusBar.Panels(3).Text = "Listening"
End Sub

Private Sub sckTCPServer_ConnectionRequest(ByVal requestID As Long)
  If sckTCPServer.State <> sckClosed Then sckTCPServer.Close
  sckTCPServer.Accept requestID
  'Display the nethood icon to
  '  indicate successful connection.
  staStatusBar.Panels(3).Picture = LoadPicture(_
    App.Path & "\nethood.ico")
  'Display the Connected status.
  staStatusBar.Panels(3).Text = "Connected"
  'Display the remote client IP address
  staStatusBar.Panels(4).Text = _
    "Remote client: " & sckTCPServer.RemoteHostIP
End Sub

Private Sub sckTCPServer_DataArrival(ByVal bytesTotal As Long)
  Dim strData As String
  sckTCPServer.GetData strData
  txtChat.Text = txtChat.Text & strData & vbCrLf
  txtChat.SelStart = Len(txtChat)
End Sub
```

```
Private Sub Toolbar1_ButtonClick(ByVal Button As _
  MSComctlLib.Button)
  Select Case Button.Key
    Case "Exit"
      Unload Me
      Unload frmClient
      Unload frmSwitchBoard
    Case Else
  End Select
End Sub

Private Sub txtChat_KeyPress(KeyAscii As Integer)
  Static strSending As String
  Dim strUserName As String
  If sckTCPServer.State <> sckConnected Then
    MsgBox _
      "Please click Connect before you send data.", _
      vbInformation, "Client Connect"
    KeyAscii = 0
    Exit Sub
  End If
  If Len(Trim$(txtUserName)) <> 0 Then
    strUserName = txtUserName
  Else
    strUserName = sckTCPServer.LocalHostName
  End If

  If KeyAscii = Asc(vbCr) Then
    sckTCPServer.SendData ">>" & strUserName & ': " _
      & strSending
    strSending = ""
  Else
    strSending = strSending & Chr(KeyAscii)
  End If
End Sub
```

Test this program on your own computer by selecting option **Both** in **frmSwitch**. Click the **Connect** button in the Client form, enter your computer name, and click OK. Figure 21 shows both Client and Server windows on the screen at the same time, with a conversation between them.

12.6 CREATING HTML HELP

12.6.1 Introduction

HTML Help represents Microsoft's latest approach to authoring Help systems. It will probably replace WinHelp and is fast becoming the Help system of choice for application designers. HTML Help is available to users of Internet Explorer 4.01 or later.

HTML Help is a set of technologies for delivering help and Web content using the *Hypertext Markup Language* (HTML). HTML Help is designed for authors or developers who create content for software, multimedia titles, intranets, extranets, or for the Internet.

Figure 21. Testing the Chat Program.

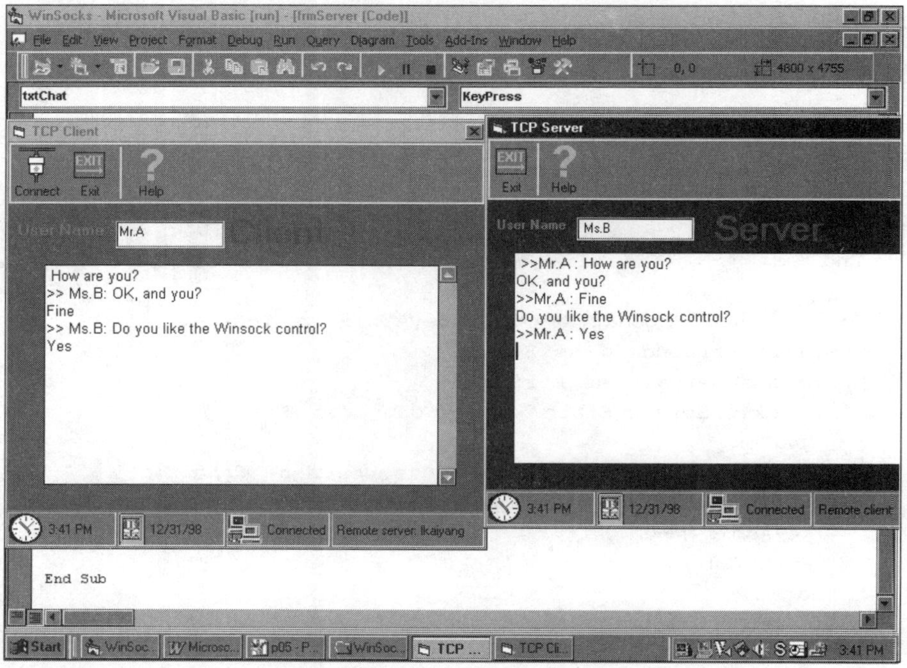

Microsoft uses HTML Help to create and publish all of its online documentation for Visual Studio 6.0.

12.6.2 Creating HTML files with Microsoft Word

In this section, we demonstrate how to create a HTML Help system with Microsoft **HTML Workshop 1.2**. *Note:* HTML Workshop 1.1 comes with Visual Basic 6.0, but you can download version 1.2 from the Microsoft Web site (www.microsoft.com).

Before creating a HTML Help system, you need to create separate HTML files for each help topic. You can use Microsoft Word, Microsoft FrontPage, Netscape, or any other HTML editor program. For the current example, we will use Word.

We're going to create several help topic files for this demonstration, saving each as HTML. In these files, if we need to insert a hyperlink in the text, we select the text we want to display as the hyperlink, and in the **Link to file or URL** box, enter the path of the file we want the hyperlink to jump to. After all topic HTML files have been created, we save them in the folder **HTMLHelp2**. We are now ready to create the HTML Help system itself:

1. In Windows, select **Help Workshop** from the **Microsoft Visual Studio 6.0 Tools** menu. The opening window will appear with a caption either as shown in Figure 22 or as "Microsoft Help Workshop".
2. Create a new help project file: From **File** menu, select **New**, select **Project**, and click on the **Next** button. Enter "BookHelp" as the project name. Click on **Finish**.
3. Click on the **Add/Remove Files** button to add the HTML file locations to a project file.

Figure 22. Loading HTML Workshop.

4. When the **Topics Files** dialog box opens, click **Add,** and select all **.HTM** files in the HTMLHelp2 folder.
5. Click on **Save all project files** and click on the **Compile** button The HTML Help Workshop displays a compilation log in the right window pane.
6. Click the **View Compiled HTML Help File** button, showing the HTML help file as in Figure 23.

12.6.3 Creating the Main Help Window

Next, we're going to create the startup help window and name it **Main**:

1. Click the **Add/Modifywindow definitions** button on the ToolBar: Type **Main** in the **Add a New Window Type** dialog, as in Figure 24.
2. Type **VB Book Help** when prompted for the **Title bar text**.
3. Select the **Navigation Pane** tab. Place a check next to **Window with navigation pane...**
4. Select **Auto sync** and select **Search Tab**. Click the OK button (see Figure 25).
5. On the next window, select the **Search** Tab and click on **Compile Full-text Search.**

Figure 23. Viewing the Compiled Help File.

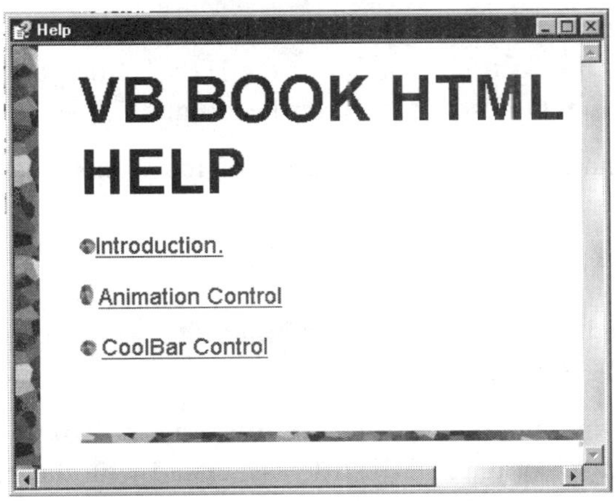

Figure 24. Adding a New Window Type.

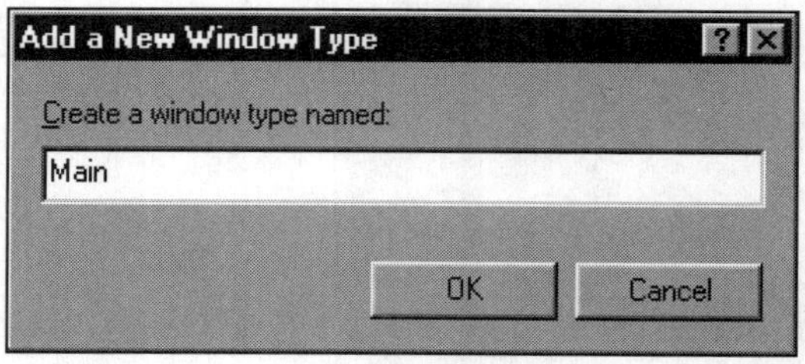

Figure 25. Setting up the Window Definition.

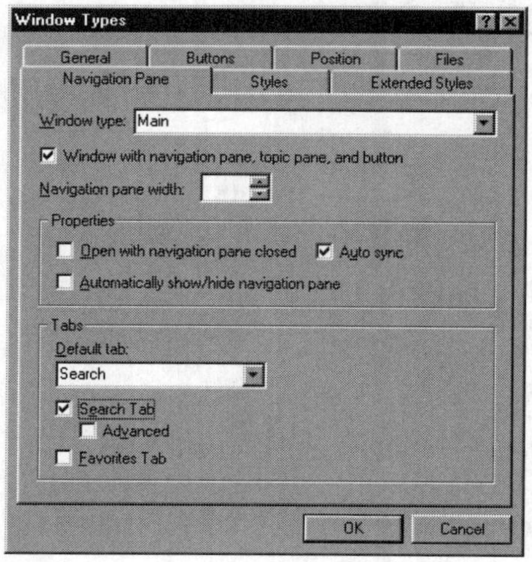

12.6.4 Creating a Table of Contents

Next, we're going to create the Contents file, in five steps:

1. In the HTML Help Workshop window, shown in Figure 26, select the **Contents** tab and choose the option to create a new contents file.
2. Click **OK**, and click **Save**.
3. Click the Contents Properties button: Clear the **Use folders instead of books** CheckBox. Click **OK**.
4. Click the **Insert a Heading** button: Type **Introduction** in the **Entry title** box, shown in Figure 27. Click the **Add** button. Select the HTML title you want to bind to the instruction. Click the **OK** button to save your heading.
5. Click the **Insert a Page** button and repeat the previous four steps (see Figure 28).

12.6.5 Creating an Index File

Step 1. Click the **Index** tab and select **Create a new index file**, as in Figure 29. Click **OK**. Use the default name INDEX.hhk.

Step 2. Click the **Insert Keyword** button: Type **Animation Control** in the **Keyword** box, as in Figure 30. Then select the HTML title associated with the keyword.

Figure 26. Creating the Help Contents.

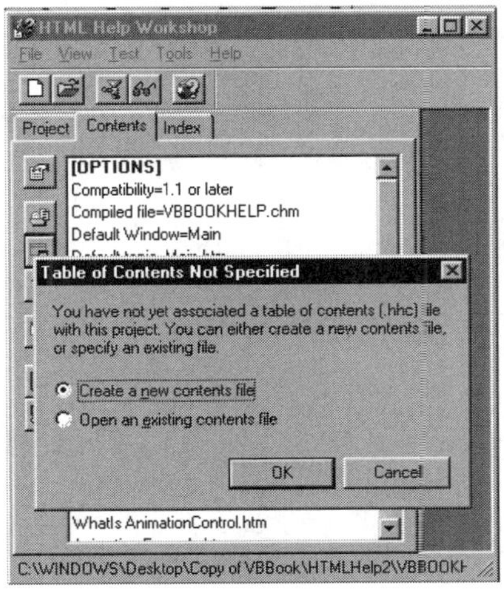

Figure 27. Inserting a Heading.

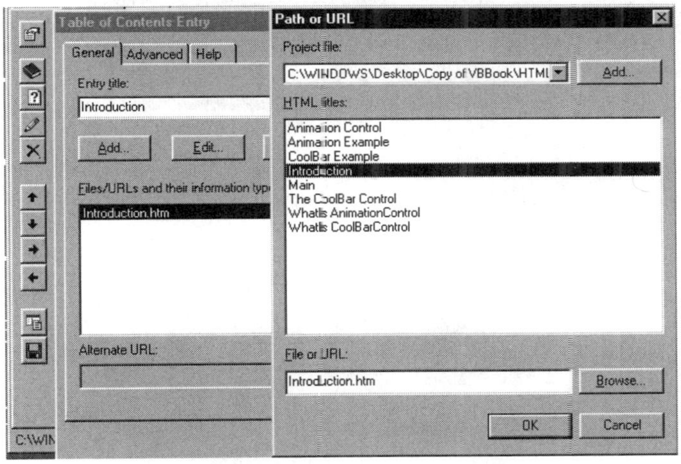

Figure 28. Inserting a Page.

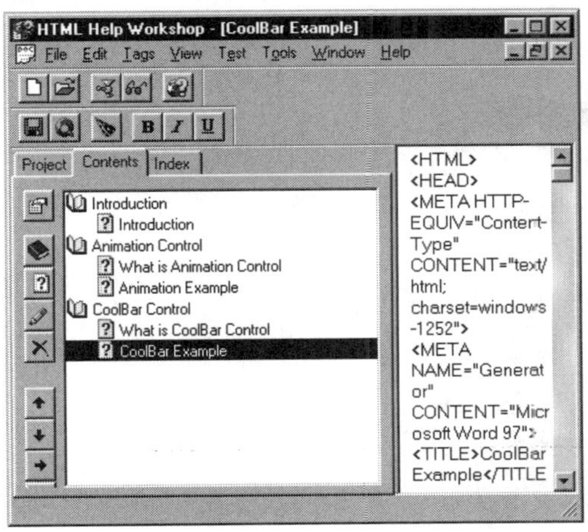

Figure 29. Creating an Index File.

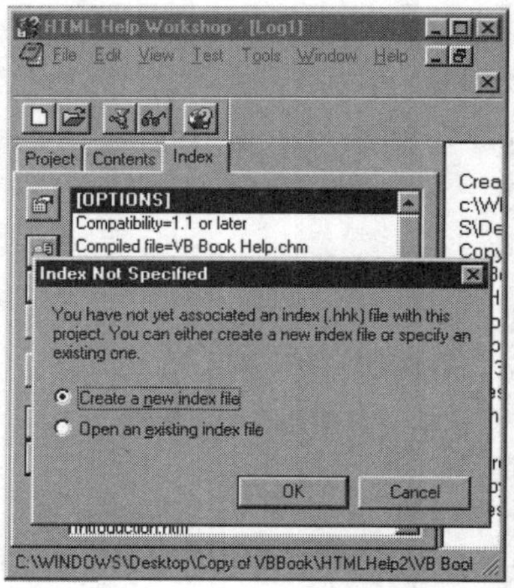

Figure 30. Inserting Keywords.

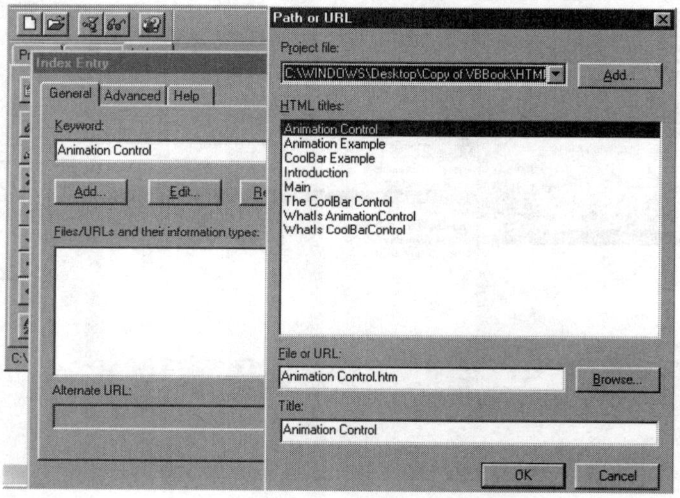

Figure 31. Setting Project Options.

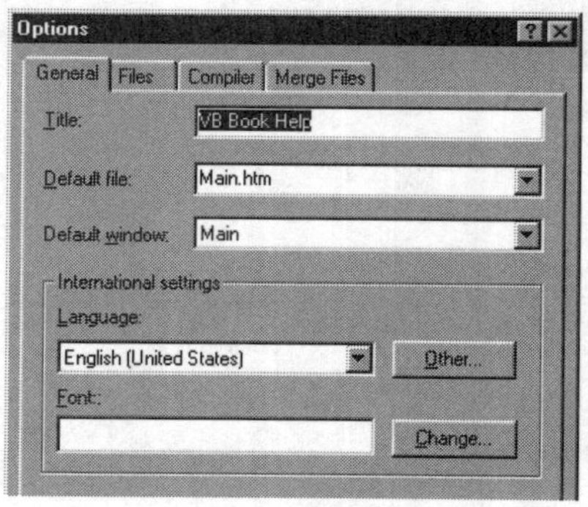

12.6.6 Compiling a Help Project

Before compiling the Help project, we need to set a few project options: First, click the **Change Project** ToolBar button: Set the project Title to **VB Book Help**, as in Figure 31. Next, select the **Compiler** tab, select the **Progress** option, and select **Compile full-text search information**. Click **OK** to save the project options. Click on the **Save All Project Files And Compile** ToolBar button to compile the project: Click the **View Compiled HTML Help File** button to view the file: Figure 32 shows the recompiled HTML Help file, VBBookHelp.chm.

Figure 32. Recompiled HTML Help File.

12.6.7 Hooking HTML Help to a Visual Basic Program

The HTML Help ActiveX control is designed to work with Internet Explorer and the **Shdocvw.dll** component. It does not include the design-time support that is necessary to use it with development tools such as Microsoft Visual Basic and C++. Linking HTML Help to a Visual Basic program is a complicated process. In the following program, we will demonstrate a simple way to display HTML help files, using an Internet Explorer object (SHDocVw.InternetExplorer).

To use an Internet Explorer object to display HTML help files, we need to create a **Frameset** (Start.htm), a **Contents navigation frame** (Hh_toc.htm), and an **Index navigation frame** (Hh_index.htm).

12.6.8 Creating a Frameset

First, we have to create a Frameset document, shown in Figure 33. Click the **File** menu, select **New**, select **HTML**, Type **Start** in the TextBox labeled "Enter the title for the HTML file".

Two-Frame HTML frameset. The following code creates a two-frame HTML frameset. It provides instructions for creating a table of contents in the left frame that jumps to topics in the right frame. Here is the HTML source code for **Start.htm**:

```
!DOCTYPE HTML PUBLIC "-//W3C//DTD HTML 3.2//EN">
<HTML>
```

```
<HEAD>
<TITLE>VB BOOK HELP</TITLE>
</HEAD>
<FRAMESET COLS="285,100%" framespacing=0  frameborder=0>
  <FRAME SRC="hh_toc.htm" name="left" scrolling="yes">
  <FRAME SRC="main.htm" name="right" scrolling="yes">
</FRAMESET>
```

Figure 33. Creating a Frameset.

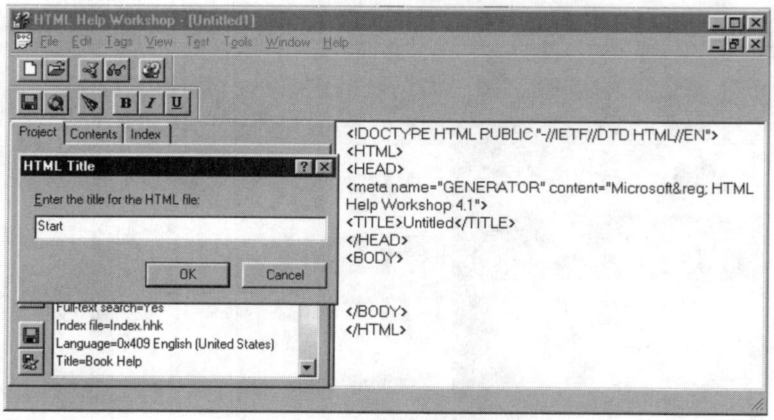

12.6.9 Contents HTML File

The Contents file displays the **Contents** button, which in turn loads **hh_toc.htm.** The **Index** button loads both **hh_index.htm** and the ActiveX control **hhctrl.ocx:**

```
<HTML>
<HEAD>
<META HTTP-EQUIV="Content-Type" CONTENT="text/html; charset=windows-
1252">
<META NAME="Generator" CONTENT="Microsoft Word 97">
<META NAME="Template" CONTENT="C:\PROGRAM FILES\MICROSOFT
OFFICE\OFFICE\html.dot">
</HEAD>
<BODY LINK="#0000ff" VLINK="#800080" BGCOLOR="#993366">
<P><!DOCTYPE HTML PUBLIC "-//W3C//DTD HTML 3.2//EN">
<SCRIPT LANGUAGE=JavaScript>
</SCRIPT>
</HEAD>
<BODY TOPMARGIN=0 LEFTMARGIN=0>
<TABLE>
<TR>
<TD><FORM ACTION=POST><INPUT TYPE=BUTTON VALUE="Contents"
ONCLICK="location = 'hh_toc.htm';" NAME="Help Topics"></FORM></TD>
<TD><FORM ACTION=POST><INPUT TYPE=BUTTON VALUE="Index" ONCLICK="location
= 'hh_index.htm';" NAME="Index"></FORM></TD>
</TR>
</TABLE>
<P>
<OBJECT
  id=hhctrl type="application/x-oleobject"
```

```
  classid="clsid:adb880a6-d8ff-11cf-9377-00aa003b7a11"
  codebase="hhctrl.ocx#Version=4,71,1111,0"
  width=250
  height=270
  >
   <PARAM name="Command" value="Contents">
   <PARAM name="Item1" value="Table of Contents.hhc">
</OBJECT>
</P></BODY>
</HTML>
```

12.6.10 Index HTML File

The Index HTML file (**hh_index.htm**) is identical to the Contents file, except that in the last OBJECT block, it displays the index rather than the contents:

```
<HTML>
<HEAD>
<META HTTP-EQUIV="Content-Type" CONTENT="text/html; charset=windows-
1252">
<META NAME="Generator" CONTENT="Microsoft Word 97">
<META NAME="Template" CONTENT="C:\PROGRAM FILES\MICROSOFT
OFFICE\OFFICE\html.dot">
</HEAD>
<BODY LINK="#0000ff" VLINK="#800080" BGCOLOR="#993366">
<P><!DOCTYPE HTML PUBLIC "-//W3C//DTD HTML 3.2//EN">
<SCRIPT LANGUAGE=JavaScript>
</SCRIPT>
</HEAD>
<BODY TOPMARGIN=0 LEFTMARGIN=0>
<TABLE>
<TR>
<TD><FORM ACTION=POST><INPUT TYPE=BUTTON VALUE="Contents"
ONCLICK="location = 'hh_toc.htm';" NAME="Help Topics"></FORM></TD>
<TD><FORM ACTION=POST><INPUT TYPE=BUTTON VALUE='Index" ONCLICK="location
= 'hh_index.htm';" NAME="Index"></FORM></TD>
</TR>
</TABLE>
<OBJECT
  id=hhctrl
  type="application/x-oleobject"
  classid="clsid:adb880a6-d8ff-11cf-9377-00aa003b7a11"
          codebase="hhctrl.ocx#Version=4,71,1111,0"
  width=248
  height=275
  >
  <PARAM name="Command" value="Index">
  <PARAM name="Item1" value="index.hhk">
</OBJECT>
</BODY>
```

12.6.11 Visual Basic Host Program

Next, let's create the Visual Basic host program, shown in Figure 34, that activates the HTML Help files. The user interface consists of a File menu, a Help menu, and two Labels.

Figure 35 shows the HTML help window activated by the program. Here is the program source code:

```
'Create an Internet Explorer object and
'use it to view display Web pages.
Public Explorer As SHDocVw.InternetExplorer

Private Sub mnuExit_Click()
  Unload Me
End Sub

Private Sub mnuHelpContents_Click()
  On Error GoTo ViewHTML_Error
  Set Explorer = New SHDocVw.InternetExplorer
  Explorer.Visible = True
  Explorer.Navigate App.Path & "/start.htm"
  Exit Sub
ViewHTML_Error:
  MsgBox "Cannot display help file: (start.htm)", , Err.Description
End Sub
```

Figure 34. VB Help Project Interface.

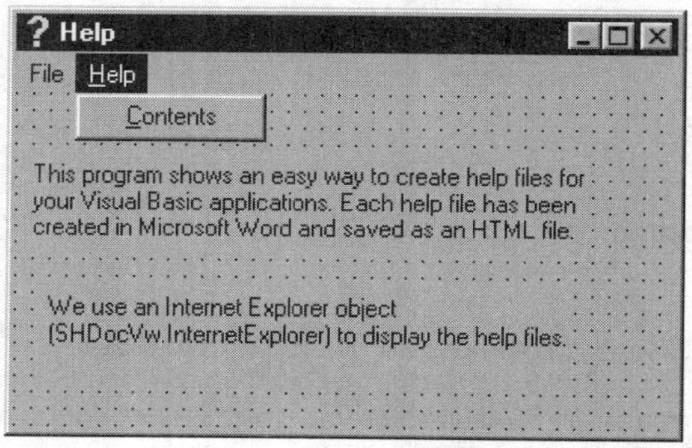

Figure 35. Calling HTML Help.

12.6.12 Advantages to Using HTML Help

There seem to be significant advantages to using HTML Help rather than WinHelp. For instance, you can launch HTML help files from Web pages. Also, animation, sound, video, and other effects are easier to add to HTML Help files. Unlike WinHelp, HTML files have no practical size limit. In general, compiled HTML Help files are much smaller than compiled WinHelp files. HTML Help files can also have active links to the Web, permitting an application's online help to reflect the most recent changes posted to the software vendor's Web site. Did we mention one disadvantage? It doesn't work with other Web browsers, so that's going to prevent some users from reading your help files.

12.7 REVIEW QUESTIONS

The following questions relate to the Internet Transfer control:

1. How is the Internet Transfer control used?
2. Which Internet Transfer control methods use the value of the URL property?
3. When is the **GetChunk** method used with the Internet Transfer control?
4. What parameters must be passed to the GetChunk method?
5. How is the Internet Transfer control's **OpenURL** method called?
6. Name several event state values that can be assigned to the Internet Transfer Control.
7. When does the Internet Transfer control raise a **StateChanged** event?
8. Why is the **StateChanged** event important?
9. How many different **state** event constants exist, and what are their names?
10. Which ActiveX object is required for viewing an HTML page?
11. How can a program display HTML pages using code?
12. How can an HTML page from the Web be saved as as an HTML file on a local computer?
13. How can an HTML page be displayed in a TextBox?
14. Which statements are required for downloading a file from an FTP site?
15. How can you tell if a file specification on an FTP site is a file or directory?
16. What program statements are used to display a directory from an FTP site?
17. How do you download a file from an FTP site to a local computer?
18. In the StateChanged event, which state indicates that a file transfer has completed?
19. Which method should be used to get data from an input buffer after a transfer is completed?

The following questions relate to DHTML:

20. What are the major differences between HTML and DHTML?
21. What is the **InnerText** property?
22. How and why is the **SPAN** tag used?

23. Name some of the differences between Visual Basic events and DHTML equivalent events.
24. How do you display text on a DHTML page?
25. How is an HTML page linked using a **Hyperlink** object?
26. How does a DHTML application store state information when moving between forms?
27. How does a DHTML application retrieve information from state variables?

The following questions relate to the Winsock control:

28. What types of applications can use the Winsock control?
29. What is the difference between the **TCP** and **UDP** protocols?
30. How does the Winsock retrieve data?
31. How does the Winsock control get remote host information?
32. How does the Winsock control indicate that it is connected to another computer?
33. What are the differences between **Server** mode and **Client** mode?

The following questions relate to HTML help:

34. Describe the overall process of displaying HMTL Help.
35. What is a **contents** file?
36. What is a **Frameset** document?
37. How is the **hhctrl.ocx** file used in the sample HTML Help application?
38. How is **SHDocVw.InternetExplorer** in the Visual Basic host program?
39. What are some advantages to using HTML Help rather than Winhelp?

12.8 PROGRAMMING EXERCISES

12.8.1 HTMLViewer - 1

Use the example program named **HTMLViewer** presented earlier in this chapter as a starting point for this exercise. Add a procedure that copies the URL for the current Web site in the Internet Explorer into the URL ComboBox (see Figure 36).

12.8.2 HTMLViewer - 2

Use the program you wrote for the previous exercise as a starting point. In this program, use a DataCombo box to hold the URLs rather than a ComboBox. When you exit the program, save all the URLs to a database table without saving any duplicate URLs. When the program runs, have it load all of the saved URLs from the database.

12.8.3 Winsock with Multiple Connections

In the Winsock example program in this chapter, the server accepts only one connection request. Modify the program to accept multiple connections (many computers to one). *Hint:* Create a control array of Winsock controls.

12.8.4 Mortgage Calculator Program

Create a DHTML application in which the user inputs the Principal, Interest, and Term for a loan, as in Figure 37. When the user clicks on the **Calculate** button, automatically display a second DHTML page with the Principal, Interest, and Term, along with the calculated monthly payment. On the second DHTML page, shown in Figure 38, the user should be able to click the **Back** button to return to the first page. The original input values should still be visible on the first page. To calculate the size of a monthly payment, you can call Visual Basic's build in Pmt function, which has the following input parameters:

```
Pmt( periodicInterestRate, numberOfPayments, principal )
```

For example, for monthly payments over 30 years on a loan of 100,000 at a yearly interest rate of 7%, the function call would be:

```
sngPaymentAmt = Pmt( (.07 / 12), (30 * 12), 100000 )
```

Figure 36. GetViewHTML Exercise.

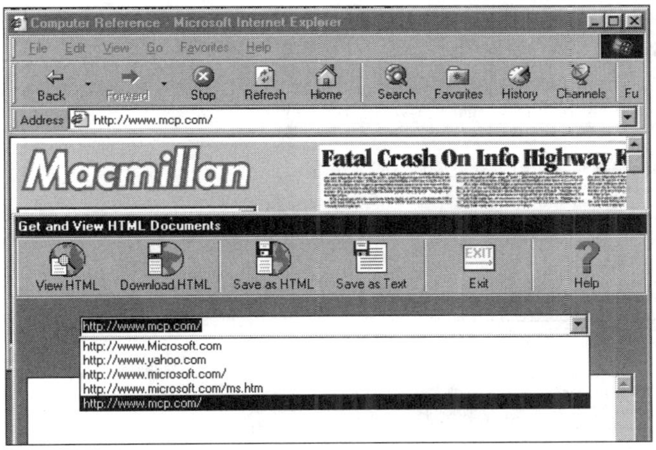

Figure 37. Mortgage Calculator, First Page.

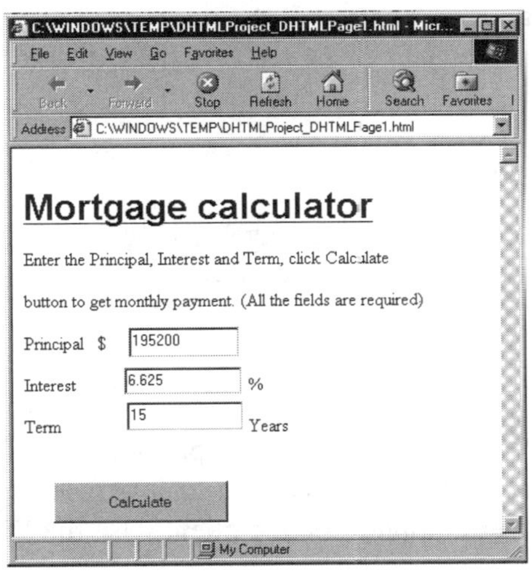

Figure 38. Mortgage Calculator, Second Page.

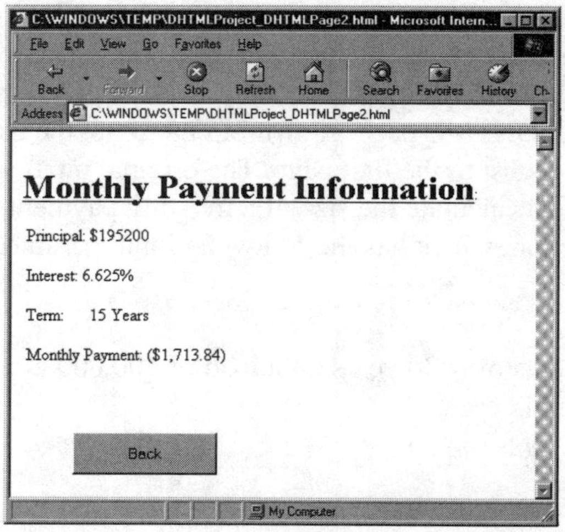

Figure 39. Testing for a Prime Number, and Factoring.

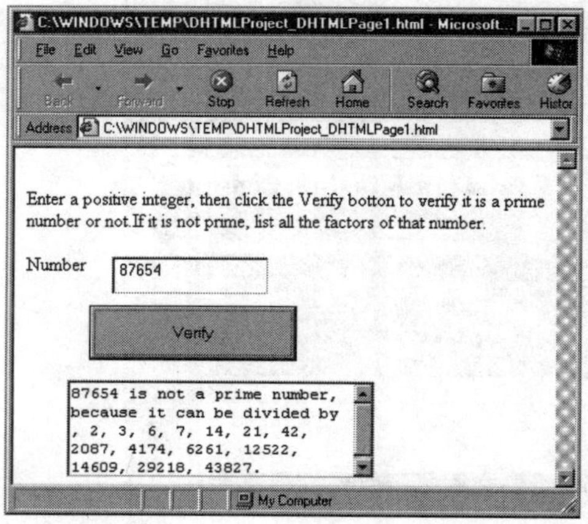

12.8.5 Factoring a Number

A prime number is a number that is only divisible by itself and 1. Create a project that can test whether or not a given positive integer is prime. If the integer is not prime, list all the factors of the number. For example, the factors of 24 are 2, 3, 4, 6, 8, and 12. See Figure 39 for a sample user interface.

12.8.6 Dynamic Changing HTML Page

Create a project that dynamically changes an HTML page's font color, font size, and underline attribute over individual paragraphs when you move the mouse over the text. An example is shown in Figure 40.

12.8.7 Tic-Tac-Toe On Networked Computers

Create a project using the Winsock control that lets two people play a Tic-Tac-Toe game across a local area network. Figure 41 shows a suggested user interface. Let one computer be the connection host, and let the other computer be the client. Use the Winsock program from this chapter as a guide.

Figure 40. Dynamic Change HTML Page.

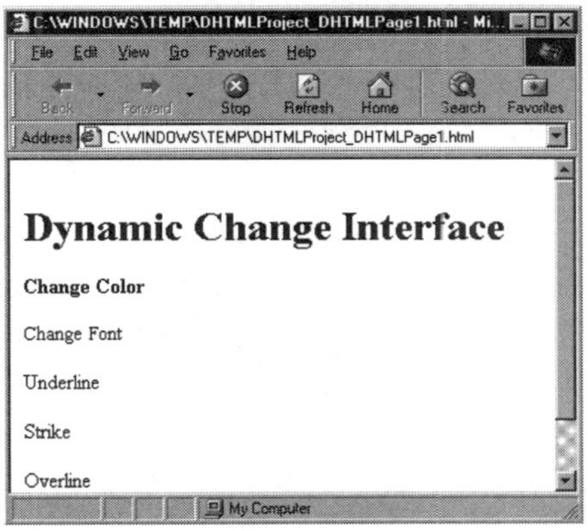

Figure 41. Tic-Tac-Toe On Two Networked Computers.

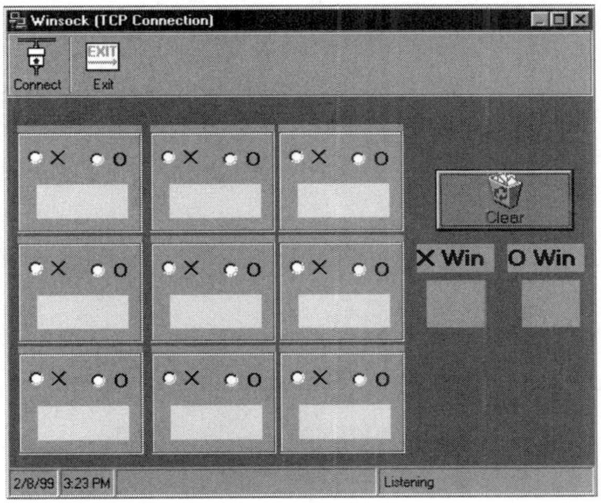

Appendix A: Visual Basic Review

Chapter Contents

Competency Review Test
Data Types, Variables, and Constants
- Data Types
- Boolean
- Byte, Integer, Long
- Single, Double, Currency
- String
- Date
- Object
- Variant
- Declared Constants
- Static Arrays
- Dynamic Arrays
- Collections
- User-Defined Types

If Statements
- Compound Expressions (And, Or, Not)
- Block IF Statement
- Using ELSE
- Select Case

Loops
- For-Next Statement
- Do-While Statement
- Do-Until Statement
- While-Wend Statement

Procedures
- Declaring a Subroutine Procedure
- Procedure Parameters
- Declaring a Function Procedure
- Passing Arguments by Reference
- Passing Arguments by Value
- Private and Public
- Optional Parameters
- Parameter Arrays

String Handling
Forms
- Form Properties
- Form Methods
- Form Events
- Sample Form-Loading Program

Standard Visual Basic Controls
- Label
- Text
- CommandButton
- OptionButton
- Frame
- CheckBox
- Image
- Line
- Timer
- ScrollBar
- ListBox and ComboBox
- Default Properties

Tools for Input-Output
- Print Method
- Format Function
- MsgBox Procedure
- MsgBox Function
- InputBox Function
- Printer Object
- Screen Object
- Application Object

Creating Menus
- Common Menu Types
- Creating a Simple Menu
- Menu Properties

Answers to the Competency Test Questions

A.1 COMPETENCY REVIEW TEST

Because this book is an advanced Visual Basic text, we assume that you already know the fundamentals of programming in Visual Basic. The following competency review test is designed to help you evaluate a basic level of competency in Visual Basic. If you have no trouble answering the questions on this test, there is a strong probability that you will be successful in understanding this book.

1. Name at least five standard data types.
2. Distinguish between variables that have module-level scope and procedure-level scope.

> In this appendix, we review the basics of Visual Basic for two reasons: First, you may have already taken a course in Visual Basic, but missed a few essential details. Second, you may already be an experienced programmer in other computer languages, and you just need a quick start before writing your first Visual Basic programs. Anything we describe can also be found in Visual Basic's online help system, with many more details than we have space for here.

3. Visual Basic allows variables to be of type *object*. Give an example of two different types of objects that can be assigned to an object variable.
4. What is the role or purpose of a variable of type *variant*?
5. What is the primary feature or characteristic of Visual Basic's dynamic array?
6. Implement the following rules in Visual Basic:
   - All employees are paid overtime if hours worked are greater than 40.
   - Union members are paid at time and three-fourths for all hours over 40.
   - Non-union members are paid at time and a half for all hours worked over 40.

   Assume that HrsWrkd contains the number of hours worked, HrlyRate contains the hourly rate of the current employee, and that UnionMember is a Boolean variable which is true if the employee is a union member and false if not. Write the code segment to compute gross pay using the variables HrsWrkd, HrlyRate, and UnionMember.
7. The integer array *Score* contains 100 entries. Use a For-Next loop as part of a code segment to compute the average of the 100 scores. Store the computed average in the variable *Average*. You may need additional variables to complete the code.
8. A list of names are stored alphabetically in the array *Name*. There are 100 entries in the list. The variable *strName* contains a name known to be stored in the list. Write the code segment using a Do While-Loop structure to locate the first occurrence of the name stored in *strName*. Display the position in the list where the match occurred.
9. What is the purpose of a Form's *Name* property?
10. Briefly describe the term *method*. Name at least two methods that are associated with a Form.
11. What is the difference between "loading" a Form and "showing" a Form?
12. How do *labels* and *TextBoxes* differ with respect to how they are typically used?
13. For what purpose is the *command button* typically used?
14. What is the purpose of the command button's *Default* property?
15. How are option buttons and check boxes alike? not alike?
16. For what purpose is a *frame* typically used?
17. How are subroutines and functions alike? not alike?
18. What is the difference between passing arguments *by reference* and *by value*?
19. Procedures may be declared as either *Public* or *Private*. What is the difference?
20. The contents of the variable Net_Pay needs to the formatted to two decimal places with a comma and dollar sign. Use the *Format* function to print the formatted value on a Form.
21. What is the purpose of the *MsgBox* procedure?
22. Including the *Option Explicit* command in your program serves what purpose?

23. What is the purpose of a control's *TabIndex* property?
24. What is the difference between the *MsgBox function* and the *MsgBox statement*?
25. A list box contains a *List* property. What values are contained in the *List* property?
26. In a list box, what is the difference between the *Clear* and *RemoveItem* methods?
27. Name the three different modes for which a sequential file can be opened.
28. For what purpose is the *On Error Goto* statement used?
29. For what purpose is the *Resume* statement used?
30. Briefly describe the use of the *Err* object with respect to error handling.

Answers to the Competency Test questions are at the end of Appendix A. The remainder of Appendix A is a general review of Visual Basic fundamentals.

A.2 DATA TYPES, VARIABLES, AND CONSTANTS

A.2.1 Data Types

The standard data types are Boolean, Byte, Integer, Long, Single, Double, Currency, String, Date, Object, and Variant. To declare a non-array variable, we use the Dim statement in one of the following forms:

```
Dim varname As type
Dim varname
```

varname is a 1-255 character identifier, starting with a letter, containing any combination of letters, numbers, and the underscore character (_); *type* is a standard Visual Basic data type, user-defined type, or class module type. The following sections contain brief descriptions of the basic data types.

A.2.2 Boolean

A boolean variable only holds values of True and False, both of which are predefined identifiers in Visual Basic. Boolean variables are ideal for holding the values of logical expressions. The following are examples of declaring and assigning values to a boolean variable:

```
Dim blnContine As Boolean
blnContinue = True
blnContinue = intScore > 0
blnContinue = (intScore > 0) AND (intCount < 20)
```

Internally, Visual Basic represents True as –1 and False as 0.

A.2.3 Byte, Integer, Long

Whole numbers can be stored in variables of type Byte, Integer, or Long. Each has a different range of possible values:

> ***Programming Tip:*** You may notice that other sources of Visual Basic programs use the following abbreviations when declaring variables, but we don't recommend doing this:
>
> ```
> Dim intScore%       'Integer
> Dim lngMiles&       'Long
> Dim sngHeight!      'Single
> Dim dblWeight#      'Double
> Dim strLastName$    'String
> ```

Byte 0 to 255
Integer –32,768 to +32,767
Long –2,147,483,648 to 2,147,483,647

The following are examples of declarations and assignments:

```
Dim bytAge As Byte
Dim intScore As Integer
Dim lngMiles as Long
bytAge = 25
intScore = 25000
lngMiles = -123456789
```

A.2.4 Single, Double, Currency

Single, Double, and Currency variables hold non-integer values. The approximate range of each is shown:

Single: -3.4×10^{38} to -1.4×10^{-45}, and 1.4×10^{-45} to 3.4×10^{38}
Double: -1.8×10^{308} to -4.9×10^{-324}, and 4.9×10^{-324} to 1.8×10^{308}
Currency: -922,337,203,685,477.5808 to 922,337,203,685,477.5807

The following are examples of declarations and assignments:

```
Dim curBudget As Currency
curBudget = 123456789012345.1234

Dim sngPayRate As Single
sngPayRate = 25.5

Dim dblVelocity as Double
dblVelocity = 1234.5678901234
```

Single variables have 7 digits of precision, so if you try to assign a more precise number, it is automatically rounded off. For example:

```
Dim sngTemperature As Single
sngTemperature = 1.2345678        'stored as  1.234568
```

Double variables have 15 digits of precision. Currency variables are ideal for financial calculations, because they can store 15 digits to the left of the decimal point and 4 digits to the right.

Real number literals can be expressed in either fixed-point or scientific (exponential) notation. For example:

```
Dim dblVelocity As Double
dblVelocity = 1.2E+15
```

A.2.5 String

The String data type in Visual Basic is, by default, a variable-length string. In the 32-bit version of Visual Basic, a String can be as long as 2^{31} characters. String literals must be surrounded by double quotes:

```
Dim strLastName As String
strLastName = "Frankenstein"
```

The & character concatenates a string to another string, a number, or numeric variable:

```
Print "You worked " & hoursWorked & " hours this week."
Print "Hello " & "there!"
```

Fixed-Length Strings. A fixed-length string, once declared, cannot change size. This type of string can be processed more quickly by Visual Basic than a variable-length string. Any extra characters assigned to the string are truncated, and if there are fewer characters than the length of the string, the string is padded with spaces at the end:

```
Dim strZipCode As String * 5
strZipCode = "33156"
strZipCode = "33156-2364"           'stored as "33156"
strZipCode = "33"                   'stored as "33   "
```

A.2.6 Date

A Date variable holds both a date and a time as a single floating-point value. The value represents a date between January 1, 0100, to December 31, 9999, and a time of day between 0:00:00 and 23:59:59. Literal dates and times must be surrounded by # characters. For example:

```
Dim dtmBirthday As Date
Dim dtmAppointment As Date
dtmBirthday = #1/22/82#
dtmAppointment = #12:06:00 PM#
dtmAppointment = #4/6/98 14:00#
```

If you try to assign a date in a different format, such as #1982/01/22#, the Visual Basic editor will transform it to the format #1/22/82#.

IsDate Function. Visual Basic provides the **IsDate** function for validating times and dates. It returns True or False, depending on whether the input expression can be converted to a valid date or time. The general format is:

```
result = IsDate( expression )
```

The expression can be a string, the text property of a Text control, or a date literal. For example:

```
If Not IsDate( txtUserDate.Text ) Then
  Debug.Print "Invalid date: " & userDate
End If
```

A.2.7 Object

Object variables can hold forms, controls, or user-defined class objects. For example, you can assign Form1 to an object variable. The following does this, and prints "Hello" on Form1:

```
Dim objAny As Object
Set objAny = Form1
objAny.Print "Hello"
```

When assigning a value to an object variable, you have to use the **Set** statement.

A.2.8 Variant

A variable of type Variant can hold nearly any value except a fixed-length string or a user-defined type. When a value is assigned to it, the value implies its type. The following example demonstrates this:

```
Dim varAny as Variant
varAny = 1234
varAny = "A big lobster"
varAny = #7/4/96#
```

You can also declare a Variant by not specifying any type:

```
Dim varAny
varAny = 1234
(etc.)
```

Variants are useful in those rare situations when you cannot predict at design time what type of value will be assigned to a variable at run time. A Variant variable also takes a little more time to process than a typed variable, because the type of data inside the Variant has to be identified before the data can be used.

The **IsEmpty** function returns True if a Variant has not been intitialized. For example, we might want to assign zero to **varAny** if it has no current value:

```
If IsEmpty( varAny ) Then varAny = 0
```

A.2.9 Declared Constants

A declared constant is assigned a value when it is declared, and keeps this value throughout the program. The constant's type can be determined by the type of value assigned to it, but explicitly declaring the type is preferred:

```
Const intWeekDays As Integer = 5
Const intDaysInWeek As Integer = 7
Const strAuthor As String = "Juan Gonzalez"
Const sngPI As Single = 3.14159
```

A.2.10 Static Arrays

There are two types of arrays in Visual Basic: static and dynamic. To declare a static array, provide the lower and upper bounds in the Dim, Private, or Public statement. The following all declare one-dimensional arrays:

```
Public strNameTable(0 To 20) As String
Private sngScores(1 To 50) As Single
Private intCoordinate(-100 To 100) As Integer
Dim strCustomers(1 To 1000) As String
Dim sngPayRates(1 To 50) As Single
Public blnStatusFlags(0 to 9) As Boolean
```

The boundary values are integers in the range of a long data type (-2^{31} to $+2^{31} - 1$). It is possible to omit the lower bound, in which case it defaults to 0. The **Option Base** statement can be used to change the default to 1. The meaning of the array declaration is clearer if you provide both the lower and upper bounds.

A.2.11 Dynamic Arrays

A dynamic array is an array one that can be redimensioned at runtime. To declare a dynamic array, use Dim, Public, or Private with no array boundaries:

```
Public strNameTable() As String
Dim intCoordinate() As Integer
Private sngScores() As Single
```

Within a procedure, use the **ReDim** statement to assign an explicit size to the array. Notice that the array's type is not included, and the boundaries can be specified by either variables or constants:

```
Private Sub MySub()
   ReDim strNameTable(1 To NameCount)
   ReDim intCoordinate(xLow To xHigh)
   ReDim sngScores(0 to 99)
   '(etc.)
End Sub
```

You can ReDim an array only once in the same procedure, but you can ReDim an array throughout a program any number of times. If you need to preserve the current contents of the array, include the **Preserve** option with ReDim. Here, for example, we expand strNameTable by 10 entries and preserve its contents:

```
ReDim Preserve strNameTable(1 To NameCount + 10)
```

The standard UBound and LBound functions return the upper and lower boundary values of an array:

```
n = LBound(strNameTable)
n = UBound(strNameTable)
```

A.2.12 Collections

Visual Basic lets you create **collections**, which are both similar to, and more powerful than arrays. You can insert a list of names into a collection, for example:

```
Dim colMyFriends As New Collection
colMyFriends.Add "Tom"
colMyFriends.Add "Sue"
colMyFriends.Add "Dan"
colMyFriends.Add "Robert"
```

There is a specialized loop statement for dealing with collections, called **For Each**. Here, for example, we iterate over **colMyFriends** and print each name:

```
Dim varPerson As Variant
For Each varPerson In colMyFriends
   Debug.Print varPerson
Next varPerson
```

You can also use a numeric index to refer to collection members. The indexes range from 1 to Count, where Count is a property stored in the collection itself. Again, we display all of the names in the Debug window:

```
Dim j As Integer
For j = 1 To colMyFriends.Count
   Debug.Print colMyFriends(j)
Next j
```

A.2.13 User-Defined Types

A user-defined type is a unique data type created by the programmer, using the **Type** and **End Type** keywords. For example, the following declaration creates a type called Student, consisting of two data members, an ID number and a last name:

```
Type Student
   lngID As Long
   strLastName As String
End Type
```

The following statements declare a Student variable and assign values to its two data members:

```
Dim udtStudent As Student
udtStudent.lngID = 123456
udtStudent.strLastName = "Ramirez"
```

User-defined types provide an enormously useful way to collect related data inside a single variable, pass the variable to procedures, and write the variable to a file. Their only drawback is that they cannot be inserted into collections.

A.3 IF STATEMENTS

A.3.1 Compound Expressions (And, Or, Not)

No Short-Circuit Evaluation. When the AND operator is used to build a compound expression, VBasic does not use short-circuit evaluation. In the following compound expression, for example, we would like to verify that count is greater than zero before using it as a divisor. Visual Basic evaluates both expressions, resulting in a runtime error when count equals zero:

```
If (intCount > 0) And (curTotalSales / intCount > 500) Then
  frmSales.Print "Average Sales Over 500"
End If
```

The expression must be rewritten as a nested-IF statement:

```
If intCount > 0 Then
  If (curTotalSales / intCount > 500) Then
    frmSales.Print "Average Sales Over 500"
  End If
End If
```

A.3.2 Block IF Statement

An IF statement always contains a boolean (True/False) expression. For example, we assign a value of True to blnOverTime when the hours worked are greater than 40:

```
If intHours > 40 Then blnOverTime = True
```

This type of IF statement is not too flexible because only a single statement can be executed after the IF condition. In most cases, we prefer to use a block-IF statement, which can be expanded to include any number of statements after the condition:

```
If intHours > 40 Then
  blnOverTime = True
  strStatus = "Overtime hours worked"
End If
```

A.3.3 Using ELSE

Often, we insert an **Else** clause in the IF statement to handle both true and false alternatives:

```
If intHours > 40 Then
  blnOverTime = True
Else
  blnOverTime = False
End If
```

The **If-ElseIf** structure can be used when there are several alternatives. Be sure to make **ElseIf** a single word. Here, we determine the special fees paid by a student based on the number of enrolled credits:

```
If intCredits < 10 Then
  curFees = 0
ElseIf intCredits < 15 Then
  curFees = 100
Else
  curFees = intCredits * 10
End If
```

If statements can be nested, but the result is often difficult to read. The following example calculates student fees based on both the credits taken and the state residency status. Use structures like this only when necessary, and be sure to indent them carefully:

```
If intCredits < 10 Then
  If blnStateResident Then
    curFees = 0
  Else
    curFees = 50
  End If
ElseIf intCredits < 15 Then
  If blnStateResident Then
    curFees = 100
  Else
    curFees = 150
  End If
Else
  If blnStateResident Then
    curfees = intCredits * 10
  Else
    curFees = intCredits * 15
  End If
End If
```

A.3.4 Select Case

The **Select Case** statement provides a convenient multiway selection structure. Its syntax is:

```
Select Case testexpression
  [Case expressionlist-n
    [statements-n]] . . .
  [Case Else
    [elsestatements]]
End Select
```

testexpression can be any numeric or string expression, *expressionlist* is a list of expressions in one of the following forms:

```
expression
expression-1 To expression-2
Is comparisonoperator expression
```

Student Credits. For example, a simple program that lets the user input the number of college credits taken by a student can use the Select Case statement to display an appropriate message. Each of the basic expression types is demonstrated here:

```
Private Sub cmdEvaluate_Click()
  Dim strStatus As String
  Select Case Val(txtCredits.Text)
    Case 0
      strStatus = "Student not enrolled"
    Case 1 To 11
      strStatus = "Part-time student"
    Case Is > 11
      strStatus = "Full-time student"
    Case Else
      strStatus = "Credits cannot be negative!"
  End Select
  lblResult.Caption = strStatus
End Sub
```

A.4 LOOPS

There are two basic types of loops: counting loops and conditional loops. A *counting* loop is most effective when the number of times that a loop must repeat can be determined either at compile time or run time. A *conditional* loop is effective when the number of repetitions is determined by some input source and cannot be calculated before the loop begins. The For-Next statement is a counting loop; the Do-While, Do-Until, and While-Wend statements are conditional loops.

A.4.1 For-Next Statement

The For-Next statement creates a counting loop. It begins at *startval*, ends at *stopval*, and increments *counter* either by 1 or an optional value stored in increment:

```
For counter = startval To stopval [Step increment]
  '...
Next [counter]
```

For example, the following loop counts forward in the sequence: 0, 1, 2, ..., 48, 49, 50:

```
For intCount = 0 To 50
  Print "count = ";intCount
Next count
```

The following loop counts backward in the sequence: 20, 19, 18, ..., 1:

```
For j = 20 To 1 Step -1
  Print samples[j];
Next j
```

The following loop counts forward in the sequence -50, -48, -46, ..., 46, 48, 50:

```
For j = -50 To 50 Step 2
  Print j
Next j
```

A.4.2 Do-While Statement

There are two versions of the Do-While statement:

Pre-Test:

```
Do While condition
  loop body
Loop
```

Post-Test:

```
Do
  loop body
Loop While condition
```

If *condition* is True, the loop repeats; if *condition* is False, the loop stops. In the Pre-test version, the loop is never executed if the condition is initially False. In the Post-test version, the loop executes at least once before the condition is tested.

This type of loop is very useful when a value is input each time the loop repeats. For example, the following loop reads from a file until the end of the file has been reached:

```
Dim strRecord As String
Dim intFilenum as Integer
'(file is opened for input....)

Do While Not EOF(intFilenum)
   Input #intFilenum, strRecord
Loop
```

The following loop iterates through an array of integers, adding each to a sum, until one of the values in the array is less than or equal to zero. If the first number equals zero, no numbers are added:

```
Dim j As Integer, intSum as Integer
Dim intList(1 to 20) as Integer
j = 0
Do While intList(j) > 0
  j = j + 1
  intSum = intSum + intList(j)
Loop
```

A.4.3 Do-Until Statement

The Do-Until statement has two forms:

Pre-Test:

```
Do Until condition
  loop body
Loop
```

Post-Test:

```
Do
  loop body
Loop Until condition
```

If *condition* is False, the loop repeats; if *condition* is True, the loop stops. In the Pre-test version, the loop is never executed if the condition is initially True. In the Post-test version, the loop executes at least once before the condition is tested.

In the following example, we repeat the loop if the current number in the array is greater than zero, and the array subscript is <= 20:

```
Dim j As Integer, intSum As Integer
Dim intList(1 to 20) As Integer
j = 1
Do
  intSum = intSum + intList(j)
  j = j + 1
Loop Until (intList(j) <= 0) Or (j > 20)
```

A.4.4 While-Wend Statement

The While-Wend loop was a part of the old Microsoft QuickBasic language, and was probably retained in Visual Basic for compatibility. It works exactly the same as a Do-While loop, in which the condition is tested before the loop body executes:

```
While condition
  '...
Wend
```

A.5 PROCEDURES

Procedures are one of the fundamental building blocks of programs, because a procedure can perform a specific task as many times as the procedure is called. Visual Basic supports three types of procedures: subroutine, function, and property. A subroutine is a procedure that does not return a value. A function procedure always returns a value. A property procedure sets or returns the value of a property in a Form or class.

To insert a procedure into your program, open a code window for a Form, code module, or class module. Use the **Add > Procedure** menu command. The dialog window shown in Figure 1 appears. In this dialog, you would enter a name for the procedure, using the same rules for naming as we mentioned for variables. The three option buttons (Sub, Function, Property) determine which type of procedure is to be created. After clicking on OK, an empty procedure is inserted at the end of the code window.

A.5.1 Declaring a Subroutine Procedure

A *sub procedure* (or simply, *procedure*) is a procedure that carries out some action but does not return a value. The general syntax for declaring a sub procedure is

```
[ Public | Private ] Sub procedureName ( parameterList )
  (local variable and constant declarations)
  (zero or more statements)
End Sub
```

where *procedureName* follows the same rules as any Visual Basic identifier, and *parameterList* is an optional list of parameters. The parentheses after the procedure name

Figure 1. Add Procedure Window.

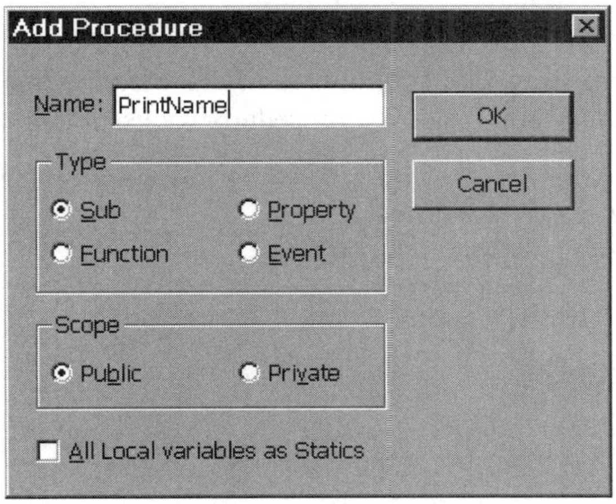

are required, even if the parameter list is empty. Public and Private refer to the scope of the procedure. A public procedure can be called from anywhere in a program, whereas a private procedure can only be called from the same Form or module.

A public sub procedure named SumArray with no parameters is declared as follows:

```
Public Sub SumArray()

End Sub
```

The parentheses at the end of the procedure name hold the procedure parameters, if any. Here is the same procedure declared with private scope:

```
Private Sub SumArray()

End Sub
```

A.5.2 Procedure Parameters

Procedure parameters are identifiers that appear in the header of a procedure definition that identify values that will be passed to the procedure. Most of the time, each parameter is assigned a data type, so Visual Basic can verify that the right types of values were passed to the procedure. A parameter list contains one or more parameters, separated by commas. Each parameter has the following syntax

```
[Optional][ByVal|ByRef][ParamArray]varname[()][As type]
```

where *type* can be Byte, Boolean, Integer, Long, Currency, Single, Double, Date, variable-length String, Object, Variant, a user-defined type, or an object type. **ParmArray** can be used only as the last item in a parameter list to indicate that the parameter is an optional array of Variant elements.

Examples. The **SumArray** procedure is declared with a single parameter called **count**, of type Integer:

```
Public Sub SumArrray(count As Integer)

End Sub
```

Or, we might declare SumArray with several parameters: the array being summed, a counter, and a variable to hold the sum. Inside the procedure, we use a loop to add the array elements:

```
Public Sub SumArray(intArray() As Integer, _
        intCount As Integer, intSum As Integer)
  Dim j As Integer
  intSum = 0
  For j = 1 To intCount
    intSum = intSum + intArray(j)
  Next j
End Sub
```

When calling a subroutine procedure in Visual Basic, do not surround the argument list with parentheses. The following statements call **SumArray** and display the sum in a message box:

```
Dim intArray(1 To 3) As Integer
Dim intSum As Integer
intArray(1) = 10
intArray(2) = 20
intArray(3) = 40
SumArray intArray, 3, intSum
MsgBox "The sum is = " & intSum
```

Terminology. Unfortunately, books and documentation are inconsistent in their use of the terms *parameter* and *argument*. In the Visual Basic documentation, procedure parameters are also called procedure arguments. In this book, we will consistently distinguish between parameters and arguments in the following way: A *parameter* appears in a procedure's declaration, whereas an *argument* is a value passed to a procedure. In the following example, **strTemp** is a parameter, and **strMsg** is an argument:

```
Public Sub Showme( strTemp As String )
  MsgBox strTemp
End Sub

Public Sub Main()
  Dim strMsg As String
  strMsg = "Passing an argument"
  ShowMe strMsg
End Sub
```

A.5.3 Declaring a Function Procedure

A *function procedure* (or simply, *function*) is a procedure that returns a value when the function is called. The general syntax is

```
[ Public | Private ] Function procedureName ( parameterList )
  As returnType
  (local variable and constant declarations)
```

```
    (statements)
    (ProcedureName = returnvalue)
End Function
```

where *procedureName* and *parameterList* are the same as for subroutine procedures, and *returnType* is the type of value that will be returned by the function.

For example, we might have declared SumArray as a function. Rather than make the sum a parameter, we can make it the function return value. The "As Integer" at the end of the line tells us that the function returns an Integer value:

```
Public Function SumArray(intArray() As Integer, _
        intCount As Integer) As Integer
   '...
End Function
```

When we implement the function, an extra variable named **intSum** is declared locally, and at the end of the function, the variable is assigned to the function name itself. This is how the function returns a value:

```
Public Function SumArray(intArray() As Integer, _
        intCount As Integer) As Integer
   Dim j As Integer, intSum As Integer
   intSum = 0
   For j = 1 To intCount
      intSum = intSum + intArray(j)
   Next j
   SumArray = intSum    '<--- function return value
End Function
```

When calling a function, surround the arguments with parentheses:

```
Dim intArray(1 To 3) As Integer, intNumVals As Integer
Dim intSum As Integer
intArray(1) = 10
intArray(2) = 20
intArray(3) = 40
intNumVals = 3
intSum = SumArray(intArray, intNumVals)
```

A.5.4 Passing Arguments by Reference

The **ByRef** keyword can be used before the name of a procedure parameter, indicating that the corresponding argument will be passed by reference. This is the default method for parameter passing in Visual Basic. The parameter inside the procedure is just another name for the object that was passed to the procedure. Any change the procedure makes to the parameter will automatically modify the argument that was passed to the procedure. Suppose, for example, that SumArray assigns zero to **intCount**:

```
Public Function SumArray(intArray() As Integer, _
        intCount As Integer) As Integer
   '...
   intCount = 0
End Function
```

Assuming that the procedure was called with an argument named **intNumVals**, we would find after the procedure call that intNumVals had also been set to zero:

```
intNumVals = 3
MsgBox SumArray(intArray, intNumVals)
' now intNumVals equals 0
```

Needless to say, this poses an obstacle to writing bug-free code, as it might be easy to forget that a parameter had been modified by a procedure. On the positive side, large objects such as arrays and Forms can be passed more efficiently by reference, because the compiler does not have to make a complete copy of the object before passing it to the called procedure.

A.5.5 Passing Arguments by Value

The **ByVal** keyword can be used before the name of a procedure parameter to assert that the corresponding argument will be passed by value. Passing arguments by value lets you avoid the side effects caused by passing by reference. When passing by value, any change to a parameter inside a procedure has no effect on the passed argument, because the procedure is only working with a copy of the original variable. In the next example, intCount is passed by value:

```
Public Function SumArray(intArray() As Integer, _
    ByVal intCount As Integer) As Integer
    '...
End Function
```

If you are unable to use ByVal in a procedure declaration, another way to pass an argument by value is to surround it with parentheses:

```
MsgBox SumArray( intArray, (intNumVals) )
```

Arrays and objects are always passed by reference. For example, if we try to pass Form1 by value, Visual Basic ignores the ByVal qualifier:

```
Public Sub SetCaption(ByVal F As Form)
  F.Caption = "This is a New Caption"
End Sub

Public Sub Main()
  Load Form1
  SetCaption Form1
  Form1.Show vbModal
End Sub
```

The parameter F is a *reference* to Form1, meaning that any modification to F is also a modification to Form1.

A.5.6 Private and Public

A procedure declared as **public** can be called from anywhere in a program. If the procedure belongs to a Form, the procedure name has to be attached to the Form name when the call is made. For example, from the Main procedure in module1.bas, we call **SumArray**, located in frmMain:

```
intSum = frmMain.SumArray( intArray, 3 )
```

On the other hand, if a public procedure is located in a code module (such as module1.bas), it can be called just by using its name:

```
intSum = SumArray( intArray, 3 )
```

A procedure declared **private** can only be called from the same Form or module. For example, all of the event procedures relating to a Form or its controls are declared private by default:

```
Private Sub Command1_Click()
  MsgBox "Command1 button was pushed"
End Sub
```

You can always change private to public. If Command1_Click were declared Public, for example, we could "push" this button from Main() in module1, although frmMain was not currently displayed:

```
Public Sub Main()
  frmMain.Command1_Click    '<-- "push" the button in frmMain
End Sub
```

A.5.7 Optional Parameters

Procedures can be declared with optional parameters. This means that one or more arguments can be omitted when the procedure is called. For example, we might have a procedure called **OpenFile** that can be called with or without a filename. If the filename is omitted, we display an InputBox and ask the user for a name:

```
Public Sub OpenFile( Optional varFilename As Variant )
  If IsMissing(varFilename) Then
    varFilename = InputBox("Name of file to open:", _
        "Opening File", "")
  End If
  '(etc...)
End Sub
```

Optional parameters must be type Variant. The standard **IsMissing** function returns True if the procedure argument has been omitted. Optional parameters must be at the end of the parameter list.

A.5.8 Parameter Arrays

The **ParamArray** keyword in a parameter list indicates that the parameter is an array of Variant parameters. This is the way that a Visual Basic procedure can have a variable-length parameter list. For example, the following **PrintItems** procedure has a parameter called **intCount** that indicates the number of parameters that will follow. The **items** array contains the rest of the parameters:

```
Private Sub PrintItems(intCount As Integer, ParamArray items())
  Dim j As Integer
  For j = 0 To intCount - 1
    Print items(j); ", ";
  Next j
End Sub
```

The procedure prints the items on the current Form. Notice that the **items** array is zero-based, and the passed arguments can be of any type. The following are examples of calls to this procedure:

```
PrintItems 3, "One", 26, Me.Caption
PrintItems 1, "Giraffe"
PrintItems 2, 126.35, 400.2
```

A.6 STRING HANDLING

Table 1 contains a list of standard Visual Basic statements, operators, and procedures that manipulate strings. Here are descriptions of the more important functions:

Asc. The Asc function provides a simple way to convert a character into its corresponding numeric ASCII code. For example, we might want to inspect the first character of a TextBox to be sure it is a digit:

```
Dim n as Integer
n = Asc( txtSalary.Text )
```

Chr. The Chr function is useful for representing non-displayable keyboard characters. Certain common character sequences are assigned predefined constants, as shown in Table 2. They can be used in any Visual Basic program, as long as **Visual Basic for Applications** has been selected in the Tools > References menu. For example, we often add a carriage-return/linefeed to the end of each line when inserting a string in a TextBox:

```
Dim strTemp As String
Dim curTotalSales As Currency
'...
strTemp = vbTab & "Monthly Income Report" & vbCrLf & _
  "-----------------------------------------" & vbCrLf & _
  "Sales of Computers......................" & _
  curTotalSales & vbCrLf
txtReport.Text = strTemp
```

Or, when printing a report, we can advance the printer to the next page by appending a Form feed character:

```
salesReport = salesReport & vbFormFeed
Printer.Print salesReport
```

CStr. The CStr function converts any expression to a string. The expression can be any valid numeric or string expression. CStr uses the international settings of Windows to perform conversions that recognize differences in numeric symbols such as decimal separators. For this reason, CStr is preferred to Str, which does not recognize international settings. The CStr function will generate a runtime error in one case: when trying to convert Null to a string.

A.7 FORMS

In this section we will discuss only the more often-used properties, methods, and event handlers associated with forms. A *property* basically behaves like a variable, or data value enclosed in the Form. A *method* is a procedure that carries out some action on the Form. An *event handler* is a procedure that is activated because of some action by the user or the operating system.

Table 1. String Statements, Procedures, and Operators.

Statement/Procedure/-Operator Syntax	Return Type	Description
+ &	String String	Concatenate two strings (+). Concatenate string to another string or numeric expression (&).
Asc(st)	Integer	Return the ASCII code of the first character in string <st>.
Chr(n)	String	Return a string containing the character that matches ASCII code in <n>.
CStr(exp)	String	Convert expression <exp> to a string.
Format(n, fst)	String	Format numeric value <n> using format string <fst>.
Instr([start,]st,srch)	Long	Find the character position of string <srch> inside string <st>, starting in position <start>. Return 0 if not found.
LCase(st)	String	Return <st> in all lowercase letters.
Left(st, n)	String	Copy <n> characters from the left side of string <st>.
Len(st)	Long	Find the length of string <st>.
result = st LIKE pattern	Boolean	Compare string <st> to <pattern>
LSet dest = source	String	Copy a <source> string to a <dest> string, left-aligned.
LTrim(st)	String	Remove all leading spaces from string <st>.
Mid(st, start, n)	String	Copy <n> characters from the middle of string <st>, starting in position <start>.
option compare Binary option compare Text	(none)	Set the default comparison method for strings to either binary or textual. Appears in module declarations.

Table 1 (cont). String Statements, Procedures, and Operators.

Right(st, n)	String	Copy <n> characters from the right side of string <st>.
RSet dest = source	String	Copy a <source> string to a <dest> string, right-aligned.
RTrim(st)	String	Remove all trailing spaces from string <st>.
Space(n)	String	Create a string containing <n> spaces.
Str(n)	String	Convert numeric value <n> into a string.
StrComp(st1,st2)	Integer	Return -1 if string <st1> less than <st2>; return 0 if <st1> equal to <st2>; return 1 if <st1> greater than <st2>.
StrConv(st, conv)	String	Convert string <st>, based on the type of conversion specified by <conv>. Sample values are vbUpperCase, vbLowerCase, vbProperCase, etc.
String(n, st)	String	Create a string containing <n> occurrences of character/string <st>.
Trim(st)	String	Remove both leading and trailing spaces from string <st>.
UCase(st)	String	Return <st> in all uppercase letters.
Val(st)	Number	Returns the numbers contained in string <st>.

Table 2. Predefined Character Sequences.

Predefined Constant	Character Sequence	Description
vbCrLf	Chr(13) & Chr(10)	Carriage-return/linefeed
vbNullChar	Chr(0)	Null character
vbCr	Chr(13)	Carriage return
vbLf	Chr(10)	Linefeed
vbBack	Chr(8)	Backspace
vbTab	Chr(9)	Tab
VbVerticalTab	Chr(11)	Vertical tab (not supported by Windows)
VbFormFeed	Chr(12)	Form feed

A.7.1 Form Properties

Of the following Form properties, some may only be set in design mode: Name, Appearance, BorderStyle, and StartupPosition.

Name. The Name property of a Form is used when referencing the Form in program code. For example, to print "Hello" on a Form whose Name property equals **Form1**, we would write:

```
Form1.Print "Hello"
```

Appearance. The Appearance property of a Form can be set to the following values in design mode.

- *Flat:* Changes the background color to the standard Windows background color.
- *3D***:** A standard Windows button face color is the default.

BackColor, ForeColor. Select the background and foreground colors for the Form. When you click on this property, a standard color pallete window will appear and you can select a color.

BorderStyle. The Borderstyle property can be set to one of the following values (predefined constants are shown in parentheses):

- *None:* The Form will have no border (*vbBSNone*).
- *Fixed single:* The Form will have a thin single-line border, and the Form cannot be resized by the user (*vbFixedSingle*).
- *Sizable:* The border is a thick line, and the user can resize the Form (*vbSizable*).
- *Fixed Dialog:* Appears as a Windows dialog box with thick borders, and cannot be resized. Has no minimize or maximize buttons by default, but you can add them back on (*vbFixedDialog*).
- *Fixed ToolWindow:* Appears similar to the Toolbox window that contains all of the Visual Basic controls. Cannot be resized (*vbFixedToolWindow*).
- *Sizable ToolWindow:* A ToolWindow that can be resized (*vbSizableToolWindow*).

Caption. The Caption property of a Form contains the text that appears on the title bar at the top of the Form. This also appears when the Form is minimized, on the Windows task bar.

Icon. The Icon property lets you select an icon that will be loaded into the Form's title bar, alongside the caption.

ControlBox. If set to True, this displays a standard Windows control box at the right side of the Form's title bar.

Font. Select the font and its properties (size, bold, underline, etc.) to be used when text is written to the Form. Under VB Help, look up the *Font* object for more details.

Left, Top, Height, Width. Set the screen position for the left side or top of the Form. Set the height and width of the Form. The unit of measurement is determined by the *ScaleMode* property, which defaults to *vbTwips*. Twips is a size measurement created for printers. There are 20 Twips per printer point and 72 printer points per inch, so there are 1440 Twips per inch.

It isn't easy to get your computer monitor to display absolute measurements. For example, a button that is 1440 Twips wide should be one inch wide on the screen. This depends on your video settings. The following table shows the actual viewing size of a 1440-Twip-wide button at various screen settings on a 19-inch monitor:

Screen Resolution	Width of Button, in Inches
640 X 480	2.5
800 X 600	2.0
1024 X 768	1.56
1152 X 864	1.38
1600 X 1200	1

MinButton, MaxButton. When these properties are True, the standard Windows minimize and maximize buttons are shown on the Form's title bar.

Moveable. When Moveable is set to True, the user can move (drag) the Form at runtime.

StartupPosition. This property sets the initial position of a Form. The values are *vbStartUpManual* (no initial setting), *vbStartUpOwner* (center within any enclosing window), *vbStartUpScreen* (center on the screen), and vbStartUpWindowsDefault (upper-left corner of screen).

Visible. If set to True, the Form will be visible to the user.

WindowState. The integer value of this property determines whether the Form will be first be displayed as *vbNormal*, *vbMinimized*, or *vbMaximized*. vbNormal is the default.

A.7.2 Form Methods

A *method* is a procedure that is attached to a specific type of object. Because a Form is a type of object, you can call Form methods. Table 3 describes a number of methods that are important when dealing with Forms.

Unload Procedure. The standard Visual Basic Unload procedure removes only the visual part of a Form from memory. The Form's properties and instance variables are still kept in memory.

The following statements, for example, load a Form called frmMain into memory, initialize one of its Label controls, show the Form, retrieve the contents of a TextBox on the Form, and unload the Form:

```
Load frmMain
frmMain.lblTitle = "Employee Payroll System"
frmMain.Show vbModal
employeeName = frmMain.txtLastName
Unload frmMain
```

This implies that when the Form was closed, the Form was simply hidden (with the Hide method), allowing us to access one of its controls. This can be a useful technique because a

Table 3. Frequently Used Form Methods.

Method	Description
Show	Display a Form (load the Form first if it is not already in memory.)
Load	Load the Form s visual portion into memory, but do not show the Form.
Hide	Remove the Form from the display, but do not unload its visual portion.
Cls	Clear all text from the Form.
Print	Display text on the Form, starting at the upper-left corner. Each call to Print writes text on a separate line.
PrintForm	Print a snapshot of the Form on the printer.
Move	Move the Form to a specific screen location.

Form may have a great deal of information that we want to use before the Form is unloaded.

Loading and Unloading Forms. To load a Form into memory without displaying it, use the Load statement. Once the Form is in memory, its properties and the values of its controls may be accessed. For example, the following statements load frmMain, modify its caption, and display it:

```
Load frmMain
frmMain.Caption = "This is frmMain"
frmMain.show vbModal
```

The Unload statement takes only the visual part of a Form out of memory.

Implicit Loading. If a Form is not yet in memory and you access one of its controls, the Form is loaded automatically (called *implicit loading*). For example, assuming that frmMain is not currently in memory, it will be loaded by the following statement:

```
frmMain.cmdCalculate.Caption = "Calculate Pay"
```

Show (Modal and Modeless). The **Show** method displays the Form as either a modal or modeless window. If a Form is shown modally, the current sequence of statements cannot continue until the Form is closed. The vbModal constant is predefined as the value 1. In the following example, frmStatus will not be shown until frmMain is closed (either by hiding it or unloading it):

```
frmMain.Show vbModal
frmStatus.Show vbModal
```

To show a Form as a *modeless* window, pass the predefined constant vbModeless as an argument to the Show method. In the following example, both forms will display simultaneously:

```
frmMain.Show vbModeless
frmStatus.Show vbModeless
' execution continues here...
```

Hide. The Hide method makes a Form disappear from the screen, but does not remove it from memory. This is useful when we still want to access data stored in the Form's controls. The following statements hide frmMain and then access the Form's Caption property:

```
frmMain.Hide
Debug.Print  frmMain.Caption
```

Cls, Print, PrintForm. The Cls method clears all text from a Form. The Print method lets one print a sequence of strings, variables, and numbers directly on a Form. The Form must be visible before the Print method is executed. The PrintForm method sends a snapshot of an entire Form to the printer. The following statements, for example, might be placed in a Form's Form_Activate event handler:

```
Private Sub Form_Activate()
   Print "Better Breakfasts, Inc."
   Print "Revision date: " & RevisionDate
   PrintForm                        'print a snapshot of the entire Form
End Sub
```

Unloaded, But Still There. Even when a Form has been unloaded, its properties and instance variables are still kept in memory. This can be an advantage if you need to retain the values of variables inside the Form, and do not want to lose them when the Form has been unloaded. On the other hand, the Form still uses up memory. The only way to completely remove a Form from memory is to assign to it a predefined value called **Nothing:**

```
Unload frmMain                'variables are still there
Set frmMain = Nothing         'now it's really gone
```

A.7.3 Form Events

When a program's startup Form is displayed the following events occurr, in order: **Initialize, Load, Activate.** When the program ends, the following events occur for any Form still on the screen, in order: **DeActivate, Unload, Terminate.**

Initialize. An **Initialize** event occurs when a Form is first created, or instantiated. The first time a Form is shown, for example, its Initialize event handler procedure executes. Or, an Initialize event will occur when a new instance of a Form is created, as in the following code:

```
Dim tempForm As Form
Set tempForm = New Form1
```

You can insert code in the Initialize event handler procedure, perhaps to open a data file associated with the Form:

```
Private Sub Form_Initialize()
  fileNum = FreeFile
  Open "myfile.txt" for input as fileNum
End Sub
```

Load. A **Load** event occurs after the visual part of a Form is being loaded into memory, but before the Form is visible. The Form_Load event handler procedure is executed immediately after the actual loading of the Form. Therefore, in this event handler, you can initalize properties of Form controls. For example, this Form_Unload handler sets both Form and control properties:

```
Private Sub Form_Load()
  Me.Caption = "Inventory Form'
  lblDate.Caption = Date
  lblCustomer.Caption = CustomerName
End Sub
```

Activate. An **Activate** event occurs when a Form becomes the active window. This can happen many times while the Form is visible, as the user can switch back and forth between forms in the same application. Each time a Form *gets the focus* (becomes active), its Activate event occurs. The Activate event does not occur, however, when the user switches between different application programs.

A Form's Activate event handler is a good place to put statements that initialize an ADO control. The following statements move adoStudents to the end of a table, get the number of records, and reset the cursor to the beginning of the table:

```
adoStudents.RecordSetMoveLast
numRecs = adoStudents.RecordSet.RecordCount
adoStudents.RecordSet.MoveFirst
```

Be sure to only place code in the Activate event handler that can be executed more than once without causing other errors in your program. Opening a file or table that is already open, for example, would cause a runtime error.

DeActivate. A **DeActivate** event occurs when a Form stops being the active window. We also call this *losing the focus.*

QueryUnload. A **QueryUnload** event occurs when a Form is about to be unloaded. The event might have been caused by the user clicking on the close button in the upper-right corner of the Form, by the application terminating, or by the Unload command in program code.

Resize. A **Resize** event occurs when the size of a Form changes. The Form might have been maximized, minimized, normalized, or the user may have resized it with the mouse. This event gives you the opportunity of adjusting other controls to match the size of the Form. For example, every time the current Form is resized, the following statements set the width of Text1 to 95% of the width of the current Form, and center Text1 on the Form:

```
Private Sub Form_Resize()
  If Me.WindowState <> vbMinimized Then
    Text1.Width = Me.Width * 0.95
    Text1.Left = (Me.Width - Text1.Width) / 2
  End If
End Sub
```

QueryUnload. A **QueryUnload** event occurs when a Form is about to be unloaded from memory. This might happen as a result of a user action, a program statement, or an event outside the application. The event handler procedure has two parameters, **Cancel** and **UnloadMode**. The first parameter, if set to True by your code inside the event handler, causes the unload operation to be cancelled. The second parameter indicates how the event was caused:

```
Private Sub Form_QueryUnload(Cancel As Integer, UnloadMode As Integer)
```

Possible values of UnloadMode are shown in Table 4.

You have the option of checking the UnloadMode value and printing an appropriate message. For example:

```
Private Sub Form_QueryUnload(Cancel As Integer, UnloadMode As Integer)
   Dim answer As Integer
   Select Case UnloadMode
      Case vbFormCode, vbFormControlMenu
         answer = MsgBox("Are you sure you want to close this window?", _
            vbQuestion & vbYesNo, "")
         If answer = vbNo Then Cancel = True
      Case vbFormMDIForm, vbFormOwner
         MsgBox "This Form's parent/owner is closing. All changes " _
                & "will be saved.", vbInformation, ""
   End Select
End Sub
```

Unload. An **Unload** event occurs after QueryUnload, just before the visual part of a Form is unloaded from memory. In the Form_Unload event handler, you might want to close files and databases and do other types of cleanup work.

Terminate. Just before a Form is destroyed, **Terminate** event occurs. The appropriate event handler is often used by programmers to release storage used by other objects, close files, and perform any other necessary cleanup. For example:

```
Private Sub Form_Terminate()
   Set colAllStudents = Nothing
End Sub
```

Table 4. UnloadMode Values.

Value	Description
vbAppTaskManager	Windows task manager is closing the application.
vbAppWindows	Current Windows session ending.
vbFormCode	Unload method invoked from code.
vbFormControlMenu	User has chosen Close command from Control menu box on Form.
vbFormMDIForm	MDI child Form is closing because the MDI Form is closing.
vbFormOwner	The owner of the Form is closing.

When a program shuts down, each Form's Terminate event occurs, whether or not the Form is loaded. A Terminate event also occurs when a Form variable is set to *Nothing*.

A.7.4 Sample Form-Loading Program

(samples: LoadForms)

To help clarify questions you might have regarding the loading and unloading of forms, their controls, and their properties, the program shown in Figure 2 provides a simple demonstration. The program consists of two forms: frmMain, the startup Form, and Form2, the Form displayed by frmMain. The command buttons on frmMain describe the various operations about to be performed. The following events occur as the program starts up:

```
Form1  Initialize
Form1  Load
Form1  Activate
```

When the user clicks on **Show Form 2**, Form2 is displayed. The following events have taken place so far, shown in the Debug window. We can see that Form1's Deactivate event occurred before Form2 became the active window:

```
Form2  Initialize
Form2  Load
Form1  Deactivate
Form2  Activate
```

On Form2, we display two counters: one shows the number of times the Form has been loaded, and the other displays the number of times the Form has been activated (the Activate event was executed). Initially, the counters are both equal to 1, shown in Figure 3.

Figure 2. Program that Loads and Shows Forms.

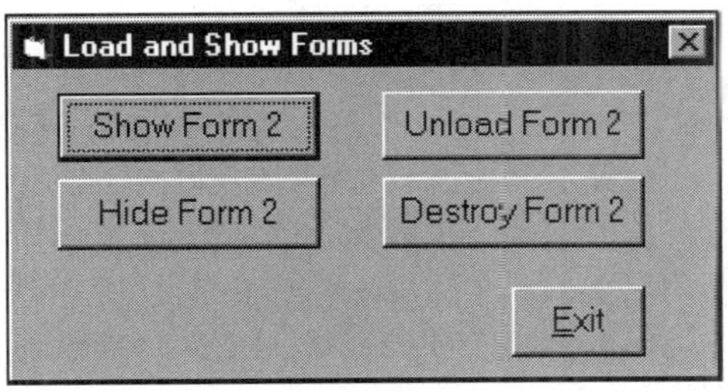

Figure 3. Showing the Number of Forms.

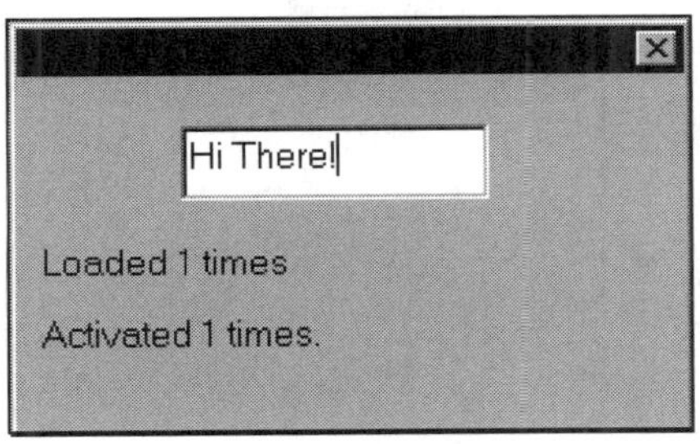

We can type a short message into Form2's TextBox, and click on the **Hide Form 2** button. The following events occur:

```
Form2  Deactivate
Form1  Activate
```

Next, we click on the **Show Form 2** button again. Form2 reappears, retaining the previous contents of the TextBox. All that has changed is that the **Activated** count now equals 2, shown in Figure 4.

Next, the user clicks on **Unload Form 2**, followed by **Show Form 2**. The following list of events shows that the Unload event took place:

```
Form2  Deactivate
Form1  Activate
Form2  Unload
Form2  Load
Form1  Deactivate
Form2  Activate
```

As we might anticipate, the TextBox has been cleared, and both counters have been incremented, shown in Figure 5.

When we click on the **Destroy Form 2** button, Form2's Terminate event occurs. When we exit the program, VB initializes Form2 again, unloads Form1, and then terminates both forms:

```
Form2  Initialize
Form1  Unload
Form1  Terminate
Form2  Terminate
```

Figure 4. Form 2 Reappears.

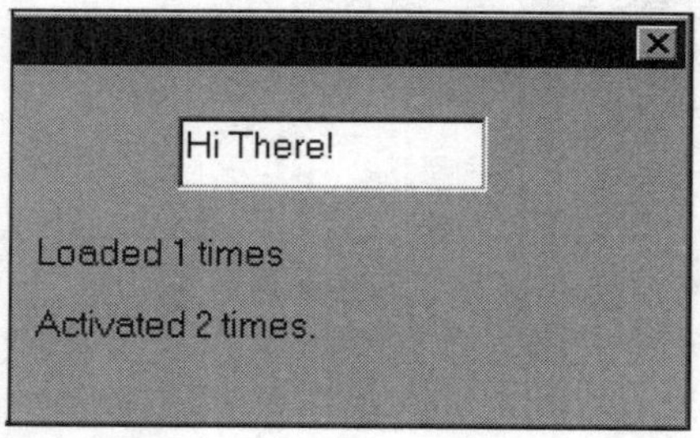

Figure 5. Form 2 Activated Again.

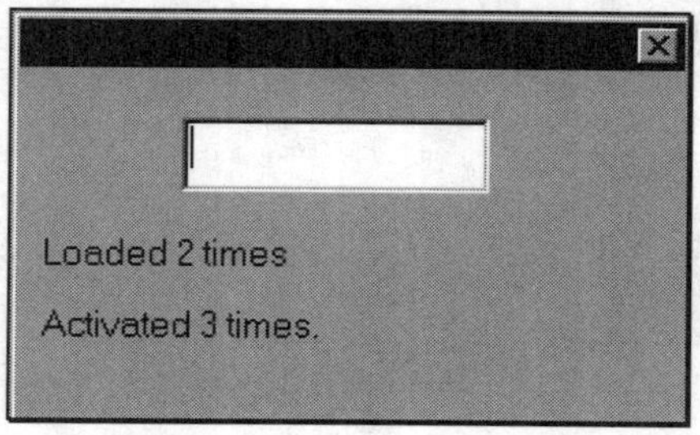

A.8 STANDARD VISUAL BASIC CONTROLS

A.8.1 Label

A Label control is used strictly for output for characters and numbers. Any value to be displayed should be assigned to its Caption property. Its Font, ForeColor, and BackColor properties are often given specific values. In general, we rarely deal with event procedures in labels. The following statement, for example, displays the current date in lblDate:

```
lblDate.Caption = Date
```

A.8.2 Text

A Text control is used primarily for input of text and numbers. It may be used for output, and at the same time allow the user to modify its contents. The Text property holds the characters that are both input and displayed. For example, we can print the contents of a text control called txtLastName on the printer:

```
Printer.Print  txtLastName.Text
```

The **Change** event alerts the program that the characters in the Text property have been modified. In the next example, the Change event handler calls the CalculatePay procedure when the contents of txtHoursWorked have changed and the value is greater than zero:

```
Private Sub txtHoursWorked_Change()
   If Val(txtHoursWorked.Text) > 0 Then
     CalculatePay
   End If
End Sub
```

Programming Tip: It's not a good idea to try to do calculations using a number typed by the user into a Text control. If the text is blank, Visual Basic will not automatically convert it into a number, and your program will stop with a *type mismatch* error. Instead, use the Val function to convert the text to a number; blank text will convert to a value of zero, which at least will not generate an error.

You can use the **MaxLength** property to limit the number of characters typed by the user into a text control. The **MultiLine** property should be set to True if you want to allow the user to type multiple lines of text. The **Locked** property can be set to True if you want to lock the contents of the TextBox and prevent it from being modified by the user. To right-justify numbers in a text control, set **Alignment** = Right Justify, and MultiLine = True. Horizontal and vertical scroll bars can be added to a text control by setting the **ScrollBars** property.

A.8.3 CommandButton

In all Windows programs, the user expects a command button to execute some action as soon as it is pressed. You can use the **Caption** property to change the text inside the button.

If the **Default** property equals True, the button will be pressed when the user presses the Enter key. If the **Cancel** property equals True, the button will be pressed when the user presses the Esc key. We often use the **Enabled** property to temporarily enable and disable command buttons. For example, the following sets cmdCalculate.Enabled based on the value of sngPayRate:

```
If sngPayRate > 0 Then
  cmdCalculate.Enabled = True
Else
  cmdCalculate.Enabled = False
End If
```

If you are clever with Boolean expressions, the foregoing can be simplified to the following:

```
cmdCalculate.Enabled = (sngpayRate > 0)
```

The **Click** event is the one we most often handle in program code. In the following, we call the CalculatePay procedure when the cmdCalculate button has been clicked by the mouse:

```
Private Sub cmdCalculate_Click()
  CalculatePay
End Sub
```

A.8.4 OptionButton

OptionButton controls are used to represent mutually exclusive choices. The Value property of an OptionButton may only be True or False. Within a group, only one OptionButton can be True, while the others are False. The Click event is the one we usually handle in program code. The following example sets sngRentalRate to 50.00 when the user clicks on the optLuxuryCar button:

```
Private Sub optLuxuryCar_Click()
  sngRentalRate = 50.00
End Sub
```

To query an OptionButton, check its **Value** property:

```
If optLuxuryCar.Value = True Then
  sngRentalRate = 50.00
End If
```

A.8.5 Frame

A Frame control is useful for grouping other controls. For example, when OptionButtons are enclosed in a Frame, they function as a single group. In the Form in Figure 6, buttons A and B form one group, while buttons X and Y form another group. This is why it is possible for both A and Y to be selected.

A.8.6 CheckBox

CheckBox controls have a Value property that can be equal to vbUnchecked(0), vbChecked (1), or vbGrayed (2). They are ideal for expressing independent options that can be Yes or

Figure 6. Option Button Groups.

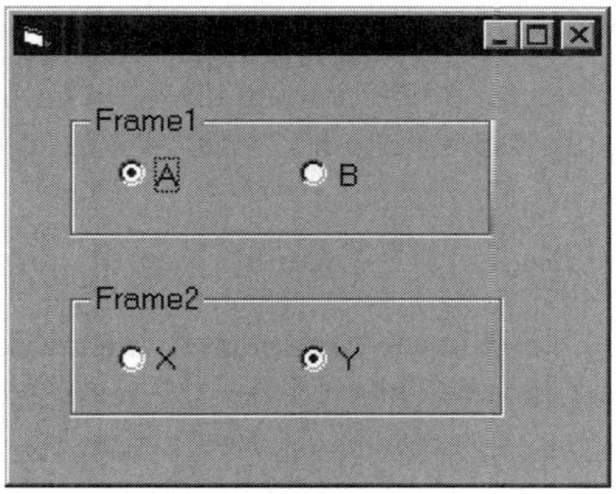

No. For example, each of the following check boxes can be checked or unchecked, as in Figure 7.

In program code we would query each CheckBox separately. For example:

```
If chkMultiCar.Value = vbChecked then sngDiscount = 0.10
If chkSafeDriver.Value = vbChecked then sngDiscount = sngDiscount + 0.15
If chkTheftProtect.Value = vbChecked then sngDiscount = sngDiscount +
0.05
```

Evaluating a CheckBox for a value of True or False does not work because Visual Basic represents True as −1 rather than 1.

A.8.7 Image

An image control displays a graphical picture on a Form. The picture might be an icon or other type of graphic file. You can set the **Picture** property in design mode to the name of a file, or you can use the **LoadPicture** function to load a file into an image control at run time:

```
imgPortrait.Picture = LoadPicture("jones.bmp")
```

Another important property is the **Stretch** property—when set to True, this property allows the image control to expand to accommodate pictures of various sizes.

Figure 7. Multiple CheckBoxes.

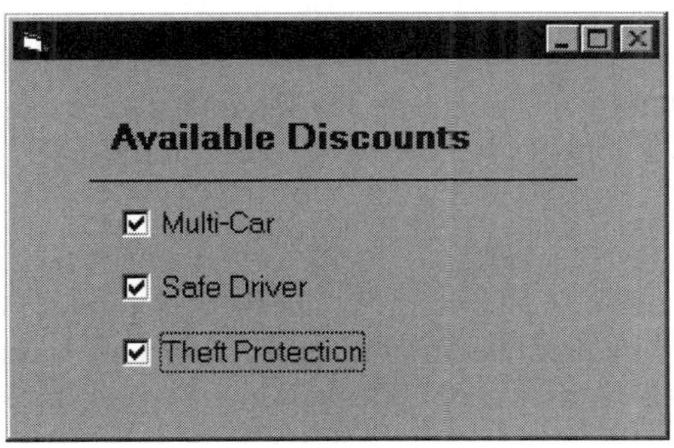

Graphics formats recognized by VB6 include bitmap (.bmp) files, icon (.ico) files, cursor (.cur) files, run-length encoded (.rle) files, metafile (.wmf) files, enhanced metafiles (.emf), GIF (.gif) files, and JPEG (.jpg) files.

An image control can also link its Picture property to an image in an ImageList control. The following statement assigns the image at index position 2 in an ImageList to an Image control called Image1:

```
Image1.Picture = ImageList1.ListImages(2).Picture
```

The following statement uses a key value in the **ListImages** collection to select an image. This is possible if a key was assigned to the image when the ImageList control was populated:

```
Image1.Picture = ImageList1.ListImages("OpenFile").Picture
```

A.8.8 Line

A Line control lets you place a line on a Form at design time. The small blocks, or handles that appear at the ends of the line can be dragged by the mouse. The **BorderWidth** property affects the width of the line. There are no events tied to line controls. The **BorderStyle** property affects the line style, being solid, dashed, dotted, and so forth. However, any line with a BorderWidth greater than 1 always displays as a solid line, regardless of its style.

A.8.9 Timer

A **Timer** control is ideal for controlling timed events, including animation. The **Interval** property measures (in milliseconds) the time between clicks. The Timer starts counting when its **Enabled** property equals True. The only event is the **Timer** event, which permits you to take action each time the timer clicks. For example, we can intialize a Timer when the current Form is loaded:

```
Private Sub Form_Load()
  Timer1.Interval = 1000
  Timer1.Enabled = True
End Sub
```

Not to be confused with Timer, the **Time** function returns the current time of day as a string. You can use a Timer control, however, to update a time display by calling the Time function once per second:

```
Private Sub Timer1_Timer()
  lblTime.Caption = Time
End Sub
```

Because the Timer control is affected by the Windows messsage queue, it cannot be expected to be precise. Think of it as an approximate measurement of time.

A.8.10 ScrollBar

The horizontal ScrollBar and vertical ScrollBar controls can be placed on a Form or other container at design time, and can be manipulated by the user. Each has a **Value** property that indicates the relative position of the button on the scroll bar. You set the **Min** and **Max** values to the smallest and largest values that the scroll bar can produced. The **SmallChange** property determines how much the button moves when the user clicks on a scroll arrow, and the **LargeChange** property determines how much the button moves when the user clicks between the button and the arrow. It is often useful to use the **Change** event to update a Label on the Form that displays the ScrollBar's current value:

```
Private Sub hsbFirst_Change()
  Label1.Caption = hsbFirst.Value
End Sub
```

A.8.11 ListBox and ComboBox

ListBox and **ComboBox** controls hold lists of strings. The strings might be the names of people, lists of inventory items, prices, state abbreviations, and so on. The items in a ListBox or ComboBox are usually related in some way. When the user selects an item by clicking on it, a **Click** event is generated. Table 5 contains a list of the ListBox and ComboBox properties that are used most often.

The **Selected** property is useful in ListBoxes that allow multiple selections by the user. In the next example, we loop through all of the ListBox items and count the number of ones that are currently selected:

```
Dim j As Integer, intCount As Integer
intCount = 0
For j = 0 To lstNames.ListCount - 1
```

Table 5. List Box and Combo Box Properties.

Property	Usage
Columns	Allows the use of multiple columns. When the first column fills with data, the second column is filled, and so on. (ListBox only)
List	An array of strings containing the items in the ListBox or ComboBox.
ListCount	A count of the items in the ListBox or ComboBox.
ListIndex	The row position (starting at 0) of the last item selected by the user.
NewIndex	The index position of the item most recently added to the list.
ItemData	Array of long integers in which each element corresponds to an item.
MultiSelect	When True, the user can select multiple items.
Selected	When True, the user selected this item.
SelCount	Returns the number of items currently selected.
Sorted	When True, the items are arranged in sorted order.
Text	A copy of the last item selected by the user.
TopIndex	Returns or sets the index of the item that appears in the top row.

```
  If lstNames.Selected(j) Then
    intCount = intCount + 1
  End If
Next j
```

The Selected property is an array in which each element corresponds to a different row of the ListBox. The **MultiSelect** property must be set to True if you want the user to make multiple selections.

The **TopIndex** property is useful when you want to use program statements to scroll a ListBox without selecting anything. The following statement, inside a Timer event handler, scrolls a ListBox downward one line each time a Timer event occurs:

```
Private Sub Timer1_Timer()
  List1.TopIndex = List1.TopIndex + 1
End Sub
```

Methods. There are three commonly-used ListBox and ComboBox methods, shown in Table 6. The following statements clear a list box and add four names:

```
lstNames.Clear
lstNames.AddItem "Joe"
lstNames.AddItem "Sam"
lstNames.AddItem "Ann"
lstNames.AddItem "Bob"
```

When the user clicks on a name, the following event handler code deletes it from the list box:

```
Private Sub lstNames_Click()
   lstNames.RemoveItem lstNames.ListIndex
End Sub
```

Using the ItemData Property. The ItemData property provides a convenient way of associating a long integer with each item in a List or Combo box. For example, you might want to save an ID number for each person listed in lstStationCrew:

```
With lstStationCrew
   .AddItem "Brooks. A."
   .ItemData(.NewIndex) = 1000
   .AddItem "Meaney, C."
   .ItemData(.NewIndex) = 1111
   .AddItem "Chao, R."
   .ItemData(.NewIndex) = 2000
End With
```

Table 6. List Box and Combo Box Methods.

Method	Usage
AddItem	Add a new item to a ListBox or ComboBox.
Clear	Remove all items.
RemoveItem	Remove one item.

Later, when the user clicks on a name, you can retrieve the employee's ID number and use it to look the person up in a database:

```
Private Sub lstStationCrew_Click()
  Dim id As Long
   id = lstStationCrew.ItemData(lstStationCrew.ListIndex)
   'search the database, using <id>...
End Sub
```

ComboBox Styles. There is one important ComboBox property that list boxes don't have: the **Style** property. It can be assigned one of three values, listed in Table 7. A *dropdown combo* is useful if an unanticipated value must be entered from time to time. The vbComboSimple style is rarely used. A dropdown list is useful when all choices are predetermined.

Table 7. Combo Box Styles.

Style Constant	Description
vbComboDropdown	Dropdown Combo: The user can select an item from the list or type a new value directly into the edit window of the combo box.
vbComboSimple	Simple Combo: The combo box does not drop down when clicked by the user. It is always visible.
vbComboDropdownList	Dropdown List: The user must select an existing item from the list; new values cannot be entered.

A.9 TOOLS FOR INPUT-OUTPUT

A.9.1 Print Method

The **Print** method may be used on either a Form or on the debug window. If you print multiple lines on a Form, the lines begin at the top line and continue to the bottom of the Form. For example:

```
For j = 1 To 20
  Form1.Print "This is line";j
Next j
```

In fact, most programs do not print directly on a Form; instead, they use Label and Text controls to display output at specific locations on the Form.

You can also print to the **Immediate** window, which appears only in the Visual Basic development environment. Once a program is compiled and run as an EXE file, debug output does not appear. The following type of statement can greatly help when debugging complicated programs:

```
Debug.Print "Hours worked = "; hoursWorked
```

A.9.2 Format Function

The **Format** function offers a powerful, flexible tool for formatting data in Visual Basic. Most of the time, you can choose from a number of standard formats when displaying numbers, dates, and times. In addition, you can create user-defined formats for numbers, dates, times, and strings. We will not discuss them here, but you can look up the topic "Format Function" in the Visual Basic help system for more information.

Formatting Numbers. When formatting a number, pass a numeric expression as the first argument, and a format string as the second argument. The function returns a string containing the formatted number:

```
resultString = Format( numExpression, "formatString" )
```

For the *formatString* parameter, you can choose among a set of predefined names. For each of the following formats shown in Table 8, we format the number **n** (containing 1234.5) and print it to the Immediate window. Many of the formats are affected by the regional settings in effect on your machine. To view the current settings in Windows, click on the Start button, select **Settings**, select **Control Panel** and click on the **Regional Settings** icon.

The **Yes/No** format displays "No" if the number is zero, and "Yes" for any other value. The **True/False** format displays "False" if the number is zero, and "True" for any other value. The **On/Off** format displays "Off" if the number is zero, and "On" for any other value. Run the following statements, for example:

```
Print Format(1, "Yes/No")       'Yes
Print Format(0, "Yes/No")       'No
Print Format(1, "On/Off")       'On
Print Format(0, "On/Off")       'Off
Print Format(1, "True/False")  'True
Print Format(0, "True/False")  'False
```

Table 8. Format Function Examples.

Format Statement	Result
`Format(n, "General Number")`	`1234.5`
`Format(n, "Currency")`	`$1,234.50`
`Format(n, "Fixed")`	`1234.50`
`Format(n, "Standard")`	`1,234.50`
`Format(n, "Percent")`	`123450.00%`
`Format(n, "Scientific")`	`1.23E+03`
`Format(n, "Yes/No")`	`Yes`
`Format(n, "True/False")`	`True`
`Format(n, "On/Off")`	`On`

The **Percent** format multiplies the number by 100 and appends a % sign.

Formatting Dates. You can also use predefined formats for dates with the Format function. Table 9 shows a sample of the current date and time formatted in a variety of ways. (The **Now** function returns the current system date and time.)

Table 9. Date and Time Formats.

Format Example	Result
`Format(Now, "General Date")`	`11/21/99 9:22:30 AM`
`Format(Now, "Long Date")`	`Thursday, November 21, 1999`
`Format(Now, "Medium Date")`	`21-Nov-99`
`Format(Now, "Short Date")`	`11/21/99`
`Format(Now, "Long Time")`	`9:22:30 AM`
`Format(Now, "Medium Time")`	`09:22 AM`
`Format(Now, "Short Time")`	`09:22`

A.9.3 MsgBox Procedure

The **MsgBox** procedure lets you pop up a small window from anywhere in a program and display a message to the user. The user has to click on the OK button to close the window before going on with the program. The general syntax is:

```
MsgBox message, options, title
```

message is a string that appears inside the message box. *Options* is an integer that specifies the type of icon and/or buttons that will appear in the box. *Title* is a string that will appear in the message box's title bar.

At the very least, you would want to pass a string containing the message as an argument to the procedure. For example:

```
MsgBox "Hours Worked must be greater than Zero."
```

This would produce the following window. Notice that by default, the project name appears in the window's title bar:

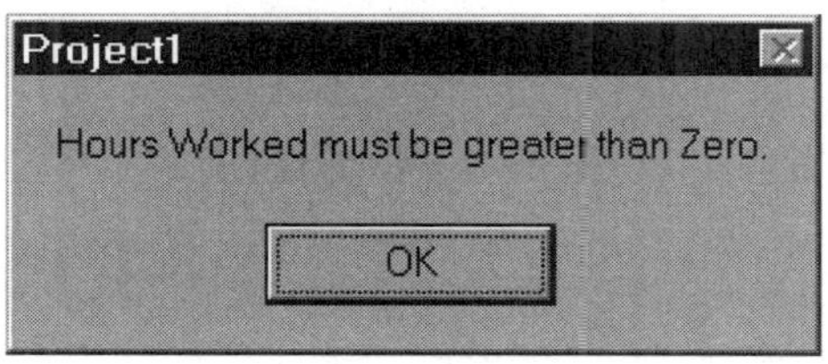

On the other hand, you might want to display an icon in the message box, as an attention-getter. The choices are:

vbCritical	Display a critical message (red circle with "X")
vbExclamation	Display a warning message (exclamation point)
vbInformation	Display an information message (letter i)
vbQuestion	Display a warning query (question mark)

For example, we will make our previous message a warning message:

```
MsgBox "Hours Worked must be greater than Zero.", _
       VbExclamation
```

Finally, we might want to change the title bar of the message box to the word "Error":

```
MsgBox "Hours Worked must be greater than Zero.", _
       vbExclamation, "Error"
```

This is the final version of our message window:

A.9.4 MsgBox Function

There are times when we also need to ask the user to confirm a question. In that case, MsgBox becomes a function and returns an integer that tells us which button the user clicked. The syntax is the same as the MsgBox procedure, except the function returns an integer value. For example, perhaps we would like to ask the user to confirm before exiting the program:

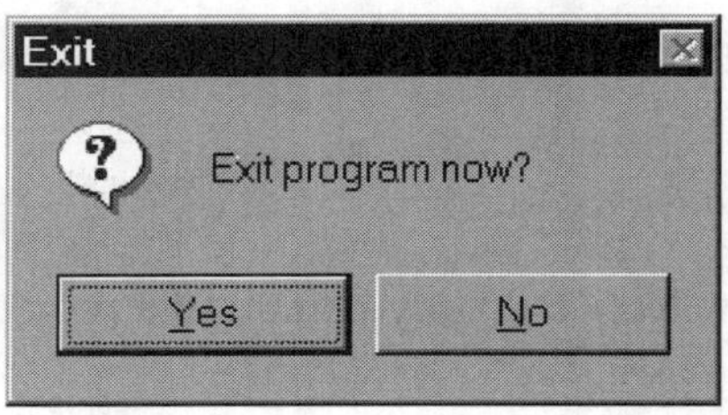

If the user clicks on the **Yes** button, the function returns a predefined integer constant called vbYes; if the **No** button is clicked, the value vbNo is returned. We can use this information in an If statement to decide whether or not the user wants to exit:

```
Private Sub cmdExit_Click()
  Dim choice As Integer
  choice = MsgBox("Exit program now?", vbYesNo _
         + vbQuestion, "Exit")
```

```
    If choice = vbYes Then Unload Me
End Sub
```

The possible return values of the MsgBox function are predefined constants, shown in Table 10. Each indicates a button pressed by the user. We also use constants to tell the function which buttons to display on the window.

The predefined MsgBox button constants are shown in Table 11. You can combine button and icon constants by adding them together. In our sample window, we used vbYesNo + vbQuestion, for example.

A.9.5 InputBox Function

Visual Basic provides a simple function called InputBox, which is an easy way to input a string from the user. Its general format is

```
retVal = InputBox( prompt, heading, default, xpos, ypos, helpfile, con-
text )
```

where the parameters are the following:

Table 10. Predefined MsgBox Return Values.

Constant	Value	Description
vbOK	1	OK button pressed
vbCancel	2	Cancel button pressed
vbAbort	3	Abort button pressed
vbRetry	4	Retry button pressed
vbIgnore	5	Ignore button pressed
vbYes	6	Yes button pressed
vbNo	7	No button pressed

Table 11. Predefined MsgBox Button Constants.

Constant	Value	Buttons Shown
VbOKOnly	0	OK button only (default)
VbOKCancel	1	OK and Cancel buttons
VbAbortRetryIgnore	2	Abort, Retry, and Ignore buttons
VbYesNoCancel	3	Yes, No, and Cancel buttons
vbYesNo	4	Yes and No buttons
vbRetryCancel	5	Retry and Cancel buttons

- *prompt* is a string that displays inside the window.
- *heading* displays in the window's title bar.
- *default* is a string placed in the user's input line.
- *xpos* is the horizontal distance from the edge of the screen to the window's left side.
- *ypos* is the vertical distance from the edge of the screen to the top of the window.
- *helpfile* is the name of a help file containing context-sensitive help.
- *context* is the help topic number inside *helpfile*.

The function's return value is the string typed by the user when the window was closed. If the user clicked on the Cancel button, the return value is an empty string. For example, let's ask the user for his/her last name. By default, the title bar contains the name of the project:

```
lastName = InputBox("What is your last name?")
```

The resulting input box is shown in Figure 8. We might also want to put a default string in an input box asking for the name of a file to be opened. If the user clicks on Cancel, the original file name is retained:

```
Dim fileName As String, temp As String
fileName = "default.txt"
temp = InputBox("Enter the name of the file to be opened:", _
    "Open File", fileName)
If Len(temp) > 0 Then fileName = temp
```

A.9.6 Printer Object

The Printer, Screen, and App objects are automatically created in a Visual Basic program. The Printer object lets you communicate with whichever printer is currently set as the default printer.

- The Orientation property orients the paper direction, and may be set to either vbPRORPortrait (vertical) or vbPRORLandscape (horizontal).
- The NewPage method ends the printing of the current page.

Figure 8. InputBox Function Example.

- The Print method prints text and numbers to the printer.
- The EndDoc method ends the printing of the current document.

The following statements, if placed inside a command button, will print the contents of a text control called txtAddress with a sideways orientation:

```
Printer.Orientation = vbPRORLandscape
Printer.Print txtAddress.Text
Printer.EndDoc
```

Of course, there are many other properties and methods. To find out about them, look under the topic "Printer Object" in the Visual Basic help system.

A.9.7 Screen Object

The Height and Width properties of the Screen object contain the height and width of the screen, measured in Twips. The following example uses these properties to center a Form on the screen:

```
Dim top As Integer, left As Integer
top = (Screen.Height - Me.Height) \ 2
left = (Screen.Width - Me.Width) \ 2
Me.Top = top
Me.Left = left
```

First, we calculate the difference between the screen height and the Form's height. Then, we calculate the difference between the screen width and the Form's width. Using this information, we set the Top and Left properties of the Form.

The MousePointer property can be used to change the mouse to an hourglass when the user has to wait for some operation to finish. For example:

```
Screen.MousePointer = vbHourglass
'  do something that takes time...
Screen.MousePointer = vbDefault
```

A.9.8 Application Object

The **App** object is a global identifier for the current program (called an *application*). You can use it to access information about the program's title, the path and name of its executable file and help files, and whether or not another instance of the application is running.

- The **PrevInstance** property equals True when another instance of the same program is currently running.
- The **Path** property equals the complete pathname of the program, from the drive letter through the directory where the program is stored.
- Version Information such as the major and minor version numbers, company name, product name, and copyright notice.

Use the Path property to reset the current drive and directory to the same location as the program's path. If your program uses Main Sub as the startup procedure, place the following statements in Main:

```
ChDrive  app.Path
ChDir    app.Path
```

Or, if your program uses a startup Form, place these statements in the Form_Load procedure.

A.10 CREATING MENUS

From the user's point of view, a command button is the simplest type of command interface. Most programs have a sufficient number of commands that it becomes impractical to activate all commands with buttons. Instead, programs generally use menus to provide a heirarchy of commands. Visual Basic provides the Menu control as the vehicle for displaying menus and responding to menu events. Any Form having a caption bar may contain a menu. In design mode, we use the Tools/Menu Editor command to create menus.

A.10.1 Common Menu Types

If appropriate to the program, the first submenu on the left is the **File** menu. It contains commands such as New, Open, Close, Save, Save As, Delete, Import, Print, and Exit. If any of your program's commands relating to files or documents seem to fit into this list, you will probably want to create a File menu.

The next menu is the **Edit** menu. Some common commands on this menu relate to Windows clipboard operations: Cut, Copy, Paste, and Clear. Find, Replace, Go To, and Bookmark commands appear on the Edit menu. Any operations that modify the current document or file can be placed on this menu.

Many programs have a **Tools** menu, an **Options** menu, a **Window** menu, and a **Help** menu. In many cases, the Options menu is the last choice on the Tools menu. The Window menu is useful for resizing, arranging, and locating individual windows that might be open at the same time. The Help menu is generally the last menu on the right.

If you want to get a feel for well-designed menu structures, look at some of the Windows applications software from Microsoft and other leading companies.

A.10.2 Creating a Simple Menu

Let's try a simple hands-on example that demonstrates the process of creating a menu. Create a project with a single Form, called **frmMain**. With frmMain displayed, click on the Tools menu and select **Menu Editor**. Each menu item must be assigned both a caption and name. For example, for the main File menu heading, we would enter the following property values:

Caption: &File
Name: mnuFile

Figure 9. Creating a File Menu.

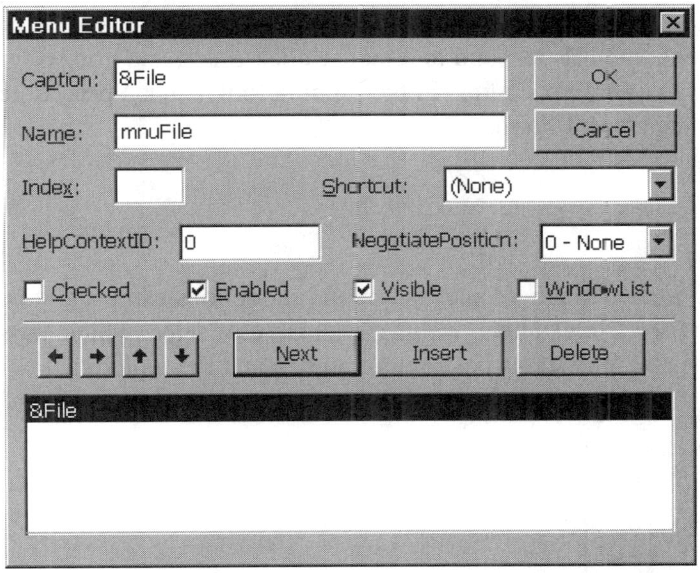

The & before the letter F will cause the letter to be underlined when the menu appears. The user will be able to activate the File menu by pressing Alt-F. Figure 9 shows the menu editor as the File menu is being created.

After entering the caption and name for a menu choice, click the **Next** button, and type the following menu choices:

Caption: E&xit
Name: mnuFileExit

But this menu choice should appear only when the user clicks on the File menu. To make this work, click on the arrow pointing to the right—this will indent the word "Exit" to the right in the window in the lower half of the menu editor.

Finally, from the Shortcut combo box, select Ctrl-X as the shortcut key for the File/Exit command. This will allow the user to activate the command more quickly. Notice that the shortcut key appears in the menu next to its matching command.

A.10.3 Menu Properties

Notice that you can decide whether each menu choice will be checked, enabled, and visible when the program starts up:

Programs typically disable or render invisible any menu choices that are not appropriate at a given time. If a file is not open, for example, most programs will disable the Edit menu. But making a menu disappear completely is an extreme step that could confuse the first-time user of a program. There are a number of other useful menu properties, shown in Table 12 which we will use in later chapters.

Menu Events. Menu controls respond to a mouse click event, and you will want to write code in the corresponding procedures. In the mnuFileExit_Click() procedure, for example, we might unload the current Form:

```
Private Sub mnuFileExit_Click()
  Unload Me
End Sub
```

Checked Menu Choices. Menu choices that represent options can usually be checked or unchecked by the user. For example, we might let the user select which parts of the current program will be visible: the status bar, the button bar, and the toolbox:

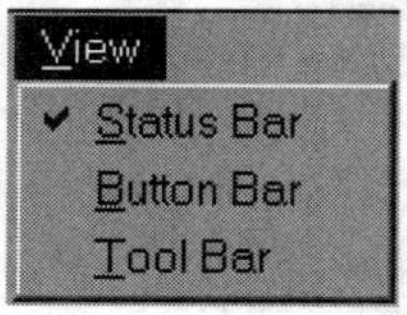

The actual checking and unchecking of these choices must be handled by code in the event handlers of these menu choices. For example, we could simply reverse the value of the Checked property for each menu choice:

Table 12. Menu Properties.

Property	Description
Caption	Required: Text that appears in the user's menu at runtime.
Checked	If True, a check appears next to the menu item when the Form is displayed.
Enabled	If True, user may click on the menu item; if False, the menu item is grayed and may not be selected by the user.
HelpContextID	An integer that refers to a matching help topic in the help file identified by the HelpFile property.
Index	Determines the item's position within a control array; not related to the item's position within the menu on the screen.
Name	Required: Identifier for menu item used in program code.
NegotiatePosition	Determines whether and how the menu appears when it is on a Form that has an OLE container control.
Shortcut	A keyboard shortcut key (such as Ctrl-S) can be assigned to the menu item.
Visible	If True, the menu item will be visible at runtime; otherwise, the item will not appear.
WindowList	If checked, the menu will display a list of open MDI (Multiple Document Interface) child forms.

```
Private Sub mnuViewStatusbar_Click()
   mnuViewStatusbar.Checked = Not mnuViewStatusbar.Checked
End Sub

Private Sub mnuViewButtonbar_Click()
   mnuViewButtonbar.Checked = Not mnuViewButtonbar.Checked
End Sub

Private Sub mnuViewToolbox_Click()
   mnuViewToolbox.Checked = Not mnuViewToolbox.Checked
End Sub
```

A.11 ANSWERS TO THE COMPETENCY TEST QUESTIONS

1. Boolean, integer, byte, long, single, double, currency, string, date, object, and variant.
2. Variables that are declared in a module's general declaration section (module-level variables) have meaning (are visible) anywhere in the module. Variables that are declared within a procedure (procedure-level variables) have meaning (are visible) only within that procedure.
3. Forms, controls, and user-defined objects.
4. A variable of type Variant can hold a value of any data type with the exception of fixed-length strings and user-defined types.
5. The dynamic array may be resized to accommodate more or less data while the programming is executing.
6. Code Segment:

```
If HrsWrkd <= 40 Then
   GrossPay = HrsWrkd * HrlyRate
Else
   If UnionMember = True Then
      GrossPay = 40 * HrlyRate + (HrsWrkd - 40) * HrlyRate * 1.75
   Else
      GrossPay = 40 * HrlyRate + (HrsWrkd - 40) * HrlyRate * 1.50
   End If
End If
```

7. Code Segment:

```
Dim Score(1 to 100) as Integer
Dim Average as Single
Dim Tot as Integer, K as Integer
For K = 1 to 100
   Tot = Tot + Score(K)
Next K
Average = Tot / 100
```

8. Code Segment:

```
K = 1
Do While (strName <> Name(K)) AND (K <=100)
   K = K + 1
Loop
Form1.Print K
```

9. A Form's Name property is used to identify the Form from within a program, typically to execute a method; e.g., Form1.Show or Form1.Print "Hello World".
10. A method is a procedure or action that is associated with an object. Unlike an event, it is not initiated by the user. Examples of methods associated with a Form include Show, Hide, Cls, and Print.
11. The *Load* statement directs Visual Basic to retrieve a Form from disk and place it in memory (it is not necessarily displayed/shown). The *Show* method directs Visual Basic to actually display (and possibly load) a Form.
12. A Label's use is restricted to output only while a TextBox may be used for both input and output.
13. The command button is used to initiate an action, to cause something to happen.
14. When the command button's Default property is set to True, pressing the Enter key is equivalent to clicking the command button.
15. Both controls are alike in that they allow the user to make a choice from a finite list. They are not alike in that option buttons are mutually exclusive - selecting one deselects all others. The user may select none, one, all, or any combination of check boxes.
16. A frame is typically used to group a set of controls such as option buttons or check boxes.
17. Subroutines and functions are alike in that they are both building-block subprogram units. They are different in that the function always returns a value to the calling program unit whereas the subroutine may return no values, one value, or many values.
18. Passing arguments by reference allows the receiving program unit to alter and return that altered value/argument to the calling program unit. Passing arguments by value means that even though the receiving program unit may alter the argument, the altered value is not returned to the calling program unit.
19. A procedure declared with the Public keyword allows the procedure to be called from anywhere in the project. A procedure declared with the Private keyword restricts procedure calls to the Form or module which contains the procedure.
20. Form1.Print Format (Net_Pay,"currency")
21. The MsgBox procedure creates a standard Windows pop up dialogue to display a message to the user.
22. Including the Option Explicit command in a program forces the explicit declaration of all variables (and their corresponding data types). This means that variables may not be used within the program unless they have been declared.

23. A control's TabIndex property determines the order in which a control receives the focus when the user uses the tab key to move from control to control.

24. The MsgBox function's return value is assigned to a variable so that the program can determine, for example, which key was pressed by the user when responding to the MsgBox dialogue. The MsgBox statement does not assign a return value to a variable and is used primarily to halt program execution until the user responds to the dialogue.

25. The List property is an array which contains the contents of the list box.

26. The Clear method removes all entries from a list box whereas the RemoveItem method removes a single entry from the list box.

27. Input, Output, and Append.

28. The On Error Goto statement is used to direct program control to a location in the program where an error-handling routine can be found. When an error occurs, the code at that location is enabled.

29. The Resume statement is used to direct Visual Basic to resume processing at the line following the one that caused an error.

30. The Err object is created whenever a runtime error occurs. The Err object's *Number* and *Description* properties are used to identify and describe the runtime error. Use of both of these properties are typically placed in an error handler.

Appendix B: Sequential and Random Files

Chapter Contents

Sequential Files
- Basic Syntax
- Reading from an Input File
- Writing to an Output File

Random access Files
- Opening a File
- Writing Records
- Reading Records
- Example: Customer Accounts Program
- Program Design
- Program Implementation

B.1 SEQUENTIAL FILES

For small amounts of information that must be used by your programs, sequential files are simple and convenient to use. Small sequential files may be read more quickly than databases, because the latter require the loading of a number of DLL libraries at run time. A "small" sequential file might be one containing only a few thousand characters or less. Another advantage to using sequential files is that they can be modified with almost any text editor, such as the DOS **Edit** program or the Windows **NotePad** program.

B.1.1 Basic Syntax

The Open Statement. The Open statement prepares a disk file for input or output. Informally, the syntax is

```
Open pathname For mode As [#]filenumber
```

where *pathname* is either a file name or a complete path and filename, starting with the drive letter. *Filenumber* is an integer that identifies the file for further input or output. *Mode* is one of the following:

- **Input**: Open an existing file for input only. Data may be read from the file, using the Input and Line Input statements.
- **Output**: Create a new file, truncating any existing file by the same name. Data may be written to the file, using the Write and Print statements.

- **Append**: Add data to the end of an existing file, or create a new file if the file does not already exist.

The file number is usually 1, 2, or 3, depending on whether or not other files are currently open, and two open files cannot share the same number. The following example opens a file called **names.txt** for input, a file called **scores.dta** for output, and a file called **logfile** for appending. Each must be assigned a different file number:

```
Open "names.txt" For Input As 1
Open "scores.dta" For Output As 2
Open "logfile" For Append As 3
```

Obtaining a File Number. The **FreeFile** function returns the next available file number, which guarantees that you will not accidentally try to use a file number that is already in use. In the following example, we call FreeFile, assign its result to fileNum, and use fileNum in the Open statement:

```
Dim fileNum as Integer
fileNum = FreeFile
Open "names.txt" for Input as fileNum
```

The Close Statement. To close a file, refer to its file number. The syntax is:

```
Close filenumber
```

If you forget to close an input file, the filenumber value cannot be used with another file, and memory used by the file is not released. If you forget to close an ouput file, data that your program has written to the file may not be saved in the file. This is because output data is written to a memory buffer and held there until the buffer is full, or the file is closed. At that time, the buffer is "flushed", meaning that the data in the buffer is physically written to disk.

B.1.2 Reading From an Input File

Example: Automobile Models File. In a car rental program, we might want to create a text file containing the names of available automobile models and their daily rental prices. This can easily be done with the Windows Notepad editor, placing each model name on a single line followed by its daily rental price on the next line:

```
Ford Aerostar
50
Mercury Villager
45
Chevrolet Cavalier
47
Dodge Aspen
50
Toyota Camry
55
Lincoln Continental
75
```

After typing this data into Notepad, we would select the **File > Save As** menu command and call the file **models.txt.** In a Visual Basic program, we would write the following statement to open the file for input:

```
Dim fileNum As Integer
fileNum = FreeFile
Open "models.txt" For Input As fileNum
```

To read a single model name from the file, we use the Input statement. This would be followed by a statement to read the corresponding price:

```
Dim modelName As String, price As Single
Input #fileNum, modelName
Input #fileNum, price
```

There are two general approaches used when opening and closing files:

- Open a file when the program starts, leave it open, and close it only when the program ends. This is an acceptable approach, unless an excessive number of files are left open at the same time. An advantage to this approach is that the current file pointer position is retained across procedure calls.
- Open and close a file within the same procedure. An advantage to this approach is that you will be more likely to remember to close the file. A disadvantage is that if the procedure is called repeatedly, some processing time is lost due to the opening and closing of the file, and the current file position is reset to the beginning of the file each time the file is opened. If the same file is being used for both input and output, the file must be closed and re-opened when switching between input and output modes.

Reading Multiple Variables. If an input file contains multiple variables, they must be separated by commas, and string values might have to be enclosed in quotation marks. The latter is particularly true when the strings contain embedded commas. In the following file, each record contains a complete customer name and an account balance. The quotes around each name tell Visual Basic to consider the name a single string value:

```
"Jones, Larry", 200.50
"Baker, Sam", 120.40
"Johnson, Susan", -50.00
(etc.)
```

The following Input statement reads a single record:

```
Input #fileNum, custName, acctBalance
```

Reading All Records. To read all records from an input file, use a looping statement that calls the EOF function to check for end of file. If each record is to be kept in memory, insert it in a ListBox, ComboBox, or array. The following procedure reads a customer name and account balance from an input file. The name is inserted in a ListBox, and the account balance is inserted in an array:

```
Private balance(0 to 100) as Single

Public Sub ReadNameFile()
  Dim fileNum As Integer, j As Integer, custName As String
```

```
    fileNum = FreeFile
    j = 0
    Open "names.txt" For Input As fileNum
    Do Until Eof(fileNum)
      Input #fileNum, custName, balance(j)
      List1.AddItem custName
      j = j + 1
    Loop
    Close fileNum
  End Sub
```

Notice from the example that **balance**, the array of customer balances, would probably be declared at the module level—this would allow it to be accessed by other procedures. Also, be sure to increment the array subscript before reading each subsequent record. The array subscript in our example was **j**.

Line Input. The Line Input statement reads an entire record, including all commas and quotes, into a single string:

```
Dim rec As String
'...
Line Input #fileNum, rec
```

The Line Input statement is particularly useful when the data is not in a standard readable format, and you need to manually separate the record into individual fields. For example, each record might contain some other type of field delimiter:

```
Jones, Larry\200.50
Adams, Bill\325.20
```

B.1.3 Writing to an Output File

A file must already be open in the Output or Append mode before data can be written to the file. There are two statements that write to sequential files: Print and Write. The **Print** statement writes data to the file exactly as it would appear on the screen. For example:

```
name = "Bob Jones"
age = 54
Print #1, lastName;",";age
```

This would store data in the file as: Bob Jones, 54

The **Write** statement, on the other hand, automatically surrounds strings with quotation marks and places a comma separator between variables:

```
name = "Bob Jones"
age = 54
Write #1, lastName,age
```

This would store data in the file as: "Bob Jones", 54

Writing All Records. To write all records from an array or ListBox to a file, set up a loop with a subscript. The following procedure writes all names from a ListBox to a file, along with the contents of an array called balance. This is the counterpart to a procedure we showed earlier called ReadNameFile:

```
Private balance(0 to 100) as Single

Public Sub WriteNameFile()
  Dim fileNum As Integer, j As Integer
  fileNum = FreeFile
  Open "names.txt" For Output As fileNum
  For j = 0 To List1.ListCount - 1
    Write #fileNum, List1.List(j), balance(j)
  Next j
  Close fileNum
End Sub
```

Programming Tip: If you are storing data in a file that will later be used as an input file, use the Write statement because it formats the data in a way that is easily readable by Visual Basic. On the other hand, if you are printing a report or some other document that will not be used as an input file for a Visual Basic program, use the Print statement.

B.2 RANDOM ACCESS FILES

Random access files provide an efficient way of storing and retrieving data in such a way that records may be modified selectively. Sequential files may only be processed in sequential record order, hence the name *sequential.* Processing begins at the first record, and continues in sequence to the last record, unless the process is halted and the file closed. A random access file, on the other hand, does not have to be processed in sequence. You can select any record, read it, and modify it in place.

There are some other important differences between sequential and random access files:

- Each record in a random access file is identified by a unique integer between 1 and 2,147,483,647, called a *record number*. Sequential files do not explicitly number their records.
- A sequential file may not be open for both input and output at the same time. Random access files, on the other hand, can be open for both operations at the same time.
- Sequential records can vary in length. Random access file records must all be the same length, for a very good reason: the physical position of any record can be found by multiplying the record number by the record length.
- Sequential records are translations of internal binary data into a text representation. Random access records require no such translation.
- When opening a random access file, the record length must be supplied by the programmer. In addition, a user-defined type is usually created that matches the layout of fields in each record. A sequential file has no such requirement. Different records may contain completely different sequences of fields.

Once a random access file has been created, changing the lengths of its records is somewhat difficult. A new record description would have to be created, a new file opened, and all records would have to be copied from the old file to the new one. When designing the record layout for a random access file, programmers will sometimes leave some slack space at the end of each record for additional data, to avoid having to undergo the time-consuming file copy process we just described. *Note:* Random access files are not database files. Databases are introduced in Chapter 5.

B.2.1 Opening a File

The general syntax for opening a random access file is

```
Open pathname For Random [Access access] As filenumber Len=reclength
```

where *pathname* is the directory path plus the filename, and *reclength* is the integer length of each record in the file. The value of *access* indicates the types of operations that will be permitted on the file: **Read**, **Write**, or **Read Write**. If *access* is omitted, Read Write is assumed. For the pathname, it is suggested that you use a distinctive filename extension such as **.rnd** to indicate that the file is a random access file.

B.2.2 Writing Records

Use the **Put** statement to write a record to a random access file. The syntax is:

```
Put filenumber, [recnumber], varname
```

where *filenumber* is the number of a file that has already been opened, *recnumber* is an integer that indicates which record is to be written, and *varname* is the name of a variable that contains the data to be written to the file.

If *recnumber* is omitted, then the record read will be either the one following the most recent Put or Get operation, or the record number returned by the most recent Seek operation. In the following statements, for example, records 10, 11, and 12 are written to the file:

```
Put 1, 10, myRec
Put 1, , myRec
Put 1, , myRec
```

If a file is empty and you write to the tenth record, space for nine empty records will automatically be saved in the file before the tenth record is inserted. This must be done, so that when a request to read the tenth record is given later on, Visual Basic can calculate the physical location of the record.

B.2.3 Reading Records

Use the **Get** statement to read a record from a random access file. The syntax is:

```
Get filenumber, [recnumber], varname
```

where *filenumber*, *recnumber*, and *varname* have the same meanings as in the Put statement. If *recnumber* is omitted, then the record read will be either the one following the most recent Put or Get operation, or the record number returned by the most recent Seek operation.

Moving the Record Pointer. The **Seek** statement can be used to position the record pointer in a random access file. Its syntax is:

```
Seek filenumber, position
```

If the next Put or Get statement does not specify a record number, the record affected will be the one positioned by calling Seek. If recNum were equal to 20 in the next example, the Get statement would read myRec from record 20:

```
Seek 1, recNum
Get 1, , myRec
```

B.3 CUSTOMER ACCOUNTS PROGRAM EXAMPLE

(samples: Customer)

Let's create a short program that keeps track of charges and payments by customers. A single random access file (customers.rnd) will store all records, using the customer ID number as the record number. We will limit ID numbers to the range 1 to 9999, to prevent the file from becoming too large. If each record were 40 bytes long, for example, the file could be as large as (40 * 9999) = 399,960 bytes.

B.3.1 Program Design

The user first enters a customer ID and clicks the Get button. If the ID is found in the file, the rest of the customer record is displayed. The main form, called **frmCustomer**, lets the user enter a customer ID, name, amount of payments, and amount of charges for each customer (see Figure 1).

New. To create a new customer record, just blank all of the fields and let the user type in all required data.

Save. To save a customer record, the user types in an ID number (between 1 and 9999), a name, total payments, total charges, and clicks the Save button. An example is shown in

Figure 1. Customer Accounts Program.

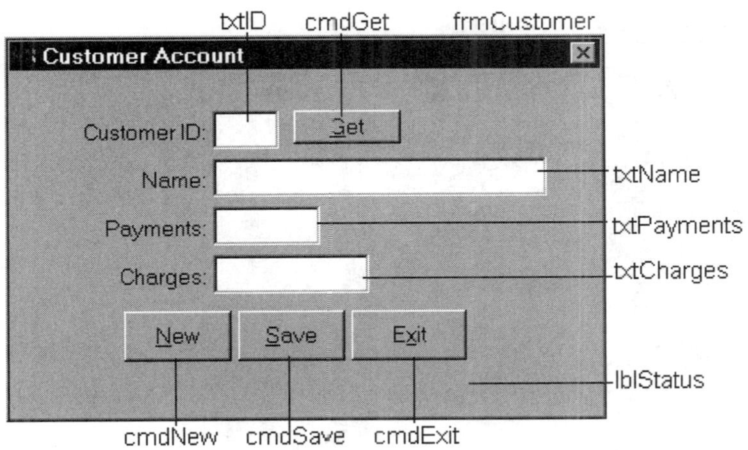

Figure 2. Each record is saved in the same random access file, using the customer ID as the record number.

Finding Records. To find an existing customer, the user enters a customer ID number and clicks on the Get button (see Figure 3). The status line at the bottom of the form indicates whether or not the record was found. Or, if the record is not found, the status line displays a message to that effect. After finding a record, the user can modify some of its fields and click the Save button to save the record.

B.3.2 Program Implementation

In the declarations section of the main form, declared constants hold the name of the random access file and the length of each record (CustomerLen). **fileNum** is the number of the open customer file:

```
Const CustomerFile As String = "customers.rnd"
Const CustomerLen As Integer = 40
Dim fileNum As Integer
```

Figure 2. Saving a New Customer.

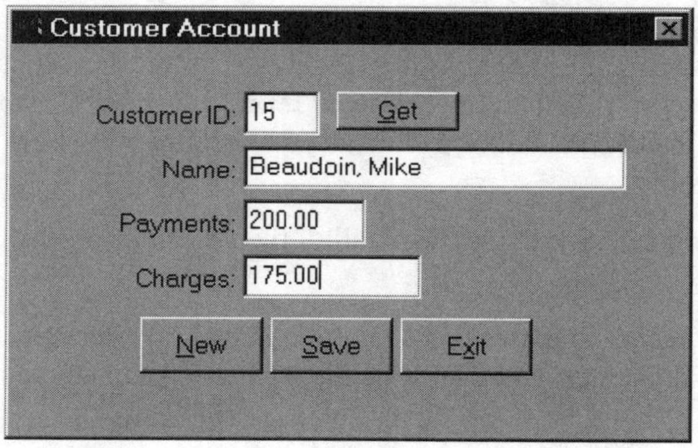

Figure 3. Searching for a Customer.

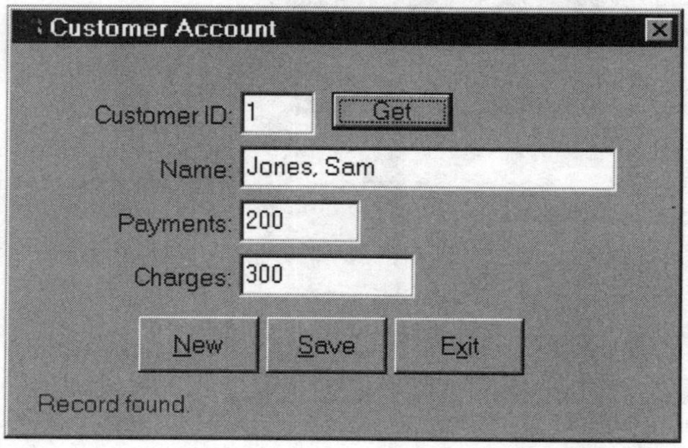

Also in the declarations section, **Customer** is declared as a user-defined type, containing all of the fields that belong in each record of the customer file. It is important to know the length of each field so the record length can be calculated:

```
Private Type Customer        ' Lengths
  id As Integer              '    2
  name As String * 20        '   20
  payments As Currency       '    8
  charges As Currency        '    8
  unused As String * 2       '    2
End Type
```

Notice that two unused bytes were left at the end of the Customer type. This allows for a small amount of expansion for additional data when needed.

We set the directory and path, get the next available file number, and open the random access file in Form_Load. The file stays open for the program's duration:

```
Private Sub Form_Load()
  ChDrive App.Path
  ChDir App.Path
  fileNum = FreeFile
  Open CustomerFile For Random As fileNum _
    Len = CustomerLen
End Sub
```

Creating a new customer record involves clearing all of the text controls on the form:

```
Private Sub cmdNew_Click()
  txtId = ""
  txtName = ""
  txtPayments = ""
  txtCharges = ""
End Sub
```

When the user clicks the **Save** button, the ID number is checked for an acceptable value. We fill in each of the fields in the Customer record variable (called cust), and write the record to the file at the position indicated by the ID number:

```
Private Sub cmdSave_Click()
   Dim cust As Customer, id As Integer
   On Error GoTo SaveRecord1
   id = Val(txtId.Text)
   If id < 1 Or id > 9999 Then
     MsgBox "Customer ID must be between 1 and 9999."
     txtId.SetFocus
     Exit Sub
   End If
   cust.id = id
   cust.name = txtName.Text
   cust.payments = Val(txtPayments.Text)
   cust.charges = Val(txtCharges.Text)
   Put fileNum, cust.id, cust
   Exit Sub
SaveRecord1:
```

```
  MsgBox Error$, vbCritical, "Error"
End Sub
```

To retrieve an existing record, the user types a record number into txtId. If the ID field in the record does not match its record number, we assume the record was never initialized:

```
Private Sub cmdGet_Click()
  Dim recNum As Integer, cust As Customer
  Dim id As Integer
  On Error GoTo GetRecord1
  id = Val(txtId.Text)
  Get fileNum, id, cust
  If cust.id <> id Then
    lblStatus = "Record not found."
    txtName.Text = ""
    txtPayments.Text = ""
    txtCharges.Text = ""
  Else
    lblStatus = "Record found."
    txtName.Text = cust.name
    txtPayments.Text = cust.payments
    txtCharges.Text = cust.charges
  End If
  Exit Sub
GetRecord1:
  MsgBox Error$, vbCritical, "Error"
End Sub
```

When the user clicks the **Exit** button, the main form unloads, triggering the Form_Unload event. We close the customer file just as the form is about to be unloaded:

```
Private Sub cmdExit_Click()
  Unload Me
End Sub

Private Sub Form_Unload(Cancel As Integer)
  Close fileNum
End Sub
```

Comments. Because this is a simple program, error checking was kept to a minimum. An improved version of the program would make sure that a record was never saved if any of its fields were blank, and each of the numeric fields would be checked for reasonable ranges of values. A nice improvement would also be to let the user select customer names from a ListBox when searching for customers.

Appendix C: Answers to Odd-Numbered Review Questions

C.1 CHAPTER 1

1. During the Design step.
3. Because choices in the design will be affected by the available resources. The design should not attempt to do something which is not possible.
5. **Prototyping** is creation of the visual part of the program (forms and controls) before writing any code.
7. Object-oriented design focuses on the physical entities that make up the application problem.
9. Doctor, Patient, Appointment, Schedule.
11. **PayRate** would be a property.
13. The addition of new features are possible without destroying the original program.
15. Special library software is used, such as **SourceSafe**, that requires modules to be checked out to only one person at a time.
17. Inadequate time and resources are devoted to testing and validation.
19. Because the process of fixing the bugs may have introduced new bugs.
21. KeyPress, KeyUp, and KeyDown.
23. File, Edit, Options, Help, Tools, View, Window, Format, Insert.
25. Choose descriptive names. Optionally, use prefixes that identify the scope and type of the variable.
27. Integer = int, Long = lng, String = str, Currency = cur, Single = sng, Boolean = bln.
29. Global, Module, Local.
31. A list is shown in Section 1.5.1.
33. A TextBox uses more memory.
35. Because VB loads modules on demand, less time will be spent loading if related procedures are in the same module.

37. Code speed, display speed, and perceived speed.
39. It takes less processing time to set and get ordinary variable values.
41. Preloaded forms can be displayed more quickly, but they also use up a lot of memory.
43. Display a splash screen while the rest of the forms are loading.

C.2 CHAPTER 2

1. The price is determined by the format (media type) and the price code.
3. By using the ListIndex property as a subscript into the titles array.
5. The album prices are numeric constants inside the CalcPrice procedure.
7. The sales tax rate would be different from state to state.
9. The Format function with a "Standard", "Currency", or "Fixed" argument value causes numeric values to print with two digits after the decimal point.
11. The **ListIndex** property of the cboSku control is essential in locating the album title.
13. The **FreeFile** function returns the next available file buffer number.
15. Version 2 lets the user purchase multiple items and add them to a ListBox representing an invoice.
17. If the user does not click on the Splash window, the Timer event will occur and the Splash window will unload.
19. The SKU number annot be blank when saving an invoice.
21. Open the file in **Append** mode.
23. When CancelError is True, a trappable error is generated when the user clicks on the Cancel button.
25. The **FileTitle** property contains just the filename with no path.
27. Assign the constant cdlOFNFileMustExist to the Flags property.
29. By assigning special constants to the Flags property.
31. The section that stores the settings for the Visual Basic programs is Hkey Current User.
33. One of the arguments passed to GetSetting is the default value to be returned by the function if a matching key cannot be found.

C.3 CHAPTER 3

1. A control array makes it easy to process the controls with a loop, and assign the same properties to all members of the array.
3. The Load statement creates a new instance of an object that may be placed in a control array. The Buttons program from this chapter is a good example.

5. Code Example:

```
Dim aForm As Form
Set aForm = frmAuthor
```

7. Code Example:

```
Dim F As Form
Set F = New frmMain
```

9. Code Example:

```
Dim j As Integer
For j = 1 To 9
   Load btn(j)
   btn(j).Caption = "Button " & j
   btn(j).Visible = True
Next j
```

11. This code assumes that all of the controls on the form have a Text property. The loop may cause a runtime error.
13. The keys in a Collection must be a string.
15. The problem with a Collection that uses last names of people as keys is that a runtime error will be generated if there are two people with the same last names.
17. A Collection can contain strings, numbers, forms, buttons, and other types of objects.
19. The parameter that is required is the member.
21. The lowest index value in a user-defined Collection is 1.
23. Because the MDI child windows are completely contained within the parent.
25. The menu on the MDI parent is replaced by the MDI child's window.

C.4 CHAPTER 4

1. Data Report Designer, Page Designer and ActiveX designer.
3. Field.
5. Number(Byte), Number (Double), Number (Long Integer), Number (Single) and Number (Integer)
7. RDO.
9. A Text field can contain from 0 to 255 characters. A Memo field can contain up to 1.2 billion characters.
11. A Jet database requires you to retrieve all records in the recordset before RecordCount returns an accurate value.
13. ConnectionString and CommandType.
15. ado.

17. The **ConnectionString** property identifies the data source connected to the ADO control.

19. DBList.

21. Yes. A Yes/No field.

23. AddNew

25. Move *n,* MoveFirst, MoveLast, MoveNext and MovePrevious.

27. No, it points just before the first row.

29. Move 5

31. The RowSource and ListField properties.

33. This can be achieved by adding "ORDER BY name" to end of the SQL query.

35. Refresh.

37. The properties that must be set are RowSource and ListField.

39. AllowAddNew.

C.5 CHAPTER 5

1. Select **Add Data Environment** from the **Project** menu.

3. True. A *Command* object contains specific information about which data are retrieved from its associated connection. The command can specify a table or SQL query.

5. Client-side and server-side.

7. No. Some Command objects execute a command and perform an update operation on the database without actually returning a Recordset object.

9. Before you can use the Data Environment designer, you must make it known to Visual Basic. Select **Components** from the **Project** menu, select the **Designers** tab, and place a check next to **Data Environment.**

11. Set mrsMyRecord = deMyDatabase.Recordsets("cmMyCommand")

13. SQL query statements.

15. adModeUnknown, adModeRead, adModeWrite and adModeReadWrite.

17. Returns the editing status of the current record.

19. RollBackTrans.

21. The EditMode property is equal to **adEditInProgress**.

23. Runtime error 3219 occurs, with the message: "The operation requested by the application is not allowed in this context."

25. SQL queries should be used whenever possible because of their superior performance.

27. **BeginTrans**, **CommitTrans**, and **RollbackTrans** methods.

29. Pessimistic locking, record by record—the provider does what is necessary to ensure successful editing of the records, usually by locking records at the data source immediately upon editing.

31. **CommitTrans** ends the current transaction and saves the changes.

33. If the user agrees by clicking on the Yes button, the **CommitTrans** method saves the changes in the database, and LoadList reloads the ListView control with the new data. On the other hand, if the user declines by clicking on the No button, the **RollbackTrans** method rolls back the transactions and the database is not modified.

C.6 CHAPTER 6

1. A *relational database management system* (RDMS) is a collection of data that is organized so that you can look at it in different ways. It contains tables, index, queries, filters, views, and validation capabilities. It is able to maintain links, or relationships between tables and to ensure that the links are consistent.

3. A column is the same as a field, but *column* is a more familiar term in relational database discussions.

5. Yes. You can assign a query string to the Recordsource property of a data control.

7. Data integrity rules, record validation rules, and field validation rules.

9. An application-independent design is general so that that multiple application programs can share the data.

11. Organize the data into tables.

13. Structured Query Language.

15. Data-Definition Language, and Data-Manipulation Language.

17. The ORDER BY clause sorts the Recordset.

19. The WHERE clause.

21. Code example:

```
SELECT LastName, FirstName FROM Employee
```

23. Code Example:

```
Call rsEmployees.Open( _
   "SELECT LastName, FirstName FROM Employee", _
      cnEmployees,,,adCmdText)
```

25. Code example:

```
SELECT * FROM Payroll
WHERE payRate BETWEEN 20 AND 30
AND hoursWorked > 40
```

27. Code example:

```
SELECT ssn, totalPoints / credits AS gpa
  FROM Transcript
```

29. The DISTINCTROW option.
31. For example, suppose one table contains three members (10,20,30) and another table contains three members (A,B,C). Then a cartesian product between these tables would consist of all possible member pairs.
33. An Inner join--this is the most common type.
35. Code example:

```
UPDATE Payroll
  Set HourlyRate = HourlyRate * 1.10
```

37. DROP TABLE Payroll
39. Code example:

```
INSERT INTO Temp
  FROM Transcript
```

41. Code Example:

```
CREATE TABLE Student
(StudentID Long,
 lastName TEXT(30),
 totalCredits SHORT)
```

C.7 CHAPTER 7

1. Right click the Project window, select **Add**, and select **Data Report**.
3. The **RptFunction** control can be configured to automatically calculate a sum, average, count, minimum value, or maximum value.
5. DataMember holds the name of the Command object providing data to the report.
7. Right click on the report, select **Insert Control**, and select **Report Title**.
9. **ExportReport**. Export the report to either HTML (for Web pages) or plain text.
11. Yes, because printing and exporting are asynchronous operations.
13. **QueryClose**
15. Right-click inside the page header area, and select **Insert Control**, and select **Current Page Number**. The symbol %p should appear in the header area.
17. Right-click anywhere in the report designer window and select "Show Report Header/ Footer". Right-click in the report footer area, and select **Function** from the **Insert Control** submenu. This places a rptFunction object in the footer area. On property windows, set Functiontype to rptFuncRCnt (counter).
19. cmStates should be copied into the group header.
21. The lowest level command (in this case, Cities) corresponds to the report detail line.

23. This approach gives us the flexibility to modify queries at runtime, based on user input.
25. No.
27. BandDisplay
29. ExpandAll
31. The first series is assigned strings that become labels for the chart's X-Axis.

C.8 CHAPTER 8

1. Algol, SmallTalk, and C++. Object Pascal was available around that time also.
3. A **class** is a definition of a data type, with properties, methods, and events.
5. The ToolBox icons are classes.
7. Yes, each instance has a separate copy of all event handlers.
9. No, unless the buttons are part of a control array.
11. Student, FirstDate, LastDate, Courses (a collection), major, gpa, credits, and advisor.
13. Inheritance.
15. Code example:

```
Dim trans As clsTranscript
```

17. Code example:

```
Set clsTranscript = Nothing
```

19. An object created inside a procedure is automatically destroyed when the procedure ends, unless another variable in a larger scope (public or module) contains a reference to the object.
21. No, the name of an instance variable must be different from any other instance variable or property in the same class.
23. Yes, two classes often have properties by the same name. The CommandButton and OptionButton classes both contain a property called Caption, for example.
25. Instance variables are usually private because we don't want class users to be able to directly modify the variables. Instead, class users call property procedures that handle the updating of instance variables.
27. To create a read-only property, omit the **Let** procedure for the property.
29. When a class object is destroyed, the Class_Terminate event occurs.
31. When a class method detects an error condition, it is usually best for it to raise an event rather than try to display its own message box..
33. A private method is called only by other methods within the same class.
35. One class object was created, and one class object exists at the end of the example. (Although st1 was set to Nothing, st2 retains a reference to the same object.)

37. The ID property verifies that the ID number is exactly six characters or digits long.
39. Each instance of the CStudentCollection class contains zero or more instances of the CStudent class.
41. No, neither class directly shows a form.
43. Each clsStudent object in the Collection is destroyed.
45. If a Collection's Item method fails to find a matching key value, a runtime error is generated.

C.9 CHAPTER 9

1. *Component software development* is the assembling of programs from tested, standardized components.
3. ActiveX provides the mechanism so that objects can work together, whether the objects are created from classes in a single program or the objects are created by external, out-of-process servers.
5. Before ActiveX was created, OLE servers were able to expose objects, methods, and properties. ActiveX is an extension of the same process.
7. ActiveX Controls, ActiveX Documents, and Code Components.
9. An ActiveX control.
11. No, they are compiled into DLL library files.
13. Code Example:
```
RaiseEvent FileError
```
15. The text in the Text control is immediately selected, as if someone had dragged a mouse ove the text.
17. The Caption and BackColor properties.
19. Just provide a Property Get procedure, and either omit the Property Let or make it Private.
21. The InitProperties event occurs.
23. We supply default properties to the WriteProperty method to reduce the size of the Form file. If a new property value is identical to the default value, Visual Basic does not save the property value.
25. When a form is opened in design mode, the ReadProperties method of the ActiveX control executes.
27. PropertyChanged must be called to allow Visual Basic to generate a WriteProperties event. This in turn causes changes to the Active X control to be saved.
29. DoctorSchedule is called a **type library** because it exposes multiple classes.
31. PublicNotCreateable means that client programs can use instances of the class only if the component creates the objects first.

33. ActiveX controls can use the Private and PrivateNotCreatable instancing properties.

35. The On Error statement should be used inside the Terminate event handler, because client programs that use the component cannot handle errors that originate from this event handler.

37. Yes, it can be run as a stand-alone executable program.

C.10 CHAPTER 10

1. It is a program or application that contains links and/or embedded copies of objects created by other programs.

3. External objects.

5. By exposing objects, the ActiveX server lets other applications create objects, call methods, and set properties using the full power of the ActiveX server. The full power of an Excel worksheet, for example, can be incorporated into a Visual Basic program.

7. (1) Select the OLE container control from the ToolBox and place a copy of it on a form. (2) Using programming statements, create instance of ActiveX objects and directly call their methods and properties.

9. Code Example:

```
Private modjWord as Word.Application
  Set modjWord = New Word.Application
```

11. Workbook, Worksheet, and Chart.

13. Yes, because Word is running in the background.

15. The object browser lists all of the class types that are available via ActiveX.

17. Yes, using the SaveToFile method.

19. Set the NegotiatePosition property of the enclosing form's menu.

21. Click on the Class property of the OLE container control.

23. This makes the controls automatically size themselves to the embedded object.

25. The main reason for using DoVerb is this: if the AutoActivate property is set to *manual*, the program can open the object by calling DoVerb.

27. The CreateLink method.

29. Visual Basic for Applications (VBA).

31. ActiveDocument.PageSetup.TopMargin = InchesToPoints(1.5)

33. Code Example:

```
Dim Excel As Excel.Application, wbook As Excel.Workbook, _
  wsheet As Excel.Worksheet
Set Excel = New Excel.Application
Set wbook = Excel.Workbooks.Add
Set wsheet = Excel.ActiveWorkbook.ActiveSheet
```

35. In the lstApplicants_Click event handler, the applicant's ID number is retrieved from the ItemData array. This ID is passed to the Find method when searching for the record.
37. The user can double click on a response topic, and the topic paragraph will appear.
39. The Check_Selections procedure verifies that an applicant was selected and at least one response topic was selected.

C.11 CHAPTER 11

1. Low-level tasks: hardware device drivers, high-speed video graphics, serial communications programming. High-level tasks: application programs, pop-up menus, printing reports, using SQL to build recordsets.
3. To handle time-critical tasks; to perform Windows programming tasks that are not directly supported by Visual Basic.
5. *Dynamic linking* allows compiled procedures to be stored in a separate file from the calling program. The procedures are loaded into memory only when called.
7. Less memory is used, and the programs can pass data to each other via the DLL.
9. The C/C++ language is the traditional language for writing DLLs, and most DLLs assume that C data types will be used as arguments.
11. Some ActiveX components are DLLs, others are stand-alone executable programs, and others are custom controls.
13. Sometimes, the name of a DLL procedure is the same as a Visual Basic keyword, or the name contains characters that would not be allowed in a Visual Basic identifier. Also, the names of Win32 API functions are slightly different frm the 16-bit API, so alias names can provide a way for the programmer to use the same names all the time.
15. Call the Windows API Sleep function.
17. A window handle is a long integer that is assigned a unique value when the window is created in memory. All Windows API functions acting on the window must refer to the window's handle.
19. It should be assigned to an array of characters.
21. It should be passed by value, unless the DLL procedure specifically asks for a pointer to an integer (notated as: int *, or long *).
23. Padding an empty string with characters forces Visual Basic to preallocate storage for the string. The API function expects the storage to be available.

C.12 CHAPTER 12

1. You can use HTTP protocol to connect to World Wide Web servers to retrieve HTML documents. Using the FTP protocol, you can log on to FTP servers, download, and upload files.

3. Retrieves data from a remote server in the StateChanged event. Use this method after invoking the *Execute* method as a *GET* operation.
5. Opens and retrieves the document at the specified URL.
7. It is triggered whenever there is a state change in the connection.
9. There are thirteen states.
11. Code sample:

```
Public Sub ViewHTML()
  On Error GoTo ViewHTML_Error
  Set Explorer = New SHDocVw.InternetExplorer
  Explorer.Visible = True
  Explorer.Navigate cboURL.Text
  Exit Sub
ViewHTML_Error:
  MsgBox "Error displaying file", , Err.Description
End Sub
```

13. Code sample:

```
Public Sub DownLoadHTML()
On Error GoTo DownLoadHTML_Error
  mstrURL = cboURL.Text
  'check for left  11 characters ("http://www.")
  'check for left 4 characters ("www.")
  If Left(mstrURL, 11) = "http://www." Or _
  Left(mstrURL, 4) = "www." Then
 'copy html document into text box
  txtDownLoad.Text = Inet1.OpenURL(mstrURL)
  Else
    MsgBox "Enter valid document name in the URL box"
  End If
  Exit Sub
DownLoadHTML_Error:
  MsgBox "Error opening URL", , Err.Description
End Sub
```

15. The last character is "/".

17. Code sample:

```
Public Sub DownloadFile()
 'Browser selecteed a file.
  Dim strFilename
 'Construct path name of file.
  mstrDirectory = Right(txtFTPAddress, Len(txtFTPAddress) _
  - Len(itcInternetBrowser.URL)) & "/" & _
  txtFTPDirectory.SelText
  mstrDirectory = Right(mstrDirectory, Len(mstrDirectory) - 1)
  strFilename = mstrDirectory
  Do
    strFilename = Right(strFilename, _
    Len(strFilename) - InStr(strFilename, "/"))
```

```
    Loop Until InStr(strFilename, "/") = 0
    'Download (Retrieve) the file.
      itcInternetBrowser.Execute , "Get " & mstrDirectory & _
      " " & mstrTempDir & strFilename
End Sub
```

19. The **GetChunk** method is used to retrieve the buffer's contents.
21. **The InnerText** property changes or retrieves the straight text between the start and end tags of the current element without affecting existing HTML tags.
23. DHTML equivalent event has on **as** prefix.
25. Sample code:

```
Hyperlink1.href = App.Path & "\lotto.htm"
```

27. Use the GetProperty functions to retrieve data.
29. The TCP protocol control is a connection-based protocol. The UDP protocol is a connectionless protocol.
31. Use RemoteHostIP property.
33. Server mode is a computer goes online waits for an incoming connection from a client. The client mode is a computer initiates a connection to a known server.
35. It is a table of content file. It contains headings and pages.
37. It is the AtiveX control loaded by hh_toc.htm and hh_index.htm.
39. We can call HTMLHelp files from within web pages. Also Animation, sound video, and other effects are much easier to add to HTMLHelp files. Unlike WinHelp, HTML has no limits to size of the Help file you can create. The completed file is just a compiled HTML file (*.chm). This file is much smaller than the compiled WinHelp files.

Index

A

ActiveControl property 113
ActiveMovie control 42
ActiveX
  code component 397
  component 350–352
  suggested reading 390
  using MS-Office code components 410
  using the Excel ActiveX server 416–417
  Visual Basic for applications 410
ActiveX control 29–43, 351–354
  ActiveX Control Wizard 369–376
  adding events 356–357
  AmbientChanged event 355
  CanPropertyChange method 358
  creating a test program 354
  delegating (properties, methods, and events) 352
  making a control data-bound 357–360
  Property Page Wizard 377–380
  property pages 377–381
  PropertyChanged method 358
  ReadProperties event 364
  resizing a control 357
  Type Library 381
  WriteProperties event 364
ActiveX Data Objects 129, 174–195
ActiveX DLL
  Instancing property 384
ActiveX document 350
ActiveX server
  creating a server 321–323
ActiveX xerver 397–399
ADO 129
ADO Connection 175
  Execute method 176
  opening a Connection 175
ADO control event 151
ADO Data control 130
  binding option buttons 132
ADO Recordset 133
  properties 177
App object
  properties 15
Application
  design 3–4
  design goals 4
  development cycle 1–5
  implementing 4–5
  testing 5–6
Application object 553
Arrays 518

B

Block IF statement 520
BookMark property 138
Boolean 514

C

Chapter exercises

AddAppointment Control 393
Adjusting ListView Column Widths 459
Biblio TreeView 208
BlendColor Program 458
Buttons Control Array 120
Changing form colors 26
Classical Music Catalog - 1 76
Cleaning Equipment Rental Wizard 72
CMotor Class 343
CMotorCollection Class 344
Computer Mail-Order Customer Data 208
Computer Mail-Order Invoice 208
Concert Hall Ticketing 205, 207, 208
Coolbar Editor 123, 124
Depreciation Schedule 74, 431
Doctors Office Appointments 205
Doctors Office Scheduling 202, 204, 205, 254, 347
DriveInfo Program 458
Dynamic Changing HTML Page 508
E-Mail Address Book 344
Express Travel Agency 27
Factoring a Number 508
Family Photo Album 432
Freight Forwarding Service 26
Glossary Program 124, 126
Hardbodies Health Club 73, 430
Health Club Class Schedule 74
HTMLViewer 506
Jumping Button Program 120
Karate School 168
Karate School MDI 458
Keeping a Window On Top 458
Kyoshi Karate 169
Kyoshi Karate School 163, 166, 297
Mail-Order Computer Sales 163, 297
Mortgage Calculator Program 507
Mozart MDI 121, 122
Mozart MDI with a ListView 123
Mozart Music 161, 162
Mozart Music Color Settings 72
Mozart Music Common Dialog 71
Mozart Music File and Directory Settings 72
Mozart Music Instruments 71, 430
Mozart Music Using a CoolBar 123
Mozart Music: CInvoice Class 344
MSChart Interactive 298
Multiple-Choice Test 28
NorthWind 295, 296, 297
Object-Oriented Glossary Program 343
Object-Oriented Time Clock 344
OptionList Control 394
Personal Stock Portfolio 433
Playing WAV Files 458
Products and Categories in a TreeView 202
Products Table in a ListView 202
Publisher ActiveX Control 395
Query Parameters 202
Saving the Student Collection 342

Searching for Books with SQL 254
Searching the Classical Music Catalog 76
Selecting and Playing WAV Files 458
Sorted Collection 121
Stellar Car Rental 253
Stellar Car Rentals 394
Student Collection 342
StudentInfo Control 393
Tic-Tac-Toe On Networked Computers 508
Time Clock Program 74
Winsock with Multiple Connections 506
Yachting Regatta 256, 345, 347
Yachting Regatta Program 254, 255
CheckBox control 542
Class
creating instances of 305
describing class relationships 328–330
event handlers 309–310
Instancing property 384
methods 310
naming conventions 305
properties 306–309
student collection example 314–318
using the Err.Raise method 313
Class modules 304–305
Classes and objects 301–310
Client-server design 318
client program 319–320
Code components 351
Code optimization 22
Coding guidelines 9–17
Indenting Code 12
Coding style
avoid default properties 15
breaking long lines 14
indenting code 12
naming controls 11
naming procedures 12
reducing code size 21
variables and constants 10–11
Collection 84–91, 519
adding objects to 86
predefined in Visual Basic 84
programmer-defined 85
removing members 88
returning references to members 87
Collection class 314–318
ComboBox control 545
Command object 172
creating 192
executing 193
CommandButton control 541
CommandType property 131
Common Dialog control 59–65
Competency Review
answers 557
Competency review test 512–514
Component Object Model (COM) 350
Component software development 350–352
Compound expressions 520
Connection object 171
ConnectionString property 130
Constants
naming conventions 10
predefined 14
Constituent controls 354
Control arrays 80–82
creating at design time 82
filling at run time 83
Controls
naming conventions 11
CoolBar control 106–111
Creating HTML HELP 495–505
compiling a Help project 501
contents HTML file 502
creating a frameset 501
creating a table of contents 498
creating the main window 497
hooking to a VB program 501
host program 503
index file 503
with Microsoft Word 496
Crystal Reports 259
CursorLocation property 176

D

DAO (Data Access Objects) 129
Data Access Objects (DAO) 129
Data consumers 131
Data Environment
creating 265
Data Environment Designer 171–174
Data Report Designer 259
Data types 514
Byte, Integer, Long 514
Date 516
declared constants 517
Object 517
Single, Double, Currency 515
static arrays 518
String 516
Variant 517
Data-bound control 131
Database
design 127
designing a database 210
filter 210
query 210
referential integrity rules 247
relational 127–133
table relations 245–247
tables 127–133
validation rules 242–244
view 210
viewing and printing reports 260
Database design 210–211
DataCombo control 153–159, 155
DataEnvironment object 171
DataField property 132
DataGrid control 153–159
DataList control 153, 154
DataRepeater control 360–361
RepeaterBindings collection 361
DataReport objects 260–262
DataSource property 132
Declared constants 517
Delete method 139
Design
goals of 4
user interface 5–6, 6, 6–7

visual 3
Designing applications 3–4
DHTML Page Designer 474
DLL procedures 437–439
API Viewer utility 439–440
Declare statement 439
declaring and calling 439–442
defining parameters 442–446
need for DLLs 437
SendMessage function 453
static and dynamic linking 438–439
Do-Until statement 523
Do-While statement 523
DoctorSchedule DLL 381–388
DoEvents 24
DragDrop
ListBox usage 9
methods 9
Dragging and dropping 9
Dynamic arrays 518
Dynamic HTML 474–476
ACME Car Rental example 483–488
events 474
GetProperty function 486
importing existing HTML pages 480–482
InnerText property 474
Lottery example 477
managing program state between DHTML pages 482–484
onclick event handler 478
PutProperty method 486

E

Err object 20
Err.Raise method 20
Error handling 17, 17–21, 18
Err object 20
Examples
ActiveX EXE Server 389–390
AddAppointment ActiveX control 361–369
attaching icons to a TreeView 105
author table (report) 265–266
automobile models file 562–564
BatchUpdate 196
blending color across a form 450–454
car rental database design 238–242
CEmployee class 306–309
client-server 318–325
College Admissions program 420–428
College Registration Wizard 58
CompanyData database 213
creating a Word document 410
creating an ActiveX DLL 381–388
Customer Accounts program 567
DataCombo and DataGrid controls 158
Disk Drive Information DLL 446–454
Doctors Office scheduling 325–340
downloading files with FTP 468
flashing a window caption 440–442
Form-loading program 539
FTP Browser program 468
GetWindowsDirectory DLL procedure 445–454
HTML Viewer program 462–468
interactively building a tree 98
linking a DataList to a DataGrid 156
ListView 91
loading a TreeView from a database 189
MDI vehicle reservations 115
medical database 172
MSChart with labels 286
music CD collection viewer 94
NorthWind Traders database 129
OLE Chart 402–405
OLE container program 406
OptionGroup ActiveX control 369–376
out-of-process component 389–391
raising employee salaries 196
registering and unregistering components 323–325
Rental Rates DLL 321–323
resizing controls on a form 89
Sales Staff 133–153, 134, 136, 139, 142, 146, 147, 149, 151, 182
Sales Staff program with SQL 146
Sales Staff with ListView 185
save/retrieve data path 68
saving a file 62
simple MSChart 285
statistical score analysis 417
Stellar Car Rental 238–242
Student class 310–314
StudentIdText ActiveX control 352–361
tab stops in a ListBox 453–454
traversing and saving a tree 103

F

Feasibility review 2
For-Next statement 522
Format function 548
Forms 531
Activate event 537
Cls method 536
DeActivate event 537
events 536–539
Hide method 536
Initialize event 536
loading and unloading 535
methods 534
Print method 536
PrintForm method 536
properties 532
QueryUnload event 537
Show method 535
Terminate event 538
Unload event 538
Frame control 542
Function procedures 526

G

GetAllSettings method. *See* Registry settings: saving and retrieving
GetSetting method. *See* Registry settings

H

Hierarchical FlexGrid control 278–284
binding to a Data Environment 279–281
displaying a report 283–285
properties and methods 281
HTML (Hypertext MarkUp Language) 474

I

IF statement with ELSE 520
IF statements 520
Image control 543
ImageHeight property 34
ImageList control 32–34
ImageWidth property 34
InputBox function 551
Internet Transfer control 462–474
  StateChanged event 471
Interviewing management and users 1

K

Keyboard
  input 7–8
  KeyDown event 7
  KeyPress event 7
  KeyUp event 7

L

Label control 541
Line continuation. *See also* Coding style
Line control 544
ListBox control 545
  using DragDrop 9
ListImage object 33
ListImages collection 33
ListView control 91–96
Loops 522–524

M

MDI applications 112–118
  ActiveControl property 113
  ActiveForm property 113
Menus
  creating 554–557
  properties 555
  standard types 8
Microsoft Access 129
Microsoft Word
  using the Macro Recorder 413–416
MIDI file 40
MouseDown event 9
Mozart Music Sales 43–52, 52–57
  program specifications 45
  user interface design 45
Mozart Music Store 2
MSChart control 285–293
  binding to an ADO control 291
  interactively filling at run time 286
MsgBox function 550
MsgBox procedure 549
Multi-User database processing 198–200
Multimedia control 40–42

O

Object variables 79–84
Object-oriented design 302–304
  implementation 303
  inheritance 304
  interface 303
  naming conventions 305
Objects
  declaring and assigning 80
OLE
  CreateEmbed method 402
  CreateLink method 405–406
  embedded Excel Worksheet 402
  embedded object 398
  embedded Word object 399–402
  linked object 398
  NegotiateMenus property 399
  NegotiatePosition property 399
  NegotiateToolbars property 401
  reading an OLE container 401
  saving an OLE container 401
OLE automation 397
OLE container 397–399
OLE Container control 399–406
OLE DB provider 130
On Error GoTo 18. *See also* Error handling
Optimization
  code optimization 22
  display optimization 23
  execution speed 22
  perceived speed optimization 23
  reducing code size 21
OptionButton control 542
Out-of-Process component 389–391

P

Predefined constants 14
Print method 547
Printer object 552
Private and Public 528
Procedure parameters 525
Procedures 524
  ByRef keyword 527
  ByVal keyword 528
  creating names for 12
  function procedures 526
  optional parameters 529
  parameter arrays 529
  parameters 525
  passing arguments by reference 527
  passing arguments by value 528
  subroutine procedures 524
Program specifications 2
ProgressBar control 31
Property pages, creating 377
Property procedure 306–309

R

Random access files 565–567
RDO (Remote Data Objects) 129
Record locking 199
Recordset
  adding, deleting, and updating 138
  adding new records 179
  ADODB Recordset 133
  BookMark property 138
  cursor 172
  CursorType property 178
  deleting records 181
  displaying images 149
  EditMode property 180

filtering records 142
Find method 147
LockType property 178
modifying existing records 180
moving the Recordset pointer 136
record locking 199
sorting records 139
transaction processing 195–198
troubleshooting error messages 182
using SQL to create a Recordset 144
RecordSource property 131
Registry settings
saving and retrieving 65–69
Relational database management system (RDMS) 210
Relational databases 127
Remote Data Objects (RDO) 129
Report
adding a footer 270
building a report application 262–265
building, using SQL 267–268
grouping by creating summary fields 273
joining tables 268
one record per page 278
ReportDesigner toolbox 260
reports with groups 270
showing from ADO Connection 275
viewing and printing 260
Resume statement 18

S

SaveSetting method. *See also* Registry settings
Saving and retrieving registry settings. *See* Registry settings
Screen object 553
Screen.MousePointer 24
ScrollBar control 544
Select Case statement 521
Sequential file 561–565
Shared database processing 199
Sort property 140
Splash screen 45
SQL language 211–228
ALTER TABLE 231
calculated columns 220
CREATE INDEX 233
CREATE TABLE 229
creating queries in Microsoft Access 228
Data Definition Language (DDL) 229–234
DDL program example 234–237
DELETE 232
DROP TABLE/INDEX 230
efficiency of 192
GROUP BY clause 218–219
HAVING clause 219
INSERT INTO 232
JOIN clause 223
logical operators 221
multiple-record append 233
ORDER BY clause 217–218
query parameters 193
SELECT statement 213
selecting from multiple tables 222
single-record append 232
structure of SQL statements 212
TOP predicate 219
UPDATE Statement 231
using SQL builder 225
WHERE clause 215–217
StatusBar control 38
String handling 530
Subroutine
declaring a subroutine procedure 524
function procedure 526
System registry. *See* Registry settings

T

Tabbed Dialog control 6, 30–31
Tabs
setting the tab order 6–7
Text control 541
Timer control 544
ToolBar control 34–38
Transaction processing 195–198
TreeView control 96–106
adding nodes 97
attaching icons to nodes 105
traversing the nodes 103

U

Update method 139
User interface design 5–6
User-defined type 519

V

Variable
naming conventions 10
Viewing the system registry 65
Visual design 3

W

While-Wend statement 524
Windows Common Controls 32
Winsock control 488–495
Wizards, creating 57–59